Romania

THE ROUGH GUIDE

D0289848

There are more than sixty Rough Guide titles covering
destinations from Amsterdam to Zimbabwe

Forthcoming titles include
Bali • Costa Rica • Majorca • Rhodes • Vietnam

Rough Guide Reference Series
Classical Music • World Music

Rough Guide Phrasebooks
Czech • French • German • Greek • Italian • Spanish

Credits

Editor:	Jo Mead
Series Editor:	Mark Ellingham
Production:	Susanne Hillen, Andy Hilliard, Link Hall and Nicola Williamson
Cartography:	Mick Bohoslawec and Melissa Flack

Acknowledgments

Dan would like to thank Ghel, Eduardo, Serge and Anna in Iaşi, and everyone at *Bucovina Estur* in Suceava.

Tim would like to thank Andrei Fluerasu, Irina Davidovici, the Farcaş family, Maria Ciceu, Isolde, Bob, James Brabazon, Emil Silvestru, Mircea Pîrlog, Ildiko Mitru, Mihail Pop, Mihail Ghizaru, Arpád Szabo, Chris Watkins, Andy Ive, Simon Broughton, Julian Ross, Martin Barlow, Charles King, David Turnock, Dennis Deletant, Tom Gallagher, Michelle Bonnel, Edward Parry, Ritchard Brazil, Tom Rathwell, Suszy Lessof, Valery Rees, Brenda Walker, Radu Munteanu, Sherban Cantacuzino, Valentina Gheorghe, Gabriela Rădulescu, Fran Weatherhead, Peter Domokos, Nick Crane, Christoph Machat, and Carolyn, who went to Canada and left me to get on with it.

Many thanks also to David Leffman, Jeanne Muchnick, Huw Molseed at Book Trust, Ellen Sarewitz for proofreading and Philip Beauvais for his excellent Bucharest updates.

This edition published 1995 by Rough Guides Ltd, 1 Mercer Street, London WC2H 9QJ.

Distributed by the Penguin Group:
Penguin Books Ltd, 27 Wrights Lane, London W8 5TZ
Penguin Books USA Inc., 375 Hudson Street, New York 10014, USA
Penguin Books Australia Ltd, 487 Maroondah Highway, PO Box 257, Ringwood, Victoria 3134, Australia
Penguin Books Canada Ltd, 10 Alcorn Avenue, Toronto, Ontario, Canada M4V 1E4
Penguin Books (NZ) Ltd, 182–190 Wairau Road, Auckland 10, New Zealand

Typeset in Linotron Univers and Century Old Style to an original design by Andrew Oliver.
Printed in the United Kingdom by Cox and Wyman Ltd (Reading).
Illustrations in Part One and Part Three by Edward Briant; illustrations on p.1 and p.305 by Henry Iles.

384p. Includes index.

A catalogue record for this book is available from the British Library.

ISBN 1-85828-097-4

Romania

THE ROUGH GUIDE

Written and researched by
Dan Richardson and Tim Burford

With additional material by
Simon Broughton

THE ROUGH GUIDES

LIST OF MAPS

MAP SYMBOLS

Symbol	Name	Symbol	Name
———	Railway	🏠	Refuge
———	Motorway	◠	Cave
———	Road	▲	Peak
- - - - -	Path	▨	National Park
– – –	Ferry route	ⵊ	Gorge
········	Waterway	⊨	Pass
▬▬▬	Chapter division boundary	✕	Airport
▬▬ ▬▬	International borders	⤫	Waterfall
········	Cable car	ⵡ	Marshland
———	Wall	ⓘ	Tourist Office
⚲	Monastery	⊠	Post Office
✡	Synagogue	Ⓜ	Underground station
⌖	Castle	▬	Building
♟	Museum	⊞	Church
∴	Ruins	⁺⁺⁺	Cemetery
△	Campsite	▨	Park

CONTENTS

Introduction viii

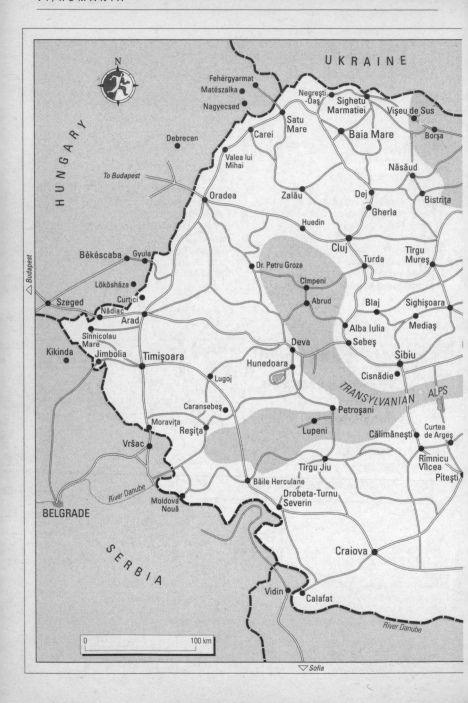

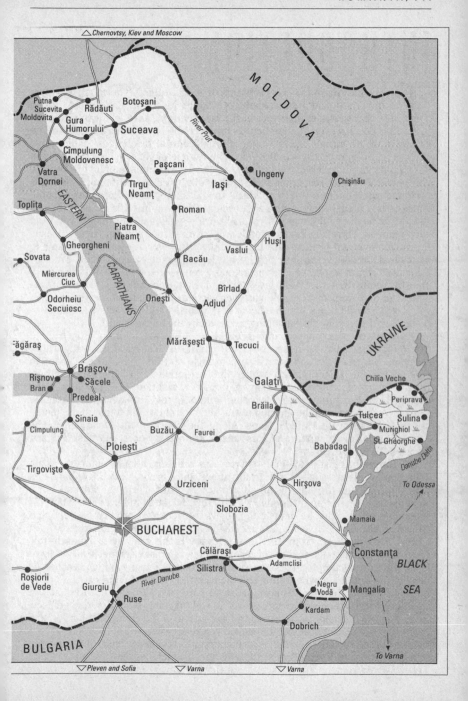

INTRODUCTION

Travel in **Romania** is as rewarding as it is challenging. The country's mountain scenery and great diversity of wildlife, its cultures and people, and a life that seems at times out of the last century, leave few who visit unaffected. However, although not as impoverished as Albania and most of the countries of the former Soviet Union, it is still one of the hardest countries of Eastern and Central Europe to travel in. The regime of Nicolae Ceauşescu drove the country to the brink of bankruptcy, and the government's efforts to provide visible fruit of 1989's revolution have further disrupted the economy; inflation is high and while there are now products in the shops, most Romanians cannot afford to buy them. Coming here on a package deal – to the Black Sea or Poiana Braşov, or on one of the many "Dracula Tours" – will effectively shield you from such realities. Travelling independently will have its frustrating moments, balancing inclinations and plans against practicalities. However, it would be a shame to let such factors deter you from at least a brief independent exploration. Much of Romania's charm lies in the less-visited, more remote regions, and it's the experience of getting there that really gives you an insight into the country. Rather than expect an easy ride, try to accept whatever happens as an adventure – encounters with Gypsies, wild bears, oafish officials and assorted odd characters are likely to be far more interesting than anything purveyed by the tourist board.

Romanians (the country's largest ethnic group) trace their ancestry back to the Romans, and have a noticeable Latin character. They are generally warm, spontaneous, anarchic, and appreciative of style and life's pleasures – sadly, in contrast to the austerity with which they're saddled. In addition to ethnic Romanians, some two million Magyars pursue a traditional lifestyle long since vanished in Hungary, while dwindling numbers of Transylvanian Germans (Saxons) reside around the fortified towns and churches built to guard the mountain passes during the Middle Ages. Along the coast, in the Delta and in the Banat there's a rich mixture of Russians, Ukrainians, Serbs, Slovaks, Bulgars, Gypsies, Turks and Tartars.

Bucharest has lost much of its charm – its wide nineteenth-century Parisian-style boulevards are choked with traffic fumes, once-grand *fin de siècle* buildings are crumbling and the suburbs are dominated by grim apartment blocks – but it remains the centre of the country's commercial and cultural life. Many of Romania's other cities are industrially blighted places that are best avoided, but Braşov, Sibiu, Cluj, Oradea and other historic towns still show glimpses of past glories. Heading north from Bucharest, **Braşov** is the gateway to Transylvania. Just twelve kilometres from the ski resort of Poiana Braşov, its medieval old town is a good introduction to the Saxon architecture of the region which reaches its peak in the fortified town of **Sibiu** and the jagged skyline of **Sighişoara**. Further north and west, the great Magyar cities of **Cluj** and **Oradea** have retained a wealth of medieval churches and streets as well as impressive Baroque edifices. Both cities lie on major international rail lines close to the Hungarian border, and could well be your first taste of Romania if you're arriving by train or road.

The best of Romania, though, is its countryside, and in particular the mountain scenery. The wild **Carpathians**, forming the frontier between the province of **Transylvania** and, to the east and south, **Moldavia** and **Wallachia**, shelter bears, stags and eagles; while the **Bucegi** and **Retezat** ranges and the **Padiş plateau** offer some of the most undisturbed and spectacular hiking opportunities in Europe. In contrast to the crowded Black Sea beaches along Romania's east coast, the waterlogged **Danube Delta** is a place set apart from the rest of the country where life has hardly changed for centuries and where boats are the only way of reaching many settlements. During spring and autumn especially, hundreds of species of birds from all over the world migrate through this region or come to breed. Almost any exploration you make among the **villages** of rural Romania will be rewarding, with sights as diverse as the log houses in Oltenia, Delta villages built of reeds, **the wooden churches of Maramureş**, and the famous **monasteries of Bucovina** painted with visions of Judgement Day. Similarly, few countries can offer such a wealth of distinctive **folk music, festivals and customs**, all still going strong in remoter areas like the Apuseni mountains, Maramureş and northern Moldavia, and in the largely Hungarian Csángó and Székelyföld regions.

When to go

The **climate** is pretty crucial in deciding where to go and when, since life can be literally at risk during winter unless you come securely booked on a skiing holiday, or fully equipped as if for a short walk in the Himalayas. Even in the capital, Bucharest, it's not always easy to find hotel rooms where the heating functions properly, and in winter, temperatures regularly fall well below freezing. Conditions improve with spring, bringing rain and wildflowers to the mountains, the softest of blue skies over Bucharest, and prompting the great migration of birds through the Delta. By May the lowlands are warming up and you might well find strong sunshine on the coast before the hordes arrive in July. Summer or early autumn is the perfect time to investigate Transylvania's festivals and hiking trails, and to see the Painted Monasteries of Bucovina, while flocks of birds return to the Delta towards the end of autumn.

AVERAGE TEMPERATURES °F (°C)			
	The Banat	**Bucharest**	**The coast**	**The mountains**
January	28 (−2)	26 (−3)	31 (−1)	33 (1)
February	33 (1)	30 (−1)	34 (1)	34 (1)
March	42 (5)	40 (4)	39 (3)	42 (6)
April	52 (11)	52 (11)	55 (13)	51 (11)
May	61 (16)	62 (17)	66 (19)	61 (16)
June	67 (20)	69 (21)	75 (24)	67 (19)
July	67 (20)	69 (23)	79 (26)	70 (21)
August	65 (18)	67 (22)	79 (26)	70 (21)
September	64 (18)	65 (18)	72 (22)	64 (18)
October	53 (12)	54 (12)	62 (17)	55 (13)
November	43 (6)	42 (5)	51 (11)	45 (7)
December	35 (1)	34 (1)	43 (6)	36 (2)

NB These are average temperatures – they can rise or fall 10°F (5°C) at midday or nightfall. Spring is short and changeable; brief showers or thunderstorms are common in the Carpathians during summer, whereas the Banat and Wallachian lowlands are prone to drought. In winter a strong, icy wind (the *crivat*) sweeps down from Russia and snow blankets most of Romania.

HELP US UPDATE

A lot of effort has gone in to ensure that this first edition of *The Rough Guide to Romania* is up-to-date and accurate. However, things can change fast in Romania: new restaurants appear, especially in Bucharest and on the coast; prices, opening hours and bus schedules are fickle; and political developments might affect your visit. Any suggestions, comments, corrections or updates towards the next edition would be much appreciated. All contributions will be credited, and the best letters will be rewarded with a copy of the new book (or any other *Rough Guide*, if you prefer). Please mark all letters "Rough Guide Romania Update" and send to:

Rough Guides, 1 Mercer Street, London WC2H 9QJ
or
Rough Guides, 375 Hudson Street, 3rd Floor, New York NY10014.

THANKS

Thanks to readers of *The Rough Guide to Eastern Europe* who wrote in with helpful comments and suggestions:

Fiona Hood, Tim Chapman, Hilary Lewis, James McCall, Tom Gallagher, Terence Rees, R. Carkett, Graham Wallace, Barrie McCormick, Stef Jansen, Chris Turton, Urs Richter, Simon Kolka, Anthony Carlisle, Julian Hall, Ian Palmer, Rupert Gude, Michael Mackey, Clive Shakespeare, P.Y. Lee, Y.M. Lee.

PART ONE

THE
BASICS

GETTING THERE FROM BRITAIN

Deciding how to get to Romania is in large part a question of choosing between a package and independent travel arrangements. If Romania is your sole destination, packages are certainly worth considering as a useful means of circumventing the hassles and frustrations of bureaucracy.

Only *TAROM* and *British Airways* offer direct flights to Romania, taking 3 hours 20 minutes, compared with around 2 days by train. Romania is included in the *InterRail* pass, a more economical way of getting there overland than buying a return ticket.

BY PLANE

The Romanian national airline is **TAROM**, for long a typical Soviet-bloc operation with little interest in its customers, but now being forced to compete and to offer a decent standard of service. It currently flies eight times a week **direct** from London Heathrow to **Bucharest** and twice weekly from London Stansted and from Manchester. Most of these planes start the day in Bucharest and return from Britain around noon; two Heathrow flights per week call at **Timişoara** en route to Bucharest. Heathrow flights are operated by Boeing 737s (or the odd new A310 Airbus), while the others still use cramped BAC 1-11s. **British Airways** has recently begun to fly four times a week from London Gatwick to Bucharest. Other European airlines serving Romania from London (*Air France*, *Austrian Airlines*, *CSA*, *LOT*, *Lufthansa*, *Malev Hungarian Airlines* and *Swissair*) require a change of plane en route.

Some charter flights are available to Romania during summer and the skiing season but you'll mostly be looking at **scheduled flights**. They are rarely the least expensive alternative, but give you the flexibility you may need. An **Apex** (Advance Purchase Excursion) ticket is the cheapest way to travel on a scheduled flight and must be reserved fourteen days in advance and include one Saturday night. Your return date must be fixed when purchasing and no subsequent changes are allowed. Currently, an Apex fare to Bucharest will cost you £349 mid-week with *British Airways* and only slightly less with *TAROM*. Eastern European airlines like *CSA*, *Malev Hungarian Airlines* and *LOT* are often cheaper – around £240 return – but usually involve delays, with connections in Prague, Budapest and Warsaw. It's always worth checking on special offers; for example, *Malev* is currently offering a 12-month ticket for £282.

If you shop around, you should be able to come up with a cheaper **discounted fare** – around £195 for a Pex one-month return with *TAROM* to Bucharest. A good place to look for discount fares is the classified travel section of papers like the *Daily Telegraph* and the *Independent* (Saturday editions), and Sundays like the *Observer*, *Sunday Times* and *Sunday Independent*, where agents advertise special deals. If you're in London, check the *Evening Standard*, *Time Out* or the free travel mag, *TNT*, found outside mainline train stations. Independent travel specialists *STA Travel* and *Campus Travel* do deals for students and anyone under 26, or can simply sell a scheduled ticket at a discount price. See the box overleaf for details of specialist Romanian flight agents.

Charter flights are in theory supposed to be sold with accommodation, but it is sometimes possible just to buy the air ticket at a discount through a travel agent. Charters have fixed and unchangeable outward and return dates, and usually a maximum stay of one month. *TAROM* offers charter flights from London Gatwick and Manchester to Constanţa in summer for the Black Sea beaches, and to Bucharest in winter for skiing, but you will need to check availability as they are sometimes suspended for a season. An average charter through an agent should cost £150–160, from Gatwick or Manchester.

AIRLINES

British Airways, 156 Regent St, London W1R 5TA; 146 New St, Birmingham B2 4HN; 19–21 St Mary's Gate, Market St, Manchester M1 1PU; 66 Gordon St, Glasgow G1 3RS; 32 Frederick St, Edinburgh EH2 2JR (all enquiries ☎0345/222111).

CSA Czechoslovak Airlines, 72 Margaret St, London W1 (☎0171/255 1898); Manchester (☎0161/498 8840).

LOT Polish Airlines, 313 Regent St, London W1R 7PE (☎0171/580 5037).

Malev Hungarian Airlines, 10 Vigo St, London W1X 1AJ (☎0171/439 0577).

TAROM, 27 New Cavendish St, London W1M 7RL (☎0171/224 3693).

DISCOUNT FLIGHT AGENTS

ACE Travel, Phoenix House, Desborough Park Rd, High Wycombe, Bucks HP12 3BQ (☎01494/463324 or 463324). *Romanian flight specialist with an office in Bucharest arranging accommodation, car rental and internal travel. Winter charter flights.*

Campus Travel, 52 Grosvenor Gardens, London SW1W 0AG (☎0171/730 3402); 541 Bristol Rd, Selly Oak, Birmingham B29 GAU (☎0121/414 1848); 39 Queen's Rd, Clifton, Bristol BS8 1QE (☎0117/929 2494); 5 Emmanuel St, Cambridge CB1 1NE(☎01223/324283); 53 Forest Rd, Edinburgh EH1 2QP (☎0131/225 6111); 166 Deansgate, Manchester M3 3FE (☎0161/833 2046); 13 High St, Oxford OX1 1DD (☎01865/242067); *Student/youth travel specialists, with branches also in YHA shops and on university campuses all over Britain.*

Council Travel, 28a Poland St, London W1V 3DB (☎0171/437 7767). *Flights and student discounts.*

East Coast Travel, 283 Archway Rd, London N6 5AA (☎0181/348 2000). *Major Romanian flight specialist (see also "Packages and Tours").*

Friendly Travel, Research House, Fraser Rd, Perivale, Mddx UB6 7AQ (☎0181/566 9040). *TAROM agent offering the very latest flight deals including charters when available.*

Intra, 44 Maple St, London W1P 5GD (☎0171/323 3305). *Specialist flight agents for Eastern Europe, also offering fly/drive deals.*

Nouvelles Frontières, 11 Blenheim St, London W1Y 9LE (☎0171/629 7772). *Long-established discount flight agent.*

Romania Travel Centre, Clayfield Mews, Newcomen Rd, Tunbridge Wells, Kent TN4 9PA (☎01892/516901). *Romanian flight agents also offering tailor-made accommodation deals.*

Russian-Romanian Travel, 13B Addison Crescent, London W14 8JR (☎0171/371 6367). *Discount flight agent for all of Eastern Europe.*

South Coast Student Travel, 61 Ditchling Rd, Brighton BN1 4SD (☎01273/570226). *Student experts but plenty to offer non-students as well.*

STA Travel, 74 Old Brompton Rd, London SW7 3LH (☎0171/581 4132); and personal callers at 117 Euston Rd, London NW1; 25 Queen's Rd, Bristol BS8 1QE (☎0117/929 4399); 38 Sidney St, Cambridge CB2 3HX (☎01223/66966); 75 Deansgate, Manchester M3 2BW (☎0161/834 0668); 28 Vicar Lane, Leeds LS1 7JH (☎0113/244 9212); 36 George St, Oxford OX1 2OJ (☎01865/792800); and at the universities of Birmingham, London, Kent and Loughborough. *Discount fares, with good deals for students and young people.*

Trailfinders, 42–48 Earls Court Rd, London W8 (☎0171/938 3366); 194 Kensington High St, London W8 (☎0171/938 3939); 58 Deansgate, Manchester M3 2FF (☎0161/839 6969). *One of the best informed and most efficient agents.*

PACKAGES AND ORGANIZED TOURS

The main advantages of **package deals** are cheap flights, free visas and assured lodgings and meals, but you have to accept that your itinerary will be planned for you and that you'll be screened from many Romanian realities. However, even if the idea of a package fills you with horror, many of the tours described below can be good spring-boards for independent travel, particularly during May and late September, when they're cheapest.

SKI PACKAGES

Almost all foreigners ski at **Poiana Braşov** (see p.127), 150km north of Bucharest, where there is little for advanced skiers, but facilities for beginners are good, with around a hundred English-speaking instructors. Prices are very reasonable, with one-week packages costing between £205 and £369 half-board. Local specialists *Balkan Holidays* are more expensive than the mass-market operators, costing between £241 and

£423. *Crystal* and *East Coast Travel* are the only British companies to offer skiing in **Sinaia** (see p.115), charging £229–329 for a week's half-board at the excellent *Caraiman* or *Palace* hotels.

Flights are from London Gatwick or Manchester (£17 supplement); the bus transfer from Otopeni to Poiana Braşov takes three and a half hours. From here excursions are available to Braşov and "Dracula's Castle" at Bran.

BEACHES, MOUNTAINS AND CYCLING

At least six British tour operators offer **beach holidays** at Mamaia, Neptun and Olimp. *East Coast Travel* manages to undercut the rest with seven nights' bed and breakfast for £175 –311; for half-board try *Balkan Holidays* and for all meals and a superior hotel, *Sunworld*. It's hard to see the point of combining Olimp with Golden

Sands in Bulgaria, but *Balkan* and *Sunworld* both offer this package (£230–421). Fourteen-night **Two Centre Holidays**, equally divided between Mamaia and Poiana Braşov, are more appealing, costing between £325 and 485. *East Coast Travel* also offers a variant of this, with a week at Neptun, three nights at Poiana Braşov and three in Tulcea (for the Danube Delta), for £394–499.

Seven-night holidays in the **Carpathian mountains**, based at Sinaia or Poiana Braşov, are offered by *Balkan Holidays* (£220–362), *East Coast Travel* (£229–350), *Enterprise* (£265–345) and *Sunworld* (£289–355). To really see the Carpathians, you might look to one of the **hiking companies**, such as *Exodus* (15 days for £580), *Footprint Adventures* (15 days from £454 without flights), *High Places* (13 days for £740) and *Sherpa* (15 days for £627–670). *High Places*

SPECIALIST TOUR OPERATORS

Airtours, Wavell House, Holcombe Rd, Helmshore, Rossendale, Lancs BB4 4NB (☎01706/260000). *Skiing packages.*

Balkan Holidays, 19 Conduit St, London W1R 9TD (☎0171/491 4499). *Romanian specialist offering skiing, Black Sea resorts, Carpathians, Transylvania and city breaks.*

British Trust for Conservation Volunteers, 36 St Mary's St, Wallingford, Oxon OX10 0EU (☎01491/39766). *Projects in the Carpathians and the Danube Delta.*

Crystal, Crystal House, The Courtyard, Arlington Rd, Surbiton, Surrey KT6 6BW (☎0181/399 5144). *Skiing packages to both Poiana Braşov and Sinaia.*

Cyclists' Touring Club, Cotterell House, 69 Meadrow, Godalming, Surrey GU7 3HS (☎01483/417217). *Cycling trips for members.*

Discover the World, The Flatt Lodge, Bewcastle, Carlisle, Cumbria CA6 6PH (☎016977/48361). *Mountain wildlife tours.*

East Coast Travel, 283 Archway Rd, Highgate, London N6 5AA (☎0181/348 2000). *Offers one of the widest choices of package deals to Romania including skiing, city breaks, fly-drives, Transylvania, Bucovina and Danube Delta tours.*

Enterprise, Owners Abroad House, Peel Cross Rd, Salford, Manchester M5 2AN (☎0161/745 7000). *Carpathian mountains, Black Sea resort and ski packages.*

Exodus, 9 Weir Rd, London SW12 0LT (☎0181/675 5550). *Hiking holidays in the Carpathians.*

Explore, 1 Frederick St, Aldershot, Hants GU11 1LQ (☎01252/319 448). *Guided tours to Maramureş, the Delta and Bucovina including some hiking.*

Footprint Adventures, 5 Malham Drive, Lincoln LN6 0XD (☎01522/690852). *Walking in the Carpathians and Bucovina, and bird-watching in the Delta.*

High Places, The Globe Works, Penistone Rd, Sheffield S6 3AE (☎01142/757500). *Hiking in the Carpathians mountains.*

Inghams, 10–18 Putney Hill, London SW15 6AX (☎0181/785 7777). *Upmarket ski operator.*

Naturetrek, Chautara, Bighton, near Alresford, Hants SO24 9RB (☎01962/733051). *Wildlife-watching holidays in the Delta and Poiana Braşov.*

Neilson, 29–31 Elmfield Rd, Bromley BR1 1LT (☎01532/394555). *Ski packages.*

Peltours, Sovereign House, 11/19 Ballards Lane, Finchley, London N3 1UX (☎0181/346 9144). *Self-drive packages to Transylvania and Bucovina, and city breaks.*

Sherpa Expeditions, 131a Heston Rd, Hounslow, Mddx TW5 0RD (☎0181/577 2717). *Specializes in hiking tours of the Carpathians.*

Sunworld, 71 Houghside Rd, Pudsey LS28 9BR (☎01132/393020). *Large selection of packages to the Black Sea resorts, Transylvania and the Carpathian mountains.*

Waymark Holidays, 44 Windsor Rd, Slough SL1 2EJ (☎01753/516477). *Mountain walking tours.*

prices are relatively high, but include more meals and extras than the others. *Footprint* also offers a fortnight's walking between the Bucovina monasteries for £477 and a week's bird-watching in the Delta for £570 (both without flights).

The *Cyclists' Touring Club* runs **cycling holidays**, for members only although not necessarily every year. In addition **wildlife holidays** are available from *Naturetrek* (£990 for ten days in the Delta and Poiana Braşov) and by *Discover the World* (£940 for ten days, mainly spent tracking wolves in the mountains), while the *British Trust for Conservation Volunteers* organizes working conservation holidays in the mountains and the Delta.

TRANSYLVANIA AND DRACULA TOURS

Several companies offer two-week **Dracula Tours**, with visits to Bucharest, Snagov, Tîrgu Mureş, Braşov and Bran Castle coupled with a week at Mamaia. *Sunworld's* tour is cheapest (£283–321), but *Balkan Holidays* also include Sibiu on their itinerary, which is well worth the extra money (£353–475); the *East Coast Travel* version costs £429–479. *Explore* offers ten-day trips which rush through Maramureş, Bucovina and the Delta (with a few half-day hikes) from £375, plus a mere £120 for flights.

The Transylvanian *Society of Dracula*, which takes a suitably ironic approach to Gothic horror, organizes more genuine **Dracula tours** – contact them at B-dul Primăverii 47, Bucharest (☎01/679.57.42), or through Bravo SA, Piaţa Unirii 1, Bucharest (☎01/614.58.03).

CITY BREAKS

City breaks are available to Bucharest, costing from £239 for two nights bed and breakfast with *Balkan Holidays*. *Peltours* and *East Coast Travel* charge this much for the flight and transfer element alone, adding from £30 per night for a twin room at the *Parc* to £92 at the *Intercontinental*.

FLY/DRIVES

Fly/drive deals vary greatly and you'll need to shop around to find something worthwhile: *East Coast Travel* offers a week's rental package for £211–£335 (£286–425 for two weeks) per person with two people sharing. This includes your air fare from London to Bucharest or Constanţa, so the car rental component can be as little as £20 each. *Intra* (see Airlines and Agents box) offers

two Transylvanian itineraries, one also taking in the Bucovina monasteries, for £765 each for two people. These include ten nights' accommodation, so are only a good deal if you would be staying in more expensive hotels anyway. See "Driving" p.26 for information on driving conditions in Romania.

See "Driving" p.26

BY TRAIN

Travelling **by train** from Britain to Romania takes around 47 hours and standard return fares are more expensive than discounted air tickets. However, with a regular ticket, stopovers are possible en route and with an ***InterRail*** pass you can take in Romania as part of a wider rail tour of Europe.

Trains depart from London's Victoria station, connecting with the Ramsgate–Ostend Jetfoil (or slower and cheaper boats from Dover) for the night train from Ostend to **Vienna**; a more costly alternative is the *Eurostar* service from London Waterloo through the Channel Tunnel. This allows you to leave London in the morning and reach **Munich** via Paris in time for the 11pm *Kalman Imre* to Bucharest. *Eurostar's* Discovery Special tickets which must be booked 14 days in advance currently cost £47.50 single to Paris; discounts on fares are now offered to *InterRail* pass holders. From Vienna there are two main choices, the *Dacia*, stopping at Sighişoara and Braşov, reaching Bucharest in early afternoon, and the *Pannonia* (originating from Prague, with carriages from Munich and Vienna on the *Kalman Imre*) which stops at Sighişoara and Braşov in the early evening, reaching Bucharest at 11pm.

TICKETS AND PASSES

A **standard return ticket** from London to Bucharest costs £365 and is valid for two months. If you're under 26 you can get a discounted *BIJ* (*Billet International Jeunesse*) ticket from *Eurotrain* or *Wasteels*, for £323, also valid for two months, which allows you to stop off along a predetermined route.

For under-26s, the most flexible way of getting from London to Romania is with an ***InterRail*** **pass**, allowing the holder free travel on most European rail lines, including Romania's. A zonal system operates, allowing you to pay only £179 for fifteen days' travel in Eastern Europe alone, or £229 for a month's travel from the Channel ports to Eastern Europe, excluding the Mediterranean

RAIL TICKET OFFICES

International Rail Centre, Victoria Station, London SW1 (☎0171/834 2345)

Eurostar, EPS House, Waterloo Station, London SE1 8SE (reservations ☎01233/617575)

Eurotrain, 52 Grosvenor Gardens, London SW1 (☎0171/730 3402)

Wasteels, Victoria Station, London SW1 (☎0171/834 7066)

BUS TICKET OFFICE

National Express Eurolines ☎0171/730 0202

and Scandinavian countries, or a maximum of £249 for a month's travel across all seven zones.

Travellers aged 26 or over can buy a more limited *InterRail 26+* ticket for £209 for fifteen days, or £269 for a month; this only covers twenty countries from the Netherlands eastwards to Turkey, although add-on tickets are available from London via Belgium.

If you're making your way to Romania **via other European cities**, you'll find that rail ticket prices drop dramatically once you're inside the Eastern bloc. From Budapest, nine services run to Romania, although only the *Pannonia*, *Balt-Orient*, *Ovidius* and *Dacia* make it all the way to Bucharest. A Budapest–Bucharest return will cost you less than £40. Other trains from Budapest run to Oradea, Tîrgu Mureş and Braşov (via the Székely Land), and to Baia Mare by a minor border crossing from Debrecen to Valea lui Mihai, for Maramureş. The *Balt-Orient* (from Berlin and Prague) passes through Transylvania in the early hours, arriving in Bucharest at 6am, and the *Ovidius* runs via Craiova, reaching Bucharest at 9.30am and Constanţa soon after noon. The *Carpaţi* travels from Warsaw via Kraków (Poland), Kosice (Slovakia) and Szolnok (Hungary) to Arad, Sibiu and Bucharest, arriving at noon.

BY BUS

There is no direct **bus service** from Britain to Romania. You can get as far as **Budapest** with *Eurolines* and then pick up a train (see above) or another bus service. The London–Budapest service departs three times a week, takes 30 hours and costs £119 return. Onward services to Transylvania are run by the Hungarian state bus company *Volán*, and by a growing number of

private operators. Return fares from Budapest range from £14 to Timişoara to £32 to Braşov.

Tickets can be booked at Népstadion station, or at *Volán* offices at Erzébet tér 1051 and Teréz korut 38, and at *Cooptourist* and IBUSZ offices. Buy your **visa** in advance of travelling, and beware that buses are more likely than trains to bear the brunt of rigorous searches and other demonstrations of official Romanian displeasure whenever tension is high.

BY CAR

Driving to Romania is really only worth considering if you have at least a month to spare, are going to Romania for an extended period, or want to take advantage of various stopovers en route.

It's important to plan ahead. The **AA** (☎01256/20123) and **RAC** (☎0345/333222) provide a comprehensive service offering general advice on all facets of driving to Romania and the names and addresses of useful contact organizations. Their European route-planning services can arrange a detailed print out of the most appropriate route to follow. Driving licence, vehicle registration documents and insurance are essential; a green card is recommended.

The best **route** is through France and Germany, Austria and Hungary, passing Frankfurt, Nürnberg, Regensburg, Linz, Vienna and Budapest, and then taking the E60 down to the Borş frontier-crossing near Oradea or the E75/E68 to Nădlac near Arad. Both **border crossings** are open 24 hours a day; most trucks use the southern route via Arad, so the surface of the Oradea–Cluj road is in better condition, and it's more scenic. With the closure of former Yugoslavia the crossing points are now very busy with trucks for Bulgaria and Turkey. There are lesser crossing points, particularly from northern Hungary towards Satu Mare, but these are less accustomed to anything but locals.

CROSSING THE CHANNEL

Most travellers use the **ferry** and **hovercraft** links between Dover and Folkestone to Calais or Boulogne, and between Ramsgate and Dunkerque. Ferry prices vary according to the time of year and, for motorists, on the size of your car. The Dover–Calais/Boulogne service, for example, starts at about £180 return low season, £220 return high season for a car with up to five passengers.

The alternative cross-Channel option is **Le Shuttle** which operates trains 24 hours a day, 365 days a year carrying cars, motorcycles, buses and their passengers through the Channel Tunnel. The journey takes 35 minutes between Folkestone and Calais. At peak times, services operate every 15 minutes, which makes advance booking unnecessary; during the night, services still run hourly.

Return **fares** for May to August are £214–308 per vehicle (passengers included) depending on the time of day you want to travel, with discounts available during the low season.

> ### CROSS-CHANNEL TICKETS
>
> **Hoverspeed**, Dover (☎01304/240101); London (☎0181/554 7061). To Boulogne and Calais.
>
> **Le Shuttle**, Customer Services Centre (☎0990/353535). To Calais.
>
> **P&O European Ferries**, Dover (☎01304/203388); Portsmouth (☎01705/772244); London (☎0181/575 8555). To Calais.
>
> **Sally Line**, Ramsgate (☎01843/595522); London (☎0181/858 1127). To Dunkerque.
>
> **Stena Sealink Line**, Ashford (☎01233/647047). To Calais and Dieppe.

GETTING THERE FROM IRELAND

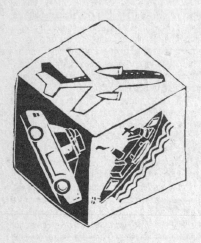

Balkantours are your best bet for **discounted tickets** (with *TAROM* via London). They also offer one-week ski packages from Belfast to Poiana Braşov for £259 and during the winter can offer flight-only charter tickets for £199. In summer, they offer a two-centre package deal flying to Varna in Bulgaria with a week in

There are no direct flights from Ireland to Romania, but both *Aer Lingus* and *British Airways* operate year-round services via other European cities.

Aer Lingus offers **scheduled flights** out of **Dublin** via Amsterdam, Brussels or London Heathrow to Bucharest for IR£608. *British Airways'* Dublin service connects with their direct Gatwick–Bucharest flight for the same fare (although buying your ticket as separate Dublin–London and London–Bucharest tickets will save you money). From **Belfast**, *British Airways* flies daily to London Heathrow with a connection via *TAROM* to Bucharest for £466 return.

> ### USEFUL ADDRESSES IN IRELAND
> #### Airlines
>
> **Aer Lingus**, 42 Grafton St, Dublin; 46 Castle St, Belfast; 2 Academy St, Cork (all enquiries ☎01232/245151 charged at local rate).
>
> **British Airways**, 60 Dawson St, Dublin (☎800/626747); Belfast (☎0345/222111).
>
> #### Agents and operators
>
> **Balkantours**, 37 Ann St, Belfast BT1 4EB (☎01232/246795); 5–6 South Great George's St, Dublin 2 (☎01679 4415).
>
> **Joe Walsh Tours**, 8–11 Baggot St, Dublin (☎01/676 3053). *General budget fares agent.*
>
> **Thomas Cook**, 118 Grafton St, Dublin (☎01/677 1721); 11 Donegall Place, Belfast (☎01232/240833). *Package holiday and flight agent, with occasional discount offers.*
>
> **USIT**, O'Connell Bridge, 19–21 Aston Quay, Dublin 2 (☎01/778 1177); 10–11 Market Parade, Cork (☎021/270900); 31a Queen St, Belfast (☎01232/242562). *Student and youth specialist for flights and trains.*

Bulgaria and a week in Neptun in Romania starting from £319. **Students** and anyone under the age of 31, should contact *USIT*, which generally has the best discount deals on flights and train tickets. For *InterRail* details see "Getting There from Britain" (p.6).

GETTING THERE FROM NORTH AMERICA

TAROM is the only airline offering direct flights to Romania from North America, but only from New York and Chicago. Using a European carrier to get to Europe is probably your best bet as you get a good choice of departure cities, reliable and comfortable service, and direct flights to London, Paris or Frankfurt with connections to Romania. All the American airlines use European carriers for the final leg of their services to Romania.

Eurail train passes are not valid in Romania itself, but North Americans are eligible to purchase five-day **rail passes** for travel within Romania, available in advance before you travel or at any major Romanian train station – for more details of these see "Getting Around" p.22.

SHOPPING FOR TICKETS

Barring special offers, the cheapest fare is usually an **Apex** ticket, although this will carry certain restrictions: you have to book – and pay – at least 21 days before departure, spend at least seven days abroad (maximum stay three months), and you tend to get penalized if you change your schedule. There are also winter **Super Apex** tickets, sometimes known as "Eurosavers" – slightly cheaper than an ordinary Apex, but limiting your stay to between 7 and 21 days. Some airlines also issue **Special Apex** tickets to people younger than 24, often extending the

AIRLINES

Air Canada in Canada, call directory inquiries, ☎1-800/555-1212, for local toll-free number; US toll-free number is ☎1-800/776-3000. *Flights to London, Frankfurt, Paris and Amsterdam for connections to Bucharest.*

Air France ☎1-800/237-2747; in Canada, ☎1-800/667-2747. *New York, Newark, Miami, Houston, Chicago, Los Angeles and San Francisco to Paris with connections to Bucharest.*

British Airways in US, ☎1-800/247-9297; in Canada ☎1-800/668-1059. *Most major US and Canadian cities to Bucharest via London.*

CSA Czechoslovak Airlines ☎1-800/223-2365. *Flights out of New York to Bucharest via Prague.*

Delta Airlines ☎1-800/241-4141; in Canada, call directory inquiries, ☎1-800/555-1212, for local

toll-free number. *New York to Frankfurt with connections to Bucharest .*

LOT Polish Airlines ☎1-800/223-0593; in Canada, ☎1-800/361-1017. *New York and Chicago to Bucharest via Warsaw.*

Lufthansa ☎1-800/645-3880; in Canada, ☎1-800/563-5954. *Flies from New York, Chicago and Toronto to Frankfurt with connections to Bucharest.*

Malev Hungarian Airlines ☎1-800/223-6884. *New York to Budapest, with connecting flights to Bucharest.*

TAROM ☎212/687-6013. *Twice a week from New York and Chicago direct to Bucharest.*

United Airlines ☎1-800/538-2929. *New York to Bucharest via London.*

DISCOUNT AGENTS, CONSOLIDATORS AND TRAVEL CLUBS

Council Travel, Head Office: 205 E 42nd St, New York, NY 10017 (☎1-800/743-1823). *Nationwide student travel organization with branches in San Francisco, Washington DC, Boston, Austin, Seattle, Chicago and Minneapolis.*

Discount Travel International, Ives Bldg, 114 Forrest Ave, Suite 205, Narberth, PA 19072 (☎1-800/334-9294). *Discount travel club.*

Encore Travel Club, 4501 Forbes Blvd, Lanham, MD 20706 (☎1-800/444-9800). *Discount travel club.*

Interworld Travel, 800 Douglass Rd, Miami, FL 33134 (☎305/443-4929). *Consolidator.*

Last Minute Travel Club, 132 Brookline Ave, Boston, MA 02215 (☎1-800/LAST MIN). *Travel club specializing in standby deals.*

Moment's Notice, 425 Madison Ave, New York, NY 10017 (☎212/486-0503). *Discount travel club.*

New Frontiers/Nouvelles Frontières, Head offices: 12 E 33rd St, New York, NY 10016 (☎1-800/366-6387); 1001 Sherbrook East, Suite 720, Montréal, PQH2L 1L3 (☎514/526-8444). *French discount travel firm. Other branches in LA, San Francisco and Québec City.*

STA Travel, Head office: 48 East 11th St, New York, NY 10003 (☎1-800/777-0112; nationwide).

Worldwide specialist in independent travel with branches in the Los Angeles, San Francisco and Boston areas.

TFI Tours International, Head office: 34 W 32nd St, New York, NY 10001 (☎1-800/745-8000). *Consolidator; other offices in Las Vegas, San Francisco, Los Angeles.*

Travac, Head office: 989 6th Ave, New York NY 10018 (☎1-800/872-8800). *Consolidator and charter broker; another branch in Orlando.*

Travel Avenue, 10 S Riverside, Suite 1404, Chicago, IL 60606 (☎1-800/333-3335). *Discount travel agent.*

Travel Cuts, Head office: 187 College St, Toronto, ON M5T 1P7 (☎416/979-2406). *Canadian student travel organization with branches all over the country.*

Travelers Advantage, 3033 S Parker Rd, Suite 900, Aurora, CO 80014 (☎1-800/548-1116). *Discount travel club.*

UniTravel, 1177 N Warson Rd, St Louis, MO 63132 (☎1-800/325-2222). *Consolidator.*

Worldwide Discount Travel Club, 1674 Meridian Ave, Miami Beach, FL 33139 (☎305/534-2082). *Discount travel club.*

maximum stay to a year. Many airlines offer youth or student fares to **under-25s**; a passport or driving licence is sufficient proof of age, though these tickets are subject to availability and can have eccentric booking conditions. It's worth remembering that most cheap return fares involve spending at least one Saturday night away and that many will only give a percentage refund if you need to cancel or alter your journey, so make sure you check the restrictions carefully before buying a ticket.

You can normally cut costs further by going through a **specialist flight agent** – either a **consolidator**, who buys up blocks of tickets from the airlines and sells them at a discount, or a **discount agent**, who wheels and deals in blocks of tickets offloaded by the airlines, and often offers special student and youth fares and a range of other travel-related services such as travel insurance, rail passes, car rentals, tours and the like. Bear in mind, though, that penalties for changing your plans can be stiff. Remember, too, that these companies make their money by

dealing in bulk – don't expect them to answer lots of questions. Some agents specialize in **charter flights**, which may be cheaper than anything available on a scheduled flight, but again departure dates are fixed and withdrawal penalties are high (check the refund policy). If you travel a lot, **discount travel clubs** are another option – the annual membership fee may be worth it for benefits such as cut-price air tickets and car rental.

Regardless of where you buy your ticket, the **fare** will depend on the season. Fares to Europe are highest from around early June to mid-September, when the weather is best; they drop during the "shoulder" seasons (mid-September to November and mid-April to early June) and you'll get the best prices during the low season, November through April (excluding Christmas and New Year when prices are hiked up and seats are at a premium). Note also that flying on weekends ordinarily adds $20–60 to the round-trip fare; the prices quoted below assume midweek travel and are exclusive of taxes.

FLIGHTS FROM THE US

Although the major European carriers offer a good choice of departure points in the US, **New York JFK** is the primary gateway. *TAROM*, offering the only direct service to Bucharest, flies out of New York for $463 low season ($563 high season). *United's* low season fare via London is $638 (high season $838). *British Airways* and *Lufthansa* offer the same low season fare but rise to $898 in summer. *CSA* is always worth trying for competitive rates, currently $598 low season ($858 high season). *Malev Hungarian Airlines* charges the same fare to Budapest, which is just 5 hours and $15 from Oradea by train. Onward flights from Budapest to Bucharest are $258.

From **Chicago** expect to pay around $578 low season ($968 high season) on *TAROM*, and $968 low season ($1028 high season) on the major European carriers. *LOT* is a good bargain possibility with a low season fare of $752 ($952 high season). Flying from the West Coast, *British Airways* and *Air France* fly out of **Los Angeles** for $858 low season ($1118 high season) via London and Paris respectively.

FLIGHTS FROM CANADA

As **Air Canada** has so many gateways in Canada, it's always worth checking into fares to London, Frankfurt, Paris or Amsterdam, and then picking up a European carrier to get you to Bucharest. Otherwise, *British Airways* and *Lufthansa* are the most frequent offering good direct flights to London and Frankfurt from several departure cities, with easy, short-layover connections to Bucharest.

Lufthansa flies out of **Toronto** to Bucharest via Frankfurt for CDN$1248 low season (CDN$1418 high season). *British Airways* serves Toronto, Vancouver and **Montréal**, with a Montréal–Bucharest fare via London of CDN$1248 low season (CDN$1388 high season).

PACKAGES AND ORGANIZED TOURS

Package tours may not sound like your kind of travel, but don't dismiss the idea out of hand. If your trip is geared around special interests, packages can avoid a lot of the hassles you might incur making the same arrangements on arrival in Romania. A package can also be great for your peace of mind, if only to ensure a worry-free first week while you're finding your feet on a longer tour.

City breaks to Bucharest start at $299 (not including air fare) – *Littoral Tours'* package includes three nights' accommodation in a five-star hotel, sightseeing, transfers and hotel taxes. They also offer **spa packages** to resorts such as Bucharest's *Flora* hotel, Black Sea resorts, the Felix Spa and Covasna Spa. Prices start at $1195 for round-trip air, hotel accommodation, all meals, complete medical examination and various treatments. The self-proclaimed health resort specialist is *Health Tours International* which offers the "original guaranteed Gerovital H3 and Aslavital treatment" at the deluxe *Cure Flora* hotel.

There are plenty of **Transylvania** tours on offer including *Littoral Tours'* "Weekend in Transylvania", a four-day/three-night private escorted tour covering Poiana Braşov, Bran Castle and Peleş Castle, with first-class accommodation and a car and English-speaking driver for $399 (not including air). Most of the other packages are **Dracula**-related, visiting places popularized in Bram Stoker's book. *Littoral Tours* has an

eight-day "Halloween Special" including round-trip air fares, all meals, costume party and bus tours starting at $1399, while *Eastern Europe Tours* offers a more personalized version with private car and driver starting from $1779.

GETTING THERE FROM AUSTRALIA & NEW ZEALAND

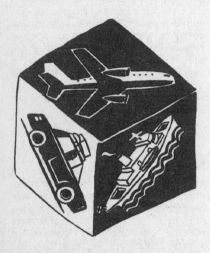

From Australia and New Zealand, there are reasonably direct services to Bucharest via Bangkok, Moscow, Rome and Singapore. The national airline, *TAROM*, has an agent in Australia only – the *Eastern Europe Travel Bureau* (see box for details).

Another option is to fly to any other European city such as Frankfurt or Vienna and travel over-land to Romania. All destinations in Europe are "common rated" – you pay the same fare what-ever your destination – so this option rarely works out cheaper than buying a discounted airfare all the way, but can be a good idea if you are visiting Romania as part of a longer trip around Europe. *Eurail* passes can be used for overland travel to countries bordering Romania but not within the country itself.

Similarly, **Round the World** tickets which take in Europe don't include Bucharest, so if you want to visit Romania on your itinerary you will have to consider an add-on fare with your main

ticket, find a cheap flight from a European discounter or travel overland.

Whatever kind of ticket you're after, first call should be to one of the **specialist travel agents** listed in the box. If you're a **student or under 26**, you should be able to undercut the fares quoted below; *STA* is a good place to start.

Each airline has its own fare structuring, though high season is usually mid-November to mid-January, shoulder March to September and low season mid-January to March and September to mid-November.

FROM AUSTRALIA

TAROM flies twice weekly to Bucharest using *Qantas* or *Thai* for the first leg to Bangkok for A$1900 low season (A$2025 high season) from all state capitals; *Aeroflot* flies to Bucharest via Moscow (A$1600/1900), also twice weekly from all state capitals; and *Alitalia* flies via Rome for A$2409/3129 from eastern Australia, A$2150/2792 from Perth.

If you're planning to travel overland via another European city, the best deals are with *Aeroflot* (as above), *Garuda* via Jakarta (A$1759/1979) and *Malaysian Air* via Kuala Lumpur (A$1814/2505).

FROM NEW ZEALAND

From **New Zealand**, *Alitalia* flies to Bucharest via Rome from NZ$2499. There's also a *Qantas–Lufthansa* combination via Singapore starting at NZ$2600. You'll get good-value flights to a range of other European destinations with *Japanese Airlines* (overnighting in Tokyo) and *Garuda*, start-ing from around NZ$2095; *Thai* from NZ$2200 and *Malaysian* from NZ$2400.

All flights, except *Qantas*, leave only from Auckland so you'll need to add on around NZ$90 for Christchurch connections.

AIRLINES

Aeroflot, 388 George St, Sydney (☎02/233 7911). No NZ office.

Air New Zealand, 5 Elizabeth St, Sydney (☎02/223 4666); cnr Customs and Queen streets, Auckland (☎09/366 2424).

Alitalia, Orient Overseas Building, 32 Bridge St, Sydney (☎02/247 7836); Floor 6, Trust Bank Building, 229 Queen St, Auckland (☎09/379 4457).

British Airways, 64 Castlereagh St, Sydney (☎02/258 3300); Dilworth Building, cnr Queen and Customs streets, Auckland (☎09/367 7500).

Garuda, 175 Clarence St, Sydney (☎02/334 9900); 120 Albert St, Auckland (☎09/366 1855).

Japanese Airlines, 17 Bligh St, Sydney (☎02/233 4500). No NZ office.

Lufthansa/Air Lauda, 143 Macquarie St, Sydney (☎02/367 3800); 109 Queen St, Auckland (☎09/303 1529).

MAS, 388 George St, Sydney (☎02/231 5066 or ☎008/269 998); Floor 12, Swanson Centre, 12–26 Swanson St, Auckland (☎09/373 2741).

Qantas, International Square, Jamison St, Sydney (☎02/957 0111 or 236 3636); Qantas House, 154 Queen St, Auckland (☎09/303 2506).

TAROM, c/o *Eastern Europe Travel Bureau* see below.

Thai, 75 –77 Pitt St, Sydney (☎02/844 0999; or 1800 9844 from July 1996; 008 221 320); Kensington Swan Building, 22 Fanshawe St, Auckland (☎09/377 3886).

SPECIALIST AND DISCOUNT AGENTS

Accent on Travel, 545 Queen St, Brisbane (☎07/3832 1777).

Adventure World, 73 Walker St, North Sydney (☎02/956 7766); 8 Victoria Ave, Perth (☎09/221 2300).

Anywhere Travel, 345 Anzac Parade, Kingsford, Sydney (☎02/663 0411).

Brisbane Discount Travel, 360 Queen St, Brisbane (☎07/3229 9211).

Budget Travel, PO Box 505, Auckland (☎09/309 4313).

Discount Travel Specialists, Shop 53, Forrest Chase, Perth (☎09/221 1400).

Eastern Europe Travel Bureau, 75 King St, Sydney (☎02/262 1144); 343 Little Collins St, Melbourne (☎03/9600 0299); 131 Elizabeth St, Brisbane (☎07/3229 9716).

Flight Centres, *Australia*: Circular Quay, Sydney (☎02/241 2422); Bourke St, Melbourne (☎03/9650 2899); plus other branches nationwide. *New*

Zealand: National Bank Towers, 205 –225 Queen St, Auckland (☎09/309 6171); Shop 1M, National Mutual Arcade, 152 Hereford St, Christchurch (☎09/379 7145); 50 –52 Willis St, Wellington (☎04/472 8101); other branches countrywide.

Gateway Travel, 48 The Boulevard, Strathfield, Sydney (☎02/745 3333).

Russia and Eastern Europe Travel, Floor 1, Room 8, 2 Hindmarsh Square, Adelaide (☎08/232 1228; ☎ 08/82332 1228 from Aug 1996).

STA Travel, *Australia*: 732 Harris St, Ultimo, Sydney (☎02/212 1255 or 281 9866); 256 Flinders St, Melbourne (☎03/9347 4711); other offices in Townsville, Cairns and state capitals. *New Zealand*: Traveller's Centre, 10 High St, Auckland (☎09/309 0458); 233 Cuba St, Wellington (☎04/385 0561); 223 High St, Christchurch (☎03/379 9098); other offices in Dunedin, Palmerston North and Hamilton.

Passport Travel, 320b Glenferrie Rd, Malvern, Melbourne (☎03/9824 7183).

From July 1996, all Sydney 7-digit numbers beginning with 2 will have 9 prefixed to them to make 8-digit numbers.

VISAS AND RED TAPE

You'll need a full passport to enter Romania, plus a visa unless you're a citizen of one of the formerly socialist states or a very few other countries such as Austria, Cyprus, Mexico, Tunisia or Turkey. British citizens must use a full ten-year passport. Visas are included in package holiday costs and issued gratis on arrival, but everyone else must pay for them either on arrival or in advance from a Romanian consulate.

A tourist visa issued on entry will cost US$33/£50, while in theory a visa issued in advance at a consulate or embassy costs US$25/£38, although in practice they are often the same price. A tourist visa is valid for a thirty-day stay, within three months of the date of issue. Transit visas (valid for three days' stay, within one month of issue) are also available and cost US$21/£32 at the border, usually more in advance.

Overstaying is an offence generally solved by means of a "tip" to the (notoriously corrupt) border police, but it is preferable to obtain a **visa extension** from any *judeţ* (county) police headquarters or the seedy, unmarked office on the first floor of Str. Nicolae Iorga 27 in Bucharest (Mon, Wed & Fri 9.30am–1pm; Tues 5.30pm–10pm; Thurs 9.30am–2pm & 5.30–8pm; Sat 9.30am–1pm). In Bucharest, you'll be sent to the *CEC* bank on Piaţa Amzei, to pay your fee (another $25 plus $6 for "urgent" service, in lei with a bank receipt for hard currency) and return with the receipt to Strada Iorga; here they may tell you to return in a day or two, although there is no reason for this and a few dollars will speed things up.

ROMANIAN EMBASSIES AND CONSULATES ABROAD

Britain 4 Palace Green, London W8 4QD (☎0171/937 9667).

Australia 333 Old South Head Rd, Bondi, Sydney, NSW (☎02/30 5718).

Austria Prinz-Eugen-Strasse 60, 1040 Vienna (☎1/505 3227)

Belgium 105 Rue Gabrielle, 1180 Brussels (☎2/345 2680).

Bulgaria Sitnyakovo 4, Sofia (☎2/707 047).

Canada 655 Rideau St, Ottawa, ON K1N 6A3 (☎613/232 5345); 111 Peter St, Suite 530, Toronto, ON M5V 2H1 (☎416/585 5802); 1111 St Urbain, Suite M-01, Montréal, PQ H2Z 1Y6 (☎514/876 1793).

Denmark Strandagervej 27, 2900 Hellerup (☎39/407 177).

France 5 Rue de l'Exposition, 75007 Paris (☎1/4062 2202).

Germany Legionsweg 14, 5300 Bonn 1 (☎228/555 860).

Hungary Thököly út. 72, 1146 Budapest (☎1/268 0271).

Ireland see Britain

Republica Moldova Vlaicu Pîrcălah 39, Chişinau (☎3732/ 227 583).

Netherlands Catsheuvel 55, 2517 KA Den Haag (☎070/354 3796).

Slovakia Frana Král' a 11, 811 05 Bratislava (☎07/491 665 or 493 562).

Sweden Östermalmsgt. 36, POB 26043, 11426 Stockholm (☎8/108 603).

Ukraine vul. Kotsyubinskoho 8, 252030 Kiev (☎044/224 5261).

USA 1607 23rd Street NW, Washington DC 20008 (☎202/332 4848 or 332 4747); 200 East 38th St, New York, NY 10016 (☎212/682 9122).

CUSTOMS

Romanian customs don't generally search tourists' luggage very closely, but they do have some byzantine **regulations**. Books in Hungarian are sometimes confiscated; Scotch whisky, Kent cigarettes and coffee are commonly used to bribe officials, but be wary of being too obvious. You can import reasonable quantities of food, clothing and medication (including contraceptives) for personal use, two cameras and one video camera, with film. If the details of your camera get written in your passport, you will have to produce it (or a police theft report) when you leave. The import or export of lei is forbidden,

and pointless, as you can't use or exchange it abroad.

On **departure**, you can again carry enough food and medicine for a 24-hour journey, and souvenirs purchased in hard currency or up to a value of L1000. These regulations are usually disregarded, and carpets and other valuable souvenirs can be removed, as long as they don't appear to be antiques. However, there are reports of travellers having to pay token fees to take their carpets out; this is not exactly legal and should be haggled downwards as far as possible. With the closure of Serbia, drug-runners from Turkey and Asia now often pass through Romania, and checks are being tightened up.

INSURANCE

Most people will find it essential to take out a good travel insurance policy. Bank and credit cards (particularly *American Express*) often give certain levels of medical or other insurance to their customers, and travel insurance may also be included if you use a major credit or charge card to pay for your trip. This can be quite comprehensive, anticipating anything from lost or stolen baggage and missed connections to charter companies going bankrupt; however certain policies (notably in North America) only cover medical costs.

If you plan to participate in **water sports** or do some **hiking**, you'll probably have to pay an

extra premium; check carefully that any insurance policy you are considering will cover you in case of an accident. Note also that very few insurers will arrange on-the-spot payments in the event of a major expense or loss; you will usually be reimbursed only after going home.

In all cases of loss or theft of goods, you will have to contact the local police to have a **report** made out so that your insurer can process the claim. This can be a tricky business in Romania since many officials outside the big cities may not be accustomed to the process, and making yourself understood can be a problem, but be persistent.

EUROPEAN COVER

In Britain and Ireland, travel insurance schemes (from around £23 a month) are sold by almost every travel agent or bank, and by specialist insurance firms. Policies issued by *Campus Travel* (see p.4 for address), *Endsleigh Insurance* (97–107 Southampton Row, London WC1; ☎0171/436 4451), *Snowcard Insurance Services* (Freepost 4135, Lower Boddington, Daventry, Northants NN11 6BR (☎01327/62805), *Frizzell Insurance* (Frizzell House, County Gates, Bournemouth, Dorset BH1 2NF; ☎01202/292 333) or *Columbus Travel Insurance* (17 Devonshire Square, London EC2; ☎0171/375 0011) are all good value.

NORTH AMERICAN COVER

In the US and Canada, insurance tends to be much more expensive, and may include medical cover only. Before buying a policy, check that you're not already covered by existing insurance plans. **Canadians** are usually covered by their provincial health plans; **students** and other holders of ISIC/teacher/youth cards are entitled to $3000 worth of accident coverage and sixty days ($100 per day) of in-patient hospital treatment for the card's period of validity. Student health coverage often extends during the vacations and for one term beyond the date of last enrolment. **Household** insurance often covers theft or loss of documents, money and valuables while overseas, though conditions and maximum amounts vary from company to company.

Only after exhausting the possibilities above might you want to contact a **specialist travel insurance company**; your travel agent can usually recommend one. *Isis* (through travel agencies) charges $50 for fifteen days, $80 for a month, $150 for three months. Two companies also worth trying are *Access America*, 6600 West Broad St, Richmond, VA 23230 (☎1-800/955-4002 or 804/285-2300), and *Travel Guard*, 1145 Clark St, Stevens Point, WI 54481 (☎1-800/826-1300 or 715/345-0505). Frequent travellers get a good deal from *Travel Assistance International* (☎1-800/821-2828), which charges $200 for a whole year's coverage (90 days maximum per trip).

None of these policies insure against **theft** of anything while overseas. North American travel policies apply only to items **lost** from, or **damaged** in, the custody of an identifiable, responsible third party – hotel porter, airline, luggage consignment, etc.

AUSTRALASIAN COVER

As in Europe, travel insurance policies are widely available through your travel agent. One of the most popular is the Cover-More "Essentials" policy offered by *CIC Insurance*. Ask your travel agent or phone head office in Sydney direct on ☎02/202-8000. As with all policies, make sure that you are covered for any sporting or outdoor activities you might be planning.

TRAVELLERS WITH DISABILITIES

Very little attention has been paid to the needs of the disabled in Romania, as in the rest of Eastern Europe. There is little sign of any major change in attitudes, and not much money to do a lot anyway. Perhaps the best solution is to book a stay in a spa (see p.19), where there should at least be a degree of level access and some awareness of the needs of those in wheelchairs.

Transport is a major problem, as public transport is almost inaccessible and cars with hand controls are not available from the car rental companies. However, it should be possible to reach Arad, Alba Iulia, Sighişoara, Braşov, Sinaia and Bucharest relatively easily by rail, reserving a place in Austrian carriages, for instance on the *Dacia* (see p.7).

As with any trip abroad, read your **travel insurance** small print carefully to make sure that people with a pre-existing medical condition are not excluded. Use your travel agent or tour operator to make your journey simpler: **airlines** or bus companies can cope better if they are expecting you. A **medical certificate** of your fitness to travel, provided by your doctor, is also extremely useful; some airlines or insurance companies may insist on it. Make sure you carry a **prescription** for any drugs you need, including the generic name in case of emergency, and spares of any special clothing or equipment as it's unlikely you'll find them in Romania.

CONTACTS
Britain
Holiday Care Service, 2 Old Bank Chambers, Station Rd, Horley, Surrey RH6 9HW (☎01293/774535). *Information on all aspects of travel.*

Mobility International, 228 Borough High St, London SE1 1JX (☎0171/403 5688). *Information, access guides, tours and exchange programmes.*

RADAR, 25 Mortimer St, London W1N 8AB (☎0171/250 3222). *Limited information on travel in Romania.*

CONTACTS (continued)

North America:

Information Center for People with Disabilities, Fort Point Place, 27–43 Wormwood St, Boston, MA 02210 (☎617/727-5540). *Clearing house for information, including travel.*

Jewish Rehabilitation Hospital, 3205 Place Alton Goldbloom, Montréal, PQ H7V 1R2 (☎514/688-9550, ext. 226). *Guidebooks and travel information.*

Kéroul, 4545 ave. Pierre de Coubertin, CP 1000 Station M, Montréal, PQ H1V 3R2 (☎512/252 3104). *Travel for mobility-impaired people.*

Mobility International USA, Box 10767, Eugene, OR 97440 (☎503/343-1284). *Information, access guides, tours and exchange programmes.*

Society for the Advancement of Travel for the Handicapped (SATH), 347 5th Avenue, New York, NY 10016 (☎212/447-7284). *Information on suitable tour operators and travel agents.*

Travel Information Service, Moss Rehabilitation Hospital, 1200 West Tabor Rd, Philadelphia, PA 19141 (☎215/456-9600). *Telephone information service and referral.*

Australia:

ACROD, PO Box 60, Curtin, ACT 2605 (☎06/682 4333).

Barrier Free Travel, 36 Wheatley St, North Bellingen, NSW 2454 (☎066/551-733).

New Zealand:

Disabled Persons Assembly, PO Box 10 –138, The Terrace, Wellington (☎04/472 2626).

COSTS, MONEY AND BANKS

Travellers will find costs low in Romania, and even when prices rise, the exchange rate soon tends to compensate. The more expensive hotels, flights, car rental and ONT excursions are priced in US dollars but must be paid for in lei, together with a receipt to show that the money has been exchanged officially. You may also need an exchange receipt to buy international train tickets, but not for internal tickets, food or any other purchase.

Travelling independently, a few **savings and reductions** are possible. *InterRail* passes are valid; **students** studying in Romania can claim a 30 percent discount on international rail and air fares, while *ISIC* and *IUS* student cards theoretically entitle you to a reduction of up to 50 percent on the price of camping, and free or reduced admission to museums. In practice the relevant officials may say no, and there's little you can do about it.

BASICS COSTS

Accommodation is likely to be your main expense, although the lowest-grade hotels charge from just $4 for a single room, $6 for a double (some hoteliers permit two people to share a single), although in first class or deluxe places you won't find any bargains. For rock-bottom budget travellers, the alternatives are cabanas ($3 per bed), or camping (around $3 per person; slightly less with a student card). Such accommodation is usually situated out of town, and can be awkward to reach by public transport.

The cost of eating out varies considerably, but you can get a **meal** with a glass of wine or beer for between $2 and $10 providing you avoid restaurants in first class or deluxe hotels, imported drinks (especially whisky) or such delicacies as caviar or sturgeon – and providing that there's a restaurant to be found. **Public transport** is cheap – it costs less than $4 to take an express train from one side of Romania to the other – but car rental involves various charges on top of the basic rate of $27 a day.

MONEY

Romania's **currency** is the leu (meaning lion; plural **lei**), which comes in coins of denominations up to 100 lei and notes up to 5000 lei (with a L10,000 note planned). Theoretically the leu is divided into 100 bani, but these fiddly little coins are no longer used and should be refused, as should any remaining L100 notes.

The exchange rate is currently around L3000 to the pound sterling (L2000 to the US dollar), and the rate seems to have stabilized at last. The leu is not an international currency, but if you want to check the current rate, the Thomas Cook European Timetable is a good place to look.

BANKS AND EXCHANGE

Changing money involves least hassle at the private exchange offices (*casa de schimb valutar*) in most towns, or at ONT offices and major hotels. Queueing and piles of documents are the norm in banks (*bancă*), and anyway they're usually only open for a few hours on weekday mornings, officially 9am–noon. Avoid the sharks hanging around the tourist hotels and exchange counters, as the risks outweigh the slim gains. Keep your exchange receipts (*borderou de schimb*), since they may be needed to pay for accommodation or international tickets, or to obtain a refund in *valuta* (hard currency) when leaving Romania. You will be asked to produce your currency exchange slips when departing the country.

It's safest to carry some of your money in **travellers' cheques**, but also wise to take plenty of **dollar bills**, some in small denominations; **deutschmarks** are also in demand, with sterling and other currencies less welcome. The private counters much prefer cash and are only now beginning to accept travellers' cheques. Banks and ONT accept all major brands of travellers' cheques, but the only brand that guarantees a speedy refund in the case of loss is *American Express*, whose Romanian agent is the main ONT office in Bucharest.

Hotels, airlines, the big car rental companies and the more upmarket stores and restaurants will usually accept **credit cards** – Diners Club, Amex, Master Card/Access and Visa – but elsewhere, plastic money is useless.

THE BLACK MARKET

There is now little profit to be made by changing money on the **black market**. The exchange rate at the street kiosks is almost as good as with the black marketeers, and it's a *much* safer deal – the police do not inspire as much fear as before 1989, so rip-off merchants are common.

If you do need to raise extra funds, you could do as the locals do, and sell your foreign goods at one of the many *consignaţie* shops. Obviously, things like personal stereos fetch a good price, as do unused trainers and other trendy gear. Goods such as whisky or coffee are ideal presents if you're invited to stay with someone.

HEALTH

No vaccinations are required to visit Romania, but hepatitis A, polio and typhoid boosters would be wise if you're planning to stay in remote areas where cooking and sanitation are sometimes none too hygienic. There's no reciprocal health agreement between Romania and Western countries, though emergency treatment (excluding drugs) is free. Don't forget to take out travel insurance (see p.15) in case of serious illness or accident. Keep all receipts so you can can reclaim the money later.

SPECIFIC HAZARDS

Beyond an occasional sore throat from traffic fumes, Romania's pollution and other environmental problems are unlikely to have much effect on any short-term visitor. **Diarrhoea** can be a problem, so stock up with *Lomotil* before you leave (remember that this treats only symptoms, not causes), besides any specific medication required. Bring **tampons and contraceptives** with you, since these are hard to find in Romania. In summer you'll also need a strong **sun block**, and very strong **insect repellant** if visiting the

Danube Delta. **Dogs** should be avoided (there's a slight risk of rabies), but **tap water** is safe to drink practically everywhere, and you'll find taps or drinking fountains at most train stations. However, there have recently been isolated outbreaks of cholera in Tîrgu Mureş and on the coast. Bottled water (*apă minerala*) is widely available.

PHARMACIES, DOCTORS & HOSPITALS

In case of minor complaints, go to a *farmacie*, where the staff are usually well trained and have the authority to prescribe drugs, and – in the big towns at least – may understand French, German or English. In theory, one pharmacy in each town should be open 24 hours, or at least display in the window an emergency number and these are listed in the *Guide*.

In Bucharest, the British and American embassies can supply the address of an English-speaking **doctor or dentist**, and there's a special clinic for treating foreigners. In emergencies dial ☎961 or ask someone to contact the local *staţia de salvare* or *prim ajutor* – the casualty and first aid stations – which should have

---

SPAS

Spa holidays are much favoured by Romanians, following the Hapsburg tradition, and the country boasts one third of all Europe's mineral springs, and 160 spa resorts (*băile*). The theory is that you stay in a resort for about eighteen days, following a prescribed course of treatment, and ideally return regularly over the next few years. However, for the tourist, if you can get cheap accommodation (best booked at a travel agency in almost any town) a spa can be a good base for a leisurely holiday. In any case it's worth bearing in mind that even the smallest spas have campsites and restaurants.

The basic treatment naturally involves drinking the **waters**, which come in an amazing variety: alkaline, chlorinated, radioactive, carbogaseous, and sodium-, iodine-, magnesium-, sulphate- or iron-bearing. In addition you can bath in hot springs or sapropelic muds, breath in foul fumes at *mofettes*, or indulge in a new generation of complementary **therapies** such as ultrasound and aerosol treatment, ultraviolet light baths, acupuncture and electrotherapy. A great deal of work has

been done to put a scientific gloss on spa treatment, and drugs such as *Pellamar*, *Gerovital H3* and *Aslavital*, said to stop and even reverse the ageing process, have been developed here. Treatment is available at all major spas, and at the *Flora* hotel in Bucharest and the *Otopeni* clinic, 2km from the airport.

The **spas** all have their own areas of specialization: Sovata is the best place for gynaecological problems; Covasna, Vatra Dornei and Buziaş deal with cardiovascular complaints; Calimăneşti-Căciulata, Slănic Moldova, Sîngeorz-Băi and Băile Olăneşti with the digestion; and others (notably Băile Herculane and Băile Felix) with a range of locomotive and rheumatic ailments. Mountain resorts such as Sinaia, Băile Tuşnad and Moneasa treat nervous complaints, not with water but with fresh air that has an ideal balance of ozone and ions. ONT distributes a booklet and makes bookings from abroad, although given current levels of business, you can save money by booking in Romania if you have time.

ambulances. Each county capital has a fairly well-equipped *Spital Judeţean*, but **hospitals** and *policlinics* in smaller towns can be dire, and most places suffer from demoralized staff and a

shortage of drugs. Foreigners are likely to receive preferential treatment, but Romanians routinely pay large tips to doctors and nurses to ensure that they're well cared for.

INFORMATION AND MAPS

Romania's national tourist office – the ONT, sometimes known abroad as *Carpaţi* – produces a range of maps, brochures and special interest booklets (on spas and folklore, for example), distributed in the appropriate languages through their offices

abroad (see box below). During the summer, ONT operates special tours for visitors including transport and accommodation along popular routes. For more details see "Getting Around" p.27.

TOURIST OFFICES

In Romania, almost all of the **county tourist offices** (OJT) have been privatized: this hasn't made a huge difference, as they were always more concerned with selling package trips to spas and beach resorts than with providing information.

Opening hours are, in theory, Mon–Fri 9am–4pm & Sat 9am–noon, but they are pretty unreliable and you'll generally have to take pot luck.

MAPS

A number of maps appear in the *Guide* section of this book, but it's always worth asking at tourist offices and hotel reception desks for a **town plan** (*plan oraşului*) or **county map** (*hartă judeţean*. Though usually of pre-revolutionary

ROMANIAN TOURIST OFFICES ABROAD

Austria 6–8 Währingerstrasse, 1090 Vienna (☎0222/343 157).

Belgium Place de Brouckère 44–46, 1000 Brussels (☎02/218 0079).

Britain 83A Marylebone High St, London W1M 3DE (☎0171/224 3692).

Denmark Vesterbrogade 55A, 1620 Copenhagen (☎31/246 219).

France 38 Ave de l'Opéra, 75002 Paris (☎1/47 42 75 46).

Germany Frankfurter Tor 5, 1034 Berlin (☎030/589 2684); Zeil 13, 6000 Frankfurt am Main (☎069/295 278).

Greece Vassilisis Sofias 33, Athens (☎01/721 3249).

Italy 100 Via Torino, 00184 Rome (☎06/488 0267).

Netherlands 165 Weteringschans, 1017 Amsterdam XD (☎020/623 9044).

Republica Moldova B-dul Ştefan cel Mare 151–153, Chişinău (☎022/222 354).

Russia Ul. Dimitria Ulianova 16/2, Moscow (☎124 2473).

Spain Calle General Pardinas 108 1G, 28006 Madrid 16 (☎91/564 0333).

Sweden Vasahuset Gamla Brogatan 33, 11120 Stockholm (☎08/210 253).

Switzerland Schweizergasse 10, 8001 Zurich (☎01/211 1730).

USA 342 Madison Ave, Suite 210, New York, NY 10173 (☎212/697-6971).

vintage, and thus featuring various communist-era street names since changed, they detail everything from monuments to filling stations, and though most are only in Romanian, they aren't hard to understand.

Among maps published outside Romania, the *Cartographia* and *Falk* maps of Bucharest are useful. Their 1:1,000,000 maps of Romania and Bulgaria, along with those produced by *Kümmerley & Frey* are also good; however the

MAP OUTLETS IN THE UK

London:
Daunt Books, 83 Marylebone High St, W1 (☎0171/224 2295).

National Map Centre, 22–24 Caxton St, SW1 (☎0171/222 4945).

Stanfords, 12–14 Long Acre, WC2 (☎0171/836 1321); 52 Grosvenor Gardens, London SW1W 0AG; 156 Regent St, London W1R 5TA.

The Travel Bookshop, 13–15 Blenheim Crescent, London W11 2EE (☎0171/229 5260).

The Traveller's Bookshop, 25 Cecil Court, WC2 (☎0171/836 9132).

Edinburgh:
Thomas Nelson and Sons Ltd, 51 York Place, EH1 3JD (☎0131/557 3011).

Glasgow:
John Smith and Sons, 57–61 St Vincent St (☎0141/221 7472).

Maps are available by **mail or phone order** from *Stanfords*, ☎0171/836 1321.

MAP OUTLETS IN NORTH AMERICA

Chicago:
Rand McNally, 444 N Michigan Ave, IL 60611 (☎312/321-1751).

Montréal:
Ulysses Travel Bookshop, 4176 St-Denis (☎514/289-0993).

New York:
British Travel Bookshop, 551 5th Ave, NY 10176 (☎1-800/448-3039 or 212/490-6688).

The Complete Traveler Bookstore, 199 Madison Ave, NY 10016 (☎212/685-9007).

Rand McNally, 150 East 52nd St, NY 10022, (☎212/758-7488).

Traveler's Bookstore, 22 West 52nd St, NY 10019 (☎212/664-0995).

San Francisco:
The Complete Traveler Bookstore, 3207 Fillmore St, CA 92123 (☎415/923-1511).

Rand McNally, 595 Market St, CA 94105 (☎415/777-3131).

Santa Barbara:
Map Link, Inc, 25 East Mason St, CA 93101 (☎805/965-4402).

Seattle:
Elliot Bay Book Company, 101 South Main St, WA 98104 (☎206/624-6600).

Toronto:
Open Air Books and Maps, 25 Toronto St, M5R 2C1 (☎416/363-0719).

Vancouver:
World Wide Books and Maps, 736A Granville St, V6Z 1G3 (☎604/687-3320).

Washington DC:
Rand McNally, 1201 Connecticut Ave NW, Washington DC 20036 (☎202/223-6751).

Note: *Rand McNally* now has 24 stores across the US: call ☎1-800/333-0136 (ext 2111) for the address of your nearest store, or for **direct mail** maps.

MAP OUTLETS IN AUSTRALIA

Adelaide:
The Map Shop, 16a Peel St, SA 5000 (☎08/231 2033; ☎08/8231 2033 from Aug 1996).

Brisbane:
Hema, 239 George St, QLD 4000 (☎07/3221 4330).

Melbourne:
Bowyangs, 372 Little Bourke St, VIC 3000 (☎03/9670 4383).

Sydney:
Travel Bookshop, 20 Bridge St, NSW 2000 (☎02/241 3554; ☎02/9241 3554 from July 1996).

Perth:
Perth Map Centre, 891 Hay St, WA 6000 (☎09/322 5733).

Erdély map published by *DIMAP* is the best available of Transylvania. This and the *Cartographia* maps are published in Hungary and cost less there, but are available through good map outlets abroad.

ONT produces free maps of the country (just about adequate for **motoring**) and others of *popasuri turistice* (campsites) and *cabane turistice* (cabanas), which are useful for hikers in particular. Hikers are also advised to seek out any remaining copies of the booklet *Invitation to the Romanian Carpathians* (*Invitaţie în Carpaţi* in its Romanian version), which contains detailed maps of the 24 main hiking areas, showing trail markings, huts, peaks etc, and briefly describing the most popular walks. There are also good **hiking maps** (*hartă turistică*) of the major mountain massifs, now being reissued by *Editura pentru Turism* and *Abeona* in Bucharest and *Editura Focul Viu* in Cluj, and as likely to be found in bookstores as in tourist offices (see p.40 for more information on hiking).

In Bucharest, street stalls outside the university are the best places for buying maps, particularly the excellent new maps of the Danube Delta (*Delta Dunării*).

GETTING AROUND

Major Romanian towns, and a huge number of small towns and villages, are most easily reached by train. The system, although more confusing than in the west of Europe, is far more approachable than the bus network, which is best used for reaching local villages around the main towns.

TRAINS

The 11,000-kilometre network of the SNCFR (*Societatea Naţională a Cailor Ferate Române*, still generally known as the **CFR** or *ChéFéRé*) covers most of the country. Although the number of cars on the roads is increasing, and bus services are widening their range, trains remain the best means for most people to get around. Consequently, they are often crowded which, coupled with the frequent lack of light, heating and water, may make long journeys somewhat purgatorial; but those who use the trains regularly often end up very much in sympathy with their rough-and-ready spirit and the generally excellent time-keeping. Many routes are extremely scenic, particularly in Transylvania, and as rail journeys are good occasions to strike up conversation with Romanians, you'll gain a lot out of ignoring any discomforts and making an effort.

You have a choice of paying more to travel fast or less to travel more slowly. **Expres** and **rapid** services, halting only at major towns, are the most expensive type of train, while **accelerats** are slightly cheaper and slower, with more frequent stops, the standard means of inter-urban travel. The painfully slow **personal** and **cursa** trains should be avoided as a rule, unless you're heading for a particular *halta* along the route. Each service has a number prefixed by a letter denoting its type – E, R, A, P or C.

Fares are more than reasonable, costing about 6000 lei (£2.20/$3.50) to travel 500km in first class. **Rail passes** are available at most train stations and cost $99 for first class travel all over Romania for a total of five days within a fifteen-day period. These can also be bought in advance of travelling, but given the low cost of fares, passes aren't really worth it.

TIMETABLES AND ROUTES

Trains generally conform pretty well to their **timetables** (*felul trenului*), which are displayed in stations and *CFR* offices (see below). The vital terms are *sosire* (sos.) and *plecare* (pl.), arrival and departure; *de la...* (from) and *pînă la...* (to); the duration of the train's stop in the station (*oprire*); and the platform or track (*linia de garare*), counting outwards from the main build-

Remember that in official publications such as timetables "î" is being replaced by "â", so that Cîmpulung will appear as Câmpulung, Sfîntu Gheorghe as Sfântu Gheorghe, and Tîrgovişte as Târgovişte.

ing. Also watch for *annulat* (cancelled), and services that only run – *circulă numai* – during certain months (eg. *între 9.V şi 8.IX* – between May 9 and September 8), or only on particular days (1 represents Monday, 2 represents Tuesday; *circula Simbata si Duminica* means the service doesn't run on Saturday or Sunday). If you're planning to travel a lot by rail, invest in the national *CFR* timetable, the *Mersul Trenurilor*, which is fairly easy to figure out, and very cheap. If you're travelling all over Europe, the Thomas Cook European Timetable, published monthly, lists the main Romanian services.

Details of main **routes** are given in the text, and summarized at the end of each chapter in the Travel Details: note that we give the total number of trains, fast and slow, in a 24-hour period, and give the totals for winter and summer where these differ greatly. As many trains run at night there may be gaps of up to seven hours in the daytime; however even where there are no direct trains there may be connections, and creative trainhopping will usually get you on your way without too long a delay.

TICKETS AND RESERVATIONS

Advance bookings for fast services are recommended, and on most such trains it's required to have a seat reservation, although if you board at a relatively minor stop you may have to take pot luck. Thus your ticket (*bilet*) will usually be accompanied by a second piece of card, indicating the service (*nr. trenului*), your carriage (*vagonul*) and reserved seat (*loc*). Return tickets (*bilet dus întors*) are rarely issued except for international services. All long distance overnight trains have **sleeping cars** (*vagon de dormit*) and couchettes (*cuşete*), for which a surcharge of a few thousand lei is levied.

Rather than queue at the station, you can book tickets at the local *Agenţia CFR* at least 24 hours in advance (allow seven days for services to the coast during summer). Addresses of offices are given in the *Guide*, and in the *CFR* timetable; opening hours vary widely, but few are open at weekends. Should you fall victim to double-

booking, ticket collectors are notoriously corrupt and a small tip can work wonders. Indeed some people never buy tickets, simply paying off the conductor every time.

PLANES

TAROM's **domestic services**, flying Tupolev-154s and other Russian-made planes, depart most days from Bucharest's Baneasă airport to Arad, Bacău, Baia Mare, Caransebeş, Cluj, Constanţa, Craiova, Iaşi, Oradea, Satu Mare, Sibiu, Suceava, Timişoara, Tîrgu Mureş and Tulcea. In summer, there are also flights to most of these places from Constanţa.

Fares for foreigners are fixed at the lei equivalent of between $30 and $54 (four times what Romanians pay), and you'll usually need your exchange receipt to prove that the money was acquired legally. Bookings should be made – preferably 36 hours in advance – at *TAROM* offices, the addresses of which appear in the *Guide*.

BUSES AND TAXIS

Bus services (run by regional ITAs) now reach virtually every village (having almost dried up before 1989, due to fuel shortages) and with a little patience will usually get you anywhere you want to go. Timetables are usually out of date, and can only be found at urban bus stations. In the countryside, knowing when and where to wait for the bus is a local art form, and on Sundays many regions have no buses at all (whereas trains run to much the same timetable seven days a week).

All towns have **local bus services**, and in the main cities you'll also find **trams** and **trolleybuses** (*tramvai* and *troleibuz*). Tickets for urban buses, trolleybuses and trams are normally sold in bunches by tobacconists and ITA street kiosks. Punch them yourself aboard the vehicle, if you can get to the machine through the crush. Most locals use season tickets, checked by plain-clothes ticket inspectors. **Information** about services seemed almost a state secret under communism, and is only slightly easier to find now. In Bucharest new bus shelters, with city transport maps, are slowly being installed.

Taxis are easy to find in towns, with lots of *Taxi-Privat* as well as state-owned vehicles. As fuel prices rise towards levels elsewhere, taxi fares keep pace, but they are still affordable for the visitor, with city-centre trips costing just a

ROMANIAN RAIL LINES

UKRAINE

HUNGARY

Sighetu Marmatiei

Satu Mare

Baia Mare

Borşa

To Budapest   Debrecen

To Budapest

Salva

To Budapest

Oradea   Zalău   Dej   Bistriţa

Huedin

Cluj   Tîrgu Mureş

Békéscaba

Dr Petru Groza

Sighişoara

Szeged

Arad   Alba Iulia   Mediaş

Kikinda   Deva   Sibiu

Timişoara   Hunedoara

Lugoj

Caransebeş   Petroşani   Curtea de Argeş

Reşiţa   Rîmnicu Vîlcea

Urşac   Oraviţa   Piteşti

Tîrgu Jiu

Băile Herculane

Drobeta-Turnu Severin

River Danube

BELGRADE

SERBIA   Piatra Olt

Craiova

Calafat

River Danube

0   100 km

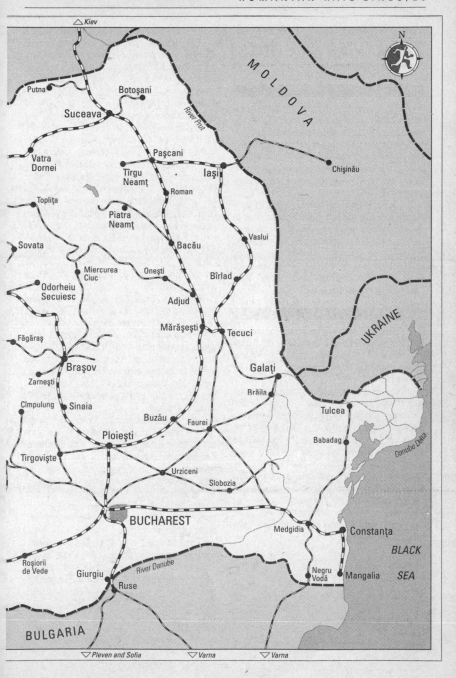

dollar or two. **Maxitaxis** are shared taxi mini-buses which run along the main thoroughfares in Bucharest and elsewhere and link various towns with their train stations.

BOATS

NAVROM, the national shipping company, maintains a small fleet of passenger boats and hydrofoils which operate principally along the arms of the Danube Delta. If business picks up, there may again be regular services between Constanța and Mangalia and, depending on the situation in Serbia, on the Danube between Turnu Severin and Ostrov.

The Danube Delta services vary greatly with the season, only operating on alternate days in winter, and you can't buy tickets in advance — you'll just have to make arrangements when you get to Tulcea. Smaller motorboats also carry passengers around Lake Bicaz in Moldavia and along the Danube–Black Sea Canal from Cernavodă to Agigea see (p.292).

DRIVING

Given the state of public transport, and its low cost, it makes little sense to travel by car unless you have a lot of business to complete in a few days — especially as the queues for fuel can be enormous.

If you do choose to drive, **regulations** are fairly standard. A national driving licence suffices, and if you don't have Green Card insurance, a month's cover can be purchased at the border, or from ADAS agencies. If you have an **accident**, you're legally obliged to await the arrival of the Poliția; drinking and driving is absolutely prohibited and severely punished. The police are now empowered to levy on-the-spot fines of up to L100,000. The most important rule is to drive on the right and overtake on the left side, while **speed limits** depend on your vehicle's cylinder capacity.

SPEED LIMITS

Type of car	Speed limit
	(built-up areas/open road)
over 1800cc.	60 /90 kph
1100 –1800cc.	60 /80 kph
under 1100cc.	60 /70 kph
jeep-type, spark ignition	60 /70 kph
jeep-type, diesel	60 /60kph

There are often long queues for **fuel** at PECO and Competrol stations, especially when rumours are flying about an imminent price rise. Most cars just use regular benzină, but super and lead-free fuel (fară plomb) are available in major cities and along the main roads from Hungary, though nowhere else. Diesel cars do not exist, but diesel fuel (motorină) is available at truck stops.

Foreign motorists belonging to organizations affiliated to the ACR (Romanian Automobile Club) receive free or cut-price **technical assistance**; and you can get motoring **information** from their Bucharest offices at Str. Tache Ionescu 27 (☎01/650.25.95) and Str. Cihoski 2 (☎01/611.04.08). For ACR breakdown services ring ☎12345. Details of car repair depots (called Auto-Service, Dacia-Service, Automechanica etc.) and provincial ACR offices are given in the Guide. The mainstays of Romanian motoring, the Dacia and the Oltcit, are based on the Renault 12 and the Citroen Visa, so spare parts for these models are easiest to come by.

Highways (Drum Național/DN) are fairly well maintained, but the quality of roads declines as you move onto county roads (Drum Judeţean) and from Drum Modernizat onto Drum Nemodernizat, which can be little more than tracks. In rural areas the danger isn't so much other motorized traffic as the risk of hitting wagons, drunks on cycles and various animals that have yet to accept the impact of the motor age. It's wiser not to drive after dark.

Other precautions include always locking the car and putting windscreen wipers in the glove compartment when not in use, since **thefts of car parts** are commonplace. If asked to pay to have your car watched, particularly overnight, it's wiser to pay up; the only alternative is to stay in an expensive hotel with supervised parking. Another street kids' racket is washing windscreens at traffic lights: most drivers wave them away and decline to pay.

Romania would be a fine country for **motorcycling**, except that the speed limit for bikes is ludicrously low: 40 kph in built up areas and only 50 kph on the open road. Helmets are compulsory and you're advised to bring vital spares as well as a tool kit.

CAR RENTAL

Western **car rental** companies such as Hertz and Europcar are now present in Bucharest (with branches at Otopeni airport) and a few other cities. Local rates start at about £17/$27 per day (£13/$21/day for a week or more), topped up by a distance charge (25 cents per km), or £49/$79 a day (£36/$57 a day for a week or more) with unlimited mileage. A hefty deposit (around £300/$500) is required, so it's as well to use your credit card here. Booking from home, you'll have to pay far more: from £46/$73 per day or £301/$482 per week, all-inclusive.

These companies use only imported cars, from Peugeot 205s up to Toyota Liteace People-movers, although *Hertz*, who work with the *ACR*, and Romanian firms like *JET Turist*, *Mercedes* and *Sebastian* may be able to lay their hands on a more inconspicuous Dacia. Renting direct from Romanian companies will save you about 20 percent on the prices quoted above.

Fly/drive deals can prove good value and it's worth checking with your travel agent as some deals add only a negligible amount on top of what you would pay for a standard air fare anyway.

CYCLING

Given the mountainous terrain and the poor state of rural roads, you'll need to be fit and self-reliant to **cycle** around Romania. Bike stores are few and far between, although most village mechanics can manage basic repairs. You're strongly advised to carry a spare tyre and a few spokes, and to check carrier nuts regularly, as the potholes and corrugations will rapidly shake them loose. A touring bike is better than a mountain bike unless you want to go off road; with the immense network of forestry roads (*drum forestiere*) and free access to the hills, genuine mountain biking is wonderful here.

If you do bring your bike, avoid cycling in **Bucharest**, where driving is such a hazardous experience anyway that you won't see bikes on the roads and drivers will have little idea how to avoid you. Carrying your bike any distance by train will be a slow business as it's unlikely you'll be allowed to take it on express services.

HITCH-HIKING

Hitch-hiking (*autostop*) is an integral part of the Romanian transport system to supplement patchy or non-existent services on backroads. It's common even on the *autostrada*, although illegal there, and it's accepted practice to pay for lifts, although this is often waived for foreigners. Hitch-hiking, however, is a risky business in any country and if you decide to travel this way, take all sensible precautions. Single women should never hitch alone, nor is hitching at night advisable.

ONT TOURS

Between mid-June and the end of September, ONT organizes **tours**, including weekends at Sinaia, Predeal and the seaside; two- or three-day excursions to Maramureş, the old Wallachian capitals, the monasteries of Bucovina, the Delta and the Prahova and Olt valleys; and jaunts around the country lasting 3, 5 or 7 days.

The three-day tour takes in Curtea de Argeş, Cozia Monastery, Sibiu, Sibiel, Braşov and Sinaia; five-day excursions add Bran Castle, Tîrgu Mureş, Sighişoara and Sovata to this list; while the week-long itinerary also includes Alba Iulia, Cluj, Bistriţa, Bicaz, and several of the Moldavian monasteries. Prices depend on the number of participants and on the types of transport and accommodation required, but as an example three people spending three days touring the Bucovina monasteries by car would pay $224 plus either $27 by sleeper train or $88 by air from Bucharest to Suceava and back; it will always be cheaper to make your own way to Suceava and book a tour there, with the possibility of latching on to a bus party.

ACCOMMODATION

Decent accommodation rarely comes cheap in Romania, in any case tourist offices tend to point visitors towards the most expensive on offer, forcing you to plead poverty before they'll divulge the location of more modestly priced establishments. There has been only minimal privatization in the hotel sector, although most outsiders agree this is the key to relaunching Romania's tourist industry, itself agreed to be one of the country's best resources for the future. However, there is an increasing degree of flexibility in the market, with private rooms available in many towns.

In summer it's safer, though rarely necessary except on the coast, to make **reservations** ahead, since cheap hotels, cabanas and cabins on campsites can get crowded. *ACR* **coupons** sold in tourist offices abroad and in offices of the Romanian Automobile Association are a system of prepaid vouchers for certain hotels throughout

Romania and these are listed in the *Guide*. Coupons entitle you to a first-class hotel room in participating establishments and you don't need to book ahead as the hotels have to keep a certain number of rooms free every day until 7pm. You will usually save money on the room over paying in cash and coupons can help to get you a room in a hotel which is "full".

HOTELS

Hotels were previously graded as deluxe, first or second class, but are now increasingly being awarded between one and five stars. All but the most luxurious of establishments display their "maximum" prices in lei (Romanians generally pay 20 percent of this figure); the top hotels show a price in dollars which is converted into lei at that day's rate. They may require you to show your exchange receipt (*buletin de schimb*), to prove that you're not paying with black-market cash.

Single rooms generally cost around two-thirds as much as a double; where none is available, expect to pay anything from half the cost of a double room to the full whack. Penny-pinching couples are sometimes permitted to share a single, while **children** sleeping in their parents' room pay 50 percent of the "third person" tariff up to the age of 6, and 70 percent between the ages of 7 and 12. Given the frequent lack of hot water it's unlikely to be worth paying extra for a private bathroom.

Hotel bars and restaurants may double as the town's nightclub (featuring dancing at the weekends), while in the foyer you can usually buy Kent or Marlboro cigarettes, whisky and ground coffee.

ACCOMMODATION PRICES

Hotels listed in this guide have been price-graded according to the scale below. Prices given are those charged for the cheapest **double room** available, which in the less expensive places usually comes without private bath or shower and without breakfast. Price codes are expressed in US dollars as the Romanian leu is not a stable currency, but you will generally pay for your room in lei.

Note that some hotels are currently closed for modernization, and others, now open, will no doubt follow in the near future. This is bound to result in higher rates when they reopen, so the prices quoted should be taken only as a guideline.

① under $10	④ $25–40	⑦ $80–135
② $10–15	⑤ $40–55	⑧ $135–190
③ $15–25	⑥ $55–80	⑨ $200 and over

MOTELS AND SPORT HOTELS

Motels (*han*) have similar facilities and prices to first class hotels, but since they're situated along main highways or beyond urban ring roads, they're not much use unless you have private transport. **Sport hotels** are an East European institution, intended for visiting teams and school groups, but now generally willing to let Westerners in. You may have to share a room, and washing facilities are likely to be primitive, but you can't argue with the bargain-basement prices ($10–15 a night).

STUDENT ROOMS

Most large towns have **student rooms** (*caminul de studenti* or *internat*) which may be rented out between July 15 and August 31. The Youth Tourism Company *CTT* (also still known by its old name of *BTT*) is responsible for bookings, but prefers groups to individuals. Before you leave Bucharest contact *CTT* head office at Str. Mendeleev 7 (☎01/614.42.00) about the possibility of booking beds in colleges around the country. We've listed regional *BTT/CTT* offices in the *Guide*, and it's worth checking them out personally to see what they can offer – note that they close very early. Even if the agency won't help, they should at least know which colleges are being used, and you might be able to secure a bed there in person. Having an *IUS* student card probably helps, but charges are minimal anyway, well under a dollar per night.

CABANAS

In the countryside, particularly in the mountainous areas favoured by hikers, there are well over a hundred **cabanas** or hikers' huts, ranging from chic alpine villas with dozens of bedrooms to fairly primitive chalets with bunk beds, a rudimentary bar and cold running water – these are the nearest equivalent to youth hostels in Romania.

Some cabanas (mainly in the Bucegi range) can be easily reached by cable car from a train station, while others are situated just a few miles from towns; however, the majority are fairly isolated, only accessible by mountain road or footpaths. Their locations are shown rather vaguely on an ONT map, *Cabane Turistice*, and more precisely on hiking maps. Mountain cabanas are supposedly forbidden to turn hikers away, but in the Făgăraş mountains, in particular, it might be wise to book in advance, by phone or through a local agency (see p.131). Beds cost about $3, slightly more if in a private room or in one of the plusher cabanas (this is about five times the rate for Romanians). The hikers' cabanas are generally friendly and useful places where you can pick up information about trails and the weather.

CAMPING

Romania has well over a hundred **campsites**, situated all over the country. You'll pay a dollar or two, and an *IUS* student card may secure a 30 – 50 percent reduction. Second-class campsites are rudimentary, and generally filthy, but first-class sites often have **cabins** or bungalows (*casute*) for rent (about $5 per head), hot showers and even a restaurant. However, water shortages seem to hit campsites especially hard, while along the coast overcrowding is a major drawback. In the mountains, certain areas may be designated as a *loc de campare* where it's permitted to pitch camp, but in fact there are few regions where you can't get away with **camping wild**. Providing you don't light fires in forests, leave litter or transgress nature reserves, officialdom turns a blind eye to campers, or, at the worst, may tell you to move along.

PRIVATE ROOMS & OTHER POSSIBILITIES

Under Ceauşescu, private accommodation ceased to be available to foreigners in the early 1970s. Now this has been reversed, and **private rooms** are increasingly available, either through agencies in cities such as Bucharest, Braşov and Sibiu (for about $15), or more informally in smaller places. In the villages there is a strong tradition of hospitality, and payment will usually be refused; but you should offer a few dollars anyway, or come armed with a few packets of coffee (easily obtained in the towns), which make very acceptable presents.

If you're travelling around a lot, you can use the **trains** to your advantage. On the long overnight journeys by *expres*, *rapid* or *accelerat* train, it only costs a couple of dollars to book a comfortable couchette (*cuşete*), allowing you to save the cost of a hotel and arrive refreshed the following morning. Couchettes (and the costlier sleeping cars, *vagon de dormit*) should be booked up to ten days beforehand using the *CFR* agencies found in virtually all towns.

EATING AND DRINKING

Under Ceauşescu the only people not driven to the black market for food were package-tourists, fed huge meals to obscure Romanian realities, and the Party elite, who had their own supply network. Nowadays visitors can either opt for the security of a package tour, confine themselves to eating in tourist hotels, or come prepared for Romanian austerity. Winter is tough everywhere, but in large towns and agricultural areas the availability and variety of food improves as the months pass, so that you can eat relatively well during the summer and autumn. Imported foods such as oranges, bananas and German yoghurts are also available, at a price. Nevertheless, if you are planning to spend some time here it might be wise to bring some concentrated, non-perishable food.

BREAKFAST AND SNACKS

Staying in a hotel, you'll normally be guaranteed **breakfast** on the premises or in a nearby café, the cost of which will be included in the charge for accommodation. Typically it's a light meal of rolls and butter (sometimes known as *ceai complet*), to which an omelette or long, unappealing-looking skinless sausages can be added. This is washed down with a large white coffee or a cup of tea.

Should you rise late, or not fancy the above, then hit the streets looking for **snacks**, known as *gustări*, which is also the Romanian word for hors

d'oeuvres. The most common are flaky pastries (*pateuri*) filled with cheese or meat, often dispensed through hatches in the walls of bakeries; brioche, a Moldavian speciality; sandwiches; a variety of spicy grilled sausages and meatballs, normally sold by street vendors and in beer gardens; and small pizzas topped with cheese and salami.

RESTAURANT MEALS

Outside the cities, you'll find most **restaurants** are in hotels or attached to them, although small private cafés are springing up in many towns. It's best to go upmarket if you can, since the choice of dishes in cheaper restaurants is limited to *cotlet* and chips, and these places tend to be thinly disguised beer-halls. At least the grisly self-service *Autoservire* canteens that Ceauşescu intended to make the mainstay of Romanian catering have largely vanished; unfortunately they've been replaced for the most part by burger bars which are little better. Fortunately, there are signs that Romanians are finally learning what pizza is meant to look and taste like. *Lacto-Vegetarian* restaurants are also vanishing – these were in any case never particularly vegetarian, but they can offer affordable food in reasonably congenial surroundings. Whatever place you settle on, always enquire "*Care feluri le serviţi astazi, vă rog?*" (What do you have today?) or "*Ce îhmi recomandaţi?*" (What do you recommend?) before taking the menu too seriously, for sometimes the only thing going is the set menu (*un meniu fix*), usually dominated by pork.

However, at smarter restaurants and *hans* (traditional inns with olde-worlde decor), there's a fair chance of finding **authentic Romanian dishes**, which can be delicious. The best known is *sarmale* – cabbage leaves stuffed with rice, meat and herbs, usually served (or sometimes baked) with sour cream; they are sometimes also made with vine leaves – *sărmăluţe in foi de viţă* – or with corn – *sarmale cu pasat*, as in Maramureş. *Mămăligă* (maize mush or polenta), often served with sour cream, is especially associated with shepherds and the authentic outdoor life. Stews (*tocane*) and other dishes often feature a sclerotic combination of meat and dairy products. *Muşchi ciobanesc* (shepherd's sirloin) is pork stuffed with ham, covered in cheese and served with mayonnaise, cucumber and herbs; while *muşchi poiana* (meadow sirloin) is beef stuffed with mushrooms, bacon, pepper and paprika, served in a vegetable purée and tomato sauce. Also watch out for **regional specialities** (*specialitățile regiunii*). Moldavia is known for its rissoles (*pîrjoale*), but also for more elaborate dishes such as *rasol moldovenesc cu hrean* (boiled pork, chicken or beef, with a sour cream and horseradish sauce), *tochitura moldovenească* (a thick stew), *rulade de pui* (chicken roulade), and *pui Cîmpulungean* (chicken stuffed with smoked bacon, sausage, garlic and vegetables). Because of Romania's Turkish past, you may find *musaka* and varieties of *pilaf*, while the German and Hungarian minorities have contributed such dishes as smoked pork with sauerkraut and Transylvanian hotpot.

VEGETARIAN FOOD

Vegetarians will have a tough time in a country where voluntarily doing without meat is simply beyond comprehension. It's hard even to get a pizza without meat. You could try asking for *ghiveci* (mixed fried veg); *ardei umpluți* (stuffed peppers); *ouă umplute picante* or *ouă umplute cu ciuperci* (eggs with a spicy filling or mushroom stuffing); *ouă romaneşti* (poached eggs); or vegetables and salads (see box overleaf). However, in practice, you're likely to end up with omelette, *mămăligă* or *caşcaval pané* (cheese fried in breadcrumbs). You can try asking for something "*fara carne, vă rog'*" (without meat, please), or check "*este cu carne*?" (does it contain meat?), but you're unlikely to get very far. Watch out, too, for the ubiquitous meat stock.

CAFÉS

Establishments called *cofetărie* serve **coffee**, cakes and ice cream. Romanians usually take their fix black and sweet in the Turkish fashion; ask for it *cu lapte* or *fără zahăr* if you prefer it with milk or without sugar. The instant varieties, called *Ness*, are usually revolting. **Cakes and desserts** are sticky and very sweet, as throughout the Balkans. Romanians enjoy pancakes and pies with various fillings; Turkish-influenced *baclava* and *cataif cu frisca* (crisp pastry soaked in syrup, filled with whipped cream); and the traditional *dulceață*, or glass of jam.

BARS

Bars are generally men-only places, and range from rough-and-ready rooms to dark dives full of prostitutes to places with a rather chintzy ice cream-parlour atmosphere. They're all usually open well into the small hours.

DRINKS

There is a great deal of drinking in Romania, as you will soon notice, and most crime is alcohol-related. The national drink is *țuică* a tasty, powerful brandy usually made of plums, taken neat. In rural areas, homemade spirits can be fearsome stuff, often twice distilled (to over 50 percent strength) to yield *palinka*, best diluted with water, and much rougher than the grape brandy (*rachiu* or *coniac*) drunk by urban sophisticates. They're all alarmingly cheap and served in large measures (usually 100 grams; ask for a *mic*, 50g, if you want less), like vodka and rum but unlike whisky, which retails for around $12 a bottle.

Most **beer** is like lager – *Silva* from Reghin, *Valea Prahova* from Azuga, *Ciucaş* from Braşov and *Eggenburger* from Baia Mare are probably the least odious brands – but you will occasionally find *bere blondă* (light ale) and *bere neagră* (brown ale). They're usually sold by the bottle (*sticlă*), and requests for *una sticlă* are assumed to be for beer.

Romania's best **wines** (and they *are* good) are *Grasca* and *Fetească Neagră* from the vineyards of Cotnari (near Iaşi) and Dealu Mare (east of Ploieşti), and the sweet dessert wines from Murfatlar; these can be obtained in the better restaurants without too much trouble. Other restaurants may just offer you a choice of red or white. Sparkling wine comes from Alba Iulia and Panciu (north of Focşani), and is very acceptable. Wine is rarely sold by the glass, but it does no harm to ask – *Serviți vinul la pahar*?

With the exception of mineral water and the universal CocaCola and Pepsi, **soft drinks** are uninviting: fruit juices are thick with sediment, and only severe dehydration justifies a resort to *sirop*.

BUYING YOUR OWN FOOD

Shopping for food is a dispiriting task, since most stores have a very limited choice of dried and bottled foodstuffs, and the few new supermarkets which have a decent range of imported foods are expensive. In addition you should check

A FOOD AND DRINK GLOSSARY

Basic foods

Brînză	cheese	Oțet	vinegar	Pîine	bread	Ciorbe	soup with
Carne	meat	Omleta	omelette	Salată	salad		sour cream
Dulciuri	desserts	Orez	rice	Sare	salt	Ulei	oil
Fructe	fruit	Ouă	eggs	Sandvici	sandwiches	Unt	butter
Iaurt	yoghurt	Pasă re	poultry	or tartina		Zahăr	sugar
Lapte	milk	Peşite	fish	Smîntînă	sour cream		
Legume	vegetables	Piper	pepper	Supe	soup		

Soups

Ciorbă de burtă	tripe soup	Ciorbă perişoare	soup with	Supă de	
Ciorbă de cartofi	potato soup		meatballs	carne cons	
Ciorbă de fasole	dried or	Ciorbă de peşte	fish soup	ommé	
	green bean	Ciorbă ţăranească	broth with	Supă de găină	chicken soup
	soup		meat and	Supă de galuşti	dumpling soup
Ciorbă de miel	lamb broth		mixed veg	Supă de roşii	tomato soup

Salads

Salată de cartofi cu ceapa	potato and onion salad	Salată de icre de crap	carp roe salad	Salată de sfeclă roşie	beetroot salad
Salată de fasole verde	green bean salad	Salată de roşii şi castraveţi	tomato and cucumber salad	Salată verde	lettuce salad

Meat and poultry

Babic (Ghiudem)	smoked (goat's meat) sausage	Patricieni	sausages (skinless)
Berbec/Oaie	mutton	Pră jit	liver
Biftec	steak	Pui	chicken
Chiftele	fried meatballs	Raţă (pe varz ă)	duck (with sauerkraut)
Curcan	turkey	Rinichii	kidneys
Gă ină	hen	Salam	salami
Ghiveci cu carne	meat and vegetable hotpot	Şniţel pané	Wiener schnitzel
		Şuncă	ham
Gîscă	goose	Tocană de carne/de purcel	meat/pork stew
Miel	lamb	Vacă	beef
Mititei	spicy sausages	Varz acră cu costiţe afumate	sauerkraut with smoked pork chops
(Pastrama de) porc	(salted and smoked) pork		

Vegetables

Ardei (gras/iute)	(green/chilli) pepper	Lă ptucă	lettuce
Cartofi	potatoes	Mază re verde	peas
Ceapă (verde)	(spring) onion	Morcovi	carrots
Ciuperci	mushrooms	Roşii	tomatoes
Conopida	cauliflower	Sfeclă roşie	beetroot
Dovleci (cu floare)	marrows (courgettes)	Spanac	spinach
Fasole (albă grasă / verde)	(broad/string) beans	Usturoi	garlic
		Varză	cabbage
Ghiveci	mixed fried veg, sometimes eaten cold	Vinete	aubergines (eggplant)

Fish and seafood

Cegă	sterlet	Icre negre	caviar	Scrumbii	herring
Chiftele de peşie	fish cakes	Midii	mussels	Şalău	pike/perch
		Nisetru	sturgeon	Ton	tuna
Crap	carp	Păstrăv	trout		

Fruit

Caise	apricots	Pepene galben	melon	Prune (uscate)	plums (prunes)
Căpşuni	strawberries	Pepene verde	watermelon	Smeură	raspberries
Cireşi	cherries	Pere	pears	Struguri	grapes
Mere	apples	Piersici	peaches		

Desserts and sweets

Baclava	baclava	Îngheţată	ice cream
Bomboane	sweets (candy)	Mascota	chocolate cake
Cataif cu frişcă	pastry soaked in syrup, topped with whipped cream	Miere	honey
		Măr in foiotaj	baked, stuffed apple
		Papanasi	cream doughnut
Clătite cu rom	pancake with rum	Pasca	Easter cake
Cozonac	brioche	Plăcinta cu brînză	cheese pie
Dulceaţă	jam (served in a glass)	Plăcinta cu mere	apple pie
		Plăcinta cu vişine	cherry pie
Ecler	éclair	Rahat	Turkish delight
Gogoşi or langoş	a kind of doughnut	Rulada rarău	Moldavian sponge and jam cake
Halva	halva		

Drinks

Apă minerală	mineral water	Bere	beer
Suc de fructe	fruit juices	Vin roşu (or alb)	red wine (or white)
Cafea mare cu lapte	white coffee	Şampanie	sparkling wine
Cafea neagră or cafea naturală	sweet black coffee	Sticla	bottle (of beer)
		ţuica	plum brandy
O ceaşcă de ceai a	cup of tea	Vodca	vodka
		Rom	rum

Common terms

Aveţi?	Do you have?	Meniu or listă	menu
Aş/am vrea	I/we would like	Micul dejun	breakfast
Anghemaht de	in a white sauce	Pahar	a glass
Cu maioneză	with a mayonaise sauce	Piureu de	mashed
		Prăjiţi	deep-fried
Cu mujdei de usturoi	in a garlic sauce	Pulpă de... la tavă	roast leg of
Fierţi	boiled	Rasol	poached
Friptură de fripţi	fried or roast	Tare/moale	hard/soft boiled
La grătar	grilled	Umpluţi	stuffed

the sell-by dates in these places, as much of the imported food has been dumped. The basics are sardines, meat paste, pickled fruit and vegetables, pasta, jam, processed cheese and biscuits. Cheese, eggs and meat can be bought in the general foodstores (alimentară), while fruit and veg should be bought in the market (piaţa) – in smaller towns and villages you'll be expected to bring your own bag. Romanian dairy products are generally of poor quality – stick to branded Brenac goods or imported Western dairy products.

The one foodstuff for which there are still queues is **bread**, but this is mainly because Romanians insist on buying it in huge quantities and all at the same time. Most, but not all, stores will sell a half-loaf to a solo traveller. Most bread is white, and not unpleasant, but it's worth asking for wholemeal bread (*pîine graham* or *pîine diatetică*). Most towns also have a *gospodină* or *cantina* selling pre-cooked meals, originally established as an aid for working mothers but equally useful to independent travellers, although you'll have to take the dish of the day.

COMMUNICATIONS

offer a poste restante service to their cardholders via their office in Bucharest (see p.78).

PHONES

The **telephone service** is at last seeing some much-needed improvements, such as a new fibre-optic link from Arad to Constanţa (linking Hungary and Turkey), thanks to loans from the World Bank and European Bank. Currently there are only 105.4 phones per 1000 people, 20 percent of the European average, with a sixteen-year waiting list for connection.

Local calls can be made from public booths, costing L20 for three minutes. You'll normally pay for the minimum three-minute call in advance, and the balance afterwards; calls are half-rate from 6pm to 6am. In addition, every town, and many villages, have a telephone and telegraph office or **PTTR**.

Modern digital exchanges and card-phones are now being installed, with which you can make **international calls** using the IDD system. In most places, you're more likely to get through from the post office (with a wait of half an hour or so, as a rule), by dialling ☎971 for the international operator, or by phoning from a deluxe hotel. Using hotel facilities inevitably means a steep service charge, so always ask the price beforehand.

In main cities there may also be a *Romtelecom* office, with direct dial phones taking phone cards, sold in the office; you can dial abroad from the orange phones. *Romtelecom* phone cards (*cartela telefonică)* currently sell for L10,000 and L20,000. Always insert with the gold lozenge foremost and facing upwards; after a few seconds you should get a sign indicating that you can start dialling.

An alternative is to use a **chargecard** issued by your home telecom company: these usually

POSTAL SERVICES

Major **post offices** are open Monday to Saturday from 7am to 8.30pm, and on Sundays from 8am to noon and, like the yellow-painted mail boxes, are marked *Poştă*. It's easier to buy **stamps** (*timbru*) and envelopes (*plic*) at tobacconists, bookstores or hotels than queue for them in post offices. The **courier** service DHL has offices in Bucharest and a few major cities such as Braşov, Constanţa and Timişoara.

Post home from Romania is very cheap, L525 regardless of letter weight, and takes about five days to Western Europe and two weeks to North America. Make sure your letters get stamped *Aeropost Romania* at the post office or write it on yourself. When sending **letters to Romania** for collection at the main post office, address them *Officiul Poştal no. 1, poşte restante* in a specific town, and make sure the last name is clearly underlined. To collect letters, you'll have to show your passport and pay a small fee. Important messages should be sent by postcard, as letters from abroad can go missing if they look as if they might contain dollars. *American Express* also

---

PHONING ROMANIA FROM ABROAD

Dial the international access code (given below) + 40 (country code) + area code (minus initial 0) + number

Australia ☎0011	New Zealand ☎00
Canada☎011	UK☎00
Ireland ☎010	USA ☎011

PHONING ABROAD FROM ROMANIA

Dial the country code (given below) + area code (minus initial 0) + number

Australia ☎0061	New Zealand ☎0064
Canada☎001	UK☎0044
Ireland ☎00353	USA ☎001

CHARGECARD ACCESS NUMBERS

BT ☎01.800.4444   AT&T's USA Direct ☎01.800.4288   MCI's WorldPhone ☎01.800.1800

ROMANIAN PHONE CODES

Alba Iulia ☎058	Braşov ☎068	Iaşi ☎032	Sibiu ☎069	Tîrgu Mureş ☎065
Arad ☎057	Cluj ☎064	Oradea ☎059	Suceava ☎030	Tulcea ☎040
Bucharest ☎01	Constanţa ☎041	Piatra Neamţ ☎033	Timişoara ☎056	

USEFUL TELEPHONE NUMBERS

All Romanian phone numbers have increased from five to six digits, and in Bucharest from six to seven digits: as a rule the numbers for the chief town of each *judeţ* or county have been prefixed with 1, while most Bucharest numbers have been prefixed with 6 (except those beginning with 25, 26, 45, 46, 77 and 78, which are prefixed with 7, and other new numbers).

☎930 directory enquiries for business numbers

☎931 and ☎932 directory enquiries for domestic numbers (A–L and M–Z respectively)

☎952 rail information

☎953 taxi

☎955 police

☎959 weather forecast

☎961 *salvarea* or rescue

☎962 emergency hospital

☎981 fire service

☎971 international operator

TIME

Romania is 2 hours ahead of GMT, 10 hours ahead of US Pacific Standard Time and 7 hours ahead of Eastern Standard Time. Clocks go forward one hour at the end of March and an hour back at the end of September.

---

give you a direct number to get through to your home operator, and charge home coinbox rates. However, chargecard calls from Romania are peculiarly expensive – a third more than neighbouring East European countries.

Faxes (*telefax*) are all the rage now, easily found around major cities, in the best hotels and in principal post offices.

THE MEDIA

Romania's **newspapers** were all housed together in the *Casa Şcinteii*, north of central Bucharest, and although there is now a free press and indeed the building has been renamed the *Casa Presei Libere*, many of them remain in the building and are controlled from there. There are supposedly 1600 titles, many of them local, and very few of any real worth. As is the case all across East-central Europe, there has been an explosion of soft (and not so soft) porn, and in addition there is an obsession with crime. Nationalist papers have a circulation of around a million, while the sensationalist tabloid *Tineretul Liber* (Free Youth) is the biggest seller, followed by *Adevarul* (The Truth – the communist party rag *Scinteia* renamed) and the most useful, *România Liberă* (Free Romania), which takes a constructive opposition line and sells 120,000.

There are a few **English-language** publications, none easily found outside Bucharest, of which the most useful is *Nine O'Clock*, a daily news sheet picked up free in hotels. Here and there you'll also come across the official tourist mag *Holidays in Romania*, which occasionally features interesting articles. In the classier hotels, Western newspapers can also be bought.

There are British, American, French and German libraries in the main cities where you can find libraries and newspapers a couple of weeks old.

Television is inescapable, never being turned off in many homes. Having been restricted to two hours a day, half of it on Ceauşescu's feats, there is now no shortage of programming. The nationwide state TV channel, and a second channel received in a few major cities, are under tight government control and have doubtless helped it to retain power at election time, just as TV played a crucial role in the overthrow of Ceauşescu. There are also one or two private local TV and radio stations whose political impartiality is like-wise suspect, and an ever-increasing number of satellite dishes picking up SKY, CNN and MTV.

For news, many Romanians tune into foreign **radio**, notably the Romanian-language broadcasts of the BBC World Service and Voice of America. The World Service also broadcasts in English; this can be found between approximately 8am and 5pm GMT on 17.64, 15.07 and 12.09MHz (17.01, 19.91 and 24.80m), and between 5 and 10pm and between 4 and 7am on 9.41, 6.20 and 6.18MHz (31.88, 48.43 and 48.54m). Reception quality varies greatly: generally, lower frequencies give better results early in the morning and late at night, higher ones in the middle of the day.

OPENING HOURS AND PUBLIC HOLIDAYS

Opening hours in Romania are notoriously unreliable. Stores are generally open from 9 or 10am to 6 or 8pm on weekdays, but may close for several hours during the middle of the day. They can also be closed at any time for deliveries or *inventar*. Supermarkets (*magazin universal*) and some food stores are open daily from 8am to 8pm, 8.30am to 1pm on Sundays. Museums open from 9am to 5pm or from 10am to 6pm, and close on Mondays and sometimes (particularly in Bucharest) on Tuesdays. Industrial workers start early and head home around 3pm; most offices are closed by 4pm.

PUBLIC HOLIDAYS
January 1 & 2
Easter Monday (Good Friday is not a holiday, but women are usually given the day off to shop and cook)
May 1
December 1 Unification of Transylvania with Romania
December 25 & 26

CHURCHES, MONASTERIES, CASTLES AND MUSEUMS

Romania's abundance of **churches** testifies to its history of religious faith – and competing faiths. In **Transylvania** these became aligned in medieval times with the ethnic stratification of society, so that the rights of "four religions" and "three Nations" were recognized (but not those of Orthodoxy and its Romanian adherents – an order stigmatized as the "Seven Deadly Sins of Transylvania"). In **Moldavia and Wallachia** Orthodoxy, supported by the boyars and princes, had a monopoly on faith, but the clergy and the Patriarchate consisted of Byzantine (and later Phanariot) Greeks more often than Romanians, and performed the liturgy and rites in incomprehensible Slavonic rather than the native tongue, as late as the nineteenth century.

This and the frequency of invasions at least partly account for the extraordinary diversity of styles. Churches range from the inspired **wooden** *biserici de lemn* in Maramureş villages to the Gothic *Hallenkirche* and austere **fortified** structures raised by the Saxons around Braşov and Sibiu. Having absorbed the **Byzantine** style of architecture in Moldavia and Wallachia, masons and architects ran riot with colour and mouldings (as at Curtea de Argeş) before producing wonderful ornamental stone facades – most notably at Iaşi's Three Hierarchs' Church, and in Wallachia, where the "Brîncoveanu style" flourished, with its porticoes and stone carving derived from native woodwork motifs.

The **frescoes** so characteristic of medieval Orthodox churches achieved their ultimate sophistication in Maramureş at the hands of largely unknown artists, and were boldly executed on the exterior walls of Suceviţa, Voroneţ and the other "Painted Monasteries" of

Bucovina, in northern Moldavia, which are today recognized as some of Europe's greatest artistic treasures. The Orthodox Church maintains dozens of **monasteries** (many in fact nunneries), the most famous, after those in Bucovina, being Snagov, where Dracula is buried, and Horez, Brîncoveanu's masterpiece.

On Sunday mornings and during the great festivals like Easter, Orthodox **services** – *slujbă* or *liturghie* – are impressive rites (which non-believers may attend without problem). Orthodox churches are often open, with old women selling tapers or praying fervently, while Roman Catholic churches allow access as far as a grille just inside the door, so that passers-by can say a quick prayer. Protestant churches are usually closed, but you can ask around for the caretaker.

Romania's most spectacular **castles** are located in Transylvania, where you'll also find towns such as Sibiu and Sighişoara, built around an inner citadel or *cetate*. Bran and Hunedoara

are both superb Gothic/Renaissance castles, while at Arad, Alba Iulia and Oradea stand three colossal Hapsburg fortresses laid out in the geometric style of the Swiss military architect Vauban. Castles, like **museums** (*muzeu*) great and small, are normally open from 9am to 5pm or 10am to 6pm daily, except on Mondays and national holidays. For visitors, many museums soon pall because of the lack of information in any language but Romanian and the identical approach to national history in every museum. **Art galleries** have a limited range of artists, but the **village museums** are interesting even without the benefit of captions; they contain peasant houses filled with artefacts, huge oil presses, watermills and other structures rescued from the the agrarian past, laid out as if in a real community. Student reductions are usually only granted to groups of ten or more, but in any case, museum **admission charges** are not high, around L400–1000.

FESTIVALS

Romanian festivals fall into four groups: those linked to the Orthodox religion, with its "Twelve Great Feasts" and hosts of lesser festivals; those marking events such as marriage, birth and death; those marking stages in the agricultural and pastoral cycle; and secular anniversaries. While the last are national holidays, and never change their date, many festivals are more mobile. The Orthodox Easter is a "moveable feast" and still reckoned according to the "Old

Style" or Julian calendar rather than the Gregorian calendar used in the West (and in Romania for secular purposes, including the date of Christmas). Rural festivals take place on a particular day, such as the first Sunday of June, the actual date of which varies from year to year, and they can also be advanced or delayed depending on the progress of the crops. Given the collapse of the tourist information system, the place to check dates is the cultural office in the county *prefectură*.

Festivals specific to particular regions are listed in the *Guide* – what follows is an overview.

WINTER FESTIVALS

Christmas (*Crăciun*) and **New Year** (*Anul Nou*) celebrations are spread over the period from December 24 to January 7, and preparations often begin as early as December 6 (St Nicholas' Day) when pigs are slaughtered for the forthcoming feasts. Groups of young men and boys meet to prepare the festival costumes and masks, and to rehearse the *colinde* – allegorical songs wishing good health and prosperity for the coming year, which they sing outside each household on Christmas Eve (*Ajun*), when the faithful exchange thin pastries called *turte* (symbolizing Christ's swaddling clothes).

In **Moldavia and Bucovina**, processions follow the *Capră* (Goat), a costumed dancer whose mask has a moveable lower jaw which he clacks in time with the music (to represent the death pangs of the old year). The week-long masked carnival in the Maramureş town of **Sighet** has similar shamanistic origins, although it has been considerably modernized.

On New Year's Eve throughout the countryside, groups of *plugăraşi* pull a plough festooned with green leaves from house to house, cutting a symbolic furrow in each yard while a *doină* calling for good health and fecundity is recited, accompanied in Transylvania by carolling, for example at **Arpaş** and **Şercaia** in Braşov county. In Tudora and the villages around Suceava, New Year's greetings are delivered by the *buhai*, a friction drum shaped like a bottomless barrel which imitates the bellowing of a bull when horse hair is drawn through the hole in a membrane. This accompanies the *Pluguşor*, a mime play of people masked as goats, little horses (*căiuţi*) and bears (*urşi*), sometimes with flute music. At dawn on New Year's Day the "little ploughmen" take over, sowing in the furrows ploughed the day before; and although the official holiday ends on January 2, villagers may keep celebrating through to Epiphany (the 6th), when **horse races** are staged in areas like the Wallachian plain and Dobrogea. January 30 is Three Hierarchs' Day, celebrated with great pomp in Iaşi's Trei Ierarhi Church, which is dedicated to the saintly trio.

A review of Gorj county's folk ensembles and miners' brass bands – the *Izvoare fermecate* or "Enchanted Water Springs" – is held on the third Sunday of **February** at Tîrgu Jiu (winter conditions permitting). Though few Romanians are nowadays devout enough to observe the traditional Lent fast, which begins seven weeks before Easter, generally in **March**, some rural folk still bake twisted loaves – *colaci* – on the 9th, Forty Saints' Day, and take them to the village church to be blessed and distributed as alms. On one weekend during the month (decided at fairly short notice) there's an early spring festival at **Hălmagiu**, called the Kiss Fair, which provides the opportunity for villagers from the Apuseni and Banat regions to socialize and trade crafts.

EASTER AND FERTILITY FESTIVALS

With the onset of spring in **April and May**, agricultural work begins in earnest, roughly coinciding with Easter, the holiest festival of the Orthodox year. Urbanization and collectivization have both affected the nature of **spring festivals**, so that **Reşiţa**'s *Alaiul primaverii* features firefighters and engineers as well as folklore ensembles within its parade of floats (throughout the first week in April). Village festivals have tended to conglomerate, so that, instead of a dozen smallish fetes, one now finds a single, large event drawing participants and visitors from across the region – for example the *Florile Oltului* (Flowers of the Olt) at **Avrig** on the second Sunday of April, attended by contingents from dozens of communities around Sibiu, some wearing the rich velvet and paste jewellery of traditional Saxon finery. Similarly, the Girl Fair at **Gurghiu**, on the second Sunday in May, is an occasion for villagers from the Gurghiul, Beica and Mureş valleys to make merry. For pomp and crowds on a larger scale, it's better to go for Braşov's Pageant of the Juni (see p.125), held on the first Sunday of May.

Though its exact dates vary, the Orthodox **Easter** (*Paşte*) also falls within the months of April and May. From *Floriile*, Palm Sunday, through the "Week of Sufferings" (*Săptămîna patimilor*, during which, it's believed, souls will ascend directly to heaven), the devout attend church services, culminating in the resurrection celebration at midnight on Easter Saturday. The cry "Christ has risen" (*Hristos o-nviat*) and the reply "Truly he has risen" (*Adevărat c-o-nviat*) resound through the candle-lit churches, full to overflowing with worshippers. With the exception of Pentecost or **Whitsun**, fifty days after Easter Sunday, subsequent Orthodox festivals are nowadays less widely observed. So, too, sadly, is the ancient Wallachian custom that allowed women to drink wine together and amuse themselves by insulting their menfolk on the third Tuesday following Easter; two days later Gypsy children dressed in leaves used to dance *Paparude* to invoke rains on the parched fields, being given coins and doused with water as they proceeded from house to house.

In southern Romania, there's a traditional belief (still held by a minority) that groups of village mimes and dancers could work magic if all the rites were correctly observed; and selected young men were initiated into the **ritual of**

Căluş. This took place in secret (the word means "gag" as well as "little horse"), and was performed by a *vătaf* who had inherited the knowledge of *descîntece* (magic charms) and the dance steps from his predecessor. On **Whit Sunday** (*Rosalia*), an odd-numbered group of these *Căluşari* began their ritual dance from house to house, accompanied by a flag-bearer and a *Mut* (a mute who traditionally wore a red phallus beneath his robe and muttered sexual invocations), thus ensuring that each household was blessed with children and a bountiful harvest, and, if need be, exorcizing anyone possessed by the spirits of departed friends and family. *Căluş* rites are still enacted in some Oltenian villages, and the *Căluşari* meet for a two-day celebration of their dancing and musical prowess at **Slatina** sometime in May (the exact date varies). There's a similar festival, the Căluşarul *Transilvanean*, in **Deva** during the second week of January, which doesn't have any particular magical significance and is nowhere near the heartland of *Căluş* country, but is nevertheless impressive.

Meanwhile, the Székely hold their Whitsun pilgrimage to Csíkszereda (Miercurea Ciuc); since they are Roman Catholics, its date is determined by the Western Christian calendar. The Székely also hold their version of the Festival of the Plough at **Băile Jigodin**, near Miercurea Ciuc, on the third Sunday of May. Once common practice, the ritual garlanding of the plough is now rare, although the *Tinjaua* or Festival of the First Ploughman (on the first Sunday of May) at **Hoteni**, in Maramureş, is similar. Thankfully the age-old **pastoral rites and feasts** marking the sorting, milking and departure of the flocks to the hills are still widespread throughout Maramureş and the **Apuseni mountains** during late April or early May, depending on local tradition and climatic factors. The best-known *Sîmbra oilor* occur on the first Sunday of May, at the **Huta pass** into Oaş (see p.254) and on the ridge of **Măgura Priei** (see p.190); but lingering snows can delay the smaller festivals, perhaps even until early July.

SUMMER FESTIVALS

The Cherry Fair at **Brîncoveneşti** on the first Sunday of **June** anticipates other harvest festivals later in the month, and the round of great **summer fairs** known as *Tîrg* or *Nedeias*. In the days before all-weather roads, these events provided the people of remote highland villages with an annual opportunity to acquire news of the outside world, and arrange deals and marriages. On the second Sunday of June, folk from some thirty Banat settlements attend the *Nedeia of Tălcălşele* at **Avram Iancu**; and another village with the same name is the base for the famous Girl Fair of **Mount Găina** (see p.185), held on the Sunday before July 20. **Fundata**'s *Nedeia of the Mountains*, theoretically on the last Sunday of June (but sometimes not until September) is the traditional gathering for people of the Braşov, Argeş and Dîmboviţa regions; while the highlanders of Oltenia have their own equivalent in the great **Polovragi Fair** (on July 15 or 20).

There are **weddings** in the villages every Saturday throughout the summer, which continue through the weekend with music, drinking and dancing. Other summer festivals perpetuate Romania's old customs and folklore: the light hearted Buying Back of the Wives at **Hodac**, and the funereal declamation of *boccas* during The King of the Fir Trees (see p.196) at **Tiha Bîrgăului** in the heart of fictional Dracula country (on the second and third Sundays of June). *Drăgaica*, the pagan pre-harvest celebration in the fields on Midsummer Day, is only practised in a few districts of Wallachia today, but *Sînzîene*, the feast of St John the Baptist on June 24, is celebrated in many places with bonfires and wreaths thrown onto roofs. The diversity of folk costumes and music within a particular area can be appreciated at events like **Şomcuta Mare**'s pastoral *Stejarul* (The Oak Tree), or the larger Rarău Mountain festival at **Ilişesti**, held respectively on the first and second Sundays of **July**.

August is probably the best month for music, with four major festivals. During the first week at **Călimăneşti** in Wallachia, the Songs of the Olt draws musicians and folklore ensembles from all over Oltenia, and coincides with a big pottery fair. On the second Sunday, people from Maramureş, Transylvania and Moldavia meet for the great *Horă* at the **Prislop Pass** to socialize, feast and dance in their finest costumes; on the same day, to the south across the mountains, the Festival of the Ceahlău Mountain is held at **Durău** near the shores of Lake Bicaz. The music of pan pipes and the bands of Gorj county (around Tîrgu Jiu) characterize another festival, At Tişmana in a Garden, where you can also find a wide range of handicrafts (for which bartering may secure better bargains than paying in lei).

This is held on August 15, the **Feast of the Assumption** or Dormition of the Virgin Mary, when there are many church festivals and pilgrimages across the country, notably at **Moisei** in Maramureş.

Reaping preoccupies many villages during **September**, giving rise to **harvest festivals**, although the custom is gradually declining. The timing of these varies with the crop, and from year to year, but you can usually rely upon At the Vintage at **Odobeşti** in the eastern Carpathians being held on the last Sunday. Earlier in the month, on the first Sunday, you can hear the panpipers of the northwest perform the Rhapsody of the Trişcaşi at **Leşu**, in Bistriţa-Năsăud county. Many of the musicians are shepherds, who also play alpine long horns and bagpipes, and compete with each other at The Vrancea Shepherd's Long Pipe, a festival held at **Odobeşti** on the third Sunday of **November**.

SPORTS AND OUTDOOR PURSUITS

Although two thirds of Romania is either plains or hills and plateaux, the country's geography is dominated by mountains, which almost enclose the "Carpathian redoubt" of Transylvania, and merge with lesser ranges bordering Moldavia and Maramureş. In such areas the scenery is usually beautiful, with pastoral valleys nestled between foothills ascending to wild crags or precipitous gorges. Much of it has escaped the ravages of hasty industrialization visible in lower-lying regions, and some areas like the Harghita mountains and the ranges north of Bistriţa and Maramureş are still essentially wildernesses, inhabited by bears and wolves and birds of prey. Throughout this area there are opportunities to pursue outdoor activities – hiking, skiing, caving or even shooting rapids in the mountains.

The Danube Delta is a totally different environment, unique for its topography – of which only one tenth is dry land – and as a wildlife habitat which attracts some three hundred species of birds during the spring and autumn migrations.

SKIING

Skiing is a popular sport in the mountains from November or December through until March, or even April, depending on conditions at the nine resorts. Foreign tour operators favour Poiana Braşov (and Sinaia) for their superior slopes and facilities, but by going through ONT or turning up on the spot you can also attend ski instruction at Borşa in Maramureş (for beginners; December to March), Păltiniş south of Sibiu, Semenic in southwestern Transylvania (November to March) or Durău/Ceahlău on the edge of Moldavia. The majority of pistes are rated "medium" or "easy" (colour-coded red or blue), but each of the major resorts has at least one difficult (black) run, and the descents from Coştila and Caraiman to Buşteni are positively hazardous. Details of the slopes, chair-lifts and snowcover at each resort are contained in a brochure from the ONT.

Ski equipment for rent at the resorts is slightly antiquated compared to the latest Western models, though otherwise serviceable; package tourists, however, get priority, so independent skiers should if possible bring their own gear. Ski rental will cost £18–24/$27–36, boots £14–17/$21–26, a lift pass £30–34/$45–50, lessons £27–35/$40–52, and a ski-pack including all the above £52–63/$78–94 for 6 days.

HIKING, CAVING AND CANOEING

The **Carpathians** – a continuation of the Alps – are the most sinuous chain of mountains in Europe; and in Romania they form a natural barrier between Transylvania and the old Regat provinces, interrupted by a few narrow passes or wide depressions. Though few of Romania's Carpathian peaks are higher than 2500m, and the majority are between 1000m and 2000m, lack of altitude is more than compensated for by the variety of geological formations and rockscapes, with mighty gorges (*cheile*) at Turda and Bicaz, and spectacular valleys cut by the Olt and Prahova rivers. Bizarrely eroded **rock formations** characterize Mount Ceahlău and karstic areas such as the Padiş plateau and the "Valley of Hell" in the Apuseni mountains, while the Bucegi range is famous for the Babele Sphinx, and the sheer walls overhanging Buşteni in the Prahova valley. Several large **caves** (*peşteri*) in the mountains with magnificent stalactites (at Chişcău, Meziad, Scarişoara and Polovragi for example) are easily accessible, but most are known only to Romania's dedicated band of pot-holers.

Dozens of **hiking trails** – signposted with red triangles, blue stripes or other markings – are shown on *Hartă Turistică* maps. Several walks are detailed in the *Guide*, while many individual ranges are minutely covered by booklets in the "Our Mountains" series – unfortunately only published in Romanian (*Munţi Nostri*) and German (*Unsere Berge*) and sporadically available from bookstores rather than tourist offices. The **Bucegi massif** is perfect for short hikes within a limited time; for it offers dramatic crags, caves and waterfalls within a few hours' walk of the cable-car, which ascends from the valley one hour's train ride from Braşov or two from the capital. To the southwest, the Retezat and Parîng mountains offer the chance of longer hikes crossing several ranges.

Several British tour operators organize all-inclusive **walking holidays** in the Carpathians (see p.5). Independent hikers should bring camping gear and food, since accommodation in mountain cabanas can't be guaranteed, and some huts don't serve meals. These **cabanas** (marked on hiking maps) are convivial places where you can learn much about the mountains; but many Romanians simply pitch camp by rivers, and providing it's not in a nature reserve, you can do the same.

USEFUL HIKING TERMS

potecă/traseu	path/route
nerecomandabil iarna	unsafe during winter
refugiu (*salvamont*)	refuge (with first aid)
şau	col (saddle)
stînca	rock
colţ	cliff
aven	doline
poiana	glade
izvors	spring
cascada	waterfall
telecabina	cable-car
teleschi	ski-drag
telescaun	chair lift
cale ferată îngustă	narrow-gauge rail line

CAVING AND CANOEING

The science and practice of **caving** owes much to a Romanian, Emil Racoviţa, who founded the world's first speleological institute at Cluj University, near the karst zone of the **Apuseni mountains**. This offers the greatest range of possibilities, from easy strolling passages to vertical shafts and flooded tunnels; there are tourist caves such as Chişcău and Meziad, big river caves such as Humpleu, Magura and Ceta-ţile Ponorului, and any number of crevices that only experts should get involved with. The other main area is the southern Banat and the **Mehedinţi massif**, with river caves such as Topolniţa, Cloşani and Comarnic.

The last major discovery was made only in 1986, at Movile in Dobrogea, and the further reaches of many other caves are still being explored by Romanian enthusiasts, and constantly yield fresh surprises. Interested groups or individuals should write to the **Racoviţa Institute**, Str. Clinicilor 5, 3400 Cluj, or Str. Frumoasa 11, 78114 Bucureşti, to enquire about co-operation and possible caves, several months in advance, stating your experience. An offer to contribute gear and a share of the costs should increase your chances of acceptance by a local club.

It's likely that the Racoviţa Institute can also put foreigners in touch with **canoeing** enthusiasts devoted to shooting the rapids: a dangerous sport practised on rivers like the Vaser in Maramureş and the Bistriţa in Bucovina, which descend steeply from their highland sources (or from caves in the karst zones). Bring all your own equipment, since there's little chance of renting or buying anything decent.

BIRDWATCHING

The best place for seeing **birdlife** is without a doubt the Danube Delta. Millions of birds winter here, or stop over during the spring and autumn migrations to northern Europe, the Mediterranean, China, Siberia and parts of Africa – a unique concentration of different species, including the Delta's own resident pelicans (slowly losing the fight against local fishermen). ONT can arrange boat tours down the main Sulina channel of the Delta, and their Tulcea or Crişan offices may sometimes be wheedled into renting small boats, which are the only means to penetrate the backwaters, where most of the birds nest. Canoes or kayaks are best for exploration, since boats with outboard motors scare the wildlife and get clogged by vegetation.

You may be able to negotiate with the local fisherman for a boat (*Pot să inchiriez o barcă?*), bearing in mind that he'll probably act as rower and guide. Doing it this way lessens your freedom of movement and is likely to be fairly time consuming.

FOOTBALL

Football's 1994 World Cup brought the Romanian team to international attention but many have been aware of their strengths ever since Steaua Bucharest, Romania's leading club, won the **European Champions' Cup** in 1986, and reached the semi-finals in 1988. Although Inter Milan allegedly offered to build a Fiat car plant in Romania in order to get their hands on Gheorghe Hagi, players have only been able to move freely to West European clubs since 1990: by 1992 nine of the national team were playing abroad, in teams ranging from Red Star Belgrade to Real Madrid. Clearly, this led to a rapid development both in their individual skills and in the national team's performance.

Romania qualified top of its group for the 1994 **World Cup**, finally going out in the quarter-final to Sweden on penalties. Since then, the manager, Iordanescu, has been promoted to major-general in the army, and the leading Romanian players have all figured in million-pound transfer deals.

Gheorghe Hagi was seen by many as the best player of the competition, although his nickname "the Maradona of the Carpathians" is due not to his footballing or handballing skills but to his insistence on wearing the no. 10 shirt. Born in Constanța, he played for the local side until a transfer to Steaua on the orders of Ceaușescu's son Valentin, who effectively ran the team. After the revolution he moved to Real Madrid for a fee of £1.8m, and after the World Cup to Barcelona. The much publicized moves of striker **Ilie Dumitrescu** and midfielder **Gica Popescu** to Tottenham Hotspur in London following the World Cup were supposedly conducted through the interpreting skills of the Spurs' player Ronnie Rosenthal, who is of Romanian–Jewish extraction.

The domestic game is dominated by Steaua Bucharest. Another Bucharest team, Dinamo, are their nearest rivals, trailed at a distance by Rapid Bucharest and Universitatea Craiova. As elsewhere in Eastern Europe, clubs have traditionally been linked to workplaces or trades; Steaua (Star) is the army team, Dinamo the police (and *Securitate*) team, and Rapid that of the rail workers.

Every town has its stadium (*stadion*), and you should be able to catch a game without problem. Tickets cost very little, and many terms, such as *meci* (match), *gol*, and *ofsaid* have been borrowed from English, although *arbitru* comes from the French for referee.

POLICE, TROUBLE AND HARASSMENT

For visitors, Romania remains generally safe: however there has been an explosion of violent crime, usually blamed on Gypsies but in fact more to do with alcohol and with the collapse of police authority. Despite this, robbery with violence is rare, and a few commonsense precautions should minimize the risk of your possessions being stolen.

You should watch out for **pickpockets**, in particular in Bucharest, where groups of Gypsies and the like hang around the Gara de Nord and the Calea Victoriei stores: a moneybelt is always advisable. Take care on overnight trains, shutting the door of your sleeper compartment securely. If your **passport** goes missing while in Bucharest, telephone your consulate immediately; anywhere else, contact the police, who'll issue a temporary visa. It's almost impossible to replace **travellers' cheques** in Romania, so these should be guarded fanatically. Thefts and other losses can be reported to the police (*poliția*) who will issue the paperwork required for insurance claims back home, though only slowly and with painstaking bureaucratic thoroughness.

THE POLICE

The **police force** has by and large been "renewed" since the revolution, and is regarded as honest if ineffectual. The **border police** however are notoriously corrupt – always keep your baggage with you when entering or leaving the country. The police lost its moral authority by playing a very minor role in the revolution, while the army established a position as guardians of freedom; thus many street patrols are composed of a policeman accompanied by a Kalashnikov-toting soldier. In rural areas the police rarely emerge from their stations except for spot-checks on cars or to bum drinks in the bars.

Unfortunately, the **Romanian Information Service** (the SRI or simply, to most people, the *Securitate*) is still on the scene, although no longer blackmailing people to report on their neighbours, friends and family. An obsession with anti-socialist activities long ago changed to a commitment to keeping the ruling elite in power, and this has not changed with the "revolution". Iliescu is even more adept than Ceaușescu at manipulating opinion and engineering provocations, and the SRI is busy. They don't normally concern themselves with tourists, but you should bear their existence in mind.

SPECIFIC OFFENCES

Foreigners are sometimes stopped and asked for **identification** (which should be carried at all times). Barring mishaps, however, this should be the extent of your dealings with the police, unless you break the law. Firstly, it's obviously safer not to become involved with the black market (see below). **Photography** is permitted everywhere except in areas designated by a sign (showing a crossed-out camera), usually near any barracks, no matter how unimportant; while **nudism** and topless bathing are forbidden except on a few beaches (although offenders are more likely to be cautioned than punished). **Camping**

wild is not allowed in nature reserves and forests, and dropping litter in theory incurs a £25 fine. **Sleeping rough** in towns is risky and will attract the *poliția*'s displeasure unless you do so in a train station and claim to be waiting for a train departing in the small hours. Should you be arrested, identify yourself, be polite and stay cool; try to avoid making a statement unless the officer speaks your language fluently; and demand to contact your consulate.

SUPPLY AND DEMAND

Bribery and corruption are rife in Romania, oiling the creaking machinery of everyday life. Bribes or tips (*ciubuc*) are the means to secure proper medical attention, a telephone, luxuries, a parking space, educational opportunities, promotions... the list is practically endless. Nor is money always involved; frequently, what happens is a reciprocal exchange of favours. Romanians refer to *pile* or "files", meaning contacts who can smooth over rough edges and expedite matters. Naturally enough this ties in with the **black market**, which is omnipresent. This has less to do with supplying illicit goods than with meeting the shortcomings of the economy.

As a visitor, you're unlikely to come into contact with this system, and as a rule the safest policy is simply not to get involved. However, if ever you can't get a room or a seat on a plane, or if you're pulled over for speeding, it's worth remembering that even one dollar can work wonders.

SEXUAL HARASSMENT

It's rare for Romanian men to subject women tourists to **sexual harassment**. Foreigners can be a different matter, since, amazing as it sounds, Turks and Greeks have taken to driving north from their repressed homelands for sex tourism – Bucharest even has a couple of strip clubs now.

As independent women travellers are rare, they're likely to be accorded some respect (if not excessive solicitude) – but also viewed with some amazement, particularly in rural areas. Most trouble is alcohol-fuelled, so avoid going alone to any but the classiest bars, especially at night and at weekends. Within earshot of other people, you should be able to scare away any local pest by shouting *lasați-ma in pace*! (Leave me alone!) or calling for the *Poliția*.

THE POSITION OF WOMEN

Romanian women carry a double burden of work and child care in a male-dominated society, and there seems little immediate prospect of changing this. Feminism, like the peace movement, was totally discredited by the hypocritical verbiage of the communists, and above all by having Elena Ceauşescu in charge of the national women's committee.

ATTITUDES TO GAYS

The communist regime was relentlessly homophobic. Sexual relations between consenting adults of the same sex were illegal; offenders were jailed or forced to submit to "voluntary treatment" including electric shocks, drugs or even castration, unless they took up the "option" of becoming an informer for the *Securitate*, a bait for other victims.

Since then things have got slightly more complicated: the government, trying to balance liberal Western opinion with more conservative public opinion, announced that homosexuality was to be legalized for men over 18, but in fact parliament voted merely to "condone" it, with seven-year prison terms still on the books for cases "causing public scandal". Nevertheless there is at least one AIDS charity in Bucharest, the *Asociaţie Româna Anti-SIDA*, working for safe sex and a more enlightened attitude on all sides.

AIDS was first identified in Romania in 1984, but the government refused to admit its existence until 1987, and took no effective measures to control the re-use of hypodermic needles before the revolution. In 1990 there were officially 1000 AIDS cases, and in late 1991, 1557 cases of HIV infection and 552 AIDS deaths were admitted; but these are certainly underestimates, as random samples suggested a figure of 130,000. These are almost all children, infected by the perverse custom of giving babies "microtransfusions", usually with dirty needles, to fortify them.

DIRECTORY

simply have a number without bothering about street names. Streets, boulevards (*bulevardul*), avenues (*calea* or *şoseaua*) and squares (*piaţa*) are commonly named after national heroes like Stephen the Great – Ştefan cel Mare – or Michael the Brave – Mihai Viteazul – or the date of an important event such as December 1, 1918, when Transylvania was united with the Old Kingdom.

CHILDREN qualify for various reductions, depending on their age. Rail transport is free for under-fives, and reduced by 50 percent for under-tens. On *TAROM* flights, children under two pay only 10 percent, and up to the age of twelve, 50 percent, providing they share a seat with an adult. In hotels, children under ten may often

ADDRESSES are written as Str. Eroilor 24, III/36 in the case of apartment buildings, ie Street (*strada*) of Heroes, the third floor of number 24, apartment 36. Some blocks have apartments back to back, in which case the entrance is also given, eg *scara B*. Outlying suburbs of Bucharest have a sector number, while in some towns, districts are known as *cartierul*, and by name, like the Schei quarter of Braşov. In small villages, houses

USEFUL THINGS TO BRING

An alarm clock, flashlight, candles, water-bottle, film, batteries, needle and thread, tampons, contraceptives, first-aid kit, ear plugs, razor blades, any prescribed medication, a supply of concentrated food for emergencies and morale boosting, and books to read.

share an adult's bed for free, or pay half of the adult cost for an extra bed in the room. In big coastal resorts and at Poiana Braşov there are kindergartens, with foreign language-speaking staff, for the benefit of holidaymakers; a few stations have a specially heated room for mothers with babies (*camera mama şi copilul*). For travellers with children, the big problems are shortages of nappies (diapers) and baby food. Local milk is not to be trusted – bring your own powdered milk. Mamaia and the main ski resorts offer the best entertainments for kids, but most large towns have a puppet theatre (*Teatrul de Păpuşi*).

CIGARETTES The most popular Western brands are Marlboro and Kent. Mysteriously, the latter had great status on the black market, although its uses as an "alternative currency" (worth $1 a packet) were over-rated. Romanian cigarettes are generally unappealing: the cheapest *Carpaţi* are of rough black tobacco; *Snagov* are milder and slightly more expensive; while the deluxe brand, *Cişmigiu*, aren't worth the extra cost. Native brands are usually filtered (*cu filtru*), and matches are called *chibrit*, while a light is *foc*.

CONSULATES AND EMBASSIES are all in Bucharest (see "Listings" p.79), and Romania has diplomatic relations with almost every country in the world. Most diplomatic buildings have Interior Ministry troops at the gate who'll demand to see your passport before permitting entry. If you've lost this, ring beforehand (and immediately, even outside working hours). Most embassies and consulates stock their national newspapers, while the US, French, German and British have reading rooms and cultural centres in Bucharest.

DEPARTURE TAX There is no departure tax in Romania.

ELECTRIC POWER is nominally delivered at 220 volts at 50Hz; plugs have two prongs 18mm apart.

FISHING Permits can be arranged through OJTs in provincial towns – the Danube Delta is an angler's paradise – and other bodies of water like Lake Bicaz and Lacu Roşu in the mountains between Moldavia and Transylvania are also rewarding.

LAUNDRIES Laundries are virtually unknown, and for travellers it's a choice between washing yourself or paying a hotel to do it.

LEFT LUGGAGE offices (*bagaje de mână*) exist in most train stations, where you'll also find left luggage lockers, which should be avoided since the locks are likely to jam. Always allow plenty of time to reclaim your baggage, especially in Bucharest and Constanţa, which are the only places where you're likely to have to show your passport.

TIME is normally two hours ahead of the UK, seven ahead of New York and ten ahead of California: clocks go forward one hour for the summer at the same time as other European countries (from the last Sunday of March to the last Sunday of September).

PART TWO

THE
GUIDE

- **CHAPTER 5**
  MARAMUREŞ
- **CHAPTER 3**
  TRANSYLVANIA
- **CHAPTER 4**
  MOLDAVIA
- **CHAPTER 6**
  THE BANAT
- **CHAPTER 2**
  WALLACHIA
- **CHAPTER 1**
  BUCHAREST
- **CHAPTER 7**
  THE DELTA
  AND THE COAST

UKRAINE

HUNGARY

MOLDOVA

UKRAINE

SERBIA

BULGARIA

Black Sea

N

CHAPTER ONE

BUCHAREST AND AROUND

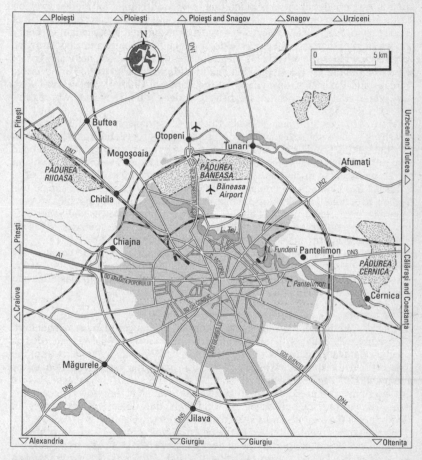

B UCHAREST (*Bucureşti*) is located only 64km from the Danube and Romania's southern border, but 600km from its northern frontier; even so almost all visitors will find themselves passing through at some point. It remains the centre of commerce and government and, with a population of over two million, is the largest city between Berlin and Athens. For much of its history its influences were primarily **Turkish**, but in the nineteenth century the city was remodelled in **French** style, and dubbed "the Paris of the East".

Between the wars, Ferdinand Lasalle described Bucharest as "a savage hotch-potch", with its Parisian boulevards and nightlife next to its slums and beggars, and today the extremes of wealth and poverty are no less evident. Life is hard in Romania, and particularly so in the misnamed "City of Joy" (*bucurie* means "pleasure" or "joy"), where fewer people have the direct access to rural relatives and the homegrown produce that makes life bearable in other Romanian cities.

On the surface the city is badly scarred by the architectural excresences of the communist period, but there is much that is worth dredging for hidden away on backstreets or just outside the centre. Overall, the city is an architectural jumble of Empire-style, concrete and disguised shantytown, softened by abundant greenery and warm, rich sunlight, where a creaking urban infrastructure and an obstructive bureaucracy block the inhabitants' natural urges towards spontaneity and *joie de vivre*. The **people** are a cosmopolitan mixture: Romanians, Gypsies, Turks, Arabs, Africans and Pakistanis, now joined by thousands of Chinese, whose triad wars have added another element to the thriving underworld of *traficanţi*, whores and beggars.

More than most European capitals, Bucharest is an insider's city. The greatest pleasures come from strolling in the secretive backstreets and from the random encounters this leads to; if you don't have time for this, it's probably best to head straight for Transylvania. **Accommodation** is more expensive in Bucharest, and you're more likely to be hassled, hustled and overcharged than elsewhere in Romania. In addition there remains the occasional risk of civil unrest; should this happen, avoid the Piaţa Revoluţiei, Piaţa Victoriei and Piaţa Universităţii, the main squares where demonstrations always converge. Though power and water cuts are now rare, hotels are overheated in summer and can be freezing in winter, when snowdrifts grip the city and the temperature plunges to -20°C (-4°F).

Bucharest is well connected by road and rail to the rest of the country, but short-distance services to the towns and villages in the immediate vicinity of the city are often limited or tortuous. However, there are some fine monasteries and mansions, notably at **Snagov**, which can be visited as day trips.

Some history

Bucharest, like Rome, has a legendary founder, in this case **Bucur**, a shepherd who supposedly built a settlement amidst the Vlăsia forest. This was recorded as a nameless "citadel on the Dîmboviţa" in 1368, and by name in an edict from the time of Vlad the Impaler. Wallachia's princes (voivodes, or *vodă* in Romanian) alternated between Tîrgovişte and Bucharest as the site of their capital, before the latter finally secured its claim in 1659, as its location at the convergence of the trade routes to Istanbul began to outweigh the defensive advantages of Tîrgovişte, in the foothills and a safer distance from the Danube.

As the boyars (nobles) moved to the city they built **palaces** and **churches** on the main streets radiating from the ill-defined centre; these streets were surfaced with timber baulks and known as "bridges" (*pod*). Although the city was subject to earthquakes and periodic attacks by Turks, Tartars, Austrians and Russians, it continued to develop, with brick houses replacing ones made of wood and clay, piped water, a municipal council from 1831, steam-powered mills from 1845, and telephones from 1884. After Romanian independence the city grew until it had a population of 380,000 in 1918; roads such as Podul Mogoşoaiei, Podul de Pămînt and Podul Calacilor were widened and paved, becoming the Calea Victoriei, Calea Plevnei and Calea Rahovei, in honour of the battles of the War of

The **telephone code** for Bucharest is ☎01, followed by seven digits. Most six-digit numbers are now prefixed with 6; those beginning with 25, 26, 45, 46, 77 and 78 are prefixed with 7, and some new numbers begin with 2 or 3.

Independence. New **boulevards** were driven through the existing street pattern in the 1890s, on the pattern of Haussmann's Paris; the first trolleybuses traversed them in 1893, and they still form the main north–south and east–west axes and a ring boulevard. Most of Bucharest's major buildings were built, many by French or French-trained architects, in the years before and after World War I.

After World War II the city doubled in population, from one to two million, and was ringed with ugly apartment buildings, first in areas such as Griviţa-Roşie which the Allies had bombed flat (aiming for the rail yards) and then on green fields, making it pointless straying more than a kilometre or so from the historic core. Finally Ceauşescu set out to impose his megalomaniac vision on the city, demolishing most of the area south of the city centre to create a new **Civic Centre**; this is unfinished and seems likely to scar the city for many years yet.

Arrival, information and city transport

Your means of travel and the time of day can greatly affect your **arrival** in Bucharest, as transport around the city, the condition of the roads and streetlighting leave much to be desired.

By train

Most international **trains** arrive after dark when Bucharest is doubly bewildering. Virtually all international and domestic services terminate at the **Gara de Nord**, a busy, squalid hive with queues for everything, where you can store luggage at the *bagaj de mina* on the concourse opposite platforms 4 and 5. Only local trains use the Gara Basarab (700m northwest of the main station), Gara Obor (northeast of the centre) and Gara Progresu (on the southern outskirts), while the Gara Băneasa (north of Piaţa Presei Libere) is used mainly by summer trains to the coast.

From the Gara de Nord, the metro can take you to Piaţa Victoriei (one stop towards Dristor 2) or to Piaţa Unirii (seven stops towards Republica), at either of which you can change onto line 2 to reach Piaţa Universităţii, the nearest stop to the heart of the city. Buses and trams from the Gara de Nord run around the centre rather than straight through it; it takes half an hour or so to walk into the centre, and taxis shouldn't cost more than a couple of dollars.

By air

International air passengers arrive at **Otopeni airport**, 16km north of the centre. Money changing facilities are available here and you can also buy entry visas across the counter. To get into the city, either give in to the friendly mob of taxi-drivers, or fight your way across the car park to find express bus #783, which departs every 30 minutes, charging L500 and terminating at the Piaţa Unirii after 30–40 minutes. Some travel companies include airport transfer in their air packages or can arrange it, so check with your agent before departure. ONT also arranges transfer by car for $20.

Internal flights land at **Băneasa airport**, just outside which you can catch bus #131, #334 or #783 or tram #5 into the centre, or bus #205 to the Gara de Nord, until around 11.30pm; night bus #414 runs to Piaţa Unirii.

By road

Buses from international destinations will drop you at the Gara de Nord. Bucharest has six bus stations, all on the edge of town, and it's unlikely you'll arrive at any of these, as they exist primarily to feed passengers from the city transport system onto buses to the surrounding villages. Private bus companies running services from other towns within Romania, such as Tîrgovişte, use the *Hotel Nord* on Calea Griviţei.

Arriving **by road** in your own vehicle is much the easiest option, although drivers should beware of potholes, cyclists, drunks and wandering animals on the "highways" at night. Approaching from Transylvania you'll pass both airports and Băneasa campsite before encountering the Şoseaua Kiseleff, which leads to the centre. The approach from Giurgiu (the point of entry from Bulgaria) is less inspiring, with a long run through high-rise suburbs until Bulevardul Dimitrie Cantemir finally reaches the Piaţa Unirii.

Information

Bucharest's main **tourist office** is 150m south of the Piaţa Romană metro station at B-dul Magheru 7 ((Mon–Fri 8am–8pm, although after 5pm you can usually only change money; Sat & Sun 8am–3pm; ☎614.51.60). The staff are not inclined to part with much information, although they'll change money, rent cars and rooms and arrange "programmes" with alacrity.

Desks in the *Intercontinental* and *Bucureşti* hotels (Mon–Fri 8am–4pm, Sat 8am–2pm) also supply tourist information, but the tendency is for visitors not bearing hard currency to be fobbed off with a poor city plan. Most of the practical information you're likely to require can be found under "Listings" (p.78). ONT's free **maps** of Bucharest are serviceable, but better ones are available from stalls on the north side of Bulevardul Republicii, by the university. One particularly interesting map, *Editura Museion* (1992) shows all the city's historic churches, museums and other monuments.

The Gara de Nord has an ONT bureau by platform 2 (opening hours as for the main office) which will change money and book private rooms, but nothing else. The board outside, which lists hotel addresses and telephone numbers, is of pre-revolutionary vintage.

City transport

Public transport is gradually becoming less chaotic, with route maps at last appearing on the new aluminium bus shelters. Most **bus** and **tram** routes avoid the central zone, apart from some express buses on the main axes, but now that the core **metro system** is open this isn't such a problem. Nevertheless, without a car you may find yourself walking a lot – no great hardship in this city of green, picturesque backwaters, although you should beware of cars, which zoom by with utter disregard for pedestrians. Road surfaces are terrible, except for the downtown thoroughfares, so that buses and trams seem set to rattle themselves to pieces, and trolleybuses frequently slip from the wires and stall. But the real problem is overcrowding. Boarding may require brute force, and "full up" can mean precisely that (at least during daytime, when doors are closed; at night, people hang from the open doorways). Once crammed inside, however, Romanians are remarkably restrained, even good-natured about their situation.

Buses and trams

There is a flat fare of L150–200 on all **trolleybuses** (*troleibuz*), **buses** (*autobuz*) and **trams** (*tramvai*), which run from dawn until midnight. As elsewhere in Eastern Europe, passengers buy tickets, singly or in bunches, in advance from street kiosks (5am–8pm), and punch them once aboard. Trams are numbered in the 1–54 series, on a red background; trolleybuses 55–99, on a green background; buses 100–399, on a blue background; night buses and those running out of the city in the 400s; and express buses (on which you pay double the normal fare, directly to the driver) in the 700s. In addition there are now private **Maxitaxis** or minibuses operating along the major arteries, which charge about double the standard fare; the current rate is posted in the window.

Bucharest's main city **bus stations** for journeys to surrounding villages and towns are Filaret, on Piaţa Filaret, in the station built in 1869 for Bucharest's first rail line, which sends buses south and southeast towards Giurgiu and Olteniţa; Băneasa, B-dul Ionescu de la Brad 1, serving Snagov, Fierbinţi and Ploieşti to the north; and Griviţa, Şos. Chitilei 221, at the *Mezeş* terminal of tram #45, serving Tîrgovişte.

KEY BUS ROUTES

• Along B-duls Magheru and Bălcescu (north–south, parallel to metro line M2): #781, #783 and #784.

• Along B-dul Dacia (east–west, north of the centre): #785, #123 and #133.

• Along B-duls Kogălniceanu and Republicii (east–west, via the university): #69 (Obor–Cotroceni), #66, #70, #85 (all Obor–Str. Pirvan, just west of Cişmigiu).

From Piaţa Rosetti (just east of the centre) other buses run east: #782 to Granitul, #63 and #506 to Obor.

The metro

The **metro** runs from 5.30am until midnight, with a flat fare of two L50 coins. Instead of ticket offices, there are kiosks at each station dispensing the correct change to drop into the turnstiles. Plans are afoot, however, to change this system to tickets. The first line (M1, shown in yellow on maps) was built to serve the new working-class suburbs, and runs east–west; the second, M2 (shown in blue), runs north–south through the centre, and the third, M3 (shown in red), branches off M1 and loops north to link the Gara de Nord with Piaţa Victoriei and Piaţa Universităţii. Although local maps indicate a change from M1 to M3 at the Gara de Nord, trains do in fact run through from Republica to Dristor 2; this may change when the branch to Laromet finally opens.

The system is decidedly not user-friendly, with poor maps and signposting and spooky lighting; however, you may be able to make out the name of the next stop from the crackly announcement as your train pulls out.

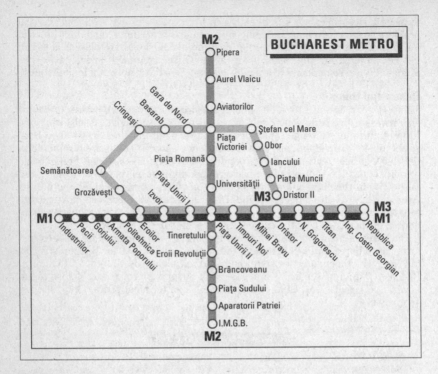

BUCHAREST METRO

Taxis

Taxis are fairly easy to find, although regular rises in the price of fuel lead to frequent protests and strikes. State-owned vehicles are generally the only ones with meters, so agree a fair price (fares are usually paid in lei) before getting into the more numerous private *taxis-particular*. For a short journey anywhere in the centre, L4000–6000 should suffice; even to travel right across the city you shouldn't pay more than L20,000 (around $10). Don't expect to get any change.

Accommodation

Most of Bucharest's **hotels** are optimistically aimed at foreign businessmen, and even the lowest-category ones aren't really economical. To make matters worse, many of the least expensive ones have either closed down for refits, or have been snapped up for their real-estate value and turned into offices. Of those that remain, their official categories range from II-A up through II and I to Luxury, although with a few notable exceptions these all fail to come up to Western standards. Hotels are found in four main areas, as listed below; most are rather run-down (if not plain sleazy), but some retain Art-Deco furnishings and an old-world feel. In addition, there's a limited selection of **private rooms** and **dormitory accommodation**, obtainable through the tourist office or your own efforts.

Hotels

Most of the hotels around the **Gara de Nord** are under the same management and charge the same prices. It's the cheapest location and the late-night ambiance is much as you'd expect in this seedy area. Around the **Piaţa Revoluţiei and the university** you're in the true heart of the city, where many of the better hotels are. If you can afford to, this is the best place to stay. The area between the **Cişmigiu Gardens and Piaţa Unirii** includes some of the most individual hotels in Bucharest, while the most pricey, privately run establishments lie out on the fringes of the inner city. In the no-man's-land to the north beyond Piaţa Presei Libere are three modern hotels (reached by bus #331 from Piaţa Lahovari), patronized by bus parties or those working at the nearby Exhibition Complex.

Around the Gara de Nord

Astoria, B-dul D. Golescu 27 (☎638.26.15 or 649.52.10). A huge Stalinist pile with an illuminated sign reading "Complex Astoria", that's trying to pass itself off as a Western-style hotel. Gloomy singles and doubles (with bathrooms); vacancies always likely. ③.

Bucegi, Str. Witing 2 (☎637.52.25 or 637.50.30). Basic but convenient, offering singles, doubles, triples and quadruples; some doubles have private bathrooms. There's also a restaurant. ②.

Cerna, B-dul D. Golescu 29 (☎637.40.87; fax 311.07.21). Small, clean, warm and not bad if you can endure the unwelcoming staff. Used by Turks in transit, with a takeaway patisserie on the ground floor. Singles and doubles only. ③.

Dunarea, Calea Griviţei 140 (☎617.32.20). Opposite the Gara de Nord, at the junction of two main roads. Singles, doubles and triples with basins; some are nice, but most are noisy. ③.

Griviţa, Calea Griviţei 130 (☎650.23.27 or 650.53.80). 200m east of the Gara de Nord. Basic singles, doubles, triples and quadruples, usually full and not the best in the area. ③.

Marna, Str. Buzeşti 3 (☎650.26.75). Just around the corner from the Griviţa – very noisy due to the trams passing by. ④.

Nord, Calea Griviţei 143 (☎650.60.81). The only luxury hotel in this area, but currently closed for refurbishment. However the exclusive "Club Nord" operates in an annexe.

Around Piaţa Revoluţiei and the university

Ambasador, B-dul Magheru 10 (☎615.90.80 or 614.61.50; fax 312.12.39). A vaguely Art-Deco Thirties block near the tourist office, rated Luxury category. Air conditioning is being installed, and its least expensive singles and doubles will become even harder to get. The bar and nightclub swarm with prostitutes. ⑥.

Athénée Palace, Str. Episcopei 1, on the northern corner of Piaţa Revoluţiei (☎614.18.11 or 614.08.99). Easily Romania's most famous hotel, with a long history of intrigue and espionage (see p.63), it is now closed for restoration by the Hilton chain (at a cost of $21m). It is unlikely to reopen before 1996, when it will be one of the most expensive in the city. ⑨.

ACCOMMODATION PRICES

Hotels listed in the *Guide* have been price-graded according to the scale below. Prices given are those charged for the cheapest double room, which in the less expensive places usually comes without private bath or shower and without breakfast. See p.28 for more details.

① under $10	④ $25–40	⑦ $80–135
② $10–15	⑤ $40–55	⑧ $135–190
③ $15–25	⑥ $55–80	⑨ $200 and over

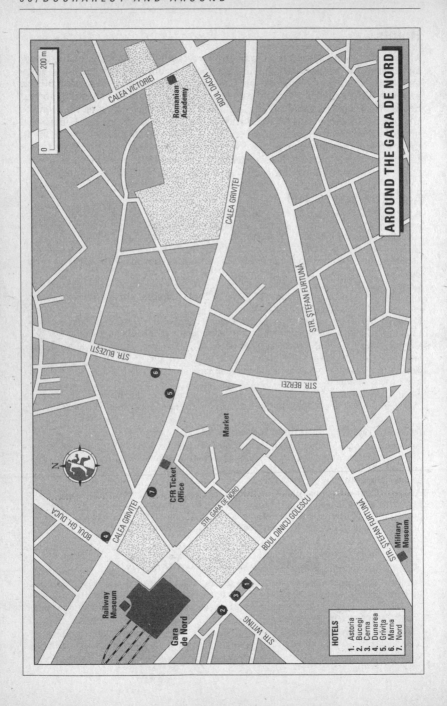

AROUND THE GARA DE NORD

200 m

CALEA VICTORIEI

BDUL DACIA

Romanian
Academy

CALEA GRIVIŢEI

STR. ŞTEFAN FURTUNĂ

STR. BUZEŞTI

STR. BERZEI

Market

CFR Ticket
Office

CALEA GRIVIŢEI

BDUL GH. DUCA

STR. GARA DE NORD

BDUL DINICU GOLESCU

STR. ŞTEFAN FURTUNĂ

Military
Museum

Railway
Museum

Gara
de Nord

STR. WITING

HOTELS
1. Astoria
2. Bucegi
3. Cerna
4. Dunarea
5. Griviţa
6. Marna
7. Nord

Banat, Piaţa Rosetti 5 (☎613.10.56). Located 400m east of Piaţa Universităţii, this slightly grubby place may soon go private and upgrade itself. ③.

Bucureşti, Calea Victoriei 63–69 (☎615.45.80 or 615.58.50; fax 312.09.27). Sited near the Piaţa Revoluţiei, this is the country's best Romanian-managed hotel, although with heavy French investment. Restaurant and grill, and most of the prostitutes from the *Athénée* seem to have moved in. ⑧.

Bulevard, B-dul Kogălniceanu 1 (☎615.33.00). A *fin de siècle* pile with Louis XIV decor, rated Cat. I. Fantastic marble and stucco in the bar and restaurant. Nightclub with cabaret. ⑦.

Capitol, Calea Victoriei 29 (☎615.80.30 or 613.94.40; fax 312.41.69). A fine turn-of-the-century building near the central post office. No singles. ⑤.

Carpaţi, Str. Matei Millo 16 (☎615.76.90, fax 312.18.57). Just north of the *Palas*. Singles and doubles with bathrooms. Bar. ④.

Continental, Calea Victoriei 56 (☎614.53.49 or 638.50.22; fax 312.01.34). Dating from 1877, better value and currently more classy than the *Bucureşti*. ⑧.

Dorobanţi, Calea Dorobanţilor 1 (☎611.82.29 or 211.54.90; fax 312.01.51). Under the same management as the *Ambasador*, though marginally better. ⑥.

Intercontinental, B-dul Bălcescu 4 (☎614.04.00; fax 312.04.86). Still the businessman's and journalist's first choice, though now rather tacky. Regarded as one of the city's main landmarks – refurbishment planned. ⑨.

Majestic, Str. Academiei 11 (☎615.59.86; fax 311.33.63). A once elegant place near the university. Singles and doubles, with bathrooms, and also studio apartments. ⑤.

Minerva 92, Str. Lt. Lemnea 2 (☎650.60.10; fax 312.39.63). Further north than the others in this group, adjacent to Bucharest's longest-established Chinese restaurant. Efficient reception, room service and air conditioning. Reservations necessary as it's usually full. ⑥.

Muntenia, Str. Academiei 21 (☎614.60.10). West of Piaţa Revoluţiei. Frequented by Greeks, with a bar and travel agencies in the hotel. Doubles and triples, with or without showers. ④.

Opera, Str. Brezoianu 37 (☎614.10.75, fax 312.52.91). Located two blocks west of the Calea Victoriei, near the Cişmigiu Gardens. Singles, doubles and studio apartments, with or without bathrooms. ④.

Palas, Str. C. Mille 18 (☎613.67.35, 615.37.10). Just west of Calea Victoriei, one block south of the *Opera*. Singles and doubles with bathrooms, with plans to go more upmarket. ④.

Between the Cişmigiu Gardens and Piaţa Unirii

Central, Str. Brezoianu 13 (☎615.56.37). Sited on the extremely noisy B-dul Kogălniceanu. Faded atmosphere; doubles and triples with bathrooms. ⑤.

Dîmboviţa, Str. Schitu Măgureanu 6 (☎615.26.17 or 615.62.44). Old-fashioned place on a quiet sidestreet by the seventeenth-century Church of Sf Ilie-Gorgan, near Izvor metro stop and the Civic Centre; some rooms overlook the House of the People. Beware of the very low bathroom doors. ④.

Hanul lui Manuc, Str. Iuliu Maniu 62 (☎613.14.15; fax 312.28.11). Simple, agreeable rooms in a famous old *caravanserai* just off Piaţa Unirii. Reservations usually required. Restaurant and wine cellar. ⑦.

Universal, Str. Gabroveni 12 (☎614.85.33). On a quiet sidestreet parallel to Str. Lipscani, to the west of B-dul Brătianu. Easily the least expensive hotel in town, if you can get in – it's used as student accommodation for most of the year. ②.

Veneţia, Piaţa Kogălniceanu 2 (☎615.91.49). Small, fairly clean, old-fashioned place with noisy basic singles, doubles and triples. Ten minutes' walk from Ceauşescu's Palace (*Casa Poporului*) and the university. ④.

North and east of the centre

Casa Victor, Str. Cîmpia Turzii 44 (☎617.76.31; fax 312.94.24). A pleasant private hotel with just five rooms, in a quiet area north of the centre (metro Aviatorilor); the fine *Bolta Rece* restaurant is on the same street. ⑥.

Flora, Str. Poligrafei 1 (☎617.44.38 or 618.46.40; fax 312.83.44). By the *Parc* and *Turist* hotels, but better in every way and aimed at a more upmarket clientele; with pool, sauna, geriatric treatment centre. ⑥.

Helveția, Str. Uruguay 29 (☎311.05.67 or 618.37.90). Bucharest's first privately built hotel – small, select, but perhaps over-ambitious, out to the north on Piața Aviatorilor. ⑧.

Lebădă, B-dul Biruinței 3 (☎624.30.12; fax 312.80.44). Inaugurated in 1987, in the former Pantelimon Monastery, later used as a TB sanatorium (and rumoured to be still infected with the bacillus); on an island in a lake, south of the suburb of Pantelimon (bus #782 to Granitul, then any bus east except #246 or #322). Tennis, bowling alley and pool. ⑧.

Parc, Str. Poligrafei 3 (☎617.65.77). This is the main hotel in Bucharest for those using *ACR* hotel coupons, and it has a pool and sauna. ⑥.

Sofitel, B-dul Exposiției 2 (☎212.29.98; fax 212.06.46). Opened in May 1994, with the linked World Trade Centre. Luxury class. ⑨.

Turist, Str. Poligrafei 5 (☎666.30.20). A tattier version of the *Parc*. ④.

Private accommodation

Private rooms can be booked at the ONT office in the Gara de Nord (where you may in any case be approached by people with the offer of a room). The main ONT office on Bulevardul Magheru won't make reservations, but simply gives you a list of addresses and tells you to negotiate with the owners. Expect to pay $15 for a centrally located double room, or less for longer stays – around $50 a week, sometimes with meals included.

Be sure to find the location on a map and find out about public transport before committing yourself; also check whether breakfast is included. Fortunately most of the suburban high-rise *blocs* are too cramped to have spare rooms, so you're likely to find yourself in an older house fairly near the centre.

Dormitory beds

Beds in student **hostels** (*căminul de studenti*) are a less certain possibility, since the booking agency *BTT* at Str. Mendeleev 5 (Mon–Fri 8am–5pm; ☎614.42.00, or 613.89.87) is more interested in groups than in individuals. You could try your luck, though, at the **N. Bălcescu Agronomical Institute** near the Casă Presei Libere (tram #3, bus #131, #205 or #783), the Lacul Tei student complex, or the **Institut Politehnic** (south of the Grozăvești metro station). Arab, African and Asian students staying at college over vacation when the hostels function (July 1– August 31) are probably the people to ask for assistance. Facilities are fairly basic in all the student halls of residence.

Camping

Camping is only feasible in summer, when the sites are sure to be open and the weather is warm enough. In any case, the facilities are pretty run down and the remoteness of the sites adds to their disadvantages. Previously, the main alternative to hotels was *Băneasa* campsite, situated out towards Otopeni airport, but this is currently being used to house Somali refugees.

The alternatives are even further from the city, in Buftea or Snagov, for example. **Buftea** is served by seven slow trains a day on the Bucharest–Ploiești line or by bus #460 from Laromet (terminus of tram #20 from Schitu Măgureanu, west of the Cișmigiu Gardens); from the roundabout on the DN1A south of the village it

BUCHAREST'S NEW STREET NAMES

If you are stuck with an out-of-date map or are trying to find a pre-revolutionary address, it is worth noting some of the street names that have changed since 1989. Confusingly the post office still operates on the old street names and letters sent to the new addresses will actually take longer to get there.

Old name	New name
B-dul Anul 1848	B-dul Brătianu
B-dul Gheorghiu-Dej	B-dul Kogălniceanu
B-dul Republicii (eastern end)	B-dul Carol I
B-dul Dimitrov	B-dul Ferdinand II
B-dul Victorie Socialismului	B-dul Unirii
B-dul Petru Groza	B-dul Eroilor Sanitari
B-dul Ilie Pintilie	B-dul Iancu de Hunedoara
B-dul Vacărești (northern part)	B-dul Mircea Vodă
Str. Nuferilor	Str. General Berthelot
Str. A. Sahia	Str. J. L. Caldcron
Str. 13 Decembrie	Str. Ion Câmpineanu
Str. Onești	Str. Dobrescu
Str. Cosmonautilor	Str. George Enescu
Str. N. Beloiannis	Str. Tache Ionescu
Str. 30 Decembrie	Str. Iuliu Maniu
Str. T. Speranță	B-dul Decebal
Piața Cosmonautilor	Piața Lahovari
Piața Scînteia	Piața Presei Libere
Piața Ilie Pintilie	Piața Sfinții Voievozi
Piața Gheorghiu-Dej	Piața Revoluției

takes 25 minutes to walk west around the lake and to the *plaja* on the right, where you can camp or sleep in a chalet.

Snagov is an excursion in its own right (see p.81), but has a campsite, too. It is harder to reach by public transport, with just three buses from the Băneasa bus station, and two local trains from the Gara de Nord on summer weekends only.

The City

The heart of the city is the **Piața Revoluției**, site of the old royal palace and the scene of Ceaușescu's downfall. It lies halfway along Bucharest's historic axis, the **Calea Victoriei**, still the main artery of city life. The majority of sights are within walking distance of here. Just to the south lies the oldest part of the city, with the remains of the original **citadel**, and south of this, beyond the River Dîmbovița, is the totally contrasting cityscape of Ceaușescu's **Centru Civic** (pronounced *Chentru Chiveek*), with its centrepiece, the monstrous **House of the People**, now perhaps the city's main tourist attraction.

Buses use the unattractive Bulevards Ana Ipătescu, Magheru, Bălcescu and Brătianu, east of the Calea; the **Piața Universității**, also the scene of major events immediately after the 1989 revolution, is the main junction along these

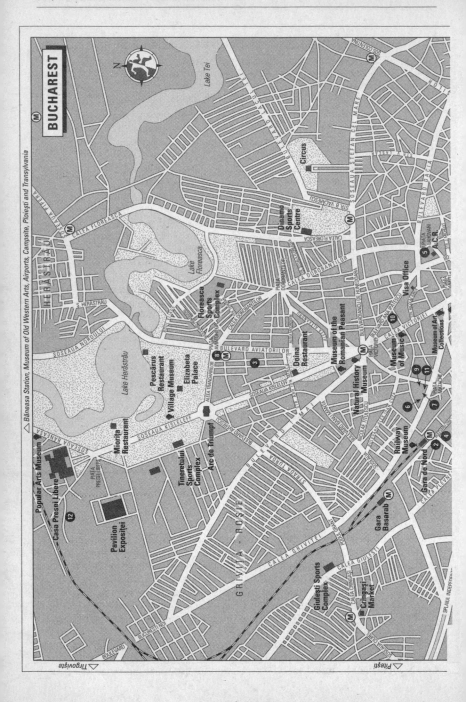

BUCHAREST

△ *Băneasa Station, Museum of Old Western Arts, Airports, Campsite, Ploieşti and Transylvania*

HERĂSTRĂU

Lake Tei

Lake Floreasca

Lake Herăstrău

CALEA FLOREASCA

SOSEAUA NORDULUI

S. HERASTRAU

SOSEAUA KISELEFF

Circus

Dinamo Sports Centre

Floreasca Sports Complex

BULEVARD AVIATORILOR

Doina Restaurant

Museum of the Romanian Peasant

Natural History Museum

Museum of Music

Museum of Art Collections

Visa Office

A.C.R.

Pescarus Restaurant

Village Museum

Elizabeta Palace

Popular Arts Museum

Casa Presei Libere

Miorita Restaurant

Arc de Triumf

Tineretului Sports Complex

Pavilion Expozitei

GRIVIŢA - ROŞIE

CALEA GRIVIŢEI

CALEA GIULEŞTI

Giuleşti Sports Complex

Grigani Market

Gara Basarab

Railway Museum

Gara de Nord

CALEA PLEVNEI

△ *Tîrgovişte*

△ *Piteşti*

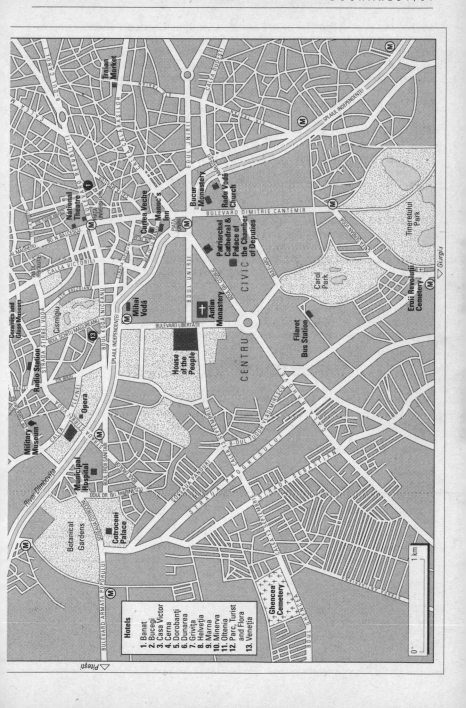

boulevards. Just west of the centre are the **Cişmigiu Gardens**, always a popular place for assignations. For a taste of the old atmosphere of the city, you need to wander north and west from here, where vine-covered facades slowly give ground to an area of dingy tenements and corner shops, and life retains a village-like slowness and intimacy. The main boulevards run north towards **Herăstrău Park**, the site of the **Village Museum**, a superb collection of buildings assembled from all over Romania.

Piaţa Revoluţiei

The **Piaţa Revoluţiei** (Square of Revolution) is a large, irregular space that was created in the 1930s to ensure a field of fire around the royal palace, in the event of revolution. While Romania's monarchy was overthrown by other means, the square fulfilled its destiny in 1989, when the Ceauşescus were forced to flee by crowds besieging Communist Party headquarters. Two days of fighting left the buildings around the square riddled with bullet holes or burnt out – with the conspicuous exception of the Central Committee building, at the centre of the storm. Romania's revolution was the most dramatic of the popular revolts that convulsed Eastern Europe in 1989, but was tainted by having been stage managed by the National Salvation Front that took power in the name of the people (see box). With many of the grand edifices that surround it still boarded up or scarred by shots, the Piaţa Revoluţei is melancholy and aimless, with bored conscripts cadging cigarettes through the railings, and BMWs cruising indifferently past down the Calea Victoriei, which crosses the square. Demonstrations still occur here, but their spirit has never recovered from the betrayal of the revolution.

THE FALL OF THE CEAUŞESCUS

The **fall of Nicolae and Elena Ceauşescu** was perfect nemesis. On the morning of December 21, 1989, an organized demonstration of support for the regime following days of rioting in Timişoara, backfired. Eight minutes into Ceauşescu's speech from the balcony of the Central Committee building, part of the 80,000-strong crowd began chanting *Ti-mi-şoa-ra, Ti-mi-şoa-ra,* and the leader's shock and fear were televised across Romania before transmissions ceased. Everyone knew that the end was nigh. Though the square was cleared by nightfall, larger crowds poured back next day, emboldened by news that the army was siding with the people in Timişoara and Bucharest. Strangely, the Ceauşescus remained inside the building until midday, when they scrambled aboard a helicopter on the roof, beginning an ignominious flight that would end with their **execution** in a barracks in Tirgovişte, on Christmas Day.

Doubts about the revolution set in when people realized that the National Salvation Front consisted of veteran communists, one of whom let slip that plans to oust the Ceauşescus had been laid months before. Among the oddities of the "official" version of the events were Iliescu's speech on the Piaţa Revoluţei at a time when *Securitate* snipers were causing mayhem, and the battle for the Interior Ministry, during which both sides ceased firing after a mysterious phone call. Given the hundreds of genuine "martyrs of the revolution", the idea that it had been a ploy to perpetuate the rule of Party bureaucrats was shocking and potentially damaging to the new regime – so the secret police were ordered to mount an investigation, which duly concluded that where manipulation *had* occurred, the Russians, Americans and Hungarians were to blame.

The Royal Palace

The most imposing of the buildings surrounding the Piaţa Revoluţiei is the former **Royal Palace**, on its northwestern corner. In 1866, the newly chosen king Carol I found pigs wallowing in mud before the original single-storeyed dwelling and when this at last burnt down in 1927, the spendthrift Carol II decided to replace it with something far more impressive. The surrounding dwellings were razed in order to build a new palace along Classical lines, with discrete side entrances to facilitate visits by Carol's mistress, Magda Lupescu, and the shady financiers who formed their *Camarilla*. A sprawling brownstone edifice with no claim to elegance, the palace was spurned as a residence by Romania's post-war rulers, Ceauşescu preferring a villa in the northern suburbs pending the completion of his own palace in the Centru Civic, while Iliescu opted to live in the Cotroceni Palace, previously used by the Party youth organization. The Royal Palace now houses the **National Art Museum**; and to its rear is the Sala Palatului, a congress and concert hall.

THE NATIONAL ART MUSEUM

The **National Art Museum** (Wed–Sun 10am–6pm) is housed in the southern wing of the palace. This building was one of those most seriously damaged in 1989, and over a hundred paintings are thought to have been destroyed. The ground floor begins with a splendid Transylvanian diptych and larger than lifesize murals from Curtea de Argeş, followed by halls of icons and embroidered boyars' garments. Of the painters exhibited on the first floor, Nicolae Grigorescu (1838–1907) gets star billing for his dark portraits and bolder, more impressionistic landscapes. Look out for the fine portraits by Gheorghe Tattarescu (1820–94), Constantin Rosenthal's revolutionary tableaux (similar to the work of Delacroix) and Theodor Aman's *Turks Massacring the Bulgarians*. Twentieth-century work seems rather more derivative, and overwhelmed by heavy gilt and marble, though Corneliu Baba's grim scenes of peasant life transcend imitation. The second floor features collections of oriental carpets, Chinese and Dutch porcelain, French furniture and tapestries, and minor works by Rembrandt, Cranach, the Breughels and Renoir.

The rest of the square

The north side of the square is filled by the **Athénée Palace Hotel**, built in 1912, one of the first buildings in Bucharest to use reinforced concrete and always one of its most prestigious hotels. The hotel, currently closed for a refit, has been a notorious hotbed of espionage since the 1930s, when the liveried staff and the characters who populated the lobby spied for Carol's police chief, and also for the Gestapo or British Intelligence. Symbolic of that fevered, corrupt era, Bucharest's elite partied through the night here while police were shooting strikers in the Red Griviţa district only a mile away. During the early 1950s the hotel was extensively refurbished as an "intelligence factory", with bugged rooms and tapped phones, to reinforce the reports of its cast of informers and prostitutes.

To the east stands the Classical-style **Romanian Athenaeum**, opened in 1888, beneath whose dome, decorated with lyres, the *George Enescu Philharmonic Orchestra* gives concerts in a rampantly *fin-de-siècle* hall. To the south, the remains of the **University Library**, totally gutted in December 1989, are now the best place to be picked up for a "student tour" of the revolutionary sights. Just behind this, at Str. Rosetti 8, is the **Theodor Aman Memorial House** (Tues–

Sun 9am–5pm), the most convenient of the various homes of notable artists dotted around the city; Aman (1831–91) trained in Paris before returning to be the first director of the Bucharest Art College. Himself a somewhat academic nationalist painter, he was a leading member of the group of Francophile intellectuals (including the painter Gheorghe Tattarescu and the sculptor Karl Storck) which dominated cultural life in the late nineteenth century. The house was built in 1868 to Aman's own designs and decorated by himself and Storck.

South of the University Library stands the **former Communist Party Central Committee building**, a Stalinist monolith that now serves as the **headquarters of the National Salvation Front**, which is really the old Communist Party in another guise. The famous **balcony** where Ceauşescu delivered his last speech is surprisingly near ground level, and quite unmarked by bullet holes. Ironically, it was from the same spot, two decades earlier, that Ceauşescu drew cheers of approval by his denunciation of the Soviet invasion of Czechoslovakia, and his vow that Romania would defend its own independence – casting himself as a "maverick Communist" whom Western leaders could embrace, an illusion that persisted almost until the end. As Romanians point out, the honourary knighthood bestowed on Ceauşescu by Buckingham Palace in 1978 was only revoked after the revolution began.

Along the Calea Victoriei

Many boyars built their residences along the Mogoşoaia Bridge, the forerunner of the **Calea Victoriei** (Avenue of Victory), and these were followed by Bucharest's most prestigious shops. This was always the city's most fashionable street, and after it was paved strolling became de rigueur, the writer Hector Bolitho recounting that "to drive down the Calea Victoriei between twelve and one o'clock will prove you a provincial or a stranger". Along the street were "huddles of low, open-fronted shops where Lyons silk and Shiraz carpets were piled in the half-darkness beside Siberian furs, English guns and Meissen porcelain", while lurking in the side streets were starving groups of unemployed, lupus-disfigured beggars and dispossessed peasants seeking justice in the capital.

The Calea still displays marked contrasts: at its northern end near the Piaţa Victoriei, it seems verdant and sleepy with touches of *ancien régime* elegance, while to the south it becomes an eclectic jumble of old apartment buildings, glass and steel facades, and shops selling cakes and western *couture* – still the setting for a promenade around noon and in the early evening. To the east and west lie Piaţa Amzei and Piaţa Sf Voievozi, two areas with busy markets.

North of Piaţa Revoluţiei

Three of the palaces along the quieter, northern end of the Calea house museums. At no. 141, a superb clamshell-shaped *porte-cochère* shades the entrance of the **Museum of Music** (Wed–Sun 10am–5pm), whose displays on the life of Romania's national composer George Enescu are not that gripping. The **Museum of Art Collections** at no. 111 (Wed–Sun 10am–6pm), occupying the early nineteenth-century Ghica Palace, houses an assortment of paintings, furniture and other antiques donated to (or confiscated by) the state. Temporary exhibitions and films also get a showing here – check the posters outside. The **Ceramics and Glass Museum** at no. 107 in the former Ştirbei Palace (1856) is small and varied; in rooms furnished with splendid mirrors, carpets, chandeliers

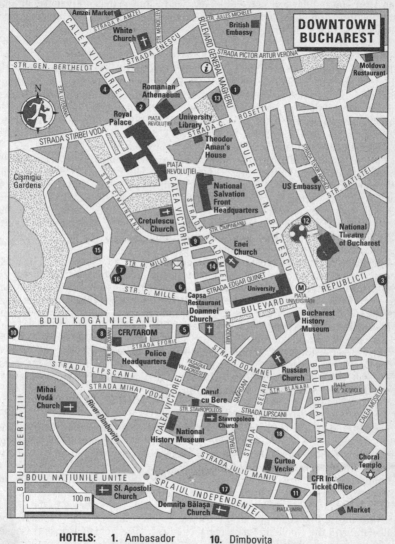

DOWNTOWN BUCHAREST

HOTELS:

1. Ambasador
2. Athénée Palace
3. Banat
4. Bucureşti
5. Bulevard
6. Capitol
7. Carpaţi
8. Central
9. Continental
10. Dîmboviţa
11. Hanul Manuc
12. Intercontinental
13. Lido
14. Majestic and Muntenia
15. Opera
16. Palas
17. Rahova
18. Universal

and tiled stoves, you can see eighteenth- and nineteenth-century Turkish and Iranian tiles, European, Japanese and Chinese porcelain, and lovely Art Deco pieces, including a Tiffany lamp.

South of Piaţa Revoluţiei

The Calea heads south from the square, past the **Creţulescu Church** fronting a tangle of streets wending west towards Cişmigiu Gardens. A venerable building, high and narrow with mock arches, elaborate carvings over the entrance, bricks laid in saw-toothed patterns around the towers, and other features of the Brîncoveanu style, the church was paid for in 1720 by the boyar Iordache Creţulescu and his wife Safta, Brîncoveanu's daughter. The church is quite battered and little remains of its frescoes by Tattarescu.

Further south, behind the Tăndărică Theatre, the **Pasagiul Victoriei** sneaks through to the **Enei Church** (also known as the *Dintr-o zi* or "(Made) In One Day" church) dating from 1702, one block further east. Shops and cinemas cluster about the junction with Bucharest's main east–west axis, Bulevardul Kogălniceanu, with the imposing **Cercul Militar** (Army House) and the *Bulevard* hotel dominating the intersection. Just beyond, an alleyway slips off to the court-yard of the picturesque **Doamnei Church** – built in 1683 and now haunted by devout grandmothers and hordes of local cats.

Further south is Bucharest's **Police Headquarters**, now surrounded by a tall fence since it was stormed by a mob in 1990, the pretext that allowed Iliescu to call in the miners to smash his student opponents. Directly opposite this, an inconspicuous portal leads into the **Pasagiul Villacrosse** (Villacrosse Passage) whose stained glass roof and gracefully curved arcade of shops gives an idea of why Bucharest once claimed to be the "Paris of the East".

Further on and left off the Calea, the small **Stavropoleos Church**, built in 1724–30, has a gorgeous, almost arabesque, facade, with a columned portico carved with delicate tracery, and lends its name to the street on which it stands. Here, too, you'll find *Carul cu Bere* (The Beer Cart), an ornately decorated tavern from 1875 (see "Eating and Drinking" p.75).

THE NATIONAL HISTORY MUSEUM

Nearing the river, the **National History Museum** (Wed–Sun 10am–6pm) looms at no. 12; this is the former Post Office building of 1900. The museum's basement exhibits Romania's national treasures: a dazzling display of gold and jewellery, from Neolithic and Dacian finds to Queen Marie's crown and the sceptres of Ferdinand I and Carol II. You'll also see plaster casts from Trajan's Column, covered with depictions of the Romans' Dacian foes.

The other floors cover Romanian history from the earliest times to the 1920s, starting with a fine collection of prehistoric goddess figures from Vadastra and Cucuteni, and the Neolithic "Hamangia Thinker". Next come Celtic and Dacian jewellery, Roman statues and armour, and medieval clothing and manuscripts. The rest of the museum traces the struggle of the three principalities towards independence and union, while the post-1920s section that formerly eulogized communism in general and Ceauşescu in particular (with two rooms full of gifts presented to him on his sixtieth birthday) is now closed. Romanian museums still tend to serve the ruling ideology, and the recent rehabilitation of the wartime dictator, Antonescu suggests that the reaction against communism may go too far in the other direction.

The Dîmboviţa

An old saying has it that whoever drinks the "sweet waters" of the **River Dîmboviţa** will never wish to be parted from Bucharest, to which one nineteenth-century traveller retorted that anyone who did "would be incapable of leaving the city for ever afterwards". Always prone to flooding, the Dîmboviţa was canalized in the 1880s and now passes underground through much of the city centre, though it is proudly displayed near the lower end of the Calea Victoriei, at Piaţa Naţiunile Unite. This marks the abrupt transition from the organic fabric of the old city to the arbitrarily imposed pattern of the Civic Centre.

The Centru Civic

In 1971 Ceauşescu visited North Korea (with Iliescu) and returned full of admiration for the grandiose avenues of Kim Il Sung's capital, Pyongyang. Thirteen years later, he set out himself to remodel Bucharest as "the first socialist capital for the new socialist man", and to create a new administrative centre which was to be "a symbolic representation of the two decades of enlightenment we have just lived through". In truth, of course, this **Centru Civic** was meant to embody the state's authority and that of Ceauşescu himself, echoing the plans for the redevelopment of Rome and Berlin under fascism.

To implement this megalomaniac vision entailed the demolition of a quarter of Bucharest's historic centre (about five square kilometres), said to be slums damaged by the 1977 earthquake, but in fact containing 9000 largely undamaged nineteenth-century houses, whose 40,000 inhabitants were expelled to the outskirts of the city. There was worldwide condemnation of this vandalism, particularly concerning the many old churches that were to be swept away; though some were in the end reprieved, they are now surrounded by huge new buildings and torn from the urban context that gave them meaning.

The core of the *Centru Civic* – occupying the former Uranus, Antim and Rahovei districts – was largely completed by 1989, just in time for the dictator's overthrow. The western end of the development now seems almost human – unlike the larger eastern extension, in the former Calaraşi, Vacăreşti and Dudeşti districts, which remains a forest of frozen cranes with an undergrowth of rusting reinforcing rods, now nicknamed "Hiroshima". The two halves are linked like a dumb-bell by **Bulevardul Unirii**, which is 4km long, 120m wide, and lined with monumental apartment buildings.

The House of the People

Dominating the entire project from the western end of Bulevardul Unirii is the colossal *Casă Poporului* or **House of the People**, the third largest building in the world after the Pentagon and the Potala. This gigantic folly epitomizes the megalomania that overtook Ceauşescu in the 1980s – here, he intended to house ministries, party organs and high functionaries' apartments. The size of the building, where the Spirei hill used to rise, is mesmerizing: each face is 270m long and 86m high, and its scale can only be grasped by comparison with the toy-like cars scuttling past below. It has twelve storeys and four underground levels (including a nuclear bunker), and reputedly contains 1100 rooms, presaged by a lobby 100m long; three assembly halls over half that length; and 4500 chandeliers (of 11,000 planned), the largest of which weighs one and a half tonnes and cost 2.5m lei.

There is marble and gold leaf everywhere (all Romanian), but the decoration was never finished due to the Ceauşescus' ever-changing whims. They were demanding patrons, allowing little more than a technical role to the architects: one staircase was rebuilt three times before they were satisfied, and a nearby apartment building survived only a few days, as Elena Ceauşescu judged it too close to the palace, whose gardens it overlooked.

The new government spent a long time agonising about an acceptable use for this huge white elephant, popularly known as the *Casă Nebunului* (Madman's House), and in 1994 it was finally decided to house the Senate and Parliament here, as well as international conferences. For a while after the revolution tourists were able to bribe their way in, by distributing packets of Kent cigarettes to the guards, but access is now much harder to arrange unless on official business. Although the Izvor metro stop is the nearest, you should start with the classic view from Piaţa Unirii.

The surviving churches

Behind the rows of new buildings are hidden various tiny Orthodox churches; elsewhere in Bucharest you'll frequently find churches in the courtyards of apartment buildings, but here they seem more disregarded and incongruous. The most striking example is the sixteenth-century **Sf Nicolai-Mihai Vodă Church**, which was moved 279m east on rails (leaving the medieval cloisters and ancillary buildings to be demolished) and now appears to have been dumped in a building site, at Str. Sapienţei 4. What's more, standing on a concrete platform, it will probably collapse when the next earthquake comes. The **Sfinţii Apostoli Church**, nearby at Str. Sf Apostoli 33A, is largely seventeenth century, while just west of the Piaţa Unirii at Calea Rahovei 3 is the eighteenth-century **Domniţa Bălaşa Church**, one of the most popular churches in the city (only saved from demolition by UNESCO funds), with an excellent choir on Sunday mornings.

On the southern side of Bulevardul Unirii, the **Antim Monastery**, a remarkably large walled complex dating from 1715 with a high-domed church and a smaller chapel, remains (minus its eastern wing) at Str. Justiţiei 64. At the top of Dealul Mitropoliei stands the **Patriarchal Cathedral**, built in 1655–68, with a later Brîncoveanu campanile and some older stone crosses with Slavonic inscriptions. Alongside are the Patriarch's Palace (built in 1875), and the **Palace of the Chamber of Deputies** (1907); the latter is generally ringed by troops, but they are less paranoid about photography than previously. There are other churches on this side of Bulevardul Dimitrie Cantemir, including **Sf Spiridon Nou** (1768, with Tattarescu paintings from 1858) at Calea Şerban Vodă 29. Just east on Bulevardul Mărăşeşti by the Dimboviţa is the **Bucur Monastery** (1743), in front of the **Radu Vodă Church** (also known as Holy Trinity or Sf Treime), founded in 1568, which was the richest monastery in the country with 8342 properties.

From the Piaţa Unirii to Piaţa Universităţii

The **Piaţa Unirii** or Square of Union, the junction of Bulevardul Unirii and Bulevardul Brătianu, is notable only as a cog in the transport system (with two metro stations, linked by a pedestrian subway), as the site of the main department store, and as the best place to view the *Casă Poporului*; otherwise it is simply an oversized expanse of concrete dominated by traffic.

The Unirea market and the synagogues

Immediately to the east of the square stands the large **Unirea market** (Mon–Sat 6am–8pm, Sun 6am–noon). This domed hall selling fish, meat and dairy produce always has terrible queues; buying fruit and vegetables from the stalls outside (which also trade on Sunday afternoons) is a less frustrating business. The fifth-floor café offers good views of the city.

In the backstreets just to the east are hidden the Jewish **Choral Temple**, Str. Sf Vineri 9, and the **Great Synagogue**, Str. Mămulari 3, where there is also a **museum** of Jewish history (Wed & Sun 9.30am–1.30pm). There are still around 7000 Jews in Bucharest, who are now reasserting their presence, but it is an ageing population.

The historic centre

Just north of the *piaţa*, a maze of streets and pleasantly decrepit houses surrounds the oldest part of Bucharest, where Prince Vlad the Impaler (other-wise known as Dracula – see p.346) built a citadel in the fifteenth century. Severely damaged during his attempt to regain the throne in 1467 (he succeeded only to be murdered a few months later), the building succumbed to earthquakes and fire and was subsequently auctioned off as wasteland. Thus the remains of the **Curtea Veche** (Old Court), at Str. Iuliu Maniu 31, are pretty modest: some walls, arches and shattered columns, which can only be viewed through the railings. Adjoining the complex is its church, the oldest in Bucharest, raised by Mircea the Shepherd in 1546–58, with the horizontal bands of brick facing and rows of small niches beneath the cornice typical of sixteenth-century Wallachian church architecture.

A few doors along from the Curtea Veche at Str. Iuliu Maniu 62, an austere white wall with barred windows conceals Bucharest's most famous establishment, **Manuc's Inn**, built as a *caravanserai* in 1808 by a wealthy Armenian, Manuc-bey Mirzaian, and now housing a hotel (see p.57), a restaurant and a *cramă* or wine cellar (daily 7am–11pm).

Immediately north is **Strada Lipscani**, a narrow street (named for the merchants from Leipzig who traded here in the eighteenth century) which is still a lively Gypsy street market ideal for buying Turkish jeans or pirated cassettes. This area is a labyrinth of little shops and cafés, interspersed with passageways like the **Hanul cu tei** at no. 63: a former *caravanserai* whose iron-doored lockups now contain a rich mixture of shops. Beware of pick-pockets in this area.

Heading north from here up Bulevardul Brătianu towards the *Intercontinental* hotel, you pass two ancient and much-loved churches: **New St George's** (now surrounded by trams), dating from 1575 and the burial place of Constantin Brîncoveanu; followed by the **Colţea Church** (1700–15), in front of the hospital of the same name and vintage.

Around the Piaţa Universităţii

The **Piaţa Universităţii** is a focus of city life and traffic, and a key site on the revolutionary history trail – there are memorials here to those killed both at Christmas 1989 and in June 1990, when the miners drove out the students who had been on hunger strike since April 30, leading to the nickname, "Piaţa Tienanmen". All this was watched by the world's journalists safely ensconced in the *Intercontinental*, nearby. Next to this rises the **National Theatre of Bucharest (TNB)**, resembling an Islamicized re-working of the Colosseum, a pet project of Elena Ceauşescu. The facade had to be rebuilt twice, and the roof once, before she was satisfied. The **School of Architecture** facing them was built in 1912–27 in neo-Brîncoveanu style, with ornate pillars, prominent, richly carved eaves and a multitude of arches. It is now notable for its rash of anti-Iliescu and pro-monarchist graffiti.

On the southwest corner of the Piaţa Universităţii is the **Bucharest History Museum** (Tues–Sun 9am–5pm), where the city's evolution is traced by means of old documents, photographs and prints; there's also a moving display about the 1989 revolution, with the school reports of some of the children killed. The neo-Gothic building, with its superb *porte-cochère*, was built as the Suţu Palace in 1833–34.

Bucharest University

Heading west, **Bucharest University** occupies the first block on Bulevardul Republicii, its forecourt thronged with students and snack-stands, while statues of illustrious pedagogues and statesmen gaze blindly at the crowds. Established in 1859 after the union of Wallachia and Moldavia, the university equipped the sons of bourgeois families to become lawyers and men of letters up until the communists took over. Technical skills and education for women were subsequently given top priority, but since the revolution, business studies and foreign languages have overtaken them in popularity.

The small, bulbous domes of the **Russian Church** appear through a gap in the cupola-topped buildings lining the southern side of the boulevard. Faced with yellow brick, art-nouveau green tiling and pixie-faced nymphs, the church has a small interior, with frescoes blackened with age and smoke, haloes glowing like golden horseshoes.

From Cişmigiu to Cotroceni

West of the Piaţa Revoluţiei, lie the **Cişmigiu Gardens** which originally belonged to a Turkish water inspector, and were bequeathed to the city in 1845 and laid out as a park. It's a tranquil place with pelicans, swans, small rowing boats and pedalos (9am–8pm in summer; about $1 per hour, and the same as a deposit) gliding around on a serpentine lake, while workers snooze beneath the trees and pensioners meet for games of chess.

The Opera and the Military Museum

The **Opera Romană** lies beyond the gardens at the western end of Bulevardul Kogălniceanu. A drab 1950s building, containing a museum of operatic costumes, scores, photographs and posters, it is overshadowed by a huge unfinished building similar to the *Casă Poporului*, which was intended to house the National History, Army and Communist Party Museums, as well as Ceauşescu's tomb. As with the *Casă Poporului*, it is now hard to know what to do with it – the most likely option is a new radio centre.

Having been displaced by the Civic Centre in 1988, the **National Military Museum** (Tues–Sun 9am–5pm), is now housed just around the corner in former barracks at Str. Ştefan Fortună 125. There are weapons, banners and uniforms galore, although Romania has rarely gone in for martial adventures. Indeed, from 1958 it was the only Warsaw Pact country without Soviet troops on its soil, and

Ceauşescu called vociferously for disarmament, announcing peace proposals and cuts in the defence budget. Post-communist Romania has contributed a chemical warfare unit to the Gulf War forces and a military hospital to the UN in Somalia, and has attempted to enforce the UN blockade against Serbian shipping on the Danube.

Cotroceni

From Piaţa Operei, across the river from the Opera, buses and trolleybuses trundle down Bulevardul Eroilor Sanitari to Cotroceni and the Botanical Gardens. The **Cotroceni Palace** was converted in 1893–1905 from a former monastery to provide a home for the newly wed Prince Ferdinand and Princess Marie, before their accession to the throne. Under communism it served as the Palace of the Pioneers (the Soviet-bloc equivalent of the Scouts), and it is now the presidential residence. Tours of one wing enter by a small door in the north wall at Şos. Cotroceni 37. Advance booking is required by phoning ☎771.32.00 or 781.75.02, with free admission on the first Tuesday of each month.

On the other side of Şoseaua Cotroceni lie the university's **Botanical Gardens**, open daily from 7am to 8pm, with the greenhouses and a museum open from 9am to 1pm on Tuesdays, Thursdays and Sundays.

Ghencea

Just south of Cotroceni (along Drumul Sării) is Bulevardul Ghencea, which leads west to the **Ghencea cemetery**. Here the Ceauşescus are buried side by side – having been buried under a pseudonym, Ceauşescu now rests beneath his own name, on the last alley on the left before the white church. There are candles and flowers left by those who feel that life was easier and simpler under his dictatorship than under "democracy". Next door is a Military Cemetery, a surreal forest of propellor blades marking the graves of airmen, even those who didn't die in crashes. Bus #173 runs along Bulevardul Ghencea from Eroii Revoluţii metro station (Mon–Fri only), and the #385 runs from Piaţa Unirii to the junction of Drumul Sării and Calea 13 Septembrie.

North to the Gara de Nord

Heading north from the Military Museum brings you to the Gara de Nord, passing a village-like neighbourhood of tiny street-corner churches and dimly lit workshops. Ivy and creepers cloak the houses – all outwardly rundown, but often concealing parquet-floored apartments with elegant antique furniture and other relics of pre-war bourgeois life.

Just west of the station, at Calea Griviţei 193, the **Railway Museum** (Tues–Fri 9am–5pm, Sun 9am–2pm), examines the history of Romanian transport from the cart to the diesel train. The country's first steam engine, built at Reşiţa in 1873, stands in the courtyard. Admission is supposedly free to *InterRail* pass holders.

The northern suburbs

The broad tree-lined Şoseaua Kiseleff runs north from Piaţa Victoriei, north of the city centre, towards the **Herăstrău Park** and the **Village Museum**, the best of Romania's open-air museums of vernacular architecture, before heading out towards the airports and the main road to Transylvania.

Piaţa Victoriei

Calea Victoriei leads into the Şoseaua Kiseleff at **Piaţa Victoriei**, where the ring boulevard dives underneath the north–south roads: on its east side stands the main government building, the **Palatul Victoria**, built in the 1930s but already with a chilly Stalinist feel to it. Opposite this are some museums: the most interesting is the **Natural History Museum** at Şoseaua Kiseleff 1 (Tues–Thurs & Sun 10am–5pm, Fri & Sat 10am–4pm), named after Grigore Antipa, the founder of Romanian icthyology; its collection of 300,000 items includes a 4.5m high skeleton of the dinosaur *Deinotherium gigantissimum*, discovered in Moldavia, and 82,000 butterflies and moths.

Behind this, at Şos. Kiseleff 3 (entrance on Str. Monetăriei), is a good little ethnographic museum, the **Muzeu Ţăranului Romǎn** (Museum of the Romanian Peasant; Tues–Sun 10am–5pm), which replaced the Museum of Party History in 1990. The **Geological Museum** (daily 10am–3pm) opposite the Natural History Museum (Şos. Kiseleff 2) is an illustration of Romania's great mineral riches, the highlight being an unlit basement room full of luminescent rocks.

THE SKOPŢI

Until their disappearance during the 1940s, the **Skopţi** coachmen, who worked along the Şoseaua Kiseleff, used to be one of the curiosities – or grotesqueries – of Bucharest. Members of a dissident religious sect founded in Russia during the seventeenth century (and related to the Lipovani of the Danube Delta), they interpreted literally the words of Christ in St Matthew's Gospel concerning eunuchs, and ritually castrated themselves in the belief that "the generative organs are the seat of all iniquities". (This was done after two years of normal married life – a period necessary to ensure the conception of future Skopţi). Driving *droshkys* pulled by black Orloff horses, the coachmen wore caftans sprouting two cords, which passengers tugged to indicate that the driver should turn left or right.

Along Şoseaua Kiseleff

The **Şoseaua Kiseleff**, a long avenue lined with lime trees, extends north from the Piaţa Victoriei. Modelled on the Parisian chaussées (though named after a Russian general), it's a product of the Francophilia that swept Romania's educated classes during the nineteenth century, and even has a triumphal arch halfway along it. The **Arc de Triumpf** was raised in 1878 for an independence parade, and patched together in 1922 for another parade to celebrate Romania's participation on the Allied side in World War I, and the benefits gained at the Versailles peace conference. In 1935–36 it was more fittingly rebuilt in stone in the style of the Arc de Triomphe in Paris.

Immediately beyond the Arc lies **Herăstrău Park**, best reached by the Aviatorilor metro station at its southeastern corner. Walks lead through formal flower beds to the shore of **Lake Herăstrău**, one of the largest of a dozen lakes strung along the River Colentina (forming a continuous line across the northern suburbs) created by Carol II to drain the unhealthy marshes that surrounded Bucharest. **Rowing** boats and **windsurfing** equipment can be rented on the shore, and curving bridges lead to a small and fragrant Island of Roses.

The residential area east of the park is one of Bucharest's most exclusive, where the communist *nomenklatura* once lived cordoned off from the masses they governed (the Ceauşescus lived in the *Vila Primavera*, at the east end of

Bulevardul Primăverii). Today it is still inhabited by technocrats, favoured artists and other members of the ruling elite.

THE VILLAGE MUSEUM

Undoubtedly one of the most worthwhile sights in Bucharest, the **Village Museum** (*Muzeul Satului*: Oct–March daily 9am–5pm; April–Sept Tues–Sun 9am–8pm & Mon 9am–5pm) at Șos. Kiseleff 28–30, is a wonderful ensemble of spiky wooden churches and peasant dwellings, including a bizarre subterranean house. Established in 1936, this fascinating collection of over three hundred houses and other structures from every region of Romania shows the extreme diversity of folk architecture.

Perhaps the most interesting are the oaken houses from Maramureş with their rope motif carvings and shingled roofing, and the beam gateways carved with suns, moons, the Tree of Life, Adam and Eve, animals and hunting scenes. Other highlights are heavily thatched dwellings from Salciua de Jos in Alba county; dugout homes from Drăghiceni (with vegetables growing on the roof) and Castranova in Oltenia; and windmills from Tulcea in the Delta. Mud-brick dwellings from the fertile plains ironically appear poorer than the homes of peasants in the less fertile highlands (where timber and stone abound); while the importance of livestock to the Székely people of Harghita county can be seen by their barns, which are taller than their houses.

Piaţa Presei Libere

The Şoseaua Kiseleff ends at **Piaţa Presei Libere** or Free Press Square, before Free Press House, a vast white Stalinist wedding-cake which was once the centre of the state propaganda industry – little seems to have changed, as the "free" publishing industry is still largely corralled into this one building. Romania's new Stock Exchange is also being set up here.

Just beyond this, by the Băneasa train station on the Bucureşti–Ploieşti Highway, stand the **Museum of Popular Arts** (Wed–Sun 9am–5pm), housed in a pseudo-fortified villa, and the **Museum of Old Western Arts** (same hours) occupied by a collection of foreign antiques. The large, dark rooms of the Popular Art Museum contain woven blankets, Transylvanian blue pottery, spinning wheels, musical instruments, furniture and beautiful peasant garments. The other building is a bizarre fusion of Tudor, Italian Renaissance and fortress-architecture, filled with hunting trophies and weapons, Flemish tapestries, Florentine furniture, and German and Swiss stained-glass windows.

THE BĂNEASA BRIDGE

The bridge immediately north of the Băneasa station, where the DN1 crosses the Colentina River, was the scene of a crucial battle in August 1944. The success of the August 23 coup against Marshal Antonescu (see p.315) meant that Hitler's oil supplies were more than halved, and is reckoned to have shortened the war in Europe by at least six months. However, at the time just 2800 Romanian troops faced between 20,000 and 30,000 Germans, mostly at Băneasa and Otopeni, but without orders due to the cutting of phone links. The bridge was held by a Romanian lieutenant and a handful of men until August 25 when Romanian reinforcements began to arrive from Craiova. Allied help finally came on the 26th when four hundred American planes bombed the German positions, and by the next day Bucharest had been cleared of German forces.

Eating, drinking and nightlife

Between the wars Bucharest was famed for its bacchanals, gourmet cuisine and Gypsy music, but this was swept away by the puritanical post-war regime, and although private enterprise is beginning to improve the situation, there is still a long way to go. Bad service and very restricted menus are still the norm, unless you want to pay a lot in hard currency, and the city is amazingly dull after dark.

Eating

The cheapest way to fuel up at midday is at one of the very few remaining lacto-vegetarian restaurants or lactobars, or the new breed of **pizzerias** and **burger-bars** that have supplanted them – these are on the main avenues and around the Gara de Nord, mostly open till around 7pm except on Sundays (though some near the station are open every day, around the clock). In the evenings the **restaurants** in the cheaper hotels are the most reliable economy option, although they may close early, around 8.30pm. The more expensive hotels provide standard international fare. **Bistro food** served in bar-style surroundings is on the increase, offering steaks, salads and home-cooked food chalked on daily changing blackboards.

For **snacks** look for holes in the walls (literally) that dispense freshly baked *pateuri cu brînzâ*, or check out the **patisseries** (*cofetărie*) which serve small portions of sticky confectionary with cola or coffee. Strangely, they often have separate sections for eating cakes and for drinking coffee, making it vary hard to do both at once. Street stalls selling filled baguettes, bananas, cola and cigarettes are also on the increase.

Food shops are now reasonably well stocked, and the **markets** (see "Listings" p.79) sell a fair variety of fruit and vegetables depending on the season. There are many new private shops and kiosks selling imported goods, especially alcohol, sweets and cigarettes; those around the Gara de Nord stay open until around 2am. If you want to buy your own food, the **delicatessens**, including *UNIC*, B-dul Magheru 19, and *Delicatesse Antoine*, at the corner of Strada Mendeleev and Strada Tache Ionescu, and also, at Calea Griviței 142 (open 24hr), opposite the Gara de Nord, are your best bet.

Pizzerias, burger bars and cafeterias

Al Fares, B-dul Libertății 118. Felafel house located close to the Casă Poporului. Open daily 10am–10pm.

Fraga & Nuris, Str. Piața Amzei 10–22. Across the road from the *Horoscop Bistro*, serving salads, burgers and omelettes. Open daily.

Horoscop Bistro, outside the Piața Amzei market. Reasonable light meals, with a tiny patio. Open Mon–Sat 7am–9pm.

Horoscop Pizzeria, B-dul Cantemir 1, Piața Unirii. Large pizzas of better than average quality with wine for L10,000.

Lacto Marna, Strada Buzești. Cheap chicken and stuffed peppers.

McMoni's, Piața Rosetti. Burgers and sandwiches for under a dollar.

Pitta Bar, just around the corner from the Piața Amzei market. Offers takeaway sausage or kebab in pitta.

Pizza Atelierului, Str. Atelierului 24. One of the better pizza restaurants.

Pizza Mini, Str. Lipscani. Situated next to the National Bank of Romania with a good range of pizzas. Also doubles as a bar. Open daily 9.30am–7pm.

Quick Master, Calea Griviței 138. Burgers and pizzas near the Gara de Nord.

Select, Aleea Alexandru 18. One of the few of the surviving *autoservires* that Ceaușescu wanted to become the mainstay of mass catering.

Patisseries

Cofetaria București, Calea Victoriei, at the side of the *Hotel București*. Gilded banquettes, delicious ice cream and cakes. Perhaps the nicest place in the city for treats. Open daily 8am–8pm.

Casablanca, on the corner of B-dul Magheru and Str. Tache Ionescu, two blocks north of the tourist office. Excellent croissants, cakes and Italian ice cream, with a range of coffees. No smoking. Open daily 8am–10pm.

Casata, B-dul Magheru. Just north of the *Efes Pub* with good pastries but lousy service.

Diplomat, Calea Dorobanților 20. Full of students from the economics faculty.

Foreign Languages Faculty Café, Str. Edgar Quinet. A fashionable spot for students, in the basement, at the rear of the university .

Lăpteria Enache, upstairs in the National Theatre, Piața Universității. A milk bar or rather, drinking-yogurt bar, with alcohol, too, and live jazz at weekends.

Panipat, Str. Rosetti 15, Calea Victoriei 204, B-dul Bălcescu and B-dul Bratiănu. Thoroughly modern franchise patisserie with good takeaway buns and pizzas and fashionably sulky staff. Open daily 8am–10pm.

Sanda, B-dul Magheru. A stand-up place, close to the *Casata*, but much friendlier.

Cofetaria Universității, B-dul Republicii, near the university. Lively, cheap and popular with students.

Cofetaria Victoriei, Calea Victoriei, near Str. Lipscani. Less grand but similar to the *București*. Open daily 8am–8pm.

Bistros and restaurants

Berlin, Str. C. Mille 4 (☎614.46.52). German trade reps usually end up here: fairly upmarket and touristy, with a floorshow most evenings, as well as an upstairs *bierkeller*. Open daily noon–7pm & 8pm–2am, bar until 3am.

Bistro Atheneu, Str. Episcopiei 3 (☎613.49.00). Right beside the Atheneum Roman Theatre, this bar with its seven or eight tables has one of the friendliest atmospheres in the city, created by Gibi, its multi-lingual owner. Always busy with Romanians and expats. Open daily 10am–midnight.

Brădet, Str. C. Davila 60 (☎638.60.14). Lebanese restaurant towards Cotroceni, a haven for vegetarians thanks to its felafel and hummus.

Caru cu Bere, Str. Stavropoleos 5 (☎613.75.60). Splendid neo-Tannhäuser decor and draught beer, with limited meals, notably *mititei* or grilled sausages famed throughout Bucharest. The name means "Beer Cart" and it rivals *Manuc's Inn* as the premier hang-out in Bucharest. Open daily 10am–10pm; folklore show Fri, Sat & Sun at 9pm. No smoking.

Casă Alba, Pădurea Băneasa (☎679.52.03). Situated in the Băneasa forest and immensely popular with the *nouveaux-riches* at weekends. Hard to get to, and harder to get back from, at any time.

Casă Capşa, Str. E. Quinet 4, entrance also at Calea Victoriei 36 (☎614.13.83 or 615.61.01). Long-established restaurant with old salon atmosphere. Good Romanian cuisine.

Casino Bucur, Str. Poenaru Bordea 2 (☎313.60.54). South of the Dîmbovița, in a beautifully decorated neo-Brîncovenesc mansion near the Centru Civic and recognizable by the limos parked by its summer garden. Pricey but worth it.

Cercul Militar, Calea Victoriei 27 (☎614.37.35). Wonderfully ornate interior and a well-placed terrace with fountain, serving good food, mainly, it seems, to wedding parties.

Doina, Şos. Kiseleff 4 (☎617.67.15). An elegant building designed by Ion Mincu, notable for Romanian dishes: pricey but good value.

DINING CLUBS

There are at least five new **private restaurants or dining clubs**, which pander unashamedly to the pretensions of Bucharest's new upwardly mobile businessmen, with overpriced drinks and underclad hostesses, but which may also offer useful facilities such as payment by credit card. They include the *Velvet*, Str. Ştirbei Vodă 2–4 (☎615.92.41); *Ilie Năstase Club*, B-dul Eliade 1 (☎679.63.85); *Felix*, B-dul Titulescu 39–49 (☎650.42.35); *Odobeşti*, Calea Moşilor 207 (☎210.47.45); and *Transilvania Club*, B-dul Carol I 76 (☎615.19.33).

Ghica–Tei, Str. Doamna Ghica 3 (☎688.26.35). Classy cuisine in the lakeside mansion of Prince Grigore Ghica, built in 1822 with later decor by Giacometti, northeast of the centre.

Hanul Manuc, Str. Iuliu Maniu 62, entrance also on Piaţa Unirii (☎613.14.15). An old merchants' *caravanserai* with indoor and outdoor dining. Service is worse outdoors, but guests indoors may be hustled out so that Iliescu and his cronies can eat in peace. Restaurant open Mon–Fri 7am–11pm, Sat & Sun 7am–midnight; also a patisserie, bar and wine cellar (daily 10am–midnight).

Hong Kong, Calea Griviţei 81 (☎659.50.25). Small, pleasant and inexpensive Chinese restaurant, 10–15 minutes' walk from the Gara de Nord. Open daily noon–11pm.

Irish Pub, B-dul Cantemir. Close to Unirii 2 metro, this is a "cook your own steak" house with self-service salads in a lively bar-style atmosphere.

Mioriţa, Şos. Kiseleff 24. Trendy and noisy, especially at weekends.

Moldova, Str. Icoanei 2, to the east of B-dul Magheru (☎611.37.82). Moldavian cuisine.

Monte Carlo, Cişmigiu Gardens (☎613.13.44). By the lake, with a covered stage – nightclub open till 4am.

Nan-Jing, Str. Lt. Lemnea 2, in the *Hotel Minerva* (☎650.60.10). Established since the 1960s, and still serving remarkably good Chinese food.

Pasagiul Victoriei. In the passage of the same name linking the Calea Victoriei and the Enei Church. Fairly slick, upmarket nest, offering caviar and other delicacies.

Pescarul, B-dul Magheru 2. Reasonable fish dishes, reasonably priced; also a snackbar. Open Mon–Sat noon–midnight.

Pescăruş, off B-dul Aviatorilor (☎679.46.40). In Herăstrău Park, specializing in fish.

Shanghai, at the junction of Str. Academiei and Str. Doamnei. One of the city's newer Chinese restaurants.

Drinking

Bars are beginning to spring up all over the city – some are rough and very basic, others quite flashy with videos and espresso machines. The larger hotels also have "night bars", often taking only hard currency and putting on tacky shows.

Bars

Bar Felix, Str. V. Lascăr (formerly Galaţi) 54. A trendy young hangout in a quiet backstreet north of B-dul Dacia – crowded and noisy.

Bulevard Bar, B-dul Kogălniceanu 1, in the Hotel Bulevard. Gorgeous *fin-de-siècle* decor, with upmarket prices and prostitutes hanging around.

Café de la Paix, corner of Piaţa Romană and Str. Eminescu. Stand-up joint selling imported booze and hot snacks to office workers and students.

Efes Pub, junction of B-dul Magheru and Str. Tache Ionescu. Owned by the eponymous Turkish brewery and advertised on TV to bring in the young consumers. Poor service and indifferent food.

Gambrinus, B-dul Kogălniceanu 18. A small, above average beerhall.
Sarpelctu Roşu, Str. Eminescu 119, corner of Str. V. Lascăr. The "Red Serpent" is a raucous place with real character, dancing and singing to Gypsy music. Serves good home-made food. Open till 3am.

Nightlife and entertainment

A fair number of the restaurants listed on p.75 feature **live acts** in the evenings; usually a quartet of Gypsies, or amplified youths playing last year's pop hits for middle-aged couples to dance to sedately. A better idea would be to try one of the places specializing in Romanian cuisine, such as the *Hanul Manuc*, *Carul cu Bere* and *Doina*, which sometimes offer good Gypsy musicians or *doina* singers, the best of whom can move diners to open-mouthed amazement by their shrieks and laments.

Discos of dubious trendiness are bursting out all over: try the *Vox Maris*, B-dul Kogălniceanu 2–4; *Bavaria 2000*, Calea Griviţei 143; *Dancing Club*, B-dul Pionerilor 16; or *Herăstrău*, Şos. Nordului 7–9; all open until at least 4am. Romanians dance well, in couples; just jigging around in the Anglo-Saxon manner is seen as not really trying.

Finding **rock concerts** largely depends on pot luck or contacts. Bucharest's *Students' Club* at Calea Plevnei 61, behind the Opera (☎615.15.58), is one place to make enquiries; another is *Club-A*, the Young Architects' Club, at Str. Blănari 14, which often features drama, foreign films and **jazz**. These are both pretty well dormant over the summer holidays.

Classical music and drama

Bucharest's cultural forte is **classical music and drama**, and several internationally acclaimed musicians have cut their teeth with the *George Enescu Philharmonic Orchestra*, which plays in the Romanian Athenaeum. Concerts and operatic productions also take place at the Opera Romană B-dul Kogălniceanu 70, the Radio Studio, Str. Berthelot 62–64, and the Opereta, B-dul Bălcescu 2, next to the National Theatre. Performances are lavish with fantastic sets and huge casts; tickets cost L1250–2000 from the venues' box offices. Outdoor concerts are held in Cişmigiu Gardens and Tineretului Park during the summer.

Most stage productions lose a lot if you don't understand Romanian, but performances at the following **theatres** might just surmount linguistic barriers: the Tăndărică Puppet Theatre, Calea Victoriei 50, and two music halls on the same street at nos. 33–35 & 174; the Comedy Theatre, Str. Măndineşti 2; and the State Jewish Theatre, Str. I. Barasch 15. In the second week of November a **festival** named after Romania's best-known playwright, Ion Luca Caragiale, brings to town the best of the year's drama from the provincial theatres. The **circus** is at Aleea Circului 15 (metro Ştefan cel Mare); like most of the theatres and concert halls it's dormant through the summer. Information should be available through your hotel reception desk or from ONT.

Cinemas

Cinemas are plentiful, both in the centre and the suburbs, showing films from all over the world, although subtitled Hollywood films are the most popular fare. A weekly poster is displayed listing what's on all over town. The main city centre cinemas are on **Bulevardul Magheru**, **Bulevardul Kogălniceanu** and the

Calea Griviţei. There are also open-air cinemas such as the *Capitol* at Str. C. Mille 13A and the *Gloria* on Bulevardul N. Grigorescu. In addition, the two branches of *Cinematecă*, at Str. Eforie 2 (☎613.04.83) and at Str. Cîmpineanu 21 (☎613.49.04), show a good selection of classic films, sometimes dubbed live by a single translator. Tickets cost around L3000.

Listings

Airlines Bookings for *TAROM* internal flights (from Băneasa airport) are handled at Str. Buzeşti 68, just off Piaţa Victoriei (☎659.41.85); for international flights (from Otopeni) go to the upstairs office at Str. Brezoianu 10, actually on Str. Domniţa Anastasia (Mon–Fri 7.30am–7pm; information ☎615.04.99; reservations ☎615.27.47; business class ☎613.03.63). Most foreign airlines have their offices on B-dul Magheru/Bălcescu or Str. Batiştei (by the *Intercontinental*): *Aeroflot*, Str. Biserica Amzei 29 (☎615.03.14); *Air France*, B-dul Bălcescu 35 (☎612.00.85); *Air Moldova*, Str. Batiştei 7 (☎312.12.58); *Austrian Airlines*, B-dul Bălcescu 7 (☎614.12.21 or 312.05.45); *Balkan*, Str. Batiştei 9 (☎312.07.11); *British Airways*, 2nd floor *Hotel Intercontinental*, B-dul Bălcescu 4; *CSA*, Str. Batiştei 3–5 (☎615.32.05 or 312.08.44); *Delta*, B-dul Unirii 33 (☎620.44.58 or 312.92.76); *El Al*, B-dul D. Cantemir (☎322.25.91); *LAR*, Str. Ştirbei Vodă 2–4 (☎615.32.06 or 615.32.76); *Lufthansa*, B-dul Magheru 18 (☎650.40.74 or 312.02.11); *Malev*, Str. G. Enescu 3 (☎312.04.27); *Romavia*, Şos. Bucureşti–Ploieşti 40 (☎633.72.63 or 633.00.30); *Sabena*, B-dul Bălcescu 24 (☎615.92.44); *Swissair*, B-dul Magheru 18 (☎312.02.38).

Airport information Otopeni airport ☎633.66.02.

American Express, ONT, B-dul Magheru 7.

Banks and exchange *National Bank of Romania*, Str. Lipscani 25; *Romanian Commercial Bank*, B-dul Carol I 12–16; *Romanian Bank for Foreign Trade (BRCE)*, Calea Victoriei 22–24; *CEC* (Savings Bank), Calea Victoriei 13; *Ion Ţriac Commercial Bank*, Str. Doamnei 12. As a rule, you're as well off using the exchange counters all over town.

Bicycle repair Str. General Berthelot 10.

Books and newspapers *Dacia*,Calea Victoriei 45, *Sadoveanu*, B-dul Magheru 6 (frequently shut), and *Eminescu*, B-dul Republicii 5, stock Romanian novels and poetry and books on native art and ethnography in English, French and German. Second-hand *anticariat* bookshops are at B-dul Brătianu 14, Str. Iuliu Maniu 54, B-dul Magheru 2, Calea Victoriei 45 and ·facing the Enei Church. There are lots of stalls on Piaţa Romană and in the Piaţa Universităţii underpass which occasionally have foreign books. The main English-language paper is called *Nine O'Clock* and on Fridays lists weekend events, theatre and opera – available free from major hotels and airline offices; you may also find the better *Times of Bucharest* in kiosks.

Car rental *Europcar* next to ONT at B-dul Magheru 7 (☎13.39.15; Mon–Fri 8am–8pm, Sat & Sun 8am–3pm) and at Otopeni (☎33.75.01; 24hr); *Hertz* at Str. T. Ionescu 27 (☎650.25.95), in the *Touring ACR* office at Str. Cihoski 2 (☎611.04.08 or 611.43.65; Mon–Fri 8am–7pm, Sat & Sun 8am–2pm) and Otopeni (☎679.52.84; daily 8am–8pm); *JET Turist*, B-dul D. Cantemir 2A (☎614.80.82/86); *Mercedes*, Str. Doamnei 12 (☎615.58.46); *Sebastian*, Calea Victoriei 135 (☎659.30.14).

Car repairs *ACR* has Technical Assistance centres at Calea Dorobanţilor 85 and Şos. Colentina 1 (☎635.41.40). *Arthur Motor Cars*, Str. Ştirbei Vodă 122 (☎615.52.75; 7.30am–8.30pm), and *Automecanica*, Str. Dreptăţii 1 (☎660.65.38; Mon–Thurs 8am–4pm, Fri 8am–2pm) are private companies that may be able to help with foreign cars. *Piese Auto* claims to have spare parts for Fiat at Calea Griviţei 212 (☎665.48.80) and for Renault at B-dul Ferdinand II 124 (☎635.00.91).

Courier services *DHL* c/o *Hotel Bucureşti*, Calea Victoriei 63–81 (☎312.26.61).

Dentist Calea Plevnei 19 (☎615.52.17).

Embassies and consulates *Australia*, Liviu Buzila, Str. Dr E. Racota 16–18 ap. 1 (☎666.69.23); *Britain*, Str. Jules Michelet 24 (Mon–Fri 9am–5pm; ☎312.03.03–05 or 615.35.71); *Bulgaria*, Str. Rabat 5 (☎633.21.50), consulate at Str. Vasile Lascar 32 (☎611.11.36); *Canada*, Str. N. Iorga 36 (☎650.61.40 or 312.03.65); *Croatia*, Str. Hristo Botev 3 4th floor apt. 14 (☎615.35.71); *Hungary*, Str. J.L. Calderon 65 (☎614.66.2 or 312.00.72); *Republica Moldova*, Aleea Alexandru 40 (☎633.04.74 or 312.97.90); *Russia*, Şos. Kiseleff 6 (☎617.01.20) (visas Str. Tuberozelor 4); *Serbia*, Calea Dorobanţilor 34 (☎611.98.71); *USA*, Str. T. Arghezi 7 (☎312.40.40 or 312.40.42).

Emergencies Ambulance ☎961; police ☎955; fire service ☎981.

Fuel The state monopoly has become a duopoly, with some *PECO* stations turned over to *Competrol*; there are now 51 filling stations in Bucharest, of which fifteen are open 24 hours. In the city centre head for Str. T. Arghezi (by the *Intercontinental*), Splaiul Independenţei (north of the Casă Poporului), Calea Dorobanţilor, Str. Brezoianu, Str. I. Mincu (behind the *Doina* restaurant) or B-dul D. Golescu (at the Gara de Nord). There are others on all main routes out of the city, notably at Băncasa and at Militari (the start of the Bucureşti–Piteşti motorway). Lead-free fuel is available at Str. Arghezi, Calea Dorobanţilor and Băneasa (all 24hr), Şos. Olteniţei 253 (8am–8pm), Piaţa Amzei (7am–9pm), Str. Schitu Măgureanu 5 (6am–4pm), and at the km36 services on the Piteşti motorway.

Football The most popular teams are the army team *Steaua Bucureşti* (B-dul Ghencea 35; tram #8 or #47, trolleybus #69), or the rail-workers' team *Locomotiv-Rapid* (Şos. Giuleşti 18; metro Cringaşi). *Dinamo* was the *Securitate* team, now renamed *Tricolor* in a vain attempt to gain popularity; but their base (Şos. Ştefan cel Mare 9; metro Ştefan cel Mare) is still known as the Dinamo stadium.

Hospitals The *Clinica Batiştei*, Str. T. Arghezi 28 (☎497-030) behind the *Intercontinental*, and the *Spital Municipal*, Splaiul Independenţei 169, are both used to dealing with foreigners, but for emergency treatment you should go to the *Spital Clinic de Urgenţa*, Calea Floreasca 8, north of the centre (☎679.43.10). Your embassy can recommend doctors speaking your language. There's a state-run Acupuncture and Homeopathy Centre at Str. Visarion 4, near Piaţa Romană.

Libraries The British Council Library, Calea Dorobanţilor 14 (Mon–Fri 10am–5pm, closed throughout August) has week-old British newspapers. The US Cultural Centre at the south end of Str. Calderon (closed July and Aug) is similar.

Markets Fresh produce is sold in the Unirii, Amzei, Obor, Cringaşi, Traian and Matache (Ilie Pintilie) markets, as well as the Aviaţei market just east of Băneasa airport; the Piaţa Amzei also has a colourful flower-market. There is a huge Sunday morning flea-market (*Tîrgul Vitan*) on Calea Vitan, fifteen minutes' walk south from the Dristor 1 metro station, alongside the Dîmboviţa embankment.

Motoring information is dispensed by *Touring ACR*, Str. Cihoski 2 (☎611.04.08 or 650.70.76; Mon–Fri 7.30am–7.30pm, Sat & Sun 8am–2.30pm), and its parent organization, the *Auto Clubul Roman* (*ACR*), Str. Tache Ionescu 25 (☎615.55.10), both near the Piaţa Romană. They sell hotel coupons and provide an insurance and breakdown service for members of foreign affiliates.

Opticians If it's an insurance job, head for *Optinova* at B-dul Unirii 5 Bloc 1-B (Mon–Fri 9am–7pm, Sat 9am–2pm); otherwise try the two *opticas* on Piaţa Lahovari, by the Opthalmic Clinic.

Pharmacies There is at least one 24-hour pharmacy in each sector of the city: Sector I (the city centre) B-dul Magheru 18 (☎659.61.15); Sector II Şos. Iancului 57 (☎653.21.72) & Şos. Colentina 1 Bl. 34 (☎635.50.10); Sector III B-dul N. Grigorescu bl. A14 (☎644.21.25); Sector IV Calea Şerban Vodă 43 (☎623.76.47); Sector V Şos. Alexandriei bl. PC 10 (☎776.27.40); Sector VI Str. Băiceni 1 (☎725.25.55) & Şos. Giulesti 123 (☎617.10.86) & Gara de Nord (☎618.20.55). In addition there are new private pharmacies, which may be better supplied, at Calea Victoriei 14, 91 & 103, Str. Ştirbei Vodă 55, B-dul Bălcescu 10 & 35, Calea Griviţei 206, B-dul 1 Mai 128 & 343, Str. V. Lascăr 129, Calea Moşilor 217 bl. 23, Şos. Mihai Bravu 12 & B-dul N. Grigorescu 49.

Photography *Kodak* are on the east side of Piaţa Unirii, *Fuji* outside ONT on B-dul Magheru, and film can also be bought in *Comturist* shops in most hotels. *Foto-Urgent* shops such as those at Str. Ion Cîmpineanu 17, Str. Radu Christian and B-dul Kogălniceanu 8 can do passport photos in hours.

Police City headquarters at Calea Victoriei 17, entrance to the north on Str. Eforiei (☎641.35.35), but for most routine matters go to the Sector 1 police station at B-dul Ana Ipătescu 22 (☎630.51.74). Traffic accidents (with damage) should be dealt with at Şos. Pantelimon 290 (☎627.30.35), Str. Drumul Taberei 44 (☎746.10.20) or Str. I. Neculce 6 (☎617.73.30).

Post office The main post office is at Calea Victoriei 37 with poste restante hidden behind at Str. Matei Millo 10 (Mon–Fri 7.30–8pm, Sat 7.30–2pm). To receive mail here, make sure it is addressed c/o *Officiul PTTR no. 1, Bucureşti*; you can also receive mail at smaller and quieter *poştas* such as Str. Garii de Nord 12, Str. T. Arghezi 37 and Str. Academiei 54.

Rail tickets *Agenţie CFR*, Str. Domniţa Anastasia 10 (Mon–Fri 7.30am–7.30pm, Sat 8am–1pm) or Calea Griviţei 139 (Mon–Sat 7.30am–7pm, Sun 7.30am–1pm); should be bought at least 24 and preferably 48 hours in advance, being sure to get a seat reservation. International tickets must be bought on the north side of Piaţa Unirii (Mon–Fri 7.30am–7pm, Sat 7.30am–noon).

Records Muzica, Calea Victoriei 41 (Mon–Fri 9am–7.30pm, Sat 9.30am–2.30pm).

Shopping Department stores: *Unirea*, Piaţa Unirii 1; *Victoria*, Calea Victoriei 17; *Cocor*, B-dul Brătianu 20; *Bucur-Obor*, Şos. Colentina 2; *Victoria*, Calea Victoriei 17; *Romarta*, Calea Victoriei 60–68 and many other branches; and *Tineretului*, B-dul Unirii 37. The "dollar shop" at Str. Episcopei 9 is useful for imported food, drink and cigarettes. *Vox Maris*, B-dul Magheru, is the best-stocked Western store.

Sports facilities The National Stadium, B-dul Muncii 43/Str. Major Coravu (stadium, ice skating); Progresul, Str. Dr. Staicovici 42, just west of the Casă Poporului (tennis); and *Floreasca*, Str. Aviator Popa Marin 2 (tennis, basketball, ice skating).

Swimming pools In the National and Dinamo stadia, as well as in hotels such as the *Bucureşti* and *Parc* – you can also swim in Lakes Floreasca (metro Aurel Vlaicu), Strauleşti (western terminus of trolleybus #97) and Băneasa (bus #131 or #205). The students' swimming place is at Ştrandul Tei, off B-dul Lacul Tei.

Travel agents *Atlantic Tur*, Calea Victoriei 202; *Horoscop*, Str. Brezoianu 10; *Meridian Tours*, Str. Ştirbei Vodă 17; *Nova Turism*, B-dul Bălcescu 21; *Paralela 45*, B-dul Kogălniceanu 7; *Romextur*, Str. Luterană 4; *SC Elvicom*, Str. N. Iorga 31; *Simpaturism*, Str. Puţu cu Plopi 18; at the north end of Cişmigiu; and *Vacanţa*, Splaiul Unirii Bl. 14–15. For international bus tickets try *Nur* (☎637.67.23), *Royal Tur* (☎312.29.80), *Toros* (☎638.48.63) and *Troy Turism* (☎637.40.87) in and around the *Cerna* and *Astoria* hotels; and *Transport Turism* (aka "Double T Tours") by the Dîmboviţa at Calea Victoria 2 (☎613.36.42).

TRAVELLING FROM BUCHAREST TO BULGARIA

Most days there are four **trains from Bucharest's Gara de Nord to Sofia**: the *Sofia* (from Moscow) at 8.30am, unnamed *accelerats* at 11.30am and 7.25pm, and the *Bulgaria* (from St Petersburg) at 9.40pm. Travelling from Bucharest, you will almost certainly be directed to the *accelerats*.

All Westerners other than Americans need a **visa** to cross into Bulgaria. Visas can be obtained at the border (see p.107), but can cost double the usual fee there; it's wiser to obtain them in advance – either before you leave home, or from Str. Rabat 5 in Bucharest (☎01/633.21.50). A tourist visa (which requires a photo) costs $30 for a thirty-day stay, and a transit visa (valid for thirty hours) $30 for single entry and $39 for double entry. It takes up to a week to issue a visa, unless you're willing to pay another $30 for same-day service.

Around Bucharest

Bucharest is surrounded by a ring of monasteries and fine country houses, most of which are popular destinations for weekend outings, but which are generally hard to reach by public transport. If you don't have wheels of your own, you may prefer to take one of the trips organized by ONT (see box below).

ONT EXCURSIONS

For visitors with ample funds and limited time, ONT (see p.52) can readily arrange **excursions from the capital**, usually half-day trips by bus or car. These eliminate the hassle of getting to places independently but rather sanitize the experience, which in some cases may fall short of the image advertised (read the small print before parting with your dollars).

Their city tour, and specialized tours of churches and museums, cost from $7 each (for ten people) to $17 (for two); five-hour trips to the Snagov, Căldărușani, Cernica and Pasarea monasteries cost between $9 and $34 each, depending on numbers. A full-day trip to Sinaia costs between $37 and $96.

Snagov and around

SNAGOV, 40km north of Bucharest, is the most popular destination: a beautiful lake with watersports facilities and a reserve for water plants (Indian waterlily, arrowhead, and also oriental beech), surrounding an island occupied by a **monastery** built in 1519. This was where King Mihai and then Ceaușescu and other high functionaries had their weekend villas, and it was the scene both of Yugoslavia's expulsion from the Warsaw Pact in 1948 and of the Hungarian leader Imre Nagy's interrogation following the Soviet invasion of 1956.

Launches motor over to the island, where monks have become resigned to visitors seeking the **tomb of Dracula**, sited in front of the church altar. Though lacking identifying inscriptions, it's likely that this is indeed the burial place of Vlad the Impaler: his murder is believed to have occurred in the forests nearby; the monks would have been predisposed to take the body, since both Dracula and his father had patronized the monastery; and there is forensic evidence. The richly dressed corpse exhumed in 1935 had been decapitated, a fate known to have overtaken Dracula, whose head was supposedly dispatched wrapped and perfumed as a gift to the Sultan. Women must be decently dressed to gain admittance here.

If you travel to Snagov by road, you pass through the area most notoriously affected by Ceaușescu's **systematization** programme. Just north of Otopeni airport **BALOTEȘTI** consists of stark modern apartment buildings to house those displaced from villages such as Dimieni, which lay just east of the airport. Vlădiceasca and Cioflinceni, on the road east to Snagov from the DN1, were bulldozed in 1988, with the inhabitants being resettled in **GHERMĂNEȘTI**, on the western outskirts of Snagov.

Practicalities

In addition to the *Hotel Măgurele* (☎01/780.22.80; ③) in the village, it's now possible to stay in private rooms or at the campsite (but beware the mosquitoes). In

SYSTEMATIZATION

Systematization was Ceauşescu's policy to do away with up to half the country's villages and move the rural population into larger centres. The concept was first developed by Nikita Krushchev in the Soviet Union in 1951, to combat the movement of younger people to the towns by **amalgamating villages** to raise the standard of rural life. Similar plans were put forward in Hungary, and in 1967 Ceauşescu reorganized Romania's local government system and announced a scheme to do away with up to 6300 villages and replace them with 120 new towns and 558 agroindustrial centres.

His declared aim (based on an original idea in Karl Marx's *The Communist Manifesto*) was "to wipe out radically the major differences between towns and villages; to bring the working and living conditions of the working people in the countryside closer to those in the towns", by herding people together into apartment buildings so that "the community fully dominates and controls the individual", and thus to produce Romania's New Man. Thankfully the project was forgotten while Ceauşescu was distracted by other prestige projects such as the Danube–Black Sea Canal and the Bucharest Civic Centre, but he relaunched it in March 1988, when he was becoming obsessed with increasing exports and paying off the national debt. Since collectivization Romania's agricultural output had declined steadily, on fertile land with one of the longest growing seasons in Europe; in 1985 the minuscule private sector produced 29 percent of the country's fruit, 14 percent of its meat and almost 20 percent of its milk. Ceauşescu was determined to **revolutionize agriculture** by increasing the growing area, while also further increasing centralization and reducing incentive and the scope for individual initiative. While the peasants had previously been able to support themselves with their own pig, cow and hens, in the new *blocs* there was to be no accommodation for animals, and to add insult to injury they were to receive derisory compensation for their demolished homes and then be charged rent.

CIOLPANI, across the lake, there's the better *Hotel Pacea* (☎01/614.99.76; ⑤) and attached Vila 23.

Although it's proposed to extend the metro all the way to Snagov, there are currently only three **buses** a day from the Băneasa bus station, and two **trains** from the Gara de Nord on summer weekends only (7.30 and 8.30am, returning at 5.10 and 8.20pm – get off at the terminus, Snagov Plajă, not Snagov Sat).

Căldăruşani

Four kilometres east of Baloteşti lies **CĂCIULAŢI**, built as a planned estate village by the Ghica family. Their villa, now the property of the Romanian Academy, was occupied by the *Securitate*, and bodies have recently been found buried in its run-down park. Trains (seven a day from Bucharest to Urziceni) halt here and at Greci, another 10km east; the latter lies a couple of kilometres south of **Căldăruşani Monastery**, otherwise beyond the reach of public transport from Bucharest. This didn't stop the world press from mobbing it when tennis stars Mariana Simionescu and Bjorn Borg were married here in 1980. The church where the wedding took place was built in 1638 by Matei Basarab and was previously noted for its school of icon-painting, established in 1787. Among the many icons displayed are eight by Grigorescu, who started painting in 1846 at the age of eight and studied here in 1854–56.

The model was to be the **Ilfov Agricultural Sector**, immediately north of Bucharest, and this was where the first evictions and demolitions took place in August 1988, with two or three days' notice being given and then shops and bus services being closed to force people out. Entire villages were removed to *blocs* in Otopeni and Ghermăneşti, where up to ten families had to share one kitchen and the sewage system had not been completed. At the same time the villagers of Buda and Ordoreanu, just south of Bucharest, were removed to Bragadiru to make way for a reservoir for the proposed Bucharest–Danube Canal and, in other villages across the nation, ugly **concrete Civic Centre buildings** began to appear in the centres of the planned New Towns. Repairs were banned in all the doomed villages and on all single-storey buildings, but these regulations were interpreted differently by the various *judeţs*. In Maramureş, the authorities, aware that greater distances to the agricultural land would be a disadvantage, allowed repair work on outlying farms and also permitted attics to count as a second storey. In the Banat, efforts were made to attract migrants to houses left by emigrating Schwabs, although these should have been demolished.

There was widespread revulsion at this scheme to uproot half of the rural populace; in August 1988 the Cluj academic **Doina Cornea** wrote an open letter (published in the West) in protest, pointing out that the villages, with their unbroken folk culture, are the spiritual centre of Romanian life, and that to demolish them would be to "strike at the very soul of the people". She was soon placed under house arrest, but the campaign abroad gathered pace. Although the Hungarian view, seeing the plan as an attack on their community, was widely accepted, it does seem clear that Ceauşescu's aim was indeed a wholesale attack on the rural way of life.

Little more had happened by the end of 1989, and the scheme was at once cancelled by the FSN; new buildings are going up all over the country, and those uprooted are returning to the sites of their villages and starting all over again.

Mogoşoaia and Potlogi

The lovely Brîncoveanu palace built in 1702 at **MOGOŞOAIA**, 10km northwest of Bucharest along the DN1, and served by local trains towards Urziceni and by bus #460/461 from Laromet, the terminal of tram #20 and trolley #97, is perhaps Romania's most important non-religious monument. It is off the official excursions list until earthquake damage has been repaired, and its neglect is a disgrace. However, the atmospheric gardens are still open and the exterior of the palace is well worth seeing. Here lies the grave of Elizabeth Asquith, daughter of the British statesman, whose epitaph reads: "My soul has regained the freedom of the night."

A good forty kilometres west of the city (on the DJ401A, between the old DN7 and the newer motorway to Piteşti) lies **POTLOGI**, a small village and site of another palace, built in 1698. Although hard to reach by public transport (look for a bus in Titu, the junction of the rail lines to Piteşti and Tîrgovişte), this is one of the most beautiful of Brîncoveanu's buildings and well worth the expedition.

travel details

Trains

Bucharest to: Arad (6 daily; 8hr 25min–10hr 20min); Baia Mare (2 daily; 11hr 30min); Braşov (18 daily; 2hr 30min–4hr 30min); Cîmpulung (1 daily; 4hr 20min); Cluj (6 daily; 7hr 30min–12hr); Constanţa (13–17 daily; 2hr 25min–5hr 20min); Craiova, via Caracal (14 daily; 2hr 20min–4hr 40min); Iaşi (9 daily; 5hr 45min–9hr 45min); Mangalia (3–6 daily; 3hr 45min–5hr); Piteşti (11 daily; 1hr 35min–2hr 50min); Ploieşti (45 daily; 39min–1hr 35min); Sibiu (7 daily; 4hr 50min–11hr 30min); Sighişoara (8 daily; 4hr 10min–7hr 10min); Snagov (summer weekends only; 1hr 10min); Suceava (8 daily; 5hr 30min–11hr 25min); Timişoara (10 daily; 7hr 20min–15hr 15min); Tîrgovişte (4 daily; 1hr 50min–2hr 15min); Tîrgu Mureş (2 daily; 7hr 40min); Tulcea (2 daily; 5–7hr).

Planes

Bucharest (Băneasa airport) to: Arad; Bacau; Baia Mare; Caransebeş; Cluj; Constanţa; Craiova; Iaşi; Oradea; Satu Mare; Sibiu; Suceava; Timişoara; Tîrgu Mureş; Tulcea.

International trains

Bucharest to: Belgrade (1 daily; 12hr 25min); Berlin (1 daily; 29hr 45min); Budapest (4 daily; 13hr 10min–15hr); Dresden (1 daily; 26hr 35min); Istanbul (1 daily; 20hr 30min): Kiev (3 daily; 25hr 20min–27hr 50min); Moscow (2 daily; 42hr 30min–44hr 50min); Prague (2 daily; 23hr–23hr 40min); Ruse (5 daily; 2hr 25min–3hr 15min); St Petersburg (1 daily; 54hr 20min); Sofia (4 daily; 10hr 20min–12hr 40min); Vienna (2 daily; 17hr 20min–18hr); Warsaw (1 daily; 28hr).

CHAPTER TWO

WALLACHIA

C enturies before the name Romania appeared on maps of Europe, foreign merchants and rulers knew vaguely of **Wallachia** – the land of the Vlachs or Wallachs, known in Romanian as *Ţară Romaneasca* – which served as a distant outpost of Christendom before being conquered by the Turks and largely forgotten about until the nineteenth century. Occasional travellers reported on the region's backwardness and the corruption of its ruling boyars, but few predicted its sudden union with Moldavia in 1859 – the first step in the creation of modern Romania. Historically subject to forces beyond their control, Wallachia's peasantry adapted and endured, whoever their master, and counted themselves lucky when ruled by an efficient tyrant such as the Impaler, who could bring the boyars to heel and repel the marauding Ottomans.

Today Wallachia, the area to the south of the Carpathian mountains, is in many ways the least interesting of Romania's three principal provinces, though many people will find themselves passing through it en route between Bucharest and Transylvania or travelling to the coast. Comprised of largely flat and featureless agricultural land, its most interesting towns are those in the foothills of the Carpathians, such as Sinaia (see p.115), Tîrgovişte and Curtea de Argeş. In addition there's a string of **monasteries**, mostly raised at the behest of "progressive" despots otherwise famed for their suppression of incessant invasions or rebellions. Industrialization has wrought huge changes around Ploieşti, Piteşti, Craiova and the coal-mining Jiu valley, all places that now have little to recommend them. Peasant life largely continues to follow the ancient pastoral or agricultural cycle in the highlands and on the Bărăgan Steppe, where pagan rites such as *Ariet* and *Căluş* are still practised.

The most rewarding part of Wallachia stretches from the ruins of **Tîrgovişte** and **Poienari** (site of **Dracula's Castle**) to the Episcopal Church at **Curtea de Argeş**, an area known as Oltenia after its chief river and littered with monuments left by Wallachia's voivodes and clerics. Unless in search of Gypsies and their music, most visitors bypass the southeast, and rightly so; but you'll find it hard to avoid the big industrialized centres of **Ploieşti**, **Piteşti** and **Craiova**, rail hubs of the region, if you're exploring in any depth.

ACCOMMODATION PRICES

Hotels listed in the *Guide* have been price-graded according to the scale below. Prices given are those charged for the cheapest double room, which in the less expensive places usually comes without private bath or shower and without breakfast. See p.28 for more details.

① under $10	④ $25–40	⑦ $80–135
② $10–15	⑤ $40–55	⑧ $135–190
③ $15–25	⑥ $55–80	⑨ $200 and over

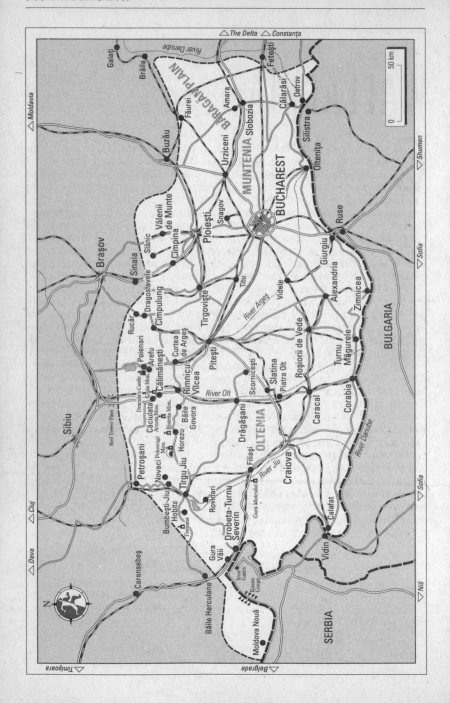

Wallachia is renowned for its **festivals**. During the third week in February, musicians gather for the *Izvoare fermecate* at **Tîrgu Jiu**; while **Polovragi** to the east is the setting for a big fair between July 15 and 20. Another fair, devoted to pottery, coincides with the Songs of the Olt festival at **Calimăneşti** during the first week in August; and at **Tismana**, pan-pipers congregate on August 15.

Ploieşti, Tîrgovişte and Piteşti

Neither **Ploieşti** nor **Piteşti** is an attractive place, but both serve as useful springboards for more enticing destinations. Ploieşti lies on the main road and rail line between Bucharest and Transylvania, with a couple of sites of interest to the north, just before crossing into Transylvania. Rail travellers may also change here for **Tîrgovişte**, the old Wallachian capital, midway between Ploieşti and Piteşti, which is reached more directly from Bucharest via the junction of Titu. Piteşti is likewise an important junction, situated astride the main routes from Bucharest to Cîmpulung and the Argeş and Olt valleys.

Ploieşti and around

As you near **PLOIEŞTI** (pronounced "Ploy-esht"), an oily smell and the eerie night-time flare of vented gases proclaim that this is Romania's biggest oil town. By the outbreak of World War I there were ten refineries here, all owned by foreign oil companies and destroyed by British agents in 1916 to deny them to the Germans; Royal Dutch Shell subsequently claimed huge damages from the Romanian government, which paid up, all its policies being driven by the need to keep on the right side of the Paris peace-makers and thus to gain Transylvania as promised. While British companies like Vickers and ICI sold out profitably to Hitler's industrialists before World War II, it was the townsfolk who paid for it, when allied aircraft carpet-bombed Ploieşti in 1944 – hence the town centre's almost total concrete uniformity.

There's little to see in town with the exception of the elegant **Princely Church** (1639) at Str. Bassarab 63, and the engagingly varied collection of clocks at Str. Sinache 1. Otherwise, Ploieşti has the usual uninspiring collection of **museums**: an art gallery at B-dul Independenţei 1; and natural science and folk art museums in the huge neoclassical Palace of Culture at Str. Catalin 1. However, the **Oil Museum**, at Str. Bagdascar 10, and **History Museum**, at Str. Toma Caragiu 10, do have interesting records of the wartime destruction of the town.

Practicalities

Trains to and from Transylvania use the Vest station, while those to and from Moldavia use Ploieşti Sud; trains to Bucharest can use either. The two stations are linked every hour or two by trains from Ploieşti Sud to Tîrgovişte and Slănic, and, more usefully, by tram #103 and bus #2, passing close to the centre. Ploieşti Nord station is on the Măneciu branch and useless except to reach Vălenii de Munte. There are two **bus stations**, on Strada Depoului to the south, and at Str. Griviţei 25 to the north. *TAROM* has an office at B-dul Republicii 17 (☎044/ 14.51.65) selling tickets for flights out of Bucharest's airports.

Ploieşti's newest **hotel** is the *Turist*, Str. Tache Ionescu 6 (☎044/12.61.01; ④), cheaper than either the *Central*, Str. Tache Ionescu 2 (☎044/12.66.41; ⑤), or

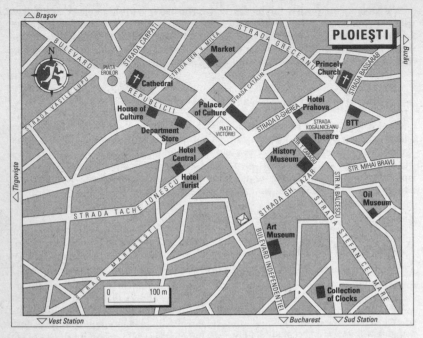

Prahova, Str. Dobrogeanu-Gherea 11 (☎044/12.68.50; ④). From June to August, *BTT* at Str. Poştei 6 (☎044/14.61.72) might have **rooms** for rent in town – an economical alternative to the **campsites** at Româneşti (11km south on the DN1 towards Bucharest), Pădurea Păuleşti (8km north on DN1 and 3km east) and Paralela 45 (with rooms, 19km north on DN1).

North of Ploieşti

The Teleajen valley runs north from Ploieşti into the foothills of the Carpathian Bend, a route followed by the DN1A, a much quieter and more relaxing alternative route to Braşov. The main stopping-place, 32km out and served by trains from Ploieşti Nord, is **VĂLENII DE MUNTE**, with a **hotel** (③) and a **museum**, in a seventeenth-century house at Str. Enescu 3 where the great historian Nicolae Iorga lived until his murder by the Iron Guard in 1940. The Valeni monastery church, founded in 1680, is at Str. Berevoieşti 4.

Just south of Vălenii, a road heads west for 11km to **SLĂNIC** (sometimes known as Slănic Prahova, to distinguish it from Slanic Moldova, to the north). Between two salty lakes (in which you can swim) rises the *Muntele de Sare* (Salt Mountain), now a spa, and previously a salt-mining centre dating from 1532. You can visit the **museum** of the salt industry in the *Casa Cămărăşiei* or former Salt Chancellery (built in 1800), and the nearby *Unirea* mine, displaying scenes from Romanian history carved in salt. Slănic lies at the end of the rail line from Ploieşti Sud via Ploieşti Vest; some of the eight daily trains do the distance in an hour and a quarter, but beware, others stop for an hour in Plopeni. Slănic does have one **hotel** (③) if you need to spend the night.

SLON, 22km north of Vălenii, is a great woodworking centre, producing barrels, spindles, spoons and shingles, as well as carpets (now mainly for Turkish companies). The village's folk dance ensemble meets on Tuesday nights, and you should be able to find **accommodation** in private rooms here. The asphalt ends in Slon, but the remains of a Roman road continue north into the hills.

The DN1A continues past Suzana nunnery (built in the eighteenth century and rebuilt in 1835–38 with icons by Tattarescu) to **CHEIA** at the head of the Teleajen valley. This is a pleasantly relaxed resort at the foot of the Ciucaş mountains, served by daily buses from Braşov, Ploieşti and Bucharest, with a **hotel** (④), **bungalows** to rent, and a **campsite**. In addition, the *Muntele Roşu* cabana lies on a side road, 7km north, at the foot of the mountains. This is a compact area of weirdly eroded conglomerate outcrops and pillars, with fine open walking country all around; the *Ciucaş* cabana, between *Muntele Roşu* and Mount Ciucaş, offers friendly but basic accommodation. From the Bratocea Pass it's downhill all the way past the *Babarunca* cabana to Săcele and Braşov (see p.121).

Cîmpina

Romania's oldest oil town, **CÎMPINA** (or Câmpina), lies on the DN1, 32km from Ploieşti, just before the mountains of the Prahova valley begin. Its only tourist sights are both on the northern outskirts. Buses meet trains and take only five minutes to haul passengers up into town; you should get off and walk to the left where they turn right onto B-dul Carol I, the main road through town. The **Nicolae Grigorescu Museum** (Tues–Sun 9am–5pm), just above the double bend at no. 166, commemorates Romania's most prolific nineteenth-century painter (1838–1907), whose talents gained him an apprenticeship at Căldăruşani Monastery at the age of sixteen and who worked with the *Barbizon* group in Paris in his twenties. Further north at no. 145 is **Haşdeu Castle**, an odd cruciform structure with battlements and buttresses, notoriously haunted, built in 1896 by an historian and linguist, Bogdan Petriceico Haşdeu. A leading figure in the 1848

THE PLOIEŞTI PLOY

In 1940, as in World War I, it was feared that Germany would occupy Romania to guarantee supplies from what was then Europe's second largest oil producer (after the Soviet Union). There was tacit support from the government of Romania, then still neutral, for Anglo-French plans to sabotage the oil wells, thus making a German invasion pointless, but due to technical problems and bad luck these never went ahead. Plan B, to block the channel through the Iron Gates, stopping the oil barges reaching Germany along the Danube, was a greater fiasco: the Germans soon found out about the British barges making their way upstream from Galaţi, supposedly in secret, and forced the Romanian authorities to expel the crews.

At this time, the RAF was based around Larissa, north of Athens, and an alternative plan was devised to attack the oil wells from here. However, it was 660km to Ploieşti over Musala, the highest peak in southeastern Europe, at the extreme limit of the range of their early Wellington bombers. Following severe maintenance problems, the plan was abandoned, and it wasn't long before the Allies were driven out of Greece itself. Finally, in June 1942 a dozen American B-24 Liberators attacked from Benghazi, and on August 1, 1943, 177 Liberators made a low-level daylight raid. One third of them were shot down, oil production was drastically cut, and the town was devastated.

revolution and then one of the progenitors of the nationalist and anti-semitic philosophy that has infected Romanian politics throughout this century, he built the castle as a memorial for his daughter Iulia who died aged nineteen. She graduated from elementary school at the age of eight, and after high school went to study in Paris; she would have been the first woman to receive a doctorate from the Sorbonne, but died of tuberculosis in 1888, leaving three volumes of plays and poetry, published after her death.

In the new centre of town to the south, the *Muntenia* **hotel** at B-dul Carol I 61 (☎044/33.30.90; ④) stands opposite the *ACR* office and a tourist agency. You'll find cheaper beds in the spa of **POIANA CÎMPINA**, 2km west of the train station, and the *casute* on the main DN1 just north at **NISTOREȘTI** and **POSADA**.

Continuing northwards from Cîmpina takes you into the **Prahova valley** with its magnificent scenery, which, although still officially in Wallachia, is described in the opening pages of the chapter on Transylvania (see p.114).

Tîrgoviște

TÎRGOVIȘTE (or Târgovişte), 50km west of Ploiești, is considerably smaller than Ploiești, with 80,000 inhabitants and factories producing equipment for the oil industry. Capital of Wallachia for more than two centuries, it gained new fame when Nicolae and Elena Ceaușescu were executed in its army barracks on Christmas Day, 1989.

The Town

Tîrgoviște's main attraction is the **Princely Court** (*Curtea Domneasca*), a mass of crumbling ramparts and rooms with a few well-preserved sections, once the royal seat of Wallachia, from where more than forty voivodes exercised their rule between 1415 and 1659. The Princely Court figured large in the life of **Dracula** (see p.346), whose bust you'll pass as you near the ruins. His early years were spent here, until he and his brother Radu were sent to Anatolia as hostages. Following the murder of his father and his eldest brother, Mircea, who was buried alive by the boyars, Vlad returned to be enthroned here in 1456, and waited for three years before taking his revenge. Invited to feast at court with their families, the boyars were half-drunk when guards suddenly grabbed them and impaled them forthwith upon stakes around town, sparing only the fittest who were marched off to labour on Dracula's castle at Poienari (see p.96). A **museum** of Dracula's life and times occupies the fifteenth-century **Sunset Tower** (*Turnul Chindiei*), although this has been closed for a long time pending repair. Nearby stands the sixteenth-century Princely Church where Dracula's successors used to attend mass, sitting upstairs in a special section screened from the congregation.

Just southeast of the Princely Court on Strada Nicolae Bălcescu (also known as Calea Domneasca) are the **Art Gallery** and **History Museum** and, further along Strada Justiței, the **museums** devoted to printing and local writers are worth a look. Back across Strada Nicolae Bălcescu, the **Stelea Monastery** was built in 1645 by Prince Vasile Lupu of Moldavia as part of a peace agreement with the Wallachian ruler, Matei Basarabs. The monastery was closed under communism but is now functioning again and its Gothic arcading and Byzantine-influenced paintings are being restored. Finally, the remains of the city walls, also erected by Matei Basarab in 1645, can be seen in places along the east side of Strada Tudor Vladimirescu.

Three kilometres northeast of town (bus #7) the graceful bulk of **Dealu Monastery** rises upon a hill. Built in 1501 with its towers above the pronaos and cornice arcades separated by cable moulding, this set the pattern for much of Wallachian church architecture until the advent of the Brîncoveanu style. Within, beneath a marble slab topped by a bronze crown, lies **the head of Michael the Brave** – severed from his shoulders within a year of Michael's conquest of Transylvania and Moldavia, putting paid to the unification of Romania for another 350 years. The inscription reads: "To him who first united our homeland, eternal glory."

Practicalities

From Tîrgovişte's **train station**, served by trains from Bucharest via Titu, and from Ploieşti, board bus #4 up Bulevardul Castanilor to reach the town centre. The new **bus station** is 1km west by the Romlux train halt; take bus #5 along Calea Cîmpulung. Eight buses a day link Bucharest (Filaret bus station) with Tîrgovişte and the Sinaia–Găeşti service also passes through.

Tîrgovişte's two **hotels** face each other across the Parcul Central. The *Turist*, Str. Victoriei 1 (☎045/61.45.65; ②), is currently the more expensive, but the *Dîmboviţa* at B-dul Libertăţii 1 (☎045/61.39.61 or 61.46.41; ①) is being refurbished and its prices will rise when it reopens. It's worth enquiring at *BTT*, St. Prieteniei Bloc H1 (☎045/63.42.24), for availability of student or private accommodation in town. The *Priseaca* **campsite** with chalets is 7km out along the Cîmpulung road; there's also a site and motel to the south at **DRAGODANA**, 6km before Găeşti.

Piteşti

PITEŞTI is an unappealing place, dominated by woodworking and petrochemical industries and their pollution, and by the Dacia factory, origin of most of Romania's cars. It is liveliest on Fridays and Saturdays, when it fulfils its traditional role as a market town for the countryfolk of the Argeş valley. The limited sights include the **Naïf Art Collection** on Pasajul Victoriei, just south of the main Art Gallery in the former town hall at B-dul Republicii 33; the **County Museum**, Str. Calinescu 44, in the turn-of-the-century prefecture building; and the **Trivale Hermitage** in Trivale Park, southwest of the centre. The seventeenth-century hermitage is nothing special, but it's a lovely twenty minutes' traffic-free walk up Strada Trivale through fine oakwoods. Alternatively, buses #2B, #5, #8 and #21 run up Strada Smeurei just to the south, leaving you in the midst of modern *blocs* just above the hermitage. If you're in the mood for parks, the Parcul Strandului

---

PITEŞTI PRISON

For many Romanians, the town of Piteşti is synonymous with its **prison**, scene under the early Stalinist regime of some of the most brutal psychiatric abuse anywhere in the Soviet bloc. In May 1948 there were mass arrests of dissident students, and from December 1949 about a thousand of them were brought here, to the so-called "Student Re-education Centre", for a programme aimed at "re-adjusting the students to communist life" and eliminating the possibility of any new opposition developing. In fact it simply set out to destroy the personality of the individual: by starvation, isolation, and above all by forcing prisoners to torture each other, breaking down all distinctions between prisoner and torturer, and thus between individual and state. "United by the evil they have both perpetrated and endured, the victim and the torturer thus become a single person. In fact, there is no longer a victim, ultimately no longer a witness", as Paul Goma put it in his book *The Dogs of Death*. Sixteen students died during this atrocious "experiment".

The programme was extended to Gherla and other prisons and the Danube–Black Sea Canal labour camps, but security was looser here and the torture was abandoned when word got out. The experiment was abandoned in 1952, when the Stalinist leader Ana Pauker was purged; it was claimed that the authorities had not been involved, and in 1954, those running the Piteşti prison were tried secretly for murder and torture. The leader of the so-called "Organization of Prisoners with Communist Convictions", Eugen Ţurcanu, and several of his henchmen were executed, while others were sentenced to forced labour for life. Nevertheless, because of the guilt of all involved, prisoners and guards, there followed a conspiracy of silence which has only been broken since 1989.

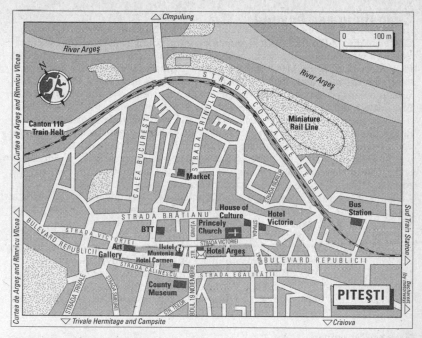

Argeş, on the bank of the Argeş at the end of Strada Riurilor, is attractive, with a miniature rail line that operates on Fridays, Saturdays and Sundays from 11am to 7pm. The **Princely Church** of Şerban Cantacuzino, built in 1656, stands on a lonely patch of grass at Str. Victoriei 7, at the south end of the main pedestrian precinct, and there is also a surviving **synagogue** at B-dul 19 Noiembrie 1, near the museum.

Practicalities

The main **train station** is Piteşti Sud, linked to the town centre by buses #2, #4, #8 and #19, although trains serving Curtea de Argeş also call at the Canton 110 halt and Piteşti Nord, in the northern suburbs. Rail tickets are available from either Piteşti Sud or the *CFR* bureau by the *Argeş* hotel. Piteşti's **bus station** is located on Strada Tîrgu din Vale, running services to Bucharest, Braşov and Calimăneşti.

Should you have a strange urge to **stay the night** before pushing on up the Argeş valley, the cheapest place in town is the *CARA Victoria* (☎048/62.25.66; ②), an Italian joint venture on Strada Brătianu at the south end of the pedestrian precinct (formerly Piaţa Lenin). The *Argeş* on the corner of Stradas Griviţei and Victoriei (☎048/62.54.50; ④) and the *Muntenia* on Piaţa Muntenia (also ☎048/62.54.50; ⑤) are the long-established state hotels, while the *Carmen*, Str. Plevnei 1 (④), is a new private establishment. It's worth enquiring at *BTT*, Str. Justiţiei 1 (☎048/62.40.00), or the **tourist office** on the north side of the *Muntenia* hotel for seasonal accommodation or to reserve chalets in the Trivale Park **campsite**.

Cîmpulung and beyond

CÎMPULUNG MUSCEL, as it is properly known, 55km from Piteşti, is overshadowed by mountains to the north, and begrimed by industries, notably the ARO four-wheel-drive factory. However the town's pedigree is impeccable, going back to pre-Roman times and including a stint as Wallachia's first capital after the voivodate was forged around 1300. Cîmpulung's main sight is the **Negru Vodă Monastery**, attributed to its namesake, the legendary fourteenth-century Black Voivode, but largely rebuilt and enlarged in 1634 and 1827 following several earthquakes. Its most striking feature is the massive gate-tower, with heavy beech gates and a twelfth-century stone carving of a doe in the vault of the entry passage; this was brought from a nearby Dominican monastery and is remarkably occidental in style. The monastery stands on Strada Negru Vodă, at no. 64, together with the **tourist office** at no. 146, the thirteenth-century **Baraţiei Church** at no. 116, Cîmpulung's **History Museum** at no. 118, and its art department at no. 136, which includes works by Grigorescu and Pallady. The ethnographic section of the museum is at Str. Republicii 5, in a fine seventeenth-century building.

If you can't afford rooms at the *Muscelul* **hotel** on Strada Negru Vodă (☎048/81.24.00; ⑤), the **tourist office** (☎048/81.24.00) will be able to give you details of the *Voina* cabana beyond the village of Lereşti north of town. Buses from the terminal on Strada I. C. Frimu (across the river, reached by a footbridge from Str. Nicu Leonard and the Cîmpulung Nord rail halt) will take you there. Voina is at the heart of the horseshoe-shaped **Iezer-Păpuşa mountains**, and there's an excellent one- or two-day hike along the ridge.

Beyond Cîmpulung

The road north from Cîmpulung into Transylvania offers plenty of excitement. Eight kilometres beyond Cîmpulung, the road merges with the route from Tîrgovişte just south of **NĂMĂEŞTI**, the site of a rock church complete with an ancient and miraculous icon and cells hewn from sandstone by sixteenth-century monks. The next two villages, **DRAGOSLAVELE** and **RUCĂR** have traditional wooden houses with verandas. Dragoslavele also has an eighteenth-century wooden church, and there's a **campsite** just beyond Rucăr. The road then continues up in a series of hairpin bends towards the Bran (or Giuvala) Pass encountering the **Bridge of the Dîmboviţa**, a spectacular gap between the Dîmboviciorei and Plaiu gorges to the north and the yet narrower Dîmboviţei gorges to the south (see p.128 for the continuation of the route beyond the Bran Pass).

Curtea de Argeş and Dracula's Castle

Wallachia's Dracula trail continues in the Argeş valley at the small town of **Curtea de Argeş**, another former capital of the region, and with the remains of the genuine Dracula's Castle at **Poienari**, in the foothills of the Făgăraş mountains.

Curtea de Argeş

CURTEA DE ARGEŞ lies some 36km northwest of Piteşti, accessible by road or rail. The town is also linked by bus to Cîmpulung, Rîmnicu Vîlcea (the gateway to the Olt defile), Braşov, Sibiu and Bucharest. The ornate Moorish-style **train** station and the **bus station** just to its south stand on Strada 1 Mai, the most direct route north to the historical sights, while a minor road heads uphill to the old town centre, just east.

Chronologically the second capital of Wallachia (after Cîmpulung and before Tîrgovişte), the **Court of Argeş** consists of a set of ruins within a wall made of boulders taken from the river, together with the oldest church in Wallachia. The complex was rebuilt by Radu Negru, the founder of Wallachia, otherwise known as Basarab I. The **Princely Church** was built in 1352 and decorated with frescoes painted in 1384; later "restoration" work has now been largely removed revealing the original frescoes, fully in the Byzantine tradition, but wonderfully alive and individual, reminiscent of Giotto rather than of the frozen poses of the Greek masters.

A more impressive but less authentic monument, the **Episcopal Church** (or monastery) of Curtea de Argeş, is sited a good kilometre north along the main road, Calea Basarabilor, reached by bus #2. It resembles the creation of an inspired confectioner given carte blanche: a boxy structure enlivened by whorls, rosettes and fancy trimmings, rising into two twisted and two octagonal belfries, each festooned with little spheres and the three-armed cross of Orthodoxy. **Manole**, the Master Builder of Curtea de Argeş, is said to have been marooned on his creation's rooftop when Neagoe Basarab ordered the scaffolding removed. Stranded on the roof, he attempted to escape with the aid of wings made from roofing shingles – only to crash to the earth, whereupon a spring gushed forth immediately.

Manole's Well stands today on the site of this spring, in the park across the road. Manole's story is perhaps a form of crude justice, however, for legend also holds that he had previously immured his wife within the walls (it being believed that *stafia* or ghosts were needed to keep buildings from collapse). However, the church you see today is not Manole's original creation of 1517 but a re-creation of 1875–76 by the Frenchman Lecomte de Nouy, who grafted on all the pseudo-Moorish accretions; he wanted to do the same to the Princely Church, only being repulsed by the historian Nicolae Iorga. The first kings of Romania and their queens are buried here, just inside the entrance, along with the church's founder, Neagoe Basarab.

Curtea de Argeş has some good **accommodation** on offer. The newly privatized *Cumpăna* in the town centre at Str. Negru Vodă 36 (②) is excellent value, and the *San Nicioară* campsite (☎048/71.37.26) up the street of the same name, opposite the Princely Court is also worth trying – a chalet for two here costs a little more than a single at the *Cumpăna*. The *Hotel Posada*, close to the church at Calea Basarabilor 27 (☎048/71.18.00; ⑤), is expensive, although it does accept *ACR* coupons.

Arefu, Poienari and around

From Curtea de Argeş, the road heads straight up the Argeş valley to **AREFU**, growing steadily more barren as it approaches the Făgăraş mountains. In 1459, the survivors of Dracula's massacre in Tîrgovişte (see p.90) were marched here to find lime kilns and brick ovens ready and were put to work building Dracula's Castle. Arefu is today a long, ramshackle village just off the valley road, with a tourist agency offering **private rooms**, which can be booked in Bucharest (☎01/666.61.95; ③).

Situated on a crag high above Arefu, **Dracula's Castle** at **POIENARI** can only be reached by climbing 1400 steps (from the hydroelectric power-station), which proves a powerful disincentive to visitors. Struggle to the top and you'll find that the citadel is suprisingly small as one third collapsed down the mountainside in 1888. The citadel is entered by a narrow wooden bridge, with the remains of two towers within. The prism-shaped one was the old keep, Vlad's residential quarters, from where, according to one legend, the Impaler's wife flung herself out of the window, declaring that she "would rather have her body rot and be eaten by the fish of the Argeş" than be captured by the Turks, who were then besieging the castle. Legend has it that Vlad himself escaped over the mountains on horseback (fooling his pursuers by shoeing his mount backwards, or affixing horseshoes that left the impression of cow-prints, according to some versions).

Poienari is only a few kilometres south of **Lake Vidra**, where the road crosses a spectacular 165-metre-high dam just before the *Casa Argeşeana* cabana. However, unless you've the means to drive over the **Transfăgărașan Highway** to Făgăraş in Transylvania (see p.130) or you're hiking around Bîlea in the **Făgăraş mountains** (see p.131), this is about as far north as you're likely to get. To the northeast of Curtea de Argeş, the village of **JGHEABURI** has a rock church with the oldest paintings in Wallachia, dating from the thirteenth and fourteenth centuries.

The Olt valley

From its Transylvanian headwaters behind the Făgăraş range, the River Olt turns southwards at the Red Tower Pass below Sibiu, carving a stupendous gorge for 50km through the Carpathians and down into Wallachia. The **Olt valley** can be approached by road or rail from the north – where it's most impressive – or by road from Piteşti, Curtea de Argeş or Tîrgu Jiu (the latter route being the longest but most scenic, see p.99). The route from the *autostradă* at Piteşti through the Olt gorge is now, with the closure of former Yugoslavia, the main truck route between Turkey and Western Europe, so it's very busy and lined with Turkish truck-stops and motels. By rail you should take northbound services from Piatra Olt on the Piteşti–Craiova line to Podu Olt and Sibiu.

Rîmnicu Vîlcea

There are more interesting places further up the Olt valley but it's worth pausing in **RÎMNICU VÎLCEA** (or Râmnicu Vâlcea), 50km beyond Piteşti, to reserve accommodation, check out the dates of the Calimăneşti festival, and pick up a map of the region. Rîmnicu Vîlcea sprawls across successive terraces above the River Olt, a typically "systematized" town, with many modern *blocs* but also many old churches. From the **train station**, it's a fairly short walk along Strada Cozia to the park adjoining Piaţa Mircea cel Bătrîn, to the south of which lies the market. The main drag, Calea lui Traian, runs along the western end of Piaţa Mircea cel Batrîn; heading north you'll pass two old churches, Sf Vineri (1557–87) and All Saints (built in 1762 in a post-Brîncoveanu style, with distinctive oblique cable mouldings that make the towers seem twisted), before reaching the **County Museum** at Calea lui Traian at no. 159, whose displays of local history stop at the 1920s. To the north the **Bishopric** (*Episcopiei*) at Str. Argeş 53 is a wonderfully tranquil complex, with three small churches set in well-kept lawns. It dates from the sixteenth century, although the main church, with its Tattarescu paintings, was only built in 1856.

Rîmnicu Vîlcea's **bus station** is south of the river, one block west of the Ostroveni rail halt, linked to the centre by Strada Coşbuc and Strada Dacia. The main **hotel** is the *Alutus* at Str. Gen. Praporgescu 43 (☎050/71.66.01; ⑤), which frequently has no running water. A cheaper alternative, with chalets as well, is the *Capela* at Aleea Castanilor 1 (also ☎050/71.51.01; ③), on the hill to the west of town, along the road beside the *Episcopiei*. The **tourist office** is in the *Hotel Alutus*, while *BTT* at Str. Gen. Praporgescu 4 (☎050/71.87.20) offers accommodation in eight student *internats* (①) across the county .

Calimăneşti-Căciulata

At **CALIMĂNEŞTI**, 15km beyond Rîmnicu Vîlcea, the renowned Songs of the Olt **folklore festival** and a **pottery fair** usually take place during the first week in August. Immediately to the north (served by Păuşa station) **CĂCIULATA** is a one-street spa lined with villas (①); the hotels are little more expensive, except for the swankier *Căciulata/Cozia/Olţul* complex (☎050/75.05.20; ⑤) to the north, at Calea lui Traian 790–794, where foreigners pay five times as much as Romanians even for car-parking. There are also campsites in both Calimăneşti (the *Seaca*) and Căciulata (the *Ştrand*).

Calimăneşti-Caciulata marks the entrance to **the Olt defile**, a deep, sinuously twisting gorge of great beauty and the site of several monasteries. Although the river was notoriously wild and dangerous here, it has now been tamed, with a series of dams, still being completed, and viaducts carry the road in places. While the main road runs along the Olt's west bank, the rail line (and a lesser road as far as Gara Turnu) follows the other side of the defile. Just beyond Căciulata, a campsite has sprouted in the vicinity of the reconstructed Arutela *castrum* (once part of Roman Dacia's eastern frontier defences, the *Limes Alutanus*).

Cozia, Turnul and beyond

A couple of kilometres along the defile, the fourteenth-century church of **Cozia Monastery** marks the advent of Byzantine architecture in Wallachia; featuring alternating bands of brick and stone, and fluted, false pillars. Cozia's completion was due to the patronage of Dracula's grandfather, Mircea the Old, who accepted Turkish suzerainty after the Crusaders' defeat at Nicopolis and now lies buried within the monastery. The church portico was added by Prince Constantin Brîncoveanu, whose name has entered Romania's architectural lexicon describing a style drawing upon folk motifs – although in this case, it's not a particularly striking example. From the belvedere nearby, there's a fine view over the Olt valley and the mountains. Across the road, the *Bolniţa* or Infirmary Church with its precious murals dates from 1543.

About 2km north, near the Mînăstirea Turnu halt, **Turnul Monastery** is based around rock cells hewn by hermits from Cozia at the end of the sixteenth century. From here it's a five to six hour walk up a trail marked by red stripes to the *Cozia* cabana, situated near the summit of the **Cozia massif**. Sheltered from northeasterly winds by the Făgăraş, this has the mildest climate of all Romania's ranges, allowing oak, walnut and wild roses to grow at altitudes of up to 1300m.

Further north along the Olt valley, there's a rail halt at **Cornetu Hermitage**, just beyond the small village of Lotru. Erected in 1666, this bizarre building is decorated with a multitude of glazed ceramics, tiles and studs. Road and rail head on towards the **Red Tower Pass** (*Turnu Roşu*), local trains halting at **MARULUI** the start of the Făgăraş traverse hiking route. The pass itself, one of the few natural breaches in the Carpathians, is marked by a ruined fortress commanding the defile, the site of many battles between Wallachian, Transylvanian, Hapsburg, Turkish and German forces over the past five centuries. Beyond lies Transylvania – change trains at Podu Olt for Braşov.

Tîrgu Jiu and around

Forewarned about **TÎRGU JIU** and the surrounding **Jiu valley**, visitors often decide to ignore them completely. From Petroşani (see p.161), Vulcan and Lupeni down to Rovinari, the valley's **brown-coal mines** support all the country's other industries. With a few exceptions it's a bleak landscape, made grimmer by slag heaps, pylons and the mining towns themselves, while the sandbanks in the river are almost solid coal dust. Under communism the miners were lauded as the aristocrats of the proletariat, but had to be placed under **martial law** in 1985, when Ceauşescu demanded ever higher output and docked pay by 50 percent when quotas weren't achieved. Since the revolution of 1989, the **miners** have been used as Iliescu's shock troops, being rushed on special trains to Bucharest to terrorize the opposition as required, and even to precipitate the resignation of prime minister Petre Roman himself.

Tîrgu Jiu is known for its great winter music gathering, the **Festival of Enchanted Water Springs** (*Izvoare fermecate*), normally staged during the third week of February, but it's a pretty uninviting time of year for visitors to be here.

The Town

The town itself is not really implicated in coal mining, but it was still raped by Ceauşescu and, leaving the train station, you risk falling into the same roadworks that have greeted visitors undisturbed since the revolution.

Nevertheless Tîrgu Jiu does hold some attractions, chiefly four monumental sculptures by **Brâncuşi**, created in the late 1930s as a war memorial for the town of his boyhood. The most noticeable (east of the rail line just north of the station) is the *Coloană fără Sfîrşit* or *Coloană Infinita* (Endless Column), a vast totem-pole of rhomboidal blocks, whose rippling form adorns many of the verandas on the old wooden houses throughout Gorj county. You'll find the other sculptures at the other end of the Calea Eroilor, which runs 1.7km west from the Endless Column to the park on the banks of the Jiu river. The *Poarta Sărutului* (Gate of the Kiss) at the entrance to the park opens onto the *Aleea Scaunilor* (Avenue of Seats), flanked by thirty stone chairs. This leads to the *Masa Tăcerii* (Table of Silence), surrounded by twelve stools (representing the continuity of the months and the traditional number of seats at a funeral feast). Brâncuşi had originally proposed a series of twelve sculptures in Tîrgu Jiu, but never completed the project. Calea Eroilor is in fact a surprisingly narrow street in a busy, dusty town, and the view east to the Endless Column is blocked by a church.

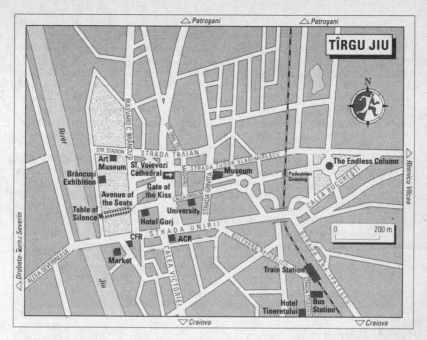

In addition, there are a couple of unremarkable little museums – the **County Museum** at Str. Griviţa 8 and, on the main road north, at B-dul 1 Mai 270, is the house where **Ecaterina Teodoroiu** was born in 1894; she died in August 1917, fighting as a man in the crucial battle of Mărăşeşti (see p.204).

Practicalities

The *Hotel Gorj* at Calea Eroilor 6 (☎053/21.48.15; ④) offers the best **accommodation** in town, as well as housing the **tourist office**. The only competition is an overpriced youth hotel, the *Tineretului*, one block south of the bus station at Str. N. Titulescu 2/6 (☎053/24.46.82; ③). The closest **campsite** lies 10km east of Tîrgu Jiu on the DN67 at Dragoeni.

The **bus terminal** at Str. Libertăţii 13 by the train station operates services to the surrounding villages as well as to Bucharest, Craiova, Deva, Drobeta-Turnu Severin and Sibiu. **Rail bookings** can be made at Bloc 2, Strada Unirii.

East of Tîrgu Jiu

Away from the industry of the Jiu valley, there are plenty of tranquil villages where traditional customs and dress are still a part of everyday life. The area east of town, with impressive **cave formations** and important **monasteries**, is also the start of several mountain hikes north into Transylvania and even the more remote sights are well served by buses from both Tîrgu Jiu and Rîmnicu Vîlcea.

CONSTANTIN BRÂNCUŞI

Arguably one of the greatest sculptors of the twentieth century, **Constantin Brâncuşi** (pronounced "Brankoosh") was born in 1876 in a peasant cottage at Hobiţa, some 28km west of Tîrgu Jiu. He came to town at the age of nine to work as an errand-boy, and later learnt the techniques of the local wood-carvers, who chiselled sinuous designs on rafters, verandas and well-heads in the region. He was sent by local boyars to art college in Craiova and then to the National School of Fine Arts in Bucharest, before leaving for Paris in 1904 with a government scholarship to the Ecole des Beaux Arts. He stayed in France for over fifty years, helping create a revolution in sculpture with his strikingly strong and simple works.

He worked as an assistant to Rodin, then, in company with Amadeo Modigliani, discovered the primitive forms of African masks and sculptures, concentrating thereafter on stripping forms down to their fundamentals. In 1920 his *Principesei X* (*Princess X* or *Principle Sex*) was banned from the Salon des Indépendents as too phallic. A different sort of scandal followed in 1926 when Brâncuşi travelled to New York taking with him one of his *Bird* series. US customs classified it as "a piece of metal" and levied import duty of $10; Brâncuşi appealed against the decision, thereby starting a critical furore which made him a household name in America. The photographer Edward Steichen gave him credibility by publicly announcing that he had bought one of his bronze *Birds in Flight* for $600 – by 1967 it was worth $175,000. Brâncuşi died in 1957, with his series of sculptures for Tîrgu Jiu unfinished, and is buried in Montparnasse cemetery in Paris.

Polovragi and around

POLOVRAGI, 48km east of Tîrgu Jiu, dominated by the Căpăţînii mountains, is home to one of the great Wallachian **fairs**. An occasion for highlanders to dress up, dance and forge deals in the old fashion, the *Nedeia* usually occurs on July 20 – but check with ONT beforehand to be sure. From the commune, a forestry road runs northwards into the mile-long Olteţu gorges, providing access to the Polovragi Monastery and cave. The **monastery**, rebuilt by Brîncoveanu, is relatively small, but the later Bolniţa Church with its fine frescoes is definitely worth the trip. Further on, lurking behind the eastern rockface at the mouth of the gorge, the **Polovragi cave** was once believed to be the abode of Zalmoxis, the Dacians' chief deity. Now fully illuminated and open for guided tours (daily 9am–5pm), it was first explored in 1860 by the French naturalist Lancelot, and is renowned for the stalactites in its "Candlesticks Gallery".

Three kilometres from the neighbouring commune of Baia de Fier, you'll find another beautiful grotto in the smaller **Galbenul gorges** (daily 9am–5pm). Although only two passages out of the **Women's cave**'s total of 10km of convolutions have been illuminated, it's an impressive sight. Halfway in, multicoloured stone columns resemble petrified wood, while in the lower passage the skeletons of 183 cave bears have been discovered. Another cave, the *Peştera Muierii* gets its name from the human skeletons – mainly those of women and children – found on its upper levels. From the cave and nearby cabana, a footpath leads up to the **Rînca tourist complex** in the Parîng mountains, 15km away. The next settlement west, **NOVACI**, marks the start of the forestry road to Rînca and on to Sebeş (see p.149). Novaci has two *hans*, on Strada Tudor Vladimirescu, and a motel just beyond town.

Horezu and the monasteries

Sixteen kilometres further east beyond Polovragi, on the main road to Rîmnicu Vîlcea, **HOREZU** is a small town set amidst orchards, sweet chestnut trees and wild lilac. It's the abode of numerous owls (*huhurezi*), hence the town's name (given as 'Hurez' on some maps). Though wooden furniture and wrought-iron objects are also produced here, Horezu is best known for its **pottery**, especially the plates, which by tradition are given as keepsakes during the wakes held following a funeral. Most of them are made by Victor Vicsoreanu, a third-generation craftsman, whose pottery is on the town's outskirts. **Accommodation** is available at the motel (050/86.07.20; ②), or the *Stejarii* campsite which also has chalets.

However, the real attraction lies a couple of miles to the northeast of town, near the little village of Romanii de Jos. The largest and finest of Wallachia's Brîncoveanu complexes, and site of the school where he created the style that bears his name, **Horez Monastery** is centred around the Great Church built in the 1690s, entered via a porchway with ten pillars and doors of carved pearwood. The colours of the interior frescoes (which include portraits of Brîncoveanu and his family) have been tarnished by the smoke from fires lit by Turkish slaves who camped here, but those in the Nuns' Refectory give a better idea of their original colours. The monastic complex also includes Dionisie's Fire-tower, a structure with finely carved columns and a stone balustrade, and set apart to the west, the small St Stephen's Hermitage.

Continuing towards Rîmnicu Vîlcea on the DN67, a left turn at Coşteşti heads 6km north to **Bistriţa Monastery**, which the boyars of Craiova endowed during the fifteenth century. As well as three sixteenth- and seventeenth-century churches, there is a cave containing two more chapels, used at the time of the Turkish wars to hide the relics of St Gregory the Decapolite – a nun will accompany you along the precipitous cliffside path to visit it. **Arnota Monastery** stands on a hill a further 4km from Bistriţa, beyond a large quarry. By financing the construction of Arnota during the seventeenth century, voivode Matei Basarab guaranteed himself a tasteful burial place within the monastery church, surrounded by fragmentary murals of his wife and chattels. As so often in this area, the porch is the work of Brîncoveanu.

Just beyond **BAILE GOROVA**, a mineral spa with campsite, 25km west of Rîmnicu Vîlcea, is **Govora Monastery**. Founded in 1494 and, predictably, rebuilt by Brîncoveanu in 1711, it is warmly regarded by Romanians as the place where the first Romanian printed book, the *Pravila de Govora*, a legal codex, rolled off the presses in 1640.

West of Tîrgu Jiu

Less than 40km west of Tîrgu Jiu on the DN67D, **TISMANA** is a complete contrast to the mining areas around, harking back to Gorj county's traditional pastoral ways. **Tismana Monastery**, 5km to the north of the village, is the oldest in Romania, founded in 1375 and surrounded by a high wall during the reign of Matei Bassarab – it served as a meeting place for rebels during the 1821 rising led by Tudor Vladimirescu. Tismana is the setting for an annual **festival of music and crafts** (At Tismana in a Garden) on August 15, where the most popular instrument is the *nai* or shepherd's pan-pipes. You'll find wooden utensils, sculptures, embroidered clothing and Oltenian rugs on sale during the festival, but the quality and range of goods has declined. There are camping chalets and a motel in the village, and a tourist complex just north of the monastery – *Hotel Tismana* ☎053/37.41.10; ③).

The DN67D continues towards the Cerna valley (see p.276) passing several interesting places en route. Just before the mining and logging town of Baia de Arama, a turn-off leads 5km northwards to **PADEŞ-CĂLUGĂRENI**, where the village men still wear **folk costume**. Piped with braid, their narrow white home-spun trousers and voluminous cloaks resemble the uniforms worn by Vladimirescu's soldiers in 1821. Picturesque **karst formations** abound in the region, particularly around **PONOARELE**, 7km south of the main road just west of Baia de Arama, including the **"Giant's Bridge"**, twenty-five metres wide by fifty long, formed when the ceiling of a large cave collapsed.

Drobeta-Turnu Severin and the Danube

Passengers aboard cruise ships between Vienna and the Black Sea approach Drobeta-Turnu Severin as nature intended – by the **River Danube**, which narrows beyond Moldova Veche and thrusts itself through the **Kazan gorge** towards Orşova, to be tamed and harnessed by the dam at the **Iron Gates**, before reaching the town. Motorists driving down from Moldova Veche or Băile Herculane can see something of this magnificent panorama (the rail journey is less scenic); but if you're coming from Tîrgu Jiu, the real landscape feast doesn't start until you reach Turnu Severin. The shortest route from Tîrgu Jiu to Drobeta-

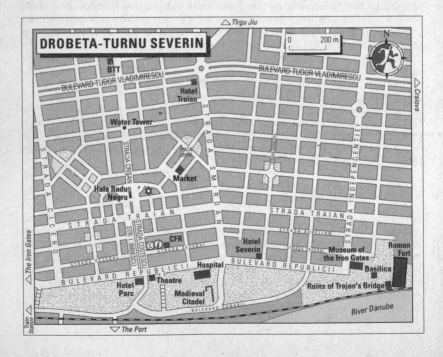

Turnu Severin is via the badly surfaced DN67, usually crowded with bulldozers. By train, you'll have to travel down to the unappealing town of **FILIAŞI** to join the Craiova–Turnu Severin line. If you're stuck between trains, there's a very cheap hotel, the *Filiaşi* (☎053/36.12.01; ①), at the far end of Strada Gării.

The Town

Nicknamed the "town of roses" for its beautiful parks, **DROBETA-TURNU SEVERIN**'s modern appearance belies its origins as the Dacian settlement of *Drobeta*, more than two millenia ago. Its Roman conquerors left more enduring landmarks, however, notably the **ruins of Trajan's bridge**, which Apollodorus of Damascus built to span the Danube at the order of the emperor in 103–105 AD. As Leigh Fermor put it, "two great stumps of his conglomerate masonry still cumbered the Romanian side", and these can be seen from the train or the grounds of the excellent **Museum of the Iron Gates** (*Portile de Fier*) at the southern end of Strada Independenţei. Nearby, also within the museum precincts, are the foundations of the fourteenth-century **Metropolitan's Basilica** and of the Roman fort guarding the bridge. Inside the museum, the aquarium holding various species from the Danube is the chief attraction, although the ethnographic, archeological and historical departments are also worth a look – the coverage of World War II has been recently reworked, although there's some way to go to bring things right up to date.

The remains of a **medieval citadel** stand between the museum and the town centre, behind the *Hotel Parc*. Stradas Bibiescu and Costescu lead north from here past the prefecture to the Hala Radu Negru, now a huge *alimentara*. Opposite is the amazingly delapidated synagogue and the site for a new Orthodox cathedral, and beyond these, the lively market on Piaţa Unirii, with stops for buses to surrounding villages.

Just east of town in **CERNEŢI** is the *cula* of Tudor Vladimirescu, now a museum dedicated to the life of the leader of the 1821 revolution.

Practicalities

BTT offers cheap dormitory **beds** in summer at Str. Crişan 25 (☎052/22.09.11; ①), but otherwise the cheapest **hotel** in town is the *Severin* at Str. Eminescu 1 (④), followed by the *Traian*, B-dul Vladimirescu 74 (☎052/21.17.60; ④) and the *Parc*, B-dul Republicii 2 (☎052/21.28.53; ⑤).

CAROL I'S ARRIVAL IN ROMANIA

One tale not told in the museum is that of the arrival of Karl Hohenzollern in Romania, an amusing vignette. Selected to be the future **King Carol I**, Hohenzollern feared kidnapping by foreign powers and thus travelled incognito by Danube steamer, masquerading as the valet of the Romanian politician Ion Brătianu, with passage booked to Odessa on the Black Sea. At Turnu Severin, Karl first set foot on Romanian soil, a "sagging jetty", whereupon the skipper yelled, "Get back on board – it's another 800 kilometres to Odessa!". Instead, Brătianu knelt in the mud to kiss the hand of his "valet" as a *droshky* hansom cab materialized, and they heard the captain exclaim, "My God, that must be the Prince of Hohenzollern".

If the **tourist office** at Str. Decebal 41 is no help, the *Parc* is the place to seek information about **riverboat services**. Services downriver to **Ostrov** and **Şimian Island** and upstream to **Moldova Veche** are however unlikely to resume until sanctions on Serbia are lifted and the temptation to sell all the fuel available on the black market is removed.

Ask at the terminal at the end of Strada Topolniţei for **buses** between Turnu Severin and Moldova Nouă. The **rail** bookings office is at Str. Decebal 43. West of Turnu Severin, the rail line runs via Gura Vaii to Orşova, and then up to Băile Herculane and Timişoara in the Banat.

Along the Danube

The Iron Gates

The Iron Gates have a formidable reputation due to the navigational hazards on this stretch of the river – eddies, whirlpools and rocks – which formerly restricted safe passage to the two hundred days of the year when the river was in spate, and meant that boats had to take aboard a pilot at Moldova. The blasting of a channel in 1896 obviated these terrors, and the building of the **largest hydro-electric dam in Europe** (excluding the former Soviet Union) at Gura Văii, 8km upstream of Drobeta-Turnu Severin, finally tamed the river.

Conceived in 1956, the hydro-electric project was undertaken as a joint venture; Romania and Yugoslavia each built a 1000MW turbine plant and locks for shipping on their respective banks, linked by a slipway dam and an international road crossing, a task that took from 1960 until 1971 and raised the river level by 33m. Romantics have deplored the results, for the dam "has turned 130 miles of the Danube into a vast pond which has swollen and blurred the course of the river beyond recognition", turning "beetling crags into mild hills", in Leigh Fermor's words. It has also reduced the Danube's peak flow, so that the pollution of Central Europe is no longer flushed out to sea but gathers here, killing fish and flora. In addition, the waters have submerged two places worthy of footnotes in history: the island of **Ada Kaleh** and old **Orşova**.

Ada Kaleh

Legend has it that the Argonauts discovered the olive tree on the island of **Ada Kaleh**, which was famous at the beginning of this century for its Muslim community, complete with mosques, bazaars and fortresses. The Turkish presence here at so late a date arose from a diplomatic oversight, for at the conference where the Ottoman withdrawal from the region was ratified, everyone forgot about Ada Kaleh, which thereby officially remained Turkish territory until much later. Before Ada Kaleh's submersion in the Danube, Eugene of Savoy's citadel and the mosque were removed and reconstructed on Şimian Island.

Orşova

Before 1918, **ORŞOVA**, 23km upstream from Turnu Severin, was the frontier crossing into the Magyar-ruled Banat, and it was nearby that Kossuth buried the Crown of St Stephen on his way into exile after the failure of the 1848–49 revolt in Hungary. However the town was flooded by the dam, and new Orşova (3km from its train station) has nothing of interest beyond a **hotel**, the *Dierna* (☎052/ 36.17.63; ④), on B-dul 1 Decembrie 1918, the main riverfront promenade. The

bus station is up the steps behind the hotel and services run to Moldova Nouă, Drobeta-Turnu Severin, Băile Herculane, Calafat and Tîrgu Jiu.

The Kazan gorge

Sixteen kilometres beyond Orşova, on either side of the village of **DUBOVA**, the sheer cliffs of the **Kazan gorge** (*Cazanele Dunării*) fall 600m into the tortuous river. Rather than attempt to cut a path through the rock, the Romans built a road by boring holes in the cliff to hold beams upon which they laid planks (roofed over to discourage Dacian ambushes). The first proper road was created on the northern side on the initiative of the nineteenth-century Hungarian statesman Count Széchenyi, but had not long been finished when the Treaty of Trianon transferred it to Romania, whereupon it was deliberately neglected and finally submerged by the rising waters. Since the building of the dam, modern roads have been built on both sides of the river, and you should by no means miss the excursion.

Moldova Veche and Moldova Nouă

Within sight of the port of **MOLDOVA VECHE**, 116km from Turnu Severin, the river divides around an island near the isolated **rock of Babakai** where, according to legend, the Turkish governor of Moldova marooned one of his seven wives, Zuleika, who had eloped with a Hungarian noble but been recaptured. Admonished to "Repent of thy sin!" (*Ba-ba-kai*) and left to die, Zuleika was rescued by her lover who later had the joy of taunting the mortally wounded governor with the news that she was alive, and had become a Christian. Another legend refers to the caves near the ruined fortress of **Golubac** just downstream on the Serbian bank of the river, where St George is said to have slain the dragon. Thereafter, its carcass has reputedly fed the swarms of bugs that infest the town of Golubac.

Moldova Veche's old quarter is largely inhabited by Serbs, obviously blond and speaking Romanian with a noticeable accent; the *blocs* to the west are inhabited by Romanians brought in when the port was developed to serve the copper and molybdenum mines inland. Nowadays half the male population is working

---

INTO SERBIA AND BULGARIA

Crossing the frontier into Serbia is easiest at the Iron Gates – you can cross by road or by local train; there's an unnamed halt by the dam (known to the Serbs as the Djerdap dam) 1km northwest of Gura Văii station proper. You can also cross to Vojvodina at **Naidăş** or **Moraviţa**, south of Timişoara – both are well served by buses for the huge numbers of smugglers and black marketeers, mostly Gypsies carrying petrol in Coke bottles, and there are also long queues of cars. In theory the *Bucureşti Express* still runs from Bucharest to Belgrade (*Beograd Dunav*) via Drobeta-Turnu Severin, Timişoara and the **Stamora Moraviţa** crossing point, but this is a thoroughly unpleasant and unpredictable place to be at the moment and getting a Serbian visa will be a problem.

Ferries across to Vidin in Bulgaria depart regularly until about 6.30pm, from **CALAFAT**, reached by road 56A from Turnu Severin, or by rail from Craiova (see overleaf). Calafat's hotel (③) and tourist office are at Str. 30 Decembrie 3; the bus terminal is on Strada Stere. For visa requirements see p.80.

abroad, which has led to some excellent little bars being set up with their earnings. There is an unmarked **hotel** (③) on the riverbank, but nothing else of interest. From the **bus station** to the east of town there are two buses a day to Orşova and five to Oraviţa, some continuing on to Timişoara, Reşiţa and Caransebeş.

The mining town of **MOLDOVA NOUĂ**, 4km inland, is also in terminal decline, and both the hotel and museum have closed.

Southern Wallachia

In many respects **southern Wallachia** is tedious, uninviting terrain, for while the Subcarpathians provide varied scenery and harbour picturesque villages, below them stretch miles of plain – dusty or muddy according to season – with state farms lost amidst fields of corn or sunflowers.

Craiova

Almost every locomotive on the tracks in Romania originally emerged from the *Electroputtere* workshops of **CRAIOVA**, a sprawling place surrounded by derricks testifying to the discovery of oil beneath what is now the chief city of Oltenia and capital of Dolj county.

Craiova's tourist attractions are few, however you may well find yourself breaking your journey here en route to Bulgaria. The **Ethnographic Museum** occupies the former governor's residence, Ban's House, at Str. Matei Basarab 14, while immediately to its north stands the church of **Sf Dumitru-Băneasa**, built in 1652, but thoroughly transformed in 1889 by Lecomte de Nouy (who did the same for the monastery of Curtea de Argeş). Craiova's best museum is the **Art Gallery** at Calea Unirii 10, with work by all of Romania's best-known artists and a few Brâncuşi sculptures (including *The Kiss*), as well as French and Dutch paintings.

The *Jiul*, Calea Bucureşti 1 (☎051/11.06.11 or 11.56.55; ⑤) is the most comfortable **hotel**, a big modern building raised in 1969, while the *Minerva* at Str.

THE *RASCOALA*

Despite its rich soil, the southern plain has traditionally been one of Romania's poorest areas, for the boyars (and worse still, their estate managers) squeezed the peasants mercilessly. Land hunger grew as the peasant population, taxes and rural unemployment increased – building up to the explosive **1907 uprising**, the *rascoala*. Triggered near Vaslui in Moldavia where Jews, believed to prey upon peasants, were the first targets, the uprising spontaneously raged southwards into Wallachia. Panic-stricken boyars flooded into Bucharest, demanding vengeance for the burning of their property – and the army obliged, quelling the ill-armed peasantry with cannon fire, and then executing "ringleaders" by the thousand. Though there's a **Museum of the Uprising** at Str. Dunării 54 in **ROŞIORI DE VEDE** (Teleorman county), the English translation of Liviu Rebreanu's novel *Uprising* is a more gripping exposition of the subject.

Kogălniceanu 3 (☎051/13.09.47 or 13.35.34; ③) is a splendidly atmospheric pile from 1902. There are chalets at the *Han Doctorul* (☎051/14.40.31) at km7 on the E74 – take bus #9 east. Alternatively you could pester *BTT* at Str. Olteţ 8 (☎051/11.73.96), in a pedestrianized area just west of the main square, for vacant college beds, particularly since both **campsites** are a long way out along the DN6 either side of town and hard to reach by public transport – the *Lunca Jiului* (Jiu Meadow) to the west, and the *Terasa Baniei* (Terrace of the Ban or Turkish governor) to the east.

Craiova's main **bus station** is conveniently placed right beside the train station, with buses to destinations as far afield as Calafat, Cîmpulung and Rîmnicu Vîlcea, and connections to the city centre via buses #1, #5, #12 and #29. Train tickets are available from the **CFR office** in the Complex Unirea on Piaţa Unirii. There are two rail lines between Craiova and **Bucharest**. The southerly route across the plain goes by way of Caracal, Roşori de Vede and Videle, and the journey to Bucharest takes about two and a half hours by express train. The alternative route via Piteşti (see p.92) runs further to the north – the sole daily express train takes four and a half hours to reach Bucharest by this slower, non-electrified, route.

Scorniceşti

If you're driving from Craiova to Bucharest, the fastest route is by DN65 (Euroroute 70) to Piteşti and then by the *autostrada*. This route takes you past a minor road at km72, leading to **SCORNICEŞTI**, the **birthplace of Nicolae Ceauşescu**. Villagers danced on his father's grave at Christmas 1989, and a museum that was until then a virtual shrine to the great *Conducator* is now likely to be totally abandoned, rather than being reworked to give a fair analysis of the dynamics of power under communism. Scorniceşti was, fittingly, one of the first new towns created under Ceauşescu's systematization programme, and has thus been drowned in concrete. Ceauşescu's birthplace is the only original building remaining in the whole town; and the only new edifice of any interest is the football stadium, one of Romania's largest.

Giurgiu

Virtually all traffic to Bulgaria from Bucharest passes through **GIURGIU**, on the Danube 64km due south of the capital by road. Trains from Bucharest's Gara de Nord take an hour and twenty minutes to crawl the 85km to Giurgiu Nord station. Giurgiu's 3km-long **Danube Bridge** (known as the Friendship Bridge under communism) was built in 1954, to carry both road and rail traffic. It's open 24 hours a day, but with the closure of the route through former Yugoslavia is now very congested. Visas are available at the crossing but it's cheaper to buy them in Bucharest (see p.80) or before you leave home.

With its notorious pollution, there's really no reason to stay in Giurgiu, but should you need to, the *Hotel Victoria* (☎046/21.25.69 or 21.34.50; ③) is at Str. Gării 1, about a hundred yards southeast of Giurgiu station (not to be confused with Giurgiu Nord, the international station), while you'll find a **campsite** on the Danube meadow (*Lunca Dunării*). For something more comfortable, try the *Giurgiu Vama*, at Str. Prieteniei 1 (☎046/22.08.95; ⑤).

A CHERNOBYL ON THE DANUBE?

Just as the Chernobyl disaster of 1986 helped to blow apart the secrecy and cynicism of the old Soviet Union, so too the **Giurgiu chemical plant** helped to drive out the old order, not in Romania but in Bulgaria. The plant opened in 1977 and later expanded with Soviet aid, solely to provide caustic soda (up to 200,000 tonnes a year) and other chlorine and sodium products for the Soviet Union. Absolutely no attention was paid to environmental issues, and emissions monitoring only began in 1984. In 1982 there were 26 escapes of gas, up to three times the safe limit, in 1984 there were 56, and in 1987, 69 – all of these drifted across the Danube, smothering the Bulgarian town of **Ruse** in a cloud of chlorine gas, producing nausea and choking coughs. Cases of lung disease in Ruse rose from just 969 per 100,000 inhabitants in 1975 to 17,386 in 1985. In 1986 almost 150,000 people received out-patient treatment for respiratory problems, and almost 5000 were detained in hospital; on average ten days' work a year per person were lost to "Ruse lung" (toxic fibrosis), and four-fifths of Ruse's young men were unfit for military service.

In 1987 there were street protests in Ruse after a chlorine cloud had hung over the city for two days; the next year a Committee for the Protection of Ruse was formed in Sofia, developing in 1989 into the Club for the Support of Glasnost and Perestroika, better known as *Ecoglasnost*, which became a forum for both dissidents and moderate Party members and spearheaded the movement for reform that finally led to the removal of the communist old guard after the fall of the Berlin Wall.

Although production has fallen dramatically, standards are still appalling; in October 1991 Bulgarian newspapers reported a fire that had killed two workers at the Giurgiu plant and had almost caused a catastrophic explosion; this had been covered up by the Romanian media for two weeks. Protests in Ruse in November, disrupting traffic to and from Romania, led to a diplomatic row between Romania and Bulgaria, but tensions have now eased, with both countries aware that neither can afford to control pollution without substantial Western aid.

travel details

Trains

Craiova to: Bucharest, via Caracal (14 daily; 2hr 10min–4hr 40min) or Piteşti (3 daily; 4hr 30min–6hr 45min); Calafat (5 daily; 2hr 20min); Drobeta-Turnu Severin (12 daily; 1hr 40min–2hr 50min); Filiaşi (21 daily; 30min–1hr); Gura Motrului (5 daily; 40–70min); Piatra Olt (10 daily; 42–86min); Piteşti (4 daily; 2hr 30min–4hr).

Drobeta-Turnu Severin to: Băile Herculane (9 daily; 40min–1hr); Caransebeş (8 daily; 2–3hr); Craiova (11 daily; 1hr 30min–3hr); Orşova (10 daily; 26–37min); Timişoara (9 daily; 3hr 6min–5hr 30min).

Piatra Olt to: Lotru (6 daily; 2hr–3hr 30min); Sibiu (4 daily; 3hr 40min–5hr 25min); Rîmnicu Vîlcea (10 daily; 1hr 25min–2hr 30min); Turnu Monastery (4 daily; 3hr 15min).

Piteşti to: Bucharest (11 daily; 1hr 40min–2hr 50min); Curtea de Argeş (5 daily; 1hr); Titu (11 daily; 53–85min).

Ploieşti to: Braşov (25 daily; 1hr 45min–2hr 45min); Bucharest (45 daily; 40min–1hr 35min); Iaşi (10 daily; 5hr–7hr 25min); Suceava (9 daily; 4hr 45min–9hr 30min); Tîrgovişte (8 daily; 1hr 30min–2hr 20min).

Tîrgovişte to: Bucharest (4 daily; 1hr 50min–2hr 15min); Ploieşti (8 daily; 1hr 40min–2hr 20min); Titu (12 daily; 45min).

Tîrgu Jiu to: Filiaşi (10 daily; 1hr 5min–2hr); Simeria (5 daily; 3hr–4hr 30min); Subcetate (5 daily; 2hr 25min–3hr 30min).

Titu to: Tîrgovişte (12 daily; 50 min).

Planes
Craiova to: Bucharest (1–2 daily).

International trains

Giurgiu Nord to: Istanbul (1 daily; 19hr 30min); Kiev (3 daily; 27hr 15min–30hr 15min); Moscow (2 daily; 44hr 20min–47hr 20min); Ruse (5 daily; 24min); St. Petersburg (1 daily; 56hr 30min); Sofia (4 daily; 8hr–9hr 15min); Thessaloniki (1 daily; 18hr 40min).

Craiova to: Belgrade (1 daily; 10hr); Budapest (1 daily; 10hr 40min).

Drobeta-Turnu Severin to: Belgrade (1 daily; 8hr 15min); Budapest (1 daily; 9hr).

International ferries

Calafat to: Vidin (Bulgaria) every 90min until 6.30pm.

CHAPTER THREE

TRANSYLVANIA

T hanks to Bram Stoker and Hollywood, **Transylvania** (Latin for "beyond the forest") is famed abroad as the homeland of Dracula, a mountainous place where storms lash medieval hamlets, while wolves – or werewolves – howl from the surrounding woods. The fictitious image is accurate up to a point: the **scenery** is breathtakingly dramatic, especially in the Prahova valley, the Turda and Bicaz gorges and around the high passes; there are spooky Gothic citadels, around Braşov and at Sibiu, Sighişoara and Bran; and there was a Vlad, born in Sighişoara, who later styled himself **Dracula**, and earned his grim nickname "The Impaler" (see p.346).

But the Dracula image is just one element of Transylvania, whose 99,837 square kilometres take in alpine meadows and peaks, caves, dense forests sheltering bears and wild boars, and lowland valleys where buffalo cool off in the rivers. **The population** is an ethnic jigsaw of Romanians, Magyars, Germans, Gypsies and others, formed over centuries of migration and colonization. Transylvania's history is still often disputed along nationalist lines, and the feelings aroused run high in both Hungary and Romania, and are routinely exploited by politicians.

Most people in Hungary view *Erdély* (their name for Transylvania) as a land "stolen" by the Romanians, where some two million Magyars face continuing harassment and subjugation by a Romanian population that they claim arrived long after the Magyars had settled the area. All Romanians assert the opposite: that Transylvania has always been rightfully theirs and that, for centuries, it was the Magyars who practised discrimination as colonialist overlords.

Since the Trianon Treaty of 1920, which placed Transylvania firmly within the Romanian state, the balance of power among the ethnic groups has shifted sharply in favour of the Romanian majority, with many peasants brought in from Moldavia and Wallachia to form a new industrial proletariat. The revolution of 1989 has allowed many Germans in particular to return, after eight centuries, to their ancestral homeland, leaving the Hungarians as the main minority group. Meanwhile Transylvania's Gypsies (*Ţigani*) still go their own way, eagerly partici-

---

ACCOMMODATION PRICES

Hotels listed in the *Guide* have been price-graded according to the scale below. Prices given are those charged for the cheapest double room, which in the less expensive places usually comes without private bath or shower and without breakfast. See p.28 for more details.

① under $10	④ $25–40	⑦ $80–135
② $10–15	⑤ $40–55	⑧ $135–190
③ $15–25	⑥ $55–80	⑨ $200 and over

pating in an economic free-for-all that they never really abandoned under communism, and largely unconcerned by growing prejudice against them. The result is an intoxicating brew of different characters, customs and places that is best taken slowly. Many towns have Saxon and Hungarian names which are used alongside the Romanian ones and these are given in brackets in the text.

Although modernization and population movements have eroded their sharp distinctions, Transylvania's historic towns still reflect the characteristics of the ethnic groups that once dominated them. Most striking of all are the *stuhls*, the former seats of Saxon power, with their medieval streets, defensive towers and fortified churches. **Sighişoara**, the most picturesque, is the Saxons' greatest legacy, followed by the citadels and churches of **Braşov** and **Sibiu**, as well as smaller Saxon settlements like **Cisnădioara**, **Hărman** and **Prejmer**. The other highlight of this southeastern corner is the castle at **Bran**, which looks just how a vampire count's castle should look. Travelling west, routes towards the Banat and Hungary pass through southwestern Transylvania, a region of mountains and moorland peppered with the citadels of the Dacians, rulers of much of Romania before the Roman conquest. To the north and east, Transylvania has a more Hungarian flavour: cities such as **Cluj** and **Tîrgu Mureş** are strongly Magyar, while **Miercurea Ciuc** and **Sfîntu Gheorghe** are the cultural centres of the Székely, an ethnic group closely related to the Magyars.

The **Carpathian mountains** are never far away in Transylvania, and for anyone fond of walking this is one of the most beautiful, least exploited regions in Europe. **Hikes** to stunning places in the Făgăraş, Apuseni and Retezat ranges can last several days, but it's perfectly feasible to make briefer yet equally dramatic forays into the Piatra Craiului or Bucegi mountains, or to one of Transylvania's many spectacular gorges.

When considering your itinerary bear in mind the **festivals** which take place across Transylvania throughout the year. May and June offer the most choice, but during months with only one or two events there's usually something happening just over the mountains in Moldavia, Maramureş or the Banat. The really special events are detailed in the text.

BRAŞOV AND SOUTHEASTERN TRANSYLVANIA

The Saxon colonists, brought to Transylvania in the twelfth century to guard the mountain passes against the Tartars, settled in the fertile land to the north of the Southern Carpathians, along the routes from Braşov to Sibiu and Sighişoara. Although many have recently returned to Germany, their **villages** remain throughout this area, with their regimented layouts and their massive **fortified churches**. Although the main highlights at **Braşov**, **Sighişoara** and **Bran** are all definitely worth seeing, one of the greatest pleasures of visiting Transylvania is the exploration of quiet backwaters and the smaller Saxon settlements with their charming wooden churches. Many of these villages, such as those in the **Burzen Land** or the **Marginimea Sibiului**, lie just a short distance from major road or rail routes, and all but the most isolated are accessible by bus or train if you have the time.

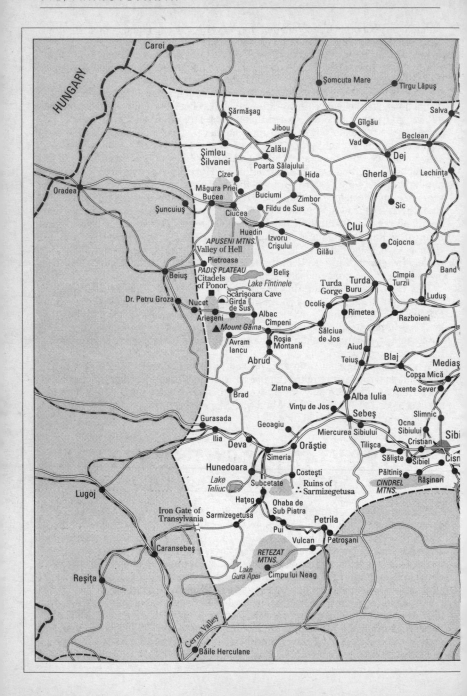

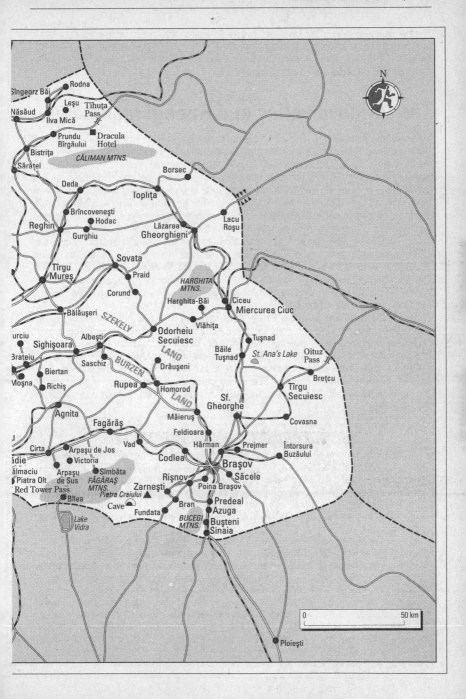

The **mountains** in this region, home to bears, chamois and eagles, provide much of the best hiking in Romania, with easy day walks in the Bucegi mountains (assisted by cable cars) and the Piatra Craiului, as well as longer expeditions through the Făgăraş and Cindrel ranges.

The Prahova valley and Bucegi mountains

Thousands of years ago, the site where Bucharest stands today was submerged by a vast sea, extending a hundred miles northwards to lap against a small island of crystalline rock. The remains of Cretaceous life-forms which flourished in the warm waters formed reefs that trapped grit as the sea level rose, holding it when the waters receded during the Neozoic period. The mountains that emerged were later shaped by glaciers which carved out the present **Prahova valley**, while streams disappeared underground and formed fantastic caves and other karstic phenomena. The valley now contains the well-maintained **DN1** which efficiently links Bucharest with Braşov. The **rail line**, too, runs straight up the valley, and express services take just two and a half hours between the cities, stopping only at Ploieşti (see p.87) and the resorts of **Sinaia** and **Predeal** en route. There are also plenty of slightly slower trains – from either Sinaia or Predeal, you can catch a slow *personal* train to **Buşteni** or Azuga, also served by some *accelerats*. A local bus links these resorts roughly hourly.

From Sinaia to Predeal the River Prahova froths white beneath the gigantic **Bucegi mountains** which overhang Buşteni with 600m of sheer escarpment, receding in grandiose slopes covered with fir, beech and rowan trees. These are the real attraction of this area: the easiest walks are those above Sinaia and Predeal, while there are more challenging hikes above Buşteni. Even if you don't stop off to hike in the range (or ride up by cable-car), the valley's upper reaches are unforgettable: sit on the west side of the train (the left, if heading north) for the best views.

HIKING IN THE BUCEGI MOUNTAINS

The Romanian-language **maps** of the *Munţii Bucegi* are invaluable for anybody seriously contemplating hiking – they shouldn't be hard to understand if you refer to our vocabulary on p.41. Most walks in the region are easy day walks with cable cars as an alternative on the steeper sections. There are plenty of **mountain cabanas** which in theory aren't allowed to turn hikers away, and if you're really stuck, the maps also locate refuges and sheepfolds (*refugiu* and *stînă*), where you may find shelter.

Snow covers **Mount Omu**, the highest point of the Bucegi (2505m), for two hundred or more days a year, but elsewhere retreats during April, leaving the meadows to a wealth of **wildflowers**. First come crocuses, snowdrops, sweet violets and ladies' gloves, followed by forget-me-nots, grape-ferns and marigolds, with violets, primroses, bellflowers, edelweiss and camomiles flourishing higher up, alongside junipers and rhododendrons. The forests shelter woodcock, hazel grouse and nightingales from the circling golden eagles, while **other wildlife** includes the Carpathian stag (around Bran), lynx, fox, rodents and wild boar. The latter, like wolves and bears, are only a potential threat to humans during the winter, or if their litters seem endangered. Above the forest, on the cliffs to the north of the massif, you may well see chamois.

Sinaia

SINAIA, 130km from Bucharest, has been dubbed the "Pearl of the Carpathians" for its magnificent mountain scenery and royal castle. Originally the preserve of a few hermits and shepherds, and later an exclusive aristocratic resort, it's nowadays full of holidaymakers keen to walk or ski in the Bucegi range.

From the casino, just above the station (where the Iron Guard murdered the Liberal leader Ion Duca in 1933, just three weeks after he had taken office as prime minister), Strada Manastirii leads up to **Sinaia Monastery**, an ensemble of little churches and courtyards. Founded by the boyar Michael Cantacuzino in 1695 and so called because it contained a stone he had brought from Mount Sinai, it superceded an earlier hermitage.

To the north lies a **park** landscaped in English fashion, where you'll find **Peleş Castle** (Wed–Sun 9am–3pm; L6000), outwardly resembling a Bavarian *Schloss*. It was built in the 1880s for Romania's imported Hohenzollern monarch, Carol I, and largely decorated by his eccentric wife Elisabeta, better known as the popular novelist Carmen Sylva, the "Romanian Sappho", who once decreed that court life at Sinaia be conducted in folk costume. The main building was followed by the **Foişor** hunting lodge and the **Pelişor** (Little Peleş) Palace, built in 1903 for Prince Ferdinand, Carol's heir. Peleş contains over 160 gloriously kitsch rooms, decorated in ebony, mother of pearl, walnut and leather – all alien to the traditional styles of Romanian art. Here Prince Carol (later crowned Carol II) met Magda Lupescu, a Jew from Iaşi who remained his mistress for forty years and became the power behind the throne, outraging Romanian society, which tended towards anti-semitism. Following the monarchy's demise in 1947, Peleş was opened to the public, with a temporary interruption when the Ceauşescus appropriated it as a "state palace", although they themselves used an Italianate villa in the grounds.

Practicalities

The **train station**, where every train from Bucharest stops, is down a flight of steps opposite the *Hotel Caraiman*. Sinaia is well served with **hotels** and has one of the very best in Romania, the *Hotel Palace*. Most hotels lie along the main street, Bulevardul Carol I, which runs south from the monastery, and their restaurants are the only places to eat. There are **campsites** north and south of Sinaia, at Vadul Cerbului and Izvorul Rece, and you're rarely far from an inexpensive hikers' cabana – the *Piscu Cîinelui* and *Schiori* cabanas are right on the outskirts of town .

Ski gear can be bought or rented in the *Hotel Montana* and at the cable car terminal on Strada Cuza Vodă.

HOTELS
Camelia, Strada Mihail Cantacuzino (☎044/31.45.55). Situated on a side street parallel to B-dul Carol I. ④.
Caraiman, B-dul Carol I 4 (☎044/31.35.51). A very classy establishment, built in 1881 in neo-Brîncovenesc style. ④.
Internaţional, Str. Avram Iancu 1 (☎044/31.38.51). This rather featureless international hotel is at the south end of town. ⑤.
Intim Str. Furnica 1 (☎044/31.17.54, x127). Semi-privatized, with excellent views over and into the monastery. ④.

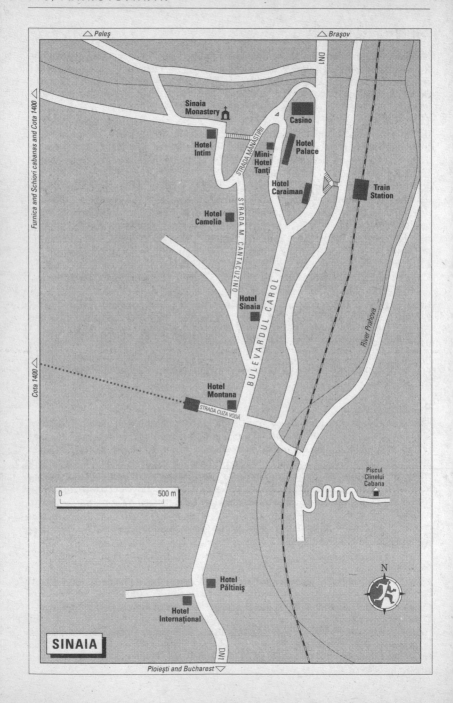

△ *Peleş* △ *Braşov*

Furnica and Schiori cabanas and Cota 1400

Cota 1400

DN1

Sinaia
Monastery

Casino

Hotel
Intim

Hotel
Palace

STRADA MĂNĂSTIRII

Mini-
Hotel
Tanţi

Hotel
Caraiman

Train
Station

STRADA M CANTACUZINO

Hotel
Camelia

BULEVARDUL CAROL I

Hotel
Sinaia

River Prahova

Hotel
Montana

STRADA CUZA VODĂ

0   500 m

Piscul
Ciinelui
Cabana

N

Hotel
Păltiniş

Hotel
Internaţional

SINAIA

DN1

Ploieşti and Bucharest ▽

Montana, B-dul Carol I 24 (☎044/31.27.50). A modern hotel built for ski packages, with disco until 3am. ④.
Palace, Str. 30 Decembrie 4 (☎044/31.20.51). Founded in 1911 and situated in the park by the casino, this gem retains the Edwardian style that made it famous. ③.
Paltiniş, B-dul Carol I 65 (☎044/31.35.55). Traditional spa-style hotel. ③.
Tanţi, Str. 30 Decembrie (☎044/31.11.51 x344). A clean and decent private mini-hotel opposite the *Palace*, well placed to pick up those who can't get in there. ④.

Mountain walks from Sinaia

From the terminal on Strada Cuza Vodă (behind the *Hotel Montana*), a cable car (Tues–Sun 9am–5pm; $2) whisks you aloft to **Cota 1400**, the roadhead halfway up the hill, site of the *Alpin* hotel and numerous cabanas. From here another cable car rises to **Cota 2000**, and a chair lift (daily except Tues 9am–5pm) to **Cota 1950**, both near the *Mioriţa* cabana, on Mount Furnica. This is the start of the taxing *Papagul* ski run back down to Cota 1400. To the south, below Cota 1950 is the *Valea Dorului* cabana, from where there's a three-hour circular walk down the Dorului valley to the beautiful tarns of **La Lacuri**, following a path marked with yellow crosses and red stripes.

Heading north, another attractive and easy walk takes you in half an hour from Mount Furnica to the half-built (but functional) *Piatra Arsă* cabana behind Mount Jepi Mari. Here, blue triangles indicate the route downwards to Buşteni (2hr maximum) via **La Scari**, a spectacular "stairway" hewn into rock, while another path (marked with blue stripes) drops westwards into the central depression of the Bucegi, reaching the *Peştera* cabana and monastery in about an hour (for routes north of *Peştera* see "Mountain walks from Buşteni" overleaf). Just west of *Peştera*, is the **Ialomiţa cave**, a four-hundred-metre grotto with a walkway in awful condition (bring a flashlight), and an unmarked path leading up through the Batrîna valley past waterfalls, the "Gorge of the Bear" and two natural bridges. Half an hour to the south lies the *Padina* cabana, from where a very rough road leads south past more caves and gorges to a camping spot near **Lake Bolboci**, eventually emerging from the Izvoraşu valley just south of Sinaia.

Buşteni

Ten kilometres further up the valley, **BUŞTENI** is a small resort overshadowed by the sheer peaks of Caraiman (2384m) and Coştila (2498m), separated by the dark Alba valley and the highest conglomerate cliffs in Europe. Caraiman is identified by a huge cross, erected as a memorial after World War I, and on Coştila there's a TV tower that looks like a space rocket. There's nothing much to Buşteni but it's a good base for the excellent walking in the surrounding mountains.

The nearest **hotel** to the train station is the *Caraiman* at Str. Libertăţii 89 (☎044/32.01.56; ③), while the *Caminul Alpin* cabana at the top of Strada Valea Albă, just north of the station, is still run in the lax old state-owned manner, with irregular opening periods. Your best bet in Buşteni is the *Silva*, south of the centre at Str. Telecabiniei 39 (☎044/32.14.12; ④) and closest to the cable car.

It's also worth enquiring at the **tourist office** at Str. Libertăţii 202 (Mon–Fri 9am–4pm, Sat 9am–noon), 150m north of the station, and at Str. Telecabiniei 46, about **private rooms** (④). The *Azuga* **campsite** just north along the main DN1, is far closer to Buşteni than to Azuga.

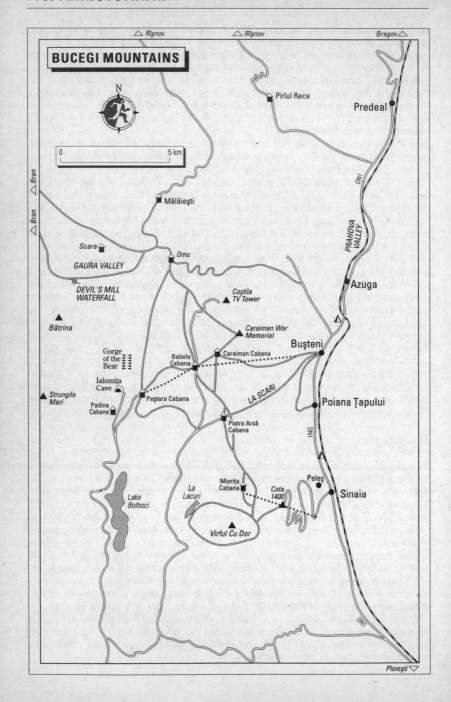

BUCEGI MOUNTAINS

Rîşnov

Rîşnov

Brașov

N

0   5 km

Bran

Bran

Bran

Piriul Rece

Predeal

DN1

PRAHOVA VALLEY

Mălăiești

Scara

GAURA VALLEY

Omu

Coştila TV Tower

Azuga

DEVIL'S MILL WATERFALL

Bătrina

Caraiman War Memorial

Gorge of the Bear

Babele Cabana

Caraiman Cabana

Bușteni

Ialomița Cave

Peştera Cabana

LA SCARI

Strungile Mari

Padina Cabana

Poiana Țapului

DN1

Piatra Arsă Cabana

Miorița Cabana

Cota 1400

Peleş

Sinaia

Lake Bolboci

La Lacuri

Virful Cu Dor

DN1

Ploiești

Mountain walks from Buzteni

From the country's oldest paper-mill and the *Hotel Silva*, an easy path marked with red dots leads past the zoo to the **Urlătoarea waterfall** and back to the road at Poiana Ţapului (2hr), while a harder footpath marked with blue crosses and a **cable car** (daily except Tues) ascend the Jepi (dwarf pine) valley to the *Caraiman* and *Babele* cabanas. *Babele* offers a panoramic view, and is only five minutes' walk from an impressive skull-like rock formation, the **Babele Sphinx**. From here you can walk in one hour or ride the cable car down to the *Peştera* cabana and monastery (see "Mountain walks from Sinaia" on p.117 for routes south and west of *Peştera*). North of *Babele*, a path marked by yellow stripes leads north to **Mount Omu** in about four hours, alternatively, from *Peştera*, a blue-striped path takes you up the Ialomiţa valley to Omu.

Though completely cloudless days are rare in the viciniy of **Mount Omu**, it is possible to see the Burzen Land, the ridge of the Piatra Craiului, and on particularly haze-free days the Făgăraş range beyond – a mountain vista of rare splendour. From the *Omul* hut (closed in winter), a path marked with blue stripes descends a glacial valley past eroded rock "chimneys" to the *Mălăieşti* chalet (2–3hr). Two other paths lead down **towards Bran**. Both take about six hours; the route indicated by yellow triangles is easier going, while the path marked with red crosses drops down the superb Gaura valley past the **Cascada Moara Dracului** (Devil's Mill waterfall) – a fitting approach to "Dracula's Castle" in the village below (see p.128).

Predeal

PREDEAL, sitting on the pass marking the official border into Transylvania, is further from the more spectacular peaks, and a centre for skiing and easy strolls. There's a reasonable choice of **accommodation** in town. The *Carmen*, just south of the station at B-dul Săulescu 121 (☎068/25.65.17; ④), can also arrange slightly cheaper rooms in villas. North of the station is the *Bulevard*, B-dul Saulescu 129 (☎068/25.60.22; ③), a neo-Brîncovenesc pile with an attractive stair- and lift-well. Further north, on Strada Trei Brazi, are the *Cirus*, an old-style ski chalet (☎068/25.60.35; ③), and the *Orizont* (☎068/25.51.50; ⑤), a modern ski-package hotel.

Ski equipment can be rented at the *Orizont* hotel and the *Cioplea* cabana (overlooking the town to the northeast), or on the main road (at no. 134), at Clăbucet-Sosire, the foot of the chair lift.

Around Predeal

The Gîrbova or **Baiului mountains** flanking the Prahova on the eastern edge of town, are the site of numerous **ski runs** – a chair lift (daily 9am–5pm) runs from Clăbucet-Sosire, ten minutes beyond the train station, to Clăbucet-Plecare. Most of the runs are graded "average", although the *Sub Teleferic* is classified as difficult, while the run southwards towards the *Gîrbova* cabana is the easiest of all.

There is good **walking** in these hills on either side of Predeal, not as dramatic as in the Bucegi but with good views to the high peaks and cliffs. There are plenty of **cabanas** to aim for: *Gîrbova* and *Susai*, within a few kilometres of Clăbucet-Plecare, and others northwest of Predeal, in the foothills of the Bucegi massif, served by buses to Trei Brazi. The latter include *Trei Brazi* itself (with a campsite nearby), *Piriu Rece* and *Poiana Secuilor* – all within walking distance of the bus terminal – and *Diham*, higher up and further south with a slalom run nearby.

Braşov

With an eye for trade and invasion routes, the medieval Saxons sited their largest settlements within a day's journey of the Carpathian passes. **BRAŞOV** (*Kronstadt*), was one of the best placed and grew prosperous and fortified as a result, and for many centuries the Saxons constituted an elite whose economic power long outlasted its feudal privileges. The communist regime wanted their own skilled working class, and to this end brought thousands of Moldavian villagers to Braşov during the 1960s, where they were drafted into the new factories and given modern housing. When the economy began collapsing in the 1980s, raised production quotas and cuts in pay at the *Red Star* and *Tractorul* factories led to the **riots of November 15, 1987**, during which the Party headquarters were sacked and a Militia officer was reportedly killed. Order was restored, but local pride in the rebellion survived, and in December 1989 there was again fighting here. Bullet holes remain as a memorial all over the facade of the university buildings at the east end of Strada Republicii, opposite the graves of some of those killed in the revolution. It seems that most of the casualties here were the victims of "friendly fire".

There are two parts to Braşov: the largely Baroque area coiled beneath Mount Tîmpa and Mount Postăvaru, and the surrounding sprawl of apartments and factories. **Old Braşov** – whose Schei quarter, Black Church and medieval ramparts provide a backdrop for the town's colourful *Pageant of the Juni* – is well worth a day's exploration; and the proximity of the Alpine resort of **Poiana Braşov**, the fortified Saxon churches of Hărman and Prejmer, and the so-called "Dracula's Castle" at Bran make Braşov an excellent base.

The best **views** of the old town are from the forested heights of **Mount Tîmpa** (967m), accessible by cable car (daily except Mon) or by various paths which wind up to the summit.

Arrival and information

Braşov is one of Romania's most important rail junctions, served by long-distance **trains** from Bucharest and the coast, Sighişoara, Cluj, Arad, and along the Făgăraş mountains from Sibiu. The train station is situated north of the old town, right in the heart of the concrete drabness of Braşov's industrial areas. Bus #4 will take you down to Parc Central (also known as Titulescu); bus tickets here are valid for two trips, with one end cancelled each journey.

There are three bus stations. **Buses** from Budapest, Focşani, Tîrgu Neamţ and Tîrgu Mureş, as well as villages to the north of Braşov, will drop you at *autogară* 1, by the train station. From Cîmpulung, Piteşti, Curtea de Argeş and Rîmnicu Vîlcea in the southwest, you'll arrive at *autogară* 2, Str. Avram Iancu 114 (bus #12 to the centre, #10 to the train station), while services from the Székely Land terminate at *autogară* 3, northeast of the main train station (trolleybus #1).

Braşov has a **tourist office** (Mon–Sat 7.30am–3.30pm; ☎14.11. 96) at the rear of the lobby of the *Hotel Carpaţi*, near Parc Central, but it deals in little more than overpriced excursions

The **telephone code** for Braşov is ☎068

Accommodation

The only reasonably priced beds are some way from town, with just a few anony-
mous and over-priced **hotels** in the centre. The *Parc* at Str. N. Iorga 2 has been
closed since 1994, but it's likely to re-open and could be worth checking on. You
might also want to consider the thirteen tourist hotels at the nearby resort of
Poiana Braşov (see p.127).

Your best option may be one of the **private rooms** (③) available through
EXO, Str. Postăvarului 6 (Mon–Sat 11am–8pm, Sun 11am–2pm; ☎14.45.91), *Kron
Tour*, Str. Bariţiu 12 (☎14.27.73), or from Bogdan Stirbu at Str. Matei Basarab 30a
(☎11.57.15) – these are likely to be in a modern *bloc*, but nowhere is too far from
the centre. People with rooms to rent also meet international express trains. *BTT*
at Str. Republicii 56 offers beds in student accommodation.

Hotels

ARO-Sport, Str. Sf Ioan 3 (☎14.28.40). Overpriced but central, in a dingy side street off B-dul
Eroilor. ④.

Capitol, B-dul Eroilor 19 (☎11.89.20). Expensive but without the veneer of class of the
Carpati. ACR coupons accepted. ⑦.

Carpaţi, B-dul Eroilor 9 (also ☎14.28.40). Still known as the *ARO-Palas* after the insurance
company that built it in 1939, this is the best hotel in town, a swanky place picketed by black-
market money-changers. ⑧.

Coroana, Str. Republicii 62 (☎14.43.30). The only hotel in town with real character, and a
pleasant restaurant from where you can watch the city's main street. ⑤.

Postăvarul, Str. Politechnicii 2 (also ☎14.43.30). Recently created by hiving off the budget
rooms of the *Coroana,* behind which it lurks. ④.

Camping

The *Dîrste* **campsite** (☎15.90.80) is about 7km from Braşov's centre, on the
Bucharest highway. To reach it, take trolleybus #3 or #6 from the centre or tram
#101 from the train station to the Saturn/Autocamion terminus on Calea
Bucureşti. From here, take the bus for Predeal which goes right past the site, or
bus #17 or #21 (for Săcele) out along the main highway until it it turns off left.
The campsite is ten minutes' walk further along the DN1 at km 160. The Dîrste
rail halt is to the north of the Săcele turning, back towards Braşov, so is of little
use. The site has reasonable facilities with hot water and two-person chalets.

You might prefer the small *Dîmbu Morii* **cabana** – another twenty minutes
beyond the campsite, or a fifteen-minute walk to the north of the Timiţu de Jos
rail halt.

The Town

The bus from the train station will set you down either at **Parc Central**, on the
edge of the old town, or on **Piaţa Sfatului**, at the heart of a Baroque townscape
that is quintessentially Germanic. The hub of Braşov's social and commercial life
is the pedestrianized **Strada Republicii** (*Purzengasse*) leading from the main
square towards the new town and the station. People stroll along its length at
noon and in the early evening – at its northeastern end are the department store
and **market,** from where you can also catch trolleybus #4 back to the train
station.

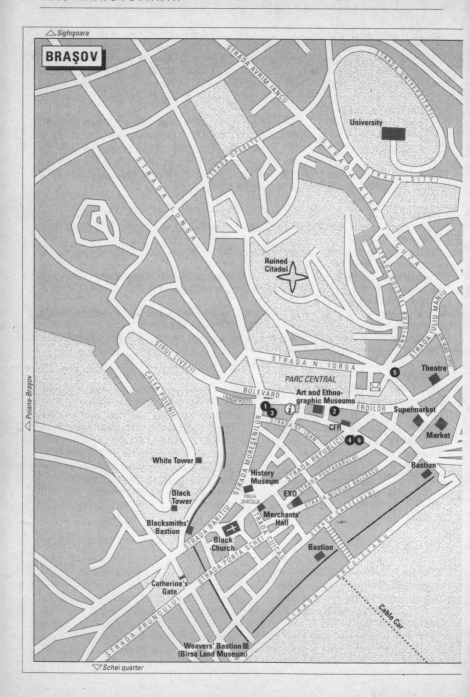

△ Sighişoara

BRAŞOV

STRADA AVRIM IANCU

STRADA OPERETE

STRADA LUNGA

STRADA UNIVERSITATII

University

STRADA ALEX

STRADA SITEI

STRADA CUZA

STRADA COLONEL BUZOIANI

Ruined Citadel

STRADA IULIU MANIU

SILVATIPE

SIRUL LIVEZII

STRADA N. IORGA

CALEA POIENII

△ Poiana-Braşov

PARC CENTRAL

5

Theatre

BULEVARD

(VADA POSTEI)

Art and Ethno-graphic Museums

EROILOR

Supermarket

1 3

(i)

2

CFR

Market

STRADA SF. IOAN

4 6

STRADA MURESENILOR

STRADA REPUBLICII

Bastion

White Tower

STRADA POSTAVARULUI

History Museum

EXO

STRADA NICOLAI BALCESCU

Black Tower

PIATA SFATULUI

STRADA CUCAS

Merchants' Hall

STRADA CASTELULUI

Blacksmiths' Bastion

STRADA BARITIU

Black Church

Bastion

STRADA PORTA SCHEI

STRADA I BRETOTEANU

Catherine's Gate

STRADA PRUNDULUI

Cable Car

Weavers' Bastion (Bîrsa Land Museum)

▽ Schei quarter

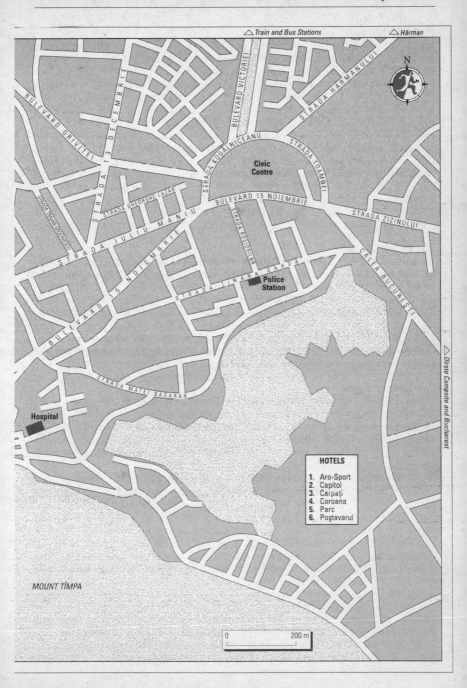

△ Train and Bus Stations   △ Härman

N

BULEVARD GRIVIȚEI

STRADA 3 DECEMBRIE

BULEVARD VICTORIEI

STRADA HARMANULUI

STRADA TOAMREI

Civic
Centre

STRADA KOGALNICEANU

STRADA GHEORGHE LAZĂR

STRADA TRAIAN GROZAVESCU

STRADA IULIU MANIU

BULEVARD 15 NOIEMBRIE

BULEVARD 15 NOIEMBRIE

STRADA PRUNDULUI

STRADA ZIZINULUI

STRADA REPUBLICII

STRADA INARA GAROA

CALEA BUCUREȘTI

Police
Station

STRADA MATEI BASARAB

Hospital

HOTELS

1. Aro-Sport
2. Capitol
3. Carpaţi
4. Coroana
5. Parc
6. Poştavarul

△ Dîrste Campsite and Bucharest

MOUNT TÎMPA

0   200 m

Piaţa Sfatului

Legend has it that when the Pied Piper enticed the children from Hamelin in Germany, they vanished underground and emerged in Transylvania near the site of Braşov's main square, now called the **Piaţa Sfatului** or Council Square. It is lined with sturdy merchants' houses, their red rooftiles tilted rakishly, presenting their shopfronts to the fifteenth-century Council House (*Rathaus* or *Casa Sfatului*), now the **History Museum** (Tues–Sun 10am–5pm). The exhibits tell the story of the Saxon guilds, who used to dominate Braşov and who met in the **Merchants' Hall** opposite. Built in the "Transylvanian Renaissance" style of the sixteenth century, this now contains craft shops, a wine-cellar and the *Cerbul Carpatin* (Carpathian Stag) restaurant. Within sight of its terrace is the town's most famous landmark, the **Black Church**, which stabs upwards like a series of daggers above the Old Pharmacy, currently being restored to house the **Ethnographic Museum**. This features a collection of local costumes, and is presently housed next to the **Art Gallery** at B-dul Eroilor 21 (Tues–Sun 10am–5pm), which has a good selection of Grigorescu, Aman and Tattarescu canvases.

The Black Church

An endearingly monstrous hall church which took almost a century (1385–1477) to complete, the **Black Church** (*Biserica Neagră*; Mon–Fri 9.30am–6pm) is so-called for its soot-blackened walls – the result of a great fire, lit by an Austrian army, that swept through Braşov in 1689. Inside, however, the church is startlingly white, with Turkish carpets hung in isolated splashes of colour along the walls of the nave – a superb collection built up from the gifts of the local merchants returning from the east. The incongruity of having Islamic prayer rugs proudly displayed in a Lutheran church never seems to have bothered anyone. **Organ recitals** on the 4000-pipe instrument are held on Wednesdays.

The fortifications

When Turkish expansion became an evident threat in the fifteenth century, the inhabitants began to fortify Braşov, assigning the defence of each bastion or rampart to a particular guild. A length of **fortress wall** runs along the foot of Mount Timpa, beneath a maze of paths and a cable car running up to the summit – fine views of the old town can be had from Strada Brediceanu, the semi-pedestrianized promenade past the lower cable car terminal.

Of the original seven **bastions** the best preserved, with three tiers of wooden galleries and meal-rooms, is that of the Weavers (*Bastionul Ţesătorilor*), on Strada Coşbuc. This now contains the **Museum of the Bîrsa Land Fortifications** (Tues–Sun 10am–4pm), where models, pictures and weaponry recall the bad old days when the surrounding region, known as the Bîrsa or Burzen Lands, was repeatedly attacked by Tartars, Turks and, on a couple of occasions, by Vlad Ţepeş. **Catherine's Gate** (which bears the coat of arms of the citadel), the **Blacksmiths' Bastion** (*Bastionul Fierarilor*) and the **Black and the White Towers** on Calea Poienii (best seen from Strada Dupa Ziduri, squeezed between stream and walls) all managed to survive these onslaughts, but the inhabitants didn't always fare so well. When Dracula attacked Braşov in 1458–60 he burnt the suburbs and impaled hundreds of captives along the heights of St Jacob's Hill to terrorize the townsfolk. Referring to allegations that Vlad dined off a holy icon surrounded by his suffering victims, his biographer Stoicescu writes that "being on campaign... the terrible Prince may not have had the time to take his meals otherwise".

THE PAGEANT OF THE JUNI

The **Pageant of the Juni** (*Sărbătoarea junilor*) is held on the first Sunday of May – under Saxon rule this was the one day in the year when the town's Romanian population could freely enter the centre. The name derives from the Latin for "young men", and on this day the town's youths dress up in costumes and, accompanied by brass bands, ride through town in groups named after famous regiments – the *Dorobanţi*, or the *Roşiori* – while the married men, or "Old Juni", bring up the rear.

The parade assembles in the morning on the **Piaţa Unirii** which forms the historic heart of Schei. It then marches to Piaţa Sfatului, returns to the Schei backstreets, and then climbs a narrow valley to the **Gorges of Pietrele lui Solomon**. Here, spectators settle down to watch the Round Dances (*Horăs*), which for the participants are really a kind of endurance test. Some of the elaborate Juni costumes are 150 years old, while one of the *Roşiori* wears a shirt sewn with 44,000 spangles that weighs 9kg – the product of four months' work by the women of Braşov.

The Schei quarter

During the heyday of Saxon rule, the Romanian-speaking population was compelled to live beyond the citadel walls, in the southwestern district of **Schei** (pronounced "Skei"). They could only enter the centre at certain times, and had to pay a toll at the gate for the privilege of selling their produce to their neighbours. Today Schei is a peaceful residential dead-end, with the peace of its Baroque streets broken only by occasional buses and children returning from school. The quarter's main sight is the **Church of St Nicholas**, on Piaţa Unirii, which was the first Orthodox church to be built in Transylvania by the voivodes of Wallachia, between 1493 and 1564. On the left as you enter the churchyard is the first Romanian-language school (1761), now a museum exhibiting the first Romanian-language textbooks, printed in Braşov in 1581.

North of the centre

North of Bulevardul Eroilor and the Parc Central is a lowish hill crowned by the overgrown **citadel ruins**, with a touristy restaurant hidden inside. To the west, Strada Lungă (Long Street) stretches interminably to the thirteenth-century **Church of St Bartholomew**, a toothy Gothic edifice under the hill where Vlad impaled his victims. This stands at the junction of the DN13 to Sighişoara and Tîrgu Mureş and the DN1 to Sibiu. The Bartolomei station, for **local trains** to Zarneşti and Sibiu, and *autogară* 2, for buses to Bran, are nearby.

Eating, drinking and entertainment

Braşov has a better than average selection of places to **eat and drink**, with good **restaurants** in the main hotels, and quite a few others worthy of mention. Chief among these are the *Cerbul Carpatin*, in the Merchants' Hall on Piaţa Sfatului, once reputed to be the best restaurant in Romania and still not bad, and the *Chinezesc*, also on the square, still possibly the best Chinese restaurant in the country. Others worth seeking out are the *Panorama* on top of Mount Tîmpa (daily 9am–10pm), the *Cetatea* in the old citadel on Dealul Cetăţii, with kitsch medieval decorations, and great views in the early evening, and a *Lactovegetarian* restaurant on Strada Gheorghe Bariţiu, by the Black Church, which is not at all vegetarian but might produce an omelette.

There are **pizzerias** at Piaţa Sfatului 1 (daily except Wed), Str. Bălcescu 2 and in the *Coroana* hotel, and a *crama* or beer-cellar, with simple Romanian food, opposite the *Postăvarul*. However the best place for a cheap and simple meal is the *Intim* at Str. Mureşenilor 4 – try the *mămăligă* (polenta). The **cafés** around Piaţa Sfatului have the best range of cakes and buns in town, while allowing you to watch the comings and goings on this lively square; the best are the *Cafea Orient* at Str. Republicii 2 and the *Casata* at Piaţa Sfatului 13.

Nightlife and entertainment

In Braşov as in the rest of Romania, **nightlife** is basically whatever happens in the restaurants attached to the hotels – Gypsy music, singing or disco depending on pot luck – although the restaurants in Poiana Braşov lay on folklore events in season. The **University** lies some distance from the centre, on the next hill east from the citadel ruins; to meet students you might try the cafés around Piaţa Sfatului or the *Casa Studenţilor* at B-dul Eroilor 29 (bring your passport, and student card if you have one).

Concerts (mostly of classical music) at the *Gh. Dima Philharmonic* at Str. Mureşenilor 25, are inexpensive and generally sold out well in advance. You can try for tickets at the booking office at Str. Republicii 4. Tickets are also on sale here for the **theatre** on Piaţa Teatrului, at the east end of Bulevardul Eroilor, and the **puppet theatre** on Strada Ciucaş.

The **Springtime Jazz and Blues Festival** takes place in early May in the theatre, and the **Golden Stag** light music festival takes over Piaţa Sfatului in September.

Listings

Bike repairs Strada N. Bălcescu 55.

Car repairs *Romanian Automobile Club*, Strada N. Iorga 13.

Exchange There are new private money-exchange offices at the junctions of Strada Republicii and B-dul Eroilor, and of Piaţa Sfatului and Strada Mureşenilor, which will accept travellers' cheques. You can also change money at the *CEC* office in the police headquarters building on Strada N. Titulescu, or at the *Banca Commerciala Romană*, Str. Republicii 45 (most services only 8.30am–noon).

Fuel If you're driving out of Braşov, the best places to fill up your tank are the fuel stations on the Făgăraş and Hărman highways, and by the Dîrste campsite on the DN1 towards Bucharest.

Pharmacy Braşov has a 24hr pharmacy at Str. Republicii 27.

Police The *judeţ* police headquarters are on Strada N. Titulescu. This is also the place for visa extensions.

Post office Str. N. Iorga 1 (daily 7am–8pm). Poste restante service available.

Shopping Braşov's department store at Str. N. Bălcescu 62 gives the impression of having been left behind by events, and you'll probably find the *consignaţie* along Strada Republicii more useful. There are two decent modern supermarkets, the *Bîrsa* opposite the market on Strada N. Bălcescu, and the *Premial* at the south end of B-dul Griviţei, as well as the older *UNIC* on Strada Mureşenilor.

Telephone office B-dul Eroiler 23 (daily 7am–9pm).

Travel agents *SimpaTurism* at Piaţa Şfatului 3 is a Western-style travel agency, booking or confirming air tickets, selling holidays and renting cars. Rail tickets can be booked at the *CFR* office, Str. Republicii 53 (Mon–Fri 7am–7.30pm). There is an office at Str. Republicii 56 which handles buses to Germany. The tourist office in the *Carpaţi* hotel will book you on excursions to "Dracula's Castle" at Bran ($28) and to the villages of Hărman and Prejmer ($20), but charges well over the odds.

Around Braşov

Braşov nestles right under the mountains and there are opportunities for hiking and skiing just a few kilometres from the city at **Poiana Brasov**. The most popular bus excursion from Braşov is to the castle of **Bran**, and in spite of the crowds it's well worth a visit. Further to the south the Bucegi mountains (see p.114) are in easy reach, and to the southwest the Făgăraş range (see p.131) contains Romania's highest peaks. Between these two lies the very distinctive ridge of the **Piatra Craiului**, a single block of limestone that offers a marvellous if tiring day's walking. A short train ride northeast of the city are two villages, **Hărman** and **Prejmer**, with remarkable moated fortress-churches. They mark the beginning of the Burzen Land (see p.133) but are included here as they are the nearest of the Saxon villages to Braşov and can be visited on organized tours if you're pushed for time.

Poiana Braşov

The resort of **POIANA BRAŞOV** is set at an altitude of 1000m, below the spectacular Mount Postavaru, 12km southwest of Braşov (bus #20 every half hour from Livada Postei, by the Parc Central). You can **ski** here from December to March on a variety of runs: *Intim* and *Drum Roşu* are the easy ones, *Lupului* and *Sub-Teleferic* the steepest. Skiing lessons are organized by the **tourist office** in the *Complex Favorit*, which also supplies guides for **hiking** all the year round. **Skiing equipment** can be rented at the *Ciucaş* and *Teleferic* hotels or at the *Sport*, where they also have climbing gear.

The **hotels** are mostly filled by package groups from Britain and elsewhere, but they may have space, especially outside the ski season. The best is the *Alpin*, closely followed by the three-star *Teleferic* and *Sport*. The others are mostly two-star establishments and all pretty similar, with the *Poiana* the only one-star hotel. If you want to find out about rooms here, it's best to approach the tourist office. They may also be able to find cheaper **rooms** in a villa or at the *Cabana Junilor*, over a kilometre along the road back to Braşov. There are also **bungalows** in the *Sat de Vacanţa* (Holiday Village). The only budget places to stay are the two **cabanas** on the high slopes of Mount Cristianu (1960m), reached by the *Kanzel* cable car and gondola – you should try to reserve beds beforehand at the tourist office here or in Braşov.

The hotels are most useful for their services, which all cost more for foreigners: **massages and sauna** at the *Alpin*, *Teleferic* and *Şoimul*; **tennis courts and equipment** from the *Poiana*; and **kindergartens** at the *Teleferic* and *Bradul* (9am–5pm) and *Ciucaş* (overnight). The *Teleferic*'s **disco** runs from 10pm to 4am, while there are indoor **swimming pools** at the *Alpin* and the *Cristal*.

The resort's **restaurants** (10am–midnight) go in for "folk" architecture and cuisine, as you'd expect with names like *Şura Dacilor* (Dacians' Shed), *Vînătorul* (Hunter) and *Coliba Haiducilor* (Outlaws' Hut); an orchestra and dancing are included at the *Capra Neagră* (Chamois), open until 1am.

Bran and around

Situated only 28km from Braşov and easily reached by bus (from Livada Postei or *autogară* 2, near the Bartolomei station), as well as on ONT's official **organized excursions**, the small town of **BRAN** commands the entrance to the pass of the same name, formerly the main route into Wallachia. A castle was built here in 1377 to safeguard this vital route, and although what's now billed as "**Dracula's Castle**" (Tues–Sun 9am–5pm) and featured on every tourist brochure and itinerary has only tenuous associations with Vlad the Impaler – it's likely he attacked it during one of his raids on the Burzen Land – the hyperbole is forgivable as Bran really looks like a vampire count's residence. Perched on a rocky bluff, it rises in tiers of towers and ramparts from the woods, against a glorious mountain background. When Ceauşescu was in his most nationalistic phase, extolling Vlad as a true Romanian hero resisting the alien hordes, the Dracula link was played up for all it was worth here, the staff used to hide in chests, which they swung open menacingly, until an American tourist dropped dead of a heart attack.

The castle has now reopened after a long period of restoration and looks much as it would have done in the time of its most famous resident, **Queen Marie of Romania**. A granddaughter of Queen Victoria, born in Edinburgh and married to Prince Ferdinand in 1892, Queen Marie soon rebelled against the confines of court life in Bucharest – riding unattended through the streets, pelting citizens with roses during the carnival, and appointing herself a colonel of the Red Hussars (*Roşiori*). Her popularity soared after she organized cholera camps in the Balkan war and appeared at the Paris peace conference in 1919, announcing that "Romania needs a face, and I have come to show mine". Marie called Bran a "pugnacious little fortress", but whether because of her spirit pervading the rooms or the profusion of flowers in the yard, it seems a welcoming abode, at odds with its forbidding exterior. A warren of spiral stairs, ghostly nooks and secret chambers filled with elaborately carved four-poster beds and throne-like chairs overhangs the courtyard. Not surprisingly, it can get horribly crowded: the trick is to arrive on the dot as the castle opens – the bus parties will be arriving as you leave.

In the grounds are some fine examples of local vernacular architecture, including a fulling mill, and by the road south, a **museum** in the former *vama* or customs house. This predictably stresses the trade links from the earliest times between the Vlachs on either side of the Carpathians, and displays examples of foreign goods including an English clock and a Canadian travelling trunk.

Practicalities

Many **buses** from Braşov's *autogară* 2 pass Bran, but there is also a private service to Bran and Moeciu (12 daily Mon–Fri, 8 on Sat & Sun) from Livada Postei, by the Parc Central in the city. From Bran there are buses almost hourly (fewer on Sundays) north to Rîşnov and Braşov, and a few south to Piteşti and Cîmpulung.

There are few **hotel** options in Bran. Across the road from the castle, beyond a tiny park and river, the *Castelul Bran* cabana offers double rooms and a long and varied menu, including large cheap brandies. In fact, the kitchen produces only sausages in the mornings, and chicken thereafter; so if you want a fancier meal or room, go to the costlier *han* (②) on the Braşov side of town. There's also a *minihotel* (②) at the fuel station further north on the Braşov road.

Private rooms (①–②) are big business here, with almost sixty local homes offering accommodation (book through *Bran IMEX*, ☎01/781.79.09 in Bucharest or ☎068/23.63.62 or 23.66.42 in Bran).

Rişnov

If you are making your own way from Braşov to Bran, you can catch a bus or the early morning train to **RÎŞNOV** (*Râşnov*) where a ruined fourteenth-century **castle** crowns one of the fir-covered hills that surround the town. Reached by steps from the courtyard of the *Casă de Cultură*, through an archway by the bus stop, this is actually the old Saxon village of *Rosenau*, with a current population of just two hundred. The church (founded in 1360) can be visited by asking at the *Pfarrhaus*, two doors along the Braşov road. There is also a good **campsite** on the other side of the citadel, on the Poiana Braşov road.

Hiking in the Piatra Craiului

Mountains dominate the skyline around Bran. To the east is the almost sheer wall of the **Bucegi range** – it takes about eight hours to climb the path from Bran to Mount Omu, where there's a cabana (see p.119). To the west, gentler slopes run up to the **Piatra Craiului**, a narrow ridge at the eastern extremity of the Făgăraş mountains. This is a limestone ridge, 20km long, known as the "Royal Rock" (*Király-kö* in Hungarian and *Königstein* in German); with karst caves along its eastern face. Carpathian bears, lynx and chamois live here, and the endemic Piatra Craiului pink grows on the northeastern side.

It is easiest to reach the Piatra from **ZĂRNEŞTI** (accessible by train from Rîşnov and Braşov, or a 4km side road from Bran). It's a fairly mundane place, although what is supposedly a bicycle factory along the road to the east of town is in fact one of Romania's largest arms factories, with a notorious accident record. From here it's under three hours' walk up the Bîrsa Mare valley to the *Plaiul Foii* cabana, the main centre for **hiking** in this area. It takes a full day to climb (following red cross markings, and using fixed cables in places) to the main ridge, 1400m above, follow red dots north along the knife-edge ridge, and then descend following yellow stripes, either to the left to Zărneşti, or right to the *Curmătura* cabana. Although you can see Romanians hiking in bikinis near the *Curmătura*, the ridge route itself is quite demanding and you should really be properly equipped with boots, waterproofs and above all plenty of water. The ridge offers fantastic views both west towards the Făgăraş range and east towards the Bucegi, while the succession of peaks and parallel strata along the ridge itself are uniquely impressive.

Fundata

Fourteen kilometres from Bran, **FUNDATA** is one of the highest villages in Romania, situated at the top of the spectacular **Bran (or Giuvala) Pass** (1290m), and there are only occasional buses through here. On the far side of the pass, the road hairpins down past a ruined castle to the karstic Podul Dîmboviţei depression, and ultimately to Cîmpulung (p.94). The village itself is little more than a scattering of small farm houses with no discernible centre other than the shop on the main road.

On the last Sunday of June each year, a big peasant **festival** – the *Nedeia Muntele* – takes place in Fundata, attracting people from three counties. The underlying purpose of the festival is to transact business: exchanges of handicrafts and livestock, and (formerly) marriages. As Fundata straddles the border between Transylvania and Wallachia, the *Nedeia* was important as a means of maintaining contacts between ethnic Romanians in the two provinces. Although the match-making aspect has disappeared, it remains a lively event with plenty of singing and dancing and a chance to see traditional costumes.

Hărman and Prejmer

Visiting the Burzen Land around Braşov on the eve of the World War II, the writer Elizabeth Kyle found churches in the Saxon villages prepared for siege as in the times of Sultan Süleyman and Vlad the Impaler. **HĂRMAN** (*Honigberg*), 12km northeast from Braşov, still looks much as she described it: situated "in a wide and lovely valley, its houses arranged in tidy squares off the main street which sweeps up towards the grim fortress that closes the vista". Inside the fortified outer walls, wooden staircases lead to the rows of Meal Rooms (*Speisesaal*) where each family stored a loaf from every baking and other supplies. Here, Kyle encountered a Saxon fräulein wearing the high, brimless *borten* denoting maidenhood, who "flung open the door, and immediately a mingled stench of ancient cheeses, mouldering ham and damp flour rushed out to meet us. From the roof rows of hams were suspended on hooks. Those nearest us looked comparatively fresh, but the highest ones were green with age." Having been informed that "some of those hams have been hanging there two hundred years", Kyle enquired why. "Because, *Gott sei Dank*, they were not required," came the answer "There was no siege."

At that time the number of Saxon "souls" in Hărman was 1500; now there are under 350, of whom perhaps seventy come to church on Sundays, usually at 9am. The church dates from the thirteenth century, with later walls and an ice-cellar with fifteenth-century frescoes.

PREJMER (*Tartlau*), further north and 3km off the main road, was similarly well prepared; a five-towered wall, 12m high, lined in the seventeenth century with four tiers of Meal Rooms, surrounds the thirteenth-century church. The entrance tower is itself protected by another fortified enclosure – the Town Hall Courtyard – added in the sixteenth and seventeenth centuries, to which the Saxons appended an arcaded corridor or Bakers' Courtyard as a Baroque flourish in less perilous times, later in the seventeenth century. This is the easiest of the Saxon churches to visit, at least if you arrive between 9am and 5pm (except Sundays), as there is a sort of concierge's lodge in the entrance passage; there is even a small museum, and some signs in English.

The land **around Hărman** was the first in the Braşov region to be collectivized (in 1950), and today Prejmer is the centre of a large agricultural cooperative, with a trout farm and textile factory. Note that the Ilieni halt is closer to the centre than Prejmer station proper (and nowhere near the village of Ilieni); almost all local trains stop at both, and fast trains at neither.

Făgăraş and around

Between 1366 and 1460, **FĂGĂRAŞ**, 54km from Braşov, and the surrounding region (the duchy of Amlaş) were under Wallachian rule. The sturdy **fortress** distinguishing the town centre was raised on the ashes of an earlier citadel, sacked by Dracula during the course of a murderous rampage from the Red

HIKING IN THE FĂGĂRAŞ MOUNTAINS

Northwest of Braşov, the DN1 and the rail line follow the River Olt across the Transylvanian plateau towards Sibiu. For much of the journey, a fringe of peaks along the southern horizon delineates the Făgăraş **mountains**. Composed mainly of crystalline schists with occasional limestone outcrops, a series of pyramid-shaped peaks linked by narrow ridges harbours more than seventy **lakes** at heights of 1800–2250m. Up to 2000m the mountainsides are covered with spruce forests sheltering deer, Carpathian bears, chamois and other **wildlife**; above this line, snow can lie until June.

Most **hiking routes** are well marked and fairly simple to follow with a *Hartă Turistică Munţii Făgăraşului* map, which can be bought in Braşov, Făgăraş or Sibiu, or in the cabanas in the mountains. If you're planning to hike, it's useful but not usually essential to **reserve accommodation**: the *Societatea Sălişte-Bîlea* at Str. Oituz 31 in Sibiu (Mon–Fri 9am–4pm; ☎069/42.10.02) handles *Bîlea Lac* and *Bîlea Cascada*, while many other huts can be booked direct. Always go well provisioned with food and water, as well as boots and waterproofs – the weather is very changeable on the ridge.

Almost invariably, the starting point is one of the settlements along the Olt valley, where route markings lead from the train stations to the mountains. All trains stop at **UCEA**, to disgorge both peasants on shopping trips and groups of climbers, who all clamber onto buses south to **VICTORIA**, dominated by its chemical works. From here a forestry track leads to the *Arpaş* cabana, and red triangles take you on past the *Turnuri* cabana (☎069/43.84.05) up to *Podragu* cabana (☎069/43.84.05) at 2136m in about nine or ten hours. The next day you can follow the **ridge path** marked with red stripes, either eastwards past Romania's highest peak, **Moldoveanu** (2544m), descending by the Sîmbăta valley to the *Complex Turistic Sîmbăta* (with a monastery, a cabana and a few buses to Făgăraş) or west to **BÎLEA** (or Bâlea), where the cabana, *Bîlea Lac*, stands surrounded on three sides by a lake, itself flanked by high cliffs. From here you can descend either by the Trans-Făgăraş Highway or by a cable car to the *Bîlea Cascada* (waterfall) cabana, and from there to the *Vama Cucului* cabana(☎069/55.07.17), Cîrtişoara and the Cîrta rail halt. In theory there are also two buses a day from *Bîlea Cascada* to Sibiu, but they cannot be relied on.

If you fancy a **longer hike**, you can continue westwards from Bîlea to climb (with the help of fixed chains) Romania's second highest peak, **Negoiu** (2535m), and onwards to descend to the train stations at Porumbacu, Avrig or Racoviţa. East, the hike to the Piatra Craiului (p.129) takes a couple of days. The approaches on the southern side arc long and tedious, but it is possible to follow the Trans-Făgăraş Highway from Bîlea or a forestry road from below the Podragu saddle to the *Cumpăna* cabana at the northern end of the sixteen-kilometre-long **Lake Vidra**, or to two more cabanas on its southeastern shore. The road continues down through the gorges past the ruins of the real Dracula's Castle, perched high above the valley just before Căpăţîneni, to Curtea de Argeş in Wallachia (p.94).

Tower Pass towards the Burzen Land, in revenge for the loss of his fiefdom. Today, the fortress houses a moderately good museum (Tues–Sun 9am–12.30pm & 1.30–5pm), as well as a fairly classy restaurant in the cellars. Despite the town's partial modernization, an old custom of **ritual insults** still prevails. On a certain day at the beginning of summer, townsfolk who bear grudges or grievances assemble on the hilltop overlooking town, and shout insults at their opponents; the aim being to vent their spleen, and hopefully become reconciled thereafter.

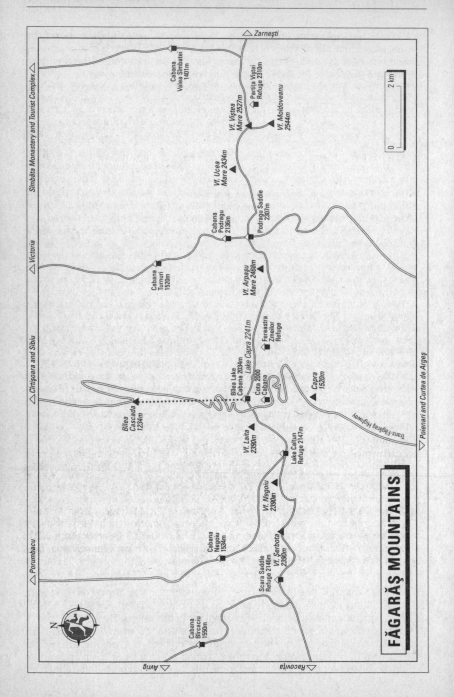

△ Zarneşti

Cabana
Valea Simbatei
1401m

Partia Viştei
Refuge 2310m

Vf. Viştea
Mare 2527m

Vf. Moldoveanu
2544m

2 km

0

Vf. Ucea
Mare 2434m

Podragu Saddle
2307m

Cabana
Podragu
2136m

Cabana
Turnuri
1520m

Vf. Arpaşu
Mare 2468m

Fereastra
Zmeilor
Refuge

Bilea Lake
Cabana 2034m

Lake Capra 2241m

Capra
1520m

Cota 2000
Cabana

Bilea
Cascada
1234m

Trans-Făgăraş Highway

▷ Poienari and Curtea de Argeş

Vf. Laita
2390m

Lake Caltun
Refuge 2147m

Vf. Negoiu
2390m

Cabana
Negoiu
1534m

Vf. Şerbota
2390m

Scara Saddle
Refuge 2146m

Cabana
Bircaciu
1550m

△ Porumbacu

◁ Cirtişoara and Sibiu

◁ Victoria

◁ Simbăta Monastery and Tourist Complex

N

FĂGĂRAŞ MOUNTAINS

▽ Avrig

▽ Racovita

Făgăraş has a **tourist office** at Str. Republicii 17, and the main **hotel**, the *Cetate*, is at Piaţa Mihai Viteazul 1 (☎068/21.17.03; ③). There is also a privately owned hotel 100m south of the *Comturist* shop at the east end of the new town centre, and the *Fîntinele* cabana on the main road 6km east of town.

Buses from Făgăraş serve the surrounding villages which have a predominantly Romanian population with a leavening of Saxons. They were ruled for a while by the princes of Wallachia, giving rise to characteristic local art forms, such as the **icons on glass** on display in the gallery at **Sîmbata Monastery**, 12km beyond Făgăraş, and still painted at Arpaşu, a further 15km along the DN1 towards Sibiu. The fifteenth-century church at **Vad**, 4km by minor road from Şercaia, at the Braşov end of the valley, also has a collection. Throughout the area, villagers still dress up in embroidered costumes for **New Year celebrations** – particularly at Şercaia, Arpaşu, Porumbacu de Jos and Porumbacu de Sus – and gather en masse together with Saxon dancers from Tilişca for the **Flowers of the Olt festival** (*Florile Oltului*) at **Avrig** on the second Sunday of April.

Beyond Avrig the road forks: the DN1 leads on past the *Fintiniţa Haiducului* (Outlaw's Spring) *han* to Sibiu; the other branch veers south to Talmaciu and on to Turnu Roşu (Red Tower) Pass into Wallachia. Travelling by rail, switch trains at Podu Olt for Piatra Olt in Wallachia; these services pass several of the monasteries in the Olt valley (see p.96).

The Burzen Land

Traditionally known by the Saxons as the **Burzen Land** or Birsenland (*Tara Birsei*), the Tîrnave plateau between Braşov and Sighişoara is dotted with the remnants of their citadels and fortified churches, and is an area popular with German visitors. Although the Székely (immediately to the north) put low walls around their places of worship and the Moldavians raised higher ones about their monasteries, it was the Transylvanian Germans who perfected this style of architecture in the fifteenth century.

Though the DN13 and the rail line north out of Braşov diverge in places due to the narrowness of the Olt valley, it's fairly easy to reach settlements en route; however there are many more in the side valleys which are well worth discovering and can only be reached by occasional buses, by car, bike or on foot.

The Saxon villages

Personal trains heading for Sighişoara stop at **FELDIOARA** (*Marienburg*), 22km from Braşov, where the Teutonic Knights, later expelled from Transylvania, built a citadel (now in ruins near the rail line at the south end of the village). The trains also stop at the riverside villages of **ROTBAV** (*Rothbach*) and **MĂIERUŞ** (*Nussbach*), both of which have fortified churches; and at **RACOŞ**, where a castle, built by the Bethlen family in 1625, is being restored. After Maieruş the road swings left across the wooded Perşani mountains, rejoining the river and the rail line where they emerge from a defile at Staţia Rupea. **RUPEA** (*Reps*), a small industrial town 4km from its train station, is dominated by a basalt hill crowned by the remains of three peasant citadels, built between the thirteenth and seventeenth centuries. The hill is also known for the springs of sulphurous, salty water which gush from it. The town is big enough to have a **hotel** (②), a local **museum** on the main square, Piaţa Republicii 191, and a bus station west of the centre.

The bus from the train station to the town of Rupea passes first through **HOMOROD** (*Hamruden*), whose church dates from 1270 with walls from the fifteenth century and a tower from the sixteenth, with three layers of paintings in the choir, all pre-Reformation. Now almost all the Saxons have left and the church is used only by a few Hungarians; it's getting very dilapidated but restoration is planned, with the help of German funds. A back road leads north from Homorod to **CAŢA** (*Katzendorf*) and **DRĂUŞENI** (*Draas*), both also with fortified churches. Beyond Rupea, the main road again diverges from the rail line, passing through **BUNEŞTI** (*Bodendorf*), where the church's **Speckturm** (Bacon Tower) is still in use as a bacon store. Ten kilometres south of here, along an unmade road, is **VISCRI** (*Deutsch-Weisskirch*), one of the most impressive of all the citadels, set, gleaming white, upon a hill. The church is largely Gothic, with walls built in 1500 and an assortment of towers from the fifteenth, seventeenth and eighteenth centuries. The mayor, Caroline Fernolend (at no. 13), is a very lively Saxon who is keen to preserve as much as possible of the Saxon culture, and there is a cottage where visitors can stay, for around $15 a night. Twenty kilometres further north, back on the main road, lies **SASCHIZ** (*Keisd*), where a hilltop citadel looks down on the village's fortified church, whose main tower shows clear earthquake damage.

Rejoining the rail line and entering the Tîrnava Mare valley you pass **ALBEŞTI** (*Weisskirch bei Schässburg*), where a small museum commemorates the life of the Hungarian poet **Petöfi Sándor**, killed nearby in battle against the Russians in 1849. As foreseen in one of his own ultra-romantic poems, Petöfi's body was never found; most likely it was trampled beyond all recognition by the Cossacks' horses, but it is also conceivable that he ended up as a prisoner in Siberia, where his remains are claimed to have been found.

Sighişoara

A forbidding silhouette of battlements and needle spires looms over **SIGHIŞOARA** (*Schässburg* to the Saxons, or *Segesvár* to the Hungarians) as the sun descends behind the hills of the Tîrnava Mare valley, and it seems fitting that this was the birthplace of Vlad Ţepeş "The Impaler" – the man known to so many as **Dracula**. Visually archaic even by Romanian standards, Sighişoara makes the perfect introduction to Transylvania: especially as the eastbound *Pannonia* and *Dacia* express trains stop here in daylight, enabling travellers to break the long journey between Budapest and Bucharest.

The old town

The old town or **citadel** dominates the newer quarters from a rocky massif whose slopes support a jumble of ancient, leaning houses, their windows sited to cover the steps leading up from Piaţa Hermann Oberth to the main gateway. Above rises the mighty **Clock Tower** where, at the stroke of midnight, a wooden figure emerges from the belfry to mark the change of day – Tuesday, the day of Mars, is represented by a soldier; Friday, by Venus, to whom a cherub profers a mirror. The tower was raised in the thirteenth and fourteenth centuries when Sighişoara became a free town controlled by craft guilds, each of which had to

finance the construction of a bastion and defend it during wartime. It has subsequently been rebuilt after earthquakes and a fire in 1676. Originally a Roman garrison town known as *Castrum Sex* (Fort Six), Sighişoara waxed rich on the proceeds of trade with Moldavia and Wallachia, as the tower's **museum** attests (Tues–Fri 9am–5.30pm, Sat & Sun 9am–3.30pm). Most of the burghers were Magyar or Saxon, and Romanians (or Vlachs as they were then called) became inferior citizens in Transylvanian towns following edicts passed in 1540. This apartheid excluded Vlachs from public office and forbade them to live in townhouses with chimneys or windows overlooking the streets, and also prohibited them from wearing furs, embroidered dress, shoes or boots.

Vlad's birthplace

In 1431 or thereabouts, in a two-storey house (no. 6) within the shadow of the Clock Tower, a woman whose name is lost to posterity gave birth to a son called Vlad, who in later life earned the title of "The Impaler". Abroad, he's better known as **Dracula**, which can be translated as "Son of the Devil", or more accurately as "Son of the Dragon" – referring to his father, **Vlad Dracul**, whom Sigismund of Hungary made a knight of the Order of the Dragon for his prowess against the Turks. When Vlad Jr was born, Vlad Dracul was merely the guard commander of the mountain passes into Wallachia, but in 1436 he secured the princely throne and moved his family to the court at Tîrgovişte. Young Vlad's privileged childhood there ended eight years later, when he and his brother Radu were sent to Anatolia as hostages for Vlad Dracul's good behaviour. There, they lived in daily fear of the silken cord with which the Ottomans strangled dignitaries – Radu sleeping his way into the favours of the Sultan while Vlad observed the Turks' use of terror, which he would later turn against them as the Impaler. Nowadays, Vlad's birthplace contains a **restaurant**, with a small **museum** of medieval weapons next door.

The churches and towers

Churches are monuments to social identity in Sighişoara, as in many old Transylvanian towns. The Saxons – whose importance here is past – have their main church on the hill's summit, closest to their *Gott*. This, the **Church on the Hill** (*Bergkirche*), is approached by an impressive covered **wooden stairway** with 175 steps and 29 landings, dating from the seventeenth century, which ascends steeply from Strada Şcolii. Ivy-grown and massively buttressed, the church has a roomy interior that seems austere despite the blue and canary yellow-painted vaulting. Some lovely stone tombs lodged near the entrance are a harbinger of the **Saxon cemetery**, a melancholy, weed-choked mass of graves spilling over the hilltop beside the ruined citadel walls.

The church, built in 1345, has been closed for restoration, and may still only be open for one hour per day, from noon to 1pm. It is tended by an old couple who inhabit the former Ropemakers' Tower together with their pigs and poultry.

Down by the Clock Tower stands the **monastery church**, also Saxon, which has a stark, whitewashed interior hung with colourful carpets as in the Black Church at Braşov, and an altar like a wooden carpet-beater. It is often closed but hosts occasional organ recitals. Of the original fourteen **towers**, named after the guilds responsible for their upkeep, nine survive, the most impressive being the hexagonal Shoemakers' Tower (*Turnul Cizmarilor*), the Tailors' Tower (*Turnul Croitorilor*) and the Tinsmiths' Tower (*Turnul Cositorarilor*), best viewed, with its fine wooden gallery, from the gateway of the Lutheran parish house (*Pfarrhaus*), below the Church on the Hill.

The lower town

The **lower town** is less picturesque than the citadel, but there's a nice ambience around the shabby centre, consisting of **Piaţa Hermann Oberth** (named after a pioneer of rocketry) and **Strada 1 Decembrie**, where townsfolk gather to consume grilled sausages, *ţuică*, Coke or watery beer, conversing in Romanian, Magyar and, occasionally, antiquated German. The number of hangouts is so small that it's easy to track down anything that's happening, while any film will be screened at the open-air cinema behind the main street. On national holidays, a brass band may perform in the citadel's Piaţa Cetăţii, and people stream up to Dealul Gării (the hill above the train station) with bottles and food. Gypsies arrive by cart, their hats crowned with flowers, to *bashavav* (play the violin), tell fortunes and pick pockets.

The area between the citadel and the river was partially cleared before 1989 for redevelopment as a Civic Centre, like that in Bucharest, and the land is still in limbo. Taking the foot bridge over the Tîrnave Mare river, you come to the Romanian **Orthodox Cathedral**, built in Byzantine style in 1937. Its gleaming white, multifaceted facade is in striking contrast to the dark interior, where blue and orange hues dominate the small panels of the iconostasis. Close by is an antique locomotive which ran on the Sibiu–Agnita–Sighişoara narrow-gauge line between 1896 and 1965.

Practicalities

The **train** and **bus stations** are north of the centre on the other side of the Tîmave Mare river. Most facilities are grouped on Strada 1 Decembrie, in the lower town. Here you'll find an OJT **tourist information** office at no. 10, the **post office** and *CFR* booking office.

Sighişoara's only **hotel** is the *Steaua* at Str. 1 Decembrie 12 (☎065/77.19.30; ③), next door to the tourist office. It has been recently privatized, with some minor refurbishment, and remains a pleasant and affordable stop-over. (*ACR* coupons are actually worth more than a room here, but they may help the staff to find a free room where none previously existed.) Otherewise, there's not a lot of choice: the *Hula Danes* **campsite**, with bungalows and tent space, is a good base for visiting more Saxon villages, 4km along the Mediaş road (take a bus rather than a train to Daneş). More convenient, if less comfortable, is the *Dealul Gării* **campsite** (with cabanas and a restaurant), on the hilltop overlooking the train station. The station underpass leads to Strada Primăverii on the north side of the tracks where you can find a footpath to the summit; a longer but easier route involves turning left from the station to cross the tracks by a bridge and following Strada Dealul Gării up the hill. You may also be able to find **private rooms** in the citadel by asking in the café around the corner from Vlad's birthplace.

There are a few good **places to eat** including the *Steaua* hotel, the campsite, the restaurant in Dracula's birthplace and a snackbar at the north end of Strada Morii.

Sighişoara to Sibiu

The main approach to Sibiu is to follow the Tîrnave Mare river west from Sighişoara. From the train or the DN14, you'll see buffalo pulling wagons or wallowing, watched by their drovers, and glimpse the towers of fortified Saxon churches in villages situated off the main road. The area south and west of Sighişoara is particularly good for leisurely exploration, its villages all accessible by bus from Sighişoara. The best of the churches are at **DAIA** (*Denndorf*), **ŞTEJĂRENII** (*Peschendorf*), **CRIŞ** (*Kreisch*), **MĂLÎNCRAV** (*Malmkrog*), **NOU SĂSESC** (*Neudorf bei Schässburg*), and **AGNITA** (*Agnethelm*), an old Saxon settlement with a grimly towered church and a small hotel. From Agnita you can travel by bus or narrow-gauge train to Sibiu, or by bus to Făgăraş through the villages of **DEALU FRUMOS** (*Schönberg*), **MERGHINDEAL** (*Mergeln*) and **CINCU** (*Gross-Schenk*), which all have imposing fortified churches.

Just off the main DN14, 26km from Sighişoara, lies the village of **BIERTAN** (*Birthälm*) which can be reached by bus from Sighişoara or Mediaş. Set high on a hill within two and a half rings of walls, linked by a splendid covered staircase, it has the best known of all the Saxon fortified churches; recently restored, it is now on UNESCO's World Heritage List. Built as late as 1516, this was the seat of Lutheran bishops, and their fine gravestones can be seen inside the towers. Buses also run down minor roads to other villages with fortified churches such as **RICHIŞ** (*Reichesdorf*, beyond Biertan), **AŢEL** (*Hetzeldorf*) to the south and **CURCIU** (*Kirtsch*) to the north; local *personal* trains enable you to stop at **BRATEIU** (*Pretai*), where there's an especially fine church and a festival, *Pe Mureš ši pe Tîrnave*, which takes place in June.

There are *Gästehäuser* or small **guesthouses** (①–②) in some of these villages, with one to six beds per room. To stay in Biertan (the most expensive by far) or Richiş, contact the Lutheran pastor, Orwin Plattner, in Biertan (☎137); in Aţel contact Stefan Pitters at no. 195 (☎105); and in Moşna (see below) Marianne Fodorean at no. 531 (☎120).

Mediaš

The only proper town on the way to Sibiu is **MEDIAŞ** (*Mediasch*), which despite the tanneries and chemical works feeding off the Tîrnava Mare valley's methane reserves, gets more prepossessing the further in you venture. Originally an Iron Age and then a Roman settlement, Mediaş was predominantly a Saxon town for many centuries, walled and with gate towers, two of which remain, on Strada Cloşca. After 1918 it began to develop an industrial and Romanian character, stemming from the construction here of Transylvania's first gas pipeline and the results of political changes after World War I.

From the **train and bus stations** on Strada Unirii, opposite the synagogue at Str. Kogălniceanu 45, follow Strada Pompierilor and then Strada Roth to the right to the town centre, **Piaţa Republicii** – characterized by its subdued café life, piles of watermelons and the **Evangelical Church**, with a 74-metre belltower slightly askew. The fifteenth-century church is a true citadel, surrounded by store-rooms, high ramparts and towers (one of which, the Tailors' Tower, served as a jail for Dracula in 1467). Inside there are Anatolian carpets, frescoes and a superb Gothic altarpiece in the style of Roger van der Weyden. The *Schullerhaus*, at no. 25 on the square, was built in 1588 and housed the Transylvanian Diet. For a limited insight into the history of the town, the **museum** is at Str. Viitorului 46 (Tues–Sun 9am–5pm), in a former monastery next to a late fifteenth-century church.

Mediaş' only **hotel** is the ugly *Central* (☎069/81.17.87 or 81.14.72; ④), at the top of Strada Pompierilor. Bus services operate from the **bus station** to Agnita, Sibiu and Tîrgu Mureş, and to all the surrounding villages. Some especially picturesque villages with fortified churches, such as **MOŞNA** (*Meschen*), lie along the road to Agnita, and camping wild is quite acceptable in the surrounding hills.

Copşa Mică and beyond

Filthy **COPŞA MICĂ**, 13km west of Mediaş, is probably Romania's most polluted town and if you're unlucky with connections you may have to change trains for Sibiu here rather than in Mediaş. A plant producing carbon-black (for dyes) was established here in 1936 and consistently left everything – plants, laundry, people – covered in soot until it was finally closed in 1993. White snow was seen here for the first time in 1994. However, the other plant here, a lead smelter, is more deadly, and has been distributing a cocktail of twenty heavy metals over the region for the last thirty years. This is now working well below capacity, and only two thousand men are left in work, with five thousand unemployed. Lead poisoning is widespread, tuberculosis and other diseases two or three times the national average, and there are about nine premature births per week; there are also said to be lots of divorces due to impotence.

Beyond Copşa Mică, the first three stops, **AXENTE SEVER**, **AGÎRBICIU** and **ŞEICA MARE**, are all close to good fortified Saxon churches, of which the first is the best. Five kilometres south of Copşa Mică (buses from Mediaş via Copşa Mică to Motiş) is **VALEA VIILOR** (*Wurmloch*), a Saxon village with a particularly fine church, the chancel of which is built up into a virtual duplicate of the tower at the opposite end.

Sibiu

"I rubbed my eyes in amazement," wrote Walter Starkie of **SIBIU** in 1929. "The town where I found myself did not seem to be in Transylvania, for it had no Romanian or Hungarian characteristics: the narrow streets and old gabled houses made me think of Nuremberg." Nowadays the illusion is harder to sustain, in a city surrounded by high-rise suburbs and virtually abandoned by the Saxons themselves, but the town is still a startling sight and home to some of Romania's best museums.

Some history

Many residents still call Sibiu *Hermannstadt*, the name given by the Transylvanian **Saxons** to their chief city. Like Braşov and other towns, it was founded by Germans whom the Hungarian King Géza II invited to colonize strategic regions of Transylvania in 1143. The first settlers were mainly from Flanders and the Mosel and Rhine lands, but with subsequent waves of emigration, the appellation *Sachsen* stuck. *Siebenbürgen*, the German name for Transylvania, derives from the original "seven towns" raised by the Saxons, of which Hermannstadt became the most powerful. Clannish, hard-working and thrifty, its inhabitants prospered and came to dominate trade between Transylvania and Wallachia, forming exclusive guilds under royal charter. Rich and privileged under the feudal system, the Saxons were envied by others and knew it. Their literature and proverbs are marked by admonitions to beware of outsiders, while a plethora of **fortifications** testifies to their historical caution. Mindful of the destruction of their first citadel by the Tartars in 1241, the townsfolk surrounded themselves during the fifteenth century with walls and forty towers; built of brick since firearms were then transforming siege warfare, they were mighty enough to repel the Turks three times. Behind these *Burgen* the Saxons linked their buildings and streets with tunnels and gateways, and set heavily grated windows to cover the stairways and corners where intruders might be ambushed. Alas for the Saxons, their citadels were no protection against the tide of history, which steadily eroded their influence from the eighteenth century on and put them in a difficult position during the Second World War. Although many bitterly resented Hitler's award of Northern Transylvania to Hungary in 1940, others relished their new status as *Volksdeutsche* and embraced Nazism. Thousands of them were conscripted into – or volunteered for – the Waffen-SS, in particular the *Prinz Eugen* division, whose atrocities in Yugoslavia inevitably brought disgrace upon the entire German community after the war. All fit men between the ages of 17 and 45, and women between 18 and 30 (30,000 in all) were deported to the Soviet Union for slave labour for between three and seven years; many did not return, and those who did found that much of their property had been confiscated.

Arrival and information

Sibiu's main **bus terminal** and **train station** are at the northwest end of town. To reach the centre, cross Piaţa 1 Decembrie 1918 (still generally known as Piaţa Gării) and follow Strada General Magheru up the hill. The main bus terminal operates services to Agnita, Mediaş, Sighişoara, Tîrgu Mureş, villages to the east such as Vurpar, and Cisnadie. For other destinations you should head west on Şoseaua Alba Iulia past the *Ştrand* (trolleybus #T3) to *autogară 2*, on Strada Autogarii (near the *Turnişor* rail halt, on the line west to Sebeş – ten minutes' walk south along the tracks). From here buses run west as far as Cluj, Tîrgu Jiu, Cîmpeni and Polovragi, although the coverage is pretty patchy.

The **airport** is in the western suburbs, and linked to town by *TAROM* bus. Heading out to the airport, *TAROM* buses leave an hour before each flight or you can take any regular bus towards Cristian.

Sibiu's **tourist office** at the corner of Strada Bălcescu and Piaţa Unirii has been closed but is likely to reopen. In the meantime, immediately behind it, at Str. Cetăţii 1 is the *Prima Ardeleana* tourist agency (daily 8am–4pm; ☎41.17.88), which sells the good *Transpress* town map. In addition Sibiu has a telephone information service, *Infotel*, on ☎43.76.68 (some English spoken).

Accommodation

There is a frustratingly narrow range of **hotels** in Sibiu, with just one very cheap option as an escape from the general mid-range mediocrity. Alternatively **private rooms** (②) can be arranged at *EXO*, Str. Bălcescu 1 (Mon–Fri 2–10pm). There is also a *complex turistic* (☎42.29.20) in the Dumbrava forest 4km to the south (trolleybus #T1 from the train station), comprising a *han*, better-quality motel and an over-priced **campsite**. In the same direction (also reached by #T1), is a small **pension** (☎42.43.04 or 48.20.31; ②), at Str. Anton Pann 12, off Calea Dumbrăvii.

Hotels

Bulevard, Piaţa Unirii 10 (☎41.21.40). More attractive than the others in this class, though with few mod cons. ④.

Continental, Calea Dumbrăvii 2 (41.69.10). A modern *bloc* formerly used by the *Securitate*, and now by tourist groups (*ACR* coupons accepted). ④.

Împăratul Romanilor, Str. Bălcescu 4 (☎41.64.90). Recently refurbished, this is far and away the best place in town, and can easily justify its prices compared to the town's other hotels. ⑤.

Parc, Str. Octavian Goga 1 (☎42.10.26). The former Party hotel, but with no great attractions other than being close to the park. ④.

The **telephone code** for Sibiu is ☎069

Podul Minciunilor (Liars' Bridge), Str. Azilului 1 (☎41.72.59). A rather grubby and cramped guesthouse, but centrally located opposite the thirteenth-century Old Women's Almshouse (*Azilul de Bătrini*). ③.

Silva, Aleea Eminescu 1 (☎44.21.41). Newly privatized place in the park behind the *Parc* hotel, and the cheapest in this price range. ④.

Sport, Str. Octavian Goga 2 (☎42.24.72). The real bargain basement option. ①.

The Town

Nothwithstanding its history, Sibiu doesn't seem a grim town. Many of the houses are painted sky blue, red, apricot or pea green, and cafés and restaurants do a busy trade along the length of the promenade. It's sprinkled with a collection of attractive **churches**, several of which you pass on your way in from the stations. On Piața 1 Decembrie 1918 there's a small Catholic chapel containing a fifteenth-century stone crucifix, while along Strada Magheru, past the old synagogue (still used in the summer by Sibiu's remaining two dozen Jews) is the Ursuline church (at the corner with Strada Avram Iancu), which dates from 1474. One block south, on Strada Șelarilor, the Franciscan church, also built in the fifteenth century, was rebuilt in the Baroque style after the roof collapsed in 1776.

The historic centre

Piața Mare is the traditional hub of public life, surrounded by the renovated premises of sixteenth- and seventeenth-century merchants, whose acumen and thrift were proverbial. The **Councillors' Tower** (*Turnul Sfatului*), built in 1588, which has been "temporarily" closed to visitors for several years, and a Baroque Jesuit church, separate Piața Mare from **Piața Mică** (Little Square) behind. You can cut through a gate below the tower, or walk left around the corner past the Baroque Brukenthal palace into the **Piața Grivița**.

The **Brukenthal Museum** (Tues–Sun 10am–5pm), partly assembled by Samuel Brukenthal, the imperial governor between 1777 and 1787, and opened in 1817 in his former palace at Piața Mare 5, stands alone as Transylvania's finest museum. Besides the best of local silverware, pottery and furniture, and various paintings by Flemish masters and by Cranach and Veronese, there's a wonderfully evocative collection of works by Transylvanian painters: mainly genre and romantic depictions of peasant life, the nobility in their crumbling castles, and wild Transylvanian landscapes, by Franz Neuhauser, Friederich Meiss, Antal Ligeti, Wellmann, Smigelschi and others. Later acquisitions include works by the best Romanian painters, such as Theodor Aman, Nicolae Grigorescu, Ștefan Luchian and Theodor Pallady.

Behind the museum is the former **Old City Hall** (*Primăria Veche*) at Str. Mitropoliei 2, built in 1475, remodelled in 1545 and now housing the **History Museum** (Tues–Sun 10am–5pm) – the courtyard is worth a look even if you choose not to go inside. Other museums in the historic centre include the **Pharmaceutical and Ethnology Museums**, Piața Mică 26 and 11 (Tues–Sun 10am–5pm), and the **Natural History Museum**, Str. Cetății 1 (same hours), which has astronomy evenings on occasional Thursdays.

In the Piața Grivița, the **Evangelical Cathedral** (Mon–Fri 9am–1pm), a massive *Hallenkirche* raised during the fourteenth and fifteenth centuries, dominates its neighbours, the Saxon *Gymnasium* (grammar school) and Theological Institute – confirming the town's pre-eminence as a centre of the Lutheran faith. The cathedral's choir is best heard on Sundays, and in summer there are

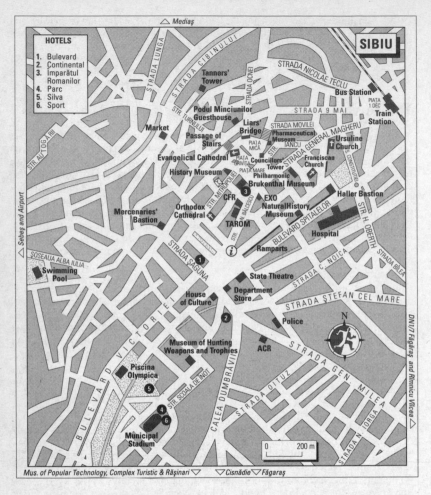

Map of Sibiu:

SIBIU

HOTELS
1. Bulevard
2. Continental
3. Împaratul Romanilor
4. Parc
5. Silva
6. Sport

Mediaş

STRADA LUNGA · STRADA CIBINULUI · STRADA OCNEI · STRADA NICOLAE TECLU

Tanners' Tower · Bus Station · PIAŢA 1 DEC · Train Station · STRADA 9 MAI

Podul Minciunilor Guesthouse · Liars' Bridge · STRADA MOVILEI · Pharmaceutical Museum · STRADA GENERAL MAGHERU

Market · Passage of Stairs · PIAŢA MICĂ · IANCU · Ursuline Church

Evangelical Cathedral · PIAŢA GRIVIŢA · Councillors' Tower · Franciscan Church

History Museum · PIAŢA MARE · Philharmonic · Brukenthal Museum

CFR · EXO · Haller Bastion

Mercenaries' Bastion · Orthodox Cathedral · STR. N. BĂLCESCU · NaturalHistory Museum · STR. H. OBERTH

TAROM · STRADA SPITALELOR

Sebeş and Airport

STR. AI. ODGARII

SOSEAUA ALBA IULIA · STRADA ŞAGUNA · BULEVARD SPITALELOR · Hospital · STRADA BÂLEA

Swimming Pool · Ramparts

1 · State Theatre · STRADA C. NOICA

House of Culture · Department Store · STRADA ŞTEFAN CEL MARE

2 · Police · N

Museum of Hunting Weapons and Trophies · ACR · STRADA GEN. MILEA

Piscina Olympica · STR. SCOALA DE INOT · STRADA OITUZ

5

4 6 · CALEA DUMBRĂVII

Municipal Stadium · STRADA N. IORGA

0 — 200 m

BULEVARD VICTORIE

DN 17 Făgăraş and Rimnicu Vîlcea

Mus. of Popular Technology, Complex Turistic & Răşinari ▽   ▽ Cisnădie ▽ Făgăraş

concerts on Romania's largest church organ on Wednesday evenings. It contains a fine collection of funerary plaques, a superb altarpiece, and in the crypt the **tomb of Mihnea the Bad**, Dracula's son and voivode of Wallachia for just one year, who was stabbed to death outside after attending Mass in 1510 (when the building was still a Catholic place of worship).

Near the cathedral, an alley sneaks off to join the **Passage of Stairs** (*Pasajul Scărilor* or *Saggasse*), which descends into the lower town overshadowed by arches and the medieval citadel wall. Just to the east of the cathedral, Strada Ocnei runs down through a kind of miniature urban canyon spanned by the elegant wrought-iron Iron Bridge (*Podul de Fier*), dating from 1859. This is nick-named the **Liars' Bridge** because of a legend that no one can tell a lie while standing upon it without the structure collapsing. However, Ceauşescu gave a speech from it and survived, although he disliked the town and never returned.

If you don't want to risk it, try instead the Cobbler's Hole (*Schüsterloch*), an alley leading from Piaţa Griviţa to Piaţa Mică 12. On the far side of the bridge, at Piaţa Mica 21, stands the **old market hall**, built in 1789, now hosting temporary art exhibitions. Another passageway leads through the Staircase Tower (no. 24) into **Strada Movilei**, a street pock-marked with medieval windows, doorways and turrets. Down in the rambling lower town are the octagonal-based **Tanners' Tower** on Strada Pulberăriei, reached via Strada Valea Mare and Strada Rimski-Korsakov, and a busy food **market** on Piaţa Cibin beside the river.

The modern centre

In Saxon times Sibiu's promenade took place along **Strada Bălcescu** (between Piaţa Mare and Piaţa Unirii) and this is still the place to find shops, offices and snacks. At no. 4 is Sibiu's oldest hotel, the *Împăratul Romanilor* (Roman Emperor), still bearing a faded resemblance to the grand establishment once patronized by the likes of Liszt, Johann Strauss and Eminescu. By then the town had out-lived its militaristic architecture – exemplified by the sixteenth-century **ramparts** and bastions along the length of Strada Cetăţii to the southeast, where three mighty **towers** were once manned by contingents of the Carpenters', Potters' and Drapers' guilds. The Haller Bastion to the northeast and the Mercenaries' Bastion to the northwest on Strada Bastionului, the last to be built in 1627, also survive. To the east of the Carpenters' Tower, the *Pulverturm* is being restored to its earlier role as the town's theatre.

With the encouragement of governor Samuel Brukenthal, Sibiu developed as a centre of intellectual life, which during the nineteenth century provided a haven for Romanians bent on raising their own people's cultural horizons. **Gheorghe Lazăr** and others opened a Romanian *Liceu* (still functioning today); Ioan Slavici and George Coşbuc edited the campaigning *Tribuna* (at Str. Bălcescu 1); and on the premises of Str. Mitropoliei 20, the first congress of **ASTRA** – an association for the propagation of Romanian culture in Transylvania – was held in October 1861. In the same street, the **Orthodox Cathedral** is an early twentieth-century copy of Haghia Sofia in Istanbul, embellished with all manner of neo-Byzantine flourishes and frescoes. The choir is fantastic, and it's worth visiting both the Evangelical and Orthodox churches during Sunday morning services to compare the different liturgical and choral styles. Beyond the cathedral you soon reach the **ASTRA Park**, where in 1905 ASTRA opened a library and museum in a fine building at Str. Lupaş 5; this leads you back to Strada Bălcescu.

Three blocks south of Piaţa Unirii, at Str. Şcoala de Înot 4, the **Museum of Hunting Weapons and Trophies** (Tues–Sun 10am–5pm), which musters stuffed animals and a fearsome armoury, is worth a visit.

Outside the centre

Further afield, near the **Zoological Gardens** in the Dumbrava forest just south-west of town, lies the **Museum of Popular Technology** (Tues–Sun 10am–5pm), perhaps the best of Romania's open-air museums. Under the Ceauşescu regime the museum faced constant political obstruction as it struggled to keep alive pride in rural traditions when the government wanted to make country life indistin-guishable from urban life – one village church actually had to be dismantled and buried for two years until it was permissible to re-erect it here. The emphasis is on folk technology, with windmills and watermills from all over the country rebuilt here in working order.

Eating and drinking

Places to eat cluster along Strada Bălcescu and around Piaţa Mare and Piaţa Unirii, although most wining and dining occurs in the main hotels. The *Împăratul Romanilor* is the best in town, noted for its Romanian cuisine and much frequented by local black marketeers, with a glitzy courtyard and a sliding roof; while the *Continental* also contains an *expres* joint.

The *Pizza Tîrgu Peştelui* on Strada Tîrgu Peştelui is one of the best private restaurants in town, although it's slightly north of the centre. You could also try the *Bufniţa* at Str. Bălcescu 45, the *Lactobar Liliacul* at no. 18, and the cafés on Piaţa Mare (of which the *Intim*, in fact at Str. Magheru 2, is non-smoking; Mon–Sat 8am–9pm). The best place for breakfast is the *Ceainăria Aroma* at Str. Bălcescu 1 (Mon–Sat 8am–9pm), which even has toasted rye sandwiches.

There's a good selection of **bars**, including the *Butoiul de Aur* (at the bottom of the *Pasajul Scărilor*, Tues–Sun 10am–10pm), a hole-in-the-wall wine cellar which sometimes serves *salam de Sibiu*, the local salami speciality; *Sibiu Vechi*, a cellar with good traditional music at Str. Papiu Ilarion 3 (Mon–Thurs & Sun 10am–midnight, Fri & Sat noon–2am); the *Crama Naţional* (down some stairs behind the old market hall on Piaţa Mică), a cheap and very cheerful place, and the *Bar Turnului* by the Councillors' Tower, good for *café frappé* and cognac. The *Royal*, at Str. Bălcescu 18, is Sibiu's trendy **nightspot** (Tues–Sun 4pm–3am).

Listings

Bike repair Str. 9 Mai 43.

Books and maps *Eminescu* bookstore, Str. Bălcescu/Str. Telefoanelor, has books (some in German) on Saxon architecture and culture. A good bet for maps is the *Luceafarul* on the corner of Calea Dumbrăvii and Str. Noica.

Car repair *ACR*, bloc 13, Str. Gen. V Milea; *Autoservice*, opposite *autogară* 2 on Şos. Alba Iulia; *Concordia*, Str. Cîmpului 13 (☎43.08.33).

Exchange Changing money isn't a problem in Sibiu as there are plenty of exchange counters. One at Str. Papiu Ilarion 12 (off Str. Bălcescu) accepts Visa cards, but at a poor rate.

Hospital On B-dul Spitalelor, opposite the Haller Bastion.

Libraries The university rectorate at B-dul Victoriei 10 houses American, British, French and German libraries (Mon–Fri 8am–4pm, except the British 10am–1pm & 2–5pm). There's also a French cultural centre and library in the *casă de cultură studenteasca* at Str. Mitropoliei, next to the *Johanniskirche*.

Pharmacy Sibiu has two 24hr pharmacies: Str. Bălcescu 53 and the private *San Marco* at Str. Nicolae Iorga 50 (to the south in the Hipodrom II quarter).

Police Str. Revoluţiei 4.

Post office The main post office is at Str. Mitropoliei 14 and has a poste restante service.

Shopping Most stores and supermarkets are on Str. Bălcescu. The main department store, the *Dumbrava*, is on the other side of Piaţa Unirii, opposite the *Continental*. For off-beat souvenirs, try the two hat stores on Str. 9 Mai, one at no. 46 (11am–2pm) which makes its Tyrolean-style hats to order only, and the other on the corner at no. 50 (8am–1pm, but often closed) which sells railmen's and officers' caps.

Sport Facilities are clustered around the open-air *Ştrand* on Şos. Alba Iulia, while you can also swim at the *Piscina Olimpică* on B-dul Victoriei. FC InterSibiu play in the Municipal Stadium in the *Parc sub Arini*.

Travel agents *CFR*, Str. Bălcescu 6 (Mon–Fri 7am–7pm) for rail bookings; *TAROM*, Str. Bălcescu 10 (Mon–Fri 7am–6pm, Sat 8am–2pm; ☎41.11.57).

Around Sibiu

Buses from the terminal by the train station serve many of the **old Saxon settlements** around Sibiu. Most of these villages have sizeable Romanian and Gypsy populations, now far outnumbering the Germans, but all have fortified churches and rows of houses presenting a solid wall to the street – hallmarks of their Saxon origins. "They have existed for seven hundred years, a mere handful, surrounded by races that have nothing in common with them, and yet they have not lost those customs that attach them to their fatherland", observed Walter Starkie in the 1920s. This remained largely true of the Saxon communities until 1989 – for example Cisnădioara, where the sight and feel of the place suggested Bavaria two hundred years ago – but the Saxons are disappearing fast, and it won't be long before their culture has vanished altogether.

The villages south of Sibiu lie in the foothills of the **Cindrel** (or Cibin) **mountains**, where enjoyable day walks and longer hikes can be taken from the small ski resort of Păltiniş. To the east and north of Sibiu, there are more Saxon villages with doughty fortress-churches, including VURPĂR (*Burgberg*), ŞURA MARE and ŞURA MICĂ (*Gross-Scheuren* and *Klein-Scheuren*), all accessible by bus, a pretty excursion through rolling hills and orchards. Half the services to Şura Mare continue on the DN14 to SLIMNIC (*Stolzenburg*), where there are the ruins of a large fourteenth-century church, while those to Şura Mica may continue to OCNA SIBIULUI (*Salzburg*), a bathing resort with fizzy, salty water which bubbles up from the lakes formed in abandoned salt-workings. Beyond the spa on the central Piaţa Traian is a solid walled church (Thurs 3–4pm) that, unusually, has a Hungarian Evangelical congregation. The spa is served by *Băile Ocna Sibiului*, a halt on the Sibiu to Copşa Mică rail line 2km north of Ocna Sibiului station proper. By the halt is a poor **campsite**, with lots of hidden charges.

Cisnădie and Cisnădioara

Two or three times an hour a bus or *maxitaxi* lurches off from Sibiu's bus station towards CISNĂDIE (*Heltau*), 10km to the south. You'll find that Cisnădie's modern outskirts quickly give way to the old Red Town (so called by the Turks both for the colour of its walls and the blood shed attempting to breach them), a convergence of streets around the **church**, whose walls are lined with the medieval equivalent of bomb shelters, where the community sought refuge during times of danger and stored a percentage of their harvest. If you ask politely, you may be taken up the massive thirteenth-century **tower:**; a succession of lofty vaults linked by creaking ladders and narrow stairways, fitted with Transylvania's first lightning conductor in 1795, and crowned by four turrets – medieval symbols of civic importance. From the belfry the view of Cisnădie's angular courtyards and red rooftops is superb, while just visible in the distance below the Cindrel mountains is the conical rock crowned by a church that overlooks Cisnădioara – legend has it that a tunnel links the two villages. On the way down, you can call in at the **Textile Museum** (Mon–Fri 8am–4pm), which has comprehensive coverage of the local household industry.

If you're keen to stay here, ask at the museum about **private rooms** (①–②) These can also be booked at the tourist offices in Sibiu and Bucharest.

From Cisnădie's centre it's a four-kilometre walk out along Strada Măgurii and the valley road, lined with poplars and orchards, west towards the striking seventy-metre-high rock that looms over **CISNĂDIOARA** (*Michelsburg*). The tiny **Romanesque church** built on its summit in 1223 frequently withstood the Tartars, villagers defending it by hurling down rocks which had previously been carried into the citadel by aspiring husbands. The custom was that no young man could marry until he had carried a heavy rock from the riverbed up the steep track, for the villagers were anxious to prevent weaklings from marrying in case they spoiled the hardy race. The church and adjoining ethnographic museum are supposedly open from Tuesday to Sunday 10am to 5pm, but you may have to ask around to find the curator.

Follow the river down through the village and you pass a few shops and rows of neat, unmistakably German houses, now used as holiday homes by the new bourgeoisie of Sibiu. There's an official **campsite** here, but you should still beware light-fingered *ţigani* wandering over the hills from their camp near Răşinari. Alternatively there are bungalows at the *Bufet Pinul* at the village limits on the road to Răşinari.

Păltiniş and the Cindrel mountains

PĂLTINIŞ, at a height of 1442m, was founded in 1894 by the *Siebenburgischer Karpatenverein* (Transylvanian Carpathian Association), the now-defunct body which opened up the Romanian Carpathians to tourism and built many of the original *cabanele*. Nowaday, Păltiniş is primarily a minor **ski resort**, but also attracts summer hikers and is linked to Sibiu by bus two or three times a day from the corner of Strada 9 Mai. Although the *Agenţia Păltiniş* has an office at Piaţa Mare 12 in Sibiu, the **accommodation** here is now privatized (or at least rented out) and you'll have to phone directly to book a bed. The choice is limited between the *Cindrelul* hotel (☎069/41.37.27; ②) and the *casa turistilor* cabana (☎069/41.60.01).

From Păltiniş, it's only two or three hours' walk, predominantly downhill, through the **Cheile Cibinului** (Cibin gorges) past Lake Cibin to the *Fîntînele*

FASCIST PHILOSOPHERS

Răşinari was the birthplace not only of the anti-semitic prime minister and poet Octavian Goga, but also, in 1911, of the philosopher **Emil Cioran**. In 1934 he published *Pe culmile disperarii* (*On the Heights of Despair*), setting out the nihilist anti-philosophy that the only valid thing to do with one's life is to end it. He continued, with a total lack of humour, to expound this view in a succession of books, but has still not quite managed to actually do away with himself. In the 1940s he supported the Iron Guard, but later in a different political climate became less extreme in his views.

Another philosopher, **Constantin Noica**, spent the last years of his life in nearby Păltiniş. Despite holding right-wing views earlier in his life and spending years in communist prisons, he never repudiated the Ceauşescu regime. With a Platonic distrust of democracy and a fascination with "the Romanian soul" and with "pure" intellectual rigour, Noica preferred to criticize Western decadence rather than Ceauşescu's dictatorship. His admirers included both prominent supporters and opponents of the regime.

cabana, following the red dots. In the morning you can push on in a couple of hours to Sibiel village (see p.148) following blue dots, or direct to Sibiel rail halt following blue crosses.

However, the route barely takes you above the tree-line, so it would be worth while trying some **longer hikes** for two or three days. One route, marked with red triangles, leads in two and a half hours to the *Gîtu Berbecului* cabana, on a forestry road along the Sadu valley and then via Negovanu Mare (2135m) in the Lotrului mountains to Voineasa in the Lotru valley (buses to Lotru station). On this route you need to camp; the more popular route into the Parîng mountains, east of Petroşani, has well-spaced cabana accommodation. This route, indicated by red stripes, follows a mountain ridge to the *Cînaia* refuge (5–6hr) and then continues over open moorland (poorly marked with red stripes and red crosses) to the *Obîrsia Lotrului* cabana, at the junction of the north–south DN67C and the east–west DN7A, both unsurfaced and open only to forestry traffic. This is the gateway to the **Parîng mountains**, an alpine area with beautiful lakes; the red crosses continue up to the main ridge, from where red stripes lead you west to Petroşani.

Răşinari

RĂŞINARI lies 12km from Sibiu on the road to Păltiniş. It's a tight-packed Romanian village with a painted Orthodox church built in 1752, and an ethnographic museum. However, it's more noteworthy for the large Gypsy encampment (*ţara*) on its southern outskirts, and the village's annual Pastoral Album **folklore festival**, held on the third Sunday of April. **Trams** run from the Dumbrava forest (trolleybus #T1 from Sibiu station) to the north end of Răşinari, while an hourly *maxitaxi* runs from opposite Sibiu's *Piscina Olimpică*, on B-dul Victoriei, through to the south end of Răşinari.

In addition to the road, a track petering out into a path (marked with red stripes) leads from Răşinari's outskirts over the mountains to Păltiniş in six to seven hours. About an hour before Păltiniş, near Mount Tomnaticu, a path marked with blue triangles turns right to the *Şanta* mountain cabana, a few kilometres east of the larger resort.

RECYCLED BUSES

The tram line from Sibiu's Pădurea Dumbrava to Răşinari closed when the vehicles finally wore out. It seemed to be totally derelict, but surprisingly re-opened in 1994. This was made possible by the provision of **cast-off trams** from Geneva, which now trundle to and fro still bearing their Swiss lettering. Additionally the **trolleybuses** of line T#1, which run from Sibiu's train station to Pădurea Dumbrava, were donated by the city of Lausanne. You may also notice that the express buses from Otopeni airport to central Bucharest also bear Geneva route maps.

These are only the most obvious examples of a trend seen throughout Romania. However, the vast majority of the second-hand **buses** running all over the country are German in origin. Most of these were cast off by east German towns when they were given old buses by west German towns; but now a second wave of buses is arriving as the east German towns throw them out too, and invest in new buses themselves.

The Mărginimea Sibiului and Sebeş

West of Sibiu, the DN1/7 and the rail line travel through the **Mărginimea Sibiului** (Borders of Sibiu) towards Sebeş. This is a fairly densely populated rural area with a lively folklore, mostly Romanian rather than Saxon, and small ethnographic museums in most villages. You'll see many flocks of sheep on the move here, with donkeys carrying the shepherds' belongings, although they are notoriously well off in this area and could easily afford four-wheel-drive vehicles; most prefer to keep to the old ways. *Personal* and *cursa* services from Sibiu halt a short distance from several settlements en route.

The routes from Braşov via Sibiu and via Sighişoara meet near **Sebeş**, at Vinţu de Jos. Road and rail routes west follow the Mureş river towards Arad between the Apuseni mountains and the Southern Carpathians and you can change trains at Simeria for Hunedoara, the Dacian citadels and southwestern Transylvania. Other trains from Vinţu de Jos head north towards Alba Iulia, Cîmpia Turzii (for the Turda gorge) and Cluj.

The villages of the Mărginimea Sibiului

The first of the accessible villages is **CRISTIAN**, also served by hourly buses from Sibiu, where a double wall protects the fourteenth-century Saxon church of *Grossau*, with its massive towers. The *Hotel Spack* (☎069/55.92.62; ③), owned by a Saxon family and kept perfectly spick and span for visitors from the Fatherland, is just north of the train station at Str. II 9.

Cristian is followed by **ORLAT** (served by buses to Gura Rîului), with its medieval castle ruins, and **SIBIEL** (3km from its train station) where there is a tradition of **witchcraft**. Traditionally – and understandably in a sheep-raising community – witches and ghosts were more feared for their attacks on livestock than on people. While blowing horns to prevent *strigoi* from stealing their ewes' milk on St George's Day, villagers also credit witches with occasional good deeds, such as magically shutting the jaws of wolves intent on ravaging their flocks. In Sibiel you'll find lovely **paintings on glass** among the collection of peasant art in the local museum. Here also is the start of a footpath which leads uphill past a ruined citadel to the *Fîntînele* cabana and through the Cibin gorges to Păltiniş in eight hours (see p.146).

SĂLIŞTE, another Mărgineni settlement, is famous for its peasant **choir**, which sings in the community centre here, and for its co-operative producing carpets and embroidered costumes. The latter are displayed in the **museum** and worn during Sălişte's "Meeting of the Youth" **festival** (December 24–31). They're more likely to appear during the course of everyday life at **TILIŞCA**, an older, more eye-catching settlement tracing its origins back to a Dacian settlement on nearby Cătănaş Hill (where there's an unremarkable ruined fort). The main road passes to the north of all of these villages after Cristian, and the stations for Sălişte and Tilişca are also several kilometres north of the villages; in addition the Sălişte *han* is 6km west of the village on the DN1/7, all of which makes public transport slightly problematical here.

However road and rail both pass through **MIERCUREA SIBIULUI** (*Reussmarkt*), a village whose name derives from the word *miercuri*, Wednesday, the traditional market day – there is still a market here on this day. In the centre is a small, well-preserved thirteenth-century church, fortified like other Saxon buildings during the fifteenth century. Trains and buses also halt 5km further on at **BĂILE MIERCUREA**, a modest spa resort with a tourist cabana.

Sebeş

The town of **SEBEŞ** (*Mühlbach*) grew up on the proceeds of the leather-working industry, trading mainly with Wallachia. In 1438 the townsfolks' biggest client, Vlad the Impaler, arrived together with the Turkish army, demanding that the town be surrendered. A number of inhabitants refused, barricading themselves in one of the towers of the (now ruined) **citadel**, which the Turks burned and stormed. The only survivor, a student aged sixteen, was then sold as a slave at Adrianople (now Edirne), but escaped twenty years later to write *Of the Religion, Manners and Infamies of the Turks* – a bestselling exposé of the bogeymen of fifteenth-century Europe – signing himself the "Nameless One of Sebeş". The **Student's Tower** (also known as the Tailors' Tower), Str. Traian 6, is thus one of the main sights of Sebeş, together with a large **Evangelical Church**, perhaps the finest Gothic church in Transylvania, largely built between 1240 and 1382, and the sixteenth-century **House of the Voivodes** next door (now housing a **museum**) where János Zápolyai (see p.311) died in 1540.

Practicalities

There is little incentive to linger in Sebeş, but should you wish to stay overnight, there's the *Hotel 9 Mai* (☎73.13.72; ③) on the street of the same name, the *Hanul Dacia* (☎73.27.43; ③) on the DN1 on the east side of town, and a **campsite** at Băile Miercurea (16km east). If you are continuing west towards Arad and the border, you'll find lots of new **motels** (②) sprouting up along the stretch of the DN7 west of Sebeş, none of them listed in any tourist leaflets and most charging the same prices.

SOUTHWESTERN TRANSYLVANIA

Over the course of millenia, the stone-age tribes that once huddled around the caves and hot springs of the Carpathian foothills developed into a cohesive society, whose evolution was crucially affected by events in **the southwest**. The stronghold of the Dacian kingdom lay in the hills south of **Orastie**, and these were ultimately conquered by Roman legions marching up from the Danube through the narrow passes known today as the Eastern Gate (*Poarta Orientală*) and the Iron Gate (*Poarta de Fier*) of Transylvania. They founded their new capital, **Roman Sarmizegetusa**, in the Haţeg depression, which became one of the earliest centres of Romanian culture in Transylvania; it's still known for the *haţegana*, a quick dance, and some of Romania's oldest and most charming churches can be found here. To the north, the region has many medieval remains left by the Hungarians whose churches and castles dominated the main route along the Mures valley to and from Hungary – **Hunedoara** is the site of the greatest medieval fortress in Romania. **Alba Iulia**, one of the most important towns of this Hungarian-influenced region, is today at the centre of Romania's expanding wine industry.

This is a different world entirely to the smoggy mining towns at the feet of the **Retezat mountains**, in the far southwest of Transylvania, whose peaks feed dozens of alpine lakes, making this perhaps the most beautiful of the Carpathian ranges. It's deservedly popular with hikers, while further to the west, **winter sports** are catching on in the **Semenic** range, peppered with beautiful caves.

Alba Iulia and around

Heading west from Medias or Sibiu, you soon leave the Saxon part of Transylvania and move into an area where Hungarian influence is more apparent. However, while a Hungarian ruling class lived here for centuries, the peasantry has always been Romanian. **ALBA IULIA**, 14km north of Sebeş, was long a centre of Hungarian power in Transylvania, both spiritual and temporal, as symbolized by the Catholic cathedral's setting in the heart of its citadel.

The Town

Alba Iulia is dominated by a huge **citadel**, in effect the upper town, laid out in the shape of a star. The **lower town** east of the citadel was partly cleared for "rationalization" in Ceauşescu's last years, but remains a mess with the redevelopment unfinished and no definite plans for its future.

The upper town

The plateau on which the **citadel** stands has been fortified since Roman times, but previous efforts must have paled before the present structure. Between 1715 and 1738, 20,000 serfs under the direction of the Italian architect Visconti built the Vauban-style fortress, which was named *Karlsburg* in honour of the reigning Hapsburg monarch. Imperial levies on the countryside did much to embitter the Romanian peasants, who turned on their (mainly Hungarian) landlords in the 1784 rising led by Horea, Cloşca and Crişan. After the uprising had been crushed, Horea and Cloşca (Crişan cheated the excecutioner by suicide) were broken on the wheel south of the citadel, an event commemorated by an obelisk standing before its richly carved Baroque main gateway, above which is Horea's death-cell.

Within the citadel, the exhaustive **Museum of Unification** embodies the credo that Romania's history has been a long search for national unity. In the ornate marble Sala Unirii facing it, Romanian delegates proclaimed Transylvania's union with the *Regat* on December 1, 1918, as the Austro-Hungarian Empire commenced its death throes. Here, too, exhibits glorify the Wallachian prince, **Michael the Brave**, who briefly united Wallachia, Transylvania and Moldavia under his crown in 1600. In a fit of pique, the Magyars later demolished his Coronation Church, so unsurprisingly the Romanians built a vast new **Orthodox Cathedral** in 1921 (where King Ferdinand and Queen Marie were crowned the year after) filled with neo-Byzantine frescoes, including portraits of Michael and his wife Stanca.

The Catholic **St Michael's Cathedral** (daily except Sat) on the opposite side of Strada Mihai Viteazu testifies to the Hungarian connection, for István I made *Gyulafehérvár* (the Magyar name for Alba Iulia) a bishopric to consolidate his hold on Transylvania. Built between 1247 and 1290 in the Romanesque style and

△ Abrud

△ Cluj

Department Store

CFR

PIAŢA 1 MAI

Hotel Transilvania

Hotel Parc

CFR

CALEA MOTILOR

BULEVARD HOREA

STRADA PRIMAVERII

STRADA

STRADA TELIA

PIAŢA EROILOR

Bethlen Palace

Museum of Unification

Sala Unirii

Hotel Cetate

Monument

Orthodox Cathedral

PIAŢA UNIRII

St. Michael's Cathedral

Horea's death-cell

STR. MIHAI VITEAZUL

BDUL TRANSILVANIEI

Princely Palace

DECEBAL

House of Culture

STRADA TRAIAN

STRADA REPUBLICII

STRADA IAŞILOR

Trinity Church

Citadel

STRADA CETĂŢII

BULEVARD 6 MARTIE

ACR

ALBA IULIA

■ Execution Site of Horea and Cloşca

0   100 m

Train and Bus Stations and Sebeş ▽

loaded with the accretions of later periods, the cathedral contains the **tomb of Hunyadi**, the greatest of Transylvania's warlords (see p.155); a century after his death this was vandalized by the Turks, still bitter at their defeats at his hands. The **Bishop's Palace** facing the entrance to St Michael's is flanked to the west by the gate to the new town, while to the east stands the former **Prince's Palace** where the Transylvanian Diets met between 1542 and 1690. On the plateau southwest of the citadel are the remains of the Roman fortress of *Apulum*, once the strongest in Dacia; 100,000 Romanians gathered here on December 1, 1918 to hear the proclamation of Romanian union, not ratified by the Trianon Treaty until 1920.

Practicalities

Everything of practical importance is found in the **lower town**. Alba Iulia's **bus and train stations** are 2km south of the centre on Strada Republicii (DN1) and linked to town by bus #12. The parallel Strada Iaşilor (between the DN1 and the rail line) makes a pleasant walk from the stations into town; turn left at the police station and post office for the citadel.

Accommodation is limited. The newest hotel in town is the *Hotel Parc* at Str. Primăverii 4, on the Parc Central (☎058/81.17.23; ⑤). The *Cetate*, in the new town to the west, at B-dul Horea 41 (☎058/82.38.04; ④), is marginally more expensive than the *Transilvania* at Piaţa Iuliu Maniu 22 (☎058/81.25.48; ④), which also contains the **tourist office**. The only other alternative is the *Dintre Sălcii* **campsite** and *han* 2km south of the bus and train stations.

Around Alba Iulia

Many of the small towns around Alba Iulia such as **Aiud** and **Teiuş** also bear witness to Hungarian supremacy and the area is easily visited on public transport. Buses run west from Alba Iulia's bus station to Arieşeni, Baia de Arieş and Cîmpeni, all beyond Abrud in the Apuseni mountains, and there are regular services north to Tîrgu Mureş, Turda and Cluj.

Zlatna

When the centre of Alba Iulia was cleared for redevelopment, the narrow-gauge rail line that ran between the town and the citadel was converted to standard-gauge and rerouted via the junction of Bărăbanţ, just north. This now heads 40km northwest to **ZLATNA**, a centre of the copper mining and smelting industries since 1774, and a rival to Copşa Mică for the title of Romania's most polluted town. In 1986 a new plant opened, tripling output, and now the soil here is too toxic to farm, and the life expectancy of the workers (who are not given helmets or gloves) is ten years less than the national average. The central government is determined to keep the plant in production, and speaks of the environmental and medical problems as "fabrications".

Zlatna also lies on the road (DN74) from Alba to Abrud, Cîmpeni and the Apuseni mountains. You may want to stop to show some kind of solidarity with Zlatna's inhabitants, although the main reason most people come here is to see the **Church of the Assumption**, built in 1424, with fifteenth- and seventeenth-century paintings.

Teiuş

Heading north from Alba, through the wine country where white *Fetească* and sparkling *Spumos* are produced, the small town of **TEIUŞ** (*Tövis*) is best known as the rail junction where you change trains for Sighişoara, and few travellers leave the station. However it has several notable old **churches**, and the further from the station you go, the better they are, and the more likely to be open. Teiuş has the usual systematized *centru civic*, about fifteen minutes' walk from the station, but otherwise the atmosphere is that of a large village, with no visitors other than Hungarians on the Hunyadi trail.

The most interesting church is Roman Catholic, built by János Hunyadi (Iancu de Hunedoara) in 1449, and rebuilt 1701–1704 in the same simple Gothic style. It lies in a tranquil location just beyond the town centre, signposted off the road to Stremţ and Rîmeţ.

Blaj

Twenty-five kilometres east of Teiuş on the main route to Sighişoara is the small town of **BLAJ**, a rail junction for the branch line to Sovata (see p.163). There's little to see, its main claim to fame being its historical status as the ark of

THE UNIATE CHURCH

In 1596 the Austrian government persuaded the Orthodox Church in Galicia (now southern Poland and Ukraine) to accept the authority and protection of the Vatican, hoping to detach them from eastern, and above all Russian, influences and to tie them more firmly to the western fold. Thus was born the **Uniate Church** (also known as the Catholic Church of the Eastern Rite, or the Greco-Catholic Church). In 1699, the synod of the Orthodox Church in Transylvania, under attack by the Hungarian Calvinist Church, also voted to accept papal authority. However the new Church failed to carry with it most Romanian Orthodox believers, and became increasingly marginal when Romania's Orthodox Church gained autonomy in the 1920s. The Uniate Church stood for independence of thought and self-reliance, as opposed to the more hierarchical and conformist Orthodox Church, so the communist regime called its million adherents "agents of imperialism" and forcibly merged them with the Orthodox Church. Uniates remained a harassed and often imprisoned minority, with no status under the 1948 and subsequent constitutions (although these recognized the existence of fourteen other denominations or "cults"), until the overthrow of communism.

The Uniates accept four key points of Catholic doctrine: the *Filioque* clause in the creed (according to which the Holy Spirit proceeds from the Father and the Son, as opposed to the Orthodox doctrine by which the Holy Spirit proceeds only from the Father; the use of wafers instead of bread in the mass; the doctrine of Purgatory (unknown in the East); and, most important of all, the supremacy of the pope. All the other points of difference – the marriage of priests, a bearded clergy, the cult of icons, different vestments, rituals and usages – remain identical to Orthodox practice.

In certain areas, such as Maramureş, there is now a considerable revival in the fortunes of the Uniate Church, although hopes that it can again revitalize the country as it did under Micu and then the *Scuola Ardeleana* or Transylvanian School around 1800 appear misplaced. The new government also supports, and is supported by, the Orthodox Church, and the Uniates are finding it a long hard struggle to even reclaim their buildings.

Romanian nationalism. When Hungary revolted against the Hapsburgs in 1848, Magyar demands to re-incorporate Transylvania within the "lands of Stephen" provoked a famous Romanian response. Forty thousand Romanians, mostly serfs, were summoned by the leader of the revolt, Avram Iancu, to Blaj, headquarters of the **Uniate Church** (see box). They gathered on the **Field of Liberty** (*Cîmpul Libertăţii*) to demand equal political rights, chanting "No decision about us, without us" (*nimic despre noi fără noi*). This event is remembered nowadays in the **museum** in the bishops' palace, Str. Armata Roşie 2, and in the semi-circle of statues on the Field of Liberty, south of the town centre.

The town itself lies midway between the Blaj and Cîmpu Libertăţii train stations, about 2km apart, and there is one hotel, the *Tîrnavele* (☎058/71.19.50; ③) at B-dul Republicii 1, right at the centre of town.

Aiud

Back on the DN1, 11km north of Teiuş, is **AIUD** (*Nagyenyed*), which boasts one of the oldest **fortresses** in Transylvania, begun in 1302, and now containing a **History Museum** (Tues–Sun 9am–5pm) and two Hungarian churches.

From the **train station**, take Strada Coşbuc, just to the left, and after the stadium turn either right then left past the prison (used to hold many former Iron Guardists after the communist takeover) to the bus station for buses into the centre, or left then right past the market to Strada Transilvania, reaching the centre in 15 minutes. The *Mureşul* **hotel** is at Str. Transilvania 3 (☎058/86.18.20; ③)), or there's a **campsite**, *Căprioara*, 5km south of town on the DN1.

The Dacian citadels, Hunedoara and Deva

The **Dacian citadels** in the mountains between Timişoara and Sibiu are less impressive than the treasures and tombs of their contemporaries, the Thracians of Bulgaria. However, this part of Transylvania does have two striking medieval structures: the ruined fortress on the Hill of the Djinn overlooking **Deva**, and the huge, practically undamaged Gothic/Renaissance castle of the Corvin family at **Hunedoara**. Deva lies on the main road and rail line linking Braşov with Timişoara and Arad, while Hunedoara is accessible by rail from Simeria or bus from Deva. The Dacian cities, however, are further off the beaten track.

Orăştie and around

The jumping-off point for the Dacian citadels is **ORĂŞTIE**, a quiet town with two cheap hotels, 38km southwest of Sebeş. Buses meet trains very reliably at the station (3km east, where you may see narrow-gauge steam engines at work in the timber sidings), but in the other direction you should allow a bit of leeway (buses every 20–30 min). From the bus terminal by the post office, follow Strada Armatei south to Piaţa Victoriei and Strada Bălcescu. To the right, off Strada Bălcescu, are the **museum** at Piaţa Vlaicu 1, whose exhibits include Dacian relics, and the old **citadel**.

The *Hotel Dacia* is at Str. Bălcescu 5 (☎054/64.19.95; ①), with a good *cofetaria* for breakfast next door. On the same street, just off Piaţa Vlaicu, the *Mini-Hotel* (②) is a good private guest house. There are also half a dozen bungalows attached to the *Poieniţa popas* restaurant just over 1km west of town on the DN7.

Further afield, four buses daily head 11km north to the spa of **GEOAGIU BAI** where there's the choice of the *Hotel Diana* (☎054/64.82.80; ③), cabanas, villas or camping space.

The Cetatea Costeşti and Dacian Sarmizegetusa

Eighteen kilometres south of Orăştie, and served by six buses a day, is the first of the Dacian citadels, the **Cetatea Costeşti**, forty minutes' walk west of the *Popas Salcîmul* campsite and *Costeşti* cabana. There are only are vague signs leading you to the three rows of earthworks grazed by cows and surrounded by birch and cherry trees.

The largest of the citadels lies deeper into the mountains, accessible by 8km of bad road leading from the hamlet of **Grădiştea de Munte**. Buses only travel as far as Costeşti. Covering an area of 3.5 hectares, 1200m above sea level, the ruins require some imagination to conjure up a picture of the former Dacian capital from the weathered walls and stumps of pillars. Archeological evidence suggests that **Sarmizegetusa** was divided into three distinct quarters: the citadel, used as a refuge by people from the surrounding residential areas during times of war; and the remains of four religious sanctuaries. Grădeştii mountain was considered sacred by the Dacians, who called it *Kogaion*, and within the sanctuaries they performed ritual sacrifices to Zamolxis, Gebeleizis and Bendis – the deities of the Earth, Heavens and Hunting. Shrewd imperialists, the Romans appropriated the shrines and re-dedicated them to Diana and other figures in their pantheon, rebuilding Sarmizegetusa after capturing it in 106AD, and stationing a detachment of the IV Legion here.

Hunedoara

HUNEDOARA (*Eisenmarkt*) would be dismissed as a smoggy, ugly iron and steel town were it not also the site of **Corvin Castle**, the greatest fortress in Romania. Leigh Fermor found its appearance "so fantastic and theatrical that, at first glance, it looks totally unreal". The castle is moated to a depth of 30m and approached by a narrow bridge upheld by tall stone piers, terminating beneath a mighty barbican, its roof bristling with spikes, overlooked by multitudes of towers, "some square and some round and all of them frilled with machicolations". Founded during the fourteenth century and rebuilt from 1453 by Iancu de Hunedoara, with a Renaissance-style wing added by Mátyás Corvinus and additions by Gabriel Bethlen in the seventeenth century, it was extensively (and tastefully) restored between 1965 and 1970. Within, the castle is an extravaganza of galleries, spiral stairways and Gothic vaulting, with an impregnable donjon and a Knights' Hall with rose-coloured marble pillars.

The castle's **museum** relates the achievements of **Iancu de Hunedoara**, the warlord known as János Hunyadi in Hungary. Legend has it that Hunyadi was the illegitimate son of King Sigismund, who gave the castle to Hunyadi's nominal father, Voicu, a Romanian noble, in 1409. Hunyadi, the "White Knight", rose largely by his own efforts – winning victory after victory against the Turks, and devastatingly routing them beneath the walls of Belgrade in 1456. Appointed voivode of Transylvania, Hunyadi subsequently became regent of Hungary and a kingmaker (responsible for the overthrow of Vlad Dracul and the coronation of Dracula, see p.346), while his own son Mátyás Corvinus rose to be one of Hungary's greatest kings.

Practicalities

The **train and bus stations** are adjacent north of the centre: to reach the castle walk south for ten minutes down the main road, Bulevardul Republicii, and turn right onto Bulevardul Libertăţii. After five minutes, cross the bridge to the right, following the *castel* signs, and you'll reach the castle in five minutes more.

Once you've seen the castle there's no reason to remain in Hunedoara unless you want to break your journey. The *Hotel Rusca* at B-dul Dacia 10 (☎054/71.20.01; ④) is conveniently situated five minutes south of the station or there's the *Cinciş* campsite with cabins on the shore of Lake Teliuc, 14km southwest of Hunedoara and served by buses to Topliţa, Hăşdău, Lunca Cernii and other villages in the Poiana Rusca hills.

Deva

The county capital, **DEVA**, gathered around a citadel, is a slightly smaller and considerably more salubrious town than Hunedoara, 16km to the south. Raised during the thirteenth century and transformed into one of Transylvania's strongest fortifications on Hunyadi's orders, the **citadel** crowns a volcanic hill in the shape of a truncated cone – supposedly the result of a stupendous battle between the djinns (spirits) of the Retezat mountains and the plain, hence the fort's old nickname, the "citadel of the Djinn". Although the mason charged with building it reputedly immured his wife in its walls, in order to guarantee his creation's indestructability, a great explosion blew the citadel apart in 1849, leaving only the ramparts and barracks. A tough climb rewards with views over the Mureş valley – which enters a defile between the Metaliferi and Poiana Rusca mountains near Deva. In the park beneath the hill, the palace of Voivode Gábor Bethlen contains a **museum** exhibiting archeological finds from the Orăştie mountains. The adjacent building houses a natural history museum, and the *prefectura* opposite, on the corner of Strada Avram Iancu, has an art gallery.

Practicalities

En route from the train station to the citadel, you pass two **hotels**, the *Bulevard* (☎054/61.47.30; ③) on the main street, the semi-pedestrianized Strada 1 Decembrie, and nearby, the *Dacia* on Piaţa Unirii (☎054/61.47.30; ④). Two better hotels stand to the east of the centre – the new *Deva* at Str. 22 Decembrie 110 (☎054/61.75.15; ⑥) and the *Sarmis* on Piaţa Victoriei (also ☎054/1.47.30; ⑤), with brothel-style decor thick with grime. In addition, Strada Aurel Vlaicu leads 5km south to the *Căprioara* cabana, a good base for walks in the Poiana Rusca hills.

The **tourist office** opposite the Bulevard hotel can book beds in mountain cabanas for you if you are heading for the Retezat range. Opposite the post office, on the corner of Strada 1 Decembrie and Strada Libertăţii, next to the *CFR* office, is a **supermarket**, one of the few food stores in Romania where you can actually select food for yourself off the shelves. The *Crocus* **pharmacy** opposite the *Hotel Sarmis* is open on Sundays, but not overnight.

Buses from the well-run bus station serve destinations in the Apuseni, such as Brad and Cîmpeni, as well as Oradea, Petroşani, Reşiţa, Rîmnicu Vîlcea, Sebeş, Timişoara and Tîrgu Jiu. All **trains** on the main line to Arad halt here, making Deva a good place to pick up services to Budapest or the further corners of Romania.

THE FESTIVAL OF THE CĂLUŞARI

Around the second week of January, Deva hosts the colourful **Festival of the Căluşari** (*Căluşerul transilvănean*) which few foreigners see. Ensembles from Wallachia and southern Transylvania perform the intricate dances and rituals originally devised to ensure good harvests and dispell the *Rusalii*. In Romanian folklore, these spirits of departed friends or relations would take possession of the living should they violate any of the taboos associated with the Week of Rusalii following Whitsun – for which the only cure was exorcism by a group of *Căluşari* led by a *vătaf* who knew the secrets of magic charms or *descîntece*. The rite was also intended to promote fertility, and in the old days the male dancers were accompanied by a mute who wore a huge red phallus beneath his robes and muttered lewd invocations. Under communism such antics were discouraged and the mute carried a more innocuous wand covered in rabbit-fur; it'll be interesting to see if the phallus reappears.

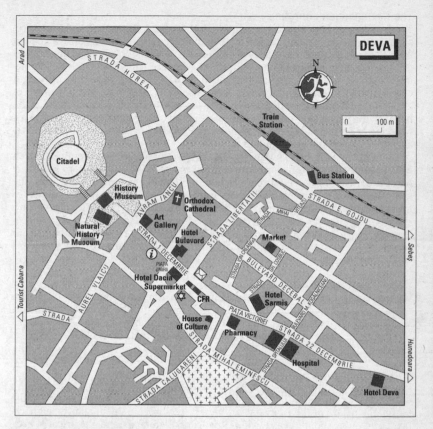

Haţeg and around

Fifteen kilometres southeast of Hunedoara, **HAŢEG** is the gateway to Transylvania's greatest Roman remains and one of the most convenient approaches to the Retezat mountains. Travelling south by rail from Hunedoara's junction, Simeria, you need to change at **Subcetate**, from where there is a 5pm train service to Haţeg and beyond to the ruins at **Roman Sarmizegetusa**. In addition to the ruins, you'll find a number of interesting **Romanesque churches** in the area immediately around Haţeg, which are reasonably well served by local buses.

There's no **accommodation** in town, although the **tourist office** on Piaţa Unirii (☎054/77.04.52) can help with bookings at the *Gura Zlata* cabana, 20km beyond Sarmizegetusa, and at cabanas further on into the mountains. To the north of Haţeg, on the DN66, the *Bucura* motel is situated right by a forestry reserve, home to a **herd of European bison**, long extinct in the wild; but there's no real reason to stop here if you're heading on to Sarmizegetusa and the mountains.

The Romanesque churches

North of Haţeg, both the rail line and the DN66 pass through **CĂLAN**. At first sight an ugly steel-making town, there is however a more pleasant spa (dating from Roman times) across the river to the east, with the lovely eleventh-century frescoed **church of Streisîngeorgiu** on its southern fringe. A couple of kilometres south of Călan, a similar church at **STREI**, dating from the thirteenth century, has fine fourteenth-century frescoes. From Silvaşu de Jos, just north of Haţeg on the road to Hunedoara, a road heads west to **Prislop Monastery**, at the head of the Silvaşului valley in the foothills of the Poiana Ruscă mountains. Founded in 1400, this is one of the oldest monasteries in Romania, but is remarkably little- known and very tranquil.

South of Haţeg is **SÎNTĂMĂRIA-ORLEA**, site of a thirteenth-century church with a fine collection of fourteenth-century murals. Twelve kilometres west of here, in **DENSUŞ**, a very strange little church has been cannibalized from the mausoleum of a fourth-century Roman army officer – most of what you see dates from the early thirteenth century, with frescoes from 1443. The south aisle is now open to the elements, but otherwise the interior is dark and gloomy, with a massive construction in the centre to support the tower's weight. Begin your search for the key at no. 15 (on the main road, east of the statue of the etymologist Ovid Densuşianu).

Roman Sarmizegetusa

Having forced the Iron Gate (see below), the Roman legions led by Trajan marched northeast to subdue the Dacian citadels in the Orăştie mountains. Within a few years they had founded towns, most notably Colonia Ulpia Traiana, to which the name of the old Dacian capital, **SARMIZEGETUSA**, was later appended. Today, the commune has a **motel** (☎054/77.73.60; ②) and **campsite** and serves as a starting point for the road to the Gura Zlata dam (see box overleaf); but its fame still derives from the nearby **Roman ruins**.

The excavated portions are only part of the original town, which contained a citadel measuring some 700m long by 500m wide. You can see the remains of the forum, the palace of the Augustales where priests were trained, and the elliptical brick and stone amphitheatre where gladiatorial combats and theatrical spectacles were staged. The **museum** (Tues–Sun) exhibits artefacts and stonework finds, and avoids mentioning the hypothesis that most of the glorified "Roman" colonists believed to have interbred with the Dacians to create the ancestors of today's Romanians were actually of Greek or Semitic origin (see p.308 for more on the Daco-Roman Continuity Theory).

The Iron Gate of Transylvania

Trains from Subcetate terminate at Sarmizegetusa, but even if you have no luck with buses it's only about 6km to Zeicani at the entrance to the **Iron Gate of Transylvania** (*Poarta de Fier a Transilvanei*), a narrow pass 700m above sea level. A monumental mace erected near Zeicani commemorates the defeat of 80,000 Turks by 15,000 Transylvanians under the command of Hunyadi in 1442, while further up the pass the Dacians had their fateful clash with the Romans in 106AD. As recorded by Roman scribes, this battle was a disaster for the Dacians: their forces were crushed, and their ruler Decebal committed suicide rather than be ignominiously paraded through the streets of Rome. The pass itself is 10km long, and while the DN68 cruises right through, rail services aren't resumed until the mining village of Bouţari on the far side.

The Retezat mountains

Although access is slightly harder than to the other Transylvanian mountain ranges, with longer walks in to the central peaks, the **Retezat massif** offers full recompense. Whereas in the Făgăraş or Piatra Craiului you find yourself for the most part following a ridge walk, with little opportunity to step aside and view the summits from a distance, here you'll find yourself surrounded by well-defined peaks, often reflected in clear alpine lakes. There is a large network of routes, so you'll meet fewer hikers and have a better chance of seeing **wildlife** such as chamois and eagles. The northwestern part of the massif is a scientific reserve; Ceausescu treated this as a private hunting reservation, but it is now being properly managed again. Entry is not allowed without permission.

Approaches to the mountains

There are three main **approaches to the Retezat**; from Roman Sarmizegetusa by a 20km road to the Gura Apci dam, on the west side of the massif; from various points along the Subcetate to Petroşani road and rail line, to the northeast; and from the West Jiu valley, to the south.

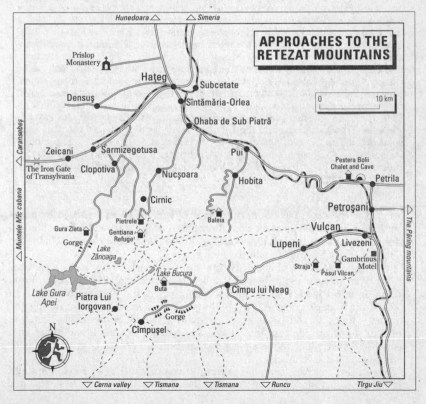

HIKING IN THE RETEZAT

FROM GURA ZLATA
The most popular hikes start from **Gura Zlata** beyond Sarmizegetusa. It's wise to reserve beds here through OJT in Deva, Haţeg or Hunedoara, since the cabana is always busy. Red stripes, blue crosses, red spots, red stripes again and blue triangles mark successive phases of the trail **between Gura Zlata and the Pietrele cabana**, going by way of Lake Zănoaga, Lake Tăul Portii and the Bucura Saddle. This hike should take nine to ten hours, but it is forbidden in winter. The Gura Zlata road continues 12km south to the "Mouth of the Water", Lake Gura Apei, from whose western extremity well-equipped hikers can follow a trail across the mountains to the **Muntele Mic cabana** in the vicinity of Caransebeş, or to Băile Herculane (allow 2 days). Heading east along the reservoir and up the Lăpuşnic valley takes you to Buta or the Bucura valley in 4 hours.

FROM CÎMPU LUI NEAG
Of the numerous **trails from Cîmpu lui Neag**, two of the most popular lead to the **Buta cabana**. Red crosses mark the quickest route (6–7 hrs), which runs through a forest of Douglas firs and up to the La Fete sheepfold, offering great views of the "karst cathedrals" en route. Red triangles indicate the longer trail (10–12 hours) to the cabana, which goes via the weirdly formed Scocului Jiului gorge, and the plateau of Piatră lui Iorgovan where you can sometimes spot chamois. A forestry road continues southwest over the watershed from the Jiu valley into the Cerna valley, and on towards **Băile Herculane**, a good two days' walk (see p.277); another path, marked with blue triangles, heads south to **Tismana** in roughly six hours (see p.101).

Buta lies in the **Little Retezat**, the limestone ridge south of the great glacial trough of the Lăpuşnic valley, which has an almost Mediterranean flora and fauna. However the best hikes take you into the crystalline **Great Retezat** to the north, past serried peaks and alpine lakes. From the south, there are two trails leading on from the *Buta* cabana: blue stripes designate a switchback path to **Cabana Pietrele** (7 hrs), dropping into the Lăpuşnic valley, leading up past the wonderful lakes of the Bucura valley and then down from a pass of 2206m past the *Gentiana* hikers' refuge; red stripes then blue triangles mark the trail from Buta to the **Baleia cabana**, going by way of the Bărbat springs and the Ciumfu waterfall (9 hrs; forbidden during winter).

The road to the dam starts from the village of **Rîu de Mori** (reached by buses from Haţeg, or a two-hour walk from Roman Sarmizegetusa) and follows the Rîul Mare valley (at least three hours' walking) to the *Gura Zlata* cabana. This is the point from which to strike out for the high peaks.

Another possible angle of attack is from the northeast, along tracks and roads leading from villages along the rail line between Subcetate and Petroşani. From **Ohaba de sub Piatră**, it's five and a half hours up to the **Pietrele cabana**, with buses (from Haţeg) going as far as Nucşoara, and even to Cîrnic during the summer – this trail and cabana can get quite crowded. Some hikers therefore prefer to start from the campsite at **Pui** and trek for six and a half hours up a steep, 23-kilometre-long mountain road to the **Baleia cabana** (see box above for hikes beyond these cabanas).

You can also approach from the **mining towns of the Upper Jiu** to the south – grim places surrounded by bleak mountains. The coalfields were first exploited during the eighteenth century and became an environmental disaster area under Ceausescu: the accident record remains appalling, and the rivers are black with coal dust. The miners are relatively well paid, but still strike periodically, seeking adequate compensation for their dire living and working conditions.

Petroşani and beyond

The largest of the mining towns is **PETROŞANI**, served by fast trains between Simeria and Tîrgu Jiu. However, unless you're interested in the history of the mines, related in a museum (Tues–Sun 10am–5pm) on Strada Bălcescu, the only reason to stop here is to stock up on food and try to reserve cabana beds through OJT, Str. Republicii 27 (☎054/54.17.33). If you need to stay overnight, there are two **hotels**, the *Petroşani* at Str. Republicii 106 (☎054/54.28.01 or 54.44.25; ③) and the cheaper and aptly named *Central* (☎054/54.35.82; ②). Less expensive accommodation lies a few kilometres out of town at the *Gambrinus* motel 5km south, the slightly more economical *Peştera Bolii* cabana to the north, and the *Rusu* cabana near the cable car into the Parîng mountains to the east (see p. 147).

Most people heading for the Retezat push straight on to the cabanas at Vulcan and Lupeni in the West Jiu valley. These are served by a branch line from Livezeni (south of Petroşani), although trains run through to and from Petroşani. From Lupeni a few buses continue up the valley to **CÎMPU LUI NEAG**, with a tourist chalet and motel (②), from where you can walk into the mountains.

THE SZÉKELY LAND AND THE EASTERN CARPATHIANS

In the ethnic patchwork of Transylvania, the eastern Carpathians are traditionally the home of the **Székely** (pronounced "Saik-ehyy"), a people closely related to the Magyars who speak a distinctive Hungarian dialect and cherish a special historic identity. For a long time it was believed that they were the descendants of Attila's Huns – who had entered the Carpathian basin in the fifth century, five hundred years before the Magyar Conquest. However, most modern historians and ethnographers believe that the Székely either attached themselves to the Magyars during the latter's long migration from the banks of the Don, or are simply the descendants of early Hungarians who pushed ever further into Transylvania, having been assigned the task of guarding the frontiers by King László in the twelfth century. Whatever the truth of their origins, the Székely feel closely akin to the Magyars who, in turn, regard them as somehow embodying the finest aspects of the ancient Magyar race, while also being rather primeval – noble savages, perhaps.

The Székely retained a nomadic, clan-based society for longer than their Magyar kindred, and were granted a large measure of autonomy. They were recognized as one of the three "Nations" of Transylvania during the Middle Ages: privileges that the Hapsburgs attempted to abolish, culminating in the massacre at Madéfalva (1764), which prompted many Székely to flee to Moldavia and Bucovina, where they founded new villages with names such as "God Help Us" and "God Receive Us". Today, their traditional costume is closer to that of the Romanian peasants, the chief difference being that the Székely tuck their white shirts in while the Romanians have them untucked and belted.

For visitors, the chief attractions of the region are likely to be the **Székely culture** and the scenery. Religion plays an important part in Székely life, as shown by the prevalence of their **walled churches**, the fervour displayed at the **Whitsun pilgrimage to Miercurea Ciuc**, and the continuing existence of Székely mystics. Traditional Székely **architecture** (blue-painted houses with carved fences and gateways, incorporating a dovecot above) can be seen in small villages throughout the *Székelyföld* (Székely Land), especially at Corund. The **landscape** gets increasingly dramatic as you move through the Harghita mountains, culminating in the Tuşnad defile and St Ana's Lake to the south, and Lacu Roşu and the Bicaz gorges just before the borders of Moldavia.

Into the Székely Land

This section describes two interconnected routes from the south into the Székely Land, starting in Sighişoara and in Braşov. **From Sighisoara** you can either head east to **Miercurea Ciuc**, the capital of the southern *Székelyföld*, or take a shorter loop to **Tîrgu Mures** via Sovata. Approaching **from Braşov** and the showpiece Saxon villages of Hărman and Prejmer (see p.130), the route follows the Olt and Mureş valleys through Sfîntu Gheorghe, Miercurea Ciuc and Gheorgheni, looping around to Tîrgu Mureş or through the Bicaz gorges into Moldavia.

Odorhei Secuiesc and around

At the end of the rail line east from Sighişoara, is **ODORHEIU SECUIESC**, western capital of the *Székelyföld*, and still known to residents by its tongue-twisting Magyar name, *Székelyudvarhely*. Unless you come for the *Seiche* **festival**, normally on the first Sunday in June, the main sights here are the fifteenth- and sixteenth-century **citadel** at the end of Strada Cetăţii (now housing an agricultural college, but you can go inside to stroll along the walls), and the two squares, Piaţa Libertăţii and Piaţa M. Aron, with three churches in a row. These are the former Franciscan monastery (1712–79, reoccupied by Clarissan nuns since the revolution), the Reformed church (1781) on an island between the two squares, and on the hill beyond, to the southeast, the Catholic church of Sf Miklós (1787–93), between the Jesuits' building of 1651 and the huge *liceul*.

The **museum** at Str. Kossuth 29 (Tues–Fri 9am–4.30pm, Sat–Sun 9am–1pm) has a fine ethnographic collection, with ceramics and *kopjafálva* (Székely funerary posts). The funerary posts, used only in the Protestant areas, bear carvings of flowers or the tools of the deceased's trade; some say that the posts hark back to the nomad days when a Magyar warrior was buried with his spear thrust into the grave. At the southern end of town, on the Sighişoara road, is the **Jesus chapel**, one of the oldest buildings in the area, built in the thirteenth century, with a coffered ceiling fitted in 1677.

Practicalities

Other than the *Tîrnava* **hotel**, near the Franciscan church on Piaţa Libertăţii 16 (☎065/21.39.63; ⑤), there is a *Sport-Hotel* (②) on Strada Parcului; and a spartan **campsite** 3km north at Băile Seiche. Odorheiu's **bus terminal** is on Strada Tîrgului, near the train station and market. Buses head north to Sovata and on to Tîrgu Mureş or east to Miercurea Ciuc.

Around Odorheiu Secuiesc

Southwest of Odorheiu is **DÎRJIU** (*Székelyderz*), a Unitarian village with a particularly fine fortified church with frescoes dating from 1419 (ask for the key next door to the church). Due west of Odorheiu, the church in **MUGENI** (*Bögöz*, near the *Dobeni* halt) dates from the fourteenth century and has valuable frescoes and a coffered ceiling, a distinguishing feature of Hungarian churches. Continuing west, on the main road and rail line to Sighişoara, the **museum** at **CRISTURU SECUIESC** (*Székelykeresztúr*) gives a detailed history of the ceramic industry, established here since 1590, with an excellent outdoor section complete with authentic chained dogs. Although buses stop in the main square, the train station and bus terminal are ten minutes' walk to the east.

East of Odorheiu Secuiesc, en route to Miercurea Ciuc, are several little resorts with low-key accommodation which are good options for breaking your journey. Four kilometres beyond the town, a badly surfaced road turns north through Brădeşti towards Gheorgheni and the isolated *Harghita-Mădăraş* cabana in the mountains. Back on the DN13A low-lying **BĂILE HOMOROD** has hot springs and a cabana used by Scouts and vacationing Trade Unionists, and both **CAPÎLNIŢA** and **VLĂHIŢA** have campsites. About 13km beyond Vlăhiţa, at the *Cabana Brădet*, a turning to the north leads up to another resort, **HARGHITA BĂI** (*Hargita-fürdö*) in the beautiful **Harghita mountains**, which has a hotel and cabana. There are occasional workers' buses up here or it's under an hour's walk from Vlăhiţa. These mountains are renowned for their abundant wildlife, including **bears**.

Corund, Praid and Sovata

CORUND (*Korond*), 25km north of Odorheiu, is famed for its green and brown **pottery**, as well as the cobalt blue introduced by the Germans in the eighteenth century. For the best choice you should poke around in the backstreet workshops (you might also find some of the carved Székely beamgates painted the traditional red and green) or turn up for the colourful **market** held on the weekend closest to August 10 every year.

For a complete change of atmosphere, push on to **PRAID** (*Parajd*), reached by local buses from both Odorheiu and Sovata. The **salt mine** at the north end of the village is still active, and there's also an underground sanatorium for chest complaints. It's a popular holiday centre, with private **rooms** (①) available from the **tourist office** at the bus stop, a fairly standard *han* just north, and a basic hotel (①) to the south.

Five kilometres further north is **SOVATA** (*Szováta*), with the resort of Sovata Bai, 3km to the east (reached by frequent local buses). It's a **bathing resort**, surrounded by beautiful forests, and based around a series of lakes that occupy old salt workings. A layer of fresh water on the surface of the lakes acts as an insulator so that the lower, salt water stays at a temperature of 30°–40°C all the year round. Sovata has four major **hotels** (④) above *Lacul Ursu*, with some villas now operating as private hotels and a growing number of *Zimmer Frei* (room free) signs along the main Strada Trandafirilor. In the lower town there's also a *han*, the *Ursul Negru* (③), the *Tivoli* cabana and campsite on Cireşul Hill, and another campsite out east along Strada Vulturului.

A single narrow-gauge **train** departs from the *Băile Sovata* station each day for Tîrgu Mureş, the regional capital. From the bus station on Strada Trandafirilor a dozen **buses** a day also run, by various routes, to Tîrgu Mureş, with other services to Sighişoara, Odorheiu, Miercurea Ciuc and Reghin.

Sfîntu Gheorghe and around

SFÎNTU GHEORGHE (*Sepsi-Szentgyörgy*), 30km northeast of Braşov, is a drab industrial town, a centre of the Romanian cigarette industry, but today at the heart of the revival of Székely culture following Ceauşescu's demise. The highlight of the town is the **museum** (Tues–Fri 9am–4pm, Sat 9am–1pm, Sun 9am–2pm) at Str. Kós Károly 10, south of the centre and a couple of kilometres west of the train station (take bus #3 or #16 and ask for the *muzeul*). Built in 1910 by **Kós Károly** (see box), the museum deals with the archeology, history and ethnography of the area, focusing on the revolution of 1848–49 (see p.313) and local figures such as Kelemen Mikes and Arón Gabor who were prominent in it.

The centre of town lies to the north of the museum, marked by the **Piaţa Libertăţii**, with a technical college by Kós to the west and the *Casa cu Arcade* (Arcaded House), the oldest building in town, to the east. North of the square, beyond the earthquake-damaged *Bodoc* hotel, Strada Körösi leads past the Romanian Information Service building to a Kós Károly house at no. 19. Continuing to the north, the cobbled Strada Şoimilor takes you into the old town, with a fine walled *Reformat* **church** built in 1547 at the top of Piaţa Kalvíny. In the cemetery, behind a Székely beamgate raised in 1981, you'll find stone versions of traditional wooden Székely graveposts, together with wooden pillars raised for each class leaving school.

Sfîntu Gheorghe's **train station** lies east of Piaţa Libertăţii, follow Strada 1 Decembrie 1918 to get to the square. The bus station is next door. There's a small private **hotel**, the *Consic* (☎067/32.69.84; ②) at B-dul Balan 31– head north from the *BTT* office, or take bus #5 from the station. The only reasonable place to eat in town is the vegetarian restaurant on Strada 1 Decembrie 1981.

KÓS KÁROLY

Kós Károly (1883–1977), or Károly Kós in the English form, was the leading architect of the Hungarian "national romantic" school, which derived its inspiration from the village architecture of Transylvania and Finland. The first is reflected in the wooden roofs, gables and balconies of his buildings, while the second appears in the stone bases and trapezoidal door frames. Fine examples of his work can be seen in Sfîntu Gheorghe and Cluj (notably the Cock Church), as well as in Budapest.

After the separation of Transylvania from Hungary, Kós, a native of Timişoara, was one of the few Hungarian intellectuals to accept the new situation and to choose to remain in Cluj and to play a leading role in Hungarian society in Transylvania. While continuing to work as an architect, he also travelled around Transylvania, recording the most characteristic buildings (of all ethnic groups) in delightful linocuts; these were published in 1929, with his own text outlining the historical influences on Transylvanian architecture, by the Transylvanian Artists' Guild, co-founded by Kós himself. In 1989 this was published in English by *Szépirodalmi Könyvkiadó* in Budapest, although it's well worth having for the linocuts even in Hungarian.

Ilieni

The old road from Sfîntu Gheorghe to Braşov runs down the right (west) bank of the Olt river to Hărman; 9km south of Sfîntu Gheorghe it passes through **ILIENI** (*Illyefalva*), served by buses to Doboli de Joss. The whitewashed **church**, built in 1782–86, dominates the whole area from its hilltop, and was beautifully restored in 1990 when the coffered roof was painted. The *Reformat* priest has also created an ecumenical conference and youth centre at the bottom of the hill, with **accommodation** in the church's defensive towers, a model farm, meat and dairy processing plants, and a children's village in which adult couples live with groups of four orphans, staying together for up to twenty years.

Covasna and around

The rail line east from Sfîntu Gheorghe to Breţcu runs close to **COVASNA**, 30km away, although the DN11 passes well to the north. Known as the "spa of the thousand springs", its Valea Zinelor (fairies' valley), to the east of town, is always busy with track-suited strollers from the **hotels** and the **campsite** along its length. Buses meet trains to take you the couple of kilometres to the modern centre of town, from where there are buses more or less hourly to the Valea Zinelor.

Covasna's main attraction is another kilometre further up the valley, an amazing inclined plane, built in 1886 as part of Romania's oldest narrow-gauge **forestry rail line**. Little is now left of the complex 760mm rail system, interconnected by funiculars, which used to serve forestry operations in the mountains of the Carpathian Bend, from the Oituz pass southwards to the Ciucaş mountains, but if you're hiking in this region you will come across its remains. You can still see waggons of timber from the logging settlement of Comandau being transferred by horse-power and lowered down the 1232-metre slope. At the bottom, the waggons continue by steam train to the main-line transfer sidings in Covasna. As other forestry lines have closed, steam locomotives have been transferred here, and there's a motley collection of machines built in Berlin, Budapest and inReşiţa as recently as the 1950s.

Covasna's only other claim to fame is as the birthplace of Sándor Körosi Csomas (1784–1842), who walked to Central Asia in 1820, visited Tibet from 1827 to 1831, and compiled the first Tibetan–English dictionary; he became the librarian to the Asiatic Society in Calcutta and is now buried in Darjeeling.

Around Covasna

The village of **ZĂBALA**, just north of Covasna on the Tîrgu Secuiesc road, boasts a sixteenth-century Székely walled church and an arboretum, while **GHELINŢA**, on a side road further north, has a walled church from around 1300, with a fine fresco. **TÎRGU SECUIESC** (*Székely Market*), almost half an hour beyond Covasna and served by trains from Sfîntu Gheorghe, was a major trading centre in medieval times and the first Székely town to be granted a charter in 1427. Today it's something of a backwater, but you can still see examples of artisans' houses dating from the sixteenth and seventeenth centuries, one of which contains the **Museum of the Corporations**, Str. Curtea 1. From here, or the end of the rail line at Breţcu, you can continue by bus over the Oituz Pass to Oneşti in Moldavia.

Băile Tuşnad and St Anne's Lake

To the north of Sfîntu Gheorghe, the River Olt has carved the beautiful **Tuşnad defile**, at the far end of which is **BĂILE TUŞNAD** (*Tusnádfürdó*), a bathing resort set amidst larch and fir woods, with three hotels and a bungalow-campsite, all easily spotted just south of the train station. To the south of the town, at Bixad, a road leads east to **St Anne's Lake** (Lacu Sf Ana) where there's a cabana popular with students. Beyond are rare peat bogs and the tiny spa of **BĂILE BÁLVÁNYOS**, also with cabana-type accommodation as well as the *Hotel Carpaţi* (☎67/36.14.49; ③). The lake, occupying a volcanic crater on Mount Ciumatu (2 hours' walk from the Tuşnad spa, following blue dot markings), is spectacularly twee and the site of a fervent **festival** on St Anne's day (July 26) – during the 1970s one festival turned into a nationalist demonstration attended by 6000 Székely. The local *Securitate* kept this a secret from their superiors, and Ceauşescu reportedly learned of it only because his son Nicu heard the story from a hitch-hiker whom he picked up in his Jaguar.

Miercurea Ciuc and around

The capital of Harghita county, **MIERCUREA CIUC** (*Szeklerburg*) is now an industrial city. The centre has been extensively rebuilt in concrete, with the wind-swept plaza of Piaţa Libertăţii at its heart. The main sight is the **Mikó citadel**, rebuilt in 1716, and now containing an excellent local **museum**, south of the centre at Str. Gh. Doja 2. Apart from this, the city's only attractions are two events.

On the third Sunday of May, the **Spring Festival** takes place at Băile Jigodin just south of town, providing an opportunity for the Székely to dress up in traditional costumes and make merry. Whit Sunday is the time of the hallowed **Székely pilgrimage to Şumuleu**, a Franciscan complex, 2km from town, founded in 1442 but largely rebuilt in the eighteenth and nineteenth centuries. The pilgrimage commemorates a Székely victory at Marasszentimre in 1442, and pilgrims garbed in black still fill the yard and church interior, singing hymns and queueing up to touch the wooden Madonna in the sanctuary. From the nearby hilltop you can see **Székely villages** dotted across the plain, either whitewashed or with old blue farmsteads.

Practicalities

Miercurea Ciuc is likely to be most useful as a place to stay the night. The best **hotel** is the *Harghita*, on Piaţa Libertăţii (☎ 067/11.60.90; ⑤); the *Bradul* at Str. N. Bălcescu 11 (☎067/11.14.93; ④) costs less, but the real bargain is the *Sport-Hotel* (①) behind it on Strada Patinoarului (Skating Rink Road), although you may have to share a room. There is also a **campsite** in Băile Jigodin.

The **bus** and **train stations** are both west of the centre, near the Odorheiu road; Ciceu station, one stop north, is the junction for the rail line across the Eastern Carpathians to Adjud. There are six buses a week to Budapest, as well as services to Braşov, Piatra Neamţ, Tîrgu Mureş and to local villages.

East into the Carpathians

Six kilometres northeast of Miercurea Ciuc by train lies **DELNIŢA** (*Csíkdelne*), where there is a fine fortified church. Three kilometres further, **NICOLEŞTI** (*Csíkszentmiklós*), also reached by buses heading for Ghimeş and the Trotuş

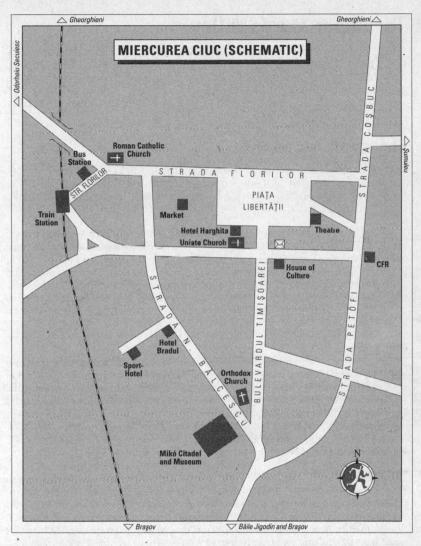

valley, has a lovely walled church on a hill, built in 1498 with Baroque additions in the 1770s. As the train hauls itself over the pass into the Trotuş valley, you'll see **Csángó settlements** (see p.204), where working watermills and blue houses with verandahs stand in orchards below steep hayfields. There are no real village centres, just a few shops in **LUNCA DE SUS** (*Gyimesfelsölok*), where there's an army base. Between Ghimeş and Palanca, is the site of the **grave of Emil Rebreanu**, executed by the Hapsburgs in 1917 for refusing to fight against Romania, and reburied here in 1922 by his more famous brother, the novelist Liviu Rebreanu.

The upper Mureş valley

From Miercurea Ciuc, a semi-circular route by both road and rail curves round through the Upper Mureş valley to the great Hungarian town of **Tîrgu Mureş**. It's a leisurely route taking in the tranquil Lacu Roşu, the untamed Caliman mountains and a plethora of attractive villages, including Gurghiu and Hoda, with renowned festivals . If you're travelling by train, you'll need to change at **Deda** for the branch line to Tîrgu Mureş.

Gheorgheni and around

Forty-five kilometres north of Miercurea Ciuc, **GHEORGHENI** (*Gyergyó-szentmiklós*) is important as a jumping-off point for **Lacu Roşu** (see below). The town's central square, Piaţa Libertăţii, is ringed with tatty buildings redolent of the era of Austro-Hungarian rule, and you'll find the **tourist office** here, on its south side.

To the north of the square, on Bulevardul Lacu Roşu, is the splendid *liceu*, completed in 1915, and to the east Strada Márton Arón leads past the Catholic church to the **museum** (Tues–Sat 9am–4.30pm, Sun 9am–1pm) on Piaţa Petöfi in a former Armenian merchants' inn. This is run by a dedicated young couple and the highlights include Székely fenceposts, weatherboards carved with shamanistic motifs brought by the Magyars from Asia, and bark salt-baskets. In the garden is a derelict steam locomotive that used to work the narrow-gauge line up to Lacu Roşu.

Practicalities

Trains arriving at Gheorgheni are met by buses to spare passengers the hike into the town centre. Getting back to the station is not so easy and you'll probably end up having to walk – about twenty minutes. The bus station is in a bleak area southwest of the *Hotel Mureş* (see below), but you can board buses on Bulevardul Lacu Roşu as they head out of town.

Gheorgheni's best **hotel** is the *Mureş* (☎065/16.19.06; ④) opposite the Trade Union House of Culture on Aleea Casei de Cultură. The cheaper *Viitorul* hotel (②) is on the south side of Piaţa Libertăţii, and there's a **campsite** 4km from town.

Lacu Roşu

Lacu Roşu (*Gyilkos-tó*), the Red Lake, lies in a small depression 25km east of Gheorgheni. It was formed in 1838 when a landslide dammed the River Bicaz, and the tips of a few pines still protrude from the water, which is rich in trout. Surrounded by lovely scenery and blessed by a yearly average of 1800 hours of sunshine, this is an ideal stop-over if you're crossing the Carpathians into Moldavia through the wild Bicaz gorges (p.212). It's a popular tourist spot and bus parties come here from all over Romania. There's good walking in the hills above the gorges, and a selection of bungalows, villas, a cabana and a campsite, although nobody seems to mind if you just pitch camp anywhere.

Lăzarea

Six kilometres north of Gheorgheni (one stop by train), the village of **LĂZAREA** (*Gyorgyószárhegy*) is worth a stop to see **Lazăr Castle**, situated just below the Franciscan monastery whose white tower is visible from the station. The castle's fine Renaissance hall and frescoed facade are being gradually restored by artists who hold a **summer camp** here each year, sleeping in the monastery cloister. Information is available in the village from the office of *Operation Villages Roumains*, the Belgian charity formed to combat Ceauşescu's systematization plans, and from the tourist office in Gheorgheni.

Topliţa and the Căliman mountains

The train line continues north from **Lazărea** to **TOPLIŢA** (*Maroshévíz*). The only sights of this third-rate spa and logging town are two wooden churches, Sf Ilie, 1km north on the main road (opposite the police station), built in 1847 and moved here in 1910, and the Doamnei Church 10km away, dating from 1658. The *Căliman* hotel at Str. Republicii 1 (☎065/14.29.43; ④), through the town centre across the river from the station, has a good cheap restaurant, but the facilities at the *Bradul* campsite, up the hill to the right of the station, are pretty dire.

To the north of the Mureş valley rise the wild, unpopulated **Căliman mountains**: a paradise for hikers, where you can walk for days without meeting a soul. The best way into the mountains from the south is probably from Rastoliţa, 30km beyond Topliţa. There's plenty of construction traffic on the road up to Secu where a dam is being built, and from here a forestry rail line runs northwest and paths head northeast to the volcanic peaks and the settlements in the huge crater beyond, leading ultimately to **Vatra Dornei**. In the narrow, rugged defile between Topliţa and Deda, retreating German soldiers made a vain attempt to ambush the advancing Red Army in 1944; the Romanian army, having suddenly changed its loyalty from the Germans to the Allies, had denied them the Carpathian passes, so the battle was largely lost before it had begun.

Now the valley is lined with various budget **places to stay**: notably the *Şoimilor* cabana, 2km west of the Stînceni Neagră rail halt, the *Doi Brazi* motel in Sălard, 3km west of Lunca Bradului station, and the *Călăoaia* cabana, 2km east of Deda-Bistra station.

Reghin and around

REGHIN, 30km from Tîrgu Mureş, is ringed by factories (notably its brewery, one of Romania's best, thanks to the pure water of the Gurghiu valley to the east of town) which have dispelled seasonal unemployment, traditionally the bane of rural life, but done nothing for the town's appearance; the only incentives to stop here are a couple of old churches and the local bus services to the villages of Gurghiu and Hodac, 20km east of town. Reghin's **bus** and **train stations** are conveniently located next door to each other on Strada Gării and there's a **tourist office** at Str. Mihai Viteazul 1.

GURGHIU and **HODA** are traditional villages of shepherds who were easily manipulated by extreme nationalists in March 1990; they were told that Hungary was set to annexe Transylvania, bussed to Tîrgu Mureş, issued with axes, pitch-forks and alcohol by the local priests and let loose on the offices of the Hungarian political party. Gurghiu is known for its **Girl Fair** (*Tîrgul de fete*) on the second Sunday of May when splendid folk costumes are brought out. At Hoda (7km beyond) the second Sunday in June sees the "Buying Back of the Wives" festival reaffirming the economic underpinnings of matrimony. To guard against a wasted journey, it's best to enquire at the tourist offices in Reghin, Gheorgheni or

Tîrgu Mureş in case the dates of these festivals change. The nearest **accommodation** is in Tîrgu Mureş, but there's no reason why you can't camp wild near the villages.

North of Reghin and served by slow trains between Tîrgu Mureş and Deda, **BRÎNCOVENEŞTI** is founded on a Roman site, with a five-towered **castle** dating from the fourteenth century, later owned by Sava Armaşul, a lieutenant of Michael the Brave. The village celebrates its most important harvest with the **Cherry Fair** (*Culesul cireşelor*) which normally takes place on the first Sunday of June. Brîncoveneşti is also the site of the first "Home for Irrecuperables" (housing handicapped orphans judged too sick or traumatized to recover) to hit the headlines in the West after Ceauşescu's fall.

Tîrgu Mureş

TÎRGU MUREŞ, now officially spelt Târgu Mureş, is still at heart *Maros Vásárhely*, one of the great Magyar cities of Transylvania, although this has been diluted by recent Romanian immigration. It has become notorious as a centre of inter-ethnic tension, due to riots in March 1990, largely stirred up by the right-wing extremists of the *Vatra* with government connivance, in which at least three died. It's also known as a centre of learning. The city's university is small, but the medical and drama schools are both renowned; under communism both of these formerly Hungarian establishments ended up teaching entirely in Romanian and consequently admitting only Romanian students, but now Hungarian-language teaching once again has equal status.

The town is also besieged by pollution from the *Azomures* fertilizer factory, near the main road and rail line to the southwest of town – it's liable to be an unpleasant experience entering or leaving town along this route.

The Town

The centre of town is **Piaţa Trandafirilor**, lined with fine Secession-style edifices, of which the most grandiose, at its west end, are the complex of the City Hall, Prefecture and Palace of Culture. These fantastic piles were built in 1912 and are typical of that era, when a self-consciously "Hungarian" style of architecture reflected Budapest's policy of Magyarizing Transylvania. Opposite the City Hall, its roof tops blazing with polychromatic, almost psychedelic, tiling, looms the **Palace of Culture**, whose stunning internal decorations required 50kg of gold. The most spectacular room is the **Hall of Mirrors**, whose stained-glass windows illustrate local myths (the caretaker should show you around, and guide tapes are available in French and German). In addition it houses a theatre, halls used for weddings (with special lotus-shaped chairs), and the **County History Museum and Art Gallery** (Tues–Fri 9am–4pm, Sat 9am–2pm, Sun 9am–1pm). This emphasizes the town's links with Moldavia, Michael the Brave and anti-Hapsburg fighters such as Avram Iancu.

Among the portraits, look out for the careworn face of György Dózsa (**Gheorghe Doja** in Romanian), a local Székely mercenary in Archbishop Bákocz's crusade, who thrust himself to the forefront in 1514 when the peasants' crusade became a radical anti-feudal uprising. After the rebellion's suppression, the aristocrats led by János Zápolyai arranged a particularly ghastly execution for

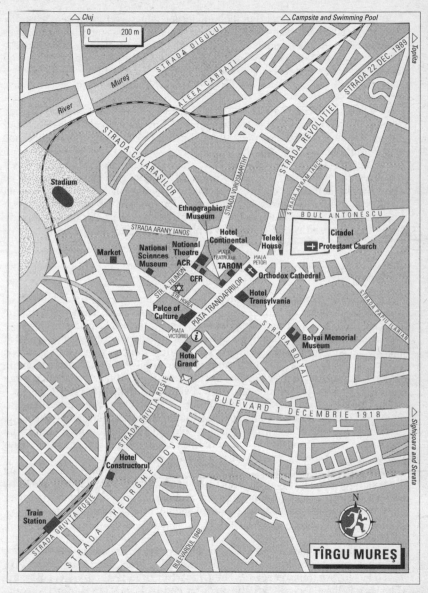

Dózsa and his followers at Timişoara (see p.272). The colourful **ethnographic section** of the museum is in the Toldalagy House at Piaţa Trandafirilor 11, a fine Baroque pile built in 1759–62, and the **natural sciences section** (same hours as the History Museum) is at Str. Horea 24, just beyond the synagogue, all rose windows and domes, at Str. Aurel Filimon 21.

At the northern end of Piaţa Trandafirilor, the neo-Byzantine **Orthodox Cathedral** (1925–34) was the Romanians' riposte to the imperialistic Magyar administrative buildings, pushing aside the more modest Baroque church of the Jesuits on its east side. Just beyond these is Piaţa Bernady György, dominated by the walls of the **citadel**, which shelter the Protestant church (built for the Dominicans in 1430 and often used by the Transylvanian Diet) and the Technical University.

Despite its longstanding role as a garrison town, Tîrgu Mureş also takes pride in its intellectual tradition; the mathematicians **Farkas Bolyai** (1775–1856) and his son **János** (1802–60), founders of non-Euclidean geometry, receive their due in the **museum** at Str. Bolyai 17 (Tues–Fri 10am–6pm, Sat 10am–1pm, Sun 10am–2pm), south of the citadel, which also houses Tîrgu Mureş's greatest treasures, the Teleki and Bolyai libraries. Count Samuel Teleki, Chancellor of Transylvania, built up a collection of 40,000 volumes, including many ancient medical and scientific texts and the works of the *philosophes* of the French Enlightenment, and opened it to the public in 1802. Another 80,000 volumes have susbsequently been added, as well as a hundred paintings by the Székely artist Nagy Imre.

Practicalities

Tîrgu Mureş, on a minor line between Razboieni and Deda, is poorly served by **rail**, although there are more *accelerat* trains these days, particularly in the summer, and a daily train to Budapest. There are also a few narrow-gauge services, including one a day to Sovata. **Buses** are often more use here, based at a large and well-organized bus station five minutes southwest of the train station at Str. Gheorghe Doja 52. There are services to all the major destinations in Transylvania as well as a weekly bus to Hungary. *TAROM* flies a triangular route from Bucharest to Tîrgu Mureş and Sibiu, twice daily Monday to Friday.

The **tourist office** at Piaţa Trandafirilor 31 is now a private travel agency, which will change travellers' cheques and Eurocheques but may not be able to do much else for you. The *TAROM* office (☎065/43.62.00) is also here at no. 6 on the square. Piaţa Trandafirilor is also the place to find food, either in the supermarket or in the several restaurants and snack bars.

Bicycles can be fixed at Str. Arany Janos 1. *ACR* on the modern plaza of Piaţa Teatrului will give you motoring information and advise on **car** repairs, while the *CFR* office, also located on the plaza, will make **train bookings** both from here and from Sighişoara, 55km south on the main line through Transylvania.

Accommodation

Turning left on Strada Griviţa Roşie out of the main train station, it takes under five minutes to reach Tîrgu Mureş's least expensive **hotel**, the *Constructorul* (①), which has its own *complex sportif*. The *Grand* (☎065/13.17.12; ⑤) is opposite the City Hall at Piaţa Victoriei 26, the western end of Piaţa Trandafirilor, with the slightly more economical *Transilvania* further along at Piaţa Trandafirilor 46 (☎065/13.33.71; ⑤). Other options are the *Continental* on Piaţa Teatrului (☎12.61.66; ⑥), the *Stejeriş* motel (☎065/13.35.09; ③) and campsite 7km along the Sighişoara road, and the *Ştrand* campsite at Aleea Carpaţi, on the River Mureş north of town take bus #14 or walk from Tîrgu Mureş Nord train station).

CLUJ AND NORTHERN TRANSYLVANIA

Cluj is the great Hungarian capital of Transylvania and a natural gateway to the region, just eight hours from Budapest by train. Largely due to the 24,000 students resident here, there is more buzz to café life than in other towns, and shops also seem better stocked than elsewhere.

The area surrounding Cluj, particularly the **Transylvanian Heath** to the east, harbours some of the richest, most varied **folk music** in Europe. Weekends are the best time to investigate villages such as **Sic, Cojocna, Rimetea** and **Izvoru Crişului**, where almost every street has its own band and there are rich pickings to be had at spring and summer festivals. Cluj is also a natural base for visiting the **Apuseni massif**, immediately to the west, with wide green pastures, easy walking and caving opportunities, particularly on the **Padiş plateau**.

To the north of the Apuseni is **Sălaj county**, a rural backwater scattered with quaint wooden churches. Further east, the historic town of **Bistriţa**, once centre of an isolated Saxon community, and today more widely known for its Dracula connections, still guards the routes into Maramures and northern Moldavia.

Cluj

With its cupolas, Baroque outcroppings and weathered *fin de siècle* backstreets, downtown **CLUJ** looks like the Hungarian provincial capital it once was. Hungarians still regret the decline of *Kolozsvár*, fondly recalled as embodying the Magyar *belle époque*, with a café society and literary reputation surpassing other cities in the Balkans. Most Romanians think otherwise: for them, Kolozsvár was the city of the Hungarian landlords until its restoration to the national patrimony in 1920, and consider Ceauşescu's addition of Napoca to its name in 1974 just recognition that their Dacian forebears settled here 1850 years ago, long before the Magyars entered Transylvania. To the Germans, who initially founded the city for the Hungarian King Geza, Cluj is *Klausenburg*, and for them, too, it had much of the glamour of the Magyars' capital. Cluj is also the birthplace of the Unitarian creed and its centre in Romania, further adding to the multi-ethnic, multi-faith cocktail.

GHEORGHE FUNAR

Gheorghe Funar, the "Mad Mayor" of Cluj, is notorious for his anti-Hungarian stance and you'll see many examples of his efforts around the city. In 1994, he renamed the central Piaţa Libertăţii, **Piaţa Unirii**, as "Unification" implies the union of Transylvania with the rest of Romania, and thus its removal from Hungary. Similarly, the lettering on the statue of Matthias Corvinus, on the main square, which used to read *Hungariae Matthias Rex*, now reads only *Matthias Rex*, and is flanked by six Romanian flags. An archeological dig was also planned (but blocked by the government) in front of the statue, presumably to provide a pretext for removing it altogether. Additionally Funar has raised a statue of Avram Iancu, the leader of the 1848 revolt against the Hungarians, near the Orthodox cathedral on Piaţa Ştefan cel Mare – this cost over a million dollars, apparently paid by businessmen including Ion Stoica of *Caritas* (see p.178), as well as by the central government.

> The **telephone code** for Cluj is ☎064

Under communism Cluj was industrialized and grew to over 300,000 inhabitants, but the city retained something of the langour and raffish undercurrents that had characterized it in former times, as well as a reputation for being anti-Ceauşescu. Now the city has a rabidly nationalist mayor, **Gheorghe Funar** (see box), who goes out of his way to offend the Magyars, still a third of the city's population, by banning all Hungarian-language signs and by constantly accusing Hungary of seeking to undermine Romania's government and regain Transylvania.

Arrival, information and accommodation

From Cluj's **train station**, it takes about twenty minutes to walk into the centre along Strada Horea, past the Mughal-style synagogue built in 1886, across the Little Someş river, where it becomes Strada Şaguna, and into the spacious **Piaţa Unirii**, the focus of the city's life. Trolleybuses #3, #4 and #9 take a loop route into the centre, going south on Strada Traian and returning on Strada Horea.

Arriving at the **airport**, by the main road just east of the city, take trolleybus #8 to Piaţa Mihai Viteazul, just east of Strada Şaguna. There are two **bus stations**, *autogară* 1, which is 4km east along B-dul 22 Decembrie, a few hundred metres before the Aurel Vlaicu trolleybus terminal (#4 from the train station, #6 from the tourist office, or #8 from Piaţa Mihai Viteazul or the airport); and *autogară* 2, just across the tracks to the north of the train station (bus #31 or #42), which serves the area to the north of the city, as well as Budapest (three buses a week).

The **tourist office** (Mon–Fri 8am–4pm; ☎17.77.78) is along the main road west from Piaţa Unirii, Strada Memorandumului, at Str. Şincai 2; take trolleybus #9 from the station. This is now privatized, but it hasn't changed much – it's always been primarily concerned with booking holidays on the coast.

Accommodation

Cluj has a wide range of **hotel** accommodation with appreciable city comforts but prices do tend to be higher than in most other towns in Romania. For student dormitory accommodation, try *BTT* at Piaţa Ştefan cel Mare 5 (☎11.80.67).

HOTELS
Astoria, Str. Horea 3 (☎13.01.66). Old-fashioned and pokey, with dubious characters hanging around. ③.
Casa Albă, Str. Racoviţa 22 (☎13.01.66). Formerly the *Feleacul*, now a very quiet and select stop-over in a small villa. ⑦.
Continental, Str. Napoca 1 (☎11.14.41). Once-grand establishment, still the classiest hotel in the centre. *ACR* coupons accepted. ④.
Delta, at *autogară* 2, north of the train station (☎13.25.07). A bus station hotel, inexpensive but grim. ①.
Melody, Piaţa Unirii 29 (☎11.74.65). Also known as the *Central*, with friendly staff, reasonable rooms, and a disco in the basement. ③.
Napoca, Str. Jósza Béla 1 (☎18.07.15). Modern building with restaurant and MTV, across the river from the Parc Central. ⑤.
Pax, Piaţa Gării 1 (☎13.61.01). Only 15 rooms (no singles), so it fills up fast. Small and gloomy, but handy for the station. ③.

Siesta, Str. Şincai 6 (☎11.55.82). No restaurant, which is actually a plus as there are no drunkards to contend with – you'll be given coupons for breakfast at the *Continental*. Recently refurbished. ④.

Sport, Str. Coşbuc 15 (☎11.67.62). Another modern building, grander than the *Napoca*, and in the Parc Central itself. *ACR* coupons accepted. ⑤.

Stadion, Str. Gen. Grigorescu 1. Located right behind the *Napoca*. ④.

Transilvania, Str. Călăraşi 1 (☎13.44.66). Luxurious modern place with indoor swimming-pool overlooking the town from Cetăţuia hill. Access only by foot (up delapidated steps) or by taxi. Formerly the Securitate's base, twelve people were supposedly gunned down on the steps in the revolution. *ACR* coupons accepted. ⑦.

Univers, Str. Tineretului 53, Cartier Gheorgheni (trolleybus #3, bus #34; ☎15.46.86). By a lake, with a marble interior, but only really convenient for truckers. ⑤.

Victoria, B-dul 22 Decembrie 56 (☎11.79.63). The Party's hotel until 1986, it specializes in rooms with double beds and no bathrooms, and is not the most salubrious of places. ④.

Vlădeasa, Str. Şaguna 20 (☎11.84.91). Pretty basic and not highly desirable, although the gallery is attractive. ③.

CAMPSITE

The **Făget campsite** is about 7km south along the DN1 towards Turda; bus #40 goes there occasionally, or failing that take bus #46 towards Cartier Zorilor until it turns off the main road, or any of the frequent buses to Feleacu and Turda, and then walk the last couple of kilometres.

There are also two **cabanas** about fifteen minutes walk from the campsite, and others at Cheile Baciului (west of Cluj on the DN1F and the rail line), and Făget-Izvor southwest on the DN1 towards Huedin.

The City

Unlike almost every other Romanian city of comparable size, Cluj avoided wide-spread demolition in order to build a Civic Centre, and the old central zone remains largely unspoilt within the line of its defensive walls. The walls have now been almost entirely demolished, although the overgrown remains of a fifteenth-century **citadel** (extended in 1715), surround the *Transilvania* hotel on Cetăţuia Hill north of the river.

Piaţa Unirii

Piaţa Unirii is the centre of the city and dotted with shops and restaurants. The square's centrepiece is **St Michael's Church** – a vast statement in stone nowadays far emptier than envisaged by the building's founders in the mid-fourteenth century, when the Catholic Magyar nobility ruled unchallenged over the city. Dwarfing the congregation in the nave, mighty pillars curve into vaulting like the roof of a forest, austerely bare of all but chiselled Magyar and Latin inscriptions.

Opposite the church, at Piaţa Unirii 30, stands the **Art Museum** (Wed–Sun 10am–5pm during restoration) housed in an eighteenth-century mansion, whose collection embraces icons, weaponry, carpets, a superb sixteenth-century altar from Jimbov, and paintings by Romanian artists, notably Grigorescu, Aman and Luchian. Many of the items were expropriated from the Magyar aristocracy, in particular the Bánffy family, who formerly lived in this house. The museum has been closed for a long period of restoration and, until the work is fully completed, you may only be admitted to temporary exhibitions in the basement.

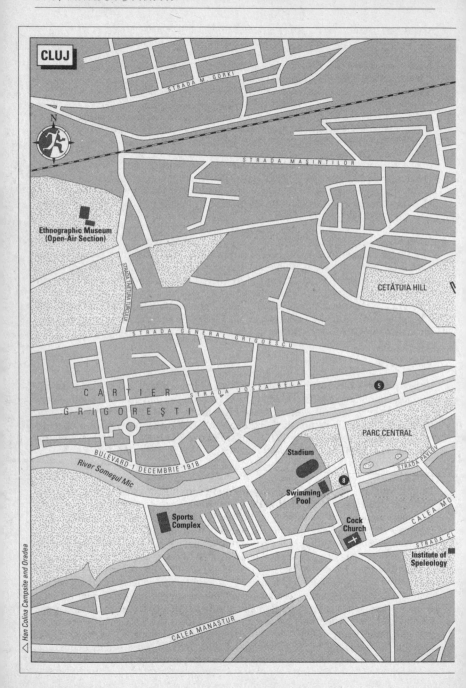

CLUJ

STRADA M. GORKI

N

STRADA MAŞINTILOR

Ethnographic Museum
(Open-Air Section)

STRADA NATURA IRCIU

CETĂŢUIA HILL

STRADA GENERAL GRIGOESCU

C A R T I E R   STRADA JOSZA BELA   ⑤

G R I G O R E Ş T I

PARC CENTRAL

STRADA PAVLOV

Stadium

BULEVARD 1 DECEMBRIE 1918

River Someşul Mic

Swimming
Pool   ⑧

CALEA MO

Sports
Complex

Cock
Church

STRADA CL

Institute of
Speleology

CALEA MANASTUR

△ Han Colina Campsite and Oradea

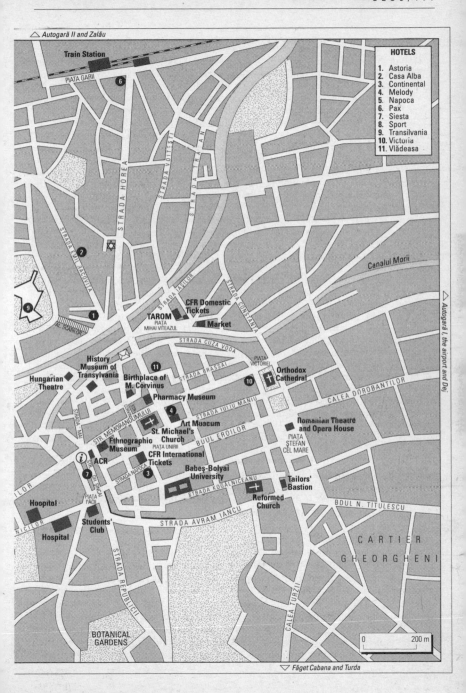

△ *Autogară II and Zalău*

Train Station

PIAŢA GARII

6

STRADA HOREA

STRADA VOMEŞTI

STRADA TRAIAN

STRADA EMINESCULUI

2

Canalul Morii

△ *Autogară I, the airport and Dej*

STRADA TAXILOR

STRADA CONSTANŢA

CFR Domestic Tickets

TAROM
PIAŢA MIHAI VITEAZUL

Market

9

1

AL. SCARILOR

STRADA CUZA VODA

PIAŢA VICTORIEI

History Museum of Transylvania

STRADA BRASSAI

Orthodox Cathedral

11

10

CALEA DOROBANTILOR

Hungarian Theatre

Birthplace of M. Corvinus

Pharmacy Museum

STRADA MEMORANDUMULUI

STRADA IULIU MANIU

Romanian Theatre and Opera House

STRADA MAI

4

Art Museum

BDUL EROILOR

PIAŢA ŞTEFAN CEL MARE

St. Michael's Church

Ethnographic Museum

PIAŢA UNIRII

CFR International Tickets

STRADA NAPOCA

3

Babeş-Bolyai University

Tailors' Bastion

i **ACR**

7

STR. BIS SUCUI

STRADA KOGALNICEANU

Reformed Church

BDUL N. TITULESCU

Hospital

PIAŢA IACII

NICILOR

Students' Club

Hospital

STRADA AVRAM IANCU

C A R T I E R

G H E O R G H E N I

STRADA REPUBLICII

CALEA TURZII

BOTANICAL GARDENS

0   200 m

▽ *Făget Cabana and Turda*

HOTELS

1. Astoria
2. Casa Alba
3. Continental
4. Melody
5. Napoca
6. Pax
7. Siesta
8. Sport
9. Transilvania
10. Victoria
11. Vlădeasa

CARITAS

One of the most bizarre episodes of post-revolutionary Romanian life is that of the **Caritas** bank, which promised investors eight times their money in a hundred days, creating a true mania throughout Transylvania and making a boomtown of Cluj for a while. In reality this was a classic pyramid investment scheme, which relied on deposits doubling every month to maintain its payments, and thus could not possibly keep going for more than a limited period. Founded in early 1992, it had three million investors by October 1993, and had moved from its offices in central Cluj to take over the municipal sports centre. Trains to Cluj carried four times their usual load, packed with peasants bringing their life savings to invest, and trains out were even more congested as they took their new televisions and microwaves home three months later. The town enjoyed goldrush prosperity, with many new shops and jobs, but it also suffered from an increase in crime.

Many similar schemes were set up elsewhere, but none enjoyed the success of *Caritas*, largely because its founder Ion Stoica had managed to use television to build an almost messianic image for himself, even claiming that he had been given the secret of success by God in order to help the poor. However, it was inevitable that things would fall apart; at the end of 1993 sixty-four *Caritas* cashiers were arrested and accused of embezzling L17 billion, and early in 1994 returns were running three months behind schedule. Stoica moved to Bucharest to drum up new business and opened branches in Snagov, Craiova and Focşani, but then vanished before finally being arrested.

There are many questions still to be answered, above all why the government allowed this patently fraudulent and probably illegal scheme to be set up in the first place and why it was allowed to continue for so long. There are many theories to do with laundering money made from drugs- or gun-running and Yugoslav sanctions-busting, or a government scheme to build an artificial boom and boost the value of the Leu by reducing the demand for dollars. This last does seem almost plausible, as the government has certainly come up with equally ingenious schemes for reducing the demand for dollars, and with at least $1 billion invested *Caritas* was quite big enough to produce macroeconomic effects in a country with exports (in 1993) of just $4.2 billion.

Further north, is the **Pharmacy Museum** (Mon–Fri 10am–4pm), in the *Hintz House* on the corner of Strada Şaguna, where Cluj's first apothecary functioned without a break from 1573 to 1948. Like the other pharmacy museums dotted across Eastern Europe, it displays ancient prescriptions and implements, as well as eighteenth-century aphrodisiac bottles.

The university area

The university area lies south of Piaţa Unirii, with Strada Napoca leading west to the **Students' Club** and the old library on Piaţa Păcii, and Strada Universităţii heading south past the Baroque church of the Piarist order to the **Babeş-Bolyai University**. Since its foundation in 1872 the university has produced scholars of the calibre of Edmund Bordeaux Székely (translator of the Dead Sea Scrolls), but has also served as an instrument of cultural oppression. Long denied an education in their own language before 1918, the Romanians promptly proscribed teaching in Hungarian once they gained the upper hand, only to hurriedly evacuate students and staff when Hitler gave northern Transylvania back to Hungary in 1940.

After liberation, separate universities were created to provide an education in the mother-tongues of each ethnic group, and for a while it seemed that inequality was a thing of the past. However, in 1959 the authorities decreed a shot-gun merger (prompting the suicides of several professors), with the predictable result that provision for higher education in Hungarian declined rapidly. This, and a similar running-down of Hungarian-language primary and secondary schooling, has convinced many Magyars that the state is bent on "de-culturizing" them. Outside the main door of the university stands a group of statues representing the **School of Transylvania** whose philological and historical researches provided fuel for the Romanian cultural resurgence of the nineteenth century and resistance to Magyarization.

At Str. Republicii 42, just south of the university, are the **Botanical Gardens** (daily 9am–9pm), the largest in the country with more than 10,000 species. They include a museum, greenhouses with tropical and desert plants, and a small Japanese garden.

Piaţa Stefan cel Mare

Strada Kogălniceanu runs east from the university, past the Reformed (Calvinist) church, built in 1487 by Mátyás Corvinus, to the restored **Tailors' Bastion**, supposedly containing a branch of the museum but always closed. The hole in the ground beyond this is to become a Uniate cathedral; until this is completed the congregation worship on Sundays in front of the statue of Matthias Corvinus on Piaţa Unirii.

North of the bastion is an elongated square, with the neat yellow and white **Romanian National Theatre and Opera** at its southern end (Piaţa Ştefan cel Mare), and the huge and startling **Orthodox Cathedral** at its northern end (Piaţa Victoriei). This looks as if it fell through a time warp from Justinian's Constantinople, but was in fact built in the 1920s, like many similar structures raised to celebrate the Romanians' triumph in Transylvania, and the neo-Byzantine stone facade hides a concrete structure. Inside, the frescoes, though religious in content, bear the ugly heavy-handedness characteristic of the 1950s, when Socialist Realism was the prescribed mode. From here, the direct route back to the centre is along the fine nineteenth-century Strada Iuliu Maniu.

UNITARIANISM

The first **Unitarian church** was founded in Cluj in 1556 by the hitherto Calvinist minister Dávid Ferenc (1520–79), and by 1568 it was already accepted as one of the four official churches of Transylvania. Unitarianism had its origins among the Italian and Spanish humanists and some of the more extreme Anabaptists, and one of its Italian leaders, Faustus Socinus (1539–1604), came to Cluj in 1578, before moving on to Kraków in 1580. There are now around 250,000 Unitarians in Romania, almost all among the Hungarian community.

Unitarianism derives its name from its rejection of the doctrine of the Trinity, as well as other basic doctrines such as the divinity of Christ, his atonement for the sins of the world, and thus the possibility of salvation. However, its significance lies in its undogmatic approach – adherents are conspicuous for their devotion to reason in matters of religion, and to civil and religious liberty, and their exercise of tolerance to all sincere forms of religious faith. They are also notable for divorcing at the drop of a hat.

West of Piaţa Unirii

The city's main east-west axis crosses the northern edge of Piaţa Unirii and heads west as Strada Memorandumului. At no. 21 is the main branch of the **Ethnographic Museum** (Tues–Sun 9am–5pm), in the palace where the Transylvanian Diet or parliament met in 1790–91. Here you can appreciate what is probably Romania's finest collection of carpets and folk costumes – from the dark herringbone patterns of the Pădureni region to the bold yellow, black and red stripes typical of Maramureş – and an even greater variety of clothing and headgear. While blouses and leggings might be predominantly black or white, women's apron-skirts and the waistcoats worn by both sexes for special occasions are brilliantly coloured. Peacock feathers serve in some areas as fans or plumes, and the love of complicated designs spills over onto distaffs, cups and masks. It also has an excellent **open-air section** (Tues–Sun 9am–4pm) to the northwest of town on the Hoia hill, with peasant houses and wooden churches from the surrounding areas; bus #37 may occasionally run from Piaţa Mihai Viteazul to the level crossing on Strada Maşinistilor, just north, but you shouldn't hold your breath waiting. A better bet is to take #27 from the station or #30 from Piaţa Unirii to Cartier Grigoreşti, and then head north from there.

The main road continues west beyond the tourist office as Calea Moţilor, and at no. 84 is the **Cock Church**, a beautiful Calvinist church built in 1913 by Kós Károly, who designed everything down to the light-fittings, all with a cock motif symbolizing St Peter's threefold denial of Christ before cock-crow.

North of Piaţa Unirii

Northwest of Piaţa Unirii, Strada Matei Corvin leads to the small fifteenth-century mansion where Hungary's greatest king was born in 1440. **Mátyás Corvinus** was the son of Iancu de Hunedoara, and thus a Romanian (although myth makes his father the illegitimate son of the Hungarian King Sigismund), but this was a virtual place of pilgrimage for Hungarians in Hapsburg days. His formidable Black Army kept the Kingdom of Hungary safe from lawlessness and foreign invasion for much of his reign (1458–90), but just 36 years later the nation was more or less wiped off the map at the battle of Mohács.

A popular lament that justice departed with his death highlights his political and military achievements; but Mátyás's reputation derives equally from his Renaissance attributes, for which his wife **Beatrix of Naples** should share the credit. By introducing him to the Renaissance culture of Italy and selecting foreign architects and craftsmen, and humanists like Bonfini to chronicle events and speeches, Beatrix was a catalyst for Hungary's own fifteenth-century Renaissance, and she personally commissioned many volumes in the *Biblioteca Corvina*. Outside St Michael's Church (completed three years before his death) a clumsy but imposing **equestrian statue** of the king tramples underfoot the crescent banner of the Turks.

Continuing north, Strada Corvin leads into Piaţa Muzeului where newly discovered Roman ruins are being excavated in the centre. The **History Museum of Transylvania** (Tues–Sun 10am–4pm) is just off this square at Str. Daicovici 2. On the first floor, strange skulls and mammoth tusks are succeeded by arrow- and spearheads charting progress from the Neolithic and Bronze Ages to the rise of the **Dacian civilization** (which reached its peak between the second century BC and the first century AD), and whose highland citadel, Sarmizegetusa, is reconstructed in models and pictures (see p.154).

Eating, drinking and entertainment

The best **food** is, as usual, in the hotels – the *Continental* is the best bet, with its splendid Baroque dining room. Elsewhere around Piaţa Unirii are the *Corvin* at no. 7 (Mon–Fri 8am–7pm, Sat 8am–2pm), the *Casablanca* pizza restaurant at no. 12 (Mon–Fri 8am–10pm, Sat & Sun 10am–10pm), the *Ursus* at no. 19, the *Gambrinus* at no. 25, and the *Someş* at no. 30 (10am–11pm); as usual, you'll probably end up choosing by opening hours, not by the menu. The *Nine Dragons* Chinese restaurant at Piaţa Muzeului 4 is also worth trying. Strada Eroilor has a disco-bar restaurant (until 11pm) at no. 49, the *P & P Ristorante* at no. 12 (Mon–Sat 7am–3pm), and a pizza takeaway at no. 26. There are also pizza takeaways on Strada Şaguna opposite the *Vlădeasa* hotel.

For traditional Romanian food and occasionally music, try the *Dacia* at Str. Memorandumului 13 (Mon–Fri 9am–10pm, Sat & Sun 10am–8pm), or the *Hubertus* at B-dul 22 Decembrie, which closes at 8pm every night. The *Pescarul* on Strada Universităţii specializes in fish dishes.

Bars include the *Gradina de Vară Boema* at Str. Iuliu Maniu 34 (daily 10am–9pm), which serves grills in a nice setting but with loud music, the *Casino* in the *Parc Central* (daytime only), as well as studenty places on Strada Napoca such as the *Bar de Zi* and the *Tineretului*. **Students** have their "House of Culture" on Piaţa Păcii, as well as other clubs at Str. Observatorului 34 and Str. Universităţii 7 (the *Bianco e Nero*).

Listings

Bicycle repair Strada Voiteşti and Piaţa Mihai Viteazul.

Bookstore The university bookstore on Piaţa Unirii has good dictionaries and books on Romanian ethnography and arts.

Car repair *ACR*, Str. 22 Decembrie 131; *Auto-Moto*, Aleea Moghioroş; *Gabism*, Str. Alvernaw 24 (7am–10pm; ☎14.52.52).

Exchange There are booths everywhere, but one worth noting is *KM 0* at Piaţa Unirii 10 (Mon–Sat 9am–6pm) which accepts Mastercard and Visa cards.

Libraries There is a British **library** in the university at Str. Avram Iancu 11, and a French *centre culturel* in the Academy building on Strada Kogălniceanu.

Markets Piaţa Mărăşeşti, to the east towards bus station 1, for basic foodstuffs, Thursdays; Piaţa Mihai Viteazul has a craft market selling work from the Apuseni highlands and the Transylvanian Heath, also Thursdays.

Pharmacy Late-night pharmacies are listed in the southeast corner of Piaţa Unirii.

Post office Strada Şaguna (Mon–Fri 7am–8pm, Sat 7am–1pm).

Shopping Cluj's main department store is on Strada Şaguna, opposite the post office. The *Iza* 24hr mini-supermarket at Str. Şaguna 34 has all kinds of fancy imported goods while the *Elvira*, on Strada Universitaţii, is more of an off-licence.

Speleological Institute The oldest speleological institute in the world, the Racoviţa, is at Str. Clinicilor 5 – pot-holers can check here for local information.

Telephone office Located directly behind the post office and also on the south side of Piaţa Unirii (daily 7am–10pm).

Travel agents Domestic rail tickets can be booked at the *Agenţie CFR* at Piaţa Mihai Viteazul 20 (Mon–Fri 8am–9pm); *CFR* international rail bookings office is at Piaţa Unirii 9 (Mon–Fri 8am–7pm), on the corner opposite the *Hotel Continental*. *TAROM* is at Piaţa Mihai Viteazul 11 (Mon–Fri 7am–2pm & 3–7pm, Sat 7am–noon; ☎13.02.34).

The Transylvanian Heath

On the whole, the **Transylvanian Heath** (*Mezőség*), surrounding Cluj, is a dull, though fertile region covered with huge prairie fields. The only reason to stop is to seek out the music that occurs spontaneously in villages, houses and sleazy smalltown bars. Finding the best – or anything at all – depends on local tip-offs and a bit of luck – it's often easy to spot musicians since so many of them are Gypsies (occasionally descended from the wandering *Lăutari* tribe) and thus noticeably darker than other people.

Bonţida, Sic, Gherla and Cojocna

In **BONŢIDA**, just off the DN1C, 27km north of Cluj, (and 4km east of the station of the same name), there's little to see but ruins. However, it's an atmospheric place, home to the remains of the Bánffy family's palace, once known as the Versailles of Transylvania, the greatest of the many Hungarian *castély* that reigned over Transylvania before World War I. The Trianon treaty marked the end of their power here, but many aristocratic families continued to live in their castles, islands of Magyar culture, in a style remarkably similar to that of the Anglo-Irish in Ireland at the same time. In March 1949, after the communist take-over, police dragged the remaining landowners away to prison and plundered their treasures, throwing uncounted books and papers onto bonfires while the houses were left to deteriorate.

One of the best places for music in this area is the village of **SIC** (*Szék*), further to the northeast. It spreads over several hills, with a number of churches and municipal buildings testifying to its former importance as a centre of salt mining. There's a high proportion of Magyars here and some Gypsies, their dwellings neatly thatched and painted blue. In defiance of Ceauşescu's breeding policies, villagers here only produced one child per family, so as not to further divide their land holdings; therefore the population is actually shrinking.

It's said that every street in Sic has its own band: typically three **musicians** on violin, *contra* and bass, sometimes with another violinist for a fuller sound. The violin plays the melody while the *contra* – often merely three-stringed – provides a chordal accompaniment with the bass. During the weekend **markets**, Gypsies inspire the villagers to wild **dances** with a stream of rough-edged music overlaying a pulsating bass rhythm. The Hungarians of Sic and other Transylvanian villages have preserved a taste for sounds evolved from the music of the ancient Magyars with Romanian *horăs* and Gypsy riffs brought from India and Central Asia woven in – indeed Sic is considered to be a kind of repository of Hungarian folk culture. Certainly, the Magyars here wear **costumes** the like of which have long disappeared into museums in Hungary: the men in narrow-brimmed, tall straw hats and blue waistcoats; and the women in leather waistcoats and black headscarves embroidered with flowers, blouses and full red pleated skirts.

The railhead for Sic is **GHERLA**, and seven buses a day run from here to the village. Gherla itself has been a centre of Armenian settlement since 1672 and was once called *Armenopolis*. The lurid green Baroque Armenian cathedral, built between 1748 and 1798, stands on Piaţa Libertăţii opposite the town's one hotel (③), reached up the stairs by the sign for the *Casă de Cultură*.

COJOCNA, 19km east of Cluj, looks and feels very different from Sic, having had a new spa town grafted onto the original village, which dates from at least 1199. Music here is less upfront and more a hybrid of Romanian tunes and Gypsy styling. There's really no need to stay at the spa hotel or campsite, since Cojocna is only a short ride from Cluj by *personal* or *cursa* trains towards Războieni and Teiuş; however, the station is a couple of kilometres west of the town.

Other excellent bands can be found in the villages of PĂLATCA (*Magyarpalatka*), VAIDA-CĂMĂRAŞ (*Vajdakamarás*), SUATU (*Magyarszovát*) and SOPORU DE CÎMPIE (*Mezőszopor*), all to the east of Cojocna, a few kilometres off the DN16 between Cluj and Reghin.

Turda

Modern TURDA (*Torda*) with its 58,000 inhabitants, mainly Magyar, produces chemicals and building materials, forcing you to penetrate a ring of filthy factories to reach its elegant centre. The main reasons for coming to town are to visit the spectacular Turda gorge, 8km to the west, and to explore the Arieş valley in the foothills of the Apuseni mountains beyond.

Turda was once one of the wealthiest towns in the country, as the grand stone houses lining its streets bear witness. The broad main square is Piaţa Republicii and on it stand two Gothic churches, one Calvinist dating from 1400 and the other Roman Catholic (1498–1504), with a Baroque interior. The latter housed meetings of the Transylvanian Diet, including the promulgation of the Edict of Turda in 1568. This recognized the equality of four faiths in Transylvania at a time when religious wars were all the rage in Europe, but merely tolerated Orthodoxy, the religion of the Vlachs, contributing to the ethnic and religious discrimination against them. Religion has a long history in Turda – fifth-century Christian tombs have been found among Roman remains and these can be seen in the museum, in the Voivodal Palace at B-dul Haşdeu 2.

Turda is well served by buses from Cluj (starting from *autogară* 1 and picking up at Piaţa Ştefan cel Mare) which drop you on Strada Gheorghe Lazăr, beyond the market to the east of Piaţa Republicii. Arriving by train at *Cîmpia Turzii* station, take bus #2 to Piaţa Republicii. Turda has one hotel, the *Potaissa* at Piaţa Republicii 6 (☎064/ 31.16.91; ③), and there's a campsite at the spa of Turda-Bai, on the site of Roman saltmines 1.5km northeast.

The Turda gorge

The Turda gorge (*Cheile Turzii*) can be reached on foot in under two hours, following red and blue cross markings southeast along the DN75 (west from the main roundabout below Piaţa Republicii). Buses towards Corneşti will take you part of the way – get off at the unmarked turning 2km beyond Mihai Viteazu, continuing north on foot for 5km. Either way you'll end up at the cabana and campsite just before the gorge itself. A footpath, marked with red stripes and crosses, runs up the gorge, overshadowed by 300-metre-high cliffs containing caves formerly used by outlaws. After about an hour, the path ends at PETREŞTII DE JOS, from where there are occasional buses back to Turda. These pass the village of SĂNDULEŞTI, where there's a fourteenth-century stone Orthodox church, a rare thing in Transylvania, as the Orthodox were then forbidden to build in stone.

The Apuseni mountains

The **Apuseni mountains**, southwest of Cluj, are bordered to the south by the Arieş valley and to the north by the Crişu Repede valley giving a variety of access points into the range, reasonably well served by public transport although you'll need plenty of time on your hands.

The **Arieş valley** runs west from Turda, between the Apuseni massif to the north, and various smaller ranges such as the Trascau and Metaliferi (Metalbearing) mountains to the south. Both the DN75 and the narrow-gauge rail line to Abrud follow the valley as far as Cîmpeni, capital of the *Moţi* highlanders. Having successfully resisted the Roman conquest, the *Moţi* moved from the valleys into the hills in the eighteenth century when the Hapsburgs attempted to conscript them into the army, and they now live all year round at up to 1400m, some of the highest settlements in Romania, in scattered groups of high-roofed thatched cottages. Along the **Crişu Repede valley**, most *accelerat* trains stop only at Huedin, Ciucea and Aleşd, but *personal* and *cursa* services open up countless opportunities for exploration by stopping at every hamlet along the line.

The Arieş valley

Travelling up the Arieş valley towards Abrud is frustrating if you're relying on the trains – they take five hours to complete the 93km journey, and there are only two services a day each way. Taking the morning train from Turda and returning by the afternoon service just about makes day trips possible. The attractive village of **RIMETEA** (*Torockó*), whose largely Hungarian population still wears traditional dress for the local fete on February 22, lies 8km south of the Buru halt. The third stop west of Buru, **OCOLIŞ**, is 2km south of the **Runcu gorge**, where there's a hike, marked with blue crosses, on to the *Muntele Băişorii* cabana. From **SĂLCIUA DE JOS**, whose festivals take place on April 4 and October 20, another three stops west, you can walk south to the **Huda lui Papară cave and the Rîmeţ gorge** (traversed either by a goat track along the cliff or through the stream itself). From the cabana and fourteenth-century **monastery** of **RÎMEŢ** at the far end of the gorge there are three buses a day to Teiuş and Aiud (see p.152).

Cîmpeni and around

CÎMPENI (*Topánfalya*), four and a half hours' ride up the valley, is the capital of the *Ţara Moţilor* and a feasible base for forays in to the mountains. There's a hotel, the *Tulnic* at Piaţa Avram Iancu 1 (☎064/77.16.97; ②) and a half-built campsite. From the town, buses run 30km northwest to **GÎRDA DE SUS**, a pretty village with old houses and a part-wooden church built in 1792, with naïve paintings inside. This is the starting point for several excellent hikes. The most popular, marked with blue stripes, begins near the **campsite** and leads through the Ordîncuşa gorges, past a mill and into a forest, emerging after three hours at the village of **GHEŢARI**. This is named after the **ice cave of Scarişoara** (*Peştera gheţarul*; daily 9am to 5pm), a few minutes' west of the village. The cave is filled with 75,000 cubic metres of ice, 15m thick, which has preserved evidence of climatic changes over the last 4000 years. At the back of the main chamber is the "church", so called because of its pillar formations, while the lower galleries, only discovered in 1950, are closed scientific reservations. From here it's five hours' walk north to the karstitic Padiş plateau (see opposite).

THE GIRL FAIR OF MUNTELE GĂINA

The **Girl Fair** (*Tîrgul de fete*) at **MUNTELE GĂINA** is the region's largest festival, and was originally a means of allowing young men who were often away with the flocks for two-thirds of the year to meet young women from other communities and – their parents willing – pursue matrimony. Naturally, would-be-weds made every effort to enhance their appeal, the girls being displayed in their finest attire, surrounded by linen, pottery and other items of dowry – even to the extent of carting along rented furniture. Nowadays this aspect of the fair has all but disappeared, but thousands still come for the music and spectacle.

The fair takes place on the last Sunday before July 20 on the flat top of Mount Găina, roughly 33km west of Cîmpeni. A special bus service transports visitors to the village of **AVRAM IANCU**, where there is a museum in the house where Avram Iancu, leader of the 1848 revolt against the Hungarians (see p.313), was born in 1824. The village hosts a large and lively fair and some people never get beyond this, but the real action is on the hilltop, and you should really be there, camping, the night before. A rough forestry road takes an 8km loop to reach the hilltop, but you can find more direct routes on foot. The biggest names in *muzică populară* appear here, with local dance ensembles, and plenty of food and drink; but there is little drunkenness and everyone behaves well, with Romanian Information Service troops (unarmed) in attendance.

The train line heads south from Cîmpeni to its penultimate stop, **ROŞIA MONTANA**, where another subterranean curiosity lies a few kilometres to the east. Evidence suggests that Transylvania was a major source of gold for the ancient world – the Romans certainly used slaves to mine these mountains and twenty-four wax tablets recording details of the operation have been found. These can be seen in the **mining museum**, the highlight of which is a 400-metre section of the winding, ancient galleries, romantically dubbed the **Citadels of Gold**, but now overwhelmed by present-day mining operations. Trains terminate at **ABRUD**, whose medieval buildings incorporate stones from earlier Roman structures. There are good bus connections from here southwest to Brad, southeast to Zlatna and Alba Iulia, and east to **BUCIUM**, 13km away. This is the centre for some thirty small mining villages and the starting point for an hour's climb to two basalt crags known as the **Detunata**. As in Slovakia and Silesia the miners here have a ceremonial "uniform", and the local folk costume combines elements of this with traditional highland wear.

The Padiş Plateau

The focal point of the Apuseni region is the **Padiş Plateau** (*Plateul Padiş*), a paradise of caves, gullies and subterranean rivers. Motorists and cyclists can approach with care from the west via Pietroasa, or from the east via Răchiţele or Poiana Horea. There are buses from Huedin to Răchiţele and Poiana Horea (two or three a day, but no service at weekends), from where it's an easy day's hike to Padiş. If you're **hiking**, it's easier to approach from Scarişoara, to the south; a track marked with blue stripes brings you in five hours to the **Cabana Padiş**, the crossroads of the plateau. This is a classic karst area, with streams vanishing underground and reappearing, and dips and hollows everywhere, all promising access to the huge cave systems that lie beneath the plateau.

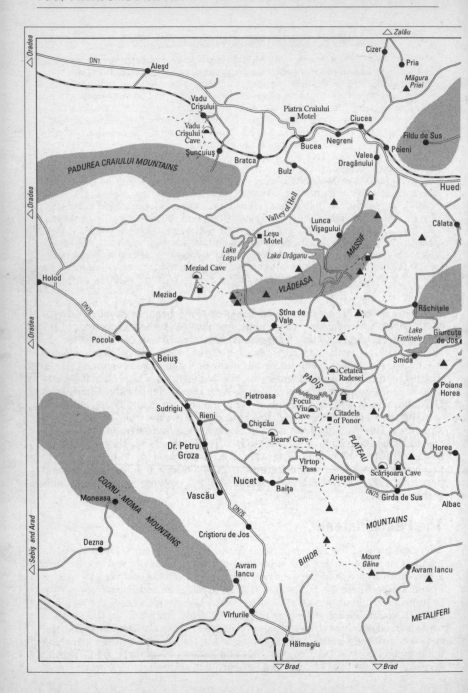

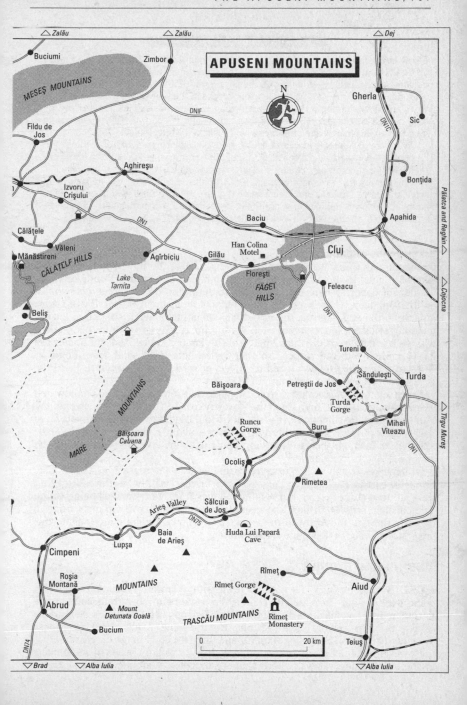

△ Zalău △ Zalău △ Dej

APUSENI MOUNTAINS

N

Buciumi
Zimbor
MEŞEŞ MOUNTAINS
Gherla
Sic
Fildu de Jos
DNIF
DNIC
Aghireşu
Bonţida
Izvoru Crişului
DN1
Baciu
Apahida
Călăţele
Văleni
Han Colina Motel
Agîrbiciu
Gilău
Floreşti
Cluj
Mănăstireni
CĂLĂŢELF HILLS
Lake Tarnita
FĂGET HILLS
Feleacu
Beliş
DN1
Tureni
Sănduleşti
Turda
Băişoara
Petreştii de Jos
MOUNTAINS
Turda Gorge
Mihai Viteazu
Băişoara Cabana
Runcu Gorge
Buru
DN1
MARE
Ocoliş
Rimetea
Arieş Valley
Sălcuia de Jos
DN75
Lupşa
Baia de Arieş
Huda Lui Papară Cave
Rîmeţ
Aiud
Cimpeni
Roşia Montană
MOUNTAINS
Rîmeţ Gorge
Abrud
Mount Detunata Goală
TRASCĂU MOUNTAINS
Rîmeţ Monastery
DN74
Bucium
Teiuş

0   20 km

▽ Brad   ▽ Alba Iulia   ▽ Alba Iulia

Pălatca and Reghin △   △ Cojocna   △ Tîrgu Mureş

KARST TOPOGRAPHY

Karst landscapes are formed by the action of rainwater on limestone. Rain picks up small amounts of carbon dioxide from the atmosphere as it falls, forming a weak carbonic acid which, when it falls on limestone rock, slowly dissolves it. Gradually, over millions of years, this causes hairline cracks in the limestone, which are steadily enlarged by running water. In its early stages, karst scenery is characterized by thin, narrow ridges and fissures; as these grow and deepen, the dry limestone is raked into wild, sharp-edged fragments and bleached white, like shards of bone.

Rivers are also affected in karst landscapes, disappearing down holes where the limestone is weakest, and flowing for miles underground, suddenly bursting from rocks where the geology changes. If an underground river widens and forms a cavern, the drips of rainwater percolating through the soil above will deposit miniscule amounts of the calcium bicarbonate that the rain has dissolved from the limestone above. Over millions of years these deposits form stalactites and stalagmites which are often coloured by traces of other minerals such as iron and copper.

Hikes on the plateau

Of the various **trails** starting from the *Padiş* cabana, the most popular, marked with blue dots, leads to the underground complex of **Cetăţile Ponorului** (the Citadels of Ponor), where the Ponor stream flows through a series of sinkholes up to 150m deep. There's a good camping spot en route at Glavoi. If you return directly to the *Padiş* cabana the round trip should take about six hours, but it's tempting to take a longer route back via the **Focu Viu** cave – a trail is marked with yellow dots from the third hollow of the Ponor Citadel, and the homeward leg is marked with red stripes. Another option is to head south from Ponor to Arieşeni (see p.267) following red triangles, or west from Focu Viu to Pietroasa (see p.266), following yellow dots and triangles.

North of the *Padiş* cabana, you can hike to **Cetatea Rădesei**; follow red stripes along a track and then the forestry road. Ten minutes beyond the Vărăşoaia pass, take another path (red dots) to the right to the citadel itself. Here you can follow the stream through a cave – slightly spooky but quite safe, although a flashlight helps. Emerging you can return over the top, seeing the various skylights from above.

Other hikes simply follow forestry roads, west to Pietroasa (marked by blue crosses), east to Răchiţele or Poiana Horea (unmarked), or northwest to **Stîna de Vale** (red stripes). This last route continues from Vărăşoaia, climbing to the Cumpănatelu saddle (1640m) and eventually turning right off the main ridge to descend through the forest to the resort (see below). Unlike most trails in this area, this six-hour walk is quite safe in winter.

Huedin and around

HUEDIN (*Bánffyhunyad*) is a small town with a largely systematized centre, 46km west of Cluj. The sixteenth-century Protestant church with its solid guard-tower survives and inside (ask at the parish office opposite), there's a delightfully wonky coffered ceiling. Huedin's one **hotel** is the modern but charmless *Vlădeasa* (☎064/25.15. 90 after 3pm; ②) and there's a good range of *cofetărie*.

However the chief reason for stopping here is to pick up buses to settlements in the surrounding valleys, where traditional customs, architecture and crafts, both Romanian and Magyar, have so far escaped obliteration by the twentieth century. Huedin's **bus station** is five minutes west of the train station and both are just five minutes north of the centre of town. Most of the surrounding villages are served by two or three buses a day during the week, but the service is virtually nonexistent at weekends.

Villages around Huedin

Heading south, the Magyars of CĂLATA (*Nagykalota*) still wear their home-made **folk costumes**, and in CĂLĂŢELE (*Kiskalota*) you'll see carved wooden home-steads. The road continues to BELIŞ (*Jósikafalva*), where a resort, with chalets and camping, is being developed beside the artificial Lake Fîntinele.

To the southeast of Huedin lies MĂNĂSTIRENI (*Magyargyerőmonostor*), with a thirteenth-century walled church whose gallery and pews were beautifully painted in the eighteenth century. Just west is VĂLENI (*Magyarvalkó*), where many of the houses have decorated mouldings. Its Gothic monastery church has a wonderful hilltop setting with a collection of carved wooden graveposts.

In the valleys to the north of Huedin there are half a dozen villages with striking **wooden churches** – examples of the Gothic-inspired *bisericii de lemn* which once reared above peasant settlements from the Tisa to the Carpathians. The most spectacular, and the nearest to Huedin, towers over FILDU DE SUS (*Felsőfüld*), a small village linked by 10km of track to Fildu de Jos (*Alsófüld*) on

---

THE CULTURE OF THE KALOTASZEG

The area immediately west of Cluj, known to Hungarians as **Kalotaszeg**, has, since the great Hungarian Millenium Exhibition of 1896, been seen by them as the place where authentic Magyar culture has survived in a less corrupted form than anywhere else. It's not uncommon here to see local people selling handicrafts by the roadside – particularly to Hungarian tourists on virtual pilgrimages to the well-springs of Magyar culture. The local **embroidery** is particularly famous; the style known as *írásos*, meaning "drawn" or "written", because the designs are drawn onto the cloth (traditionally with a mixture of milk and soot) before embroidering. They are usually stylized leaves and flowers, in one bold colour (usually bright red) on a white background.

The Calvinist churches of these villages are noted for their **coffered ceilings**, made up of square panels (often called "cassettes"), beautifully painted in the eighteenth century, like the pews and galleries, in a naïve style similar to the embroidery. The architects of the "national romantic" school, led by Károly Kós (see p.164), were strongly influenced by Transylvanian village architecture, as well as by that of the Finns, the Magyars' only relations.

The composers **Béla Bartók and Zoltán Kodály** put together fine collections of Transylvanian handicrafts, and Bartók's collection of carved furniture from Izvoru Crişului (*Körösfő*) can be seen in his home in Budapest. However their main object was to collect the **folk music** of Transylvania; starting in 1907, they managed, despite local suspicion of the "monster" (their apparatus for recording onto phonograph cylinders), to record and catalogue thousands of melodies, setting high standards of musical ethnography while discovering a rich vein of inspiration for their own compositions. Bartók believed that a genuine peasant melody was "quite as much a masterpiece in miniature as a Bach fugue or a Mozart sonata... a classic example of the expression of a musical thought in its most conceivably concise form, with the avoidance of all that is superfluous".

the Huedin–Zalău road. Built in 1727, it was painted in 1860, with scenes of Daniel in the den with some wonderful grinning lions. Other churches lie to the north, along the main road from Cluj to Zalău; the oldest, erected during the sixteenth century, is at **ZIMBOR** (*Magyarzsombor*). Later churches show developing flourishes including carved wooden gates, such as those at **SÎNMIHAIU ALMAŞULUI** (*Almásszentmihály*). From here a minor road heads for Jibou, past **HIDA** (*Hídalmás*), 4km north, and **RACÎŞ** (*Almásrákos*), a further 6km, whose churches are distinguished by carved columns and old murals.

Ciucea and beyond

Twenty kilometres west by train or along the DN1 from Huedin is **CIUCEA** (*Csucsa*). At the east end of the village is a **museum** (Tues–Sun 10am–5pm) dedicated to the poet and politician **Octavian Goga** (see box). The Hungarian poet **Endre Ady** lived in the village until 1917, and after his death, Goga bought his house and had a sixteenth-century **wooden church** from Gălpîia brought here. Later still Goga's own mausoleum was built in the grounds.

The Measurement of the Milk at Măgura Priei

Like pastoral folk in Bulgaria, Spain and Greece, the Romanian highlanders entrust their sheep and goats to shepherds, who spend summer in the high pastures protecting the flock from bears and wolves and making cheeses for the community's winter sustenance. In Romania, this has given rise to *Măsurisul laptelui* (Measurement of the Milk festivals), held in the villages around Ciucea, on the slopes of **Măgura Priei**, the highest ridge in the Mezeş range.

At dawn on the first Sunday in May, the shepherds bring the flocks, which have spent a couple of days grazing on the new grass in the hills, to meet the villagers in a glade where the "measurement" takes place. The she-goats are milked by women and the ewes are milked by shepherds – the yield of each family's animals is measured to determine the quota of cheese that they will receive at season's end. The ritual is accompanied by much feasting and dancing.

Măgura Priei is only a couple of kilometres north of the road from Ciucea to Românaşi, but most people approach from **PRIA**, to the north. The daily bus from Zalău to Ciucea will drop you at the turning, just north of Cizer, from where it's about 4km to the village. Camping is the best bet as the only tourist **accommodation** in the region consists of a hotel in **POIENI**, 7km east of Ciucea, and two cabana/campsites, one 5km east of Ciucea, south of the Valea Drăganului train halt, and the other between Zalău and Românaşi.

South into the mountains

Two dramatically named valleys run south into the Apuseni mountains on either side of Ciucea. To the east, the **Valea Drăganului** (Devil's valley) runs south from the halt and *complex turistic* of the same name. A daily bus runs from Huedin as far as Lunca Vişagului, from where you can follow the forestry road south past a reservoir before following the track marked with blue crosses west to Stîna de Vale (see p.265). The road down the **Valea Iadului** (Hell valley) turns off the DN1 at the Piatra Craiului train station, by the wooden church of Bucea, and just east of the *Piatra Craiului* motel. Civilization ends after 25km, at the *Leşu* motel, by the artificial lake of the same name; it's another 20km, past the Iadolina waterfall, to Stîna de Vale.

ENDRE ADY AND OCTAVIAN GOGA

Ady Endre, as he is known by the Magyars, was the great figure of early modernist poetry in Hungary. Born in 1877 in Érmindszent (now named Ady Endre) in Satu Mare county, he went to Paris in 1904, where he came into contact with Symbolist poetry, and returned to Hungary as a radical and exciting new poet. He stood against chauvinism and narrow nationalism, but his poetry was not always properly focused. Married in 1915, he continued womanizing until he died, weakened by syphilis, in 1919.

His near contemporary **Octavian Goga** was born in Răşinari, near Sibiu, in 1881, and studied at the Hungarian *liceu* in Sibiu and at Budapest University. However, while writing mainly for the magazine *Luceafarul*, he identified himself with the quest for Transylvanian independence from Hungary, and was imprisoned, then sentenced to death *in absentia* and further accused of raising legions from POWs in Russia to fight the Hapsburgs. In 1919 he married and travelled under a false name through Bolshevik Russia to be Vice-President of the National Committee for the Union of the Romanians, lobbying successfully at the Versailles peace conference. For the 1937 elections Iuliu Maniu made a pact with the Iron Guard, but the king outmanoeuvred them by installing Goga as prime minister of a coalition government headed by the anti-semitic National League of Christian Defence; he lasted six chaotic weeks before the king dismissed him for insulting his mistress. Nevertheless his romantic poetry, "full of soil and peasant values", is still admired in Romania.

One *accelerat* a day and all local trains stop at **ŞUNCUIUŞ** (*Vársonkolyos*) 23km west of Ciucea and 10km south of the DN1. From here a track leads east to the **Peştera Vintului** (Cave of the Wind). The cave's 42km of passages are on four levels and have taken years to explore; access has been restricted to experienced cavers, but it's possible that part of the cave will soon be opened to the public. The Racoviţa Institute in Cluj (see p.181) are the best people to ask.

From Şuncuiuş you can walk west along the river and the rail line to the next halt, Peştera and the **Vadu Crişului** cave; ask at the cabana across the footbridge about visiting the cave. The cave is also accessible from Vadu Crişului (*Rév*), a village just south of the DN1, traditionally known for producing unglazed red and white pottery; it's a two-kilometre walk through the gorge. Beyond Vadu Crişului, the road and the rail line run together across the plain to Oradea, the gateway to the Banat.

Northern Transylvania

The two counties of **Sălaj** and **Bistriţa-Năsăud**, covering the swath of ranges from the Apuseni mountains to the Eastern Carpathians, are historically referred to as **Northern Transylvania**, the tract of territory which Hitler ordered to be handed over to his Hungarian allies. If you're travelling from Cluj to Maramureş, or eastwards over the Carpathians into Moldavia, road and rail routes are fast and direct, but it's well worth considering detours or stopovers in this little-visited region.

Into Maramureş, express trains run via Dej to Jibou in just over two hours, then on to Baia Mare. The quickest road route is north to Baia Mare along the DN1C. **Into Moldavia,** trains from Cluj travel via Năsăud and the Ilva valley to

NORTHERN TRANSYLVANIA

On August 30, 1941, needing Hungarian support in his new offensive against the Soviet Union, Hitler's **Vienna Diktat** forced Romania to cede 43,492 square kilometres and 2.6 million people in northern Transylvania to Hungary. The new border ran south of Oradea, Huedin, Cluj, Tîrgu Mureş and Sfîntu Gheorghe and west of Tîrgu Secuiesc, and then more or less along the watershed of the Eastern Carpathians east of Miercurea Ciuc and Gheorgheni, west of Bicaz and Vatra Dornei, to the border of what is now Ukrainian Transcarpathia, then Hungarian, northeast of Borşa. The border is still a living memory in these areas, and locals will be able to show you the earthworks that used to mark it.

Over 10,000 Romanians, government servants and intellectuals such as teachers, lawyers and priests, were expelled in cattle trucks, some at just two hours' notice, and others after being subjected to mock executions. Atrocities were committed by the Horthyist police, with 89 killed in the village of Treznea and 157 in Ip, both in Sălaj county, and this was repeated after the more extreme Sztójay Döme government took power in Budapest in March 1944 and the Hungarians, Hitler's last allies, retreated before the Red Army.

Vatra Dornei and past several of the Painted Monasteries. The DN17 heads east from Dej to Bistriţa and through the Bîrgau valley to Vatra Dornei. Bistriţa and Năsăud, 20km apart, are linked by frequent buses, so it's easy to hop from one route to the other.

Dej and around

You may need to change trains at **DEJ**, 46km from Cluj, en route for Baia Mare. From the main *Dej Călători* station it's a good kilometre into the town centre, which consists essentially of Piaţa Bobîlna dominated by the mighty **Reformed Church**, built in late Gothic style between 1453 and 1536. On the same square, in the Town Hall, is the **Municipal Museum** , featuring the usual local history and a room dedicated to the surrounding salt industry.

Dej has two **hotels**, the *Bucegi* at Str. 1 Mai 1 (☎060/21.25.80; ③) which only has shared bathrooms, and the *Someş* at Piaţa Mărăşeşti 1 (☎060/21.33.30; ⑤). The **bus station** is at Str. Bistriţei 2, north of the centre.

Around Dej

Dej lies on the edge of Sălaj county, one of the least-known areas of Romania, despite boasting at least sixty-sixsurviving **wooden churches**. Accommodation in the region is scarce and you'll have to be prepared to start early to see a village or festival then move on, or else be prepared to camp out. The best of the churches is at **FILDU DE SUS**, most easily reached from Huedin (see p.188).

You'll see some wooden churches from the train as it winds its way up the Someş valley between Dej and Jibou. The most interesting are at **BÎRSĂU MARE**, **FODORA** (immediately south across the river), **PODIŞU** (reached from Ileanda station by a hand-hauled ferry) and **RĂSTOCI** (west of its station). Across the river from the station of Căpîlna pe Someş lies **VAD**, now a tiny village but once seat of one of the first Orthodox bishoprics in Transylvania, founded by 1523. The stone church was built by Ştefan cel Mare and shows Moldavian influences.

Zalău and around

You'll need to change trains at Jibou for the county capital, **ZALĂU**. Sălaj is a very scattered rural area, and Zalău is just a small country town with a large industrial fringe grafted on since World War II. There's nothing of interest in town beyond the county **museum** at Str. Pieței 9 (Tues–Sun 10am–6pm), and its art section not far south at Str. Doja 6. However, the ruins of Roman *Porolissum*, built to defend the northernmost limit of Roman Dacia, are immediately south of the village of Moigrad, 12km east. Here the Praetorian Gate has been rebuilt, and you can still see the remains of the *vallum* that blocked the valley, as well as an amphitheatre and the ruins of an earlier Dacian citadel on the adjacent hill.

Zalău has two **hotels**, just to the north of the museum: the *Porolissum*, on Piața 1 Decembric 1918 (☎060/61.52.20; ④), and immediately behind it the much more welcoming *Meses* (☎060/61.47.20; ②). The **bus station** is about twenty minutes' walk north of the centre at Str. Mihai Viteazul 54, and the **train station** is much further north, at the south end of the village of Crișeni; bus #1 links them both to the centre, taking about 15 minutes from the train station.

Around Zalău

A couple of buses a day run south to **BUCIUMI**, an old Romanian settlement noted for its local costumes and choral and flute music, which celebrates its festival on August 15, the Assumption of the Virgin. Rising to the west are the Meseș (or Meszes) hills – rugged highlands that host the *Măgura Priei* shepherds' festival on the first Sunday of May (see p.190).

Heading northwest from Zalău, the first **wooden church** is at **SIGHETU SILVANIEI**; from Șarmășag station turn left and walk for about fifty minutes, then take the unmarked and unsurfaced road on the right. The church, built in about 1632, is small and simple, with a new basilica recently added. In addition, a village **fair** takes place here beneath Michael's Oak on the second Sunday of July. **DERȘIDA**, two stops beyond Șarmășag, has a fine eighteenth-century wooden church, and there's another one at **CORUND**, 8km southeast of the Supur railway halt, with a fete on January 14 and 15. After **ACÎȘ**, which has a Romanesque church, the main road continues northwards to Satu Mare (44km), while the rail line veers west to Carei, where you can pick up trains to Oradea as well as to Satu Mare and Baia Mare in Maramureș.

Heading southwest from Șarmășag towards Oradea, will take you to **ȘIMLEU SILVANEI**, the main centre of western Sălaj, where there are fifteenth-century castle ruins. There is **accommodation** at the spa of **BOGHIȘ** 15km south. Continuing south from here there are several remote villages in the foothills of the Plopiș massif – **SÎRBI** and **TUSA** have good wooden churches. **BULGARI**, 25km north of Zalău has a small wooden church, rebuilt in 1783, with a unique rounded apse, as well as attractive but worn paintings. Ask for the key at no. 106 (at the entrance to the village) or no. 56 (the priest's house, just below the church).

Năsăud and the Someș Mare valley

Twenty-five kilometres northeast of Dej, the small town of **NĂSĂUD**, is at the heart of a region where villagers still wear their traditional embroidered waistcoats and blouses. A selection of these is on display in the **museum** on Strada Granicerilor. There is a **hotel** on the main Piața Libertății, if you want to break your journey.

Just 5km south of town along the Bistriţa road is the birthplace of **Liviu Rebreanu** (1885–1944), whose novels *Ion, Uprising* and *The Forest of the Hanged* give a panoramic view of Romanian society before the First World War – the village is now named after its most eminent son.

The Someş Mare valley

Heading east from Năsăud, **ILVA MICĂ** is the junction for a minor branch line up towards the Rodna mountains and provides access to the shabby spa of **SÎNGEORZ-BAI**, with hotels and cabanas, a good starting-point for hikes north into the Rodna massif. The line terminates at the mining town of Rodna Veche, 7km short of **ŞANŢ**. This attractive village of wooden houses with open verandas and shingled roofs is noted for its elaborate **wedding celebrations** (usually at weekends).

One of the best **festivals** in the region is held at **LEŞU**, on the first Sunday of September. The "Rhapsody of the Trişcaşi" brings together pipers from the counties of Bistriţa-Năsăud, Vîlcea and Maramureş, and is a great opportunity to hear *nai* (pan-pipe) music. The few local services towards Vatra Dornei stop at the Leşu Ilvei halt eight minutes after leaving Ilva Mică; from here you may have to walk the 4km east up the valley.

Bistriţa and the Bîrgău valley

Bram Stoker used the landscape of the forested Bîrgău valley as the setting for Dracula's castle. Stoker never visited Romania, though he read widely in the British Museum Library in London and accurately described the hills covered with orchards that surround the town of **BISTRIŢA**, where Jonathan Harker received the first hints that something was amiss. Remains of human settlements from Neolithic times have been found here, although the earliest records of the town coincide with the arrival of Saxon settlers. Nowadays, Bistriţa's appearance is predominantly modern, and for evidence of its folk traditions you have to investigate the museum or, preferably, the neighbouring Bîrgău valley. Getting to Bistriţa by road is quite straightforward, but the rail journey may involve changing at Sărăţel, just southeast of Beclean on the line to Deda and Braşov.

From the Bistriţa Nord station and the bus station, head south on Strada Gării and then east on Strada Şincai to reach Piaţa Centrală, dominated by a great Saxon Evangelical **church**. Built in the Gothic style in the fourteenth century, this was given Renaissance features, including a 76.5-metre tower, in 1563 by Petrus Italus, who also introduced the Renaissance style to Moldavia. On the north side of Piaţa Centrală, the arcaded **Şugălete** buildings (occupied by merchants in the fifteenth century) give a partial impression of how the town must have looked in its medieval heyday. At Str. Dornei 5 you'll find the *Casa Argintarului*, a stone-framed Renaissance silversmith's house now housing the **Art Gallery**, and continuing east, on Piaţa Unirii, is the Orthodox church, dating from 1280 (with fourteenth-century additions). Beyond it, in a former barracks at Str. Gen. Balăn 81, the **County Museum** has a collection of Thracian bronze-ware, Celtic artefacts, products of the Saxon guilds, mills and presses. Like Braşov and Sibiu, Bistriţa used to be heavily fortified, but successive fires during the nineteenth century have left only vestiges of the fourteenth-century citadel along Strada Kogălniceanu and Strada Teodoroiu, including the **Coopers' Tower** (*Turnul Dogarilor*) in the Parc Municipal.

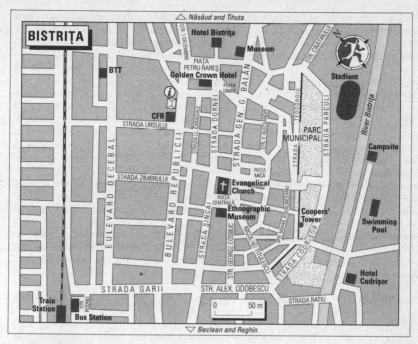

Practicalities

Exploiting the Dracula connection, blood-red alcoholic "Elixir Dracula" and bear salami are sold in the **hotel** at Piaţa Petru Rareş 4 (☎063/21.26.27; ⑦) called the *Coroana de aur* (Golden Crown) after the inn where Harker was warned not to travel on St George's Day: "Do you not know that tonight, when the clock strikes midnight, all the evil things in the world will have full sway?" Less costly options are the *Bistriţa* opposite at Str. Petru Rareş 2 (☎063/21.21.55; ④), and the *Codrişor* on Strada Onişor (☎063/21.62.07; ③). There's also the Codrişor **campsite** which has bungalows for rent.

Bistriţa's **tourist office**, B-dul Republicii 7A, can arrange excursions to, and reservations at, the Dracula Hotel (see overleaf). They will also be able to confirm the dates of festivals at Leşu and the Bîrgau villages, as well as the **International Folklore Festival** held in Bistriţa itself in the second week of August. The *CFR* agency and post office are located right by the tourist office, and the *TAROM* agency is in the *Coroana de Aur*.

The Bîrgău valley

Buses up the valley to Vatra Dornei in Moldavia leave Bistriţa three times a day. Trains go only as far as Prundu Bîrgăului (where there is a hotel), from where it's another 60km to Vatra Dornei, including the 1200m Tihuţa Pass. Since lifts may be few and wolves have occasionally attacked solitary humans after dark at the pass, car-less travellers should think twice before attempting the final stretch; drivers, too, should bear in mind the possibility that snow might block the road at its highest point.

The scenery in the **Bîrgău valley** is awe-inspiring, with sheer mountain faces and forests of fir trees, and its villages are living monuments to a way of life unchanged for centuries. The ceramics, woodcarvings and folk dress displayed in the museum at **LIVEZELE**, 8km from Bistriţa and served by local bus #3, are part of everyday life in other villages further up the valley. In **JOSENII BÎRGĂULUI**, 8km on, black pottery is manufactured and old fulling mills and cottages remain in use. **PRUNDU BÎRGĂULUI**, site of a paper mill since 1768, is the site of the *Ţăinari* (Raftsmen's Festival) on March 28–29, when unmarried men crown their sheepskin jackets with a small hat buried beneath a plume of peacock feathers. On St George's Day (April 23), it's customary for young men to light bonfires over which unmarried girls jump – only one attempt is permitted, success portending marriage within the year, while failure is taken to mean another year of maidenhood.

From Prundu Bîrgăului it's less than 1km to **TIHA BÎRGĂULUI**, which some years (check with the tourist office in Bistriţa first) hosts an interesting event on the third Sunday of June. Traditionally, the peasantry viewed death as a long journey into another world not much different from this life, requiring an accounting of one's deeds in this world as a prelude to new experiences in the next. This was the duty of the deceased's relatives and friends. The **festival of Regele Brazilor** is an opportunity to hear the traditional songs, and the part-stereotyped, part-improvised lamentations known as *bochet*.

Climbing steadily as it heads eastwards, the DN17 passes the village of Piatra Fîntînele and the **Dracula Hotel** (or *Hotel Tihuţa* ☎063/26.68.41; ③), which outwardly resembles a forbidding castle. In the novel, Dracula's abode was located two days' journey from the "Borgo (Bîrgau) Pass" by van Helsing's carriage, or one night's in the Count's calèche. In fact this hotel was built in 1983, to serve a few ski-slopes. Just beyond lies the **Tihuţa pass**, often blocked by snow between late October or early November and mid-May. The surrounding ranges harbour more **bears** than in any other part of Europe, as well as red deer, boars and **wolves**, and the view from the pass of the green "crests" or *obcinele* of Bucovina to the northeast and the volcanic Căliman mountains to the southeast is marvellous. The road descends past the picturesque village of Poiana Stampei to **Vatra Dornei** (see p.239).

travel details

Trains

Alba Iulia to: Arad (4 daily; 2hr 40min–5hr); Cluj (7 daily; 1hr 50min–2hr 50min); Deva (8 daily; 50min–1hr 30min); Sebeş (1 daily; 35min); Sibiu (1 daily; 1hr 55min); Simeria (8 daily; 50min–1hr 25min); Teiuş (20 daily; 30min); Timişoara (4 daily; 4hr 30min); Tîrgu Mureş (1 daily; 2hr); Vinţu de Jos (18 daily; 10 min); Zlatna (4 daily; 1hr 39min).

Beclean pe Someş to: Baia Mare (2 daily; 2hr 40min–4hr); Bistriţa (6 daily; 40min–1hr); Cluj (4 daily; 1hr 10min–2hr 30min); Deda (5 daily; 1hr 10min–2hr); Dej (8 daily; 20–45min); Sărăţel (11 daily; 20–40 min); Sighet (3 daily; 4–5hr 10min); Suceava (3 daily; 5hr 20min–5hr 40min).

Bistriţa Nord to: Bistriţa Bîrgăului (3 daily; 1hr 5min); Bucharest (1 daily; 9hr 15min); Cluj (3 daily; 1hr 45min–3hr 30min); Luduş (3 daily; 3hr 45min); Prundu Bîrgăului (3 daily; 50min); Sărăţel (14 daily; 20min).

Blaj to: Cluj (8 daily; 1hr 50min–3hr); Copşa Mică (19 daily; 20–45 min); Sighişoara (18 daily; 1hr–2hr 10min); Teiuş (18 daily; 30min).

Braşov to: Baia Mare (3 daily; 8hr 20min–8hr 45min); Băile Tuşnad (9 daily; 1hr–1hr 40min); Bucharest (18 daily; 2hr 30min–4hr 30min); Ciceu (8 daily; 1hr 25min–2hr 15min); Cluj (8 daily; 4hr 40min–12hr); Deda (6 daily; 3hr 40min–5hr 30min); Făgăraş (11 daily; 55min–1hr 35min);

Hărman (8 daily; 11min); Miercurea Ciuc (10 daily; 1hr 25min–2hr 15min); Prejmer (8 daily; 30min); Rîşnov (6 daily; 30min); Sibiu (8 daily; 2hr 10min–3hr 10min); Zărneşti (6 daily; 45min).

Ciceu to: Adjud (4 daily; 2hr 50min–3hr 40min); Baia Mare (2 daily; 6hr 40min–8hr 40min); Braşov (10 daily; 1hr 40min–2hr 35min); Cluj (1 daily; 4hr 40min); Deda (8 daily; 2–3hr); Ghimeş (7 daily; 1hr–1hr 20min); Iaşi (2 daily; 6hr); Miercurea Ciuc (16 daily; 10min).

Cîmpia Turzii to: Cluj (21 daily; 50min–1hr 25min); Teiuş (19 daily; 40min–1hr).

Cluj to: Baia Mare (1 daily; 3hr 10min); Braşov (8 daily; 4hr 50min–8hr); Bucharest (8 daily; 7hr 40min–12hr 50min); Cojocna (7 daily; 30min); Constanţa (1 daily, summer only; 12hr 15min); Dej (15 daily; 50min–1hr 30min); Galaţi (1 daily; 10hr 15min); Huedin (11 daily; 50min–1hr 30min); Iaşi (3 daily; 9hr–9hr 25min); Oradea (10 daily; 2hr 10min–4hr 25min); Războieni (21 daily; 1hr–1hr 30min); Rîmnicu Vîlcea (1 daily; 5hr 50min); Salva (6 daily; 1hr 40min–2hr 50min); Sighet (2 daily; 5hr 25min–7hr 15min); Sighişoara (8 daily; 3hr–4hr 40min); Suceava (3 daily; 6hr 40min–7hr).

Copşa Mică to: Blaj (19 daily; 25–45min); Braşov (12 daily; 2hr 25min–4hr 35min); Cluj (9 daily; 2hr 15min–3hr 35min); Mediaş (20 daily; 15min); Sighişoara (16 daily; 40min–1hr 15min); Sibiu (9 daily; 45min–1hr 10min); Teiuş (12 daily; 40min–1hr 10min).

Deda to: Beclean pe Someş (4 daily; 1hr 10min–1hr 40min); Braşov (7 daily; 3hr 50min–5hr 30min); Brîncoveneşti (8 daily; 30min); Cluj (1 daily, 2hr 25min); Reghin (9 daily; 20–40min); Tîrgu Mureş (9 daily; 45min–1hr 20min).

Dej Calatori to: Baia Mare (3–4 daily; 2hr 5min–3hr 5min); Beclean pe Someş (7 daily; 20–40min); Bistriţa (3 daily; 1hr 30min); Cluj (15 daily; 50min–1hr 35min); Ilva Mică (8 daily; 1hr 20min–2hr 10min); Jibou (7 daily; 1hr 10min–1hr 50min); Năsăud (8 daily; 55min–1hr 35min); Salva (10 daily; 45min–1hr 20min); Sighet (2 daily; 4hr 30min–5hr 45min); Zalău (4 daily; 2hr–2hr 40min).

Deva to: Alba Iulia (9 daily; 55min–1hr 40min); Arad (6 daily; 1hr 50min–4hr 30min); Brad (3 daily; 1hr 15min); Cluj (3 daily; 3hr–3hr 15min); Ineu (1 daily; 3hr 15min); Sibiu (4 daily; 2hr–3hr 40min); Sighişoara (3 daily; 2hr 25min); Timişoara (6 daily; 2hr 50min–3hr 10min); Tîrgu Mureş (1 daily; 3hr 20min).

Făgăraş to: Braşov (11 daily; 1hr–1hr 50min); Craiova (1 daily; 5hr 15min); Deva (3 daily; 3hr

40min–4hr 20min); Podu Olt (7 daily; 1hr–1hr 40min); Sibiu (11 daily; 1hr 15min–2hr 10min).

Hunedoara to: Bucharest (1 daily; 8hr); Cluj (1 daily; 3hr 35min); Simeria (11 daily; 25–40min); Teiuş (4 daily; 2hr–2hr 45min).

Jibou to: Baia Mare (7 daily; 50min–1hr 35min); Carei (4 daily; 1hr 45min–3hr 15min); Şarmăşag (8 daily; 55min–1hr 30min); Zalău (12 daily; 30–50min).

Miercurea Ciuc to: Adjud (2 daily; 3hr 5min–3hr 30min); Braşov (10 daily; 1hr 25min–2hr 25min); Dej (3 daily; 3hr 50min–4hr 50min); Gheorgheni (7 daily; 1hr–1hr 20min).

Podu Olt to: Braşov (5 daily; 2hr 25min–3hr 20min); Lotru (7 daily; 1hr–1hr 30min); Rîmnicu Vîlcea (7 daily; 1hr 35min–2hr 25min); Sibiu (16 daily; 25–40min); Turnu Monastery (6 daily; 1hr 25min–1hr 45min).

Războieni to: Alud (17 daily; 30min); Cluj (20 daily; 1hr 5min–1hr 45min); Teiuş (21 daily; 25–45min); Tîrgu Mureş (11 daily; 55min–1hr 40min); Vinţu de Jos (8 daily; 1hr–1hr 30min).

Sărăţel to: Beclean pe Someş (11 daily; 25–40min); Bistriţa (14 daily; 20min); Deda (7 daily; 50min–1hr 20min); Luduş (3 daily; 3hr 25min).

Sfîntu Gheorghe to: Baia Mare (2 daily; 8hr 10min); Băile Tuşnad (11 daily; 35–50min); Braşov (14 daily; 30min–1hr); Deda (6 daily; 3hr 15min–4hr 35min); Hărman (8 daily; 30–50min); Miercurea Ciuc (11 daily; 1hr–1hr 30min); Prejmer (9 daily; 30min).

Sibiu to: Agnita (2 daily; 3hr); Bucharest (7 daily; 4hr 50min–11hr 30 min); Cluj (2 daily; 3hr 25min–3hr 40min); Copşa Mică (5 daily; 50–1hr 10min); Craiova (3 daily; 4hr 40min–6hr 30min); Deva (4 daily; 2hr 15min–3hr 35min); Mediaş (3 daily; 1hr 30min–2hr 20min); Piteşti (1 daily; 5hr 45min); Podu Olt (17 daily; 25–40min); Rîmnicu Vîlcea (5 daily; 2hr 5min–3hr); Sălişte (9 daily; 30–55min); Sibiel (7 daily; 30min); Simeria (4 daily; 1hr 55min–3hr 10min); Vinţu de Jos (9 daily; 1hr 30min–2hr 10min).

Sighişoara to: Braşov (14 daily; 1hr 40min–3hr 30min); Bucharest (8 daily; 4hr 10min–7hr 10min); Cluj (8 daily; 3hr–4hr 45min); Copşa Mică (16 daily; 45min–1hr 50min); Mediaş (18 daily; 35–1hr 5min); Odorheiu Secuiesc (3 daily; 1hr 15min); Rupea (9 daily; 50–1hr 30min).

Simeria to: Alba Iulia (11 daily; 50–1hr 35min); Arad (7 daily; 1hr 50min–4hr 50min); Deva (31 daily; 10min); Hunedoara (9 daily; 25–40min); Petroşani (9 daily; 1hr 40min–2hr 40min); Sibiu (4

daily; 2–3hr); Subcetate (12 daily; 30–1hr 5min); Teiuş (12 daily; 1–2hr); Tîrgu Jiu (5 daily; 2hr 55min–4hr 30min); Vinţu de Jos (13 daily; 40min–1hr 10min).

Subcetate to: Haţeg (2 daily; 11min); Petroşani (9 daily; 1hr 10min–1hr 40min); Sarmizegetusa (2 daily; 55min); Simeria (13 daily; 30–1hr 5min); Tîrgu Jiu (5 daily; 2hr 20min–3hr 30min).

Teiuş to: Aiud (18 daily; 15min); Alba Iulia (20 daily; 20–40min); Cluj (18 daily; 1hr 30min–2hr 20min); Războieni (21 daily; 20–45min); Simeria (8 daily; 1hr 10min–1hr 50min); Vinţu de Jos (17 daily; 30–45min).

Tîrgu Mureş to: Cluj (2 daily; 2hr 15min); Deda (10 daily; 1hr–1hr 20min); Galaţi (1 daily; 9hr); Iaşi (1 daily; 9hr 40min); Lechinţa (1 daily; 4hr 40min); Războieni (11 daily; 55min–1hr 35min); Reghin (10 daily; 35–50min); Sovata (1 daily; 3hr 30min); Timişoara (1 daily; 6hr 35min).

Turda to: Abrud (2 daily; 4hr 45min–5hr); Buru (2 daily; 55–1hr 10min); Lupşa (2 daily; 3hr 30min–3hr 45min).

Vinţu de Jos to: Alba Iulia (18 daily; 10min); Simeria (13 daily; 40–1hr 15min); Sibiu (9 daily; 1hr 35min–2hr 5min); Teiuş (17 daily; 30–50min).

Zalău Nord to: Carei (4 daily; 1hr 15min–2hr 30min); Cluj (1 daily; 3hr); Dej (3 daily; 2hr–2hr 50min); Jibou (11 daily; 30–50min; Satu Mare (1 daily; 2hr 10min).

Zlatna to: Alba Iulia (4 daily; 1hr 20min).

Planes

Cluj, **Sibiu** and **Tîrgu Mureş** to: Bucharest (1–2 daily) and Constanţa (during the summer only).

International trains

Braşov to: Berlin (1 daily; 26hr 50min); Budapest (4 daily; 10hr 35min–14hr 20min); Dresden (1 daily; 24hr 40min); Munich (1 daily; 20hr); Prague (2 daily; 20hr 30min); Vienna (2 daily; 14hr 40min–15hr 15min); Warsaw (1 daily; 25hr 15min).

Cluj to: Budapest (2 daily; 8hr).

Deva to: Berlin (1 daily; 22hr 40min); Budapest (3 daily; 6hr 35min–7hr 5min); Dresden (1 daily; 20hr 30min); Munich (1 daily; 16hr); Prague (2 daily; 16hr 30min); Vienna (2 daily; 10hr 40min–11hr 20min); Warsaw (1 daily; 20hr 30min).

Miercurea Ciuc to: Budapest (1 daily; 13hr).

Sibiu to: Warsaw (1 daily; 23hr).

Tîrgu Mureş to: Budapest (1 daily; 10hr 20min).

CHAPTER FOUR

MOLDAVIA

Give me, O God, the Moldavian's wisdom last.

— Romanian proverb

The "wisdom" of **Moldavia** is not easy to define. The region, more than others in Romania, has experienced invasions, tumult, oppression and corruption, instilling in its people a fatalistic attitude. Throughout the centuries of Turkish domination, Moldavians burned lamps before the icons of a glorious past – embodied in the hero figure of Stephen the Great – and awaited its resurrection. It seemed to begin in the nineteenth century, with a flowering of art, liberal politics and land reform, but the wheel kept turning – through a bloody uprising and its suppression, fascist and communist terror, and a sham revolution – until the present, stagnant Nineties, when icon-burnishing is as fashionable as ever.

Moldavia's complex **history** is best understood in relation to the cities of Iaşi and Suceava, the former capitals of the region, and you'll find more details under the individual city accounts. Moldavia used to be twice its present size, having at various times included Bessarabia (the land beyond the River Prut) and Northern Bucovina (on the edge of the Carpathians). Both territories were annexed by Stalin in 1940, severing cultural and family ties; these have revived since the fall of communism, especially between Moldavia and the former Bessarabia – now the sovereign Republic of Moldova.

For travellers, Moldavia gets more interesting the further north you go, and the difficulty of some journeys can, perversely, add to the attraction of your final destination. This is particularly true of the jewels in the Moldavian crown, the **Painted Monasteries of Southern Bucovina**. Secluded in valleys near the Ukrainian border, their medieval frescoes of redemption and damnation blaze in polychromatic splendour at the misty, fir-clad hills. **Voroneţ** and **Suceviţa** boast peerless examples of the *Last Judgement* and the *Ladder of Virtue*; **Moldoviţa** is famous for its *Siege of Constantinople*, while **Humor** and **Putna** have a quieter charm. Though all are more or less accessible from the regional capital, **Suceava**, many visitors opt for ONT **tours** from Bucharest (see *Basics* p.271), although it's far less expensive to make your own way to Suceava and book a tour there (see p.224).

As in Wallachia, most towns and cities have been marred by hideous *blocs* and factories, and only **Iaşi** holds any great appeal, having numerous churches and monasteries from its heyday as the Moldavian capital, and a charm that puts Bucharest to shame. By contrast, the countryside looks fantastic, with picturesque **villages** dwarfed by the flanks of the Carpathians. Just over halfway to Suceava, **Neamţ county** contains Moldavia's largest **convents** – **Agapia** and **Văratec** – and the weirdly shaped **Ceahlău massif**, a paradise for hikers and climbers. While backwaters such as the Magyar-speaking **Csángó region** are worth investigating if you're seriously into rural life, the most approachable and rewarding aspect are local **festivals**. Aside from winter fairs, the main ones are at Ilişeşti (July), Durău (August), Iaşi (October) and Odobeşti (November).

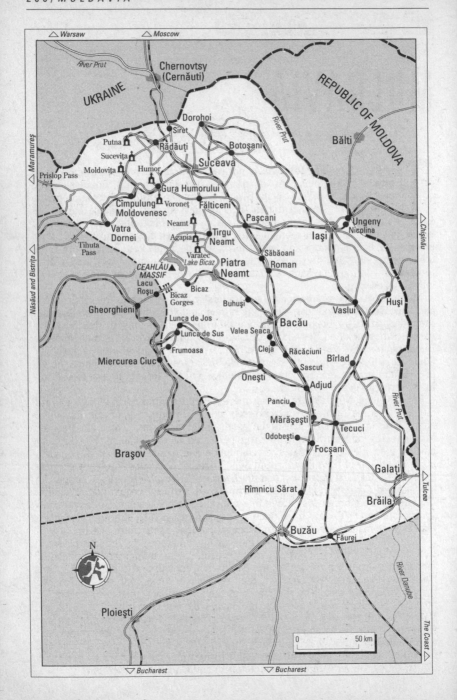

Most visitors aim straight for northern Moldavia, where the attractions are. **Flights** from Bucharest (and Constanţa in summer) are the fastest way of reaching Iaşi or Suceava. The main rail line runs north to Suceava and Ukraine; **trains** to Brăila and Galaţi branch off at Buzău, and most of those to Iaşi at Mărăşeşti. Almost all services halt at Adjud, the junction for the Csángó region, and all stop at Bacău, the springboard for Neamţ county. **Motorists** heading north along the DN2 should note that although the road is designated on maps as Euro-route 85, it's actually a country road where horse-drawn waggons without lights are a major hazard at night.

Most towns offer a choice of hotels, but you can't assume the same of villages, where you'll be lucky to find any **accommodation** at all. The situation is best in summer, when cabanas and campsites open in many rural areas, as do roadside **restaurants** catering to motorists.

Brăila and Galaţi

Lying well off the main route through Moldavia, close to the Danube Delta, **Brăila** and **Galaţi** are seldom visited by tourists, and only then while en route to or from Tulcea, the Delta "capital". Both were once ports where the Orient and Occident colluded in exporting Romania's agricultural wealth; now they are backwaters and monuments to economic failure. Brăila's docks are almost moribund – though the town remains surprisingly nice – while Galaţi is blighted by bankrupt industries. Moving on to Tulcea entails an unenviable choice between an early morning bus from Brăila or a thrice-weekly ferry from Galaţi; both towns are linked to Bucharest by fast train.

Brăila

Despite its reputation for being run by the Turkish mafia, **BRĂILA** seems a restful, pleasantly gone-to-seed Danubian town, laid out in concentric streets radiating from the port esplanade. A settlement since time immemorial, Brăila was first recorded as Wallachia's principal harbour in the Spanish *Libro de conoscimento* of 1350. After three centuries under Turkish occupation, it resumed shipping the harvests of the Bărăgan Plain to the rest of Europe, creating huge fortunes for a few landlords who built elegant villas here. At that time, Brăila had the largest Gypsy population of any town in Europe; most were in domestic service (generally as slaves, before Gypsy slavery was abolished in 1855) or lived by entertaining the *gadjé*. The villas have long crumbled but the Gypsies remain.

Arrival and information

From Brăila's **train station**, catch bus #4 or #10 outside, or walk 1km down Strada Victoriei to the tree-lined Bulevard Independenței; bear right as far as Piața Hristo Botev, and then left along Strada Mihai Eminescu to Piața Trajan. The **bus station** on Strada Siret, 150m from the train station, is of no use to tourists except for its daily bus to Tulcea (7.30am).

Don't bother with the **tourist office** on Calea Călărașilor (Mon–Fri 8am–8pm, Sat & Sun 9am–3pm; ☎039/63.30.98) just past the *Centru Civic*, although *BTT* (Mon–Fri 8am–4pm; ☎039/63.39.61) across the road at no. 56, and *CFR* (Mon–Fri 7.30am–7pm, Sat 7.30am–1pm) at B-dul Independenței 1 can be of help with accommodation and train tickets. There's a *PTTR* office (Mon–Sat 7.30am–8pm, Sun 7am–2.30pm) with direct-dial intercity phones on the corner of Piața Hristo Botev and Strada 1 Decembrie 1918, the continuation of Strada Eminescu which has a large **market** further on.

Accommodation

Belvedere, Piața Independenței 1 (☎039/63.52.70). In the *Centru Civic*, overlooking the river. Modern and comfy, with a decent restaurant. ④.

Delta, Str. M. Eminescu 56 (☎039/61.16.10 or 61.16.09). Fairly cheery doubles with shared bathrooms, on the main street. ②.

Pescărus, Str. M. Eminescu 17 (☎039/61.16.59). Atmospherically archaic, with huge rooms and shared cold-water facilities. ①.

Sport, Str. D. Boltineanu 4 (☎039/64.37.63). Nondescript building down the first turning to the right off Calea Galați, leading off Piața Trajan. ③.

Tineret, Calea Călărașilor 56 (☎039/63.64.00 or 63.64.80). Agreeable enough, if you can find it round the side of a white building with curved balconies; *BTT* is next door. ④.

Traian, Piața Trajan 1 (☎039/63.56.25). Shabby high-rise building, but a refit is imminent. Takes *ACR* coupons. ④.

The Town

An attractive melange of Empire-style facades in pastel colours, and sidewalks paved with Dobrudjan granite, the old centre radiates from **Piața Traian**, a leafy expanse named after the Roman emperor Trajan. Trajan's bust is mounted on a tall plinth, admired by a sculpted peasant and his son, the father gesturing as if to say, "This is your Daco-Roman heritage". Nearby stands the **Archangel Church**, originally built as a mosque by the Turks; its freestanding belfry was added later. The wrought-iron **clocktower** adorned with the old town's ship emblem is regarded by locals as the highlight of the town's sights. Sepia photos of Brăila in its heyday appear in the **History Museum** (Tues–Sun 10am–6pm) on the corner of Piața Trajan and Calea Galați.

Leading from the square, Strada Eminescu, bedecked with colourful pots of flowers, is the main shopping street. To the northwest of Piața Trajan, another major axis, Calea Călărașilor, intersects with Bulevardul Independenței at the start of the **Centru Civic**, where broad steps and dry fountains flanked by abstract bird sculptures descend to a riverside beach. En route, you'll pass a large **Greek Orthodox church** built by the community that dominated the shipping business before World War II, and a **statue of Ecaterina Teodoriu**, the heroine of the battle of Mărășești, waving a pistol at the end of Bulevardul Independenței.

The side street beside the *Hotel Traian*, leads to the **waterfront**, with its mournful array of rusting freighters and patrol boats, solitary fishermen and drunks. The far shore is a Delta-esque landscape of reedbeds, oaks and willows, full of birds and rodents. Though an irregular **car ferry** sails up the "Old" branch of the Danube to Măcin, on the road to Tulcea, motorists would do better to cross the river by bridge, outside town.

Eating, drinking and entertainment

Snack-vendors operate on Piaţa Traian and the adjacent stretch of Strada Eminescu, where the *Restaurant Lotca* (8am–10pm), decorated with ships and offering fish, is preferable to **eating** in the *Hotel Traian*, and easier than trekking out to the smarter restaurant in the *Hotel Belvedere* (7.30am–10pm; closed Mon). For breakfast, try the *Self Trading Company* café on Strada Eminescu opposite the *Hotel Pescărus*. Avoid the *Traian*'s basement bar, which poses as a nightclub and wildly overcharges on the grounds of having a few bored hookers and an empty stage. It's cheaper to **drink** upstairs or in the basement of the *Lotcha*. On Saturdays there's a **disco** (10pm–2am) in the *Cinema Bulevard*, at B-dul Independenţei 57.

Galaţi

GALAŢI grew up as a port on the confluence of the River Danube and Moldavia's inland waterways, the Siret and the Prut. In Bram Stoker's *Dracula*, Jonathan Harker and Godalming come here to catch a steamer up the Siret and Bistriţa rivers, to Dracula's castle at the Bîrgău Pass. In real life, Galaţi was associated with such figures as Alexandru Ioan Cuza – a local magistrate when he was unexpectedly elected Prince of Moldavia – and with the future Victorian hero, Gordon of Khartoum, who was posted here as an obscure officer in 1872.

Badly bombed in 1944, Galaţi was largely rebuilt as a series of numbingly identical apartment buildings and swelled to its present size during the 1960s, when Romania's largest **iron and steel works** were constructed here. For Gheorghiu-Dej and Ceauşescu, this enterprise was the prerequisite for Romania's emergence as a fully industrialized nation, and a symbolic and concrete assertion of independence from the Warsaw Pact, which preferred Romania to remain a largely agricultural country. To finance the Galaţi *combinat* and other projects, Ceauşescu borrowed 12 billion dollars from the West; when the products didn't sell, this could only be repaid by exporting food and yet more food. To make matters worse, the factory not only consumed energy and generated pollution with equal profligacy, but relied on imported iron ore – the only mineral resource lacking in Romania. It is kept half-going today simply because the political costs of closure are too high.

Practicalities

In a town where your main objective is to leave, it makes sense to stay as close as possible to the *Gara fluvială*, from where **ferries and a hydrofoil to Tulcea** depart (Mon, Wed & Fri at 8.45am). Try to book tickets the day before, or turn up early and expect a scrum. Galaţi's **train station** lies to the east of the town centre – besides fast trains to Brăila and Bucharest, there are services to Iaşi and into Transylvania. *CFR* is located at Str. Brăilei bloc BR2; *BTT* at Str. Domnească 11, bloc P1. The most convenient **hotels** are the *Dunareă*, Str. Domnească 3 (☎036/41.80.41; ④), and *Galaţi*, Str. Domnească 12 (☎036/46.00.40; ④), near the bottom end of Bulevardul Republicii, which runs north through the centre.

From Buzău to Bacău

Sadly, the main route northeast from Bucharest, the DN2, is a miserable adver-
tisement for Moldavia, as hideously modernized towns succeed one another up
the Siret valley without even the sight of the Carpathians to lift your spirits until
you're halfway to Suceava. There's little reason to stop anywhere along the way
unless you're envisaging a detour into the wine-growing or Csángó regions of the
Subcarpathians.

That said, you might consider visiting **BUZĂU**, 115km from Bucharest, on the
last Sunday in June, when it holds a kitsch **festival** derived from the ancient rite
of *Drăgaica*. Once widespread in rural Romania, this Midsummer Day's custom
required young girls wearing crowns and hoods to go singing and dancing into
the fields to verify the readiness of the wheat for harvesting. In town, however,
they can only go through the motions.

FOCŞANI, 75km further north, is even uglier than Buzău, but has buses and
trains to the **wine-growing regions** of Odobeşti and Panciu. **ODOBEŞTI**
produces the yellow wine that was Ceauşescu's favourite tipple, and is noted for
its **festivals**. The grape harvest is celebrated in late September, while on the third
Sunday of November, the musically inclined shepherds of Vrancea county gather
to entertain each other with performances on alpine horns and pan-pipes. At
PANCIU, they make sparkling wines.

In Romania, the rail junction of **MĂRĂŞEŞTI** is remembered for a savage
battle in the summer of 1917, when German forces advancing on Iaşi were halted
by Romanian troops, determined to preserve the last unoccupied region of their
country. On the outskirts of town, a giant **mausoleum** containing the remains of
6000 dead is the site of **military parades** on public holidays and the anniversary
of the battle.

The Csángó region

Csángó means "wanderer" in Hungarian, an appellation given by the Székely to
the religious dissenters among them who fled over the Carpathians from
Transylvania in the fifteenth century, to be joined by war refugees in the seventeenth and eighteenth centuries. Once there were some forty **Csángó villages** in
Moldavia, a few as far east as the Dneistr river, but today their community has
contracted into a hard core of about 60,000 people living between Adjud and
Bacău, and in the Ghimeş district at the upper end of the Trotuş valley. Most
rural Csángó are fiercely conservative and fervently religious, wear folk costume
and speak a Magyar dialect; their music is harsher and sadder than that of their
Magyar kinsfolk in Transylvania.

Mutual suspicions and long memories of the Ghimeş uprising of 1934 made
this a sensitive area in communist times. While allowing them to farm and raise
sheep outside the collectives, the Party tried to dilute the Csángó by settling
Romanians in new industrial towns like Oneşti, and to stifle their culture. Though
things are a lot freer now, the region is still unexplored so far as **tourism** goes,
and has almost no infrastructure. Should you decide to spend any time here,
come prepared to camp (or negotiate for a bed), with ample supplies.

The most rewarding area is the upper part of the **Trotuş valley**, beyond the
ugly chemical town of Oneşti (formerly named "Gheorghiu Gheorghiu-Dej", after

Ceauşescu's predecessor). **GHIMEŞ** – or Ghimeş-Faget – is the largest of four Csángó settlements in the valley, and unusual for having a Gypsy population that is totally integrated into village life. It has a strong musical tradition and hosts a **winter fair** on January 20–21. Another village worth investigating, with a similar musical heritage, is **FRUMOASA** (Beautiful), only 9km from the Transylvanian town of Miercurea Ciuc (see p.166). **ADJUD**, on the main Bucharest–Suceava line, is the junction for the branch line to Ghimeş, served by several slow trains daily, while on weekdays Frumoasa is directly accessible by bus from Bacău. There should also be the odd bus or at least hitchable traffic along the valley, enabling you to reach **LUNCA DE JOS** and **LUNCA DE SUS** on the borders with Transylvania (see p.167).

The lowland Csángó settlements are less isolated and distinctive, being only a few miles west of the main route between Adjud and Bacău, from where there are several buses daily to **CLEJA** and **VALEA SEACA**, and slow trains halting at **SASCUT** and **RĂCĂIUNI**. There's a **motel** (②) on the main road near Răcăiuni.

Bacău

BACĂU is a large town with little to recommend it except its hotels, telephone office and transport services – the latter enabling you to reach more interesting places like the Csángó or Neamţ county. First industrialized in the mid-nineteenth century, it now has a huge chemical *combinat* on the outskirts, and a modernized *centru* vastly out of scale with its backstreets. Aside from a neo-Byzantine church at one end of the main street, Strada Nicolae Bălcescu, and the Brîncoveanu-style **Bacovia Theatre** further along, the only evidence that Bacău is older than a century is the ruined **Princely Court**, off Strada 9 Mai. Surrounded by apartment buildings, the enclosure contains the Church of the Virgin founded by Stephen the Great's son, Alexandru, and a circular tower, similarly over-restored in 1973. The **Museum of History and Fine Arts** (Tues–Sun 10am–6pm) at Str. Soimului 23 exhibits prehistoric and Dacian artefacts, and works by Theodor Aman, Nicolae Grigorescu and others.

Arrival and information

To reach the centre from the **train station**, catch any bus marked *centru* or head up Strada Eminescu, to the right of the *magazin* across the road, which eventually leads to a park opposite the *Hotel Moldova*, where the two central axes converge. Bacău is on the mainline between Bucharest and Suceava, and the junction for a branch line serving Piatra Neamţ and Bicaz (near the Ceahlău massif). The **bus depot** is 15 minutes' walk along Strada Unirii from the centre, operating buses to the Csángó villages of Cleja, Valea Seaca and Frumoasa, as well as Braşov in Transylvania and Vatra Dornei in northern Moldavia.

Most services in town are on Strada Nicolae Bălcescu: the **tourist office** (Mon–Fri 7.30am–7pm, Sat 8am–1pm) is next to *CFR* (Mon–Fri 7.30am–8pm; ☎034/14.63.40), along from the *Romtelecom* office (daily 7am–10pm) with direct-dial international phones, while *TAROM* (Mon–Sat 7am–8pm; ☎034/11.14.62) is across the road. The Pasajul Revoluţei at the side of *Romtelecom* leads to *BTT* (Mon–Thurs 8am–4.30pm, Fri 8am–2pm; ☎034/13.49.66) on Strada Mihai Viteazu, two blocks behind which is the central **market**. The town's emergency **hospital** (☎034/13.40.00) is the best-equipped in Neamţ county.

Accommodation

Bistriţa, Str. Luminii 3 (☎034/13.35.44). Beige Stalinist low-rise near the *Casa Culturii*. Rather gloomy, with shared bathrooms. ②.

Central, Str. N. Bălcescu 2 (☎034/13.48.37). Tucked away beside the Bacoiva Theatre, this old-fashioned place has a pseudo-Gothic hall that almost compensates for the spartan rooms and facilities. ③.

Decebal, Str. Ignita Sancu Sturza 2 (☎034/14.62.11). A concrete monster at the far end of Strada Bălcescu, only marginally better than the *Moldova*. ④.

Dumbrava, Str. Eliberarii 2 (☎034/14.38.38). Head on 150m past the *Bistriţa* and turn right at the "Carex" sign to find this decent Sixties place with a snazzy foyer. ③.

Moldova, Str. N. Bălcescu 16 (☎034/14.63.22). A high-rise building with a bizarre foyer out of *Barbarella*. Its disco and bingo hall make this Bacău's main nightspot. Takes *ACR* coupons. ③.

Neamţ county

Neamţ county is the only real attraction between Bucharest and the old Moldavian capitals of Iaşi and Suceava. Although its towns – **Piatra Neamţ** and **Tîrgu Neamţ** – are nothing special, they serve as jumping-off points for the historic monasteries of **Neamţ**, **Agapia** and **Văratec**, set in wooded foothills that turn gloriously red and gold in autumn. Further to the northwest rises the **Ceahlău massif**, whose magnificent views and bizarrely weathered outcrops make this one of the finest hiking spots in Romania.

Without a car, you're faced with the question of which town makes a better base for excursions. Tîrgu Neamţ is closer to the sights and runs a few more buses than Piatra Neamţ; the latter, in contrast, offers a better choice of places to eat and the certainty of a bed. The two towns, 40km apart, are linked by hourly **buses**, but only half of them run via Baltatesti, the turn-off for Văratec and Agapia. On Sundays, there are fewer services to the monasteries and none to Ceahlău.

Piatra Neamţ

Nestled in the Carpathian foothills where the River Bistriţa emerges into the Cracau basin, **PIATRA NEAMŢ** is one of Romania's oldest settlements, inhabited by a string of Neolithic and Bronze Age cultures, and the Dacians, whose citadel has been excavated on a nearby hilltop. The town was first recorded in 1453 under the name of Piatra lui Craciun (Christmas Rock); its present title may refer to the German (*Neamt*) merchants who once traded here, or derive from the old Romanian word for an extended family or nation – *Neam*. As one of Moldavia's earliest industrial centres, the town later played a major role in the general strike of 1919, and was one of the few places where the communists were able to sabotage production during World War II. That said, Piatra has little to attract visitors beyond a medieval church and a better-than-average collection of prehistoric relics.

The Town

Today, Piatra Neamţ features every style of communist architecture from dismal low-rises to the pseudo-malls that mushroomed in the 1980s. What's left of the old town is clustered around **Piaţa Libertăţii**. The **Church of St John** originally formed part of a Princely Court, of which only vestiges remain. Erected by

Stephen the Great in 1497–98, hard on the heels of his seminal church at Neamț Monastery, it set a pattern for Moldavian church architecture thereafter. The upper part is girdled by niches outlined in coloured brick, which on later churches held saintly images. Beside the door, a votive inscription by his son Bogdan presages a host of tacky modern paintings of Stephen inside, where a dusty case of valuables justifies an entry charge. Nearby stands a slender Gothic **Belltower** with a witch's hat brim, constructed in 1499.

Off to the left are a Brîncoveanu-style mansion containing the **Art Museum** (Tues–Sun 10am–5pm) with work by local painters, and a smaller building that combines folk architecture with Art Nouveau, housing an **Ethnographic Museum** (same hours). On the far side of the square, some vaulted **ruins of the Princely Court** have been laid bare by a shaft dug into the slope below the Petru Rareş Liceé, but it's hard to see much through the gate, which seems to be permanently locked. There are several attractive **old villas** on Strada Ştefan cel Mare, off to the left; Elena Cuza, the widow of the deposed leader, Alexandru Ioan Cuza (see p.313), lived at no. 55 until her death in 1909.

The **History Museum** (Tues–Sun 9am–5pm) on the corner of Strada Eminescu devotes its ground floor to ancient relics. The left-hand section features a lifesize replica of a Stone Age hut furnished with wolfskins and grindstones, and fertility charms and pottery created by the Cucuteni culture (c.3000–2000 BC). Finds across the corridor include a Bronze Age tomb complete with skeleton, and a curious Iron Age figure dubbed the *Cavalier scit* (Seated Rider). Upstairs, the Romanian aptitude for woodcarving is exemplified by a "knitted cable" throne and an exquisite door with the Moldavian crest entwined in foliage. On Bulevardul

Republicii, the small wooden **house of Calistrat Hogas** (Tues–Sun 10am–5pm), is now a memorial museum to the writer (1847–1918) who praised the charms of Neamţ county when the town still consisted of Alpine-style chalets.

Practicalities

You can walk up the tree-lined Bulevardul Republicii from the **train station** to the downtown area in about ten minutes, passing *BTT* (Mon–Fri 9am–4pm, Sat 10am–2pm) en route. As well as serving the monasteries, **buses** run from Piatra Neamţ through the Bicaz gorges to Gheorgeni and Braşov in Transylvania, and to Cîmpulung Moldovonesc, Gura Humorlui and Iaşi.

Since the **tourist office** amounts to a monoglot receptionist in the *Hotel Bulevard*, any of the other hotels are as likely to be able to give you information. *TAROM* (Mon–Fri 7.30am–noon) and *CFR* (Mon–Fri 7am–7.30pm) are on the corner of the mall that runs along Strada Alexandru cel Bun. You can **change money** in the *Hotel Ceahlău* (Mon–Fri 9am–5pm, Sat 9am–noon) or the *Petrudava* store (Mon–Fri 8am–7pm, Sat 9am–1pm) around the corner from the *Hotel Central*.

Piatra Neamţ's three **hotels** all have private bathrooms, and include breakfast. Just 200m from the train station, *Hotel Bulevard*, B-dul Republicii 38–40 (☎033/21.62.30; ③), is a drab 1950s shoebox, and in the centre of town, a gloomy highrise streaked with damp houses the *Hotel Central*, B-dul Republicii 26 (☎033/21.64.14 or 21.62.30; ④) – *ACR* coupons accepted. The best of this poor bunch, with decent rooms and views, is *Hotel Ceahlău* at Piaţa Ştefan cel Mare 1 (☎033/21.99.90; ③), which also takes *ACR* coupons. There's a **campsite**, *Ştrand Camping* (or *Bîtca Doamnei*) on Aleea Tineretului (☎033/21.12.16; ①–②), a wooded summer-only site with huts. To get there, walk along Strada Bistriţei till you reach the footbridge (1km), or drive across the road bridge downriver.

Hotel **restaurants** come a poor second to the *Lacto-Vegetarian Restaurant Garofiţa* (daily 7am–10pm) in the mall, which, despite its name, mainly offers meat dishes and often features "Hunters' Nights", with bear and stag on the menu. For pizzas or burgers, try the *Rotisserie* (Mon–Sat 9am–11pm) on the corner of Bulevardul Decebal and Strada Titu Maiorescu. There are **bars** in the *Central* and *Ceahlău* hotels, and outside the station, while in summer, local youths pack the nightly *Little Italy* **disco** near the campsite.

Agapia and Văratec

The rolling countryside west of the road between Piatra and Tîrgu Neamţ provides an idyllic setting for Romania's largest convents: **Agapia**, with 300 nuns, and **Văratec**, with 280. Each comprises a walled convent and a village of nuns, up the road from an agricultural commune of the same name. The nuns live in cosy houses with pale blue, fretted eaves and glassed-in verandahs; some were built for them by their families and are rented to tourists in summertime – the income going to the convent, which supports scores of nuns in their old age. Taking photos within the convents is not allowed.

You can get to the convents from Piatra Neamţ, which has two daily buses to Agapia, or Tîrgu Neamţ, which has four services daily to Agapia and two to Văratec. They normally wait 30 minutes before starting back, giving you time for a quick look at the convent. To visit both sites, it's quicker to walk between the two rather than return to town for another bus out. If you miss the last bus back and you don't fancy staying at Agapia or Văratec, walk or hitch the 5km back to the main road, and wait for one of the regular buses between Tîrgu Neamţ and Piatra Neamţ.

Agapia

Agapia Monastery actually consists of two convents several miles apart; most visitors are content to visit only the main complex of **Agapia din Vale** (Agapia-in-the-Valley), at the end of a muddy village of houses with covered steps. The walls and gatetower aim to conceal rather than to protect; inside is a whitewashed enclosure around a cheerful garden. When prayers are due, one of the nuns beats an insistent rhythm on a wooden tocsin; another plays the pan-pipes, followed by a medley of bells, some deep and slow, others high and fast.

The monastery **church** was built in 1642–44, by Prince Basil the Wolf's brother, Gavril Coci. Its helmet-shaped cupola, covered in green shingles, mimics that of the gatetower. During renovations in the 1850s, the interior was repainted by Nicolae Grigorescu, the foremost religious artist of the day. Off to the right is a **museum** of icons and vestments from the seventeenth and eighteenth centuries (daily 10am–7pm). Downhill by the Topolniţa stream stands another, **wooden church** with three shingled domes and a modern gatetower.

Agapia din Deal (Agapia-on-the-Hill) or Agapia Veche (Old Agapia) is a smaller, more tranquil convent, high up a wooded slope about half an hour's walk from Agapia din Vale; turn right at the unmarked junction after ten minutes. Another trail from Agapia din Vale leads to Văratec (see below). The *Hanul Agapia* on the road to Agapia din Vale has **rooms** (②).

Văratec

Hedgerows line the narrow road winding through Văratec commune to the pretty nuns' village and **Văratec Monastery**, its whitewashed walls and balconies enclosing a lovely garden shaded by cedars. The novices inhabit two-storey buildings named after saints, while the older nuns live in cottages, next to a **museum** of icons (Tues–Sun 10am–6pm), and an **embroidery school** established by Queen Marie in 1934. It's an odd but not unfitting site for the **grave of Veronica Micle**, the poetess loved by Eminescu, who couldn't afford to marry her after the death of her despised husband (see p.219).

Văratec was founded in the eighteenth century, round a church that no longer exists; the site of its altar is marked by a pond with a statue of an angel. The present **church**, built in 1808, is plain and simple, culminating in two bell-shaped domes and six chimneys. Given harsh winters, the nuns have sensibly installed stoves in the narthex, which is barely separated from the nave by a pair of columns.

In fine weather, it's a pleasant **walk from Văratec to Agapia**; the seven-kilometre trail through the woods takes one and a half hours, starting by house no. 219, back down the road from Văratec Monastery. Another trail, marked by blue dots, leads **to Siha hermitage** (2hr), built into the cliffs near the cave of St Teodora, hidden by strange outcrops. A backroad connects Siha to the **Sihistria and Secu hermitages**, and from there to the main road (10km) between Tîrgu Neamţ and Ceahlău, a few kilometres west of the turn off for Neamţ Monastery (see overleaf).

The *Hotel Filiorou*, a family-run bed-and-breakfast in Văratec commune, 1.5km from the monastery, has pleasant **rooms** (②).

Tîrgu Neamţ

TÎRGU NEAMŢ (German Market) is smaller and duller than Piatra, discouraging you from straying far. The main Bulevardul Eminescu has a cluster of signposts that implies several museums in the vicinity – all of which are actually outside town, except for the **house of Veronica Micle** (Tues–Sun 10am–4pm) on the corner of Strada Cetăţii, nearby.

The town's saving grace is the Neamţ **citadel** (Tues–Sun 10am–6pm), Moldavia's finest ruined castle, 1km along Strada Cetăţii and then 15 minutes' slog uphill. Founded by Petru Muşat in the fourteenth century, it was beefed up by Stephen just in time to withstand a siege by Mohammed II in 1496. Later, it was partly demolished on the orders of the Turks by Prince Cantacuzino, but once again saw service in the war between Moldavia and Poland at the end of the seventeenth century. You approach by a long curving wooden **bridge** raised on pillars high above a moat; the final stretch was designed to flip enemies down into an oubliette. Within the **bailey**, a warren of roofless chambers that used to be an arsenal, courthouse and baths, surround a deep well ringed by battlements that survey the Neamţ valley for miles around. The citadel is visible from the road to Neamţ Monastery, but far more impressive at close quarters. Lower down the hillside are the remains of an outer wall, added by Stephen.

Practicalities

Tîrgu's **train station** is tucked away in the backstreets – five trains daily link the town with Paşcani, the interchange for Iaşi and Suceava. The **bus station** on Strada Cuza Vodă operates services to the monasteries and Ceahlău, Reghin, Topliţa and Braşov in Transylvania and Gura Humourlui and Vatra Dornei in northern Moldavia.

The main drawback to spending much time in Tîrgu Neamţ is the lack of **accommodation**. Following the closure of the *Hotel Plaieşu* at the end of Bulevardul Ştefan cel Mare for long-term repairs, the only place to stay is the *Hanul Casa Arcaşului* (②) at the foot of the hill below the citadel, which can't be depended on outside of summer. There's nowhere to **eat** except for a pizza den and a *cofetărie* on Ştefan cel Mare that are usually closed, or the **market** off Bulevardul Eminescu – although **bars** operate round the clock near the bus station.

Neamţ Monastery

Neamţ Monastery is the oldest in Moldavia and its chief centre of Orthodox culture; it is also the largest men's monastery in Romania, with seventy monks and dozens of seminary students. The original hermitage, founded by Petru Muşat, was rebuilt in the early fifteenth century by Alexander the Good, with fortifications and a printing house that protected Neamţ and spread its influence. Under Stephen the Great, its new church became a prototype for Moldavian churches throughout the sixteenth century, and its school of miniaturists and illuminators led the field.

Outwardly, Neamţ resembles a fortress, with high stone walls and an octagonal corner tower (there used to be four). On the inside of the gatetower, a painted Eye of the Saviour sternly regards the monks' cells with their verandahs wreathed in red and green ivy, and the seminary students in black tunics milling around the garden. Totally rebuilt by Stephen in 1497, to celebrate a victory over the Poles, the sweeping roof of the church overhangs blind arches inset with lozenges and glazed bricks, on a long and otherwise bare facade. Its trefoil windows barely illuminate the interior, where pilgrims kneel amidst the smell of mothballs and candlewax. At the back of the compound is a smaller church dating from 1826, containing frescoes of the Nativity and the Resurrection.

Outside the monastery stands a large onion-domed **pavilion** for *Aghiastmatar*, the "Blessing of the water" on Epiphany. In pre-war Bucharest, a similar ritual was performed beside the River Dîmboviţa, attended by the king, patriarch and other dignitaries. A wooden cross was cast into the icy river, whereupon the faithful, dressed in white, dived in to retreive it before the patriarch officially blessed the water, which was then taken home in bottles for use in times of illness.

The turn-off for the monastery is 12km west of Tîrgu Neamţ, shortly after the commune of Vînatori-Neamţ that straggles along route 15B. There are several **buses** daily from Tîrgu Neamţ and one or two from Piatra, but the schedules change too often to be posted, so you'll have to ask. To get back, it may be worth begging a lift as far as the main road, where buses pass by more frequently. Should need arise, there are **rooms** (②) and a summer **campsite** with huts (①) at the *Hanul Braniște*, 9km from Tîrgu Neamţ on the road to Ceahlău.

The Ceahlău massif

Aptly designated on local maps as a *zona abrupt*, the **Ceahlău massif** (*Masivul Ceahlău*) rises above neighbouring ranges in eroded crags whose fantastic shapes were anthropomorphized in folk tales and inspired Eminescu's poem, *The Ghosts*. The Dacians believed that Ceahlău was the abode of their supreme deity, Zamolxis, and that the gods transformed the daughter of King Decebalus into the Dochia peak. The massif is composed of Mesozoic cretaceous sediments – especially conglomerates, which form pillar-like outcrops – and covered with stratified belts of beech, fir and spruce, with dwarf pine and juniper above 1700m. Its **wildlife** includes black nanny-goats, mountain-cocks, bears and boars, and the majestic Carpathian stag.

Ceahlău's isolation is emphasized by the huge, artificial **Lake Bicaz** (Lacul Izvoru Muntelei) that half-encircles its foothills. A hydroelectric **dam** (*baraj*), built in 1950, rises at the southern end, 3km from **BICAZ**, accessible by train from Piatra Neamţ, or by any bus bound for the Bicaz gorges. During summer, there are **boat trips** from the dam to the Pîrîul Mare landing stage below Ceahlău itself. The lake is rich in **fish**, including rainbow trout, and there's a good **campsite** with huts (①) midway between the dam and the village of Potoci.

At the other end of the reservoir, the route from Tîrgu Neamţ to Durău and the mountain road from Vatra Dornei converge at **POIANA LARGULUI**, where it's feasible to **change buses** if you're prepared to wait a few hours. The local **campsite** is awful, but there's a decent new site, *Popas Petru Vodă*, at the Argel Pass, 12km uphill towards Tîrgu Neamţ.

Hiking above Durău

The main base for **hiking** in the massif is **DURĂU**, on the northeastern side, which can be reached by bus from Piatra Neamţ or Tîrgu Neamţ, and has four **hotels** (②–③) and a cabana, with a **tourist office** in the *Hotel Durău*. On the second Sunday in August, Durău hosts the **Ceahlău Feast**, an opportunity for shepherds to parade their finery, which attracts many tourists. From December to March, **skiing** replaces hiking as the main activity around the resort, which also boasts a small nineteenth-century **hermitage** (*schit*) with naturalistic paintings by Nicolae Tonitza, who used local backgrounds for his biblical scenes.

Otherwise, there's nothing to keep you from pressing on to the *Fîntînele* cabana, 45 minutes' walk on the red-striped trail starting from the bus station. A longer route (marked by blue crosses, then red crosses and finally yellow triangles) also runs there via the **Duruitoarea cascade**, which falls a total of 25m in two stages.

From Fîntînele, the red-striped route ascends within sight of the Panaghia rocks and Toaca peak to a plateau with glorious views and the *Dochia* cabana (1750m), two hours later. It continues south via several massive **rock pillars** to Poiana Maicilor, where the red-striped route turns downstream to the *Izvoru Muntelui* cabana and the Bicaz road, while another trail marked with blue crosses runs on to Neagra village, on the road to the **Bicaz gorges** (see below). Either takes about two hours, starting from Dochia.

Into Transylvania and north to Vatra Dornei

To the north and south of the massif, steep valleys culminating in a gorge or a pass allow two routes **into Transylvania**. The northern one crosses a 1112-metre-high pass beyond the alpine spa of Borsec, before descending to Topliţa, in the upper Mureş valley. Although it's a scenic journey, the infrequency of buses from Tîrgu Neamţ to Topliţa may dissuade you from stopping over on the way (see p.169).

A better route runs through the **Bicaz gorges** (*Cheile Bicazului*), 25km upriver from Bicaz, past the lovely village of **BICAZ ARDELEAN**, which has a **wooden church** dating from 1829 and holds a **festival** on the first Sunday in April. Sheer limestone cliffs rise to a height of 200–300m above the river, pressing so close around the "Neck of Hell" (*Gîtul Iadului*) that the road is hewn directly into the rockface. The *Cheile Bicazului* cabana, amid the gorges, marks the start of several **hiking** trails, and a longer one ascends from Lacu Roşu to the *Piatra Singuratică* (Lonely Rock) cabana. **Buses** from Piatra Neamţ, Tîrgu Neamţ and Bicaz travel this way en route to Gheorgheni (see p.168).

Alternatively, you can head north to **Vatra Dornei** (see p.239), by bus from Tîrgu Neamţ. The 136-kilometre journey takes four hours following the River Bistriţa through a narrow, twisting valley hemmed in by fir-covered peaks. About 20km before Vatra Dornei, you'll see the well-signposted *Cabana Zurgeni*, across the river, from where a trail leads to the heart of the Rarău massif (see p.238).

Iaşi

IAŞI (pronounced "Yash"), the cultural capital of Moldavia, is by far the nicest city in the region, and the only one where you're likely to want to stay a while. Its university, theatre and resident orchestra rival those of Bucharest – which was merely a crude market town when Iaşi became a princely seat – and give it an air of sophistication enhanced by a large contingent of foreign students. Cementing its place in the nation's heart, Romanians associate Iaşi with the poet, Eminescu; Moldavians esteem it as the burial place of St Paraschiva; and several million smokers depend on the city for producing *Carpaţii*, the country's cheapest brand of cigarettes.

The **telephone code** for Iaşi is ☎032

Despite lying east of the main route northwards through Moldavia, Iaşi is accessible by direct **trains** from the capital (6–7hr) or from Brăila and Galaţi; frequent services from Paşcani, the junction on the Bacău–Piatra Neamţ–Suceava line; **buses** from most towns in Moldavia; and daily **flights** from Bucharest (and Constanţa during summer).

Some history

Iaşi's ascendancy dates from the 1560s, when the Moldavian *hospodars* (princes) gave up the practice of maintaining courts in several towns, and settled permanently in Iaşi. This coincided with Moldavia's gradual decline into a Turkish satellite, ruled by despots who endowed Iaşi with churches and monasteries to trumpet their earthly glory and ensure their immortal salvation. **Basil the Wolf** (1634–53) promulgated a penal code whereby rapists were raped and arsonists burned alive – but he also founded a printing press and school, which led to the flowering of Moldavian literature during the brief reign of the enlightened **Dimitrie Cantemir** (1710–11).

After Cantemir's death, Moldavia fell under the control of Greek **Phanariots** – originally from the Phanar district of Constantinople – who administered it on behalf of the Ottoman Empire, chose and deposed the nominally ruling princes (of whom there were 36 between 1711 and 1821), and eventually usurped the throne for themselves. The boyars adopted Turkish dress and competed to win the favour of the Phanariots, who alone could recommend their promotion to the Sultan. As Ottoman power weakened, this dismal saga was interrupted by the surprise election of Prince **Alexandru Ioan Cuza**, who clinched the unification of Moldavia and Wallachia in 1859, with the diplomatic support of France. In the new *Regat*, Cuza founded universities at Iaşi and Bucharest, introduced compulsory schooling for both sexes, and secularized monastic property, which then accounted for a fifth of Moldavia. Finally, his emancipation of the serfs so enraged landowners and military circles that in 1866 they overthrew Cuza and restored the *status ante quo* – but kept the *Regat*.

The latter half of the nineteenth century was a fertile time for **intellectual life** in Iaşi, where the *Junimea* literary circle attracted such talents as **Mihai Eminescu** and **Ion Creangă**, who, like the historian, **Nicolae Iorga**, became national figures. Their Romanian nationalism was more romantic than chauvinist, but unwittingly paved the way for a deadlier version in the Greater Romania that was created to reward the *Regat* for its sacrifices in **World War I**, when most of the country was occupied by the Germans, and the government was evacuated to Iaşi. With its borders enlarged to include Bessarabia and Bucovina, Moldavia inherited large minorities of non-Romanian-speaking Jews, Ukrainians and Gypsies, aggravating ethnic and class tensions in a region devastated by war.

During the 1920s, Iaşi became notorious for **anti-semitism**, spearheaded by a professor whose League of Christian National Defence virtually closed the university to Jews (who comprised over a third of the population), and later spawned the Iron Guard (see box overleaf). Their chief scapegoat was **Magda Lupescu**, a local Jewess who became King Carol's mistress and was widely hated for amassing a fortune by shady speculations. In 1940, they both fled abroad in a train stuffed with loot.

THE IRON GUARD AND ROMÂNIA MARE

Moldavia and Iaşi have long been associated with the far right of Romanian politics. The most ardent member of Iaşi's League of Christian National Defence was **Corneiliu Codreanu**, who went on to found the Legion of the Archangel St Michael in the early 1930s, better known as the **Iron Guard**. Wearing green shirts with bags of Romanian soil around their necks, the *Legionari* chased away village bailiffs to the approbation of the peasantry, and murdered politicians deemed to be insufficiently nationalistic, until Marshal Antonescu jailed its leaders and Codreanu was shot "trying to escape". His followers fled to Berlin; when allowed back home, they helped carry out the Nazis' genocidal "Final Solution," in Romania.

After the war, the communists employed ex-*Legionari* as thugs against the social-ists and the National Peasant Party, whom they regarded as their real enemies. Following the 1989 revolution, fascism has been making a comeback with the **România Mare** (Greater Romania) party of **Vadim Tudor**, which ascribes all the nation's problems to a conspiracy of Jews, Magyars, Gypsies and everyone else who isn't a "pure" Romanian. Their headquarters in Iaşi is rather bizarrely shared with the Ecology party.

Arrival, information and accommodation

Arriving at Iaşi's main **train station**, you can either catch tram #3, #8, #9 or #11, or walk uphill past the ornamental tower on the corner of Strada Gării, and bear right along Strada Arcu to reach the central square, Piaţa Unirii (10–15min). Flights are usually met by *TAROM* buses; a taxi into town from the **airport** costs $2–5. For the two daily flights to Bucharest, the bus departs two hours earlier from outside *TAROM* at Str. Arcu 3. The intercity **bus station** is 300m along Şoseaua Arcu, within walking distance of downtown, serving Braşov, Cîmpulung Moldovenesc, Piatra Neamţ and Tulcea; there are also services to Chişinău and Bălţi, across the border in Moldova.

Iaşi's **tourist office** in the *Centru Civic* (Mon–Fri 8am–3pm; ☎11.43.64) has a helpful English-speaking member of staff, but if you just want to **change money**, the *Cambio Exchange* on Strada C. Negru (Mon–Sat 9am–6pm, Sun 10am–1pm), off the main street opposite the Church of the Three Hierarchs, offers a better rate. Likewise, the most recent **map** of the city (combined with a plan of the Moldovan capital, Chişinău) is available from the bookshop opposite *CFR* on Piaţa Unirii, rather than from the tourist office.

Accommodation

Iaşi has **hotels** to suit every taste and budget, although those on Piaţa Unirii are really the only convenient ones. **Student accommodation** for groups is theoreti-cally available from *BTT* (Mon–Sat 8am–4pm; ☎11.36.65), in the *Hotel Orizont*'s lobby, but in practice they aren't keen to help. Individuals might find students prepared to let them sleep in one of the many *caminul di studenti* located around the university on B-dul Copou, 1km northwest of the centre. **Camping Ciric** (☎17.35.20), by a lake north of town, is only open over summer, when hourly buses run there from Tîrgul Cocou, outside the Golia Monastery. There are also cabins (②) here in a wooded setting, but the filthy toilets are a big deterrent.
Bucium Motel (☎14.07.12), on the Vaslui road, 12km from town. Open all year, with a summer campsite. Only worth considering if you have a car. ②.

Continental, Str. Cuza Vodă 2 (☎11.43.20). Old-fashioned and a bit noisy, but not unpleasant. This is the least expensive downtown hotel and has rooms with or without private bathrooms. ③.

Moldova, Str. A. Panu 29–31 (☎14.22.25). Comfortable but soulless building amidst the *Centru Civic*, with a restaurant and two bars. Breakfast included. Takes *ACR* coupons. ⑤.

Orizont, Str. G. Ureche 2 (☎11.27.00). Small complex, around the far side of the *Moldova*. ④.

Sport, Str. Sfîntu Lazar 76 (☎13.78.17). Behind a bank 500m downhill from the Palace of Culture. The cheapest place in town – no singles or frills. ③.

Traian, Piaţa Unirii 1 (☎14.33.30). Atmospheric nineteenth-century establishment that's still quite elegant and only a little more expensive than the *Continental*. All rooms with baths or showers; breakfast included. Accepts *ACR* coupons. ④.

Unirea, Piaţa Unirii 5 (☎14.21.10). High-rise Sixties building that's showing its age. All rooms with private baths; breakfast included. Takes *ACR* coupons. ⑤.

The Town

Many of the sights of Iaşi can be found on the streets radiating from the **Piaţa Unirii** (Square of Union), whose bronze **statue of Cuza** (see box on p.213) has been reduced to pygmy status by the *Hotel Unirea* and a shopping precinct leading up to Bulevardul Independenţei. Strada Lăpuşneanu, running off by the *Hotel Traian*, leads to Cuza's old house at no. 14. Here, the **Union Museum** (Tues–Sun 10am–5pm) boasts a coffee set emblazoned with an imperial *N* – symbolizing Napoleon III's support for unification – and glosses over Cuza's *opéra-bouffe* downfall. Bursting into his bedroom, soldiers found him making love to the King of Serbia's daughter-in-law; when pressed to sign a decree of abdication, he objected, "But I haven't got a pen". "We have thought of that", they said, producing a pen and ink; whereupon Cuza rose from bed complaining of the lack of a table. "I will offer myself", said a colonel, presenting his back to forestall further procrastination . . . and so Cuza signed and went into exile. He died in Heidelberg in 1873.

Along Ştefan cel Mare

Iaşi's traditional interplay of civil and religious authority is symbolized by a parade of edifices along **Strada Ştefan cel Mare** – where florid public buildings face grandiose churches. The huge colonnaded **Metropolitan Cathedral**, built in the 1830s, dominates the neighbouring Metropolitan's Palace and Theological College, and dwarfs worshippers with its cavernous interior, painted by Tattarescu. The cathedral overflows in mid-October, when thousands come to kneel before the blue and gold bier containing the **relics of St Paraschiva** (c.980–1050). Venerated as the patron saint of Moldavia, households, harvests, traders and travellers, Iaşi's St Paraschiva seems to be a conflation of four Orthodox martyrs of that name. Nearby stands the Old Metropolitan **Church of St George**, raised in 1761; the pillars of its porch are carved with symbolic animal reliefs, in the post-Brîncoveanu style of Wallachia.

Across the road behind an elegant park, the French-eclectic **National Theatre**, built by the Viennese architects Felner and Helmer in the 1890s, is named after its founder and first director, Vasile Alecsandri (1821–90) who, owing to a lack of plays in Romanian, had to write much of its initial repertory. He is duly honoured by a statue outside the theatre, and its auditorium is one of the most beautiful in the country.

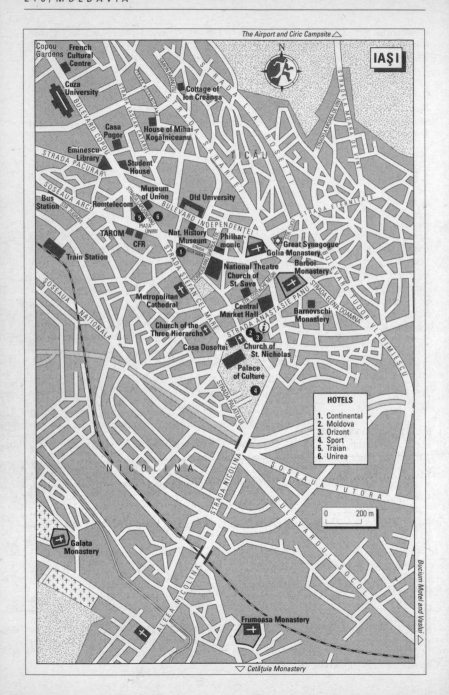

The Airport and Ciric Campsite △

IAŞI

Copou Gardens
French Cultural Centre
Cuza University
Cottage of Ion Creangă
Casa Pogor
House of Mihai Kogălniceanu
Eminescu Library
STRADA PACURARI
Student House
Museum of Union
Old University
Bus Station
Romtelecom
SOSEAUA ARCU
TAROM
CFR
Nat. History Museum
Philhar-monic
Train Station
Great Synagogue
Golia Monastery
Barboi Monastery
National Theatre
Church of St. Sava
Metropolitan Cathedral
SOSEAUA NATIONALA
Central Market Hall
Barnovschi Monastery
Church of the Three Hierarchs
Casa Dosoftei
Church of St. Nicholas
Palace of Culture

HOTELS
1. Continental
2. Moldova
3. Orizont
4. Sport
5. Traian
6. Unirea

N I C O L I N A

0   200 m

Galata Monastery

Frumoasa Monastery

△ Cetăţuia Monastery

Bucium Motel and Vaslui △

Further along Strada Ştefan cel Mare stands the famous **Church of the Three Hierarchs** (*Trei Ierarhi*), its exterior carved all over with chevrons, meanders and rosettes as intricate as lace. When completed in 1639 – perhaps by the Armenian master-builder, Ianache Etisi – Basil the Wolf had the exterior gilded, desiring it to surpass all other churches in splendour. Aside from its unique carvings, the church follows the classic Byzantine tribolate plan, with two octagonal drums mounted above the naos and pronaos in the Moldavian fashion. Visiting hours enable you to view the **sarcophagi of Dimitrie Cantemir and Alexandru Cuza** (daily 9am–1pm & 3–7pm); otherwise, the church only opens for services (Mon–Sat 5.30am & 5.30pm, Sun 8am). The nearby abbot's house contains a **museum** of religious art (Tues–Sun 10am–4pm).

By backtracking and turning off onto Strada Costache Negru, you can also find the contemporaneous – yet quite different – **Church of St Sava**, whose earth-coloured walls and red pantiles give it the look of an Andean village church. Its massive, squat belltower is doubly impressive for being devoid of ornamentation. Unfortunately, you can't go inside.

The Palace of Culture and around

At the southern end of Ştefan cel Mare, an equestrian **statue of Stephen the Great** and a cross to the martyrs of the revolution are overshadowed by the stupendous **Palace of Culture** (*Palatul Culturii*) – a Neo-Gothic pile built between 1890 and 1926 as a government centre, which houses four museums (Tues–Sun 10am–5pm). Its spired tower and pinnacled wings presage a vast lobby awash with mosaics, stained glass and armorial reliefs, dominated by a magnificent double staircase. You can admire the decor free of charge, but separate tickets are required for entry to each museum. Currently, only two are open.

The corridor on the right of the lobby leads to a **Polytechnical Museum** of music boxes, symphoniums and orchestrions. Depending on the number of visitors, the curators might demonstrate the ingenious Popper's Bianca which anticipated the motion-picture show. Upstairs, casts of antique statues line the way to an **Ethnographic Museum** exhibiting woven skirts and embroidered waistcoats, six-foot-long Moldavian alpine horns, hollow trunks used as beehives, and oil-presses the size of trees. Should they reopen, the **Moldavian History Museum** is notable for its vaulted *Sala Voievozilor*, containing the portraits of dozens of rulers, while the **Museum of Art** has a fine collection of post-1919 Colourist works, such as Pallady's *Nude on a Yellow Background*.

Two much-restored relics of Iaşi's past stand between the Palace and the *Centru Civic*. Having housed a press that spread the words of the cleric and scholar, Metropolitan Dosoftei (a statue of whom sits outside), the arcaded seventeenth-century **Casa Dosoftei** makes a fitting but dull **Museum of Old Moldavian Literature** (Tues–Sun 10am–5pm). The Phanariot policy of using Iaşi's presses to spread Greek as the language of Orthodox ritual had the unintended result of displacing the ossified Old Slavonic tongue from this position, clearing the way for intellectuals to agitate for the use of their own language, Romanian. Next door is a copy of the **Church of St Nicholas** built by Stephen in 1491, which the French architect Lecomte de Noüy pulled down and rebuilt in 1888–1904, its svelte facade masking a hermetic world of carved pews and gilded frescoes.

The Centru Civic and Golia Monastery

Due to the array of administrative buildings that already existed on Ştefan cel Mare, the architects of Iaşi's *Centru Civic* wisely focused on consumer aspirations instead, hence the modernistic **Central Market Hall** (*Hala Centrală*) and the rounded **Scala complex** on the other side of Strada Anastasie Panu. Further along, an unfinished department store allows a glimpse of the former **Barnovschi Monastery**, founded by Prince Barnovschi in 1627, and now reduced to a pale buff church with a shingled porch and onion-spire, flanked by a gatetower.

Another monument to feudal ambition has fared better in a walled garden with a tall Byzantine gatetower, at the far end of the main road. The **Barboi Monastery** still bears the name of its seventeenth-century founder, Urşu Barboi, but its Church of Peter and Paul was built in the 1840s by Dimitrie Sturza, who is buried in the pronaos. Notice the overhead gallery, for the choir.

North of the *Centru Civic*, protected by a 30-metre-tall gatetower and rounded corner bastions, the **Golia Monastery** is a peaceful haven in the heart of Iaşi, whose dozen monks enjoy a rose garden dotted with shrines. Founded in the 1560s by Chancellor Ion Golia, the monastery was fortified by Basil the Wolf, who began a new **Church of the Ascension**, completed by his son Ştefaniţa in 1660. A striking mixture of Byzantine, Classical and Russian architecture, the church boasts of its associations with Tsarist Russia, having been visited by Peter the Great in 1711, and serving as the burial-place for the **viscera of Prince Potemkin**, Catherine the Great's favourite. The organs were removed so that Potemkin's body could be preserved and returned home after he died in 1791, having caught a fever in Iaşi and defied doctors' orders by wolfing huge meals, starting with smoked goose and wine for breakfast.

Along Bulevardul Independenţei

Bulevardul Independenţei, a drab thoroughfare linking the monastery with Strada Lăpuşneanu, has a few sights worth noting. Between an apartment building and a clump of kiosks near the start of the boulevard, you can see the Star of David atop the **Great Synagogue** – a sad misnomer for this lowly domed edifice founded in 1671 and restored in the 1970s (shortly before most of its congregation left for Israel), which now shows little sign of being used.

Further up the boulevard at no. 72, the **Natural History Museum** (Tues, Thurs & Sat 9am–3pm, Wed, Fri & Sun 9am–4pm) occupies the eighteenth-century Russet House, where the election of Cuza as Prince of Moldavia took place in 1859, in the Elephant Hall. It then belonged to the Society of Physicians and Naturalists, who opened their mineral, flora and fauna collections to the public in 1834, making this one of the first such museums in Romania. Across the road stands the **Old University** (now the University of Medicine and Pharmacology), a Baroque pile that was constructed between 1795 and 1806 as a palace for the Callamachis, and given to the university in 1860. Alongside rises the spooky **gatetower** of the St Spiridon Monastery (which now serves as a hospital); the old **church** contains the tomb of its founder, Grigore Ghica, whose head was sent giftwrapped to the Sultan, for harbouring treasonous thoughts.

The boulevard finally leads to the **Independence Monument**, a statuesque woman striding forth ahead of billowing drapery, sculpted by Gabriela and Gheorghe Adoc in 1980. From here you can head past a big **outdoor market** towards the University district (see below) or return to Piaţa Unirii via the shopping precinct behind the *Hotel Unirea*.

Copou

Copou, the university district, lies northwest of the centre, out along the boulevard of the same name, where trams (#1, #4, #8 & #13) rattle uphill with students hanging out of the doors. The foot of the hill is distinguished by a Stalinesque **Student House** (*Casa Studenţilor*) with bas reliefs of musical youth, alongside a small park overlooked by crumbling **statues of Moldavian princes** (Dragoş, Alexander the Good, Basil the Wolf and Dimitrie Cantemir), and the colonnaded **Eminescu Library**. Working here as a librarian, Eminescu could nip across the road for meetings of the *Junimea* literary society (1863–85) in the **Casa Pogor**. The house belonged to Vasile Pogor, a co-founder of the society who isn't included in the canon of writers honoured by statues outside, but is duly mentioned in the **Museum of Moldavian Literature** on the premises.

Further uphill, **Cuza University**, an Empire-style edifice built by Louis Blanc in the 1890s, acts as an umbrella for 26 faculties and eight research institutes of the Romanian Academy. Nearby are the tranquil **Copou Gardens**, where Eminescu meditated under a favourite lime tree. The park is full of ponds, with an Alley of Busts of the notables who once frequented it, an obelisk to the dead of World War I, and an **exhibition centre** (Tues–Sun 10am–5pm) featuring a section on Eminescu (see box below).

Ţicău

Ţicău is a pretty, hilly, old residential quarter, east of the university area, where two memorial museums (Tues–Sun 10am–5pm) provide an excuse for a ramble. At no. 15 on the street that now bears his name, the **house of Mihai Kogălniceanu** commemorates the orator and journalist (1817–91) who was banned from lecturing for lambasting "oppression by an ignorant aristocracy", and who fled to Hapsburg Bucovina in 1848, but returned to help secure Cuza's election and serve as foreign minister. More entertaining is the adobe *Bojdeuca* or **cottage of Ion Creangă**, at Str. Barnutiu 11, which displays first editions and prints of his works, including stills from films made from them. A defrocked priest and failed teacher, Creangă (1837–89) wrote *Recollections of Childhood* and fairy tales like the *Giants of Irunica*, finally achieving success just before he died.

MIHAI EMINESCU

Mihai Eminescu, Romania's "national poet", was born in Botosani (1850) in northern Moldavia and schooled in Cernăuţi, the capital of Hapsburg Bucovina. At the age of sixteen, he gave his surname, Eminovici, the characteristic Romanian ending -*escu* and became a prompter for a troupe of actors, until his parents packed him off to study law in Vienna and Berlin. Returning to Iaşi in 1874, he found a job as a librarian, joined *Junimea* literary society, and had a tortured affair with the poetess Veronica Micle, the wife of the university rector. After the rector's demise, Eminescu decided that he was too poor to marry her and took an editorial job in Bucharest to drown his grief. Overwork led to a mental breakdown in 1883, and from then on until his death six years later, periods of madness alternated with lucid intervals. He is best remembered for *Luceafărul*, a 96-stanza ballad of love, and the *Evening Star*, which unfortunately doesn't translate well into other languages.

The Frumoasa, Cetățuia and Galata monasteries

A more ambitious way to stretch your legs is to visit the **monasteries** in the Nicolina district, beyond the fetid stream of the same name. Catch tram #9 downhill past the Palace of Culture and out along Strada Nicolina; cresting the flyover, you'll see the Cetățuia and Galata monasteries on separate hilltops, and a modern church with a prow-like spire in the valley, where you should alight. From here, either follow the side street uphill past a cemetery, to reach Galata; or cross the main road, head down through apartment buildings and over the tracks to find Frumoasa Monastery and the trail to Cetățuia. If you're to intending to visit all three, it's best to see Cetățuia – which requires the most effort – before Galata.

The "Beautiful" or **Frumoasa Monastery** looks anything but that – having been derelict for decades – but it remains an imposing sight, on a low plateau surrounded by ruined walls. Founded by the ill-fated Grigore Ghica in 1773, Frumoasa differs from the other monasteries owing to a ponderous form of Neoclassism that found favour when the complex was reconstructed in the early nineteenth century. Its belltower is capped by a black dome that vies for mastery of the skyline with two bell-shaped, brown cupolas atop the church. Although unsafe to enter, they deserve a look from the outside.

At the far end of Strada Cetățuia, you'll find a truck park with a path climbing to the summit of a hill. This is also accessible by road – the path is quicker but a hard slog. Here, the "Fortified" or **Cetățuia Monastery** seems remote from Iași; on misty days, the city is blotted out, and all you can see are moors. Its high walls conceal a harmonious ensemble of white stone buildings with rakish black roofs, interspersed by dwarf pines and centred on a church that's similar to the *Trei Ierarhi* in town, but less richly carved. In the nave are buried Prince Gheorghe Ghica and his wife, who founded the monastery in 1669–72; it was restored in 1930 on the initiative of the historian, Nicolae Iorga.

The **Galata Monastery** on Miroslavei hill, across the valley, is likewise entered by a fortified gatetower. On the right are the ruins of the original monks' quarters and Turkish bath, beside a newer building (1800) in use today. Its church has a typically Moldavian plan, with an enclosed porch and narthex preceding the nave. Galata was founded in 1583 by Prince Petru Șchiopul, who is buried in the nave with his daughter, Despina. Lower down the hill are an elaborate Neo-Brîncoveanu war memorial erected in 1920, and steps down to Aleea Nicolina, which runs past ramshackle cottages and browsing goats, to rejoin the main road.

Eating, drinking and entertainment

The *Traian, Unirea* and *Moldova* hotels have **restaurants** which stay open till 11pm (with bands after 8pm); the *Traian*'s is the nicest, though the menu is much the same at all of them. Definitely the best place to eat is the private *Select Restaurant*, opposite the *Continental*, which offers a wide range of tasty dishes (try the chicken stuffed with mushrooms – *pui umplut cu ciuperci*) and claims to be open 24 hours. Providing you're careful to watch what you drink, it's not too expensive. You'll find various joints dispensing pizza, *mititei* (spicy sausages) and other **snacks** in the vicinity of Piața Unirii, Strada Lăpușneanu, and the university.

There are fairly seedy **bars** in all the hotels. The *Unirea* has a café-bar with a terrace on the thirteenth floor, affording fine views of the city; the *Moldova*'s night bar (10pm–4am) offers a disco of sorts; while the *Traian*'s swarms with Arabs seeking prostitutes. Romanian students frequent the **billiard hall** in the *Scala complex* on the corner of Strada A. Panu, opposite the Central Market Hall. Further back down this side street is the *Dream Club* (Fri & Sat 7.0pm–4am, Sun 7.30pm–2am), Iaşi's liveliest **disco**, where the admission fee and cover charge will set you back about $3. Another trendy hangout is the *Geletari Bar Arlechino* (8am–midnight; closed Tues), located on the stretch of Ştefan cel Mare between Piaţa Unirii and the Metropolitan Church, which serves Italian **ice cream** and imported alcohol.

Entertainment

Iaşi's big event is the **St Paraschiva festival week** (*Sarbatorile Iaşului*) in October, when people from all over Moldavia flood into town to pay homage to the saint buried in the Metropolitan Church. The exact date varies every year, but the most important day is always on a Friday in the middle of the month. In a more folkloric vein, there's a **Festival of Winter Customs** on the first Sunday in January, and a week-long **Ceramics Fair** (*Tîrgul de Ceramica Cucuteni 5000*) towards the end of June. The French Cultural Centre (Mon–Sat 9am–6pm) at B-dul Copou 26 organizes **French Days of Culture** during the summer.

Lovers of classical music should try to attend a performance of the **Moldavian Philharmonic**, the best orchestra in Romania after Bucharest's (which usually poaches its finest soloists). You'll find it on Strada Cuza Vodă behind the National Theatre. Tickets are available at the box office, or from the *Agenţia Teatrală* near the junction of Ştefan cel Mare and Piaţa Unirii.

Listings

Airline office *TAROM* is at Str. Arcu 3 (Mon–Fri 7am–7pm, Sat 7am–noon; ☎11.52.39).

Airport ☎17.81.26 for information.

Car repairs *ACR* (☎13.01.77).

Dentist *Centru Medical Apollonia* at the Piaţa Unirii end of Str. Ştefan cel Mare (Mon–Fri 4–8pm, Sat 8am–noon).

Exchange *Cambio Exchange*, Str. C. Negru (Mon–Sat 9am–6pm, Sun 10am–1pm).

Fuel There are 24hr fuel stations on Şos. Păcurari and Şos. Bucium.

Hospital on the corner of Str. L. Catargi and Str. Berthelot (☎14.06.90).

Photography You can buy film and get photos developed at the well-signposted *Kodak* place on Str. Ştefan cel Mare.

Post office In the *Romtelecom* building on Str. Lăpuşneanu (daily 7am–8pm).

Shopping The *Galerile Anticvariat* at Str. Lăpuşneanu 24 is a good place to browse for antique souvenirs and secondhand books in foreign languages. For food, try the Central Market Hall (Mon 7am–3pm; Tues–Fri 6am–8pm; Sat 7am–6pm) on Str. A. Panu or the outdoor market on Bulevardul Independenţei uphill behind the *Hotel Unirea*.

Telephones Direct-dial international phones are available at *Romtelecom* on Str. Lăpuşneanu (daily 7am–8pm), and in the lobby of the *Hotel Traian*.

Train tickets *CFR* is on the south side of Piaţa Unirii (Mon–Fri 8am–8pm; ☎14.76.73); the section upstairs handles bookings for the *Prietenia* night train to Chişinău in Moldova, for which foreigners must already have a visa.

Suceava and around

Confronted with the belching factories sprawling across the river, it's difficult to imagine **SUCEAVA**, 150km northwest of Iaşi, as an old princely capital. Its heyday more or less coincided with the reign of **Stephen the Great** (1457–1504), who warred ceaselessly against Moldavia's invaders – principally the Turks, then advancing confidently after capturing Constantinople – and won all but two of the thirty-six battles he fought. This record prompted Pope Sixtus IV to dub him the "Athlete of Christ" – a rare tribute to a non-Catholic, which wasn't extended to Stephen's cousin Vlad the Impaler, who massacred 45,000 of the infidel during one year alone.

While Stephen's successors, **Bogdan the One-Eyed** and **Petru Rareş**, maintained the tradition of endowing a church or monastery after every battle, they proved less successful against the Turks, who ravaged Suceava several times. Eclipsed by Iaşi as the capital, its last moment of glory was in 1600, when **Michael the Brave** (*Mihai Viteazu*) completed his campaign to unite the principalities by marching unopposed into Suceava's Princely Citadel. In terms of national pride, the nadir of its fortunes was the long period of **Hapsburg rule** over northern Moldavia (1775–1918), although this allowed Suceava to prosper as a trading centre between the highland and lowland areas.

Under communism, this traditional role was deemed backward and remedied by hasty **industrialization** – the consequences of which now blight the town. Its wood-processing and tanning plants have poisoned miles of the river, while the "Suceava syndrome" of malformed babies has been linked to air **pollution** from the artificial fibres factory. Sadly, like many towns in Romania, Suceava can neither afford to scrap its noxious economic mainstays, nor better exploit the wealth of raw materials in the region.

From a visitor's standpoint, Suceava is primarily a base for **excursions to the Painted Monasteries** (see p.230), which are the only reason to spend much time here. The town's own sights can be covered in a day.

Arrival, information and accommodation

You'll probably arrive at one of the **train stations** in the industrial zone across the river: the **Gara Suceava** (or Gara Burdujeni), linked to the centre by trolleybus #2, and **Suceava Nord** (bus #1 or trolleybus #3 or #5) seem the likeliest bets, as the third station, **Suceava Vest**, chiefly handles freight. Seats on the *accelerat* services to Cluj and Timişoara should be reserved a day in advance at *CFR* on Piaţa 22 Decembrie (Mon–Fri 7am–8pm).

Air passengers are met at the **airport** by buses for the eight-kilometre transfer into town. The *TAROM* office is on Piaţa 22 Decembrie (Mon–Sat 7am–8pm) and the airport bus leaves from outside two hours before each flight.

Most **buses** and trolleybuses stop at the top of the hill near the corner of the main square, Piaţa 22 Decembrie. Local buses run to Dragomirna Monastery, Arbore and Solca (see p.227), and on weekdays to Rădăuţi, the connection for the

---

The **telephone code** for Suceava is ☎030

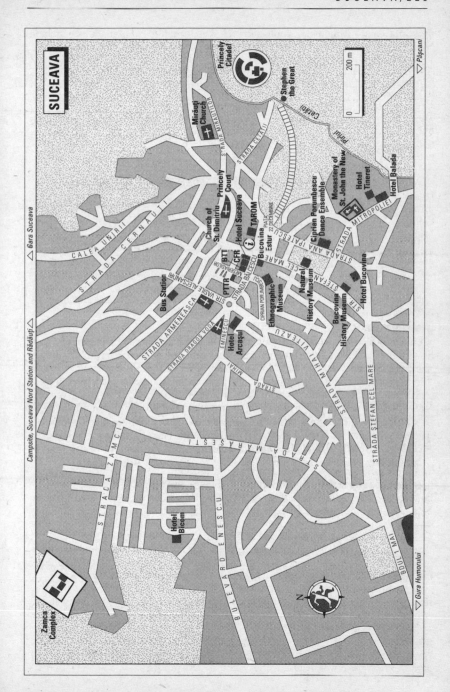

SUCEAVA

Princely Citadel

Stephen the Great

Mirăuți Church

Church of St. Dimitriu

Princely Court

Hotel Suceava

TAROM

Monastery of St. John the New

Hotel Tineret

Hotel Balada

Ciprian Porumbescu Dance Ensemble

Bucovina Estur

BTT

CFR

PTTR

Bus Station

Natural History Museum

Ethnographic Museum

Bucovina History Museum

Hotel Bucovina

Hotel Arcaşul

Hotel Bicom

Zamca Complex

△ Bara Suceava

Campsite, Suceava Nord Station and Rădăuți △

▽ Gura Humorului

▽ Gura Humorului

▽ Pașcani

200 m

0

CALEA UNIRII

STRADA CERNĂUȚI

STR. RADU MIRĂUTILOR

STRADA PETRU

STR VASILE ALECSANDRI

STRADA ARMENEASCA

STRADA DRAGOȘ VODĂ

STRADA MIHAI EMINESCU

MATEI CORVIN

BULEVARDUL ENESCU

STRADA A. MĂRĂȘEȘTI

STRADA C. ZAMCII

STRADA ȘTEFAN CEL MARE

MITROPOLIEI

STRADA ANA IPĂTESCU

STR. ȘTEFAN CEL MARE

MIHAI VITEAZU

BD L 1 MAI

N

Sucevița and Moldovița monasteries. Longer-range destinations include Cîmpulung, Vatra Dornei, Tîrgu Neamț, Brașov and Cernăuți, in Ukraine.

The ONT **tourist office** (Mon–Fri 8am–3.30pm; ☎22.12.97) is also on Piața 22 Decembrie and is useless except for changing money. Happily, an excellent substitute lies just across the square – *Bucovina Estur* (Mon–Fri 9am–5pm, Sat 9am–3pm; ☎22.32.59), whose keen, English-speaking staff supply information, rent private rooms, and offer tailor-made tours of the monasteries for half the cost of the ONT excursion. The *PTTR* office – which doesn't have direct-dial **phones** – occupies a large building on the corner of Strada Bălcescu and Strada Meseriașilor.

TOURS TO THE PAINTED MONASTERIES

Given that everyone comes to Suceava to visit the **Painted Monasteries** (see p.230) and public transport is limited – it's not surprising that many visitors opt for organized **tours**. *Bucovina Estur* provides a car with a driver and a guide for a 250-kilometre-tour covering **Putna**, **Sucevița**, **Moldovița** and **Voroneț** for $106, irrespective of the number of people. You can also devise your own itinerary, based on a standard rate per kilometre and a charge for the guide over 24 hours. As the staff are knowledgeable and charming, and the whole deal costs far less than a poor tour from ONT that might not even materialize, there's really no contest.

Accommodation

Considering what you get, Suceava's **hotels** are pretty overpriced, and low-budget travellers have little choice other than the *Hotel Tineret*. BTT, on the corner of Strada Meseriașilor (Mon–Fri 8am–8pm; ☎21.52.35) can book rooms in the *Tineret* for slightly less than you'd pay on the spot. For solo travellers in particular, the best option is a **private room** in the centre, through *Bucovina Estur*; $25 per person gets you a clean, warm room and three good meals a day.

Camping is not a good option in Suceava. *Suceava Camping*, Str. Cernăuți 1, has been derelict for some time, but it's possible the site might have been revived – it's down a path behind the *Dacia Service* depot at the bottom of the road in from Suceava Nord station.

Arcașul, Str. Mihai Viteazu 4–6 (☎21.09.44). Dour Sixties low-rise near the centre. Breakfast included. ⑤.

Balada, Str. Mitropoliei 3 (☎22.31.98). Smart private hotel boasting satellite TV, downhill from the Monastery of St John the New. Some rooms have double beds and balconies. Breakfast included. ④.

Bicom, Str. Narciselor 10 (☎21.68.81). Another comfy private hotel, with its own hot-water supply, in a quiet suburb 20 minutes' walk from the centre. ④.

Bucovina, B-dul A. Ipatescu 5 (☎21.70.48). Typical Seventies high-rise on the edge of the centre. All rooms with private baths and cable TV; breakfast included. Accepts *ACR* coupons. ⑤.

Gloria, Str. V. Bumbac 4 (☎21.01.48). Similar to the *Arcașul*, but located behind the County Prefecture on Str. Bălcescu. Doubles only, some with kitchens. ④.

Suceava, Str. N. Bălcescu 4 (☎22.24.97). Overpriced and nondescript, but dead central. All rooms with baths or showers; breakfast included. Takes *ACR* coupons. ④.

Tineret, Str. Mitropoliei 5 (☎21.58.86). Located behind the *Balada*, where you'll spot its *BTT* sign. Tolerably basic, with doubles, dorms and shared bathrooms. ①–②.

The Town

Most of Suceava's sights relate to its past as a princely capital, and are easily reached. Just behind the bus stop near the main square, kids scramble over the ruined **Princely Court** (*Curţii Domneşti*), which amounts to very little other than the **Church of St Dimitriu**. A typical Moldavian-style church of the sixteenth century, built by Petru Rareş, its facade features a double row of niche-bound saints, and the drum is ornamented with coloured tiles. The freestanding bell-tower, added thirty years later, bears the Moldavian crest (see box below). At weekends, visitors may encounter **funerals** where the deceased is laid out in an open coffin, amidst candles and loaves of bread, while a horse-drawn hearse waits outside. Corteges often parade around Piaţa 22 Decembrie – as do wedding parties; sometimes one follows another.

By heading up the side street you'll find Suceava's **market**, which is busiest on Thursdays, when cartloads of peasants roll into town to sell their produce. Many wear items of traditional dress such as fur-lined leather or sheepskin waistcoats (*pieptar*), wrap-around skirts (*catriniţă*) or white woollen pantaloons (*iţari*). Further examples – and finer embroideries and crafts rarely seen nowadays – are exhibited in an **Ethnographic Museum** at Str. Ciprian Porumbescu 5 (Mon & Wed–Sun 10am–6pm). The half-timbered building is the oldest civil edifice in Suceava county, and served as an inn during the seventeenth century.

At Str. Ştefan cel Mare 33, the **Bucovina History Museum** (Tues–Sun 10am–8pm) begins with the usual array of Bronze Age amphorae, and works stolidly through medieval times and the independence struggles until 1945, whereupon a slew of paintings replaces the exhibits once devoted to Ceauşescu. The main attraction is a lifesize **model of Stephen's throne room**, with richly costumed figures of the monarch, his wife and boyars. A **Natural History Museum** (Tues–Sun 10am–6pm) full of stuffed wildlife stands further up the road at no. 23.

The Monastery of St John the New

Downhill from Bulevardul Ana Ipatescu, the **Monastery of St John the New** (*Manasteria Sf Ioan cel Nou*) can be located by its colourful steeple, striped with blue, black and yellow chevrons. Started by Prince Bogdan in 1514 and finished by his son Ştefanita in 1522, its monumental **Church of St George** was intended to replace the Mirăuţi Church (see below) as Suceava's Metropolitan cathedral, so no expense was spared. The facade was once covered with **frescoes** like the Painted Monasteries of Bucovina, but, sadly, only the *Tree of Jesse* and a fragment of the *Last Judgement* remain.

PRINCE DRAGOŞ AND THE AUROCH

Churches throughout Moldavia display the emblem of the medieval principality: an auroch's head and a sun, moon and star. This symbolizes the legend of **Prince Dragoş**, who is said to have hunted a giant **auroch** or *zimbru* (a descendant of the wild cattle of the Pleistocene era, larger than a bison) all the way across the mountains from Poland, until he cornered it by a river and slew the beast after a fight lasting from dawn to dusk (hence the Morning Star, sun and moon). In honour of his favourite hunting dog, **Molda** – who also perished – Dragoş bestowed her name on the River Moldova, and adopted as his own totem the auroch – the mightiest animal in the Carpathians until it became extinct in the Middle Ages.

Inside, worshippers prostrate themselves before the coffin holding the **relics of St John the New**, whose martyrdom is depicted on the wall of a small **chapel** near the church. Arrested for preaching in Turkish-occupied Moldavia, he was dragged through the streets of Cetăţii Alba behind a horse, and slashed to death by enraged Muslims. The monastery serves as the headquarters of the **Patriarchate of Suceava and Bucovina**, besides which, there is also a pavilion for the blessing of holy water (stored in 230-litre drums, for the faithful to take away in bottles).

The Princely Citadel and the Mirăuţi Church

Suceava's most impressive monument is the **Princely Citadel** (Tues–Sun 10am–6pm) atop a hill overlooking the centre. Also known as *Scaun* (seat or throne), the citadel was founded in the fourteenth century by Petru Muşat I – who moved the capital from Siret to Suceava – and strengthened by Alexander the Good. Stephen the Great added the moat, curtain walls and bastions that enabled it to defy Mohammed II, the victor of Constantinople, in 1476. Although blown up in 1675, much of the three-storey keep and the outyling chambers remain; from the ramparts, there's a fine view of Suceava and the Mirăuti Church, across the valley.

To reach the citadel, descend through the park opposite the main square; cross the bridge into the woods and follow the path uphill to the giant equestrian **statue of Stephen the Great**, unveiled in 1977; the bas-reliefs on the pedestal depict the battle of Vaslui, against the Turks. From here, several paths lead to the citadel, slightly further on and about 20 minutes' walk from the centre.

WINTER AND SUMMER FESTIVALS AT ILIŞEŞTI

Many villages in northern Moldavia still hold **winter festivities** that mingle pagan and Christian rites. Preparations for Christmas become obvious on St Nicholas's Day (December 6), when people butcher pigs for the feast beside the roads – not a sight for the squeamish. Women get to work baking pies and the special pastries called *turte*, symbolizing Christ's swaddling clothes, while the men rehearse songs and dances. On Christmas Eve (*Ajun*), boys go from house to house singing *colinde* that combine felicitations with risque innuendoes, accompanied by an instrument which mimics the bellowing of a bull. After days of feasting and dancing, the climax comes on New Year's Eve day, when the **Goat** (*Capra*) is unleashed. Garbed in black and red, with a goat's head mask which he clacks to the music of drums and flutes, the *Capra* whips through the streets the **Bear** (*Urşi*), who symbolizes the forces of nature and dances until he drops, only reviving when other dancers – dressed as lancers, Turks or "Little Horses" – appear. Then a brass band starts playing and everyone begins downing *ţuicăs* and dancing, setting the pattern for a binge that will last all night.

The easiest place to experience these festivities is the commune of **ILIŞEŞTI**, 19km west of Suceava – which also hosts a **summer folklore festival**, "From the Rarău Mountain" (*De sub montale Rarău*), on the second Sunday of July. Ensembles from three counties – Bacău, Neamţ and Maramureş – participate, and it's a chance to enjoy *horăs* and shepherds' dances, fiddles, flutes and alpine horns, and a panoply of costumes.

Without a car, Ilişeşti is best reached from Suceava by **bus** (3–4 daily; 1hr), as the nearest train halts, Stroieşti and Păltinoasa, are up to 9km away. There's a **motel-campsite** (①–②) 6km down the road to Păltinoasa.

Returning to town, you can take another path through the woods to emerge near the **Mirăuţi Church**. Likewise founded by Petru Muşat, this was originally the Metropolitan cathedral, where the early princes of Moldavia were crowned. Its facade is decorated with blind arches and a sawtoothed cornice sandwiched between thick cable mouldings, while below the eaves are frescoes of saints, added in the nineteenth century. The church is currently closed for restoration.

The Zamca complex
Another, more neglected ruin straddles a plateau on the northwest edge of town, 25 minutes' walk from the centre. Surrounded by a dry moat and overgrown earthworks, the **Zamca complex** was founded as a monastery in 1606, and later fortified with ramparts and a gatetower. Its church combines Gothic and Classical elements with oriental motifs, introduced by Armenian settlers – but is so derelict that you can't enter. Much of the compound is planted with cabbages, belonging to a family squatting in the three-storey *clişarniţa*, where dignitaries were once accommodated. Though not much from a monumental standpoint, the site has a desolate grandeur at dusk.

Eating, drinking and entertainment

Eating out boils down to a choice between the cavernous **restaurants** in the *Suceava*, *Bucovina* and *Arcaşul* hotels; the dark, old-fashioned *National* (daily 7.30am–11pm) at Str. Bălcescu 3; and the sleazy *Bucureşti* (daily 6am–8pm) on the corner of the main square. With a car, it's better to eat at the *Casa Bucovina*, 1km from downtown Suceava on the road to Rădăuţi. Otherwise, there are several **fast-food** outlets near the market.

Aside from a **disco** in the *Casa Culturii* on the main square (Thurs–Sun 7pm–2am), and the cinema, the youth of Suceava have little else to do but drink and smooch in parks after dark. The **Ciprian Porumbescu Dance Ensemble** on Bulevardul Ana Ipatescu is often away on tour, but sure to appear at the "From the Rarău Mountain" **folklore festival** at Ilişeşti, in July (see box opposite).

Dragomirna Monastery

The nearest of the monasteries to Suceava is the (unpainted) Dragomirna convent, 4km beyond the village of **Mitocul Dragomirnei**, 12km north of town. On weekdays, **buses** to the village leave about 6am, 11.50am and 3pm; at weekends at 8.30am and 3.20pm; in each case, starting the return journey to Suceava roughly half an hour after they arrive. If you're **driving** or hitching, be sure to take the left-hand road where it forks at the iron *Mitocoul Dragomirnei* sign; buses stop 750m further along. Rolling plains conceal the monastery until the last moment – much of the surrounding land is farmed by the nuns.

Massively walled like a fortress, the **Dragomirna Monastery** (daily 9am–5pm) was founded in 1602 by Metropolitan Anastasie Crimca, who designed its **church**. Crimca is thought to have suffered from the same eye defect as El Greco, which might explain its extraordinary proportions: the church is 42m high but only 9.6m wide. Its white stone facade is encircled by a thick cable moulding, below a double row of pendentive arches; the trefoil windows reflect the influence of Polish Gothic architecture, with which Crimca was familiar. Its octagonal tower, resting on two star-shaped pedestals, is carved with meanders and rosettes, like the Church of the Three Hierarchs in Iaşi. The pronaos contains several pre-Christian tombs, brought here from the Black Sea coast, while Crimca himself is buried in the nave; his portrait is visible on the pillar to the left as you walk through. The star-vaulted nave is covered in dark blue, red and gold frescoes (some with buildings in the background, which was uncommon then); its iconostasis comes from the Socola Monastery.

The complex also contains a smaller church with an open porch in the Wallachian style, modernized living quarters for the seventy nuns, and a **museum** harbouring seven illuminated manuscripts which (together with 19 others in Romania and abroad) are the only surviving products of the school of illuminators founded by Crimca, who was a talented artist himself. The defensive **walls** and towers were added in 1627 by Prince Miron Barnovschi, owing to the threat of foreign invasions. These were so frequent that wooden village churches were sometimes mounted on wheels so that they could be towed away to safety.

While the **campsite** outside seems to have shut for good, up to four women visitors at a time can **stay at the convent**. The lodgings are comfortable (but lacking hot water), and the ambience is tranquil. Would-be guests must book a week before, through *Bucovina Estur* in Suceava.

Arbore and Solca

Though **Arbore and Solca** are often grouped together with the Painted Monasteries, neither of them have ever been more than a village church, and only Arbore has the external frescoes characteristic of the genre. Such quibbles aside, however, their kinship in form and spirit is undeniable. Getting there (and back) by **public transport** takes most of the day, and precludes carrying on to any of the other monasteries. Buses from Suceava either run directly to Solca, or take a roundabout route to Arbore, via Rădăuţi and Solca. On weekdays, the last bus back from Solca passes through Arbore about 6.15pm.

Arbore

Opposite the cemetery on the road through **ARBORE**, 33km from Suceava, stands a **church** built in 1503 by one of Stephen's generals, Luca Arbore, who owned the village. While its wooden stockade and stone belltower are rustic enough, its frescoed walls and sweeping roof are as majestic as any monastic edifice. Like the Painted Monasteries, its murals follow iconic conventions inherited from Byzantium, which designated subjects for each wall, arranged in rows according to their hierachical significance. This is obvious on the apses, where the angels and seraphim appear at the top; archangels and biblical saints below; then martyrs; and lastly a row of cultural propagators or military saints.

As usual, the images on the exposed northern side of the church have been obliterated by the weather, and the best-preserved **frescoes** are found on the relatively sheltered south and west walls. The former is covered by eight rows of scenes from Genesis and the *Lives of the Saints*, where some colours have faded, while others remain as lustrous as medieval miniatures. Red, yellow, pink and ochre counterpoint the prevailing green, of which five shades and 47 hues have been identified. The eaves and buttresses have protected half of the *Last Judgement*, which consigns "heathens" awaiting hell to the top right-hand corner; from the sixteenth century onwards, Christian Armenians joined the Turks, Jews and Tartars in perdition, as Romanian merchants felt threatened by their competition.

Since the church is only open for services, you're unlikely to be able to view Arbore's tomb, beneath a canopy in the pronaos, nor his votive portrait. In the courtyard lie two heavy, hollowed-out stone **slabs used for mixing colours**, after the walls had been rendered with charcoal and lamp-black. As a glance at most Romanian buildings makes plain, the key to the frescoes' durability has been lost; the artists worked in secret and left no records. Though scientists from MIT and Tokyo University have managed to identify thirty substances – including animal size, vinegar, egg, gall and honey – ten ingredients still elude discovery. Since duplicating the paint is impossible, restorers can only hope to stabilize what's left of the frescoes.

Solca

Moldavian fortified monasteries were usually sited at the head of a valley to form a defensive bottleneck against the Turks or Tartars, who hated fighting in confined spaces. The exact spot was decided by shooting arrows from a nearby hilltop; where the first one landed, they dug for a water source that was henceforth deemed holy; the second arrow determined the location of the altar; the third the belfry, and so on. After the monastery was finished, they raised crosses on the hill from where the arrows had been fired.

All these conventions were observed at **SOLCA**, 8km up the valley, where the church built in 1612–20 was fortified like a monastery due to its strategic location on the edge of the highlands. Though lacking any monks' quarters, it was meant to be garrisoned in times of crisis – there are cellars for storing gunpowder and holes in the wall for supporting the archers' galleries. The **church** is tall and heavily buttressed, with the characteristically Moldavian octagonal belfry on a double star-shaped base, straddling a steep roof (newly retiled in red, purple, white and yellow – like that of the gatetower). In the courtyard there's a wooden cross in honour of the martyrs of the revolution, where funeral cakes are blessed and prayers are said at Easter.

The beauty of the scene is only marred by the foul smokestacks of Solca's **beer factory**, next door. Villagers once boasted of the product and of their pure spring water, but nowadays sadly acknowledge that the quality of both has declined. Otherwise, most people are employed in forestry and raise animals in their backyards.

Should you feel like a day or two in the country, exploring the woods or **skiing** in wintertime, it's possible to stay with the Strugariu family, at Str. Gheorghe Doja 30A. Their house near the church has warm **rooms** and hot water; hearty meals are included. Book a week in advance through *Bucovina Estur* in Suceava. There's a grubby **restaurant** (10am–8pm; closed Tues) in the *Complex Commercial* near the metal bridge.

Rădăuţi and Marginea

The dreary market town of **RĂDĂUŢI** (pronounced Ra-dah-*oots*) could be ignored but for its role in the local transport network, which bridges the gap betweeen Putna and the Painted Monasteries of Suceviţa and Moldoviţa. However, in the event of having to wait for a connection, you can check out a few sights in the centre. The **Bogdana Church** is the oldest in Moldavia, having been erected by Bogdan Vodă (1359–65), who forged the principality and made Rădăuţi its capital. Though it was the patriarchal seat before this moved to Suceava, the church is a simple building, without any frills; Bogdan's tomb lies in the nave.

The **Ethnographic Museum** (daily 8am–4pm) a few blocks away on the corner of Strada Republicii has a fine collection of local costumes, and artefacts whose ingenuity is epitomized by a water-powered fulling mill for beating cloth. By washing textiles up to twenty times, Bucovinan women produced embroidered blouses whose colours remain fresh 100 years later. The stripe on their skirts indicated whether they were married (blue) or not (red). Off hall 9, you can visit the *atelier* of Constantin Colibaba and his sons, who continue a tradition of ceramics painted with birds and flowers in green, yellow and brown; items can be bought in the workshop.

Rădăuţi itself is only worth visiting on Thursdays or Fridays, when it hosts a **bazaar** attended by peasants from the surrounding villages, and Ukrainians trying to earn money by selling their family hierlooms. To add to the mayhem on Fridays, there's also **car spares market** that draws people from all over Moldavia. By the same token, this is the worst time to try to change buses or get a room in town.

The *Hotel Nordic* (☎030/41.66.40; ③) across the road from the museum has a panelled lobby that ill prepares visitors for the dingy **rooms** and cold-water facilities upstairs. If you have a car, it's better to go for the *Popasul Vladul Vladichii* (☎030/46.44.09; ①), 3km outside town on the Suceava road, which has huts open all year, and a twenty-four hour bar and **restaurant** from April to September. Rădăuţi's **bus station** is 200m down the road from the *Hotel Nordic*. Aside from buses to the monasteries of Suceviţa and Moldoviţa there are services to Suceava, Cîmpulung and Tîrgu Neamţ. Putna Monastery is accessible by regular **trains** up the branch line from Rădăuţi.

Marginea

The commune of **MARGINEA**, on the road between Rădăuţi and Suceviţa, is traditionally known for producing **black pottery**, as featured in Rădăuţi's Ethnographic Museum. If you're curious to see it being made, the *atelier* (Mon–Fri 9am–5pm) is on the main road opposite a metal sign in the form of a pot (not to be confused with the giant 3-D ceramic pot down the road). Motorists should note that Marginea is also linked by a side road to Solca (see p.229) and Putna (see p.232). The latter route passes through **VOITINEL**, which is notable for being entirely populated by **Gypsies** – the only such village in Suceava county. Should you need **accommodation**, the *Motel Vicov* (☎030/46.41.38; ③) in **GĂLĂNEŞTI** will go to the trouble of warming up a room if you contact them in advance (their phone number is a fax number, too). It also has a **restaurant** (daily 10am–9pm).

The Painted Monasteries of Southern Bucovina

The **Painted Monasteries of Southern Bucovina** are rightfully acclaimed as masterpieces of art and architecture, steeped in history and perfectly in harmony with their surroundings. Founded in the fifteenth and sixteenth centuries, they were citadels of Orthodoxy in an era overshadowed by the threat of infidel invaders. **Metropolitan Roşca** is credited with the idea of covering the churches' outer walls with paintings of biblical events and apocrypha, for the benefit of the illiterate faithful. These **frescoes**, billboards from the late medieval world, are

essentially Byzantine, but infused with the vitality of folk art and mythology. Though little is known about the artists – who guarded their trade secrets by working in seclusion – their skills were such that the paintings are still fresh after 450 years' exposure. Remarkably, the layer of colour is only 0.25mm thick, in contrast to Italian frescoes, where the paint is absorbed deep into the plaster.

If forced to choose between them, the prize for monumental compositions goes to **Voroneţ**, whose *Last Judgement* surpasses any of the other examples of this subject, or to **Suceviţa**, for its unique *Ladder of Virtue* and a splendid *Tree of Jesse*. However, **Moldoviţa** is a better all-rounder, with a fine *Last Judgement* and *Tree of Jesse* and a brilliant *Siege of Constantinople*, while **Humor** has the most tranquil atmosphere. In addition, there is **Putna Monastery**, which doesn't have any frescoes, but is still mightily impressive, housing the tomb of Stephen the Great. The churches at Arbore and Solca (see p.228) could also be included on the circuit if you have a car.

The monasteries are scattered across a region divided by imposing hills or "crests" (*obcine*) branching off from the Carpathians – and also by history. When the Hapsburgs annexed northern Moldavia in 1774, they coined the name *Bucovina* – "beech covered land" – to describe their new acquisition, which they governed from Cernăuți. Romania recovered Bucovina after World War I, but in 1940 the northern half was occupied by the Soviet Union and incorporated into Ukraine – which still retains it. Thus, Romanians speak of **Southern Bucovina** to describe what is actually the far north of Moldavia – implying that Bucovina might be reunited one day. Names aside, the scenery is wonderful, with misty valleys and rivers spilled down from rocky shoulders heaving up beneath a cloak of beech and fir. The woods are at their loveliest in May and autumn.

Visiting the monasteries
Without a car, visiting the monasteries is a time-consuming business, so many tourists opt for **excursions** run by agencies in Suceava (see p.224), which enable you to see all four Painted Monasteries plus Putna in a long day. Otherwise, **getting there** involves striking out by train from Suceava or by bus from Rădăuți, and staying overnight at each location. (Moldovița and Sucevița are also accessible by bus from Cîmpulung.) The routings make it hard to get from one monastery to another without backtracking, although this can be avoided by **hiking** across the hills at certain points. **Accommodation** presents less difficulties since there are enough hotels and campsites to make camping wild unnecessary – but the choice of **food** is limited, so you'd be wise to stock up in Suceava.

Though the monasteries have no set **visiting hours**, you can assume they'll be open 9am–5pm daily, except for their museums, which are closed on Monday. There is a modest **admission charge**, plus a surcharge ($3) for cameras or videos. As working convents or monasteries, they prohibit smoking, and will turn away visitors whose **dress** offends Orthodox sensibilities.

Putna

Putna lacks the external murals of the Painted Monasteries, but as the first of the great religious monuments of Southern Bucovina and the burial place of Stephen the Great it seems a good place to start, with the advantage of being accessible by train from Suceava or Rădăuți. The slow ride past meandering rivers and fir-clad hills whets your appetite for **PUTNA** village – a wonderful jigsaw of wooden houses with carved gables and shingled roofs. Head uphill from the station till you reach the main road, and bear left; the monastery is at the end of a tree-lined drive, 1km further on.

In 1466, Stephen chose the site of **Putna Monastery** by firing an arrow from the steep hill that now bears a white cross. The monastery was rebuilt by Stephen after it burnt down in 1480; ravaged by war in the seventeenth century and repaired in the eighteenth; only to be damaged by an earthquake and restored again in 1902. Its walls and belltower were plainly intended for defence; in less troubled times, they emphasize Putna's status as a patriotic reliquary, with a statue of Eminescu inside the entrance to identify the national poet with Moldavia's national hero.

The **church** is plain and strong, its facade defined by cable mouldings, blind arcades and trefoil windows, while the interior follows the usual configuration of three chambers: the sanctuary (or naos), containing the altar and iconostasis at its eastern end; the nave (or pronaos); and the narthex, just inside the porch – although at Putna, the porch has also been enclosed to form an esonarthex. Prince Bogdan the One-Eyed, the wife of Petru Rareș and Stephen's daughter and nephew are buried in the narthex, which is separated from the nave by two thick cable-moulded columns. Here, a graceful arch and a hanging votive lamp distinguish the **tomb of Stephen the Great** (right) from those of his two wives (both called Maria). Unusually for an Orthodox church, the interior is unpainted, but illuminated by stained-glass windows.

Outside stand three **bells**, the largest of which (cast in 1484) was only used to herald events such as royal deaths, and was last rung in 1918 when it was heard in Suceava. Hidden from the communists for almost fifty years, it only came to light after the revolution. The middle bell traditionally served for everyday use, while the end one was the gift of an archimandrate who repaired its sixteenth-century precursor. At the rear of the yard stands a tower that was used as a treasury in medieval times; the monks' cells along the wall date from 1856. Antique embroidery, silver psalters and illuminated manuscripts are exhibited in a small **museum** (Tues–Sun 10am–5pm).

Uphill and slightly to the east of the monastery, there's a curious hollowed-out rock with a door and window, reputedly once the **cell of Daniil the Hermit** – a monk who was indirectly responsible for the foundation of Suceviţa Monastery (see below). The **wooden church** back along the main road is supposed to have been raised by Dragoş Vodă, and moved to its present location by Stephen.

Practicalities

Basic double and quadruple **rooms** are available at the *Cabana Turistica Putna* (☎030/104; ①), near the wooden church, which is open year round and charges by the bed. There is also a summer **campsite** with huts (①) and a **restaurant**, closer to the monastery. Owing to a lack of **buses** from Putna, travelling on to the Painted Monasteries entails catching a train to Rădăuţi, and a bus from there.

From Putna, **hiking to Suceviţa Monastery** takes about three hours. Pick up the route (marked by blue crosses) from Putna station rather than at the monastery (where several trails converge). After following the main valley for about an hour, ignore the turn-off to the left near a hut and a bridge, but take the next turning on the right, cross another bridge and carry on round to the left, which will bring you out at Canton Silvic 13. From here, stick to the forestry track up to Strulinoasa Sud, which deteriorates into a pony trail as it approaches the watershed, but improves once it descends into an open valley. You should reach the monastery about an hour and half after crossing the watershed.

Suceviţa

Suceviţa Monastery – the last and grandest of the monastic complexes – owes nothing to Stephen or his heirs, being a monument to the boyars Iremia Movilă, his brother Simion (who succeeded him as *hospodar*), and his widow, Elisabeta – who poisoned Simion so that her own sons might inherit the throne. Their first foundation was a village church (now surrounded by a graveyard), followed by the monastery church in 1584, and its walls, towers and belfry in stages thereafter. Massively built, with whitewashed walls and steep grey roofs, the fortifications enhance the grandeur of the church, whose **frescoes** – painted in 1596 by two brothers – offset brilliant reds and blues by an undercoat of emerald green.

Entering the monastery, you're confronted by a glorious *Ladder of Virtue* covering the northern wall, which is less eroded than usual owing to the colossal eaves. Flights of angels assist the righteous to paradise (*rai*), while sinners fall through the rungs into the arms of a grinning demon. The message is reiterated by the *Last Judgement* beneath the porch – reputedly left unfinished because the artist fell from the scaffolding and died – where angels sound the last trump and smite heathens with swords, as Turks and Jews lament, and the Devil gloats in the bottom right-hand corner. Outside the porch, you'll see the two-headed Beast of the Apocalypse, and angels pouring rivers of fire and treading the grapes of wrath. Also notice the iron ox-collar hanging by the doorway, which is beaten to summon the monks to prayer.

The *Tree of Jesse* on the south wall symbolizes the continuity between the Old and the New Testament, being a literal depiction of the prophecy in Isaiah that the Messiah will spring "from the stem of Jesse". This lush composition on a dark blue background amounts to a biblical Who's Who, with an ancestral tree of prophets culminating in the Holy Family. *The Veil* represents Mary as a Byzantine empress, beneath a red veil held by angels, while the *Hymn to the Virgin* is illustrated with Italianate buildings and people in oriental dress. Alongside is a frieze of ancient philosophers clad in Byzantine cloaks; Plato bears a coffin and a pile of bones on his head, in tribute to his meditations on life and death. As usual, the hierachy of angels, prophets, apostles and martyrs covers the curved apse at the eastern end.

Inside the narthex, the lives of the saints end with them being burnt, boiled, dismembered or decapitated – a gory catalogue relieved by rams, suns and other zodiacal symbols. As usual, the frescoes in the nave are blackened by candle-smoke, but you can still discern a votive picture of Elisabeta and her children on the wall to the right. Ironically, her ambitions for them came to nought as she died in a Sultan's harem – "by God's will", a chronicler noted sanctimoniously. Iremia and Simion are buried nearby.

By climbing the **hill** behind the village church's graveyard, you can see the complex as a whole, and appreciate its magnificent setting at the foot of the surrounding hills, carpeted with firs and lush pastures.

Practicalities

Suceviţa lies midway between Moldoviţa Monastery on the far side of the Ciumîrna Pass, and Rădăuţi to the east. From Rădăuţi there are four buses daily. If time is short, get the mid-morning bus to Suceviţa, visit the monastery, and then catch the Cîmpulung-bound service that passes through around 3.45pm and runs over the mountains to Vatra Moldoviţei – enabling you to visit two monasteries in one day.

Rooms are available at the *Hanul Suceviţa* (☎030/141; ①), 300m down the road from the monastery towards Rădăuţi – which also has a **restaurant** (daily noon–9pm) and a summer **campsite** with huts – or 3km uphill in the direction of Moldoviţa, where the private *Popaşul Turistic Bucovina* (☎030/165; ③) offers similar huts and fewer rooms.

Moldoviţa

Approaching from Suceviţa over the Ciumîrna Pass, you'll come upon the monastery shortly before **VATRA MOLDOVIŢEI** village. **Moldoviţa Monastery** is a smaller complex than Suceviţa but equally well defended, its ivy-clad walls enclosing white stone buildings with lustrous black shingled roofs. The monastery was founded in 1532 by Stephen's illegitimate son, Petru Rareş, during whose reign the Turks finally compelled Moldavia to pay tribute and acknowledge Ottoman suzerainity. Its **frescoes** were painted by Toma of Suceava in 1537, at a time when Petru Rareş still hoped to resist, despite the inexorability of the Turkish advance since the fall of Constantinople in 1453.

To raise morale, the Turkish siege was conflated with an earlier, failed attempt by the Persians in 626. A delightfully revisionist *Siege of Constantinople* along the bottom of the south wall depicts the Christians routing the infidel with arrow and cannons and the help of miraculous icons being paraded around the ramparts. Illustrated above is the *Hymn to the Virgin* composed by Metropolitan Sergius in thanksgiving for her intervention, while further along is a lovely *Tree of Jesse*, with dozens of figures entwined in foliage. All the compositions are set on an intense blue background.

The open porch contains a fine *Last Judgement* showing a crowd of dignitaries growing agitated as a demon drags one of their number (said to be Herod) towards the fires below, where Satan sits on a scaly creature – incised with oddly formal nineteenth-century German graffiti. Within the church, saints and martyrs are decapitated en masse around the narthex – where Bishop Efrem is buried – and the nave, whose doorway bears an expressive *Mary with Jesus*. Also notice the mural of Petru Rareş, his wife and sons presenting the monastery to Jesus, on the right as you enter the naos.

Nuns' cells line one side of the compound, while in the northwest corner rises an imposing two-storey *clisarniţa* with a circular tower. This contains a **museum** of monastic treasures (Tues–Sun 10am–6pm) including a silver-chased Evangelistry presented by Catherine the Great and the wooden throne of Petru Rareş, a bust of whom has been erected outside.

Practicalities

The village of Vatra Moldoviţei can be reached by **bus** from Rădăuţi or Suceviţa, or from Cîmpulung. Another option is to catch a **train** from Vama (on the Suceava–Gura Humorlui–Cîmpulung line), up a branch line that runs along Vatra Moldoviţei's main street – unfortunately, only one train leaves Vama at a reasonable hour (currently 3.15pm). There's a basic **motel** (✆030/33.61.80; ②) at the turn-off for Suceviţa, while some villagers rent **rooms** (①) on request.

Gura Humorlui, Voroneţ and Humor

The last two Painted Monasteries lie a few kilometres either side of **GURA HUMORLUI**, a small logging town accessible by bus or train from Suceava or Cîmpulung, which has just enough facilities to make a tolerable base. The bus and train stations are adjacent to each other and you should check on **buses to Voroneţ and Humor** as soon as you arrive. The current timetables make it hard to visit both monasteries in the same day unless you walk to Voroneţ and back in the morning, and then catch a bus to Humor, which is further away. Gura Humorlui is also linked by bus to Arbore, Iaşi and Piatra Neamţ.

From the bus station, the main road, Strada Ştefan cel Mare, lies straight ahead. The turn-off for Voronet is 750m to the left, while the centre of town is in the other direction. *CFR* (Mon–Fri 8am–3pm) is near the **market**, before the road forks at Piaţa Republicii, whose unfinished multi-storey building is the town's landmark. The road to Humor leads off the left of the square.

The most reliable place **to stay** in Gura Humorlui is the *Hotel Carpati* on Strada 9 Mai (☎030/23.21.03; ②), found by bearing right at the fork by Piaţa Republicii and then up the side street opposite the Catholic church. Private **rooms** (②) are advertised on the corner of Strada Ştefan cel Mare and the Voroneţ road, but ferocious dogs may deny you access, in which case it's best to press on to the *Voroneţ* cabana, which is open over the summer, near the bridge 1km down the village road. Alternatively, you could opt to stay at Humor instead (see opposite). The 24-hour *Restaurant Anacalina* is a better bet for **eating** than any of the drunken dens off Piaţa Republicii.

Voroneţ Monastery

On a fine day, it's no hardship to walk to Voroneţ from Gura Humorlui. The turning is clearly signposted, and there's no chance of going astray on the valley road (4km). At the fork, take the right-hand route to the monastery, entered by a gate near the cemetery. There are two convenient places to eat nearby.

Ion Neculce's chronicle records that Stephen founded **Voroneţ Monastery** in 1488 to fulfil a pledge to the hermit Daniil, who had previously assured the despondent *hospodar* that, should he undertake a campaign against the Turks, he would be successful. The Turks were duly forced back across the Danube, and Voroneţ was erected in three months; chronologically, it comes between Putna and Neamţ Monastery. Its superb **frescoes** – added at the behest of Metropolitan Rosca in 1547–50 – have led to Voroneţ being dubbed the "Oriental Sistine Chapel", and put "Voroneţ blue" into the lexicon of art alongside Titian red and Veronese green. Obtained from lapis lazuli, this colour is most intense on a rainy day, just before sunset.

The church was designed to be entered via a door in the southern wall, with a closed esonarthex replacing the usual open porch, thus creating an unbroken surface along the western wall. Here is painted a magnificent *Last Judgement*, probably the finest single composition among the Painted Monasteries. Fish-tailed bulls, unicorns and other zodiacal symbols form a frieze below the eaves, beneath which Christ sits in majesty above a chair symbolizing the "Toll Gates of the Air", where the deceased are judged and prayers for their souls counted. On either side are those in limbo, the Turks and Tartars destined for perdition. Beneath them, devils and angels push sinners into the flames, while two angels sound the last trump on alpine horns. In response, graves open and wild animals come bearing the limbs they have devoured – all except the deer (a symbol of innocence) and the elephant (no threat in Romania). Amusingly, there's a crush of righteous souls at the gates of the Garden of Eden.

Weather has damaged the frescoes along the north-facing wall, but you can still distinguish Adam and Eve, the first childbirth, the discovery of fire and the invention of ploughing and writing. Also notice *Adam's Deed*, illustrating the myth that Adam made a compact with Satan. The south wall is covered by three compositions: comic-strip scenes from the lives of St Nicholas and St John on the buttress; a *Tree of Jesse*; and a register of saints and philosophers where, as usual, Plato is depicted with a coffin-load of bones.

Inside, the walls and ceiling of the esonarthex are painted with martyrdoms and miracles. The second row from the bottom on the left depicts St Elijah in his "chariot of fire", intent on zapping devils with his God-given powers. According to native folklore, God promptly had second thoughts and restricted Elijah's activities to his name-day. On the right-hand sides of the gloomy narthex and star-vaulted sanctuary are the **tomb of Daniil** the hermit, and a fresco of Stephen, his wife Maria Voichita and their son Bogdan presenting the monastery to Christ. After 1786, the surrounding monks' cells disappeared and the monastery was dissolved. Aside from its church, only the **belltower** remains.

Humor Monastery
In another valley 6km north of town, the wooden village of **MĂNĂSTERIA HUMOR** straggles towards its namesake, **Humor Monastery** (1530). Unlike the other complexes, Humor is protected by a wooden stockade rather than a stone rampart, and lacks a spire over the naos – indicating that it was founded by a boyar instead of by a *hospodar*, namely Teodor Bubuiog, the Chancellor of Petru Rareș, who is buried here with his wife Anastasia. The prevailing hues of the **frescoes** at Humor are reddish brown (from oriental madder pigment), but rich blues and greens also appear.

The *Last Judgement* on the wall beneath the unusual open porch is similar to that at Voroneț, with the significant difference that the Devil is portrayed as the Scarlet Woman (though this patch is now so faint that you can't tell, anyway). Such misogyny had its counterpart in the peasant conception of hell (*iad*) – said to be a cavern upheld by seven old women who during their lifetimes had surpassed Satan in wickedness. Since the women are mortal, the legend goes, *Dracul* (the Devil) must constantly search the world for replacements (and never fails to find them). The *Tree of Jesse* along the northern wall has been virtually effaced by erosion, but restorers are busy touching up the *Hymn to the Virgin* on the south front. Like its namesake at Voroneț, this depicts her miraculous intervention at the siege of Constantinople by the Persians – although the enemy has been changed into Turks to make a propaganda point. Morale may have been stiffened, but neither murals nor the stone watchtower added by Basil the Wolf could save Humor from marauding Turks, and the monastery was eventually declared derelict in the eighteenth century. It is now a small convent. On a nearby hillock stands another church, used by the villagers.

As an alternative to **staying** in town, you can enjoy bed and board at *La Maison du Bucovine* (☎030/172; ②), around the left of the stockade; or try to locate *Palma Camping*, off to the left past a school back along the road from the monastery. They speak French at both places.

Since buses are so infrequent, **hitching** into Gura Humorlui is common practice. A few buses in the other direction continue up the Humor valley to the long, strung-out village of **POIANA MICULUI**, from which there are three **trails to Sucevița**; the easiest one (marked by blue stripes) follows a forestry track and takes about five hours.

Cîmpulung Moldovenesc and Vatra Dornei

Cîmpulung Moldovenesc and **Vatra Dornei** are chiefly of interest as bases for **hiking** in the Rarău and Giumalău massifs, and as way-stations en route to Transylvania or Maramureș, with Vatra Dornei serving as a springboard for reaching several **festivals** just across the Carpathians. There's less reason to come out of season – particularly once the snow arrives, a month or two earlier than in the lowlands. Both towns are situated along the main train line from Suceava to Cluj.

Cîmpulung and the Rarău massif

CÎMPULUNG MOLDOVENESC ("Moldavian settlement in the long field") is a logging town with a modern centre and some old wooden houses in the backstreets. Being strung out along the valley, it has two **train stations** – don't alight at Cîmpulung Est by mistake. To reach the centre, bear left, then right, and left along Calea Transilvanei, the main street, which subsequently becomes Calea Bucovinei. The **Museum of Wooden Art** (Tues–Sun 9am–5pm) on the corner at no. 10 displays alpine horns, fiddles, looms, sledges and throne-like chairs, all beautifully carved. Cîmpulung also boasts Professor Tugui's vast **collection of wooden spoons**, at Str. Gheorghe Popovici 3 – however this kitsch delight is closed at the time of writing. A block behind the pseudo-medieval **church** with a tiled steeple you'll find the market with a small **Ukrainian bazaar**, and the bus station.

The **tourist office** (Mon–Fri 7am–3pm) is in the lobby of the high-rise *Hotel Zimbru*, across the square from *CFR* (Mon–Fri 8am–3pm), while a hundred metres or so further on, there's an old-fashioned *PTTR* (Mon–Fri 7am–9pm) on the corner of Strada Dimitrie Cantemir. Don't miss the impressively kitsch bronze **statue of Dragoş Vodă and the auroch**, locked in mortal combat, on the square across the road.

Out-of-season **accommodation** is limited to the clean, warm *Hotel Zimbru* (☎030/31.24.41; ④), Calea Bucovinei 1–3, or the smaller, private *Hotel Minion* (☎030/31.15.81; ④), 300m along Strada D. Cantemir, which has cable TV. By carrying on to the end of the road and bearing right, you'll see the summer-only *BTT* complex of chalets (①); the *Deia* cabana lies 3km up the trail nearby, and is likewise only open in summer. Both hotels have **restaurants** (the *Minion*'s is better), while the *Brasserie Select* on Strada Porumbescu, diagonally opposite the church, is the place for drinking.

Four **buses** daily run to Vatra Moldoviţei, near Moldoviţa Monastery, and to Rădăuţi, via Suceviţa Monastery; there are also daily services to Iaşi and Piatra Neamţ.

The Rarău massif

The **Rarău massif** to the south of Cîmpulung is said to be unlucky owing to an ancient curse, nonetheless, it remains a popular **hiking** spot, its dense spruce forests harbouring lynx, bears, roebuck and other **wildlife**. Most visitors base themselves at the *Rarău* cabana, 14km and 3–4 hours' walk up the road from Cîmpulung Est station. From here, a trail (4hr) marked by red triangles leads past the **Pietrele Doamnei** (Princess's Rocks), three huge Mesozoic limestone towers, to reach the ancient **Slatioara Secular forest** of fifty-metre-high firs and spruces. Another, red-striped route runs southwest from *Rarău* to the *Giumalau* cabana (3–4hr), from where you can hike on to Vatra Dornei via the Obcina Mică peak (5–6hr). None of these trails are feasible in winter.

The road **to Vatra Dornei** crosses the Mestecanis Pass (1099m) by way of two villages with Ukrainian-style **wooden churches**, to enter the Bistriţa valley at IACOBENI, where trains usually halt after emerging from a tunnel below the pass. Should you need to stop for the night, there's a cabana in Mestecanis and a *han* (①) in Iacobeni.

Vatra Dornei and beyond

VATRA DORNEI is another logging town-cum-resort that has been a spa since Hapsburg times, and dabbled in skiing since the Seventies. From Vatra Dornei Băi station, you can spot the ochre-and-white Baroque **casino** that once diverted visitors, but now lies derelict. To the right of the park is the *Baza de Tratament* offering **balneological therapy** involving turf mud and various mineral waters. Spa treatments are bookable at *Dorna Turism*, opposite the *Hotel Rarău*, which contains another agency, *BVT* (☎030/37.37.09), that can arrange **horse-riding**.

The old centre of town lies in the other direction from the station, along Strada Lucefărul and the road at the far end, Strada Eminescu. Off to the right along Eminescu, the clocktowered County Council building contains a humdrum **Enthnographic Museum** (Tues–Sun 10am–6pm); while 200m to the left, a derelict Moorish-style **synagogue** (no. 54) is followed by the signposted start of a long hiking **trail to the Rotunda Pass** in the Rodna mountains (21–22hr). Ask locals to point you towards the **chair-lift** (*telescaun*) up to the 1300-metre-high Dealul Negrii (summer 9am–6pm; winter 9am–4pm; closed Mon), a popular **skiing** spot to the southwest of town.

Accommodation ranges from backstreet villas and flats – rentable through *BVT* – to the overblown *Calimani* (☎030/37.39.21; ④) and *Bradul* (☎030/ 37.39.21; ④) hotels and the smaller *Rarău* (☎030/37.37.09; ③), around the *Baza*. In summer, there are also cabins at *Autotourist Camping*, near the start of the hiking trail to the Rotunda Pass. Of the three hotel **restaurants**, the *Rarău*'s is the liveliest. The *Western Restaurant* in the building that resembles the casino, further along Strada Oborului, is really a **disco** (10pm–3am), while the self-styled motel at the top of the hill behind the park is actually a weird **bar** full of hunting trophies.

On to Maramureş and Transylvania

From Vatra Dornei, you can head south towards **Neamţ county**, northwest into **Maramureş**, or west into **Transylvania**. Buses to Piatra Neamt and Tîrgu Neamţ follow the scenic Bistriţa valley down to Poiana Largului, at the northern end of Lake Bicaz, in the vicinity of the Ceahlău massif (see p.211).

The route to Maramureş heads up the valley past such lovely villages as **CIOCANEŞTI**, where the houses are perched on hillocks, and **BOTOS**, which has a new **wooden church** in the Ukrainian style: very broad and square, with one large and four small cupolas. There's a **hotel** (②–③) with cabins north of **CÎRLIBABA**, 8km before the road forks towards the Rotunda Pass into Transylvania, and the **Prislop Pass** into Maramureş, where the Horă at Prislop **festival** occurs on the second Sunday in August (see p.257). One bus daily crosses the mountains to Vişeu in Maramureş, while four others run as far as Cîrlibaba, from where you could probably hitch over the pass.

Of the three routes into Transylvania, the most dramatic is via the **Tihuta Pass** – otherwise known as the Bîrgău Pass, where Bram Stoker located Dracula's castle (see p.196). Buses from Vatra Dornei run through the pass en route to Bistriţa. Travelling **by train**, instead, you'll take a more northerly route via Ilva Mică; the Ilvei Lesu halt, one stop before, is within walking distance of Leşu (see p.194). The third route crosses the 1271-metre-high **Rotunda Pass**, which is prone to blizzards and untravelled by buses.

travel details

Trains

Adjud to: Braşov (2 daily; 5hr 15min); Ghimeş (4–7 daily; 1hr 55min–2hr 50min); Miercurea Ciuc (4 daily; 3hr 15min–4hr); Suceava (10 daily; 2hr 30min–5hr 10min); Tîrgu Mureş (1 daily; 6hr 30min).

Bacău to: Bicaz (6 daily; 1hr 30min–2hr 30min); Piatra Neamţ (11 daily; 55min–1hr 35min); Suceava (11 daily; 1hr 45min–4hr 10min).

Bîrlad to: Galaţi (6 daily; 2hr 50min–3hr 7min); Iaşi (12 daily; 1hr 45min–3hr).

Galaţi to: Bîrlad (6 daily; 2hr 40min); Braşov (1 daily; 6hr); Constanţa (2 daily; 4hr–6hr 25min); Iaşi (2 daily; 4–6hr); Mărăşeşti (8 daily; 1hr 50min–2hr 50min); Oradea (1 daily; 13hr 14min); Tîrgu Mureş (1 daily; 9hr).

Iaşi to: Braşov (2 daily; 8hr–8hr 25min); Bucharest (9 daily; 5hr 45min–9hr 45min); Cluj (3 daily; 9hr); Constanţa (1 daily; 7hr 35min); Craiova (1 daily; 14hr 50min); Suceava (5 daily; 2–3hr); Timişoara (4 daily; 15hr–16hr 20min); Tîrgu Mureş (1 daily; 9hr 40min).

Mărăşeşti to: Tecuci/Tecuci Nord (15 daily; 19–25min); Galaţi (8 daily; 1hr 45min–3hr); Iaşi (6 daily; 2hr 45min–4hr 45min); Suceava (7 daily; 3hr–5hr 10min).

Paşcani to: Iaşi (15 daily; 1hr–1hr 20min; also 5 daily from Paşcani Triaj; 1 hour); Suceava (22 daily; 42–80min); Tîrgu Neamţ (5 daily; 45min).

Suceava/Suceava Nord to: Bucharest (8 daily; 5hr 30min–11hr 25min); Cîmpulung Moldovenesc (10 daily; 1hr 30min–2hr); Cluj (3 daily; 6hr 30min–7hr); Iaşi (5 daily; 2hr–2hr 40min); Ilva Mică (5 daily; 4hr 10min–5hr); Putna (6 daily; 2hr 20min); Rădăuţi (7 daily; 1hr 15min); Timişoara (3 daily; 12hr 45min–13hr 30min); Vama (9 daily; 1hr 10min–1hr 25min); Vatra Dornei (7 daily; 2hr 35min–3hr).

Tecuci/Tecuci Nord to: Bîrlad (11 daily; 35–1 hr 10min); Galaţi (11 daily; 1hr 25min–2hr 25min); Iaşi (10 daily; 2hr 20min–4hr 20min).

Vama to: Moldoviţa (3 daily; 45min).

Vatra Dornei to: Cluj (4 daily; 3hr 50min–5hr 15min); Iaşi (3 daily; 5hr); Suceava (7 daily; 2hr 25min–3hr 15min).

Planes

Bacău to: Bucharest (1 daily; 30min).

Iaşi to: Bucharest (1 daily; 1hr).

Suceava to: Bucharest (Mon–Fri 2 daily, Sat & Sun 1 daily; 1hr); Constanţa (summer only; 1 daily; 45min).

International trains

Iaşi to: Chişinau (3 daily; 5hr 45min–7hr 20min); Kiev (1 daily; 21hr 20min); Moscow (1 daily; 38hr 30min); Sofia (1 daily; 18hr).

Suceava Nord to: Kiev (2 daily; 19hr); Moscow (1 daily; 36hr 10min); Saint Petersburg (1 daily; 48hr); Sofia (2 daily; 17hr–18hr 30min).

CHAPTER FIVE

MARAMUREŞ

Romania has been likened to a country with one foot in the industrial future and the other in the Middle Ages – still an accurate enough characterization of its northwestern counties. Within 30km of heavily industrialized Baia Mare, thickly forested mountains and rough roads maintain scores of villages in a state of almost medieval isolation, amidst a landscape of rounded hills with clumps of oak and beech and scattered flocks of sheep. One nineteenth-century traveller compared it to an arcadian vision of England pervaded with "a feeling of remoteness", and since **Maramureş**, unlike other regions, was never conquered by the Romans, some features of life appear to have changed little since Dacian times.

This is certainly true of many of the **villages**, which are the main reason for visiting the area. The majority of buildings are made of wood by craftsmen whose skill is renowned, and the inhabitants produce virtually everything that they wear, use and eat – and if not, do without. Nowhere else in Europe do **folk costumes** persist so strongly, the women weaving boldly striped *catriniţa* aprons, with cloth from the water-powered fulling mills (*piuă*), and embroidering intricate designs on the wide-sleeved cotton blouses worn by both sexes – most conspicuously during markets and **festivals**, when the villages blaze with colourful attire. On Sundays people promenade and there may be a public dance, either in the street or on a purpose-built wooden platform. Just as people wear the medieval rawhide *opinchi* footwear or archaic felt boots bound with thongs, so villagers have retained their traditional **religion** (a mixture of pagan beliefs and the Uniate rite), their myths and codes of behaviour. Large families, personal integrity and skilled work are all esteemed; the Church and community exert powerful sanctions against transgressors, and men are wont to react to perceived slights on their honour by drawing knives (which in some villages are eschewed at table, being reserved for butchering animals, whittling wood and fighting).

Above all, perhaps, there's the marvellous **woodwork** of Maramureş – carvings decorate the eaves, doorways and windows of houses lining each village main street. Every household subsists with its livestock and barns within a compound fenced with timber, brush or lattice-work, and entered via a beamed

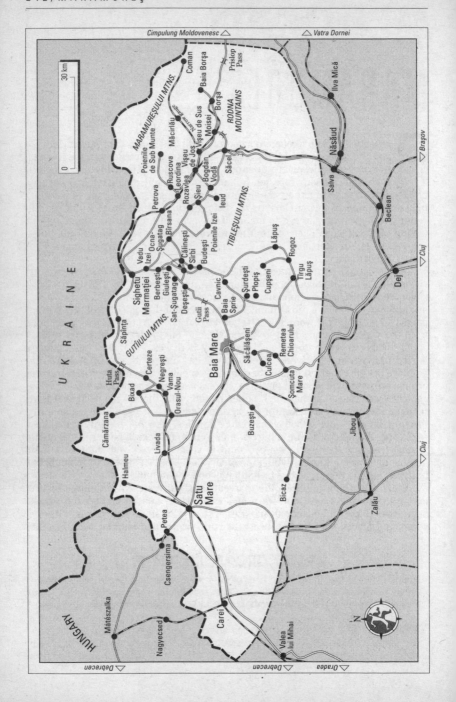

gateway (*poarta*), the size of which indicates the family's prosperity. Many are elaborately carved with the "tree of life", astrological symbols, human figures and animals, and there seems to be no slackening in productivity. The most elaborate structures are the *biserici de lemn* or **wooden churches**, mostly built during the eighteenth century when this Gothic-inspired architecture reached its height. Originally founded upon huge blocks of wood rather than stone, they rear up into fairytale spires or crouch beneath humpbacked roofs like fugitives from Transylvania, generally sited on the highest ground in the village to escape seasonal mud.

Satu Mare and **Baia Mare**, the two largest towns in the area, both accessible by plane or sleeper train from Bucharest, are nothing special. If you're coming from Hungary, you can drive across from Csengersima to Petea (15km from Satu Mare), or catch the three daily local trains from Vásárosnamény and Matészalka to Carei or from Debrecen to Valea lui Mihai, and switch onto northbound services. There are also daily buses from Debrecen to Satu Mare and one a week (on Saturdays) from Budapest and Nyíregyháza to Satu Mare and Baia Mare.

The best base from which to explore the villages and churches of Maramureş is Baia Mare, which also boasts an excellent village museum. **Public transport** in the region is patchy with only limited buses to the outlying villages. The best solution is to rent a car, otherwise try at least to see the beautiful church paintings at **Rogoz** and **Deseşti**, the towering wooden church at **Şurdeşti**, the frescoes and icons of **Călineşti** and **Budeşti** and the quirky "Merry Cemetery" at **Săpînţa**. Further afield in the Iza valley, the visions of hell painted inside the church at **Poienile Izei** are the most individual images you will see in Maramureş, while the frescoes at **Ieud** are the most famous. Maramureş also offers hiking in the peaceful **Rodna mountains** on the borders with Moldavia and Ukraine.

Satu Mare

When the diplomats at Versailles signed the Treaty of Trianon they drew an arbitrary line across the old Hungarian county of Szabolcs-Szatmár and left the provincial capital of Szatmárnémeti in Romanian hands. Renamed **SATU MARE** ("Big Village") and shorn of its traditional links with the Great Plain, the town lost its original function as a trading post along the River Someş, shipping salt from Ocna Dejului downstream to Vásárosnamény on the Tisza, but retained a sizeable Hungarian population.

The centre of town is Piaţa Libertăţii with a fire tower, raised in 1904 and resembling a Turkish minaret, peering over its north side. There's little to detain you – the **Historical and Ethnographic Museum** at B-dul Lucaciu 21 (Tues–Fri & Sun 10am–6pm, Sat 10am–2pm), on the corner of Bulevardul Traian, the road in from the train and bus stations, has the usual mixture of folk costumes and Daco-Roman remains, while the **Art Gallery** at Piaţa Libertăţii 21 (same hours) features the work of local artist Aurel Popp (1879–1960).

Practicalities

Satu Mare's main **hotels**, the Secessionist-style *Dacia* (☎061/71.42.76; ④) and modern *Aurora* (☎061/73.62.16 or 71.49.46; ④), are on Piaţa Libertăţii, with the

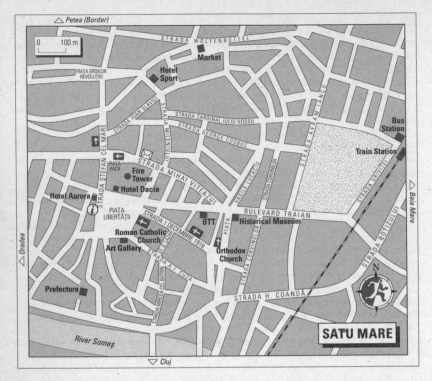

STRADA WOLFENBUTTEL
Petea (Border)
0   100 m
PIAŢA EROILOR REVOLUTIEI
Hotel Sport
Market
STRADA IOAN SLAVICI
STRADA MILENIULUI
STRADA CARDINAL IULIU HOSSU
STRADA GEORGE COSBUC
STRADA AVRAM IANCU
Bus Station
Train Station
STRADA STEFAN CEL MARE
PIAŢA PACII
Fire Tower
STRADA MIHAI VITEAZUL
Hotel Dacia
STRADA CORVINILOR
CASTLE LUCACIU
STRADA GRIVITEI
Baia Mare
Hotel Aurora
PIAŢA LIBERTĂŢII
STRADA I DECEMBRIE 1918
BTT
PIAŢA
Historical Museum
BULEVARD TRAIAN
Oradea
Roman Catholic Church
Art Gallery
STRADA A.I. CUZA
STRADA LUPENI
Orthodox Church
STRADA CORVINILOR
STRADA BOTIZULUI
Prefecture
STRADA MIRCEA CEL BATRIN
STRADA H. COANDĂ
N
River Someş
SATU MARE
Cluj

Sport at Str. Mileniului 25 (☎061/71.29.59; ④). The *Aurora* also houses the **tourist office**. *BTT* at Calea Traian 7 (☎061/73.79.15) might be able to rustle up dormitory beds if you can't afford the hotel rates. Satu Mare's **campsite** is 5km east in Păuleşti, and, if you're driving, there's also the option of the *Amelia* motel (☎061/73.23.98; ②), 14km south in Mădăraş. In addition to the **restaurants** in the hotels, the town's Swabian (German) minority boasts a *bierkeller* (Mon–Fri 9am–5pm, Sun 9am–2pm).

With **trains** leaving for Baia Mare every two to three hours there's little reason to stay. *TAROM* has its office at Piaţa 25 Octombrie 9 (☎061/71.78.59), selling tickets for flights to Bucharest.

Baia Mare

BAIA MARE ("Big Mine") is Romania's largest non-ferrous metals centre. Mining mania has waxed and waned here since the fourteenth century when, under its Hungarian name of Nagybánya, it was the Magyar monarchs' chief source of gold bullion. The main reason for staying here is to prepare for expeditions into the surrounding countryside, but it's an attractive town with a variety of museums to pass the time.

The Town

The **old town** is clustered around the main Piaţa Libertăţii, 2km east of the station and reached by frequent buses and maxitaxis along Bulevardul Bucureşti. The thick-walled **house of Iancu de Hunedoara**, fifteenth-century Regent of Hungary, is on the square at no. 18, known as the Casa Elizabeta. The cathedral lies to the south of the square – the 50-metre-high **Stephen's Tower**, begun in 1446, was originally part of the cathedral until it was replaced in 1717 by the present Baroque pile. The **Art Gallery**, behind the cathedral at Str. 1 Mai 8, exhibits eighteenth- and nineteenth-century paintings on wood and glass, and a number of canvases by artists of the Nagybánya School, which transformed Hungarian art at the beginning of the twentieth century, by introducing Impressionist influences. Most of the work is now in Budapest, however, and the stuff here is attributed to the "Baia Mare School" – a sly piece of Romanian revisionism. 1996 will see the School's centenary; look out for major shows both here and in Budapest.

Mining and minting are both heavily represented in the **County Museum**, just north of Piaţa Libertăţii at Str. Monetăriei 1. This has been closed for some time due to lack of funds, but it's worth seeing the Mint Tower (*Bastionul Monetăriei*) incorporated in the museum building, as well as the medieval Strada Monetăriei itself and the *Reformat* church (1809) at its junction with Strada Podul Viilor.

Strada Dr Vasile Lucaciu, running east from Piaţa Libertăţii, has some old buildings with cellars entered from the street. At the far end of Strada Olarilor (which follows the line of the old city walls), just south of the Art Gallery, is Piaţa Izvoarelor, where the fifteenth-century Butchers' Bastion (*Bastionul Măcelarilor*) overlooks the market-place where the outlaw Pintea Viteazul was shot in 1703.

Baia Mare's main tourist attraction is its **Village Museum** with over a hundred examples of peasant houses, watermills and other buildings from the surrounding region, and a seventeenth-century wooden church (from the village of Chechiş, just to the south). Many of these are extremely eye-catching, and if you don't have time to visit the villages, this museum is the next best thing. With it, on Florilor hill north of the river, are the **Ethnographic Museum** and the **zoo**.

Practicalities

Baia Mare's **tourist office** (Mon–Fri 10am–6pm, Sat 10am–4pm) to the north of Piaţa Revoluţiei has a good map of the region, which is essential if you are planning on touring the villages. The tourist office can usually help if you want to **rent a car**, otherwise find out all you can about local **buses** and accommodation in the hinterland here. Bus services for Sighet usually depart from the main terminal near the train station. Five buses a day from Baia Mare continue from Sighet to Borşa, and there are also hourly services to Tîrgu Lăpuş, as well as a couple to Zalău, Cluj and Oradea. The *TAROM* office is at B-dul Bucureşti 5 (☎062/41.16.24).

For **car repairs**, head for the *ACR* yard at Str. 8 Martie 1, east of town at the turning north to the Firiza dam, and there are other garages along Bulevardul Independenţei, towards Satu Mare. Baia Mare boasts a genuine **launderette** with self-service washing machines, possibly the only one in Romania, just north of the train station on Bulevardul Decebal.

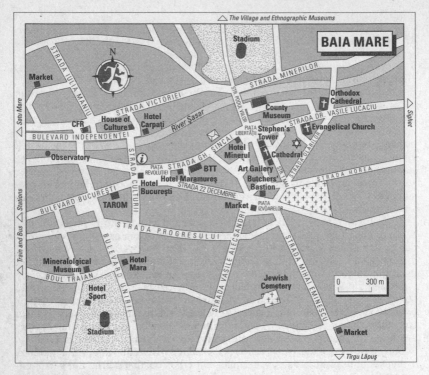

Accommodation

Baia Mare has a good selection of **hotels** and *BTT*, Str. Şincai 29, may also be able to arrange cheaper lodgings in town. The *han* on Dealul Florilor, above the Village Museum, is currently only a restaurant but is building an extension with bedrooms. Further afield, to the west on the Satu Mare road are the *Apa Sărăta* (Salty Water) **cabana and campsite** (7km out by city buses #6, #7, #13 and #29, at the east end of Tăuţii Măgherăuş, just before the unmarked turning south to the airport) and the *Doi Porumboi* (Two Pigeons) campsite (18km). The *Doi Veveriţe* (Two Squirrels) cabana lies 10km to the southwest, on the DN1C towards Şomcuta Mare. Finally, two small cabanas can be reached by a road northeast into the Igniş mountains, the *Bodi-Ferneziu* (on a hill 2km west of the road) and the *Baraj-Firiza* at a dam 10km north by bus #18.

Bucureşti, on Piaţa Revoluţiei at Str. Culturii 4 (☎062/41.63.01). A standard tourist hotel, but not unreasonably priced. ④.

Carpaţi, B-dul Independenţei 2 (☎062/41.48.12). Privatized but not radically transformed from the norm. ④.

Mara, B-dul Unirii 11 (☎062/43.66.60). Has a foyer fit for a luxury hotel but distinctly ordinary rooms. ④.

Maramureş, Str. Şincai 37 (☎062/41.65.55) Overpriced hotel frequented by businessmen and foreign groups. ④.

Minerul, Piaţa Libertăţii 7 (☎062/41.60.56). The most attractive hotel in town with an excellent central location. ③.

Sport, B-dul Unirii 14a, but actually one block west on Strada Transilvaniei (☎062/43.49.00). By far the least expensive place in town, a classic sport hotel intended for visiting teams. Plenty of space unless there's a big tournament on. ①.

Into the countryside

East of Baia Mare, the going gets harder – many of the villages are well off the main roads, and are awkward to reach without private **transport** when you'll have to rely upon hitching or the overcrowded buses that run once a day to most villages. Private cars are scarce so be prepared for intermittent lifts or short rides between villages in the back of waggons or vans. Cycling is a great way to get the most out of a visit to Maramureş, but mountain bikes might be preferable on some of the back roads. There are **hotels** in Borşa, Ocna Şugatag and Sighet, but otherwise come prepared to camp wild, with plenty of food supplies. If you get really stuck in a village, ask the priest (*popă* or *preot*) for advice – try to repay any hospitality with gifts (tea and coffee are ideal).

Codrul, Chioarul and Lăpuş

Maramureş proper lies to the north of Baia Mare, beyond the Gutîi pass, while to the south of Baia Mare are three similar ethnographic zones, which were part of Someş county until it was dismembered in the 1968 reforms. The southwestern corner of the county, beyond the Someş river, is known as **Codrul**, the area immediately south of Baia Mare is **Chioarul**, and further east is **Lăpuş**. Folk costumes are similar to those of Maramureş, though with tall straw hats, and here too there are fine wooden churches.

The most accessible village of Codrul is **BUZEŞTI**, 30km west of Baia Mare, with a wooden church built in 1739, the bulbous steeple of which bears witness, despite its poor condition, to the penetration of Baroque influences into this area, while the four corner pinnacles echo the Gothic towers of both Transylvania and Hungary. Much more remote, in the far extremity of the county, is **BICAZ**, also with an Orthodox church dated (in Cyrillic script) 1723 and with paintings from the same period. As in Buzeşti, a new church has been built here and the old one is decaying, although repairs are planned.

Many of the villages of Chioarul have old churches, but perhaps the most interesting is at **SĂCĂLĂŞENI**, only 10km south of Baia Mare. Although rebuilt at the end of the seventeenth century, it originally dates from 1442, with a carved doorway and paintings from 1865. **CULCEA**, just to the southwest, has a church from 1720 with plastered walls; 6km further south is **REMETEA CHIOARULUI**, which has a fine church (1800) but is better known as the starting point for walks through the gorge of the Lăpuş river to the Chioarului citadel. Ten kilometres further, on the DN1C, is **ŞOMCUTA MARE**, where choirs and bands assemble for the *Stejarul* **festival** on the first or third Sunday of July – you'll find a **campsite** with bungalows 6km north on the DN1C in Finteş forest.

The centre of the Lăpuş area is the small town of **TÎRGU LĂPUŞ** (Lăpuş Market) which has a hotel, the *Lăpuşul* (☎062/46.42.17; ②). The wooden Church of the Dormition dates from 1661 and boasts walls that are both painted and carved; the oldest murals are those in the pronaos, dating from c.1697, and the icons include the first works of Radu Munteanu. **CUPŞENI** is one of the most

WOODEN CHURCHES

There is a strong tradition of building **wooden churches** right across Eastern Europe, from Karelia and northern Russia all the way to the Adriatic, but in terms of both quality and quantity the richest examples are in Maramureş. From 1278 the Orthodox Romanians were forbidden by their Catholic Hungarian overlords to build churches in stone, and so used wood to ape Gothic developments.

In general, the walls are built of blockwork (squared-off logs laid horizontally) with intricate joints, cantilevered out in places to form brackets or consoles supporting the eaves. However, here Western techniques such as raftering and timber-framing allow the high roofs and steeples that are characteristic of the area, rather than the tent roofs or stepped cupolas used to the north. Following the **standard Orthodox ground-plan**, the main roof covers narthex and naos and a lower one the sanctuary; the naos usually has a barrel vault, while the narthex has a low planked ceiling under the tower, its weight transmitted by rafters to the walls; thus there are no pillars, although there is a wall between narthex and naos. The roof is always shingled and in many cases is in fact double, allowing clerestory windows high in the nave walls, while the lower roof can be extended at the west end to form a porch.

Most of the Maramureş churches were rebuilt after the last Tartar raid in 1717, acquiring large porches and tall towers, often with four corner-pinnacles, clearly derived from the masonry architecture of the Transylvanian cities. Inside, almost every church now has a choir gallery above the west part of the naos, always a later addition, as shown by the way it is superimposed on the **wall paintings**. These extraordinary works of art were produced by local artists in the eighteenth and early nineteenth centuries, combining the icon tradition with pagan motifs and topical propaganda. They broadly follow the standard Orthodox layout, with the Incarnation and Eucharist in the sanctuary (for the priest's edification), the Last Judgement and moralistic parables such as the Wise and Foolish Virgins in the narthex (where the women stand), and the Passion in the naos; however the treatment of the latter changed in the nineteenth century as the Uniate Church gained in strength, with more emphasis on the Ascension and the Evangelists. Sixteenth-century icons (such as those found in Budeşti) show northern Moldavian influence; the seventeenth-century Moisei school was the first to show the imprint of the Renaissance, and from the late eighteenth century, Baroque influences were added. The first of the major painters was **Alexandru Ponehalski**, who worked in the 1750s, 1760s and 1770s in Călineşti and Budeşti, in a naïf post-Byzantine style with blocks of colour in black outlines. From 1767 to the 1780s, **Radu Munteanu** worked around his native Lăpuş and in Botiza, Glod and Deseşti, painting in a freer and more imaginative manner. In the first decade of the nineteenth century, **Toader Hodor** and **Ion Plohod** worked in Bîrsana, Corneşti, Valeni and Naneşti, in a far more Baroque style.

Since 1989 there has been a **renaissance of the Uniate or Greco-Catholic faith**, repressed under communism and forcibly merged with the Romanian Orthodox Church; many parishes have reverted to Greco-Catholicism, reclaiming their churches, while in other villages one church is now Orthodox and the other Uniate. In addition many villages have started to build large new churches; because services are so long, it's not possible to cope with demand by having several services on a Sunday, and thus most of the women and children have to remain outside the small wooden churches, following proceedings inside either by pressing an ear to the wall or by a small loudspeaker. The appearance of the new churches will make it more and more likely that you'll find the wooden churches locked up, even on a Sunday – it's never hard to find the key-holder, but the fabric of the buildings will doubtless start to deteriorate. Remember that people **dress conservatively** here, and shorts are not appropriate, particularly for visiting churches.

idyllic villages in the region and home of some of its best carpenters. Here, the upper church, built in 1600, has a fine tower but badly damaged paintings, and the tiny lower church, moved here from Peteritea in 1847 by the Uniates, was beautifully painted in 1848 by Radu Munteanu.

However, the best examples in this area are the two churches in **ROGOZ**, 5km east of Tîrgu Lăpuş. This is a prosperous village with a growing population; local custom forbids divorce or abortion, so there are five or six children per family. Not surprisingly, a modern church has been built here, too, but the old churches are well maintained. The one to the right (built around 1695 in Suciu de Sus and moved here in 1893) is Uniate, and the one to the left is Orthodox. Built of elm some time between 1661 and 1701, the latter is unique for its naturalistic horse-head consoles (as opposed to the more usual dovetail design) supporting the roof at the west end, and for the asymmetric roof, with a larger overhang to the north to shelter a table where paupers were fed by the parish. Some of the paintings by Radu Munteanu were painted over in the 1830s, but even so this remains one of the most beautifully painted churches: look out for a *Last Judgement*, to the left inside the door, and the *Creation* and the *Good Samaritan*, on the naos ceiling. There are four buses a day from Baia Mare, heading for Băiuţ or Grosii Tibleşului, as well as local services from Tîrgu Lăpuş.

Şurdeşti and Plopiş

The small mining town of **BAIA SPRIE**, noted for its autumn **Chestnut Carnival**, and for a wooden-roofed Orthodox church (dating from 1793) behind the Town Hall (built in 1739), lies 10km from Baia Mare along the Sighet road. From here you can detour off the main road to reach some classic Maramureş villages, on the fringes of the Chioar district. Just south of **ŞURDEŞTI** – pronounced "Shure-desht" – a magnificent Uniate **wooden church** (built in 1724 or 1738) rises from a hill above a stream. Clad in thousands of oak shingles, its 45-metre-high tower is the tallest wooden structure in Europe and three times the length of the church itself; you can climb up into the tower and roof space from the porch. Inside the church, which someone from the painted house near the stream will unlock for you, there are remarkable wall paintings (1810–11), and also interesting late eighteenth-century icons.

PLOPIŞ, a kilometre or so away across the fields, has a similar, though slightly smaller, church, built between 1798 and 1805, which likewise features four corner turrets on its spire, a feature of many wooden churches here and in the Erdőhát region of Hungary. If you continue north along the minor road, it eventually leads through the mining town of Cavnic, over the **Neteda Pass** (1039m) and down to **Budeşti** (see p.252); there are seven buses a day from Baia Mare to Cavnic via Şurdeşti, but to go further you'll have to hitch a ride in a mine vehicle, simply a portakabin on a truck chassis.

Along the Baia Mare–Sighet road

Continuing from Baia Sprie, the main DN18 passes a turning to the *Şuior* and *Mogoşa* cabanas, a couple of kilometres to the east, and zig-zags up to the 1109-metre-high **Guţîi Pass** (with an inn, named after the outlaw Pintea Viteazul) before descending into the Mara valley, past the splendidly carved houses and gateways of **MARA**.

The wooden church at **DESEŞTI**, 30km from Baia Mare, is hidden among some trees to the left, above the road and the trackbed of a disused forestry rail line, now used as a cycle track. Though the spire has been clad in sheet metal since a lightning strike, this is a fine example of the "double roof" or clerestory style which enabled the builders to construct windows high up inside the nave to increase the illumination. Nonetheless, it's dark inside and even with candles you'll find it hard to pick out the marvellous **wall paintings**. Executed by Radu Munteanu in 1780, they seem more primitive yet less stylized than the frescoes in the Moldavian monasteries which were painted some 200 years earlier. Boldly coloured in red, yellow and white, the figures of saints and martyrs are contrasted with shady-looking groups of Jews, Turks, Germans, Tartars and Franks. The frescoes also include folk-style geometric and floral motifs, while the inscriptions are in the Cyrillic alphabet (since Old Church Slavonic remained the liturgical language of Romanian Orthodoxy until the nineteenth century), but many of the paintings are flaking and peeling and may soon be lost unless something is done.

Hărniceşti, Giuleşti and around

The next church, also dating from 1770, is in the village of **HĂRNICEŞTI**; in 1942 the apse was widened, and in 1952 the porch was added, so that now the tower seems disproportionately short. The church stands just north of the junction of a back road east towards Ocna Şugatag and Budeşti; two buses a day from Baia Mare to Ocna Şugatag take this road through **HOTENI**, known for its *Tînjaua* **festival**, held on the first or second Sunday of May. As in many of the villages of the Mara valley, this is a celebration of the First Ploughman, a fertility rite that dates back at least to Roman times.

Continuing along the main road towards Sighet, you reach **SATŞUGATAG**, with another fine church beside the road. Built in 1642, and now in some need of repair, it's accompanied by a graveyard containing a number of beautiful stout wooden crosses, and some picturesque cottages. To the right, a minor road leads off to Ocna Şugatag, Călineşti, Sîrbi and Budeşti, with another right turn 2km north leading to **MĂNĂSTIREA GIULEŞTI**, a tiny village with a tiny church, founded in 1653 and now shared by Orthodox and Uniate congregations; it boasts fine paintings from 1653 and 1783, as well as late eighteenth-century icons by Alexandru Ponehalski.

The main road continues northwards to **GIULEŞTI** proper, which, like many of these villages, has an ancient **watermill** (*moara*). Its two mill wheels are driven by water sluiced off a fast-flowing stream, the drive shafts running into a building where the miller can control the wheel with a kind of tension brake. The two millstones grind wheat and corn, with the miller traditionally taking one cupful of each hopper-load. Everything is made of wood, down to the little channels siphoning off water to lubricate the spindles of the wheels, and it doubles as a fulling mill, the wheel turning a spindle driving levers which cause wooden mallets to beat the cloth.

Further north, on the edge of **BERBEŞTI**, a carved wooden crucifix (*troiţa*), at least three hundred years old, stands beside the road adorned with four mourning figures and symbols of the sun and moon. Similar wayside crosses can be found in Moldavia, sometimes inscribed *Doamne, apara-ma de dracul* (Lord, protect me from the devil), for traditionally travel was considered a hazardous undertaking. Tuesday was an unlucky day on which no journeys were made nor

MARAMUREŞ FUNERALS

The **cult of the dead**, central in Romanian culture, is particularly well developed in Maramureş, where the rituals to be observed after a death are fixed and elaborate; if anything is omitted, it is believed that the soul will return as a ghost or even a vampire. The church bells are rung thrice daily for three days while the deceased lies at home, a period during which neighbours pay their respects and women (but not men) lament the deceased in improvised rhymed couplets that are also shouted at weddings, dances and other social events.

When the priest arrives at the house on the third day, the wailing and lamenting reach a climax before he blesses a bucketful of water, extinguishes a candle in it, and consecrates the house with a cross left etched on the wall for a year. The coffin is carried by six married male relatives or friends, stopping for prayers (the priest being paid for each stop) at crossroads, bridges and any other feature along the way, and then at the church for absolution. The funeral itself is relatively swift, with everyone present throwing soil into the grave and being given a small loaf with a candle and a red-painted egg, as at Easter. These must also be given to passers-by, and tourists, who would give great offence if they refused. These knot-shaped loaves or *colaci* bear the inscription NI KA ("Jesus Christ is victorious") which is stamped in the dough by a special seal called a *pecetar*. These may only be used by a widow or some other "clean woman"; the stamp is standard, but the handle, usually wooden, can be elaborately carved with motifs such as the "Endless Column" (or *axis mundi*), the tree of life, wolf's teeth or a crucifix.

Three days later there is another *pomană* or memorial meal, when bread is again given to church officials and all present; after nine days nine widows spend the day fasting and praying around the deceased's shirt; six weeks and six months after the funeral the absolution is repeated, with another meal, as the dead must be given food and drink, and after a year a feast is given for all the family's dead. The Uniates also remember their dead on All Souls' Day, which is not an Orthodox festival. Mourning lasts for one year, during which time the close family may not attend weddings or dances and women wear black. As elsewhere in Romania, *şergare* or embroidered napkins are hung over icons in the church or over plates on house walls in memory of the dead.

Marriage and reproduction are seen as essential in Maramureş, so much so that if a person of marriageable age (in fact from eight years old, the age of first confession) dies unmarried a **Marriage of the Dead** or *nunta mortului* is held. A black flag is carried, and the deceased and a bridesmaid or flag-carrier (best man) are in wedding costume, although everyone else is in mourning garb. In the case of a man, there is a stand-in bride, while for a woman the bride's crown is used symbolically.

important work begun, and it was believed that after sundown ghosts and vampires (*strigoi*) roamed, seeking victims. From Berbeşti, the DN18 continues to Vadu Izei, the mouth of the Iza valley (see p.254), and Sighet (see overleaf).

The Cosău valley

South of Berbeşti, a minor road turns off to the right at Fereşti, and leads up the Cosău valley to several picturesque villages (perhaps the most interesting of all from a ethnographic point of view), which can also be approached from the south, crossing the Neteda Pass (see p.249), from the west, using the road via Hoteni, or from Bîrsana, to the east.

Across the river from Fereşti is **CORNEŞTI**, where there's an early eight-eenth-century church and another **watermill**, which also serves as a laundry. Women beat clothes with carved wooden laundry bats beside the river, often improvising songs and verses as they work. There's a distinctive local technique called singing "with knots", in which the voice is modulated by tapping the glottis while the singer doesn't breathe for lengthy periods. Certain instruments are also peculiar to Maramureş, for example the *cetera*, a fiddle with a half-size bridge, producing a very penetrating note, the *zongoră*, a guitar, often with three strings, used to mark the rhythm, and the *dobă*, a kind of drum.

Călineşti and Budeşti

Continuing south you come to three villages about 4km apart, with two **wooden churches** apiece. At **CĂLINEŞTI**, the beautiful *Susan* or upper church, just north of the junction, was built in 1784. Its companion, the seventeenth-century *Josan* (lower) or *Caieni* church, is very special, one of the loveliest in Maramureş, with its huge nineteenth-century porch and internal paintings by Ponehalski from 1754. It's best reached by a path across the fields next to house no. 385, on the road east to Bîrsana. **SÎRBI** has two small and unassuming wooden churches (the *Susan* to the north, built in 1667, and the *Josan*, built in 1703) and some fine water mills.

Beyond this is **BUDEŞTI**, a large village but one of the least spoiled in Maramureş. The *Josan* church, in the centre of the village (by a memorial to the dead of the 1989 revolution), was built in 1643 and contains frescoes, icons on wood by Ponehalski, and the coat of mail of Pintea Viteazul (the outlaw Pintea the Brave). The *Susan* or upper church dates from 1586 and has particularly fine paint-ings from the 1760s, also by· Ponehalski. The building has been gradually extended westwards, so that the tower is now almost central. From here there is a particularly fine walk through idyllic countryside to Hoteni via **BREB**, a small village with a hideous new church and a particularly lovely and tranquil wooden church (dated 1531 by local tradition), hidden away in the valley. Budeşti can be reached by four **buses** a day from Sighet taking the high road via **OCNA ŞUGATAG**, a former salt-mining centre that is now a small spa, with a **hotel** (③) and **campsite** (to the north), as well as shops and a weekly **market** on Thursdays.

Sighetu Marmaţiei and around

SIGHET (as it's generally known) stands just a few kilometres from the Ukrainian border; although Westerners can't cross here, it still has the air of a frontier town, with churches of almost every denomination. When the territory to the north was called Ruthenia, the easternmost province of Czechoslovakia, Sighet was a famous smuggling town. An overgrown monument to the Jews rounded up by the Hungarian gendarmerie and deported in 1944 stands at the end of Strada Mureşan, off Piaţa Libertăţii, the more westerly of the town's two imposing squares.

Today Sighet is a peaceful modern town with 40,000 inhabitants, where you can see residents of the surrounding villages in local costume, especially on the first Monday of the month when the livestock market takes place. The town is famed for its **winter carnival** when many of the participants wear extraordinary shamanistic costumes and masks; unfortunately few foreign visitors are around to witness this in the week after Christmas.

The Town

The **Maramureş Ethnographic Museum** at Str. Bogdan Voda 1 exhibits pottery, woodcarvings, masks and wall rugs (*scoarte*), and has an open-air section – the **Village Museum** – situated on Dobăieş hill on the town's eastern outskirts (30 minutes' walk, or get off bus #1 by the bridge and School no. 5, and walk northeast for five minutes up Strada Muzeului). Here you can see dozens of houses, farm buildings and churches collected from the Iza valley – an essential sight if you're intending to give the real thing a miss. If the **Art Gallery** at Str. Mihali de Apşa 17 is shut, you can enquire at the museum.

On Strada Barnuțiu, just off the main drag, stands the former **prison**, now marked with plaques listing the 51 prominent figures who died here in the purges of the early 1950s; these included bishops such as Marton Aron, academics such as Gheorghe Brătianu, government ministers and politicians such as Iuliu Maniu, leader of the Peasants' Party. Its 72 cells held about 180 members of the pre-war establishment, at least two-thirds of them aged over sixty; they were brought here presumably so that they could be rapidly spirited away into the Soviet Union if the communist regime was threatened. The prison now calls itself the International Centre for Study of Totalitarianism, and a museum is planned.

Practicalities

You'll find the **tourist office** on Piața Libertății, opposite the *Tisa* **hotel** at no. 8 (☎062/51.26.45; ③), one of Romania's more pleasant and friendly hotels. To the west, Strada Eminescu leads to the grubby chalet-style *Marmația* in the Grădina Morii park by the river (☎062/51.22.41; ⑤). There's a footbridge across the Iza from here to Solovan hill, where you can easily camp wild. In the other direction, 4km east on the DN18, is the overpriced *Teplița* motel (☎062/51.28.15; ⑤).

The surrounding villages are served by at least one **bus** a day, usually at about 4pm, from the terminal opposite the train station at Str. Iuliu Maniu 1. **Trains** east from Sighet reverse at the Ukrainian border before following the Vişeu valley up to Vişeu de Jos – a less absorbing route than along the Iza but still scenic, particularly around the village of Petrova. From Vişeu de Jos there are trains to Borşa and up the Vaser valley (see p.256), but most services continue south towards Salva and Beclean, the junctions for trains to Suceava, Cluj and Braşov. This route is described in more detail on p.258.

Săpînța

SĂPÎNȚA (or Săpânța), 16km northwest of Sighet, is served by five buses a day, including those to Baia Mare and Satu Mare via the Huta Pass and Negreşti. This village has achieved a star on every tourist map, largely thanks to the work of Stan Ion Pătraş. Its **Merry Cemetery** (*Cimitir vesel*) features beautifully worked, colourfully painted headboards carved with portraits of the deceased or scenes from their lives (chosen by relatives), and inscribed with witty limericks (composed by Patraş as he saw fit). Some are terse – "who sought money to amass, could not escape Death, alas!" – while a suprising number bespeak violent deaths, like the villager killed by a "bloody Hungarian" during the last war, or a mother's final message to her son: "Griga, may you pardoned be, even though you did stab me". Patraş himself died in 1977 but left two apprentices, Turda Toader and Vasile Stan, to continue the funerary masterwork. The village is now lined with handicraft stalls, and is becoming rather too accustomed to busloads of tourists making a stop for half an hour and then rushing on.

The Oaş depression

Beyond Săpînţa, the road turns south towards Satu Mare, entering the **Oaş** depression via the **Huta Pass** (587m). In this region shepherds assemble on the first Sunday of May for the **festival of Sîmbra Oilor** when barren ewes are separated from the others and the milk yield is measured. Whether this process – known as *Ruptul Sterpelor* – occurs in May (as in Maramureş) or early July (as it does further south), the participants dress for the occasion in waist-length sheep-skin *cojoc*, covered in embroidery and tassels, or fluffy woollen overcoats called *guba*, and heartily consume fiery Maramureş brandy and sweet whey cheese.

Most of the shepherds come from villages beyond the *Sîmbra Oilor* cabana on the other side of the pass: such as **HUTA-CERTEZE** and **CERTEZE**. In both villages, you may see people wearing traditional Oaş **folk costumes**, also widely worn during the **festival** on September 1 at **NEGREŞTI**, the largest settlement in the region. The **Oaş Museum**, at the north end of the main Strada Victoriei, has been closed for restoration but has a good display of local ethnography. There's also a small open-air museum on Strada Livezilor, to the south beyond the bridge, which has half a dozen blue-painted houses and a wooden church. Oaş is sometimes billed as an undiscovered Maramureş, but most of the local men now work or trade abroad, so that the roads are lined with new bungalows and traditional costume is little worn except in the remotest villages such as **CAMARZANA**.

The only **accommodation** in Negreşti is the *Oşanul* hotel at Str. Victoriei 89 (☎062/85.11.62; ④). The other hotels in Oaş are the *Valea-Mariei* (☎062/85.07.50; ②), 5km north of **VAMA**, a ceramics centre, and the *Călineşti* (☎062/85.14.00; ②) in **CĂLINEŞTI-OAŞ**, by a reservoir 15km west of Negreşti.

The Iza valley

Some of the loveliest villages and wooden churches in Maramureş are situated in the **Iza valley**, which extends for roughly 60km to the Rodna mountains forming the frontier with Moldavia. Most of the villages along the Iza and in the side valleys have a daily bus from Sighet, and there are several buses to Vişeu and Borşa, most following the DJ186 along the Iza rather than the DN18 along the Rona and Vişeu valleys. Although there's no tourist accommodation and virtually no shops along the valley until Săcel, you could also hike it in a couple of days.

Bîrsana and Rozavlea

VADU IZEI, where the valley road turns off the main road to Baia Mare, is well known as the workplace of Gheorghe Borodi, who carves monumental **gateways** erected by Maramureş families as status symbols. The church at **BÎRSANA**, 15km from Vadu Izei, is small and neat and perfectly positioned atop a hillock in the middle of the village. The florid paintings, among the best in Maramureş, were done in 1720, soon after the church's construction, and in 1806, by Hodor Toador and Ion Plohod, with icons on wood by Hodor Toador – the narthex is adorned with saints and processional images, while the naos is painted with Old and New Testament scenes, each in its own decorative medallion.

Being a hinterland region, Maramureș remained vulnerable to attacks by nomadic tribes until the eighteenth century, and the wooden church at **ROZAVLEA**, 26km further on, was built of fir beams in 1717, just after the last Tartar invasion. Its magnificent double roof was recently restored and looks a little new, but will doubtless weather nicely.

Poienile Izei

Southwest of Rozavlea, an execrable 12-kilometre-long track into the hills leads to the village of **POIENILE IZEI** (The Meadows of the Iza). Anyone in the house above the new church will unlock the old church (1604) for visitors. Inside, it is filled with **nightmarish paintings**, its walls red with the fires of Hell, wherein dozens of sinners have their vulnerable white bodies tortured by demons (*draci*) with goat-like heads and clawed feet. A woman is being pressed with a hot iron, a man is hung from a butcher's hook by his tongue, while others are furrowed by sharp ploughs or casually sawn in two. Beneath it all processions of sinners are driven into the mouth of Hell – an enormous bird's head with fiery nostrils.

These pictures constitute an **illustrated rule book** too terrifying to disobey, whose message is still understood by the villagers. A huge pair of bellows is used to inflict punishment for farting in church, while the woman being ironed had burnt the priest's robes while pressing them. Women violating traditional morality face torments in the afterlife: adultresses are courted by loathsome demons and a woman who aborted children is forced to eat them. These Hell scenes presumably formed the nasty part of a huge *Day of Judgement* in the narthex, which has half disappeared. Opposite are paintings of gardens and distant city-scapes in a sort of Gothic *Book of Hours*-style, seemingly executed at a later date. Murals in the nave are badly damaged and soot-blackened, but from the balcony you can recognize Adam and Eve, the Fall, and episodes from the lives of Christ and John the Baptist.

Ieud and beyond

Back in the Iza valley, about 5km further southeast, a turn-off at Gura Ieudului leads upstream to the village of **IEUD**, 3km south. Lanes fenced with lattices run between the houses, clustered within their courtyards, and during summer the air is pervaded by the scent of lady's-mantle, a plant mixed with elder and wormwood to make "face water", which was also used for baths to invigorate weak children. Divorce is virtually unknown in this religious and traditional village; thus about fifty of Ieud's women are "heroine mothers", having borne fourteen children each, and nigh on half the population of 5000 is of school age. It was Ieud artisans, supervised by the master carpenter Ion Țiplea, who restored Manuc's Inn in Bucharest some years ago, and the tradition of woodworking has been maintained since the superb Orthodox **Church on the Hill** was first raised here in 1364. Supposedly the oldest church in Maramureș (though largely rebuilt in the eighteenth century), with a double roof and tiny windows, it housed the Ieud Codex (now in the Romanian Academy in Bucharest), the earliest known document in the Romanian language. It has perhaps the best-known paintings of any Maramureș church, executed by Alexandru Ponehalski in 1782; look out for Abraham, Isaac and Jacob welcoming people in their arms, in the pronaos. Ask opposite the *bufet* or *Textile-Incaltimente* shop for the church key, and have a look at the ingenious removable ratchet used to open the bolt in the main door. Ieud's lower church, the Uniate *Val* or *Şes* church, was built in 1718 and has an immensely high roofline and, unusually, no porch; there are few wall paintings left, but the icons on glass and iconostasis are valuable.

BOGDAN VODĂ, formerly known as Cuhea, is one of the valley's main villages, standing on the road leading to Moldavia, and has long-standing ties with that region. The local voivode, Bogdan, left from here to march over the mountains, supposedly to hunt bison, and founded the Moldavian state in 1359 – the influence of Ştefan and other Moldavian rulers seems to have imparted a semi-Byzantine style to the frescoes inside Bogdan Vodă's church. The building materials used in 1722 were typical of Maramureş, however: thick fir beams rather than the stone used at Putna and other Moldavian monasteries. From here a rough road leads to Vişeu de Jos in the next valley north (see below), while the main road continues on to **SĂCEL** and meets the DN17C, running south to Salva and Bistriţa.

The Vişeu valley and the Rodna mountains

The River Vişeu is fed by numerous sources in the wooded highlands above the **Vişeu valley** and surrounded by mountains that merge with the "crests" of Bucovina and the higher peaks of Chornohora in Ukraine. Buses along the main road from Sighet are rare, but all trains from Sighet stop at the **picturesque villages** of **PETROVA** and **LEORDINA**. Just beyond, near Ruscova, a track leads 18km upriver to the Ukrainian-populated village of **POIENILE DE SUB MUNTE**, which is even more beautiful. The evening fast **trains** from Sighet turn southwards at **VIŞEU DE JOS**, passing through Săcel en route to Salva; and five trains a day run up a branch line from Vişeu de Jos through Vişeu de Sus and Moisei to the alpine resort of Borşa.

From **VIŞEU DE SUS**, a larger settlement than its namesake, with the grotty *Cerbul* hotel at Str. Spiru Haret 2 (②), early birds can catch the 7am **logging train** up the steep **Vaser valley**. Hauled by a vintage steam engine, it carries lumberjacks (*butinarii*) up to their camps near the Ukrainian border, and at 3pm begins the journey back down from Coman. Bears and deer drink from the river, unperturbed by the trains and loggers, while in the mountain forests live stags, elusive lynxes, and also wolves, a dozen or so of whom are shot each winter when the packs become too ravenous. The Vaser river, rich in trout and umber, descends rapidly through the 50-kilometre long valley, and its whirling waters have begun to attract **kayaking** enthusiasts to logging settlements like **MĂCIRLĂU**, from where there's a very rugged trail over the Jupania ridge of the Maramureş mountains to Baia Borşa.

The large village of **MOISEI**, 12km beyond Vişeu de Sus, lies beneath the foothills of the Rodna massif, whose peaks are often still snowy while fruit is ripening in the village's orchards. Though its present existence is bucolic, within living memory Moisei suffered a tragedy that's become a symbol of atrocity and martyred innocence in Romania. In October 1944, retreating Hungarian troops machine-gunned twenty-nine villagers and set Moisei ablaze – a massacre commemorated by a circle of twelve stone figures by Vida Geza with faces modelled upon those of two of the victims and of the masks that are worn during festivals in Maramureş. This stands at the eastern end of this very long village, opposite a small museum.

Today, Moisei's peaceful existence is exemplified by its womenfolk – spinning wool as they walk down the lane, or working in the fields with their babies nearby, hung in cradles from trees. A couple of kilometres along a side valley south of the village stands a monastery, scene of a major pilgrimage on August 15, the Feast of the Assumption. There's a wooden church here, dating from 1672, and **accommodation** in a *han* at the pass to the south.

The branch line ends 2km west of Borşa, 9km east of Moisei; maxitaxis run from the station through the town of Borşa to Baia Borşa, just to the north, the centre for all the mines in the surrounding hills. Most services are in **BORŞA** itself, including the *Iezer* hotel on Strada Victoriei (③), as well as a wooden church rebuilt in 1718 and hidden away north of the road west of the centre. Pre-1939 travellers describe this as a centre of Jewish merchants, living from forestry and trade with Moldavia by the road over the Prislop Pass, about 12km east. Roughly 2km before the pass you'll find the **Borşa Complex ski resort** with villas, the *Hanul Butinarilor* chalet and the *Cascada* and *Stibina* (⑤) hotels.

Hiking in the Rodna mountains

The Rodnas are one of Romania's best **hiking** areas, largely because you are sure to have them virtually to yourself. The easiest way into the mountains is either by the chair-lift from the Borşa Complex (not generally active outside the ski season) or from the 1416m **Prislop Pass**; from here you can head either north into the Maramureş mountains, wild and largely unvisited, although scarred by mining and forestry, or south into the Rodnas. Following red triangles, then blue stripes, it should take you two hours at most to reach the main crest at the Gărgălău saddle, from where you can follow red stripes east to the Rotunda Pass and ultimately Vatra Dornei (see p.239), or west into the highest part of the massif. Four and a half hours will get you to **LA CRUCE**, where you can turn right to follow blue stripes up to the automatic weather station on the summit of **Mount Pietrosul** (2303m), ninety minutes away. There are great views in all directions, particularly deep into Ukraine to the north. Borşa is 1600m below, and it takes another two and a half hours to get back there.

Apart from camping, the only place to sleep in the mountains is the *Puzdrele* cabana – two to three hours' trek from the hamlet of Poiana Borşa, following the route marked by blue triangles, which continues to the main ridge in a couple of hours. With a map, you can hike on south and down towards the Someş Mare valley and Năsăud (see p.193) in a couple of days, camping wild en route.

Into Moldavia

Just before the Prislop Pass, linking Maramureş with **Moldavia**, you'll see a monument marking the site where the last Tartar raid was finally driven off in 1717. At the pass stands an inn behind which a major festival, the **Horă at Prislop**, takes place on the first or second Sunday in August every year, attracting thousands of participants and spectators. Although not a major part of the displays here, the Round Dance or *Horă* still has the power to draw onlookers into the rhythmically stepping, swaying and stamping circles. The *Horă* used to serve as a sanction in village society – local miscreants seeking to enter the circle were shamed when the dancing immediately ceased, and only resumed when they withdrew.

On the far side of the pass, the road runs down the lovely Bistriţa valley to Cîmpulung Moldovenesc (see p.238), from where you can reach Suceava and several of the Painted Monasteries by rail. Two buses run per day from Vişeu to Vatra Dornei; you can change either there or at Iacobeni for trains to Cîmpulung Moldovenesc. Travelling **to Transylvania**, four trains a day link Vişeu de Jos with **SALVA**, a busy junction on the line from Cluj to Vatra Dornei and Suceava.

travel details

Trains

Baia Mare to: Beclean pe Someş (2 or 3 daily; 2hr 50min–4hr 10min); Braşov (2 or 3 daily; 8hr 25min–9hr 45min); Bucharest (2 daily; 11hr 15min–11hr 40min); Cluj (2 daily; 3hr 25min–5hr); Dej (4 or 5 daily; 2hr 20min–3hr 25min); Jibou (7 or 8 daily; 50 min–1hr 30min); Satu Mare (8 or 9 daily; 1hr–1hr 30min); Timişoara (1 daily; 6hr 30min).

Salva to: Bucharest (1 daily; 8hr 40min); Cluj (6 or 7 daily; 1hr 40min–2hr 40min); Dej (9 or 10 daily; 45min–1hr 25min); Ilva Mica (12 daily; 30–45min); Sighet (4 daily; 3hr 30min–4hr 25min); Vişeu de Jos (4 daily; 1hr 40min–2hr 15min).

Satu Mare to: Baia Mare (8 or 9 daily; 1hr–1hr 35min); Bucharest (3 daily; 13hr–19hr 45min); Negreşti (4 daily; 1hr 30min).

Sighet to: Bucharest (1 daily; 12hr 20min); Salva (4 daily; 3hr 25min–4hr 35min); Vişeu de Jos (6 daily; 1hr 45min–2hr 15min).

Vişeu de Jos to: Borşa (5 daily; 45min); Bucharest (1 daily; 10hr 30min); Sighet (6 daily; 1hr 45min–2hr 10min); Vişeu de Sus (5 daily; 15min).

Planes

Baia Mare and Satu Mare (planes serve both on a triangular route): Bucharest (2 daily; 1hr); Constanţa (summer only; 1 daily; 1hr 15min).

International trains

Baia Mare to: Budapest (1 daily; 8hr 45min).

Carei to: Mátészalka (2 daily; 2hr).

Valea lui Mihai to: Debrecen (2 daily; 1hr 30min).

CHAPTER SIX

THE BANAT

The **Banat** (*Bánság* in Hungarian) is the historical term for the western marches of Romania between the Timiş and Mureş rivers, but it has come to include also the *Crişana*, or the county of Oradea, on the Crişul Repede river. It has much in common with Hungary's Great Plain and ex-Yugoslavia's Vojvodina region, sharing similar featureless scenery, great rivers and chunks of history, with an intermingling of different ethnic groups. The frontiers were finally settled according to the principle of national self-determination at the Versailles conference of 1918–20, each country's delegates arriving bearing reams of demographic maps and statistics to support their claims. During the communist era, policies towards ethnic minorities were generous in Hungary and Yugoslavia, and comparatively fair in Romania until the 1960s, from when an increasingly hard line caused a haemorrhaging of the population, particularly of ethnic Magyars; around 80,000 left in both 1988 and 1989, as liberalization gained pace in Hungary but things went downhill fast in Romania. The Schwab Germans, who originally settled in this area when the marshes were drained and resettled after the expulsion of the Turks, have almost all emigrated to Germany since 1989. Nevertheless many villages of Slovaks, Serbs, Magyars and other minority groups remain here.

From the visitor's point of view, the cities of **Oradea**, **Arad** and **Timişoara** overshadow the rest of the Banat – partly on their own merits, but also because each town dominates a route between Transylvania and Hungary or Serbia, and provides access to most other places of interest in the region. When you're tired of such sights and café life as the cities have to offer, you'll find the western ranges of the **Apuseni mountains** with their **stalactite caves, wooden churches** and village **festivals** within easy reach, while Belgrade, Debrecen, Szeged, Cluj, Sibiu and other major cities are only a few hours away.

Oradea and around

Situated on the banks of the Criş Repede river, with a population of 200,000, **ORADEA**, is close to the site of Bihara – the capital of a Vlach voivode, Menumorut, who resisted Hungarian claims on the region during the tenth century – and bears the stamp of its subsequent rulers. Founded around a monastery, the medieval town of *Nagyvárad* (as the Magyars still call it) prospered during the reign of **Mátyás Corvinus**, who was raised at the Bishop's court here, and later acquired a mammoth Vauban-style citadel and the wealth of stately neoclassical, Baroque and Secession piles which constitute Oradea's most characteristic feature.

Oradea is the capital of **Bihor county**, known as the "Land of Hot Waters", for its profusion of thermal springs, which have been exploited to create **spas; Băile Felix**, 8km from the city, is the most developed.

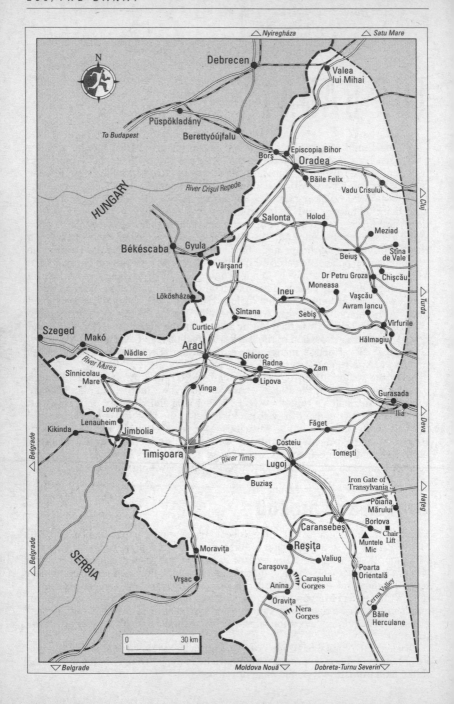

ACCOMMODATION PRICES		

Hotels listed in the *Guide* have been price-graded according to the scale below. Prices given are those charged for the cheapest double room, which in the less expensive places usually comes without private bath or shower and without breakfast. See p.28 for more details.

① under $10	④ $25–40	⑦ $80–135
② $10–15	⑤ $40–55	⑧ $135–190
③ $15–25	⑥ $55–80	⑨ $200 and over

Arrival, information and accommodation

Oradea, is situated 16km from **BORŞ**, the 24-hour checkpoint on the DN1 (E60) at the border with **Hungary**; and a mere 6km from **EPISCOPIA BIHOR**, where international trains clear customs. By rail, it's 4 hours and 45 minutes from **Budapest** on the *Partium, Claudiopolis, Corona* and *Varadinium* expresses – the first two of which arrive in Oradea at noon and 6pm, enabling you to find a room before nightfall.

Trams #1 and #4 take you south from the **train station** along the main Calea Republicii continuing along Strada Gen. Magheru where the Calea swings right towards Piaţa Republicii. Oradea is an important junction for international trains to Prague and Kraków as well as Budapest – all international tickets must be bought at the *CFR* office on Calea Republicii (Mon–Fri 8am–6pm).

There are two **bus terminals**, one southeast of the centre at Str. Războieni 81 linked to the centre by bus #13, and the main one immediately adjacent to the Oradea Est train halt, served by tram #2. They operate services to and from Beiuş, Abrud, Deva and Alba Iulia; and Hungary, via Debrecen. Direct buses for Budapest leave from the *Crişana* department store on Calea Republicii.

The **airport** is on the edge of town on the Calea Aradului and flights (from Bucharest and Constanţa) are met by *TAROM* buses. Tickets can be bought at *TAROM*'s office at Piaţa Republicii 2 (Mon–Fri 7am–7pm, Sat 9am–2pm; ☎059/ 13.19.18), from where buses leave seventy minutes before each flight.

Information

Oradea's **tourist offices** include the *Crişul* in the foyer of the *Transilvania* hotel and *Lucon* at Str. Moşoiu 1 (which both offer daytrips to Hungary) and *CIG* at Str. Moscovei 8 (day trips to Uzhgorod and Mukachevo in Ukraine, as well as deals to Hungary, Poland and Istanbul). OJT, in the *Hotel Dacia* or at Băile Felix, may be able to fix you up with excursions to Stîna de Vale, the Bears' Cave at Chişcău and various folklore events in the Apuseni mountains, although most of these can be reached without their help.

Accommodation

Oradea has a reasonable selection of hotels, although you might consider checking out the hotels in the spa of Băile Felix (see p.264). Otherwise, the alternatives are a **dormitory bed** from the County Youth and Sport Office, at Str. Vulcan 11 or the **chalets** and **campsites** beside the river at **TILEAGD**, 19km east of town along the DN1, and in the spa of **BĂILE 1 MAI**.

Astoria, Str. Teatrului 1 (☎059/13.07.45). Nothing special and rather overpriced. ④.

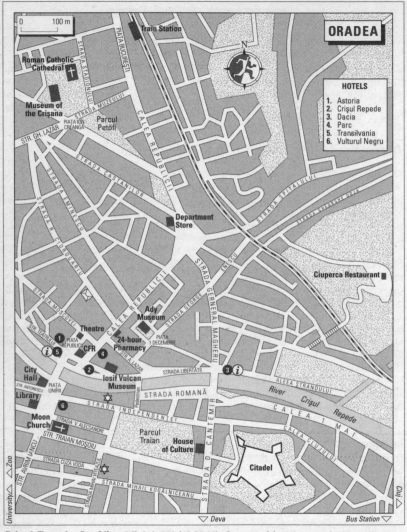

ORADEA

HOTELS
1. Astoria
2. Crișul Repede
3. Dacia
4. Parc
5. Transilvania
6. Vulturul Negru

Crișul Repede, Str. Libertății 6 (☎059/13.25.09). In a good location overlooking the river and close to the central squares, but fairly ordinary. ③.

Dacia, Aleea Ștrandului (☎059/11.86.56). The best hotel in town, frequented by businessmen and tour groups. ⑤.

Parc, Calea Republicii 5 (☎059/11.16.99). A friendly place on the city's main pedestrianized street. ③.

Transilvania, Str. Teatrului 2 (☎059/13.05.08). Good value for money. ③.

Vulturul Negru, Str. Independenței 1 (☎059/13.54.17). The least expensive of Oradea's hotels, in a highly atmospheric building – the first stop in Romania for generations of backpackers. ③.

The City

The city's most famous sights are in the north of town, just west of the train station, alongside Strada Stadionului. Countless serfs toiled from 1752 to 1780 to build Romania's largest Roman Catholic **Cathedral**, all Baroque gold leaf, marble and choirboys, with a huge organ (see posters for details of concerts). Their labour was doubtless also exploited to build the vast U-shaped **Bishop's Palace**, with its 100 rooms and 365 windows (1762–77, modelled on the Belvedere Palace in Vienna), in the same leafy park which also has three giant Californian Redwoods. The palace now serves as the **Museum of the Crişana** (Tues, Thurs, Sat 10am–3pm; Wed, Fri, Sun 10am–6pm) whose highlights are a series of **engravings by Albrecht Dürer** (his father was born in a nearby village), and a collection of 14,000 traditional painted eggs from Bihor and Bucovina; in Bihor the technique involves painting patterns such as wheels and zig-zags in bee's wax and then dipping the egg into an onion skin dye to produce simple white and ochre patterns, while in Bucovina several layers and dyes are used to produce more complex patterns and colours.

Heading south, Calea Republicii becomes a pedestrianized promenade as it nears the river, lined with shops, *cofetărie*, cinemas and plenty of ostentatious Secession buildings. It eventually opens onto **Piaţa Republicii**, dominated by the State Theatre (opened in 1900), a typically pompous design by the Viennese duo, Helmer and Fellner.

Just to the east are are two **memorial houses**, of little interest to the average visitor. One, in the tiny Traian Park (Mon, Wed, Fri 10am–3pm; Tues, Thurs, Sun 10am–2pm), commemorates the Magyar poet **Endre Ady** (see p.191) who lived in Oradea for four years and, unusually for his era, opposed Hungarian chauvinism towards the Romanians; the other, at Str. Vulcan 16, remembers **Josif Vulcan**, who lived here between 1880 and 1906 and edited the literary magazine *Familia* (in which Mihai Eminescu made his debut).

South of the river

Apart from the nondescript church half-blocking the north side of **Piaţa Unirii** across the Crişul Repede river, most of the buildings around this square were designed to maximize the impact of the waterfront. The former **City Hall** is a monumental restatement of well-worn classical themes to which the architects added a fun touch: chimes that play the March of Avram Iancu every hour. Given that the Austro-Hungarians were still in control when the building was raised in 1902–03, it seems odd that they chose to commemorate Iancu – a Romanian revolutionary whose agitation inspired the protest on the "Field of Liberty" at Blaj in 1848 (see p.152), and who then took to the hills with a guerrilla band, harassing Magyar troops and landlords and urging the serfs to revolt. Next to this stands the **City Library**, a more spectacular piece of architecture from 1905.

Facing these across Piaţa Victoriei is an ornate Secession-style edifice of 1908 with the splendid name of the **Vulturul Negru** or "Black Eagle". Running through this, an arcade with a stained glass roof connects three neighbouring streets. Part of the complex is occupied by a hotel that could have sprung from the pages of a Graham Greene thriller – an ill-lit labyrinth of rooms and corridors inhabited by brooding staff and a furtive clientele (see above). To the south, Oradea's main Orthodox church, built in 1792, marks the stylistic transition from Baroque to neo-classical, but is better known as the **Moon Church** after the large sphere mounted beneath its clock, which rotates to indicate the lunar phases over a period of 28 days. There are also no less than three imposing **synagogues** nearby: on Strada Independenţei opposite the *Vulturul Negru*; just east at Strada Mihai Viteazul 2; and just west on Piaţa Rahovei. Oradea was a great centre of Jewish settlement, and in December 1927 Codreanu's League of the Archangel Michael (soon to become the Iron Guard) held a congress here having been brought free in special trains – they wrecked four synagogues before leaving.

To the east, beyond Piaţa 1 Decembrie, rises the imposing bulk of Oradea's **citadel**, a Renaissance stronghold enlarged during the eighteenth century by Italian disciples of the Swiss military architect Vauban. Pentagonal in shape, with bastions guarding each corner, the citadel used to be additionally protected by a moat filled with warm water from the Peţa, which never froze. Although the external walls seem very dilapidated, the citadel is now the traffic police headquarters, and is busy with people seeking driving tests and number plates.

Heading south from Piaţa Unirii, Strada Avram Iancu becomes Calea Armatei Romăne, with a **Military Museum** (Tues–Sun 10am–4pm) on the left at no. 22 and the University on the right: the third gateway into this attractive leafy campus leads to a **wooden church**, built in Letca in 1760 and moved here in 1991 to be the chapel of the theological faculty. With its new porch and radiators, it no longer has the authentic atmosphere of a village church, but on the other hand it is usually open, and you can also climb up into the tower. Returning north, Strada Matei Basarab leads left to the **zoo** (daily 8am–8pm), which has monkeys, yaks, lions, llamas, various varieties of pheasant, as well as native Romanian animals such as wolves, goats, owls and squirrels.

Eating, drinking and entertainment

The best hotel **restaurants** are in the *Dacia* and *Transilvania* hotels but there's a fair choice of other places. Calea Republicii and the streets leading off it have plenty of cafés, including the *Oradea*, Str. Vulcan 1, and the *Cocoşul de Aur* at Str. Grigorescu 2. The *Olivery* at Str. Moscovei 12, tries to be a real restaurant, serving breakfast, lunch and dinner. There's also a Chinese, *Tian Tang*, opposite the *Parc* hotel on Calea Republicii; a *Lactovegetarian* at Calea Republicii 11; the adjacent *Globus* hamburger joint; and the *Ciuperca* with its outdoor terrace on Viilor hill. The bar in the *Astoria* hotel is the smart place to go **drinking**, while there are several other bars along Strada Vulcan.

If you want to buy your own food, you'll find the *Promesc* and UNIC **supermarkets** (respectively under the *Parc* hotel and on the corner of Strada Eminescu), and a private **bakery** at Str. Mihai Viteazul 5 for hot fresh bread.

The town's **Philharmonic Orchestra**, housed at Piaţa 1 Decembrie 10 (tickets from Str. Moscovei 5), is well regarded, while children might enjoy performances at the **Puppet Theatre**, Str. Alecsandri 9 (*Vulturul Negru* arcade).

The spas

The spa town of **BĂILE FELIX**, 8km southwest of Oradea, along DN76 offers a **thermal pool** (8am–6pm) surrounded by mock-rustic buildings and a park containing a wooden church, and a plethora of modern hotels. It's served by tram #4 from Oradea's train station or bus #12 from the Moon Church to the end of the line at **NUFARUL**, and then bus #14 or a train towards Mierlau. The best of the

hotels is the *Internaţional* (☎059/26.14.45; ⑤)), followed by the *Lotus* (☎059/13.43.55; ④)), *Nufarul* (☎26.11.42; ④)) and the overpriced *Termal* (☎059/26.12.14; ④)), but there's also inexpensive accommodation at the *Muncel* (☎059/26.14.60; ②)) by the Beiuş turning. Many of Băile Felix's hotels are home to the students of Oradea's Evangelical College, the first to be founded in Eastern Europe, but there is usually plenty of space during the summer holidays. A similar but less developed spa is **BĂILE 1 MAI** (Întîi Mai), reached by bus #15 from Nufarul, turning off the DN76 just before Băile Felix, which has a **campsite** (with *casute*) but fewer hotels.

Both places offer healing **mud-baths**, either in sapropelic fossil gunge or the local peat bog, and dips in pools fed by the warm and slightly radioactive River Peţa, in which the **thermal lotus** (*Nymphaea lotus var. thermalis*), otherwise found only in the Nile Delta, has survived since the Tertiary Period.

The western flanks of the Apuseni mountains

Villages, festivals and hiking in the **Apuseni mountains** are generally described in the chapter on Transylvania (see p.184); what follows is a quick run-down of attractions along the mountains' **western approaches**, starting from Oradea. Most attractions lie close to the DN76, but trains to Beiuş and Vaşcău now take a very roundabout route, following the main Arad line through **SALONTA**, birthplace of the Hungarian poet Arany János (1817–82), remembered in a museum (Tues–Sun 10am–4pm) in a tower built in 1630 on the main square.

Beiuş and around

The small town of **BEIUŞ**, 55km from Oradea, has Baptist, Greek Catholic, Roman Catholic and Orthodox churches cheek-by-jowl in the centre. However, its main attraction is as a jumping-off point for the impressive stalactite **caves of Meziad and Chişcău**. Minibus excursions are organized for around $20 a head by the *Crişul Negru* **tourist agency** (Mon–Fri 8am–3.30pm; ☎059/21.16.01) housed in the **hotel** at Str. Ioan Ciordaş 2 (☎059/21.18.09; ④)), just north of the central Piaţa Vulcan. If you're killing time, the folk art and ceramics in the town's **Ethnographic Museum** (Tues–Sun 10am–5pm) are worth seeing.

From the bus station, next to the train station on the southern edge of town, **buses** run twice daily except Sundays to the village of **MEZIAD**, 10km northeast of Beiuş. The famous **cave**, with its huge entrance arch, is a further 3km away. It was first explored in 1859; in the 1960s a road was built, and 25,000 visitors a year came here until the even more spectacular cave at Chişcău (see overleaf) opened in 1980. Guides shepherd parties around the cave, commenting on the stalactites and other features of this warren with a total length of almost 5km; the hour-long tours occur whenever they feel like it between 9am and 6pm every day.

In summer, buses run from Beiuş to **STÎNA DE VALE** (or Stâna de Vale), a modest alpine resort at 1100m with **rooms**, **chalets** and a **campsite** serving the hiking fraternity. Between November and April, the resort's three **ski slopes** are open and lessons for beginners are available. From here, it's about five hours' walk to the *Padiş* cabana (see p.185), taking a path marked with red stripes which runs via the Poieni peak, the Cumpănăţelu saddle and the Vărăşoaia clearing. Experienced walkers might prefer the more challenging trail to Meziad (6–8hr, marked by blue triangles; not recommended in winter or bad weather). With many twists and turns around karstitic features, this follows the ridge above the Iad valley, surmounting the Piatra Tisei peak before descending to the tourist chalet below.

Buses leave Beiuş twice a day (Sundays excepted) for **CHIŞCĂU** ("Keesh-cow"). Accidentally discovered by local quarry-workers in 1975, the cave here was found to contain dozens of Neolithic ursine skeletons – hence its name, the **Bears' Cave** (*Peştera Urşilor*). You're obliged to take a one-hour guided tour (Tues–Sun 10am–6pm), but the experience is not to be missed: this is the only Romanian cave up to Western standards of presentation and lighting. The rock formations of the 488-metre-long upper gallery – shaped like castles, wraiths and beasts – are accompanied by the sound of water crashing into subterranean pools; the lower gallery is closed.

Into the mountains .

Access to Chişcău is via a road leading off the route from Sudrigiu to **PIETROASA**, a picturesque village on the upper reaches of the Crişul Pietros. Water-powered saw-mills still operate here and the older residents wear traditional Bihor costume. Each year, on a Sunday in August, the villagers troop 8km north up the Aleu valley for the **festival** of *Bulciugul de Valea Aleu*. Buses run from Beiuş to Pietroasa, but do not continue along the forest road up to the **Padiş plateau** near the "Citadels of Ponor" (see p.188). The hiking trail to the *Padiş* cabana, marked with blue crosses, follows the road for the most part; after about 5km, a path designated by yellow triangles, diverges south to the Focul Viu cave, near Ponor.

You can also approach the plateau along **the road to Gîrda de Sus** and the Scarişoara Ice Cave (see p.184). Some way south of the Pietroasa turning, **RIENI** is worth a look for its **wooden church**, just west of the village, by the train halt. Built in 1753 the church is now slightly run-down, with lots of woodpecker damage, but is interesting for its doorway and the spire, like one slipped over another, typical of this area. However, the best part of the journey comes once you leave the DN76 and the rail line beyond the small industrial town of **DR PETRU GROZA** and head eastwards. Dr Petru Groza (also known as Ştei,

DR PETRU GROZA

A delegate at the Assembly of Alba Iulia in 1918, **Groza** (1884–1958) was an important politician before and after World War II. With the Communist Party banned since 1924, it was he who in 1933 founded the agrarian party (based in Deva) known as the Ploughmen's Front, which was literally a front for the communists. Imposed as prime minister of the coalition government in 1945, after communist agents provocateurs had gunned down communist demonstrators to discredit the democratic parties then leading the government, it was his job to organize elections in 1946 to establish the communists in power. Unfortunately the people voted overwhelmingly against them, so after three days' delay, totally false results were issued, and in mid-1947 the remaining leaders of the democratic parties were arrested.

Groza tried to moderate the nationalism of the Communist Party leader Gheorghiu-Dej; however on December 30, 1947 he visited King Mihai with him to force the king's abdication. He showed the Dowager Queen his pistol, joking that he wouldn't let the king do to him what he'd done to Antonescu. His eventual dismissal was viewed as a harbinger of the regime's crack-down on Romania's Magyar minority.

though not yet formally renamed) offers accommodation at the *Bihorul* hotel (☎059/31.06.15; ③), near the train and bus stations. The village of **BĂIŢA** just past Nucet has several caves nearby and holds a lively **fair** on the last Sunday in September; while on the far side of the 1160m Vîrtop Pass lies **ARIEŞENI**, with its traditional dwellings and wooden church. There's a campsite here, as at **GÎRDA DE SUS** a further 8km down the road, from which it's two to three hours' walk north to the Scarişoara Ice Cave.

The branch line from Oradea terminates at **VAŞCĂU**, but the DN76 continues through the mountains for 32km until it joins the Arad–Brad road and rail line at the village of **VÎRFURILE**. En route, just south of Criştioru de Jos, a rough track leaves the main road and leads 30km east to the village of **AVRAM IANCU** below **Mount Găina**, where the famous *Girl Fair* occurs every year (see p.185). There are several more festivals in the villages around Vîrfurile, but these are easier to approach from Arad (see p.270).

Arad and around

ARAD is a fine city of impressive buildings dominated by its eighteenth-century **citadel**. As a major rail junction, connections are good both to international destinations and within Romania, with many of the nearby **villages** in the foothills of the Apuseni mountains reachable via branch lines.

Arrival, information and accommodation

Like Oradea, 117km to the north, Arad lies just inside the border with Hungary. Approaching from Hungary, motorists enter Romania at **NĂDLAC** (on the E68 from Szeged), 40km away, or at **VĂRŞAND**, to the north halfway to Oradea; travelling by rail, you'll cross over from Lőkösháza to **CURTICI**. The *Pannonia* express reaches Arad at 2.30pm, while the other major services all arrive during the night.

The **train station** and **bus terminal** lie in the north of the city on Calea Aurel Vlaicu, both handling international and local services. Local buses are of little interest, but there are daily international connections with Szeged in Hungary and less frequent services to and from Budapest. Buses to Germany are run by the travel agencies in the *Central* and *Mureşul* hotels.

Arad's **airport** is in the western suburbs, with flights four times a week to and from Bucharest. *TAROM*'s office is at the southern end of Bulevardul Revoluţiei at Str. Unirii 1, by the State Theatre (Mon–Fri 7am–7pm, Sat 9am–2pm; ☎057/61.15.67).

The **tourist office** at B-dul Revoluţiei 72 isn't particularly helpful and you'll probably get as much help from the foyers of the larger hotels. There's a 24-hour **pharmacy** nearby at B-dul Revoluţiei 80 and an *ACR* office at Str. 1 Decembrie 1918.

Accommodation

If you're looking for budget accommodation, you'll need to head for the *Subcetate* **campsite**, with cabins, just south of the citadel at Piaţa 13 Martiri 13 (☎057/21.13.14; ②); this is largely used by busloads of Georgian and Ukrainian trade-tourists, but the owner is keen to attract Western tourists. In addition the *Sălaşul de la Răscruce* (Abode at the Crossroads) chalet and campsite (with bungalows) is situated 7km west of town along the Nădlac road; and there's a small family-owned campsite on Strada Voinicilor, to the east along the road to Lipova.

Arad, Str. Armata Poporului 9 (☎057/21.36.63). Reasonable hotel situated in the former *Securitate* headquarters – you can ask to see the cells in the basement. ④.

Ardealul, B-dul Revoluției 98 (☎057/21.18.40). The most interesting hotel in Arad, this former coaching inn incorporates a large hall (now a cinema) where Liszt, Brahms, Johann Strauss and Pablo Casals all performed. However it has no single rooms, and unusually offers no reduction on the price of a double. ③.

Astoria, B-dul Revoluției 79 (☎057/21.66.50). A slick place aimed at foreign tourists and businessmen. ⑤.

Central, Strada Horia, off B-dul Revoluției. Sullen staff even though this is a semi-privatized hotel. ④.

Mureșul, B-dul Revoluției 88 (☎057/21.15.40). Pleasantly tatty at the moment, but soon to be restored and upgraded with a view to privatization. ④.

Parc, Str. Dragalina 25 (☎057/21.66.81). Comfortable and largely indistinguishable from the *Astoria*. ⑤.

The City

Arad's main **Bulevard Revoluției** is lined with the city's most impressive buildings; above all the **City Hall** (1876) at no. 75, the **State Theatre** (1874) at no. 103, closing off its southern end, and the massive turn-of-the-century **Roman Catholic church** nearby, with a domed entrance hall. Behind the theatre is a series of squares including Piața Avram Iancu, just off which, at Strada Gh. Lazar 2, is the **Old Theatre**, built in 1817 and extensively renovated in 1993, where Eminescu and many famous actors worked. The main **market** lies west of Piața Avram Iancu next to the Baroque Romanian Orthodox cathedral (1865).

Arad's chief sight is its huge **citadel** commanding a loop of the River Mureș, facing the sprawling town on the west bank. Shaped like a six-pointed star with its ramparts and bastions obliquely sited to provide overlapping fields of fire, the citadel was the "state of the art" in fortifications when it was constructed between 1762 and 1783 in the style of Vauban. It proved something of a white elephant from its inception, since the Turks against whom it was ostensibly raised had already been pushed out of the Pannonian basin in 1718; but its three levels of underground casements provided the Hapsburgs with a ready-made prison following the suppression of the 1848 revolution. It remains a barracks to this day, and can only be admired from a distance.

From 1718 the Hapsburgs had deliberately settled Swabians, Slovaks, Serbs and Romanians in the devastated, depopulated area known as the *Partium*, and excluded Magyars from this strategic region so as to facilitate its assimilation into their empire. But despite this, Arad's population rose up against Hapsburg rule several times in 1848–49. The revolt was finally crushed with the help of Tsarist Russia, and the Hapsburgs made an example of the ringleaders by executing thirteen generals, mostly Hungarian, outside the fortress walls – an event commemorated by a **monument** at the entrance to the campsite, just south.

The execution features prominently in the **Museum** housed within the eclectic **Palace of Culture** (1913), on Piața George Enescu behind the City Hall, which is also home to Arad's Philharmonic Orchestra. In the library building at Str. Stejarului (or Str. Gh. Popă) 2, you'll find the **Art Gallery**, which features furniture from the seventeenth century on.

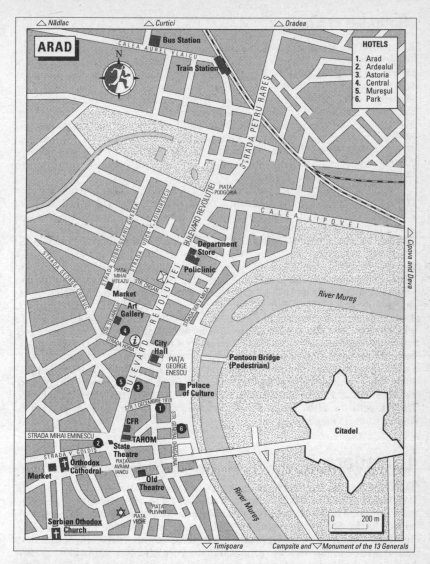

△ Nădlac   △ Curtici   △ Oradea

ARAD

CALEA AUREL VLAICU

Bus Station

Train Station

STRADA PETRU RAREȘ

HOTELS

1. Arad
2. Ardealul
3. Astoria
4. Central
5. Mureșul
6. Park

PIAȚA PODGORIA

CALEA LIPOVEI

△ Cipova and Deva

Department Store

BULEVARD REVOLUȚIEI

STRADA TUDOR VLADIMIRESCU

Policlinic

STRADA DOBROGEANU GHERTA

PIAȚA MIHAI VITEAZU

River Mureș

STR CRIȘAN

Market

STRADA GEORGE COȘBUC

Art Gallery

STRADA EPISCOPIEI

STRADA DINU LIPATTI

STRADA STILEARIU

4 ℹ

STRADA HORIA

City Hall

BULEVARD REVOLUȚIEI

PIAȚA GEORGE ENESCU

Pontoon Bridge (Pedestrian)

5 3

Palace of Culture

STR 1 DECEMBRIE 1918

1

CFR

STRADA GENERAL DRĂGALINA

6

Citadel

STRADA MIHAI EMINESCU

TAROM

2

State Theatre

STRADA V. GOLDIȘ

PIAȚA AVRAM IANCU

Orthodox Cathedral

†

Market

Old Theatre

River Mureș

PIAȚA PLEVNEI

PIAȚA VECHE

Serbian Othodox Church

†

0   200 m

▽ Timișoara   Campsite and ▽ Monument of the 13 Generals

Eating and drinking

Of the hotel **restaurants**, the *Astoria*'s has the best reputation, but you'll find plenty of other options on Bulevardul Revoluției particularly clustered around the southern end between the *Astoria* and the State Theatre. Two of the more interesting places are the *Zarandul* at B-dul Revoluției 89, which serves regional cuisine, and *Macul Roșu* at the north end of the main street, specializing in fish. The outdoor **market** in Piața Mihai Viteazu sells bread, cheese and fruit.

Northeast of Arad

From Arad, it's possible to reach a number of villages noted for their **festivals**, either by road, or by branch rail lines. The commune of **SÎNTANA**, 7km east of the Arad–Oradea highway, hosts a festival called *Sărbătoarea Iorgovanului* on the last Sunday of May. By rail, it's a 35-minute journey on any train from Arad towards Oradea or Brad. Although the festival is nowadays an excuse for dancing, music and dressing up in traditional costumes, it originated as a parish fair, like the one on February 1 at **PÎNCOTA**, 15km east and another thirty minutes by train towards Ineu and Brad. Thirty-eight kilometres beyond Pîncota past **INEU**, where there's a hotel (②) and a castle (1295–1645), the commune of **BÎRSA** (or Bârsa) is noted for pottery and has its own fête, *Sărbătoarea Druştelor*, on the first Sunday in April.

Continuing towards Brad, you'll come to **VÎRFURILE** at the junction with the DN76 from Oradea. A minor road runs 6km north from here to the small village of **AVRAM IANCU** (not to be confused with the other village of the same name just over the mountains), where people from thirty mountain villages gather for the *Nedeia of Tăcaşele* on the second Sunday of June. Besides being an occasion for trade and socializing, this large **fair** provides a chance for musicians to play together, and the *Nedeia* is an excellent time to hear *cetera* (fiddles), *nai* (pan-pipes) and *buciume* or *tulnic* (alpine horns). The connection between new life and stirring lust probably underlies a good many spring festivals, and it's one that the delightfully named **Kiss Fair** (*Tîrgul sărutului*) at **HĂLMAGIU** acknowledges. Traditionally, the event allows young men and women to cast around for a spouse while their elders discuss crops and the fecundity of livestock. You can easily reach the village, two stops beyond Vîrfurile on the line to Brad; the date of the festival (during March) varies, although Arad's tourist office might know.

Accommodation is thin on the ground in this area. Other than the hotel at Ineu, there's one at **SEBIŞ** (②), just west of Bîrsa, and a *han* and campsite at **DEZNA** 12km further north. Continuing on the DN76 towards Transylvania, **BRAD**, with the *Hotel Crişul Alb* at Str. Minerilor 10 (③), is only thirty kilometres from Hălmagiu.

Timişoara

TIMIŞOARA has long been the most prosperous and advanced of the cities of the Banat, and still boasts the country's premier technical university. It claims to have been one of the first places in the world to have horse-drawn trams (1869), as well as the first in "Romania" to have a public water supply (the same year), but these days it's best known as the **birthplace of the 1989 revolution**, and still sees itself as the only true guardian of the revolution's spirit, swiftly hijacked by the neo-communists of Bucharest.

Close to the border with Serbia, and the only other Romanian airport besides Bucharest operating scheduled international flights, Timişoara is a major travel hub. **Approaching from Serbia** isn't the most likely of routes at the moment, but the border crossings are open and busy with black-marketeers. The E70 from Belgrade enters Romania at **MORAVIŢA**, 61km south of Timişoara. The daily *Bucureşti Express* from Belgrade is the only direct train service from Serbia, but arrives in Timişoara at midnight.

The **telephone code** for Timişoara is ☎056

Arrival, information and acommodation

Timişoara's main **train station**, Timişoara Nord, is a fifteen-minute walk west of the centre along Bulevardul Republicii. The **bus station** is across the canal from the train station and one block west, at Str. Reşiţa 54, next to the best of Timişoara's markets. It operates services to and from Oraviţa and Moldova Nouă, on the Danube, as well as Brad, Hunedoara, Petroşani and Tîrgu Jiu. See "Listings" on p.274 for details of international bus companies.

The **airport**, for international and domestic flights, is east of the city. *TAROM* buses passengers into town 30 minutes after the arrival of every flight; for departures, buses leave their office on Bulevardul Revoluţiei 90 minutes before each flight.

Information

The **tourist office** at Str. Piatra Craiului 3 has been privatized and is now the *Cardinal's Exchange* change bureau (Mon–Fri 8am–4pm, Sat 9am–noon), but they are friendly and still have a stock of pre-1989 town plans to give away. There's another branch, at B-dul Republicii 6, which is also an official *Europcar* car rental agency.

Accommodation

Timişoara has plenty of rather soulless upmarket **hotels**, but if you're on a tight budget *CTT* at B-dul Revoluţiei 1989 26 (☎13.31.48) can offer **dormitory beds**. There's a **campsite** with bungalows on Aleea Pădurea Verde, 4km out in the Green Forest. The simplest way to get here is by trolleybus #11, which terminates just beyond the 24-hour *PECO* filling stations on Calea Dorobanţilor (DN6) and the turning north to the campsite.

Banatul, B-dul Republicii 5 (☎13.60.30, 13.77.72 or 13.78.55). Good value and convenient for the train station. ③.

Central, Str. Lenau 6 (☎11.76.70) A dull modern building, but the staff are welcoming. ④.

Continental, B-dul Revoluţiei 1989 2 (☎13.41.40). The former *Securitate* hotel, used by business men and tour groups. ④.

International, B-dul C. D. Loga 44 (☎13.34.12 or 19.01.93). Built as a villa for Ceauşescu, this was converted to an upmarket hotel in 1990. Much of it is used as office space, and there's stylish atrium displaying photographs of the 1989 revolution on the balcony. ⑧.

Nord, B-dul Gen. Dragalina 47 (☎11.23.08). Opposite the train station, this is a typical cheap station hotel. ③.

Timişoara, Str. Mărăşeşti 1 (☎13.78.15). A good-quality hotel reasonably priced; *ACR* coupons accepted. ⑤.

The City

The city now called Timişoara originally grew up around a Magyar fortress, *Castrum Temesiensis*, at the marshy confluence of the Timiş and Bega rivers, and from the fourteenth century onwards functioned as the capital of the Banat – hence the old name for the region, the *Banat of Temesvár*. As a stronghold it played a crucial role during the 1514 uprising and Hunyadi's campaigns against

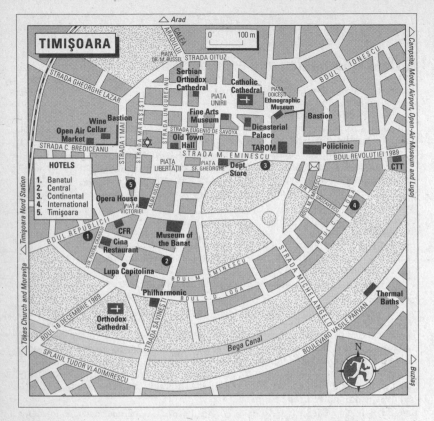

the Turks, who in 1552 conquered the town, from where they ruled the surrounding *pashalik* until 1716. The Hapsburgs who ejected them proved to be relatively benign masters over the next two centuries, the period when *Temeschwar* (as they called it) acquired many of its current features.

Piaţa Libertăţii and around

The city centre is a network of carefully planned streets and squares radiating from **Piaţa Libertăţii**, which boasts a substantial Baroque **Town Hall** (1734) on its north side. The square was the setting for the particularly gruesome **execution of György Dózsa** (Gheorghe Doja), leader of the peasant uprising that swept across Hungary and Transylvania in 1514. The terrified nobility eventually rallied behind János Zápolyai and defeated the peasants beneath the walls of Timişoara. Dózsa, a former mercenary of Székely origin, was put to death on the main square, where an iron throne and crown for the "King of the Serfs" were both heated until red-hot. Then, Dózsa was seated and "crowned" before his body was torn asunder by pincers; some of his followers were starved, compelled to watch his torture and then force-fed parts of the charred corpse, before themselves being executed, while others were hanged above the gates of Oradea, Alba Iulia and Buda as a deterrent.

Northeast of the square, the huge but dull **Dicasterial Palace** at the east end of Strada Eugenio de Savoya, a complex of 450 rooms built for the Hapsburg bureaucracy of the nineteenth century, is worth a look for its sheer bulk, if you're passing. The **Museum of the Banat** lies to the south of Piaţa Libertăţii (Tues–Sun 10am–5pm), occupying the castle raised in 1316 by the Hungarian monarch Charles Robert and later extended by Hunyadi. Warlords and rebels figure prominently in the large historical section; the museum also exhibits nearly 21,000 stuffed birds and mounted butterflies.

Northeast of Piaţa Libertăţii, **Piaţa Unirii** is a splendid traffic-free showpiece of Baroque urban design, with a plague column raised in 1740, and the former prefecture of 1754. The **Museum of Fine Arts** at no. 1 on the square, displaying work by minor Italian, German and Flemish masters, is overshadowed by the monumental Roman Catholic and Serbian Orthodox **cathedrals**. Built between 1736 and 1754, the former, to the east, is a fine example of Austrian Baroque, by Fischer von Erlach of Vienna. The **Romanian Orthodox cathedral** (1936–46) constructed after the signing of the Treaty of Trianon, stands between Piaţa Victoriei and the river, well to the south, blending neo-Byzantine and Moldavian architectural elements and exhibiting a fine collection of eighteenth-century Banat icons in its basement. Many of the protesters gunned down during the 1989 uprising were killed in front of this cathedral and there are memorials and candles outside.

In 1868 the municipality purchased the redundant citadel (previously redesigned after Vauban, as in Arad and Oradea) from the Hapsburg government, and demolished all but two sections, loosely known as the **Bastions**, to the west and east of Piaţa Unirii. The western section contains a wine cellar called *Timişoara 700* (in honour of the city's 700th anniversary in 1969), and to the east, the entrance at Str. Hector 2 admits you to a beer and wine bar; just west another section is occupied by the exhibition on the 1989 revolution (see box overleaf) and the **Ethnographic Museum** at Str. Popa Şapcă 4 (Tues–Sun 10am–5pm). Varied folk costumes and coloured charts illustrate the region's ethnic diversity, but in an anodyne fashion – there's no mention of the thousands of Serbs exiled to the Dobrogea in 1951 when the Party turned hostile towards Tito's Yugoslavia, which radically altered the Banat's ethnic make-up. In addition, the museum has an **open-air section** just outside town, where old Banat homesteads and workshops have been reassembled in the **Pădurea Verde** (Green Forest) – take buses #24, #26, #27, #30 and #35 east along the DN6.

Eating, drinking and entertainment

Timişoara has a good selection of **restaurants**, fast-food places, cafés and food markets, especially along Bulevardul 16 Decembrie 1989 and around Piaţa Libertăţii. The *Bulevard*, on the corner of Piaţa Victoriei and Bulevardul Republicii, opposite the Opera House, is one of Timişoara's more established restaurants, serving traditional Romanian dishes, and there's a busy beer garden here, too. **Patisseries** are popular with the locals – the best are *Violeta*, B-dul 30 Decembrie 6; *Trandafirul*, Str. Eminescu 5; *Flora* on the Bega Canal at Splaiul Vladimirescu; and the *Cofetaria Unirea* on Piaţa Unirii.

The city's grand nineteenth-century entertainment venues include an **Opera House** and three **theatres** – two of which stage plays in German (Str. Mărăşeşti 2) and Hungarian (Str. Alba Iulia 2). The concert hall of the **Banat**

LÁSZLO TÖKES AND THE REVOLUTION OF 1989

Despite doubts about the authenticity of the **events of December 1989** in Bucharest (see p.62), Timişoara's popular uprising is still regarded as the catalyst of the revolution. The spark was lit to the southwest of the centre, when crowds gathered to prevent the internal exile of the *reformat* pastor **Lászlo Tökes**.

Pastor Lászlo Tökes comes from a distinguished dynasty of Reformed (Calvinist) churchmen. Born in 1952, he followed his father into the priesthood, but was soon in trouble for **teaching Hungarian culture and history** to his parishioners in Dej; after two years without a job, he was posted to Timişoara in 1986. Here he became increasingly outspoken in his **criticism of the government** and the church authorities, while stressing that he spoke not only for Hungarians but also for the **equally oppressed Romanians**. In particular he protested against the systematization programme, denouncing it on Hungarian television in July 1989. This led to an increasingly vicious campaign against him by the local *Securitate*, spreading slanderous rumours about him, smashing his windows and harassing his family and friends, which culminated in the murder in September 1989 of one of the church elders.

Lászlo Papp, Bishop of Oradea, a government placeman, agreed that he should be transferred to the tiny village of Mineu, north of Zalău, but he refused to leave his parish and resisted legal moves to **evict** him. Being officially deemed unemployed, he lost his ration book, but his parishioners brought him food despite continuing harassment. Eventually he was **removed to Mineu** on December 17, and stayed there until the 22nd; the fact that it took so long for a police state to shift him, and that the eviction was so clearly signalled and then delayed for a day or two, is cited as evidence that plotters against Ceauşescu were deliberately trying to stir up a rising. After the removal of Tökes, **riots** erupted on the streets of Timişoara, culminating in Ceauşescu's order for the army to open fire on protesters.

The new National Salvation Front tried to co-opt Tökes onto its council, with other dissidents, but he soon asserted his independence; appropriately, in March 1990 he took over the job of Bishop Papp, who fled to France. Tökes has continued to speak up for the interests of the Hungarian minority, and Romanian nationalists have always accused him of being an agent of the Hungarian government and of the CIA.

There is now a **plaque** on the plain apartment building at Str. Timotei Ciprariu 1 (left off B-dul 16 Decembrie 1989), where the eviction took place – Tökes's church was on the first floor. There are also two **displays** of photographs and other mementoes of the events of December 16 to 22, 1989, one in the *International* hotel, and another, rough and ready but with gripping photos, in the old fortifications on Strada Hector, to the rear of the Ethnographic Museum.

Philharmonic is at B-dul Victoriei 2. **Dancing** often take place in restaurants like the *Cina* at Str. Piatra Craiului 4, or in the *Continental*, *Timişoara* and *Central* hotels' restaurants.

Listings

Airline office *TAROM*, B-dul Revoluţiei 1989 3 (☎19.01.50).

Bus company (international services) *Priamus*, B-dul 16 Decembrie 1989 (☎11.81.56), at the end of Strada T. Ciprariu.

Car repairs *ACR*, at the *Timiş* motel, Calea Dorobanţilor 94 (☎11.23.45); *Autoservice* on the Lugoj road or at Intrarea Doinei 2, off Calea Aradului.

Car rental *Europcar*, B-dul Republicii 6 (Mon–Fri 8am–4pm, Sat 9am–noon).

Exchange *Cardinal's Exchange*, B-dul Republicii 6 (Mon–Fri 8am–4pm, Sat 9am–noon).

Fuel There are 24-hour *PECO* fuel stations on Calea Dorobanţilor (DN6) out towards the Green Forest.

Health centre *Policlinic*, B-dul Revoluţiei 1989, 9.

Post office B-dul Revoluţiei 1989, 2, opposite the *Policlinic*.

Pharmacy Piaţa Victoriei (Mon–Fri 7.30am–8.30pm, Sat 8am–8pm, Sun 8am–2pm)

Bookstore, on the corner of Piaţa Victoriei and Strada Măciesilor. Stocks English and French books and magazines.

Newspapers Foreign newspapers can be bought at the main post office (until 3pm).

Train tickets *CFR* is at B-dul Republicii 1 (Mon–Fri 8am–8pm).

The Timiş valley

The main rail line and the DN6 follow the River Timiş southwest from Timişoara towards Băile Herculane and Wallachia, passing through the small Hapsburg towns of **Lugoj** and **Caransebeş**. From Caransebeş, there is easy access into the **mountains**, either west into the Semenic massif, or east to Muntele Mic, Ţarcu, Godeanu and ultimately the Retezat range to the east.

Lugoj and around

LUGOJ, 63km from Timişoara, is notable above all as the birthplace of several Romanian musicians, including the opera singer Traian Grozăvescu, and the composers Tiberiu Coriolan Brediceanu and Ion Vidu. The train station, hotels and main services are all west of the River Timiş, while, across the Iron Bridge, you'll find the **Uniate Cathedral** on Piaţa Republicii which has some fine neo-Byzantine paintings, and nearby, on Piaţa Victoriei, the Orthodox **Church of the Assumption**, a hall-church by the younger Fischer von Erlach, one of the most important Baroque buildings of the Banat.

Lugoj is a peaceful place to stop over. There are two **hotels** on Strada Mocioni, in the centre of town, the *Dacia* at no.7 (☎056/31.28.40; ③) and the *Timiş* at no.39 (☎056/31.31.50; ④). In addition there is a new hotel, the *Făget*, state-owned but built for foreign businessmen (⑤), with plans for a swimming pool, tennis courts and horse riding. This is 3km out along the road to Faget and Deva (the DN68A), served by buses #2 and #7 (peak hours only).

Even more peaceful is **COŞTEIU**, 7km north, served by local buses on the Timişoara road, or by slow trains towards Ilia. There's a bathing place here by the river, and chalets and tent space at the *Parc* **campsite**.

Caransebeş and the Muntele Mic

CARANSEBEŞ lies beneath the mountains at the confluence of the Timiş and Sebeş rivers, around which Gypsies, the *Zlatari*, used to pan for gold. Having served as the Banat's judicial centre during the Middle Ages, Caransebeş, commanding communications through the Eastern Gate, inevitably became a Hapsburg garrison town – hence the outcrops of *belle époque* buildings among the pre-fabricated structures of the socialist era. There's little to occupy you here today, but you may well be passing through or need to stay the night if you're heading for the mountains. The **bus terminal** is on Splaiul Sebeşului, over the Sebeş river, with two daily buses to Borlova for **Muntele Mic** (see below).

Caransebeş is served by **planes** on the Bucharest–Arad route and you'll find the *TAROM* office at Str. Mihai Viteazul 3 (☎056/51.30.63). Most **trains** arrive at the main station well north of town, from where it's twenty minutes' walk into the centre (although local services also stop 2km further south at the Caransebeş halt, west of the centre). The bus from the station runs along Strada Bălcescu (DN6), and terminates just before the bridge over the Sebeş river. For the town centre, you should head back to the north and turn right at the spiky neo-Gothic synagogue. Beyond the pedestrianized Strada Mihai Viteazul is the leafy **Piaţa Dragolina**, where you'll see two lions flanking a memorial to locally born General Ion Dragolina, who died at the head of his troops in the Jiu Valley in 1916. On the far side of the square is the **County Museum of Ethnography and the Border Regiment** in the eighteenth-century barracks (entrance to the left on Strada Cazărmii).

You'll find the *Tibiscum*, the town's only **hotel**, by the stadium on Strada Baba Novac (☎056/51.12.55; ②), to the west down the steps from the south end of the rail bridge.

Borlova and the Muntele Mic

BORLOVA, 13km from Caransebeş, is noted for its embroideries and peasant weddings, and holds a **festival**, *Măsurişul laptelui*, around April 23 every year, but most visitors pass straight through en route to the **Muntele Mic** (Little Mountain) resort. The resort can be reached by staff bus or a ten-kilometre walk from Borlova, followed by a chair-lift ride. Due to the heavy snowfalls in the area, you can **ski** here from late autumn until late spring and there are also good **hiking** trails. The resort consists of one **hotel** (③) and a series of less expensive villas and chalets. You can walk north to the Muntele Mic itself (1hr) or south to the weather station at 2190m atop Mount Ţarcu (3hr); from here suitably equipped hikers can take trails heading eastwards towards Lake Gura Apei and the Retezat mountains (following red stripes), or southwards to Godeanu and the Cerna valley (red dots) – be prepared for an overnight expedition (a tent is essential), and this route is not recommended during winter. From Muntele Mic, there's also a route (following blue stripes) to **POIANA MĂRULUI**, to the east, from where three buses a day head back to Caransebeş via Oţelu Roşu.

The Cerna valley

Most trains from Caransebeş run north to Timişoara, or south to Orşova and Turnu Severin on the Danube (see p.102), but there are also branch services west to Reşiţa and east to Bouţari. Continuing south by road or rail, you pass through the **Poarta Orientalia** or Eastern Gate of Transylvania before reaching **Băile Herculane** and its spa at the bottom of the **Cerna valley**. The middle and upper reaches of the valley itself are still much as Patrick Leigh Fermor described them when he travelled through the region in the 1930s: "a wilderness of green moss and grey creepers with ivy-clad water-mills rotting along the banks and streams tumbling through the shadows", illuminated by "shafts of lemon-coloured light". Among the butterflies and birds that proliferate here you might see rollers, which the Romanians call *Dumbrăveancă*, "one who loves oakwoods".

Băile Herculane and around

BĂILE HERCULANE gets its name from the Roman legend that Hercules cured the wounds inflicted by the Hydra by bathing here, and the nine springs with their varied mineral content and temperature (38°–60°C) are used to treat a wide range of disorders. During the nineteenth century, royal patronage made *Herkulesbad* one of Europe's most fashionable watering-holes. Today, several ugly modern hotels have arisen among the elegant buildings, but the resort remains busy and surprisingly affordable.

Other than wallowing in the renowned **Apollo Baths**, Băile Herculane's chief attraction is its surroundings – statuesque limestone peaks clothed in lush vegetation and riddled with caves. You can bath for free in the **Seven Hot Springs** (*Șapte Izvoare Calde*) about 35 minutes' walk upstream just beyond the Cerna rapids, while another two hours' hiking will bring you to the white **Gisella's Cross** from where there are magnificent views. From here, an unmarked path leads you in thirty minutes to a spectacular 300m precipice with boulders strewn about the forest of black pines. Other paths provide access to the vaporous **Steam Cave** on Ciorci hill (1hr 30min), the **Outlaws' Cave** where Stone Age tribes once sheltered (30min), and the **Mount Domogled nature reserve** with Mediterranean species of trees and flowers and more than 1300 varieties of butterfly (4hr).

It's roughly 40km from Băile Herculane to the watershed of the Cerna river, on a forestry road that continues to Cîmpușel and the Jiu valley (a path marked with red stripes runs parallel along the ridge to the north to Piatra lui Iorgovan in the **Retezat mountains** – allow one or two days; see p.160).

Practicalities

Băile Herculane's **train station** is 5km from the spa but bus #1 runs every half hour from the station to the central Piața Hercules. If you're arriving by **bus** from another town however, you'll be dropped at a dusty yard over a kilometre short of the centre. There's a good range of hotel **accommodation** both in the centre and in the modern satellite spa of **PECINIȘCA**, towards the train station. Băile Herculane's *Apollo* (②), *Decebal* (②) and *Cerna* (②) are all excellent value, while the *Belvedere* on Str. N. Stoica Hațeg (④) is one of the spa's more upmarket hotels. There are no less than four **campsites**: the *Plopii Fara Sat* at the train station, the *Pecinișca* and *Flora* along the road into town, and one at the Seven Hot Springs, all very crowded in season.

Reșița and the Semenic range

People have been beating iron into shape around **REȘIȚA**, 40km from Caransebeș, since Dacian times. The foundry can trace its history back to 1771 and steam locomotives have been manufactured here since 1873; if you're entering town on the Timișoara road, Bulevardul Revoluției din Decembrie, you'll pass a **collection of locomotives** outside the Reșița Nouă train halt. Local steelworkers have a long tradition of militancy detailed in the **museum** at Str. Văliugului 103, and take pride of place in the *Alaiul Primăverii* **spring parade**. Besides this event (normally held during the first week in April), the town also hosts the **Bîrzava Song Festival** some time in August.

However, Reşiţa is otherwise distinctly unattractive and most travellers continue straight on to the mountains. If you do have to stay, the *Semenic* **hotel** stands on the central plaza (☎056/41.34.80; ④), but if you're considering attending either of the festivals, it's cheaper to stay outside town at Semenic or Crivaia (see below) or at one of the three **cabanas**, the *Constructorul, Splendid* or *Turist* on Lake Secu 13km east. If you're planning on doing some hiking, Reşiţa is a good place to stock up on food. There's a good **market**, by the Sud train station, and a **supermarket**, the *Comtimalimenta* on the plaza.

Into the mountains

Reşiţa's **bus station** on Strada Traian Lalescu operates fairly regular services out to **VĂLIUG**, the starting point for excursions into the **Semenic mountains**. From here, one road leads 3km south to **CRIVAIA** , where there are **bungalows** and a **campsite**, while another leads to the terminal of the chair-lift up to **SEMENIC** which has chalet-style **accommodation**. Pistes at Semenic are graded from "difficult" to "very easy", and are normally fit for **skiing** from November until April. The 11.30am bus from Reşiţa runs to Văliug, Crivaia and Semenic, and to **Trei Ape**, an artificial lake with a chalet, and returns at 4pm.

Although the massif is lower and less rugged than others in the Carpathians, it still offers the chance of good **hiking**. One of the most popular treks is from Semenic west through Crivaia to the Comarnic Cave, and on to the **Caraşului Gorges** (10–11 hours; blue stripe markings). Situated just before the eastern entrance to the gorges, the **Comarnic Cave** is the Banat's largest grotto, with a spectacular array of rock "veils" and calcite crystals distributed around its 400 metres of galleries on two levels (guided tours until 3pm). The gorges themselves are extremely wild and muddy (good boots are required) and harbour several more caves, of which *Popovăţ* (likewise open for tours) to the south is the most impressive. If you don't fancy hiking here from Semenic or Crivaia, the gorges can also be entered near **CARAŞOVA**, a village on the main road 16km south of Reşiţa. However they may be impassable in part, in which case you should follow the blue stripes onwards from Comarnic to the hamlet of **PROLAZ**, and pick up the route through the gorges there.

Oraviţa and on to Moldova Nouă

From Reşiţa, the DN58 continues south to the coal-mining towns of **ANINA** and **STEIERDORF**, from where the DN57B leads east to Băile Herculane and west to **ORAVIŢA**, the historic centre of the former Caras county, close by the border with Serbia. It's a curiously long thin town stretching east from the bus and train stations, and home to Romania's oldest **theatre**, between the end of the one-way system and the police station at Str. Eminescu 18 (note this is some 3km from the train station). Built between 1789 and 1817, the theatre is no longer used for plays, but houses the town **museum** (Mon–Fri 8am–5pm), commemorating the German community that brought the Industrial Revolution to this corner of the Austro-Hungarian Empire, as well as the surprising number of local writers and Eminescu himself, who came here as prompter with a theatre company in 1868. There's a **chalet** another couple of kilometres east, and a **hotel** (③) by the filling station on the main road north out of town.

Oravița is virtually the end of the rail line's penetration into the *Banat Romanesc*, the southwestern-most corner of Romania, but buses continue to Moldova Nouă (see p.105), including at least five a day owned by private companies, cheaper and slightly more comfortable than the state buses. These run either via the **NAIDĂŞ border crossing** into the Vojvodina (now almost entirely swallowed up by Greater Serbia), or via **SASCA ROMÂNĂ**, base for the **Nera gorges** (Cheile Nerei) immediately to the east. In the other direction, seven private buses a day run from Oravița to Timișoara, as well as several to Reşiţa, two to Băile Herculane, and one to Caransebeş.

travel details

Trains

Arad to: Baia Mare (1 daily; 5hr 40min); Brad (4 daily; 3hr 25min–5hr); Braşov (5 daily; 5hr 50min–7hr 40min); Bucharest (6 daily; 8hr 25min–10hr 20min); Deva (9 daily; 1hr 45min–3hr 15min); Hălmagiu (3 daily; 4hr); Oradea (5 daily; 2hr–2hr 50min); Satu Mare (1 daily; 4hr 30min); Sebiş (6 daily; 1hr 45min–2hr 30min); Sibiu (3 daily; 4hr 15min–7hr); Sighişoara (3 daily; 4hr 15min); Sîntana (16 daily; 20–40min); Timișoara (10 daily; 50min–1hr 20min); Vîrfurile (3 daily; 3hr 40min).

Caransebeş to: Băile Herculane (11 daily; 1hr 10min–1hr 50min); Drobeta-Turnu Severin (8 daily; 2hr–3hr); Lugoj (12 daily; 30min–1hr); Orşova (11 daily; 1hr 30min–2hr 15min); Reşiţa (8 daily; 50min–1hr 25min); Timișoara (12 daily; 1hr 15min–2hr 25min).

Oradea to: Arad (5 daily; 1hr 50min–2hr 45min); Baia Mare (1 daily; 3hr 30min); Beiuş (2 daily; 4hr 40min); Ciucea (9 daily; 1hr 15min–2hr 40min); Cluj (8 daily; 2hr 25min–4hr 25min); Dr Petru Groza (2 daily; 5hr); Iaşi (1 daily; 11hr 45min); Satu Mare (5 daily; 1hr 50min–3hr 20min); Suceava (1 daily; 9hr 30min); Timișoara (5 daily; 3hr–4hr 10min); Tîrgu Mureş (1 daily; 4hr 50min).

Timişoara to: Bucharest (8 daily; 7hr–14hr 35min); Buziaş (7 daily; 40min–1hr); Caransebeş (12 daily; 1hr 10min–2hr 45min); Lugoj (15 daily; 40min–1hr 30min); Oravița (2 daily; 2hr 42min–3hr 45min); Reşiţa (4 daily; 2hr–2hr 45min); Sînnicolau Mare (4 daily; 2hr).

Planes

Arad to: Bucharest (1 daily; 1hr).

Caransebeş to: Bucharest (1 daily; 50min).

Oradea to: Bucharest (3 daily; 1hr).

Timişoara to: Bucharest (3 daily; 1hr).

International trains

Arad to: Berlin (1 daily; 20hr 50min); Budapest (4 daily; 4hr 30min–5hr 15min); Munich (1 daily; 14hr 10min); Prague (2 daily; 14hr 40min); Vienna (2 daily; 8hr 50min–9hr 30min); Warsaw (1 daily; 19hr).

Curtici to: Békéscsaba, Hungary (2 daily; 1hr).

Jimbolia to: Kikinda, Serbia (2 daily; 20min).

Oradea to: Budapest (4 daily; 5hr 30min).

Stamora Moraviţa to: Vrsac, Serbia (3 daily; 20min).

Timişoara to: Belgrade (1 daily; 4hr 40min); Budapest (1 daily; 5hr 20min).

CHAPTER SEVEN

THE DELTA AND THE COAST

n theory, the **Danube Delta** and Romania's **Black Sea coast** have a lot going for them. The Delta, a vast area of reeds and shifting land, provides a unique habitat for over three hundred species of birds (many of them found nowhere else in Europe), as well as a host of other creatures. The coast is blessed with abundant sunshine, warm water and sandy beaches, and when you've had enough of that, there are numerous Roman remains plus the occasional mosque to visit.

However, don't come expecting an unspoilt and effortless paradise. Although the **Delta wildlife** is as rich as you could wish, it mostly chooses to nest away from the main arms (*braţi*) of the river – in particular, the one flowing from the Delta capital of **Tulcea** down to **Crişan**, where ONT tour groups are taken. To really appreciate the diversity of birdlife, you'll need to pay one of the fishermen to row you into the backwaters and lakes; negotiations can be time-consuming, so if you're seriously bent on bird-watching, be prepared to spend at least a week here. Real enthusiasts should bring their own canoes.

Much of the coast has been ravaged by industry or tourism, or both, and it can get so overcrowded between June and September that the only way to avoid endless hassles over transport, rooms and meals is to book a package holiday from home to **Mamaia, Neptun, Venus** or one of the other resorts. There's more of a relaxed atmosphere about the city of **Constanţa** though, which boasts lots of sights in the old quarter around the seaport, originally established by the ancient Greeks.

Getting to both the Delta and the coast is fairly simple. During the summer, *TAROM* usually operates direct charter **flights** from a variety of European cities including London, to Constanţa. Both Constanţa and Tulcea are linked by plane to Bucharest, and in the summer, there are flights to Constanţa at least weekly from all of Romania's major regional airports. If you're coming by train from Bucharest, services to Constanţa and Mangalia on the coast are fairly fast and frequent, but very overcrowded in season. Book well in advance (the return journey, too, if possible), changing at Medgidia for the Delta if there's no direct service to Babadag or Tulcea. In summer many extra services run from regional centres to Mangalia, often overnight. Driving will be eventually be made easier by a new toll motorway between Bucharest and Constanţa, but little of it is likely to be open before 1997.

ACCOMMODATION PRICES

Hotels listed in the *Guide* have been price-graded according to the scale below. Prices given are those charged for the cheapest double room, which in the less expensive places usually comes without private bath or shower and without breakfast. See p.28 for more details.

① under $10	④ $25–40	⑦ $80–135
② $10–15	⑤ $40–55	⑧ $135–190
③ $15–25	⑥ $55–80	⑨ $200 and over

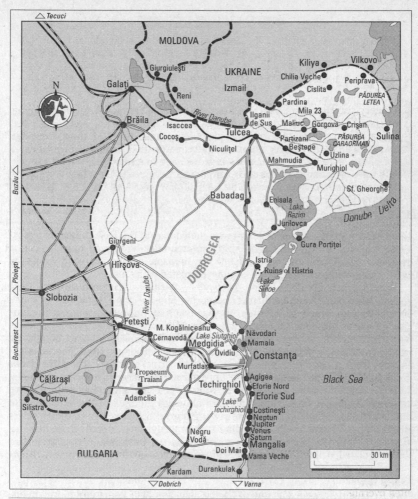

THE DANUBE DELTA

Every year the River Danube dumps seventy million tonnes of alluvium into the **Danube Delta** (*Delta Dunării*), Europe's youngest, most restless landscape. Near the regional capital, **Tulcea**, the river splits into three branches (named after their respective ports, Chilia, Sulina and Sfîntu Gheorghe), dividing the Delta into large areas of reeds and marsh, over 4000 square kilometres in all, of which only nine percent remains permanently above the water. This is the **grind** – tongues of accumulated silt supporting oak trees, willows and poplars twined round with climbing plants – as distinct from the **plaur**, or floating reed islands, which amount to some 700 square kilometres. Over time the distinction is a fine one, for the movement caused by spring and autumn floods splits, merges and

---

THE LIPOVANI

Formerly dispersed all over the Delta, the **Lipovani**, descendants of the Old Believers who left Russia in the eighteenth century to avoid persecution, are now only found at Mila 23 and at two villages on Lacul Razim, Jurilovca and Sarichioi. Once easy to recognize by their on-shore garb of tall hats and black cloaks, they gave up this costume in the early twentieth century, but can still be identified by their blond hair, beards and blue eyes.

Adapting to their watery environment, the Lipovani became skilled **fishermen** and gardeners, speaking a Russian dialect amongst themselves but equally fluent in Romanian. Since you're likely to rely upon Lipovani boatmen to guide you through the confusing side channels (*gîrla*), be prepared for their fundamentalist abhorrence of the "Devil's weed", tobacco. However, any contact with them will like as not involve partaking of **vodka**, their consumption of which is legendary. Normally, a single glass circulates incessantly, each drinker knocking back the contents before replenishing it and passing it on.

---

often destroys these forms making any detailed map of the Delta outdated almost as soon as it's drawn. Although fishing communities have lived here for centuries, it's an inhospitable environment for humans: a Siberian wind howls all winter long, while in summer the area is inundated with flies.

Yet it's a paradise for wildlife, particularly **birds**, which pass through from China, India and Mongolia during the spring and autumn migrations, or come from Africa to breed in summer. Besides herons, glossy ibises, cormorants, golden eagles, avocets, shelduck and other Mediterranean breeds, the Delta is visited by reed buntings, white-tailed eagles and various European songbirds; whooper swans, plovers, arctic grebes, cranes and half-snipes from Siberia; Saker falcons from Mongolia; egrets, mute swans, cormorants and mandarin ducks from China; and its remoter lakes support Europe's largest **pelican colonies**. Otters, mink, muskrat, foxes, boars, wolves, polecats and other **animals** live upon the abundant small game and **fish**; although the bulk of the latter goes to the fishermen, for whom the caviar-bearing sturgeon that spawn in these waters are the most valuable catch. According to their rarity, species receive the designation *peste tot în Deltă* (common everywhere); *parţial* (mainly in certain areas); or *izolat* (isolated, usually only on reservations) on maps of the Delta.

Delta tours

The Delta is rightly seen as one of the greatest assets of Romania's tourist industry, and private companies (notably *ATBAD*, at Str. Babadag 11, Tulcea; ☎040/ 51.41.14) are moving in to the area, mostly offering **packages** in floating hotels in the heart of the Delta. In the face of growing tourism, the entire area was declared a **Biosphere Reserve** in 1990, with over 500 square kilometres strictly protected.

Most **tours** stick to the main axes, from which most of the wildlife has been scared off. ONT's two-day trip from Constanţa – including a visit to Tulcea, a hydrofoil ride to Crişan, lodgings at the hotel there, and a short exploration of the backwaters by fisherman's canoe – is reasonable value for $48. However, be wary of the so-called Delta tour organized by ONT from Bucharest ($85) which includes very little time actually spent on the water. *BTT* operate their own trips into the Delta, either by boat from their pontoon by Tulcea's Art Museum or by helicopter to their base at Lacul Roşu, south of Sulina. If you want to travel independently around the Delta, you can make all the necessary arrangements in Tulcea (see p.285).

Tulcea

TULCEA has been tagged as the "Gateway to the Delta" ever since ancient Greek traders established a **port** here – it was recorded by Herodotus, and later by Ovid, who used the town's Roman name, *Aegyssus*. Its maritime significance was slight until the closing stages of the period of Ottoman domination (1420–1878), when other powers suddenly perceived it as commercially and strategically important. Tulcea then entered a cycle of rapid development and calamitous slumps. Nowadays, the outskirts of the town are heavily industrialized and the port is too shallow for large modern freighters, but it's still the chief access point for passenger vessels entering the Delta. Tulcea is also host to two **festivals**, the International Folk Festival of the Danubian Countries, in August, and a winter carnival in December.

The Town

The town is clustered along the south bank of the Danube. To the northeast of the central **Piaţa Republicii**, on the corner of Strada Sahia and Strada 9 Mai, is the **Art Museum** (Tues–Sun 9am–5pm) whose fine collection of paintings and contemporary sculpture includes Impressionistic female nudes by Pallady; Iosif

▽ *Babdag and Constanţa*

Iser's and Theodor Aman's fanciful "Turkish" scenes; and Delta landscapes by Sirbu and Stavrov. You'll also see Igolesco's *Balchik*, painted at a time when Romania ruled the southern Dobrogea (regained by Bulgaria in 1940). The village of Balchik (Balčik) was a thriving artistic community, so loved by Queen Marie that, although she had to be buried with her husband in Curtea de Argeş, she asked for her heart to be buried in Balchik. When the southern Dobrogea was handed over to Bulgaria, it was brought back to Romania in a casket which spent the communist period in the National History Museum in Bucharest. Its final resting place has still to be decided.

Strada 14 Noiembrie heads north from Piaţa Republicii **to** the nineteenth-century **Azizie Mosque**, a very ordinary-looking building like a school with a minaret. Having been fairly inconspicuous under communism, the local Turkish women are now more visible, in bright gypsy colours with baggy trousers. Beyond the mosque, Strada Gloriei runs through a pretty area of small white houses with gardens ending at the **Parcul Monumentului**, where you'll find the town's **Roman remains**, an **obelisk** to the dead of the 1877–78 war, and the **History Museum** (Tues–Sun 10am–5pm) with a collection of Roman, Greek, Byzantine and medieval coins.

Back in the centre, the **Ethnographic Museum** on Strada 9 Mai (Tues–Sun 10am–4.30pm) has displays on the varied groups inhabiting the Delta and the Tulcea region. On the far side of the systematized Piaţa Civică, is the **Natural History Museum**, Str. Progresului 32 (Tues–Sun 10am–4.30pm); equipped with multilingual guides and captions, it explains all about the Delta as an ecosystem, and houses an excellent **aquarium** of fish from the region.

Practicalities

Tulcea's **train station** is on the western edge of town, and it's an easy walk from here along the waterfront, to Piaţa Republicii, passing the **bus station** and *NAVROM* **ferry terminal** and office on the way. Tulcea is linked to Bucharest, Braşov, Cluj, Iaşi and Constanţa by train, but it's a slow journey down to the main junction at Medgidia. The best way to travel to and from Bucharest is to use the hydrofoil link with Galaţi to the northwest which enables you to pick up express train services (see p.203).

There's no official tourist office but you can try for **tourist information** in the main hotels; the **Biosphere Reserve** is at Str. Păcii 20 (☎040/51.52.77), and plans to open an information centre. You'll find **TAROM** (10am–5pm; ☎040/51.12.27) across Strada Isaccei from the *Delta* hotel; flights usually operate a triangular route to Bucharest via Constanţa, three times weekly in winter and six times a week in summer. Most **travel agencies** in town are only concerned with Delta trips, but those in the *NAVROM* ticket-hall and on Piaţa Republicii also sell tickets for **boats to Izmail**, in Ukraine (about $10 for a day-trip); it's wise to have your Ukrainian visa in advance, as it'll cost you $10 a day if issued on arrival. Boats leave at 8am and take two hours, so you can easily be in Odessa by the evening.

Accommodation is fairly limited in Tulcea with just three main hotels: the *Delta* at Str. Isaccei 2 (☎040/51.47.20; ⑤); the *Egreta* at Str. Păcii 1 (☎040/51.71.03; ④); and the *Europolis* (formerly the *Tulcea*) at Str. Păcii 20 (☎040/51.24.43; ④) – all relatively pricey and characterless. Budget options include the lodgings at the Seamen's Union (*Sindicatul Marinarilor*), by the river west of the train station (②), the *Han Trei Stele* on Strada Carpaţi, behind the market (②), and the *Tineretului* at Str. Isaccei 24 in Ciuperci Park (☎040/55.07.30; ②) – reception is on the first floor. This is the polluted end of town, thanks to the smoke belching from the aluminium plant just west. **BTT**, almost opposite the Natural History Museum on Strada Kogălniceanu (8am–4pm), might be able to find you a bed in a student dormitory.

The main **market**, good for buying snacks and provisions for trips into the Delta, is just south of the centre down Strada Păcii (beyond the barn-like church of St George). The "Ukrainian market", just south of Strada Isaccei (halfway to the station) is largely a venue for trading in imported goods, although you'll find some food here, too.

TRAVELLING IN THE DELTA

A **permit** is needed to enter the RBDD (Danube Delta Biosphere Reserve), which covers everywhere you might find yourself. This is most easily obtained in Tulcea from the manager of the *Delta* hotel (mezzanine floor). The basic permit costs under a dollar, with supplementary charges for boating and fishing; organized groups have to pay about twenty times as much, and are limited to seven fixed routes (which change slightly from year to year).

In addition to the three main arms (*braţi*) of the Danube, there are **routes** from Tulcea via the **Canal Mila 35** and Gîrla Şontea to the villages of Pardina and Mila 23, and via the **Canal Litcov** to Crişan (both parallel to the Sulina arm); from Mila 23 to Lacul Trei Iezere and Chilia Veche; from Mila 23 to Letea via the **Canal Magearu**; from Crişan southeast to Caraorman, Lacul Roşu and Sulina; from the Sfîntu Gheorghe arm to Lacul Razim via the **Canal Dranov**; and from Jurilovca to Gura Portiţei. If you want to explore beyond these routes, take a compass and a detailed **map**, available in Tulcea and Bucharest; the green map published by *CTT* in 1992 has English text and shows the Biosphere Reserve's strictly protected zones, which must be avoided.

DeltaRom, which owns the **hotels** in Crişan, Maliuc and Sulina, also owns the *Delta* hotel in Tulcea, so it makes sense to ask here about reservations. Buy **essential supplies** like bread, canned food, fruit and cheese in the market in Tulcea; candles, a big container for drinking water, and plenty of mosquito repellent are also vital.

Predictably, there's a certain amount of hassle and confusion involved in buying **tickets** from *NAVROM*'s office on the waterfront (Mon–Sat 8am–8pm, Sun 8am–3pm), since they're only sold half an hour before the boat sails, due to connecting with boats from Galaţi. In summer *NAVROM* operates daily **services** along each main arm of the Delta leaving Tulcea at 1.30pm for Periprava, Sulina and Sfîntu Gheorghe. Hydrofoils also connect Galaţi with Tulcea continuing to Sulina at 9.30am and returning at 1pm. In winter, boats head downstream on Monday, Wednesday and Friday, returning the next day. As a rule services to Sulina sail from no. 1 (the westernmost) or no. 3, those to Periprava from no. 2, and those to Sfîntu Gheorghe from no. 4. The hydrofoils are swift and business-like vessels (in theory there's a 10kg luggage limit, but they're not bothered about backpacks), but the ferries are far more fun; lumbering vessels crammed with people and piled high with dinghies, rods and camping gear, and greeted at every jetty-stop along their route by crowds of kids selling melons and fish.

Into the Delta

The following sections cover each arm of the Delta in turn, and then the Lake Razim region. If you just want to take a trip down to the sea and back, **Sfîntu Gheorghe** is preferable to Sulina, as it's less built up, it's easier to camp wild or find private rooms, and above all you can take a quick look at the Delta on foot without having to cross the Danube or hike too far. Note that many of the **telephone numbers** given in this section are only reachable via the operator.

Tulcea to Periprava

The **Chilia arm** of the river (*Braţul Chilia*), which branches off upstream from Tulcea and marks the border with Ukraine, carries 58 percent of the Danube's water, but very little tourist traffic. For travellers, there are four major drawbacks to this route: boats will only carry you to **PERIPRAVA** (100km from Tulcea but still 30km from the Black Sea); there are poor prospects of finding smaller boats heading into the interior from there; there is a total lack of tourist accommodation; and Periprava marks the centre of the area worst affected by Ceauşescu's project to drain the Delta and turn it into agricultural land. One way to see a little of this route is to travel as far as **CEATALCHIOI**, 20km from Tulcea, then walk 10km to **TUDOR VLADIMIRESCU**, from where a **ferry** crosses the river every hour back to Tulcea, docking opposite the *ACR* office. Small settlements such as these are involved in the gathering of **reeds**, which are used to build Delta houses and to obtain cellulose, a raw material for diverse industries. The cutting, which stimulates the reeds to grow up to 2.5m in two months, can only be done by hand, a task performed by thousands of prisoners during the Stalinist era, including priests, ex-*Legionari*, former captains of industry, and purged *Securisti*. The reeds stifle most of the other plants around them but provide a warm, wind-free shelter for countless small birds, rodents and amphibia.

Around Periprava

In the days when Bessarabia was part of Romania, **CHILIA VECHE**, 25km west of Periprava, was merely a suburb of Chilia (now Ukrainian Kiliya) across the river. As a Moldavian fort, Chilia's moment of fame came in 1476 when it repelled a Turkish invasion; at that time it was just 5km from the coast, today it is 40km away. The hamlet of **CÎŞLIŢA**, 8km distant, lies at the end of a picturesque track, unuseable at many times of the year, which runs through an old forest frequented by **foxes** and **wild boar**.

Lake Roşca, roughly 10km to the south of **BABINA** on the Cernovca tributary between Chilia Veche and Periprava, harbours geese, egrets, storks and Europe's largest **pelican colony**; but very few small boats travel this way. Immediately to the south of Periprava is the **Pădurea Letea** – a forest of oaks tangled with lianas, now a strict reserve, that's a haven for falcons, owls, white-tailed eagles, and wildcats as well as snakes. The forest is surrounded by **sand-dunes** where tortoises, lizards and 1800 species of insects live.

Tulcea to Sulina

Between 1862 and 1902 the **Sulina arm** (*Braţul Sulina*) was shortened from 92km to 63km, by the digging of long straight sections. Constant dredging and

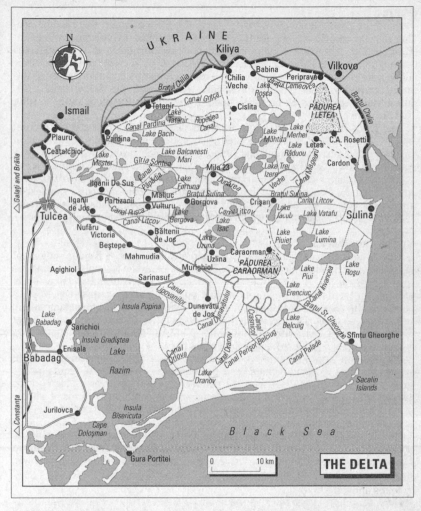

THE DELTA

groynes running 10km out to sea still enable 7000-tonne freighters to take this route from Tulcea, and the additional tourist traffic makes this the busiest and least serene of the Danube's branches. However, it has the advantages of a tourist infrastructure and several settlements where there's a fair chance of renting boats to visit a variety of wildlife habitats. The journey from Tulcea to Sulina takes an hour and a half by hydrofoil or four hours by ferry, but there's not much point in staying on until the end – Sulina is a very dismal seaport and there are a couple of much better destinations en route. Travellers who come equipped to explore the Delta by **canoe** face turbulence from the wakes of passing ships on the main waterway, but beyond **Ilganii de Sus** you can escape into calmer backwaters, broken by the odd rapid, leading to the inland lakes.

Maliuc

Beyond the river's fork, 12km from Tulcea, there's a **cabana** with accommodation for 40 people at **ILGANII DE SUS**, opposite the fishing village of **PARTIZANI**. It's worth enquiring here about renting boats to visit two lakes further to the north, **Meşter** and **Lunga**. **MALIUC** on the left bank of the river, 12km further on, is a larger place, with a research station and a **Museum of the Reed Industry**. There's also a **campsite and hotel**, the *Salcia* (☎991; ④). Fishermen here might be prevailed upon to row you to the mute swans nesting on **Lake Furtuna**.

The reeds in this area provide a home for fast-breeding great crested grebes; solitary and less successful red-necked grebes; bearded reedlings, which nest in piles of cut reeds; and herons and little egrets, which favour nests in the overhanging willow trees. From Lake Mester or the Păpădia channel, **canoeists** can follow the Gîrla Şontea into the original Dunărea Veche branch of the river, leading to Mila 23 (see below), although there are powerful currents, submerged roots and aquatic plants (*rizac*), and a series of small rapids. Nearby **Lake Gorgova** is rich in carp and sheat fish, and frequented by eastern flossy ibises.

Crişan and Mila 23

CRIŞAN is the main tourist centre along the Sulina arm. A fishing settlement following the shoreline for 7km, its administrative centre is a couple of kilometres to the north at **MILA 23** on the "old" branch of the Danube. Passenger boats stop on the south bank at Crişan, almost opposite the **monument** at Mila 13 (marking the distance from the sea), unveiled by Carol I in 1894 to inaugurate the new canal sections. On the north bank before Mila 14 are the *Lebădă* **hotel** (☎991; ④) and a **campsite** with bungalows but no running water; should you wish to it's quite feasible to camp wild around here.

Mila 23 is a large village of reed cottages (rebuilt after a flood in the 1960s), where the men fish and women tend the gardens of vegetables, plums, pears, grapes and quinces, and look after the poultry, pigs and beehives. Golden orioles (which nest in pear trees) and bladder-frogs are the commonest forms of wildlife around here – the **pelicans** have been driven further north to Lake Merhei and south to Lake Iacob. You can easily walk to the southern end of Lake Iacob following the dyke. Mila 23 is the starting point for **excursions** to most of the surrounding lakes; beyond the Canal Crişan to the south, the **Pădurea Caraorman forest** is now a strict reserve (protecting **wildlife** such as owls, eagles, falcons, wildcats, boars and wolves).

Sulina

Ever since it was recorded by a Byzantine scribe in 950, **SULINA** has depended on shipping. Genoese vessels used to call here during the fourteenth century, while throughout the period of Ottoman power it was less a trading port than a nest of pirates who preyed upon shipping in the Black Sea. From 1900, Sulina was a free port, and later it became the headquarters of the International Danube Commission established by the great powers after the First World War. But world recession and larger vessels emptied the port within a decade, so that by 1940 John Lehmann found "a hopeless, sinking feeling" in a place where "people get stranded, feel themselves abandoned by civilization, take to drink, and waste into a half-animal existence". The state has tried to sustain Sulina, though economics remain opposed: expensive annual dredging is required to enable even small- and medium-capacity ships to enter, while large-capacity freighters can now bypass the Delta altogether by taking the Danube–Black Sea Canal. Ceaușescu's solution was to establish a dump here in 1987 for imported industrial waste; however dioxins leaked out and polluted the Bulgarian coast, and radioactive leaks were spotted by the *Mir* space station, forcing a clean-up that undoubtedly cost far more than the $2m earned.

Unless you like shabby bars and decaying waterfronts there's nothing to draw you except for the **Old Lighthouse**, built in 1802, and the **cemeteries**, between the town and the sea, which offer an evocative record of all the nationalities who lived and died here in the days of the free port. Greeks dominated business, but there was also a large British contingent, now resident in the Anglican cemetery. If you get stranded here, there's the *Sulina* **hotel** (☎040/54.30.17; ⑤) or the *Europolis* (③), about 200m to the right of the landing stage as you disembark.

Tulcea to Sfîntu Gheorghe

The Delta's oldest, most winding arm is the least used by freighters and fishing boats; nevertheless it carries a fair amount of tourist traffic, and unlike other parts of the Delta, some settlements can also be reached from Tulcea by bus. At **VICTORIA**, 12km by road from Tulcea, it's worth trying to find a fisherman to row you across the river and into the water lily-smothered Litcov Canal, while the five hills of **BEȘTEPE**, 8km further on give a wonderful **panoramic view** of the Delta. Ferries call at **MAHMUDHIA**, which boasts the *Plaur* restaurant, a grimy **motel**, and vestiges of the Roman-Byzantine citadel of Salsovia just to the west; the Byzantine Emperor Constantine had his co-ruler Licinus killed here, seizing absolute power himself.

The best plan, however, is to take the road to **MURIGHIOL**. Six buses a day come here from Tulcea, on a circular route via either Mahmudia or Sarinasuf. One bus in each direction continues east from Murighiol to **DUNAVĂȚ** and can drop you at the turning to the gleaming white oasis of the *Pelican* **hotel** (☎17; ④) and **campsite** (with chalets), otherwise you have to get off at the shell of the planned *Centru Civic* and walk 3km, turning left just before the last house in the village. If you plan to visit Sfîntu Gheorghe as well, it's easier to go there direct by boat and stop here on the way back, to continue by road or river.

Murighiol has its natural attractions – namely black-winged stilts, avocets and red-crested pochards nesting around the salt lakes nearby. From here, it should be possible to rent a boat and travel through the backwaters to **UZLINA**, which is otherwise accessible by ferry. This fishing village is the scientific centre of the Biosphere Reserve and the Cousteau Foundation; the Isac and Uzlina lakes to the north are a protected **pelican colony**. Continuing downstream, the new channel is edged by high levees, but the meanders of the old channel are tree-lined and populated by deer, boar, foxes, water snakes, black ibis and egrets.

SFÎNTU GHEORGHE (Saint George), 64km downriver from Murighiol, lives by fishing. The most prized catch is **sturgeon**, whose eggs are exported as **black caviar** (*icre negre*). **Private rooms** are available here, or you can camp wild. There's even entertainment provided by a band in the square at weekends, and by a floating disco-bar. From Sfîntu Gheorghe, you can take boat trips into the Ivancea Canal to Lacu Roșu, or out to the Sacalin islands at the river's mouth, inhabited by goosanders, red-breasted geese, and goldeneyes.

Around Lake Razim

Birdlife buffs should also consider **Lake Razim**, whose waters are separated from the Black Sea by two long, tongue-like *grinds*. The **Insula Popina**, a nesting-ground for two types of shelduck, is now a closed reserve. In November and December, Lake Razim's western shoreline is invaded by a million white-fronted geese and 20,000 red-breasted geese (half the world population), which come from arctic Russia and stay here, or around Istria further to the south, until the reedbeds freeze.

Babadag

From Tulcea, the DN22 and the rail line head south through the eroded Paleozoic hills of the Dealurile Tulcei to **BABADAG**, a town of 9000 people. From the **train station** it's fifteen minutes' walk down Strada Rahovei and Strada Stejarului to the **Mosque of Ali Ghazi** at Str. Geamiei 14, the oldest mosque in Romania, dating from 1522. There is a visible Turkish minority here, but the mosque is now disused. At the north end of the town's one-way system is the *Dumbrava* **hotel** (☎040/56.13.02; ②); in addition the *Doi Iepuraşi* **cabana and campsite** is 6km south of town along the DN22, by the *Codru* rail halt. The town also has some good seedy **bars**, including the *Taj Mahal* and the *Crama Expres*. Its facilities make Babadag a useful base for exploring the west shore of Lake Razim; buses to Enisala and Jurilovca leave from behind the mosque.

Enisala, Jurilovca and Gura Portiţei

A quiet place with reed cottages, **ENISALA** lies 8km from Babadag and about 1km from the **ruined Heracleia citadel** which overlooks Lake Razim. Built by Genoese merchants during the thirteenth century on the site of an earlier Byzantine fortress, the citadel is now abandoned, although the shoreline is busy with wading birds.

The village of **JURILOVCA** further down the coast merits more attention, and there's accommodation at the *Albatros* **hotel** (③). Trawling the rich fishing grounds of Lake Goloviţa, fishermen bring their catch to Jurilovca for weighing. Sturgeon is the most valu '.!e of the 31 species of fish harvested, but **carp** accounts for the bulk of the catch. They move up into the shallows to spawn, and the Chinese variety, introduced during Romania's honeymoon with the People's Republic in the 1960s, has since supplanted the indigenous species due to its greater voracity and fertility. Romanians, Lipovani (served by two Lipovani-Orthodox churches, one of them wooden) and a few Muslim Turks and Tartars co-exist quite happily here, as witnessed by the small **Ethnographic Museum**; unlike Transylvania, the Delta has never really been noted for ethnic rivalry.

Around Jurilovca there are vestiges of a second- to sixth-century Greek citadel on Cape Doloşman facing **Bisericuţa Island** which has medieval ruins. From the town, you can take motorboat trips out to **GURA PORTIŢEI**, which consists of a few Lipovani reed huts, with a **campsite, chalets** and a **restaurant**, sited on a spit of land between Lake Razim and the sea. Before 1989 it was one of the few places where the *Securitate* could be left behind for a week or two, and remains a popular spot for the non-conformist intelligentsia, and the starting point for excursions to the **Periteasca-Leahova seabird reserve**, just north.

Istria

Heading south, towards the coastal resorts, you'll pass through **ISTRIA**. Eight kilometres east of the train halt is the **ruined Greek city of Histria** with its shattered temples to diverse deities. The ruins cover a fairly small area despite the fact that this was the most important of the Greek settlements along the coast during the fifth and sixth centuries; within a few hundred years, alluvial deposits and sand smothered the port and the town was abandoned. In the vicinity of the ruins you'll find a **campsite** with chalets; while another lies further south along the road to Năvodari at **NUNTAŞI**.

THE COAST

Romania's **Black Sea coast** (the *litoral*) holds the promise of white beaches, dazzling water and an average of ten to twelve hours of sunshine a day between May and October, but this is countered by the logistical nightmare of a million people flocking to the resorts during the season. At peak times competition for rooms and food can be intense, and overcrowded trains and buses can make getting around very difficult. Curiously, this doesn't seem to be the case with **Constanţa**, a relaxed seaport-cum-riviera-town, dotted with Turkish, Byzantine and Roman remains and the proud possessor of a superb archeological museum.

To get the best out of resorts like **Mamaia, Neptun, Venus, Saturn** or **Mangalia**, there's really no sensible alternative to **package tours** – you'll find the main operators listed in *Basics*. Despite significant differences between packages, they all guarantee a room and minimize extraneous hassles. The cost of accommodation and air fare in such deals works out far less than you would pay should you try to do the whole thing independently. However, if you don't come on a tour, travel agencies in just about any town on the coast offer rooms in bungalows or less comfortable hotels. *CTT* can book rooms for students at the **Costineşti International Youth Camp** (see p.301). The only resort you should actively avoid is **Năvodari**, which is irredeemably horrible. If you're looking for somewhere as yet "undeveloped", try **Doi Mai** and **Vama Veche**, just a few miles from the Bulgarian border, or **Gura Portiţei** in the Delta (see opposite).

The Dobrogea and the Danube–Black Sea Canal

The overland approaches to Constanţa cross one part or another of the bleak northern **Dobrogea**. It's difficult to think of any reason for stopping here, but the changes wrought over the last forty years certainly merit some explanation. Driving on the DN2A, you'll cross the Danube at **GIURGENI** and see orchards and fields planted on what used to be pestilential marshland; but this transformation is nothing compared to the great works further to the south, starting at Cernavodă, where the rail line crosses the Danube on what was Europe's longest bridge when it opened in 1895. There's also a modern road bridge here, linking the DN3A and the DN22C, which provide the most direct road route to Constanţa, parallel to the rail line and the **Danube–Black Sea Canal**.

Cernavodă

CERNAVODĂ, whose name rather ominously translates as "Black Water", was chosen as the site of Romania's first **nuclear power station**. A Canadian-designed reactor was chosen, and Ceauşescu was personally involved – having inspected a similar CANDU reactor in Canada in 1985, he returned home and immediately criticized managers for using too much concrete at Cernavodă. In addition there were major problems with inadequate welding, so that it now seems that only one of the five reactors proposed will finally come into service, supposedly during 1995.

Cernavodă is also the western entrance to the **Danube–Black Sea Canal**. Opened to shipping in 1984, the canal put Cernavodă a mere 60km from the Black Sea, rather than 400km via the Delta which, in any case, is impassable for larger freighters. It offers obvious savings in fuel and time, but realizing a profit after the huge investment depends on European economic revival, and particularly on an end to the conflict in former Yugoslavia and on the success of the new Rhein–Main and Nürnberg–Regensburg canals. Charlemagne's vision of a 3000km-long waterway linking Rotterdam with the Black Sea finally came to fruition in 1993, although soaring costs and environmental protests in Bavaria had stalled the final stage of the project for ten years.

Along the canal

According to ONT, it's now possible to travel by motorboat from Cernavodă to Agigea along the canal, which would allow you a good look at this awesomely ugly feat of engineering. However, the service rarely runs, but all trains through the Dobrogea stop at the town of **MEDGIDIA** (junction for Tulcea and Negru Vodă, the crossing-point to Bulgaria) on the canal, while slow trains and irregular cruise boats halt at the canal-side wine-producing town of **BASARABI** and its eastern suburb of **MURFATLAR**. Constanţa's tourist office organizes excursions

---

THE CANAL OF DEATH

Work on the **Danube–Black Sea Canal** started in 1949, when the Party launched this "hero project", and writers like Petru Dumitriu (who made his name with a book on the canal, *Dustless Highway*) waxed lyrical about the transformation of humble peasants into class-conscious proletarians through the camaraderie of the construction site. But as Dumitriu acknowledged after his defection in 1960, the *Canalul Mortii* as it came to be known, claimed the lives of over 100,000 workers, the bulk of whom were actually there under duress. **Forced labour** was permitted from 1950, and six-month sentences were doled out without trial by the Ministry of the Interior; those affected included Uniate priests and tens of thousands of peasants who resisted collectivization. From 1952 these were joined by relatives of prisoners, war criminals and those who had try to flee abroad.

In 1953, after untold suffering and the realization that the chosen route (through the 84-metre-high Canara Hills towards Năvodari, north of Constanţa) was plain crazy, the project was abandoned. When work was resumed in 1973, a new route was selected and the canal was successfully pushed eastwards to join the sea at Agigea, south of Constanţa. However it carries less than ten percent of the predicted traffic and may well be remembered as another of Ceauşescu's follies.

to Murfatlar, of which the shortest and best value for money is the four-hour wine-tasting tour which includes a visit to the **museum** with its old presses, reliefs of Dionysos and withered vines.

Dug into the hills near Murfatlar is the **Rupestral complex**, consisting of six small churches and a few rooms linked by passageways. Discovered in 1957, the complex was created during the ninth to eleventh centuries, and there are Greek and Slavonic inscriptions and pictures of humans and animals inscribed on its rock walls. **VALU LUI TRAIAN**, on the rail line 4km east of Murfatlar has a **campsite**.

Adamclisi and Ostrov

If you're interested in ancient monuments you might consider detouring south from Cernavodă or Medgidia to visit the Roman remains near **ADAMCLISI**. Just north of the DN3 and the village of Adamclisi rises an arresting marble structure, a reconstruction of the **Tropaeum Traiani**. The original was erected in 109 AD to celebrate Trajan's conquest of the Dacians, and every facet reflects unabashed militarism, not least the dedication to Mars Ultor. The trophy-statue – an armoured, faceless warrior – gazes over the plateau from a height of 30m, on a hexagonal plinth rising from a base, 32m in diameter. Carved around the side of the base are 49 **bas-reliefs** or metopes (originally, there were 54), portraying the Roman campaign. Each of the six groups of metopes is comprised of a marching scene, a battle, and a tableau representing victory over the enemy, an identical arrangement underlies scenes XXXVI–XLII of Trajan's Column in Rome, created to mark the same triumph over the Dacians. Around the statue are other **ruins** of buildings once inhabited by the legionary garrison or serving religious or funerary purposes. Unfortunately, there's no tourist accommodation in the vicinity; public **buses** do run from Cernavodă and Medgidia (heading for Băneasa and Ostrov), but you may prefer the security of a bus trip from the coast.

Into Bulgaria

Sixty kilometres west of Adamclisi along the DN3 is the small border town of **OSTROV**, where you can cross over to the Bulgarian town of **Silistra**. Ostrov has a **campsite** with chalets, near the jetty for ferries to **CĂLĂRAȘI** on the north bank of the Danube. Although the **VAMA VECHE crossing** (see p.303) is more suitable if you're driving down the coast to **Varna**, it's also possible to enter Bulgaria from **NEGRU VODĂ** at the south end of the DN38. All three crossings are open 24 hours a day. By rail, *accelerats* travel from Constanța via Medgidia and the crossing at Negru Vodă to **Kardam** and **Dobrich**. Make sure you get your Bulgarian **visa** in Bucharest or before leaving home.

Constanța

Most visitors first encounter the Black Sea coast at **CONSTANȚA**: a busy riviera town and Romania's principal port. Its ancient precursor *Tomis* was supposedly founded by survivors of a battle with the Argonauts, following the capture of the Golden Fleece; centuries later the great Latin poet **Ovid** was exiled here from 8 AD until his death in 17 AD. The town is an attractive mix of Greco-Roman remains, Turkish mosques and crisp modern boulevards, swept and watered

> The **telephone code** for Constanţa and the Black Sea resorts is ☎041

daily by Gypsy women. However, since 1989, Constanţa has gained notoriety as the world's child AIDS capital, while also increasingly falling under the sway of Gypsy and Turkish racketeers.

Arrival, information and accommodation

Constanţa is served by **Mihail Kogălniceanu airport**, 25km northwest, from where it's a half-hour journey into the centre by *TAROM* bus (or any bus on the DN2A between Constanţa and Hîrşova). *TAROM*'s office is at Str. Ştefan cel Mare 15 (☎61.40.66).

The **train station** and *Autogară Sud*, the **bus station** serving destinations south of Constanţa, as well as Varna and Istanbul, are 2km west of the centre, to which they are linked by Bulevardul Republicii and trolleybuses #40 and #43. Trolleybus #40 continues north to the southern fringe of Mamaia, and #43 runs parallel past *Autogară Nord*, where you'll arrive from places north along the coast. Train tickets are sold at the *CFR agenţia*, Aleea Vasile Canarache 4 (Mon–Fri 7am–7pm, Sat 7am–1pm), overlooking the new port, and you will need to book several days in advance during the summer.

Occasionally a **steamer**, the *Dierna*, sails up the coast from Mangalia, docking at the *portul turistic* just north of Constanţa's old quarter, but this is not a regular service.

Information

Constanţa has two **tourist offices**, ONT at B-dul Tomis 74 (Mon–Fri 8am–7pm) and the privately run *Litoral* on the same street at no. 46. Both are keen to sign visitors up for **excursions**, and some are worth considering. The enormous *Tropaeum Traiani* monument at Adamclisi (see p.293) is relatively inaccessible and a four-hour organized trip is the easiest way to see it. ONT's two-day Delta Tour, taking in some of the backwaters near Crişan, can also simplify transport problems.

Accommodation

There's not a great choice of **hotels** in Constanţa itself, so at peak times you might have to find a room in one of the beach resorts to the north and south of town. The least expensive places in town are the *Tineretului* at B-dul Tomis 24 (☎61.35.90; ④) and *Continental* at B-dul Republicii 20 (☎61.56.60; ④). The only alternatives are the *Palace* at Str. Opreanu 5 (☎61.46.96; ⑤), with a beautifully cool and quiet marble foyer, and the *Intim* at Str. Titulescu 9 (☎61.78.14; ⑥), an old establishment, once the *Hotel d'Angleterre*, where Eminescu stayed briefly in 1882. **Private rooms** can be obtained from *Danubius* at B-dul Republicii 22–34 (☎67.01.29).

Otherwise, *CTT*, at B-dul Tomis 22 (☎61.52.62), might be able to arrange **dormitory beds** during summer, along with holidays at the International Youth Camp in Costineşti. The closest **campsites** are on the outskirts of Mamaia and Eforie Nord (see p.299 & p.300). If you're hoping for a bungalow there, or a room in any of the other resorts, ask at the tourist offices.

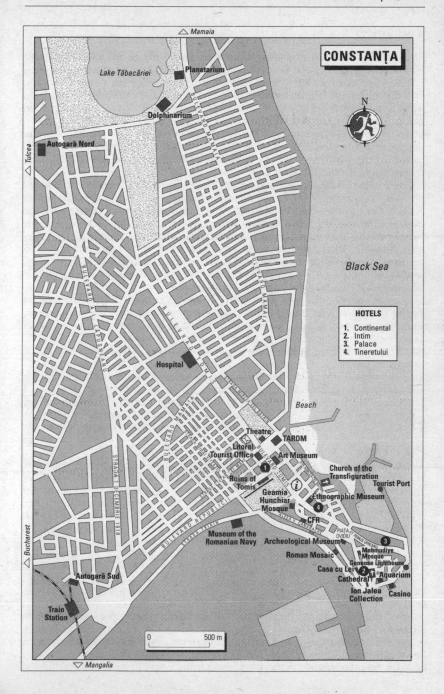

CONSTANȚA

Black Sea

HOTELS
1. Continental
2. Intim
3. Palace
4. Tineretului

△ Mamaia

Lake Tăbacăriei

Planetarium

Dolphinarium

△ Tulcea

Autogară Nord

Hospital

Beach

Theatre
TAROM
Litoral
Tourist Office
Art Museum
Ruins of Tomis
Church of the Transfiguration
Tourist Port
Geamia Hunchiar Mosque
Ethnographic Museum
CFR
Museum of the Romanian Navy
Archeological Museum
PIAȚA OVIDIU
Roman Mosaic
Mahmudiye Mosque
Geneose Lighthouse
Casa cu Lei
Aquarium
△ Bucharest
Cathedral
Casino
Ion Jalea Collection
Autogară Sud
Train Station

STRADA 1 DECEMBRIE 1919

BULEVARD A. LAPUSNEANU

BULEVARD TOMIS

BULEVARD MAMAIA

BULEVARD REPUBLICII

0   500 m

▽ Mangalia

The Town

The pivotal point of the new town is the junction of **Bulevardul Republicii and Bulevardul Tomis**. Here, under a mural of the Dobrogea's archeological sites, you'll find sections of ancient walls, serried amphorae and other **ruins of Tomis**. Whether or not the Argonauts came here first, *Tomis* was settled by Greeks from Miletus in the sixth century BC as an annexe to Histria, which it later superseded before being incorporated within the Roman empire as *Pontus Sinister* at the beginning of the Christian era. The most prominent remains are those of the defensive wall created in the third and fourth centuries and the Butchers' Tower, raised in the sixth century by Byzantine colonists who revived *Tomis* and renamed it to honour Constantine.

South of the archeological park, Strada Traian overlooks the commercial *portul maritim*, and provides an appropriate setting for the **Museum of the Romanian Navy** at no. 53 (Tues–Sun 10am–6pm). The title is slightly misleading, since the museum includes models of Greek triremes that sailed long before the name "Romania" existed, and photographs recording the unexpected visit of the battleship *Potemkin*, whose mutinous sailors disembarked at Constanța in July 1905 and scattered. Extensive material on the wartime exploits of the Red Navy serves to obscure the role of Romania's own navy during the last war – supporting the occupation of Odessa and aiding the Nazi fleet.

Back on Bulevardul Tomis, north of Bulevardul Republicii, the **Art Museum** at no. 82 (Wed–Sun 9am–5pm), has the usual sampling of Aman and Grigorescu, including painters of the Dobrogean landscape, such as Iosif Iser, Ştefan Dumitrescu and Francisc Şirato, around the first-floor gallery. South at no. 32, you'll find the **Ethnographic Museum** (Wed–Sun 10am–6pm), which has a fine display of colourful Dobrogean rugs and folk costumes. The museum stands almost opposite the **Geamia Hunchiar**, a small mosque built in in 1869, surmounting a tangle of dingy coffee houses, kebab and pizza joints. A couple of blocks east, at Str. Mircea cel Bătrîn 36, is the **Church of the Transfiguration**, dating from 1865 when the Greek community at last got permission from the Ottoman rulers for a church, and brought a monk from Athos to decorate it.

Piaţa Ovidiu

Piaţa Ovidiu, at the southern end of Bulevardul Tomis, is the central square of the old quarter. A statue of Ovid gazes mournfully down, as he might well have done when he was exiled from Rome by Emperor Augustus in 8 AD (probably for intriguing at court and writing *The Art of Love*). Marooned in backwater *Tomis* where he found the natives uncouth and the winters appalling, Ovid spent his last years unsuccessfully petitioning emperors for his return, and composing his melancholy *Tristia*:

> *Rain cannot pit it, sunlight fails in burning*
> *This snow. One drift succeeds another here.*
> *The north wind hardens it, making it eternal;*
> *It spreads in drifts through all the bitter year.*

Also on the square, Constanţa's **Archeological and National History Museum** (Wed–Sun 10am–6pm; 8pm in summer) has an excellent collection, especially of statues of deities, displayed in the hall just left of the entrance. A menhir of a Hamangia-culture Earth Goddess, complete with battle-axes, occupies the first room; while in the lower section you'll find Fortuna and Pontos, the protectors of *Tomis*; an Aedicula carved with the chillingly lovely Nemesis twins, goddesses of Revenge and Universal Equilibrium; and other statues, including the mysterious **Glykon Serpent**. Though considered to have been carved during the second century like the others, the Glykon statue is unique and extraordinary, being about the size of a squatting toddler, with an antelope's head, human hair and ears, and a gracefully coiled serpentine body ending in a lion's tail.

Outside the museum you can see a display of funerary inscriptions, and to its rear a modern structure encloses a fine **Roman mosaic**, more than 600 metres square. It was discovered 5m below street level in 1959, and may have once graced a third- to fourth-century commercial building, or even the upper hall of the Roman *thermae*, whose outer walls, their archways sealed, can be seen from Aleea Canarache.

South of Piața Ovidiu

From **Piața Ovidiu**, it's a short walk south to the **Mahmudiye Mosque** (9.30am–5.30pm), whose 50m-high minaret is a feature of the skyline and offers a great view of the town and harbour. Built in 1910, the first reinforced-concrete building in Romania, it's the seat of the Mufti, the spiritual head of Romania's 55,000 Muslims (Turks and Tartars by origin), who live along the coast of the Dobrogea. Further south along Strada Muzeelor are the fancy **Orthodox Cathedral** of SS. Peter and Paul, an early design by Ion Mincu, and at the street's end, opposite more ruins of ancient *Tomis*, the **Ion Jalea collection of sculptures** bequeathed by the artist (May–Oct daily 8am–8pm; Nov–April Wed–Sun 9am–5pm). Jalea, born in Tulcea in 1887, generally produced conventional and academic sculptures for the state, being forced to produce monumental equestrian work such as that of Mircea cel Bătrîn in Tulcea's main square.

On the **waterfront**, the former **Casino** stands on a jutting promenade. Originally erected as a pavilion for Queen Elizabeta (Carmen Sylva) in 1904, it is now a restaurant. During a visit in 1914 by the Russian Imperial family, who had arrived by yacht with vague intentions of marrying a daughter to Prince Carol, it was the venue for a disastrous gala performance of mystical allegories by little girls, which ended in smashed scenery and broken limbs. Despite a *Te Deum* in the cathedral and an amicable spitting contest between the two parties, the Russians sailed away less than a day later.

The tanks of the **Aquarium** (daily 9am–4pm), opposite the Casino, contain 4500 species of aquatic life from the Dobrogean lakes, the Delta and the Black Sea. Just beyond, you can see the so-called **Genoese Lighthouse**, erected in 1860 in memory of the thirteenth- and fourteenth-century mariners who tried to revive the port.

The beach and Lake Tăbăcăriei

Visitors with children or a low tolerance of museums often head straight for the **beach** behind the Art Museum, spread beneath a terraced cliff north of the *port turistic*. Another popular spot is the park surrounding **Lake Tăbăcăriei**, between Constanța and Mamaia: trolleybus #40 runs along Bulevardul Mamaia, to the east of the park, and #43 heads up Bulevardul Alexandru Lapușneanu, to its west, both starting from the train station. The #40 passes a more than usually depressing **dolphinarium** (9am–7pm) and a **planetarium** (same hours) at the southeastern corner of the park; from the nearby Tăbăcăriei Wharf a **miniature train** carries children around the lake. **Luna Park**, north of the lake, has various rides and games, including bowling, and there is an **ice-skating** rink on the edge of the Pioneers' Park, also the site of Constanţa's football stadium.

Eating and drinking

Most hotels have **restaurants** on the premises, but, for once, there are plenty of other places to choose from in town. The most popular include the *Cazino* in the Casino; the very stylish *Casa cu Lei* ("House with Lions", so named after the statues flanking its doorway) at Str. Titulescu 1 and the *Pescăruşul Argintiu* at Str. Vasile Alexandri 7, a fish restaurant with a kebab and felafel joint, near the Ethnographic Museum. There's a Chinese restaurant, the *Bei-Con*, at the corner of Republicii and Tomis (daily 10am–midnight), an Italian, the *Venezia*, at Str. Mircea cel Bătrîn 5, and the French *Restaurant au Coq Simpa* opposite the Post Office on Strada Ştefan cel Mare (daily 11am–midnight). Piaţa Ovidiu's best eating place is the *Victoria*, while the *Terasa Colonadelor*, just east of the Museum of the Romanian Navy, is particularly worth visiting for its summer garden.

In the backstreets of the old town, especially around the Hunchiar mosque, you'll find various seedy yet appealing **bars**; perhaps more civilized, though still in a tatty area, is the *Club B*, at Str. Mircea cel Bătrîn 15. Restaurants such as the *Cazino* and *Casa cu Lei* also have excellent terraces, great for a beer at sundown.

Mamaia and around

MAMAIA, 6km north of Constanţa, is Romania's best-known coastal resort, and the majority of package tourists end up here. The **beach** of fine, almost white sand, fringed with olive trees, is Mamaia's greatest asset, while its gentle gradient and the absence of currents and strong tides make it particularly safe for children. Legend has it that the gods created the beach to reunite a kidnapped princess with her daughter, who was abandoned on the sea shore wailing "Mamaia, Mamaia!"; but the name could equally be derived from *Mamakioi*, meaning "village of butter" in Turkish.

HOTEL PRICES ON THE BLACK SEA COAST

In all the resorts along the Black Sea coast, the traditional rigid **pricing structure** has begun to fragment, but most of the hotels in each resort are still owned by one state holding company, with all their hotels in each category charging the same. Two-star hotels generally charge the equivalent of $15–20 a night in season for a double room (②–③), and three-star hotels up to three times that (④–⑥); there are very few one- or four-star establishments. **Private hotels** tend to cost slightly more than than state hotels, but are usually worth it. You should be sure which meals are included, and also bear in mind that prices in July and August are up to 20 percent higher than in June and September; at other times most hotels are closed.

Very few hotels are used to the concept of anyone turning up independently, rather than in a group, and it may take them a while to work out what to charge (probably around 20 percent over the group rate); foreigners can find themselves paying up to six times the rate for Romanians. Each resort has a *dispecerat cazare* or **accommodation office**, responsible for allocating lone arrivals: this can work out less costly, though not always, and is usually the only way to get a self-catering villa.

The resort

Ranged along a narrow spit of land between the Black Sea and Lake Siutghiol, most of Mamaia's 55 **hotels** are within 100m of the beach. Approaching by trolleybus from Constanţa, you'll have to change from the #40 to the #47 at the *Pescarie* terminal; one stop north, the resort begins with the thirteen-storey *Parc* hotel. The main street curves away from here around the shore of the lake, packed with tennis and basketball courts, restaurants and discos, passing clusters of mainly two-star hotels as well as Mamaia's only one-star establishments, the *Pescăruş* (☎83.16.73; ②) and *Delfin* (☎83.16.40; ②).

North of the main watersports area, just beyond the casino, are a couple of good privatized hotels, the *Condor* (☎83.11.42; ④) and *Albatros* (☎83.10.47; ④). Continuing north, you pass the *Rex* (☎83.15.95; ⑦), Mamaia's only four-star hotel, Club Med's exclusive *Thalassa* complex, and most of the hotels used by British package companies. The resort ends with a few newer three-star places (by a small naturist enclosure), and then a **campsite**, the *Turist*; from here it's about 5km up the road to the equally crowded *Hanul Piraţilor* site. If you do arrive without a room reservation (see box opposite), the **accommodation offices** in the south wing of the *Bucureşti* hotel, in the middle of the resort (☎83.11.40, 83.11.52 or 83.11.68) are your best bet – they will accept *ACR* vouchers.

Mamaia has ample **sporting facilities**, but unless your package deal includes rental charges, all activities and equipment must be paid for in hard currency at the following dollar-equivalent rates, standard along the coast: waterskiing ($20/hour); yachting ($10/hour); surf boards ($3/hour, 5 hours for $11). Fifty minutes on a tennis court costs $2 (10 sessions for $15.50), and $1.50 gets you the use of a racquet and two balls for one hour.

Nightlife consists of glitzy cabaret most nights at the *Melody* and *Orient* nightclubs, folklore displays at the *Orient* and *Hanul Piraţilor* and nightly discos the *Perla*, *Select* and *Delta* hotels.

> The **telephone code** for Constanţa and the Black Sea resorts is ☎041

Ovid's Island and beyond

From Mamaia, regular motorboat trips run to **Ovid's Island**, where there's a suitably rustic restaurant, the *Insula Ovidiu*, at the northern end of **Lake Siutghiol**. Also known by the easier name of Lacul Mamaia, the lake was formed when a river's outlet silted up, and for many centuries it was a watering hole for herds of sheep and cows brought down from the Carpathians – hence the origin of *Siutghiol*, "Lake of Milk" in Turkish.

It's inadvisable to travel much further north, since **NĂVODARI** looms on the horizon. The beach here must have been lovely once, but with characteristic concern for the environment, a gigantic, reeking superphosphates plant has been constructed nearby, its pipelines running through the **campsite** which, unbelievably, has been designated a children's resort. Beyond Năvodari a minor road heads north past Lake Nuntaşi and its **campsite** to the Greek ruins at Histria (see p.291).

Agigea to Vama Veche

Just south of Constanța, the road and rail line cross the new Danube–Black Sea Canal where it meets the coast at the **Agigea port complex**. Beyond this, the array of resorts extending to **Mangalia** is another facet of Romania's progress over the last twenty years – modern complexes created where only scrubland or rundown villages existed before. Except for the fact that most are situated along a clifftop overlooking the beach, they are fairly similar to their prototype, Mamaia, to the north. You can reach them by **local buses** from Constanța, or by **trains** along the rail line to Mangalia, although all transport is crowded in summer. If it's operating, the *Dierna* **steamer** is probably the most civilized way to reach Mangalia.

Around Lake Techirghiol

Trains and buses #10, #11 and #12 run 14km south from Constanța to **EFORIE NORD**. Founded in 1899 by Bucharest's Eforia hospital, Eforie Nord clambers along a clifftop 15–20m above its beach. The resort is, however, best known for its therapeutic **black mud** scooped from the shores of **Lake Techirghiol**, whose mineral-saturated waters got the lake its name, derived from *tekir*, Turkish for "salt" or "bitter". **Therapeutic baths** by the lake (south of the train station) specialize in treating rheumatic disorders and the after-effects of polio; while on the lake's single-sex nudist beaches people plaster themselves with mud, wait until it cracks (happily exposing themselves to passing trains), and then jostle good humouredly beneath the showers.

The resort itself basically comprises two parallel streets, Bulevardul Tudor Vladimirescu, running along the cliff-top, and Bulevardul Republicii, where you'll find the bus stops, stores and offices. Eforie Nord is an older-style resort, with plenty of **villas**, allocated by the **tourist office** at B-dul Republicii 13 (☎74.11.88), as well as the rather faceless hotels needed for mass tourism. Most **hotels** are two-star but there are some good bargains, and due to the baths you are more likely to find them open out of season here than elsewhere. The *Decebal* (☎61.82.12; ③) is the station hotel, but is far better than that implies, while the *Traian* (☎74.18.08; ②), next door, and the *Hefaistos* (☎74.29.46; ②) on Strada 23 August, are both excellent value for money. Inland is the three-star *Europa* (☎74.29.90; ⑤), where you can use *ACR* vouchers and **rent cars**.

Of the two **campsites**, the nicer is the *Meduza*, just inland at the northern end of Bulevardul Vladimirescu; the *Șincai*, along Strada 23 August towards Techirghiol, is much more run down. There are plenty of **restaurants** in town, of which the *Nunta Zamfirei* and *Berbec* are famous for their folklore shows.

Although there's nowhere to stay, it's a nice trip around the lake to **TECHIRGHIOL** (terminus of bus #11), where there are three hundred Muslim families (Turks and Tartars by origin) among the village's population. Bizarrely, there's a wooden church here, transplanted from Vișeu in Maramureș.

Compared to its northern neighbour, **EFORIE SUD** now seems like the town that died – locals insist that the five decrepit seaside **hotels** on Strada Dezrobirii will reopen, but each year it seems less likely. The large *Cosmos* **campsite** is squalid, and there is also a selection of rather unappealing hotels and villas along Strada Negru Vodă and Strada Dr Cantacuzino, squeezed between the train station (by Lake Techirghiol) and the sea.

South to Mangalia

Bus #10 from Constanţa terminates in **TUZLA**, immediately south of Eforie Sud; bus #12 continues on to Mangalia every thirty minutes, however it follows the main road for the most part, so that resorts between here and Mangalia are best reached by train. Even express trains slow to a crawl between Constanţa and Mangalia, taking an hour to cover the 43km. From mid-June to mid-September extra services are laid on, providing an almost continuous service along the coast, with reservations required only west of Constanţa.

The eight kilometres of beach immediately north of Mangalia are now lined with the modern hotels of the new resorts, all given mythological names, that have arisen in the last three decades. The stretch of cliffs to their north is broken only by the former fishing village of **COSTINEŞTI**, now the site of Romania's principal **International Youth Camp**, with a fine sandy beach sheltered to the north by Cape Tuzla. This is run by the *Compania de Turism pentru Tineret* (Youth Tourism Company), and until 1989 only young people booked through *CTT* (or *BTT* as it then was) could stay here. Things have now changed and **accommodation** is open to all. It's best to book before coming; if you haven't, arrive early and head across the car park to the *birou cazare*, where you can ask about accommodation in *casute* and villas. Alternatively you can try the **hotels** to the south of the beach. The *Forum* (☎74.28.55; ④) is a friendly modern place, but the *Azur* refuses to take stray foreigners. A jazz festival is held at the end of August or early September.

Eight kilometres further south by rail is **NEPTUN**; from here bus #15 runs along the coast to Mangalia. Neptun was built in 1960 between the Comorova forest and the sea, ensuring a lush setting for the artificial lakes and dispersed villas that make this the most desirable of the Black Sea resorts. Shopping centres, discos, sports facilities and hotels here are a cut above the Romanian average, as also in the satellite resort of **OLIMP**, just north; originally an enclave for the communist *nomenklatura*, this is still frequented by the country's elite as well as Western package tourists.

Most **rooms** are still assigned to package tourists, however, so if you're hoping to get something through the *dispecerat cazare* opposite Neptun's *Hotel Decebal* you could well be disappointed. The best hotel is the *Neptun* (☎73.10.20; ⑥) but the others are not much cheaper. *ACR* vouchers are accepted at the *Transilvania*, *Belvedere* and *Amfiteatru* hotels, and in summer you can **rent cars** at the *Belvedere*. There's a **campsite** at the north end of Olimp, and another tiny site with bungalows at the south end of Neptun, by the *Autoservice* yard. The best **restaurants** are the *Calul Balan*, right at the southern end of Neptun, and the *Insula* (specializing in fish) on the lake behind the *Neptun* hotel. Tourist excursions on offer include banquets in Ceauşescu's former holiday home, the *Vila Nufarul*, on a lake deep in the woods inland.

The four resorts to the south are more uniform, and the hotels are mainly state-owned two-star places, although some have been privatized. The first, immediately abutting Neptun, is **JUPITER**, which rubs shoulders with the forest and has a gently sloping beach with fine sand. Centred on the artificial Lake Tismana, this is more youth-orientated, with 2000 places available in the *Zodiac* and *Liliacul* **campsites**. **Rooms** are available day or night from the *dispecerat cazare* (☎73.11.84) at the southern end of the resort, next to a video-bar. Nightlife focuses on the *Paradis* bar/disco and the *Zodiac* holiday village.

Imagine Mayan architects called upon to design Palm Beach and you'll get some idea of the pyramidical complexes that are the most striking feature of **AURORA**, the most recent resort, set on the cape of the same name southeast of Jupiter. Small and elegantly designed compared to the other resorts, Aurora has ten **hotels** (④) named after jewels, all very popular with students at Easter and in the low season.

There's a barely perceptible gap before **VENUS**, which is broadly similar to Jupiter, with several man-made semi-circular beaches, a disco and two main **bars**, the *Calipso* and *Auto-Night-Club*. There are four private **hotels**, the *Dana* (☎73.15.03; ③), *Felicia* (☎73.16.07; ③), *Silvia* (☎73.16.06; ③) and *Adriana* (☎73.15.06; ③), of which the *Silvia* is the most lively, with a 24-hour bar and shop and plans for refurbishment. Venus also has a *dispecerat cazare* (☎73.16.74) if you need help with accommodation. At the south end of the resort is a **campsite** and, just inland, **stables** where you can hire horses for exploring the forest, inhabited by roe-deer, grouse and pheasants.

A reed-fringed lake lies between Venus and **SATURN**, a high-rise resort with various grades of **hotels**, a large but run-down **campsite** and two **holiday villages**, the *Dunărea* and *Delta*. You can play tennis, minigolf or bowls, or dine to music at the *Balada*, *Prahova* or *Mercur* restaurants. As in Venus, *CFR* shares premises with the post office, and for accommodation you should call ☎75.19.83.

Mangalia and beyond

The modern suburbs of **MANGALIA** are close to swallowing up Saturn, and in fact Mangalia's **train station** is nearer to Saturn than to the centre of town. As with Constanța, Mangalia's appearance of modernity belies its ancient origin – the Greeks founded their city of *Callatis* here during the sixth century BC, when population pressure impelled them to colonize the Black Sea coast.

Heading south from the station and turning left at the first roundabout, you'll reach the *Mangalia* hotel (☎75.20.52; ⑤). Behind, in Parc Stadionului, are the **ruins of Callatis**, which include sarcophagi and the vestiges of a Christian basilica, and beyond, at Şos. Constanței 19 (the road from the roundabout to the centre), is the **Archeological Museum** (9am–6pm). Just south of the small town centre on Strada Oituz stands the **Sultan Esmahan Mosque**, built in 1590 and surrounded by a Muslim graveyard. There are medicinal baths on the town's outskirts beside Lake Mangalia, utilizing radioactive sulphurous hot springs to treat various muscular and neurological afflictions.

Mangalia's other **hotels**, the *Zenit* (③), *Astra* (③) and *Orion* (③), are along the promenade between the *Mangalia* and the harbour, where the *Dierna* steamer docks behind the long breakwater. Mangalia's **campsite** is north of town – from the train station turn left, then right after five minutes at the *Saturn* sign.

Doi Mai and Vama Veche

The laid-back villages of **DOI MAI** and **VAMA VECHE**, traditionally the haunts of artists, intellectuals and non-conformists, lie further south down the coast from Mangalia; bus #14 runs roughly every ninety minutes. Neither village has a hotel, but almost every house provides **private accommodation** or you can **camp** in the dunes. Doi Mai (Second of May) has two **restaurants** and an *alimentară*, but its beach (which does have free showers) is crammed between a naval dockyard and an anti-aircraft battery.

Under communism Vama Veche (Old Customs Post), just short of the border with Bulgaria, was closed to all but staff of Cluj University or those who could claim some vague affiliation with it; it became a haven for non-conformists, who could escape the surveillance of the *Securitate* here. There was always some skinny-dipping, but now wearing clothes is the exception rather than the rule on the beach. There are no facilities at all, other than a bar/canteen where you can order meals a day in advance.

travel details

Trains

Constanţa to: Braşov (2 daily; 5hr 30min–9hr); Bucharest (13–17 daily; 2hr 25min–5hr 20min); Medgidia (24–27 daily; 29–58min); Suceava (1 daily; 7hr 30min); Tîrgu Jiu (1 daily; 7hr); Tulcea (2 daily; 4hr–4hr 22min).

Medgidia to: Babadag (6 daily; 1hr 50min–2hr 20min); Bucharest (9–11 daily; 2hr 10min–4hr 10min); Istria (4 daily; 1hr 20min); Mangalia (4–8 daily; 1hr 40min–2hr 50min); Negru Vodă (5 daily; 1hr 10min–1hr 25min); Suceava (1 daily; 7hr); Tulcea (6 daily; 2hr 30min–3hr 10min).

Hydrofoils

Tulcea to: Galaţi (daily in summer; 1hr 30min); Periprava (daily in summer; 2hr 30min); Sf. Gheorge (daily in summer; 2hr); Sulina (daily in summer; 1hr 30min).

Ferries

Tulcea to: Galaţi (daily in summer; 3hr 15min); Periprava (daily in summer; 5hr 30min); Sf. Gheorge (daily in summer; 5hr); Sulina (daily in summer; 4hr).

Cruises between **Constanţa** and **Mangalia** during the summer, as advertised.

Planes

Constanţa to: Bucharest (1–2 daily; 45min); Arad, Bacau, Cluj, Iaşi, Oradea, Satu Mare, Sibiu, Suceava, Tîrgu Mureş (1 daily during the summer).

Tulcea to: Bucharest (1–2 daily; 45min).

International trains

Constanţa to: Budapest (1 daily; 16hr); Chişinau (1 daily; 13hr 35min); Dobrich (2 daily; 5hr 15min).

PART THREE

THE
CONTEXTS

THE HISTORICAL FRAMEWORK

Although inhabited since prehistoric times, Romania only achieved statehood during the nineteenth century, and Transylvania, one third of its present territory, was acquired as recently as 1920. Hence, much of Romania's history is that of its disparate parts – Dobrogea, the Banat, Bessarabia, Maramureş and, above all, the principalities of Moldavia, Wallachia and Transylvania.

ORIGINS: GREEKS, DACIANS & ROMANS (4000 BC–271 AD)

Despite the discovery of bones, weapons and implements within Carpathian caves, very little is known about the nomadic hunter-gatherers of the early **Stone Age**. With the recession of the glaciers, humans seem to have established their first settlements in Dobrogea, where the excavation of a Neolithic village at Habaşeşti and the discovery of numerous statues suggest that the tribes – known to archeologists as the **Hamangia Culture** – probably had a matriarchal society, worshipping fertility goddesses and the great Earth Mother.

Other cultures followed in the Bronze and Iron Ages, followed by the Celts of the **Hallstadt and La Tène cultures** who arrived from Asia in the last millennium BC; meanwhile during the sixth and seventh centuries BC,

Greek traders established ports along the Black Sea coast, the ruins of which can still be seen at Histria, Constanţa (*Tomis*), Mangalia (*Callatis*) and other sites. Commerce flourished between the Black Sea and Aegean ports, but the interior remained basically unknown to the Greeks until 514 BC, when a Persian fleet under Darius attempted to expel the Scythians from their new settlements along the Danube. In 335 BC Alexander the Great crossed the Danube, defeating the Getae but failing to subdue them; in 292 BC his successor Lysimachus was captured by the Getae ruler Dromichaetes, only to be lectured on the value of peace and sent home.

The chronicler Herodotus had reported in the sixth century BC that of the numerous and disunited tribes of **Thracians** who inhabited the mountains on both sides of the river, the "bravest and most righteous" were those subsequently known as the "Geto-Dacians". The term Thracians is now taken as an umbrella term for the mix of original East Balkan tribes and incoming central European tribes then inhabiting this area, including the Getae on the Danube, the Dacians to their north, the Thracians proper to the south, and the Illyrians in present-day Albania.

Over the centuries these related tribes gradually coalesced and were brought under a centralized authority, so that by the first century BC a single leader, Burebista (82–44 BC), ruled a short-lived **Dacian empire**, occupying the territory of modern-day Romania and the entire western seaboard of the Black Sea. It's assumed that, besides believing in a traditional mother goddess, the Getae and Dacians practised sun worship to a certain extent, and accorded semi-divine status to their chieftains, who ruled as priest-kings. Agriculture – and a pastoral lifestyle in the highlands – provided the basis for the Dacian society, at the apex of which was the religious and political capital, **Sarmizegetusa**, located in the Orăştie mountains. Digs have revealed Dacian settlements as far afield as Maramureş and Mount Ceahlău, and the sheer size of the kingdom contributed to its fragmentation after Burebista's demise.

A ROMAN COLONY

Before **Decebal** (87–106 AD) managed to reunite the kingdom, the lower reaches of the

Danube had already been conquered by the **Romans**, who then began to expand northwards. The Dacians resisted, but were defeated during the course of two campaigns (in 101–2 and 105–6) by the Emperor Trajan (98–117). Although the Apuseni mountains and Maramureş were never subdued, most regions fell under Roman hegemony, maintained by the building of roads linking the garrison posts and trading towns. Besides the capital, *Ulpa Traiana*, important Roman towns included *Apulum* (Alba Iulia), *Napoca* (Cluj), *Drobeta* (Turnu Severin) and *Porolissum* (Zalău). For the **colonization of Dacia** (so rich and important a colony that it was known as *Dacia Felix* or Happy Dacia), settlers were brought from imperial territories as far afield as Greece and Spain and – on the evidence of shrines to Isis and Mithras – from Egypt and Persia. Later, the adoption of Christianity as the official religion led to its acceptance in Dacia, at least superficially; and in Hadrian's time the region was divided into two provinces to make its administration easier. With increasing incursions by nomadic Asian tribes such as the Goths in the third century, however, the defence of Dacia became too costly, and in 271 Emperor Aurelian ordered the withdrawal of Roman legions and administrators from the region.

THE AGE OF MIGRATIONS & DACO-ROMAN CONTINUITY

The Romans' departure was immediately followed by the arrival of other nomadic peoples sweeping out of Asia and on into western Europe during the **Age of Migrations**, including the Huns (4th and 5th centuries), Avars (6th century), Slavs (7th century) and Bulgars (7th century, along the coast en route to Bulgaria). The low-lying regions were greatly exposed to these invasions, whereas high mountains protected the region later to be called Transylvania. Excavations there have yielded coins bearing Roman inscriptions ranging from the time of Aurelian to the beginning of the fifth century, suggesting that the settlements continued to trade with the empire despite the Roman withdrawal – one of the arguments used to buttress the "Continuity Theory".

First propounded by Dimitri Cantemir (see below), and elaborated later in the eighteenth century to draw together the Moldavian and Wallachian peoples, and later the Transylvanians, the **Daco-Roman Continuity Theory** holds that the Romanian people descended from the Roman settlers and the indigenous Dacians, who interbred and formed a hybrid culture. Since the poorer colonists (as opposed to rich ones, officials and troops) were likely to have remained following the imperial withdrawal, this process of formation continued for longer than the relatively brief period of Roman occupation (about 160 years) would suggest, and thus had a lasting impact on the culture of the population. Documentary evidence for this is, not surprisingly, practically non-existent, but Romanian philologists point to numerous words in their language derived from Latin; in particular, terms refering to pastoral activities (the mainstay of the Dacian lifestyle) and Christian worship. While some Romanians boast loudly about their Roman heritage, however, many of the imperial settlers would have been not free Romans but former slaves and soldiers, many of them Greeks and Arabs.

The theory would be of academic interest only were it not entwined with the dispute, now centuries old, between the Magyars and Romanians over the **occupation of Transylvania**. By claiming this racial and cultural continuity, and their uninterrupted residence within the Carpathian redoubt, Romanians assert their original, rightful ownership of Transylvania, and dismiss their rivals as usurpers. Conversely, the Magyars (who had first passed through as just another Asiatic horde around 896 before settling in the Pannonian basin, now Hungary) claim that their occupation of the "land beyond the forest" (from about 997 to 1038) met little resistance, and that the indigenous people were of Slavic stock, Pechenegs and Cumans owing their loyalty to the Bulgars (who had actually managed to repel the next tribal wave coming from Asia, the Avars, and forged an empire that by 812 included all of Romania). According to Magyar historians, **Vlachs** (Romanians) are first mentioned in Transylvania around 1222, as groups of these nomadic pastoralists crossed the Carpathians, having wandered over the course of centuries from their original "homeland" in Macedonia and Illyria. This, together with other evidence (such as the Slavic rather than Latin derivation of the names of places and rivers), undermines the Romanian claim to prior occupation – or so Hungarian scholars argue.

THE MEDIEVAL PRINCIPALITIES

TRANSYLVANIA

Whatever the indigenous population's identity, István I (Saint Stephen) and later monarchs of the Árpád dynasty such as Geza II gradually extended **Hungarian rule over Transylvania**, using foreigners to bolster their own settlements around the Mureş and Someş rivers, which allowed the region's mineral wealth to be shipped west. Besides subduing local Cumans, Bulgars and Vlachs, the colonists had to withstand frequent invasions by the **Tartars** (or Mongols), nomadic warriors who devastated much of Eastern Europe in 1241–42 and over the next five centuries.

While the Teutonic Knights invited to colonize the Bîrsa Land (around Braşov) in 1211 were evicted in 1225 for defying Andrew II, other groups of Germans – subsequently known as **Saxons** – built up powerful market towns like *Hermannstadt* (Sibiu) and *Kronstadt* (Braşov), which were granted self-government as "seats" (*sedes* or *stuhle*). Another ethnic group, the **Székely**, acted as the vanguard of colonization, moving during the thirteenth century from their settlements in the Bihor region to the eastern marches, where they too were allowed relative autonomy.

Unlike the Székely, who originally held land in common and enjoyed "noble" status, the Hungarians in Transylvania were either classed as plebs liable to all manner of dues and taxes, or as members of the tax-exempt nobility. This group dominated **the feudal system**, being represented alongside the Saxon and Székely "nations" (*Natio*) on the Diet which advised the principality's military and civil leader, the **Voivode**, who acted for the Hungarian king. During the Árpád dynasty, Diets included *knezes* drawn from the Romanian-speaking Vlachs who, even then, may have constituted the majority of Transylvania's population. From the mid-fourteenth century onwards, however, Vlachs faced increasing **discrimination**, being gradually excluded from areas inhabited by Saxons or Magyars, and barred from public office. Besides the mistrust sown by Bogdan Vodă's rebellion in Maramureş (see below),

religion played an important part in this process. Whereas the Vlachs were Orthodox (barring a few apostate nobles), the other communities adhered to the Catholic church, which sought to undermine Orthodoxy throughout the Balkans. Over time, these divisions of class, race and religion coalesced into a kind of medieval apartheid system, which was to bedevil Transylvania's inhabitants for centuries to come.

WALLACHIA AND DOBROGEA

On the far side of the Carpathians, fully fledged principalities emerged somewhat later. Chronicles attribute the foundation of **Wallachia** (Vlahia or the *Ţara Românéasca*) to Negru Vodă (known as Basarab I), who made Cîmpulung its first capital in 1290 and beat off the Hungarians at the battle of Posada in 1330; but some confusion exists as to whether they refer to his fourteenth-century successor Radu Negru, who consolidated princely power and likewise belonged to the Basarab dynasty. The shift in Wallachia's capitals over the centuries – from Cîmpulung in the highlands down to Curtea de Argeş and Tîrgovişte in the foothills and then Bucharest on the plain – expressed a cautious emergence from the safety of the mountains. Oppression, anarchy and piety were commonplace: the tithes and *robot* squeezed from the enserfed masses allowed the land-owning **boyars** to pursue their favourite occupations – endowing Orthodox churches and engineering coups against the ruling voivodes. In centuries to come, the average duration of their reigns dropped to less than three years.

Important trade routes linking Poland with the Black Sea passed through Wallachia, but commerce was entirely in the hands of Germans, Poles, Greeks and Jews. Though lavishly endowed, Wallachia's **Orthodox church** was subordinated to the Bulgarian and Byzantine patriarchates, writing its scriptures and conducting its rituals in Old Slavonic rather than the vernacular tongue. This was in part a legacy of Bulgar rule during the eighth and ninth centuries, but also reflected the policy of Wallachia's rulers, who tended to look south across the Danube for allies against the powerful kingdom of Hungary. These allies themselves faced a dangerous threat in the expansionist Ottoman Turks, and were soon to be wiped from the map for centuries.

MOLDAVIA AND BESSARABIA

From Maramureş, where attempts to enforce Hungarian rule provoked resistance amongst the indigenous population, communities followed the rebel leader **Bogdan Vodă** over the Carpathians in 1359. Their settlements around the headwaters of the Moldova were the cradle of a new principality, **Moldavia**, which emerged in the 1360s; but the process of occupying the hills and steppes beyond the Carpathians had begun centuries earlier, more or less spontaneously. Groups of Romanian-speaking pastoralists and farmers gradually crossed the River Prut, moving on to the Dnestr where they encountered Ukrainians who called them "Volokhi". The Moldavian capital gradually shifted eastwards from Rădăuţi to Suceava, and then southwards to Iaşi when safety permitted. **Alexander the Good** (Alexandre cel Bun; 1400–32) may have gained his honorary title by ousting Turks from the eastern marches, though it could well have been bestowed by the Basarab family whom he made feudal lords of the region subsequently known as **Bessarabia**; or retrospectively by Moldavia's peasantry who suffered during the prolonged, violent anarchy that followed Alexandru's death. Besides Tartar invasions and rebellious boyars, Moldavia faced the threat of ambitious neighbouring powers – the kingdoms of Hungary and Poland on the western and northern borders, and the growing menace of the Turks to the south.

OTTOMANS, NATIONES AND PHANARIOTS

From the mid-fourteenth century onwards, the fate of the Balkan countries was determined by the **Ottoman empire** of the Seljuk Turks, which spread inexorably northwards, inflicting a shattering defeat on Serbia at Kosovo in 1389 and finally subjugating Bulgaria in 1393. Being preoccupied with digesting these gains, the Ottomans accepted a huge payment from **Mircea the Old** (Mircea cel Bătrîn; 1386–1418) in return for ceasing their rampage through Wallachia in 1395. Appeals to the Pope and the Holy Roman Emperor Sigismund, King of Hungary and Bohemia, led to the dispatch of a crusading army, which through its own folly was crushed at Nicopolis on the Danube in 1396. This and subsequent Christian defeats

left the Turks entrenched along the lower Danube, compelling Mircea to acknowledge Ottoman suzerainty in 1417. By surrendering the fertile **Dobrogea** region and paying tribute, outright occupation was avoided and Wallachia's ruling class retained their positions; but henceforth both rulers and ruled were confronted with the alternatives of submission or resistance to an overwhelming force.

Even before the fall of Constantinople in 1453, Wallachia, Moldavia and Transylvania had become Christendom's front line of **resistance to the Turks**, and indeed, with Russia, the only Orthodox Christian states remaining free. Throughout the fifteenth century, the principalities' history is overshadowed by this struggle and the names of their military leaders. The Transylvanian voivode **Iancu de Hunedoara** (János Hunyadi) defeated the Turks near Alba Iulia and Sibiu in 1441–42, before becoming regent of Hungary in 1446 and leading multinational armies to victory at Niş and Belgrade, where he died of a fever in 1456. Iancu's son **Mátyás Corvinus** (1458–90, also known as Hunyadi Mátyás or Matei Corvin) became Hungary's great Renaissance king and continued to resist the Turks. Conflicting Polish and Hungarian ambitions periodically caused fighting between the principalities, whose rulers were as likely to betray each other as to collaborate, while the Sultans' willingness to accept tribute and appeasement allowed sporadic truces, and a particularly peaceful interlude under Neagoe Basarab of Wallachia (1512–21). The Ottomans were dislodged from southern Bessarabia by **Stephen the Great** (Ştefan cel Mare) of Moldavia and temporarily checked by the fortresses of Chilia and Cetatea Alba (now deep in Ukraine), but their resurgence under Bajazid II, and peace treaties signed with the Turks by Poland, Hungary and Venice in the 1470s and 1480s, presaged the demise of Moldavian independence, as was apparent to Stephen by the end of his embattled reign (1457–1504). Due to Wallachia's greater vulnerablity, its rulers generally preferred to pay off the Turks rather than resist them; **Vlad Ţepeş** (The Impaler – see p.346) being a notable exception from 1456 until his death in 1476.

In **Transylvania**, the least exposed region, the **Bobîlna peasant uprising** of 1437, under Antal Budai Nagy, rocked the feudal order. To safeguard their privileges, the Magyar nobility concluded a pact known as the **Union of Three Nations** with the Saxon and Székely leaders, whereby each party or *Natio* agreed to recognize and defend the rights of the others. As a consequence, the Vlachs were relegated to the position of "those who do not possess the right of citizenship. . .but are merely tolerated by grace", and a spate of decrees followed, effectively prohibiting them from holding public office or residing in the Saxon and Magyar towns. The increasing exploitation of the Magyar peasantry led to another uprising under György Dózsa in 1514, savagely repressed by voivode **János Zápolyai** (1510–40), who imposed the onerous *Werbőczy Code* or *Tripartium*, in 1517. This feudal version of apartheid was reinforced during the sixteenth century when Transylvania became a stronghold of the **religious reformation**. While the *Nationes* averted sectarian strife by decreeing equal rights in 1556 for the Calvinist, Lutheran, Catholic and Unitarian faiths to which their members subscribed, both the Edict of Turda (1568) and the Diet of 1571 merely tolerated the existence of Orthodoxy, the religion of the Vlach population.

The crushing defeat of Hungary by Suleyman the Magnificent at **Mohács** (1526) and the Turkish occupation of Buda (1541) exacerbated the **isolation of the principalities**. Although the Hapsburg dynasty of Austria laid claim to what was left of Hungary after Mohács, Zápolyai managed to play them off against the Ottomans, and thus maintain a precarious autonomy for Transylvania, even gaining control of Hungary east of the River Tisza (the *Partium*) in 1538; and successors such as István Báthori (1571–81, who was elected King of Poland from 1575 and drove back Ivan the Terrible), and Zsigmond Báthori (1581–97) were able to maintain this independence. In **Moldavia**, however, **Petru Rareş** could only hold his throne (1527–38 and 1541–56) by breathtaking duplicity and improvisations, while his successors plumbed even further depths.

SHORT-LIVED UNIFICATION

Understandably, Romanian historiography has scant regard for such figures, and prefers to highlight the achievements of **Michael the Brave** (Mihai Viteazul, often known in Wallachia as Mihai Bravul). Crowned ruler of Wallachia by the boyars in 1593, his triumphs against the Turks in 1595 were followed by the overthrow of Andrew Báthori in Transylvania in 1599 and a lightning campaign across the Carpathians in 1600 to secure him the Moldavian throne. This opportunist and short-lived **union of the principalities** under one crown – which fragmented immediately following his murder in 1601 – has subsequently been presented as a triumph of Romanian nationalism, and evidence suggests that the Vlachs in Transylvania welcomed Mihai as a liberator. However, although he improved the status of the Vlach nobles and the Orthodox church in Transylvania, he did nothing for the serfs, and the *Nationes* kept their privileges.

Between 1604 and 1657 Transylvania attained genuine independence from the Hapsburgs and Ottomans, although the region was rarely at peace. István Bocskai (1604–06) pushed its border westwards, and "Crazy" Gábor Báthori (1608–13) promoted himself to prince and pursued a vendetta against the Saxon towns until overthrown by **Gábor Bethlen**, whose encouragement of cultural and economic development and resistance to the tide of counter-Reformation made his reign (1613–29) a golden age by most standards.

From the 1630s onwards, **Moldavia and Wallachia** avoided direct occupation as Turkish *pashaliks* by accepting Ottoman "advisers". These Greek families – the Ghicas, Cantacuzinos, Rosettis, Ducas and others – originated from the Phanar district of Constantinople, and hence collectively became known as the **Phanariots**. In Moldavia, they encouraged the Orthodox church to abandon **Old Slavonic** as the language of the scriptures and ritual in favour of Greek; but this policy had the unintended result of stimulating a move towards the Romanian language, using books printed at Govora and Iaşi. This presaged a minor cultural renaissance – particularly in the field of architecture – during a period of relative stability provided by the reigns of **Matei Basarab** (1633–54), **Şerban Cantacuzino** (1678–88), **Constantin Brîncoveanu** (1688–1714) in Wallachia and **Dimitri Cantemir** (1710–11) in Moldavia. After brutally terminating the reigns of the last two, the Turks dispensed with native rulers, and began appointing **Phanariot princes** instead. These were purely concerned with plundering the principalities to pay the huge bribes necessary to remain in good standing at court, and enrich themselves before relinquishing what was essentially a franchise to make money, and returning home. Their rapaciousness and more than seventy changes of ruler in Moldavia and Wallachia between 1711 and 1821 beggared both regions, and gave rise to the proverb that "madmen rejoice when the rulers change".

THE STRUGGLE FOR INDEPENDENCE & UNIFICATION

From 1683, when the siege of Vienna was broken, the alliance of Christian powers known as the "Holy League" succeeded in **driving the Turks out of Hungary**, Croatia and Slavonia; in 1686 Budapest was retaken, in 1687 the second battle of Mohács reversed the result of the first encounter, in 1688 Belgrade was retaken, and in 1691 the battle of Slankamen established the frontier along the line of the Danube and Sava Rivers, and thus **Hapsburg control of Transylvania**. In 1697 the great general Prince Eugen of Savoy took command of the Hapsburg forces, and in the Treaty of Karlowitz of 1699 the Turks accepted their claims to all of Transylvania except for the Banat of Temesvár. The Turks attempted a comeback in 1714, but were finally driven from Hungary and the Banat in 1718. Thereafter, the **decline of Ottoman power** in the Balkans continued, and while nationalist movements struggled to free their countries during the nineteenth century, the main European powers became increasingly preoccupied with the "**Eastern question**" – which of them should inherit the Ottomans' influence? Foreign interests were generally entangled with local ones, so that the principalities' internal conflicts between the old nobility, the bourgeoisie and the peasantry could have repercussions on an international level, and vice versa.

This first became apparent in **Transylvania**, where Hapsburg recognition of the privileged "three Nations and four religions" – as established by the *Leopoldine Diploma* of 1691 – was followed by attempts to undermine this status quo, principally directed against the Hungarian nobility. As Catholics and imperialists, the Hapsburg monarchy persuaded the Orthodox clergy in Transylvania to accept papal authority, and promised that Vlachs who joined the **Uniate Church** (see p.153) would be granted equality with the *Nationes*. Although the Diet's opposition ensured the retraction of this promise in 1701, Bishop Ioan Inocenţiu Micu and the intellectuals of the "Transylvanian School" (*Şcoala Ardealana*) agitated for equal rights and articulated the Vlachs' growing consciousness of being **Romanians**. By far the largest ethnic group, they now began to assert their "original claim" on Transylvania and solidarity with their kinsfolk across the Carpathians. The future Joseph II toured Transylvania incognito and begged his mother, the Empress Maria Teresa (1740–80), to protect the Romanians from discrimination. In 1781 he issued an edict of religious toleration before dissolving the monasteries and embarking upon the abolition of serfdom. All this came too late, however, to prevent the great peasant rebellion led by **Horea, Crişan and Cloşca** in 1784–85. Its crushing only stimulated efforts to attain liberation by constitutional means – such as the famous *Supplex Libellus Valachorum* petition of 1791, which was approved by the emperor but predictably rejected by the Transylvanian Diet.

The gradual development of liberal and nationalist movements in **Moldavia and Wallachia** stemmed from a variety of causes. The ideals of the Romantic movement and the French Revolution gained hold amongst the intelligentsia and many young boyars, while the success of Serbian and Greek independence movements and the emergence of capitalist structures in the principalities showed that Turkish dominance and feudalism were in decline. A rebellion in support of the Greek independence struggle organized by the Phanariot Alexandre Ypsilanti attracted little following within Moldavia, but the example inspired a major uprising against Phanariot rule in Wallachia in 1821, led by **Tudor Vladimirescu**. Although defeated, this uprising persuaded the Turks that it was high time for the **end of Phanariot rule** in 1824, and the restoration of power to native boyars.

THE RISE OF RUSSIA AND WORLD WAR I

As the power of the Ottomans declined, that of **Tsarist Russia** grew. Fired by imperialist and Panslavist ideals and fear of Hapsburg encroachment (manifest in 1774, when Austria annexed the region henceforth known as **Bucovina**), Russia presented itself in 1779 as the guardian of the Ottomans' Christian subjects, and expanded its territories towards the Balkans as well as into the Caucasus and Central Asia. In 1792 Russian forces reached the River Dnestr; one Russo-Turkish war led to the annexation of Bessarabia in 1812, and another to the Treaty of Adrianople (1829), by which Moldavia and Wallachia became Russian protectorates. The Tsarist governor **General Kiseleff** was in no sense a revolutionary, but he introduced liberal reforms and assemblies in both principalities under the terms of the *Règlement organique*, which remained in force after the Russians withdrew in 1834, having selected two rulers. Of these, Michael Sturdza in Moldavia was the more despotic but also the more energetic, levying heavy taxes to construct roads, dikes, hospitals and schools.

Given the boyars' dominance of the assemblies, economic development took precedence over the political and social reforms demanded by sections of the liberal bourgeoisie, particularly the growing number of Romanians who had studied in France. The **democratic movement** which emerged in both principalities – led by **Nicolae Golescu, Ion Brătianu, Nicolae Bălcescu and Mihail Kogălniceanu** – campaigned against the *Règlement* and for the unification of Moldavia and Wallachia, which was anticipated by the removal of customs barriers between the two in 1846. These movements briefly came to power in 1848, the **Year of Revolutions**, which heightened nationalist consciousness in the principalities and amongst the Romanians of Transylvania (see below).

Armed intervention by Russia, now claiming to be "the gendarme of Europe", restored the status quo ante; the Congress of Paris, ending the Crimean War in 1856, reaffirmed Turkish rule, although Russia was obliged to return part of Bessarabia to Moldavia. Thus the nationalist cause was thwarted until January 1859, when the assemblies of Moldavia and Wallachia were persuaded to elect a single ruler, **Alexandru Ioan Cuza**, thereby circumventing the restrictions imposed to prevent their **unification**. French support enabled the United Principalities (renamed Rumania in 1862) to weather Hapsburg hostility, and the govern-

ment embarked on a series of reforms, the most important of which were the **abolition of serfdom** and the expropriation of the huge monastic estates. Although the peasants were still bound to pay for the land "given" to them (and, as a result, fell into greater debt than before), these measures enraged the landowning classes and other conservative elements, who forced Cuza's abdication in 1866. They selected the German Prince Karl of Hohenzollern to become Prince Carol I, and a fully-fledged king in 1881. In 1877 yet another Russo-Turkish war broke out, and Carol personally led a Romanian army into Bulgaria to help the Russians, suffering huge losses in taking Pleven and the Shipka Pass; as a result the Treaty of Berlin, ending the war in 1878, forced Turkey to recognize **Romanian independence** (declared on May 9, 1877) and to cede Northern Dobrogea to Romania (then known as Rumania).

Events in **Transylvania** followed a different course during the nineteenth century. There, popular support for the 1848 revolution split along nationalist lines. Whereas the abolition of serfdom was universally welcomed by the peasantry, the Romanian population opposed the Diet's unification of Transylvania with Hungary, which Magyars of all classes greeted with enthusiasm; the Saxons were lukewarm on both issues. Following protest meetings at Blaj, **Avram Iancu** formed Romanian guerilla bands to oppose the Hungarians; belated attempts by Kossuth and Bălcescu to compromise on the issue of Romanian rights came too late to create a united front against the Tsarist armies which invaded Transylvania on behalf of the Hapsburgs. As in Hungary, the Hapsburgs introduced martial law and widespread repression in the aftermath of the revolution.

As a result of the *Ausgleich* or Compromise of 1867 which established the Dual Monarchy of the Austro-Hungarian Empire, the Transylvanian Diet was abolished and the region became part of "Greater Hungary", ruled directly from Budapest. The governments of **Kalman Tisza** (1875–90) and his successors pursued a policy of **"Magyarization"** in Transylvania, as in Slovakia and elsewhere, although Bucovina and Maramureş remained under Austrian rule and avoided the worst of this. Laws passed in 1879 and 1883 made Hungarian the official language, and a barrage of laws relating to education and the press were passed in an effort to undermine Romanian culture. The cultural association **ASTRA**, founded in 1861, acted in its defence until the establishment of the **National Party** in 1881, which maintained close links with kindred parties across the Carpathians.

The influence of foreign capitalism increased enormously around the turn of the century, as Rumania's mineral wealth – particularly its oil – inspired competition amongst the great powers. While liberal and conservative politicians engaged in ritualistic parliamentary squabbles, however, nothing was done about the worsening impoverishment of the people. Peasant grievances exploded in the **răscoala** of 1907 – a nationwide uprising which was savagely crushed (with at least 10,000 deaths) and then followed by a series of limited, ineffectual agrarian reforms.

Rumania's acquisition of territory south of the Danube in 1878 was one of the many bones of contention underlying the **Balkan Wars** that embroiled Rumania, Bulgaria, Serbia, Macedonia and Greece. Rumania sat out the first Balkan War (1912–13), but joined the alliance against Bulgaria in 1913 and gained the southern part of Dobrogea. King Carol signed a secret pact with the Central Powers; however he died in 1914 and was succeeded by his nephew Ferdinand, married to the Duke of Edinburgh's daughter, Marie. Thus when Rumania entered **World War I** in August 1916, it joined the Triple Entente and attacked the Austro-Hungarian forces in Transylvania. After brief advances, the tide turned against Rumania, as Bulgarian and German forces crossed the Danube and captured all of Wallachia (including Bucharest) and much of Moldavia; desperate defence at Mărăşti, Mărăşeşti and the Oituz Pass, aided by French, Russian and even British advisors, finally averted total collapse, but the demise of Russia forced Rumania to sign an onerous peace treaty in May 1918. By October, however, the collapse of the Central Powers on the Western Front reversed this situation entirely. The Austro-Hungarian empire rapidly fragmented as its subject races established their own states with the support of the Entente and President Woodrow Wilson: Rumanian armies advanced into Transylvania, and then on into Hungary to overthrow the short-lived communist régime of Béla Kun in August 1919. On December 1, 1918 the Romanian assembly of Alba Iulia declared **Transylvania's union with Rumania** to scenes of wild acclaim. The Romanian population of Bessarabia, set free by the Russian Revolution, had already declared their union with Rumania in March 1918, followed in November by Bucovina.

Despite furious opposition, above all from the Hungarians, this was subsequently upheld by the Entente powers and the **Treaty of Trianon** in 1920, as a reward both for fighting on the "right side" (the winning side) in the war and for being such a firm bulwark against Bolshevism. Rumania doubled both in population and territory, while Hungary lost half of its population and two thirds of its territory, the source of great resentment ever since. The "successor states" of Rumania, Czechoslovakia and Yugoslavia formed the "Little Entente", defensive alliances against Hungarian revanchism, cemented by a Franco-Rumanian treaty in 1926.

"GREATER ROMANIA" (1921–44)

The country's enlarged territory was dignified by the adoption of the name **Greater Romania**, but the lives of the mass of the population hardly improved. The expropriation of Hungarian estates in Transylvania affected not only the nobility, but smallholders as well; Hungarian employees, no matter how lowly, of the rail lines, the post office, or any government body were dismissed on such a scale that Romanian immigrants had to be brought in from Moldavia and Wallachia. Equally the many peasants who expected to benefit from the **agrarian reform** of 1921 were rapidly disillusioned when speculators and boyars appropriated much of the land by financial manipulation.

Romania was governed by the **National Liberal Party**, favoured by King Ferdinand, but soon standing for little except holding on to power for its own sake: it pursued nationalist and populist policies, damaging the economy by discriminating against foreign investors. On Ferdinand's death in 1927, they were dismissed and replaced by the National Peasant Party, which in 1928 won the only remotely fair election in this period. Despite its parliamentary majority and its genuinely reforming and honest policies, the National Peasant government, led by **Iuliu Maniu**, pursued conservative policies, constrained by falling demand for Romanian exports following the world economic crisis of 1929, vested interests and entrenched corruption.

However it was a bizarre moral issue that led to the government's fall: in 1930, after a three-year regency, **Carol II** came to the throne and at once broke a promise to put aside his divorced Jewish mistress, Magda Lupescu. The puritan Maniu resigned and the government fell apart. Carol exploited the constitution of 1923, giving the king the right to dissolve parliament and call elections at will; a totally corrupt system soon developed whereby the government would fix elections by every means possible, only to be dismissed and replaced by the opposition when the king had tired of them. Between 1930 and 1940 there were no less than twenty-five separate governments, leading to the collapse of the political parties themselves. Strikes in the oil and rail industries in 1933 were put down by armed force; Carol set up his own "youth movement", and soon began routine phone-tapping by the *siguranţa*, the *Securitate*'s predecessor.

THE IRON GUARD AND WORLD WAR II

A **fascist movement** also established itself, particularly in Bessarabia, which had a long tradition of anti-Semitism. The main fascist party was the Legion of the Archangel Michael, founded in 1927 and known from 1929 as the **Iron Guard**, which inherited much of the National Peasant Party's rural support. The green-shirted Legionaries extolled the soil, death and a mystical form of Orthodoxy, and fought street battles against Jews and followers of other political parties, as well as murdering four current or former prime ministers. In 1937 the anti-Semitic National League of Christian Defence was installed in power by the king, but the prime minister, the poet Octavian Goga (see p.191), at once insulted Lupescu and was dismissed in February 1938, after just six weeks in power. This at last provoked Carol to ban all political parties (other than his own National Renaissance Front) and set up a royal dictatorship (soon to be endorsed by a fixed plebiscite); the Legionary leader **Corneliu Codreanu** was killed in November "while trying to escape".

Carol did not want to be driven into the arms of Hitler, desperately seeking closer economic ties with the West. However it was too late; in February 1939 Germany demanded a monopoly of Romanian exports in return for a guarantee of its borders, and in March agreed an oil-for-arms deal. In April, Carol obtained feeble guarantees from Britain and France, but in August the equilibrium was shattered by the Nazi-Soviet Non-Aggression Pact. In June 1940 a Soviet ultimatum led to the annexation of Bessarabia and northern Bucovina, and, two months later, Hitler forced Carol to cede Northern Transylvania to Germany's ally, Hungary, and southern Dobrogea to Bulgaria. On September 6, unable to maintain his position after giving away such huge portions of Romanian territory, Carol fled with Lupescu and his spoils, leaving his son **Mihai**, then nineteen years old, to take over the throne.

Mihai accepted the formation of a Legionary government, led by Codreanu's successor Horia Sima and by **Marshal Ion Antonescu**, who styled himself *Conducator* ("leader", equivalent to *Führer*) but had little influence over local legionary groups who unleashed an orgy of violence against Jews and liberals. To ensure himself a stable and productive ally, Hitler forced Antonescu to curb the Iron Guard; he began to disarm it, provoking an armed uprising (and the savage butchery of two hundred Jews in Bucharest) in January 1941, only suppressed by the army after a fierce struggle.

Romania entered **World War II** in June 1941, joining the Nazi invasion of Russia, with the objective of regaining Bessarabia and northern Bucovina. Romanian troops took Odessa and joined in the attacks on Sevastopol and Stalingrad, taking heavy casualties. Jews and Gypsies in Bessarabia, Bucovina and the Hungarian-controlled area of Transylvania were rounded up and deported for slave labour and then to extermination camps. By 1943, however, the Red Army was advancing fast, and Antonescu began to look for a way to abandon Hitler and change sides. Opposition to the war mounted as the Russians drew nearer, and on August 23, 1944 a **royal/military coup** overthrew the Antonescu regime just as they crossed the border – a date commemorated until 1989 as Liberation Day, although it took until October 25 to clear the Germans from the country.

THE HOLOCAUST IN ROMANIA

In 1939 Romania had the third greatest **Jewish population** in Europe after Poland and the Soviet Union. Most lived in Bessarabia, Bucovina and parts of northern Moldavia, notably around Dorohoi. Bessarabia and northern Bucovina were ceded to the Soviet Union in June 1940, as demanded by Hitler, and at least fifty Jews were killed in Dorohoi by retreating Romanian troops. On June 22, 1941, Romania declared war on the Soviet Union, but action did not commence on this front until July 3, so the troops filled the interval by carrying out an awful pogrom in Iaşi, killing about 8000 Jews. As the army advanced (with units of the German *Einsatzgruppe D* following), there were many more massacres; at least 33,000 Jews died in Bessarabia and Bucovina between June 22 and September 1, 1941.

Deportations to Transnistria, the conquered territory beyond the River Dnestr, began in earnest on September 16; in addition to the atrocities in the camps, 18,000 to 22,000 died in transit. Between November 21 and 29, 1941 all 48,000 Jews held in the Bogdanovka camp in southern Transnistria were killed; another 18,000 were killed in the Dumanovka camp.

In July 1942, the Germans began to press hard for the Jews of Wallachia, Moldavia and southern Transylvania to be deported to the camps, following those of Hungarian-controlled Northern Transylvania. This was agreed but then refused after lobbying by neutral diplomats and the Papal Nuncio, although it was probably due to the fact that the Jews were still vital to the functioning of the economy. In November 1942 it was agreed that Romanian Jews in Germany should be sent to the German death camps.

By November 1942, when the Allies launched their attack at El Alamein and the Operation Torch landings in North Africa, and it was likely that Stalingrad would be held by the Soviets, Romania was thinking of changing sides. The **World Jewish Congress** (in Geneva) proposed a **plan** to save 70,000 Romanian Jews, and possibly 1.3 million more in Eastern Europe, by paying the Romanian government twelve shillings per head to allow them to leave by ship for Palestine. This was blocked by opposition from anti-Semites in the US State Department and from Britain, worried about the reaction of Arabs to further Jewish immigration to Palestine, as well as by the practical problems inherent in sending money to a Nazi ally. Thirteen boats did leave, with 13,000 refugees, but two sank (with 1,163 on board) and others were stopped by Turkey, under pressure from both Britain and Germany.

In 1944, Antonescu, negotiating secretly in Stockholm for an exit from the war, began a **limited repatriation** from the camps of Transnistria, bringing back 1500 in December 1943 and 1846 orphans by March 1944. He warned the Germans not to kill Jews as they retreated; nevertheless a final thousand Jews were killed in Tiraspol jail. On March 20, 1944 the Red Army reached the Dnestr, and the worst of the nightmare ended. In Antonescu's trial in May 1946 it was said, "if the Jews of Romania are still alive, they owe it to Marshal Antonescu", who claimed to have saved about 275,000 Jews by his policy of keeping them for extermination at home. Overall between 264,900 and 470,000 Romanian Jews, and 36,000 Gypsies died in the war; 428,000 Jews survived or returned alive.

THE PEOPLE'S REPUBLIC (1944–65)

While the Romanian army subordinated itself to Soviet command, and fought alongside the Red Army to push the Nazis out of Transylvania, Hungary and Czechoslovakia, the struggle to determine the state of **post-war Romania** was already under way. The Yalta agreement put Romania firmly within the Soviet sphere, but the Western powers maintained observers in Bucharest, requiring a veneer of democratic process. The first government formed by King Mihai was a broad coalition, with communists only playing a minor role, but gradually, due largely to the presence of the Red Army and

veiled threats of annexation, the communists and their fellow-travellers, such as the Ploughmen's Front, increased their influence. In March 1945, a new coalition was installed under the premiership of **Dr. Petru Groza** (leader of the Ploughmen's Front); again this included politicians from the pre-war parties as a sop to conservative opinion and the West, but the key posts were occupied by **communists**. The land reform of 1945 benefited millions of peasants at the expense of the Saxons and Swabians of Transylvania and the Banat, who had become the biggest landowners since the dispossession of the Magyars, while women were enfranchised for the first time in 1946, their votes supposedly contributing to the election of another ostensibly "balanced" government. In fact, while virtually every device ever used to rig an election was brought into play, it seems that the communists and their allies only received about 20 percent of the votes: nevertheless it was announced that they had received almost 80 percent, and the takeover steamed on regardless.

Like Groza's first administration, this included leading capitalists and former Guardists, whom the communists initially wooed, since their first aim was to eliminate the left and centre parties. The leadership of the National Peasant Party played into their hands by secretly meeting US officials, enabling them to be disposed of on espionage charges in 1947, while other parties were forcibly merged with the communists. On December 30, 1947 **King Mihai was forced to abdicate** and Romania was declared a **People's Republic**.

Antonescu and up to 60,000 others were executed after highly irregular trials in 1946 and 1947. Eighty thousand arrests followed in an effort to overcome peasant resistance to **collectivization** (a reversal of the earlier agrarian reform), with many more in the simultaneous campaign to "liquidate" the Uniate Church. The **nationalization** of industries, banks and utilities in June 1948 placed the main economic levers in communist hands; thereafter the bourgeoisie was assailed on all fronts, and the Party openly declared its intention to reshape society by applying Stalinist policies. While vital sectors of the proletariat were favoured to secure their loyalty, **police terror** was used against real or potential opponents, with victims incarcerated in prisons like Jilava and Piteşti, or conscripted for reed-cutting in the Delta or work on the Danube–Black Sea Canal, the "Canal Mortii" which claimed over 100,000 lives before being abandoned in 1953.

The communist party itself was split by bitter conflicts between its "Muscovite" wing (those who had spent the war in Moscow, led by Ana Pauker and Vasile Luca) and the "nationalists", themselves split between the "prison-communists" and the "secretariat-communists", who had remained free and in hiding. In 1952 the prison-communists emerged on top, under **Gheorghe Gheorghiu-Dej**, General Secretary of the party's Central Committee since 1948, who had retained

Stalin's confidence largely because the secretariat group were too ideologically flexible, while Pauker and her group were simply too Jewish. The purging of 192,000 members was however quickly followed by Stalin's death in 1953: Gheorghiu-Dej took great exception to reformist trends in the USSR, and stuck grimly to the Stalinist true faith. Disagreeing with the role of "breadbasket" assigned to the country by the Eastern bloc trade organization, Comecon, he followed a Stalinist policy of developing heavy industry, claiming the impossible growth rate of 13 percent per year.

The USSR, having annexed Bessarabia once more, had given parts of it to Ukraine and created the puppet **republic of Moldova** from the rest. Therefore Gheorghiu-Dej's increasing refusal to follow the Moscow line was a great success domestically, tapping into a vein of popular nationalism that was exploited more systematically by Ceauşescu, his successor. By arresting the leadership of the left-wing Hungarian People's Alliance and establishing an "Autonomous Hungarian Region" in the Székely Land in 1952, Gheorghiu-Dej simultaneously decapitated the Magyar political organization in Transylvania while erecting a facade of minority rights.

In March 1965 Gheorghiu-Dej died, and was soon succeeded by **Nicolae Ceauşescu**, until then a little-known party hack, who was able by 1969 to out-manoeuvre his rivals in the collective leadership and establish undisputed power.

"YEARS OF LIGHT": THE CEAUŞESCU ERA

There seems little doubt that for the first few years of his rule, Ceauşescu was **genuinely popular**, and might even have been able to win an election: he encouraged a cultural thaw, put food and consumer goods into the shops, denounced security police excesses (blaming them on Gheorghiu-Dej), and above all denounced the Warsaw Pact invasion of Czechoslovakia in 1968. His **independent foreign policy** gained Romania the reputation of being the "maverick" state of the Eastern bloc, maintaining links with Albania, China and Israel after the USSR and its satellites had severed relations, building links with West Germany, criticizing the invasion of Afghanistan in 1979, and defying the Soviet boycott by sending a team to the Los Angeles Olympics in 1984.

Rewards included state visits to Britain and the USA, admittance to the GATT, IMF and World Bank, and trade deals with the EC and USA.

However he soon reverted to tried and tested methods of control as the shops emptied again and his **economic failure** became obvious. Ceauşescu stuck throughout to the Stalinist belief in heavy industry, and throughout the 1970s the country's **industrialization programme** absorbed 30 percent of GNP, and $10,200m in foreign loans. Because quality was always inadequate, little could be exported, but Ceauşescu became obsessed in the 1980s with the need to repay Western loans. Living standards plummeted as all but a minimal amount of food was exported, and the population was obliged to work harder and harder for less and less. Amazingly, all the foreign debt was repaid by 1989, although there was no prospect of any improvement in living standards thereafter.

Ceauşescu was convinced that the key to industrial growth lay in **building a larger workforce**, and therefore as early as 1966 he banned abortions and contraception for any married woman under 40 with less than four children (in 1972 the limits were raised to 45 and five). It was only in the 1980s, when developing paranoia and his personality cult put him increasingly out of touch with ordinary people, that he introduced the "**Baby Police**" and compulsory gynecological examinations, to ensure that women were not trying to avoid their "patriotic duty". Unmarried people and married couples without children were penalized by higher taxes. Ceauşescu also **discriminated against the minorities**, trying to persuade them to assimilate with the Romanian populace; it became increasingly hard to get an education or to buy books in Hungarian or German, or to communicate with relatives abroad, while families were pressured to give their children Romanian names.

The two million-plus Magyars (including the Székely and Csángós) bore the brunt of this chauvinism, causing a notable worsening of diplomatic relations with Hungary. Neither this nor criticism of the treatment of the Gypsy population worried Ceauşescu, but he tried to keep on the right side of the German and Israeli governments, which purchased exit visas for ethnic Germans and Jews in Romania for substantial sums in hard currencies.

There were other equally appalling **abuses of human rights**, all of which got worse through the 1980s: the **systematization** programme for rural redevelopment, censorship, the "typewriter law" (requiring that every machine be registered with the police) and the constant repression of the **Securitate** or secret police, which produced an atmosphere of ubiquitous fear and distrust even between members of the same family, as up to one in four of the population was rumoured to be an informer, and virtually every home was supposed to be bugged. Increasingly, key posts were allocated to relatives of the Ceauşescus, while all other senior figures were rotated every few years between jobs and between Bucharest and the provinces, to prevent anyone building up an independent powerbase and being able to challenge for power.

In the **1980s** everything went downhill rapidly, as Ceauşescu was insulated by his subordinates from the truth about the country's economic collapse. Food, electricity, lightbulbs, everything was in short supply, but Ceauşescu and Elena pushed on with megalomaniac projects such as the Palace of the People in Bucharest, the Danube–Black Sea Canal (again) and the village systematization programme. Just as Gheorghiu-Dej had rejected Moscow's policy changes after Stalin's death, so too Ceauşescu made plain his opposition to *glasnost*, and it began to be rumoured that Gorbachev would be glad to be rid of the increasingly erratic Romanian leader.

Throughout 1987 there were muffled reports of student strikes, and in November food and heating shortages and the introduction of a seven-day week at the Red Flag tractor factory in Braşov led to unexpected **anti-Ceauşescu riots**. Silviu Brucan, ambassador to the United Nations and United States from 1956–62, and others then issued a statement to the Western press warning that "the cup of privation is now full and the workers no longer accept that they can be treated like obedient servants". Again in March 1989 they wrote an open letter to Ceauşescu, urging an end to systematization and human rights abuses. Ceauşescu's response was to send them into internal exile and rush food and *Securitate* to the cities. At the Party congress of November 1989 he rejected any change in economic or social policies and was re-elected unanimously, as usual.

THE REVOLUTION

By **December 1989** the situation in Romania was so desperate that it seemed impossible for Ceauşescu not to bow to the **wave of change** that had swept over the whole of Eastern Europe: yet he refused to even acknowledge its existence, beyond being convinced that Gorbachev and Bush were conspiring to remove him from power. Indeed most observers felt that change would not come until Ceauşescu had died, an event expected sooner rather than later.

However, the people of Romania were aware of events in the other countries of East-Central Europe, thanks to the BBC and Radio Free Europe. The people of **Timişoara** could receive Hungarian and Yugoslav television and radio as well, and it was here that the forces of change finally broke loose. A turbulent priest of the Hungarian Calvinist church, **Lászlo Tökes**, had become such a thorn in the establishment's side that he was to be forcibly removed from Timişoara to a tiny village in the back of beyond; the order for his transfer had been given in March but he had refused to leave his congregation. Tökes was due to be evicted on December 15; his congregation massed outside the church to prevent this, but he was nevertheless removed in the early hours of the 17th.

Both Hungarians and Romanians were already protesting on the streets, and this now turned into a **riot**. Ceauşescu ordered that this should be halted by any means necessary; protestors were met with bullets, and for a while the streets were cleared. However from Monday, December 18, the factories around town went on strike and by the 20th the centre of town was filled with up to 100,000 protestors, **demanding Ceauşescu's resignation**, while the army chose to withdraw rather than launch a massacre.

Nicolae Ceauşescu, feeling that the crisis had been contained, went as planned to Iran on the 18th, to sign an arms deal, and unwisely left Elena in charge: she insisted on further savage and counter-productive action. When Ceauşescu returned from Iran on the evening of the 20th he ordered a crack-down on the "hooligan elements" in Timişoara, thinking that he could still manipulate the usual knee-jerk nationalist reactions (he blamed all disturbances on Hungarian interference). However, the young soldiers in Timişoara, finding that

they were faced with Romanians as well as Hungarians, refused to shoot.

Ceauşescu also called for a massive show of support by supposedly tame crowds in **Bucharest** the next day, December 21. Over 100,000 people were brought from their workplaces to Piaţa Republicii (now Piaţa Revoluţiei) to hear him speak, although he was soon interrupted by shouts of "Timişoara!" and the singing of "Romanians Awake". Television screens went blank, but not before the whole nation had seen the look of incredulity and confusion on his face as he realized that his regime was finished. The police and *Securitate* opened fire but were unable to clear the crowds from the city centre, partly because the Minister of Defence, **General Vasile Milea**, ordered the army not to shoot. On the morning of December 22, Ceauşescu had Milea shot, but this merely precipitated the defection of many army units to the side of the protestors. By noon the crowds had broken into the Party's Central Committee building, and the **Ceauşescus fled by helicopter** from the roof.

It's fairly clear what happened to them, but much less clear what was going on behind the scenes. They flew to their villa at Snagov and then on to a military airfield near Titu, before hijacking a car and finally being arrested in Tîrgovişte. They were held in the military barracks there, and when the news of their capture proved insufficient to stop loyal *Securitate* units firing on the crowds, they were tried and **executed on Christmas Day**. The "trial" was a farce, with no doubt of the outcome, but most Romanians felt it was justified and necessary to end the fighting.

Meanwhile in Bucharest, and in other cities such as Braşov, Arad and Sibiu where there had been demonstrations and street-fighting, army and police units were changing sides; it's unclear at what point their leadership had decided to abandon Ceauşescu, but evidence suggests that it was earlier rather than later. Nor is it clear at what point the **National Salvation Front** (*Frontul Salvării Naţonale* or FSN), which emerged to take power from December 22, had been formed: there are many conflicting accounts, but it seems certain that a coup of some kind had been prepared before the disturbances in Timişoara. The FSN was supposedly formed in the Central Committee building on the afternoon of December 22 by a

ILIESCU AND THE NEW REGIME

Born in 1930 to communist parents, **Ion Iliescu** spent World War II in internment, and then studied in Moscow at the same time as Gorbachev: rumours about their relationship later did him no harm at all, although there's no evidence that they met. Returning to Romania, he made his way up the party ladder, joining the Central Committee in 1964; already he was seen as the newly appointed Ceauşescu's heir apparent. In 1971 he accompanied him to China and North Korea; Ceauşescu came home full of enthusiasm both for the Cultural Revolution and for the totalitarian architecture of Pyongyang, but Iliescu disagreed and was sent to an unimportant job in Timişoara.

Although this has since been presented as a break both with Ceauşescu and with communist ideology, too, it's clear that he continued to be on friendly terms with the President, and in 1979 he returned as director of the National Water Council and a member of the Political Executive Council (*politburo*). It's claimed that from 1982 Iliescu, General Militaru and Virgil Magureanu were plotting against Ceauşescu, and in 1984 there was supposedly a coup attempt. Iliescu was again demoted in 1984 after disagreeing with the boss about the Danube–Black Sea Canal, being dropped from the Political Executive Council and the Party's Central Committee (after 19 years' service) and appointed director of the state Technical Publishing House.

It is odd that from now on he was consistently spoken of as the only possible candidate to **succeed Ceauşescu**; yet he was never a dissident and did nothing to put himself forward beyond building private links with the party and military hierarchy. It's said that the generals required a seasoned politician at the helm, rather than a group of poets and intellectuals, before they would support the revolution.

Since 1989, Iliescu, with his affable smile and his aura of competence and experience, has been seen as **a figure of stability and continuity**, while also benefiting electorally from the gratitude due to the overthrower of Ceauşescu. He disowned Marxism, but for a long time showed no understanding of anything but authoritarianism, using standard phrases about "fascist elements" and "foreign agents", and continuing at first to call people "comrade". Since then he has kept power by employing familiar methods of manipulation mixed with strong-arm tactics, which has usually worked domestically while losing support abroad.

Around two-thirds of the *Securitate*'s manpower were taken on again by the new SRI, and it has continued to operate in much the same way as before 1989, with opposition leaders (especially defectors from the FSN) being bugged and harassed. Around 40 percent of the successful private companies in Bucharest are run by former *Securisti*. Up to a third of the population are supposed to have been *Securitate* informers (and between one and five million files are still shut), and a sixth of the population were members of the Party. As a result of such general guilt there is much less stigma attached to people's past records than elsewhere in Eastern Europe.

Nevertheless there's a strong feeling that those at the top not only got away with murder, but have in fact profited to a ridiculous extent from the new dispensation. Only twenty-five communist officials were jailed for offences committed prior to the revolution, and the last of these were released in September 1994. There were no trials for offences committed during the revolution itself, and there has still been no explanation of events. Although it was the army who, on the surface, deposed Ceauşescu, it seems likely that Iliescu is more deeply in the debt of the *Securitate*.

group of people who had gathered there independently, but clearly many of them were already in contact. The key figures were Party members who had been side-lined by Ceauşescu, and **Ion Iliescu** was soon named as president; his prime minister was **Petre Roman**, an up-and-coming member of the younger generation of communists.

It seems that around a thousand people died in the revolution and the "terrorist" phase that lasted until January 18; although, initially, both the new government and the Hungarian media published inflated death tolls of 10,000 or more.

FREE ROMANIA

It did not take long after the Ceauşescus' execution for the **FSN to consolidate its power**; almost at once it reversed its pledge not to run as a party in the elections due in May 1990. It was soon evident that revolutionary idealists were being elbowed aside by the former governing élite, who had no intention of leaving office. Supporters of other parties demanded the **removal of ex-communists** from the government and began regular protests in Bucharest; these were disrupted by miners from the Jiu Valley, bribed and duped by the government to act as their enforcers.

From April 22, Bucharest's Piaţa Universit-ăţii was occupied by **students** protesting against the ex-communists and demanding an end to state control of TV. They began a hunger-strike on April 30, and on June 13 the police cleared the square of the *golani* or hooli-gans, as they proudly called themselves. The police were in turn attacked, perhaps by *provocateurs*, and the next day **10,000 miners** arrived in town on special trains. They were greeted by Iliescu and taken by plain-clothes agents to set upon the *golani* who had returned to the square and to ransack university, news-paper and opposition party offices. They terror-ized the city until June 16, leaving at least seven dead and 296 injured. The reaction abroad was dismay, with the US suspending non-humanitarian aid and boycotting Iliescu's inauguration as president. At home, the nation went into shock, and remained cowed for the next year while the economy collapsed.

In the meantime, on May 20, the FSN had easily won **Romania's first free elections**, garnering 66.5 percent of the vote, while Iliescu won 85 percent of the vote for presi-dent. The actual voting was deemed fair enough by international observers, even though a million more votes were cast than were on the register, supposedly "due to the enthu-siasm of the people for democracy". However the FSN's domination of the airwaves had won them the election well before the actual voting. Most urban intellectuals soon took to referring to December 1989 as the "so-called revolu-tion", and it was increasingly taken for granted that nothing much had changed in the political life of the country.

Economic reform got under way slowly, but some adjustment was unavoidable as the country was rocked by the inevitable opening to Western imports and by the world recession. **Food rationing** had been ended as soon as the FSN took power, together with systematiza-tion, the registration of typewriters, and the bans on abortion, contraception and contacts with foreigners, and the new government took care to empty the warehouses and fill the shops with food. Food subsidies were not cut until November 1990, and the state-controlled **prices rose** steadily from then on, until they were finally freed altogether in May 1993.

Imports rose by 48 percent in 1990, and exports fell by 42 percent (due in part to agricultural produce being kept for home consumers), while **inflation** rose from 65 percent in 1990 to almost 300 percent in 1993.

In September 1991, the **miners**, although still better off than most Romanians, went on strike for more pay and then rampaged again through Bucharest. The prime minister, Roman, was forced to resign, and was replaced by another technocrat, **Teodor Stolojan**, who continued with broadly reformist policies. Opposition gains in local elections in February 1992 fuelled the fears of conservatives within the FSN, leading to their leaving the party to form the Democratic Front of National Salvation (renamed the Party of Social Democracy of Romania in 1993), led by Iliescu. Roman's wing became the Democratic Party or PD (FSN). The government became a coalition, with the PDSR kept in office by minority parties, and opposed by another coalition known as the Democratic Convention.

A **second general election** was held in September 1992, after the adoption of a new constitution; Romania is now a **presidential democracy**, in which the prime minister has little autonomy. Iliescu won 61 percent of the vote for the presidency, but his party won just 28 percent; the Democratic Convention had 20 percent, Roman's FSN 10 percent, and the main Romanian nationalist party and the Hungarian Democratic Union of Romania each took 7.5 percent. The opposition refused to form a government, so Iliescu selected **Nicolae Văcăroiu**, formerly head of taxation in the Finance Ministry, to lead another government of technocrats kept in power by the FDSN and an unholy alliance of neo-communists and extreme nationalists. Since then the govern-ment has survived a succession of parliamen-tary votes of confidence and strikes by miners, rail workers and other key groups, managing for the most part to avoid inflationary wage rises. The **need for aid and a fear of international isolation** have kept the govern-ment on a reformist course, although key reformers periodically resign, frustrated by the struggle against the conservatives. In February 1993, an agreement was reached for associa-tion with the European Union; in October, Romania became the last Eastern Bloc state to join the Council of Europe; and in January 1994 it was the first to sign the Partnership for Peace. The granting of Most Favoured Nation status by the USA in November 1993 led to huge cuts in tariffs, although the nascent private sector was slow to take advantage of the export opportunities. Although there had still been no mass privatization of state industries, the private sector now contributed 3.6m jobs and 30 percent of official economic activity.

A particularly welcome sign was Iliescu's support from mid-1994 for the **tight fiscal policies** of the National Bank's governor Mugur Isarescu, which halved inflation to 6 percent per month and allowed the leu to actually rise slightly against the dollar. The official exchange rate matched the black market rate, and businesses were able to obtain as much hard currency as they required for imports and investment, having previously only been able to get a third of their needs through official channels. The reward was substantial loan support

from the World Bank and IMF, but up to $3.5bn is needed if restructuring and privatization are to proceed.

Iliescu's support for economic reform does not extend to **land reform**, although Văcăroiu and his government see returning land to the people as the best way to revitalize agriculture. The president urged the courts not to issue property deeds, but even so by early 1993 four million had been issued. Parliament refused to allow foreigners to buy land, and this has sometimes been interpreted as including any company with foreign investors.

Nevertheless the corner has been turned: industrial output in 1994 was about 10 percent higher than in 1993, and exports in the first half of 1994 were 38 percent higher than in the first half of 1993. Unemployment has stabilized at 11 percent, and inflation is falling, to 80 percent in 1994 and half that in 1995, while in mid-1994 real incomes rose for the first time in many years.

THE KING

Many people now look to **the King** for an escape from the vile intrigues of the "democratic" politicians. **Mihai** was born in 1921 and ruled from 1927 to 1930 and from 1940 to 1947; he earned his people's respect by his role in the coup of August 23, 1944, when he dismissed Marshal Antonescu and had him locked in a safe, and by his attempts to maintain democratic government afterwards. His **abdication** was precipitated, in part, by attending the wedding of Britain's present Queen Elizabeth and Prince Philip in November 1947, meeting Princess Anne of Bourbon-Parma, and returning home engaged to be married. Faced with the prospect of a continuing dynasty, the communists were forced to drive him out. He and his wife lived as market gardeners in England until 1956, when Mihai became a test pilot and then a broker in Switzerland.

Since 1989, he has tried several times to visit the royal graves in Curtea de Argeş, and the government's repeated refusal to allow this is an indication of its sense of illegitimacy. In April 1990 he was refused a visa, and although at Christmas 1990 he was granted a visa (travelling on a Danish diplomatic passport), he was stopped on the motorway and deported twelve hours after arriving at Otopeni. At Easter in 1992 he was permitted a visit, which drew large crowds, but has not been allowed to return since; in October 1994 he again arrived at Otopeni but was put straight back onto the plane.

Royalist graffiti is widespread, and in opinion polls up to 20 percent now want Mihai's return. The opposition parties are in favour of a referendum on the subject, although few of them are actively monarchist.

CHRONOLOGY OF MONUMENTS

pre-4000 BC	Tribes roam the valleys and plains.	Remains of bones and weapons found at Băile Herculane.
4000 BC	Earliest settlements on the Dobrogea.	Habaşeşti Neolithic village; "Hamangia Culture" carvings include **goddess figures** and the **"Hamangia Thinker"**.
3000 BC	Copper-working in Transylvania.	Axes, adzes etc. exhibited in Cluj History Museum.
C7–C6 BC	Coast colonized by **Greek** trading ports (ruled by Roman and Byzantine empires from C1 AD onwards).	Walls dating from foundation of **Histria** (675 BC), **Tomis** and **Callatis** (C6 BC) overlaid with **Roman and Byzantine** remains, including a fine mosaic floor at Constanţa.
C3 BC –C1 AD	**Dacians** inhabit area of present day Romania; ruled by Burebista in C1 BC, and Decebal (87–106 AD).	**Goldwork** (C3 BC). Excavations of many earthworks, citadels and sanctuaries, including **Sarmizegetusa**, the Dacian capital in the Orăştie mountains.
101–271	**Roman conquest** of Dacia (completed 106) produces a fusion of cultures: the Daco-Romans, held to be the ancestors of the Romanian people.	**Trajan's Bridge** at Drobeta–Turnu Severin, forts and the ruins of **Ulpa Traiana** show the Roman line of advance. The **Tropaeum Traiani** at Adamclissi commemorates the Roman victory.
271–C9	Goths, Huns, Avars and Bulgars carve successive empires here; Slavs begin to settle from 567.	Inscriptions, coins and burial remains either support the **Theory of Daco-Romanian Continuity** or don't; the debates continue.
896–C13	**Magyars** gradually wrest control of Transylvania from native voivodes; **Saxons** settle there after 1143; and in 1224 migrate into eastern Transylvania.	Indigenous structures – the **Bihara Citadel** near Oradea, the **Rupestral Complex** (C9–11) at Basarabi – and those of the newcomers: eg. **Cîrţa Székely Monastery**, the "Passage of Stairs" in Sibiu, and parts of some **walled towns**.
C13	Radu Negru founds the Bassarab dynasty and the principality of **Wallachia** south of the Carpathians. Tartars invade Transylvania in 1241 and 1284, giving impetus to the building of walls and citadels.	**Negru Vodă Monastery** founded in 1215 at Cîmpulung, the first Wallachian capital, together with many churches (walled during the C15). The one at **Cisnadioara** (c.1200) and **St. Michael's Cathedral** in Alba Iulia are examples of C13 **Romanesque architecture**.
C14	East of the Carpathians, Bogdan Vodă founds the principality of **Moldavia** (1364) with Rădăuţi as its capital.	**Citadels** of **Făgăraş** and **Rîşnov** (rebuilt C15). The Court at **Curtea de Argeş** (c.1370) precedes **Cozia Church** which marks the advent of **Byzantine architecture** in Wallachia. Styles in the north are divergent – eg. the wooden Church on the Hill at **Ieud** (c.1364) and Rădăuţi's **Bogdana Church**. Brasov's **Black Church**, the first phase of St. Michael's in Cluj, and **Bran Castle** (1377) exemplify Transylvanian **Gothic architecture**.

C15

Turkish expansion is checked by Hunyadi in Transylvania, Vlad Ţepeş in Wallachia and Ştefan the Great in Moldavia. After the 1437 Bobîlna peasant uprising the Magyar nobility, Saxons and Székely form the **Union of Three Nations** to defend their privileges.

Bistriţa Monastery founded in Moldavia (1407). **Hărman, Prejmer** and other **fortified churches**, the **castles at Lazar, Poienari and Hunedoara** and the strengthening of the **walls around Sighişoara, Cluj and Sibiu** are all monuments to a period of violence and insecurity. Ştefan founds the **monasteries** of **Voroneţ** (1488), **Neamţ** (1497) and **Putna** (1504) in Moldavia.

C16

Peasant uprising of 1514. Following the Ottoman and Hapsburg partition of Hungary, Transylvania struggles to stay independent, while Moldavia and Wallachia acknowledge Ottoman suzerainty.

Monasteries of **Arbore, Humor, Moldoviţa** and **Suceviţa** are built; soon, their walls and those of Voroneţ are painted with magnificent **frescoes**.The **Episcopal Church** at Curtea de Argeş (1517) rises above the limitations of Byzantine architecture in Wallachia; while Sibiu's Councillors' Tower and the **Sighişoara citadel** are typical of C16 Saxon buildings in Transylvania.

C17

In 1600, **Michael the Brave** briefly unites Moldavia, Wallachia and Transylvania. Moldavia and Wallachia have a respite from misrule during the reigns of Vasile Lupu (1633–52) and **Constantin Brîncoveanu** (1688–1714) but later succumb to the **Phanariots**, while Transylvania has its "Golden Age" under Gabor Bethlen (1613–29).

Between the construction of Dragomirna and Cetă ţuia monasteries, **Moldavian church architecture** reaches its apogee with the building of Iaşi's **Trei Ierarhi** (1639), covered in intricate stone-carvings. In Wallachia, the monasteries of Arnota, Gorova and Polovragi precede **Horez Monastery** (1691–93), the largest, most impressive example of **Brîncoveanu-style architecture**, which also characterizes Sinaia Monastery (1695).

C18

The Ottomans withdraw in 1718. Serbs and Swabians settle in the Banat. In 1784 a peasant uprising occurs in Transylvania. The Romanians' petition for political equality is rejected in 1791.

Despite the Creţelescu Church in the Brîncoveanu style, the C18 is more notable for the construction of splendid **wooden churches in** Maramureş at **Rozaulea, Bogdan Vodă Şurdeşti** – and many **Baroque churches, palaces and cathedrals**, eg. in Oradea, Cluj, Sibiu and Timişoara. Huge **Vauban-style citadels** are raised at Arad, Alba Iulia and Oradea.

C19

Magyars revolt against Hapsburg rule and declare the union of Transylvania with Hungary despite Romanian opposition (1848–49). In 1859 **Moldavia and Wallachia** unite to form Romania, while after 1868 the Hungarians pursue a policy of **"Magyarization"** in Transylvania.

In Bucharest, the construction of the Şos. Kiseleff and the Calea Victoriei reflects **French influence**; Manuc's Inn, the Şuţu Palace and many new buildings are founded in the capital and after 1859 universities are established at Iaşi and Bucharest. Sibiu's Podul de Fier, the Brukenthal Museum, electric street lighting in Timişoara, the building of rail lines and a channel through the Iron Gates are all aspects of **modernization** affecting Transylvania. Monumental buildings in Iaşi, Tîrgu Mureş etc. embody the era's assertive nationalism.

1907	**Peasant uprising** in Romania.	Ploieşti oilfields developed by foreign capital. The Mosque at Constanţa is the first **ferro-concrete** structure (1910).
1918	**Union of Transylvania with Romania**; confirmed by the Trianon Treaty (1920) despite Magyar opposition.	**Monumental Orthodox Cathedrals** constructed in Alba Iulia, Tîrgu Mureş, Timişoara, Cluj etc. to celebrate the status of "Greater Romania" in the 1920s. In the '30s, the Royal Palace and the **Arc de Triumpf** are built in the capital.
1944	Romania liberated from Nazis.	Damage caused by Allied bombs is rapidly repaired and **high-rise blocks** are built to meet the housing shortage (eg. in Ploieşti and Bucharest).
1949	Establishment of **Communist Party** rule..	Romania's **industrialization** and the style of architecture are strongly **Soviet-influenced** – eg. the Casa Scinteii and the first, abortive attempt to dig the Danube–Black Sea Canal using forced labour. The **Friendship Bridge** (completed in 1954) and the **Iron Gates dam** (1971) are both joint nationalist ventures with neighbouring socialist countries; while the Galaţi steel mill and the coastal **tourist complexes** have a Western input. The **Danube–Black Sea Canal** is opened in 1984. Subsequent major construction projects included **Otopeni airport**, the **Metro** and the **Centru Civic** in the capital; the Dîmboviţa canal; and Romania's first **nuclear power station** at Cernavodă on the Danube.
1965	**Ceauşescu** becomes leader following the death of Gheorghiu-Dej, and pursues a nationalist economic policy contrary to the wishes of Comecon, which is reluctant to help. This persuades **Ceauşescu** to seek credit and technical assistance from the West.	
1977	Earthquake in Bucharest.	
1989	**Ceauşescu overthrown**. Romania's first free elections held.	Even before the revolution there was a boom in building churches and private houses in the villages.

ROMANIA'S MINORITIES

While Wallachia and Moldavia are largely monocultural, Transylvania has always been pluralistic and multi-ethnic. Although there is a specifically Transylvanian culture and sensibility common to all the races living there, there are still those who seek to make political capital by setting one race against another. For visitors, of course, this multi-ethnic mix is at the heart of Transylvania's charm.

THE MAGYARS

Transylvania (including the Banat) was ruled by Hungary for several centuries, and when it was united with Romania after World War I Hungary lost half its population and two-thirds of its area. Although Slovakia and Croatia were also lost, it's Transylvania which has always been the focus of Hungarian desires; there are still about two million **Magyars** or Hungarians in Romania.

The Hungarians had treated their subject peoples badly, denying them their linguistic and cultural rights, and inevitably the Romanians, once they were in charge, behaved in a similar manner. Things became far worse in Ceauşescu's later years, and eventually Magyars began to flee across the border to Hungary, the first refugees from one Warsaw Pact state to another. Around 10,000 fled in 1987 and double that in 1988, when demonstrations in Budapest against oppression in Romania (and especially the systematization programme) played a key part in the movement towards political reform at home. In late 1989 hundreds of refugees were crossing the border every day, despite many more being caught by border guards; in 1990, 17,000 emigrated legally, but numbers have since declined.

Normal civil rights were in theory restored, with Hungarian-language education widely available, but as Magyars asserted their rights there was a reaction in the Romanian community, feeding nationalist parties such as the Party of Romanian National Unity and *Vatră Romanească*, whose policy is "to make Romanians masters in their own home". These parties keep the government in power, and so new laws are proposed to curtail Hungarian-language education; the Democratic Union of Hungarians in Romania, the largest opposition party but effectively powerless, launched a campaign of civil disobedience against this in 1994.

There are in fact three Transylvanian Magyar communities, the Székely and the Csangó to the east, and the regular Magyars who settled later in the west. All remain strong and confident of their cultural identity, and there is little likelihood of a further exodus.

THE GERMANS

In contrast to the permanence of the Hungarians, there are now few **Germans** left in the country. The Saxon community in Transylvania dates back to 1143, when they were invited to guard the Transylvanian passes by King Geza II of Hungary; they developed a unique culture of their own, and grew prosperous by dominating the trade routes to Asia. They were granted self-government, based on their seven chief towns of Hermannstadt (now Sibiu), Kronstadt (Braşov), Schassbürg (Sighişoara), Klausenburg (Cluj), Mühlbach (Sebeş), Mediasch (Mediaş), and Bistritz (Bistriţa). As the Tartar threat was superseded by that from the Turks, these became fortified cities, while every village has a walled church, often with storage chambers for food in case of siege. From the eighteenth century, the Saxons (actually of Mosel-Frankish origin) were joined by other German colonists: the *Schwaben* or Swabians, who moved into the areas of the Banat recently vacated by the Turks, and the *Ländler* in Transylvania and Bucovina.

The population reached a maximum of about 650,000 in the 1930s. After World War II some Germans were expelled from Bucovina and Dobrogea, and, between 1945 and 1950, 75,000 men and women, accused of pro-Hitler sympathies, were taken for slave labour in the Soviet Union. Many of them had their property confiscated and this was not returned to them after 1989 when land was decollectivized. German law guarantees citizenship to all those of German origin, and in the 1980s the then West German government began to buy 10,000 exit visas a year. Thus the Saxon community was already slipping away when the revolution came; since then, however, it has almost entirely vaporized, leaving just one or two old folks in villages dominated by Romanians and Gypsies. There are now under 20,000 Germans in Romania; after thirty generations, the Saxon culture is virtually extinct.

THE JEWS

The history of Romania's **Jews** is similar to that of the Germans. Again there were two communities, the Sephardim, living along the Danube and speaking Ladino, and the Ashkenazim, the Yiddish-speaking Jews spread right across Central Europe, with many in Bucovina and Maramureş. Jews have been in Romania since Roman times, with more coming in the eighth and ninth centuries after the collapse of the Jewish Khazar empire, also in 1367 and in 1648 when they were expelled from Hungary and Poland. Most settled in Bessarabia and Bucovina, and prospered there; the community peaked around 1924, when it numbered 800,000. Romania was one of the few parts of the world where Jews were allowed to own land and form self-sufficient rural communities.

Although the Turks had treated them fairly, independent Romania increasingly treated Jews as foreigners rather than citizens, and they began to emigrate, above all to North America. The 1907 revolt was strongly anti-Semitic, and was followed by the rise of the Iron Guard and other nationalist parties; during **World War II** the Jewish population was butchered (see box on p.316), leaving only 428,000 Jews in Romania by 1947.

In the glorious new world of communism, the people were to be one without ethnic distinction, and all national minorities' organizations were disbanded in 1953. However Stalin was always anti-Semitic, and after the purging in 1952 of Romania's Jewish Foreign Minister, Ana Pauker, the climate turned against Romania's Jews again. Ceauşescu was happy to **sell Jews to Israel** for up to $3000 for each exit visa; at least 300,000 had left by 1989. Moses Rosen, Chief Rabbi from 1947 as well as a parliamentary deputy, performed a dazzling balancing act, travelling to the US every year to argue for the continuation of Much Favoured Nation status in order to gain exit visas for his flock. Additionally the American Joint Distribution Committee, not allowed to operate anywhere else in Eastern Europe, was able to spend $4m a year on the welfare of Romania's Jewish community. Rosen died in 1994, leaving Romania's anti-Semitism largely unaffected by the revolution.

THE GYPSIES

For most **Gypsies** or *Rom*, life is worse today than under Ceauşescu. They are attacked for not working, but also for smuggling and for the other shady deals by which they earn a living. State television always focuses on Gypsies in opposition demonstrations to discredit the opposition by association; but there has been an equal rise in ethnic consciousness among the *Rom*, and there are now five *Romani* newspapers.

Gypsies left northern India in the tenth and eleventh centuries and arrived in Europe around 1407, at the same period as the Tartar invasions. Almost at once many were enslaved, and, in the sixteenth century, came the first great period of **persecution**, matched only by the Nazi holocaust. In Wallachia and Moldavia Gypsies were divided into two main groups, the *Lăieşi* or "members of a horde", free to roam, and the *vătraşi* or settled Gypsies. The latter were slaves, working as grooms, servants, cooks and farm labourers, as well as being musicians. In 1837 the politician Mihail Kogălniceanu, who campaigned on their behalf, wrote: "On the streets of the Iaşi of my youth, I saw human beings wearing chains on their arms and legs, others with iron clamps around their foreheads, and still others with metal collars about their necks. Cruel beatings, and other punishments such as starvation, being hung in the snow or the frozen river, such was the fate of the wretched Gypsy."

Wallachia and Moldavia **freed their Gypsies** between 1837 and 1856: many in fact stayed with their original owners, but many also emigrated, reaching Germany in the early 1860s, France in 1867, Britain and the Netherlands in 1868, and North America by 1881. This is usually seen as a direct result of their emancipation from slavery, but the movement west had in fact begun some decades earlier. The economic system that made slavery viable had begun to break down as cheap grain imports from North America flooded Europe, and inevitably the boyars would in any case have cast them off before long.

At least 20,000 Gypsies were **deported to Transnistria** by Antonescu's regime during World War II, and a higher proportion died than in any other European country. The communist regime confiscated Gypsies' carts and forced them to settle on the edges of villages; in 1956 38 percent of Gypsies over the age of 8 were illiterate, but by 1966 almost all their children at least went to elementary school. In 1981 there were an estimated 1.8m Gypsies in Romania, and there are now over 2m, almost 10 percent of the population and **Europe's largest minority**. Around 40 percent of them no longer speak *Romani* and these consider themselves barely *Rom*; perhaps 10 percent are still nomadic, although they usually spend the winter camped at a permanent settlement.

There is increasing **discrimination** against Gypsies, and widespread antipathy towards them; given their great increase in numbers and visibility, they are now the universal scapegoats. They have received very little international aid and discrimination against them, particularly in employment, has inevitably pushed many into crime. Perhaps more alarming is the great rise in **crime against Gypsies**; there have been many instances of fights leading to mobs burning down Gypsy houses and driving them out of villages, and at least eight Gypsies have been killed in racist attacks since 1989. In almost every case village authorities have condoned the attacks, police have kept away, and there have been no arrests.

GYPSY CULTURE

The Gypsies left India to escape the caste system, and today their society is divided into clearly defined groups of uniform equality. There are around forty **tribes or groups** in Romania, including the *argintari* (jewellers), *boldeni* (flowersellers), *căldărari* (tin/coppersmiths), *curara* (sievemakers), *fierari* (blacksmiths), *grăstari* or *lovari* (horsedealers), *lăutari* (musicians), *poitori* (whitewashers), *lingurari* (makers of spoons and other wooden utensils), *rudari* (miners), *slătari* or *aurari* (goldwashers), and *ursari* (bearleaders and tinkers). There is also a general division into *corturari* (nomadic tent-dwellers) and *vătraşi* (settled).

Gypsy concepts of propriety are, with their language, their most obvious Indian heritage; everything is defined as either *wuzho* (clean), or *marime* or *mochadi* (unclean). **Involvement** with non-Gypsies (*gadjé*) is seen as risky (especially sharing food or having sex with them), and in particular the upper half of the body is regarded as clean while the lower half is not. Thus upper-body excretions such as spittle are seen as clean and may be used to wash wounds, and upper clothes must be washed separately from lower clothes.

As soon as a girl reaches puberty she must wear a long skirt and a separate top, washed separately and not with men's or children's clothes. Women are not allowed to cook while menstruating or during pregnancy. Women don't cut their hair, which is always bound, and once they are married it must always be covered with a *diklo* or headscarf. **Marriage** (seen as a cure for epilepsy and mental retardation) takes place in a girl's early teens, bringing an end to her education. Red and green are lucky colours, so a bride will wear red and a baby will wear a red band on its wrist, while black is used only for mourning.

Cutlery and crockery are potentially unclean, so Gypsies eat with their hands and prefer disposable cups and plates; the greatest insult is to refuse someone's food. As in India, to be fat is to be seen as wealthy and lucky, although women also carry their wealth with them in the form of huge Hapsburg gold coins. Friday is a day of fasting, when no animal products are eaten.

OTHER MINORITIES

There are many **other ethnic groups** in Romania, and not only in Transylvania. Around 70,000 **Ukrainians** live in Maramureş and Bucovina, and 45,000 **Russians** (mostly Lipovani) live in the Danube Delta, Dobrogea and Moldavia. Almost as many **Serbs** live at the other end of the country, in the Banat, having fled from Turkish domination in the eighteenth and nineteenth centuries, and there are about 18,000 **Slovaks** in the same area, descendants of colonists brought into the area after the Turks had gone. Muslim descendants of the Turks and Tartars themselves still live on the Black Sea coast, around 23,000 of them, with 10,000 Bulgarians in the same area. In the thirteenth century, the **Armenian** diaspora reached Moldavia, and later moved on into Transylvania, settling in isolated but prosperous communities in towns such as Suceava, Brăila, Constanţa, Dumbrăveni, Gheorgheni and

Gherla; now they are almost totally assimilated, although their churches survive, some with Hungarian priests.

The **Aroumanians**, are a group of ethnic Romanians who lived in Bulgaria and near Thessaloniki for many centuries as prosperous merchants with their own Romanian-language schools and culture, almost all returned to Romania between the World Wars, and they have virtually vanished as a recognizable culture, although their weaving (dark red geometrical patterns on a black background) can still be seen in museums.

RELIGION

As everywhere in the world, ethnic differences are reflected in **religion**; the Romanian majority follows the **Romanian Orthodox** creed, which like the other Orthodox Churches is a hierarchical body not given to free thought or questioning dogma or authority. Under Ceauşescu the Church did everything it was asked to, and positively discouraged dissidence. Some Romanians in Transylvania, and particularly in Maramureş, follow the **Uniate** creed (see p.153), which was regarded by the communists as untrustworthy and was forcibly merged with the Orthodox Church.

The Hungarian population is divided more or less equally between the **Roman Catholic** and **Calvinist** (*Reformat*) faiths; the Calvinist Church was pretty much under the communist thumb, but the Catholics had the strength to resist and to keep its integrity. The Schwab and Ländler Germans are also Roman Catholics, while the Saxons, Catholics when they arrived in Romania, later embraced **Lutheranism**, although a few are Seventh-Day Adventists. In addition about 1 percent of the population, mainly around Cluj and Turda, are **Unitarian** (see p.179), and since 1989 the Baptists and other evangelical Churches have been making great gains, mostly among people who are disorientated by change and the loss of certainty and stability in society.

ENVIRONMENTAL AND SOCIAL PROBLEMS

In Romania there is little that really compares with the environmental devastation of wide swathes of southern Poland, the northern Czech Republic, and eastern Ukraine, but even so the country did suffer, and there are many industrial plants that cause immense damage in their immediate neighbourhood. While the bulk of the damage was inflicted during the communist period, it should be stressed that some of the worst offenders, such as Copşa Mică's carbon-black plant and the Valea Călugărească fertilizer plant (east of Ploieşti), were built in the capitalist period, and the Reşiţa and Hunedoara steelworks and the Zlatna copper smelter date back to the eighteenth century.

Romania's mammoth increase in industrial output over the last five decades – production of steel rose from 280,000 tonnes in 1938 to 13,790,000t in 1985, and of fertiliser from just 5900t in 1950 to 1,199,200 tonnes in 1985 – was achieved by a total disregard for any considerations other than **maximizing production** as fast as possible. Thus industrial injuries are commonplace, and energy consumption is triple Western levels per unit of output, the most notorious example being the Slatina aluminium smelter, whose 1989 electricity consumption was equal to Romania's total domestic consumption. Industrial pollution is calculated to affect 10 percent of the population, and 20 percent of the country's territory.

The most polluted sites now are Copşa Mică, Zlatna and Baia Mare, all of which produce acid rain and a cocktail of up to ten heavy metals that run straight into the water system. In **Zlatna**, where a new plant was opened in 1986, sulphur dioxide emissions are above the legal maximum 30 percent of the time and dust emissions 63 percent of the time, while life expectancy in the area is ten years below the average, and falling. In **Baia Mare**, 50,000 tonnes of sulphur dioxide are pumped out every year, together with 3000 tonnes of metal dust, both well over safe levels. Almost as bad are the artificial fibre factories of **Brăila**

and **Suceava** – the latter giving rise to "Suceava Syndrome", a unique respiratory and nervous complaint that has led to many malformed babies. In 1987, the chemical plant in **Giurgiu** produced clouds of chlorine that floated across the Danube to blanket the Bulgarian town of Ruse (see p.108), and there are fertilizer and petrochemical plants in Arad, Dej, Făgăraş Năvodari, Piteşti, Ploieşti, Tîrgu Mureş, all producing illegal levels of hydrocarbons and inorganic compounds. In **Bucharest**, total emissions have fallen by a third since 1989, due to industrial recession; in some industrial areas ammonia levels are still nine times the legal limit and lead two hundred times the limit, but throughout the city nitrous oxides and lead (in car fumes) and dust are the main problems.

Additionally, the **use of fertilizers, pesticides and insecticides** has caused problems, damaging 900,000 hectares of agricultural land and entering the drinking water supply. The Ialomiţa and Someş rivers are entirely dead, as are the Dîmboviţa below Bucharest, the Olt below Slatina, the Jiu below Craiova, the Mureş below Arad, the Siret below Suceava, and the Bistriţa below Piatra Neamţ; in all 3300km (18 percent of Romania's rivers) fall into this category.

Due to the damming of the Iron Gates and the dyking of the Danube flood plain, the **Danube's flow** through the Delta is reduced by 50 cubic kilometres per annum, leading to algal blooms and lower fish yields. In places the river is only oxygenated to a depth of 10m, and the Delta may be entirely dead within a decade unless water flows can be speeded up.

At one time Ceauşescu did take an interest in pollution problems, with **environmental protection laws** passed in 1967, 1973 and 1976, and a National Council for the Protection of the Environment created in 1975, although without a budget of its own. The Braşov cement works were closed (after the creation of new capacity elsewhere) and the Bucharest abattoir and incinerator were moved to the outer suburbs. In the 1980s, however, he became more obsessed with expanding industrial capacity, and environmental data became increasingly secret. Water quality has been monitored since 1960, and air quality since 1973; but little use was made of this information before 1989.

After the revolution, a new **Ministry of Waters, Woods and Environmental Protection** was created, with the aim of reducing pollution by a fifth by 1995, and bringing it down to European levels soon after the year 2000. Two ecological parties were set up, gaining 4 percent of the vote in the 1990 elections (half of it in Bucharest), giving them a senator each and twenty deputies between them. A new environment law has been stuck in parliament for over a year, but an ordinance on atmospheric pollution was passed in August 1993; this means that potential investors can at least calculate future environmental costs, although not as yet past liabilities.

Much the same applied to the **protection of historical monuments**, with useful legislation being passed before 1977, when the Historical Monuments Administration was disbanded for daring to oppose Ceauşescu's plans for Bucharest's Civic Centre. There was no effective protection from then until 1989, and many towns have simply been gutted. In February 1990, the Administration for Historical Monuments, Sites and Areas was set up, but again the required legislation is stuck in parliament, and there is no state funding. Most conservation to date has been achieved with funding from the Church, or, in the case of **Saxon monuments**, from Germany. **Biertan** and the **Bucovina and Horez monasteries** are to become UNESCO World Heritage sites.

Ceauşescu was also determined to have his own **nuclear power station** at Cernavodă, on the Danube, and chose a 700MW Canadian design rather than that used at Chernobyl and all over the Soviet bloc. Construction standards were so appalling that a third of welded joints in pipes failed stress tests, and since 1989 it has had to be more or less totally rebuilt. One reactor is finally due to open in 1995.

HEALTH PROBLEMS

As a result, in part, of these environmental conditions, Romania also has serious **health problems**. Socio-economic factors also contribute: bad housing in some parts of Bucharest leads to children suffering three times the level of respiratory disease found in other parts of the city, and in 10 percent of settlements, **water supplies** are under one hundred litres per day per head, with water being cut off for five or more hours a day in major towns such as Caracal, Slatina, Ploieşti, Constanţa, Iaşi, Cernavodă and Craiova. The average family spends 56 percent of its income on food, but their **diet** contains on average only 2832 calories (less even than in the late 1980s); 10 percent of children aged 10–14 are anaemic.

In the 1960s, **average life expectancy** was similar to that in Western Europe, but has since fallen behind. It dropped from 71 in 1989 to 69 in 1992, behind every European state except Albania and Slovakia, though still seven years longer than in Russia. **Cancer rates** are rapidly overtaking those in Western Europe, with breast cancer doubling in twenty years, and cervical cancer rates six times those in Greece, Italy and Spain. An explosion in lung cancer is not far off, due to a massive post-war rise in smoking. Respiratory diseases are common and the incidence of tuberculosis is the highest in Europe (93 cases per 100,000).

HIV has been present since 1984, but was not officially accepted until 1987; there were 1321 cases in early 1991, 1230 of them in children under twelve, almost all caused by injections with infected needles.

In 1967 Ceauşescu introduced his notorious laws designed to boost **Romania's birthrate**; these were briefly effective, but soon fertility began to drop, and continued to do so even as the laws became more draconian. By 1983 the birthrate was back to its 1966 level of 14.3 per thousand, and has continued to fall. **Infant mortality**, at 24.3 per 1000 live births in 1993, remains very high, almost triple the average for the developed nations of the OECD. This high rate is due to lack of medical equipment, congenital abnormalities (due in part to pollution), and low birth weight, and these also lead to a high mortality rate among children aged 1 to 4.

HEALTH SERVICE REFORM

Romania's **healthcare system** needs fundamental reform: health spending amounts to only 3 percent of GNP, and is not a priority for the government. Nevertheless the World Bank is leading a reform project, driven by the urgent need to improve health. Romania has plenty of well-trained **doctors**, and, with the opening of private medical schools, there will soon be an oversupply. However, there is a great shortage of **nurses** as training was halted altogether between 1978 and 1990. There are still only a thousand **psychologists** in Romania as psychology was seen as subversive under Ceaușescu, and there are no **geriatric specialists** at all, while the geriatric population is soon to double.

Most of those working in the health service are deeply demoralized, leading to a poor attitude to patients; in theory doctors earn less than half the average salary, but in practice the gifts and backhanders that fuel the system may bring their earnings up to double the average. The system is hierarchical and hospital-centred; there are no job interviews – those doctors qualifying with top marks get prestigious jobs in hospitals while the worst are assigned to local *dispensars* or clinics. These are depressing and underfunded places, usually referring patients to a *policlinic* (for outpatient care) or hospital; this is very inefficient, and a major shift to primary and preventative health care (including comprehensive family planning) is essential.

ORPHANS AND AID

The result of Ceaușescu's scheme to increase the workforce has been that many women have had children that they could not possibly afford to bring up, and, as is well known, these have been abandoned in dire state **orphanages**, grossly under-staffed and under-funded, with staff so desensitized that children were left to yell and to bang their heads against the wall. Reared with no mental stimulation, it's not surprising that many orphans were diagnosed (at three years old) as mentally handicapped and left without education in "Institutes for the Irrecuperable".

The Western media was saturated with distressing images of these orphanages, causing a massive popular reaction, particularly in Germany, and emergency **aid and volunteers** flooded into Romania. Today, relief agencies focus on long-term strategies with emphasis on training and helping the Romanians to help themselves. There are still blackspots – **old people's homes** are even worse than the orphanages, but little work has been done there, and little aid of any kind has reached southern Wallachia.

Childless Romanian couples are reluctant to **adopt** as most orphans are Gypsies and therefore not wanted. However, interest from the West was considerable; at least 10,000 had been adopted by foreigners by July 1991, when adoptions were abruptly halted, in order to prevent the sale of babies. Since then there have only been a handful of international adoptions a year, all handled by the Romanian Adoption Commission. However, there are still cases of babies being bought and smuggled out – in 1994, a British couple were arrested for this but released from custody after government intervention.

Ion Țiriac (once Boris Becker's coach) has opened his own orphanage in his home town of Brașov, and is running TV ads for funds; these

AID AGENCIES

There is still relief work to be done in Romania, but it is best achieved by working through the main established **agencies**, which are gradually absorbing most of the new charities set up in 1990. These work with church bodies and other established structures in Romania, and are co-ordinated by the **Romania Information Centre** at Southampton University in England (☎01703/551328) and the **Interdepartmental Commission for Co-ordination and Support of Humanitarian Activities** (*Comisia Interdepartamentala pentru Coordonarea și Sprijinirea Activităților Umanitare*, Str Ministerului 1–3, Bucharest 70107 (☎01/613.75.44 or 615.02.00 ext. 384)

Contact addresses

The Adopted Romanian Children's Society, 150 Montague Mansions, London W1H 1LA.

Christian Childrens' Fund of Great Britain (Romania), 52 Bedford Row, London WC1R 4LR or FREEPOST WC1R 4BR (☎0171/831 7145).

Relief Fund for Romania, 7th floor, 54–62 Regent St, London W1R 5PJ (☎0171/439 4052).

Romanian Orphanage Trust, 21 Garlick Hill, London EC4V 2AU (☎0171/248 2424).

World Vision UK, 599 Avebury Boulevard, Central Milton Keynes MK9 3PG (☎01908/841 000).

will not raise much money in Romania but are a useful first step in consciousness-raising. Efforts are being concentrated on encouraging people to take orphans home for weekend visits, to give them love and show them life outside the orphanages. The problem of unwanted children remains, and will do so until there is comprehensive family planning.

WILDLIFE

Despite Romania's industrial pollution problems, much of the countryside is surprisingly unspoilt, and as you climb up into the hills you enter a world where pesticides and fertilizers have never been used and where meadows are full of an amazing variety of wild flowers – a land-scape representative of Europe two or three centuries ago.

HABITAT

One third of Romania is mountain, largely forested, and this is where most of the more interesting flora and fauna are to be found. One third of the country is hill and plateau, with a fair quantity of woodland remaining, and one third is plain, mostly intensively farmed.

The **Carpathian mountains** form an arc sweeping south from Ukraine and around Transylvania to end on the Danube at the Iron Gates. At lower levels they are mostly covered with oak and hornbeam, with, up to about 1400m, an association of beech mixed with common silver fir and sycamore known as Carpathian Beech Forest (*Fagetum carpaticum*). Spruce begins to appear at about 1000m, and is dominant from 1400m to 1700m. Above this comes the lower alpine zone, characterized by dwarf pine and other stunted bushes, and then, from 1900m, the higher alpine zone of grass, creeping shrubs, lichen, moss and ultimately bare rock.

Elsewhere, particularly on the **Transylvanian plateau**, there is much more oak and beech forest, although much has been cleared for fields. To the east there are vast grassy steppes, the western end of the immensely fertile Chernozem or "black earth" belt that stretches east for 4000km to Novosibirsk.

In the **southwest** of the country, near the Iron Gates of the Danube, the climate is more Mediterranean, with Turkey and downy oaks, Banat pine and sun-loving plant species on the limestone rocks of the Mehedinţi and Little Retezat massifs.

The **Danube Delta** is a unique habitat, described in detail on p.281. Formed from the massive quantity of sediments brought down the river, it provides an ideal stopping-point for millions of migrating birds, as well as a home for many reptiles and other animals.

Nature reserves have existed in Romania since 1930, and there are now 586 in all, including individual caves, rocks and even trees. The first National Park was created in 1935 in the Retezat mountains; although the Scientific Reservation in the western part of this park was treated by Ceauşescu as a private bear hunting reserve. The Retezat and Rodna mountains and the Danube Delta have been named as part of UNESCO's worldwide network of Biosphere reserves, and at least ten other national parks are to be designated as a result of the government's Environment Bill. These include the Bicaz and Nera gorges, the Cerna valley, and the Apuseni, Bucegi, and Căliman mountains.

FLORA

The **mountain meadows** of Romania are a riot of wild flowers in the spring. The timing of this varies with the altitude, so that any time from April to July you should be able to find spectacular scenes of clover, hawkweed, burdock, fritillary and ox-eye daisy covered in butterflies, and, at higher levels, gentians, white false helleborine, globeflower and crocus. **Alpine plants** include campanulas, saxifrage, orchids, alpine buttercup, pinks, and, in a few places, edelweiss.

In the warmer **southwest** of the country, the Turda gorge is an especial sun-trap, with rarities such as *Allium obliquum, Aconitum fissurae, Hieracium tordanum* and various species of *Dianthus*, while there are other rare varieties of *Hieracium* in the Retezat Scientific Reservation, and orchids, lilies and *Carduus* varieties on the limestone of the Little Retezat.

The **Danube Delta** is home to 1150 plant species, which fall into three main categories. The floating islets that occupy much of the Delta's area are largely composed of reeds (80 percent *phragmites*), with mace reed, sedge, Dutch rush, yellow water-flag, water fern, water dock, water forget-me-not, water hemlock, and brook mint. In the still backwaters, wholly submerged waterweeds include water-milfoil, hornwort, and water-thyme; while floating on the surface you'll find water plantain, arrowhead, duckweed, water soldier, white and yellow waterlily, frog bit, marsh thistle, and épi d'eau. The river banks are home to white willow, poplar, alder, and ash; while the more mature forests of Letea and Caraorman also contain oak trees, elm and aspen and shrubs such as blackthorn, hawthorn and dog rose. The Romanian peony can be found along the coast nearby.

BIRDS

Permanent residents are relatively rare in the **Danube Delta**, with only around 44 species remaining all year round. These include white-tailed eagle, cormorant, greylag goose, mute swan, griffon vulture, great crested grebe, bittern, shelduck, mallard and kingfisher.

The twin peaks of ornithological interest in the Delta come from the end of March to early May, and from August to October, when millions of **migratory birds** (at least a hundred species) pass through in all directions: osprey, plovers, arctic grebes, cranes and half-snipes from Siberia; Saker falcons from Mongolia; and egrets and mandarin ducks from China.

From mid-May to mid-July, another hundred-plus species of birds, most of which have wintered in Africa, come to **breed** here and in the great lakes immediately to the south. Europe's largest colonies of white and Dalmatian pelicans, 60 percent of the world population of pygmy cormorants, and over 12,000 night herons, squacco herons and purple herons nest here, together with marsh harriers, black-winged stilts, glossy ibises, spoonbills, curlews and avocets. The coastal plains attract griffon vultures, short-toed eagles and the hobby.

In **winter**, the number of visiting birds is reduced but still amazing. Main visitors include most of the European population of great white herons (or egrets), 20,000 red-breasted geese (almost half the world population), 50,000 white-fronted geese, and 30,000 red-crested pochard, with smaller quantities of other ducks such as pintail, goldeneye, wigeon, teal, smew, red- and black-throated divers and Manx shearwater.

Away from the coast, on the **plains** inland, you may still find the great bustard, while summer visitors include the stridently coloured roller and bee-eater, the equally exotic-looking hoopoe, the imperial eagle, red-footed falcon and lesser grey shrike. The calandra lark, the largest European lark, lives all year round on the Bărăgan steppe.

Other than in the Delta, the biggest and most dramatic birds are usually to be seen in the **mountains**, above all the golden eagle and the raven, while in the **forests** lurk large game birds such as the capercaillie, hazel grouse, and (in the north) black grouse. Easiest to spot are nutcrackers, jays and woodpeckers (particularly the black and three-toed species in conifers, and great spotted, middle spotted and white-backed species in deciduous trees).

The forests are also home to raptors including buzzards, sparrowhawks, hen harriers and eagle owls. Nightingales visit deciduous woods in summer, and you're also likely to see storks, in particular the white stork, whose large nests are characteristically built in the heart of human habitations, on telephone poles and chimneys.

ANIMALS

The largest mammals live in the montane forests. Having been protected under Ceauşescu, for his own personal hunting, there are now many thousands of **brown bear** in Romania, particularly in the eastern Carpathians. Although they are beginning to raid garbage bins in Poiana Braşov, they are generally afraid of humans and will keep well clear unless you come between a female and her cubs in April or May.

The Carpathian **red deer** is found mainly in the northern spruce forests, where the stags' mating cries resound through the valleys in September and October; it is often possible to observe their ritual conflicts from a distance.

Above the treeline, the most visible mammal is the **chamois**, the mountain goat which can be seen grazing in flocks with a lone male perched on the skyline to keep watch. **Wild boar** are found in the lower forests (including the Delta), and can weigh 200kg, almost as much as a red deer stag. They appear mostly at night, and can leave a clearing looking as if it has been badly ploughed when they have finished digging for roots. They too have a reputation for aggression when protecting their young in the springtime.

Wolves, though fairly thinly spread, inhabit the hilly forested parts of the country, and the Letea area of the Delta. They are blamed for attacks on sheep and are hunted in winter, when their tracks can be followed in the snow. Smaller forest mammals include fox, wild cat, polecat, marten, weasel, stoat and red squirrel, while the Delta is home to otter, enot, coypu, mink and muskrat.

The most frequently seen **amphibia** are salamanders (not unusual after rain), while **snakes** include the grass snake, horned adder and (less common) adder. The warm weather of the southern Banat and the Delta sandbanks provides a suitable environment for **tortoises** and **lizards**.

Romania's rivers are home to seventy species of **fish**, mainly trout, dace, grayling, barbel and carp. The stiller waters of the Delta shelter another fifty species; the main channels are home to perch, pike and sheatfish, and to many types of sturgeon, sterlet and the related sevruga, as well as the Danube mackerel. Most of these species are in decline due to pollution, over-fishing and eutrophication of the water due to algal blooms.

MUSIC

The Carpathian mountains trace a cultural fault-line across Romania that separates Central Europe from the Balkans, sharply dividing the musical styles on either side. Of course such borders are rarely impermeable; the same language is spoken on either side and there is plenty of cultural and musical cross-fertilization. The many strands of Romanian music are extraordinarily varied and archaic, preserving almost archeological layers of development, from the "medieval" music at the extremities in Ghimeş and Maramureş, to the "Renaissance" sounds of Mezőség and the more sophisticated music of Kalotaszeg.

Tours to study Romanian folk **dance** are organized by the Doina Foundation (*Stichting Doina*), c/o Silviu Ciuciumiş, Aarhuispad 22, 3067 PR Rotterdam, Netherlands (☎10/421 86 22), which also helps organize an annual Balkan festival in Zetten and sells flutes, boots, costumes and icons.

THAT OLD TRANSYLVANIAN SWING

If you want to experience a real living European folk tradition, there's no beating **Transylvania**. Home to an age-old ethnic mix, the region's music is extraordinary: wild melodies and dances that are played all night, especially at weddings. Although many Transylvanian villages were collectivized in the communist

years, their spirit remained relatively resilient to the changes. The region's music, certainly, survived intact, and it's still a part of everyday life. The older people know the old songs and still use them to express their own personal feelings.

The composers Bartók and Kodály found Transylvania the most fertile area for their folk-song collecting trips in the first decades of this century, and they recognized that the **rich mix of nationalities** here had a lot to do with it. Transylvania has been home to Romanians, Hungarians, Saxons, Gypsies and other nationalities for hundreds of years. For these communities music is part of their national identity, yet it is also part of a unified and distinctly Transylvanian culture. The Romanian music of Transylvania is closer to Hungarian than it is to the Romanian music in the rest of the country. And the Hungarian music of Transylvania sounds much more Romanian than the music of Hungary proper.

In fact within Transylvania the Romanians and Hungarians share many melodies and dances. It takes a very experienced ear to tell the difference and even then a particular melody may be described as Hungarian in one village and Romanian in another just over the hill. The Romanian dances often have a slightly less regular rhythm than the Hungarian, but often the only difference between one tune and another is the language in which it is sung. There's even a unique recording of an old man from the village of Dimbău (Küküllődombó) singing a song with the first half of each line in Hungarian and the second half in Romanian

Transylvania is much more **Central European** in character and architecture than the other parts of Romania, and Transylvanian Romanians tend to consider themselves more "civilized" than their compatriots in Moldavia and Wallachia. The music of Transylvania sounds much less Balkan than that from over the Carpathians; it might seem wild and exotic, but it is recognizably part of a Central European tradition with added spice from its geographical location.

The traditional ensemble is a **string trio** – a violin, viola (*contra*) and a double bass, plus a cimbalom (*tambal*) in certain parts of Transylvania. The *primás*, the first violinist, plays the melody and leads the musicians from one dance into another while the *contra* and bass are the accompaniment and rhythm sections of the band. The *contra* has only three strings and a flat bridge so it only plays chords, and it's the deep sawing of the bass and the rhythmic spring of the *contra* that gives Transylvanian music its particular sound. Often the bands are expanded with a second violin or an extra *contra* to give more volume at a noisy wedding with hundreds of guests.

WEDDING PARTIES

Music in Transylvania serves a social function – nobody would dream of sitting down and listening to it at a concert. In some areas there are still regular weekly dances, but everywhere the music is played at weddings, sometimes at funerals and at other occasions, including when soldiers go off to the army, and around Christmas.

Wedding parties last a couple of days and often take place in a specially constructed wedding "tent" built from wooden beams and tree fronds. The place is strung with ribbons and fir branches, tables are piled high with garish cakes and bottles of *țuică* and fresh courses are brought round at regular intervals. There's a space cleared for dancing and on a platform is the band of musicians sawing and scraping away at battered old fiddles, and a bass making the most mesmerizing sound. The bride and groom, stuck up on their high table, look a little fed up while everybody else has the time of their lives.

Wedding **customs** vary slightly from region to region but generally the band starts things off at the bride's or groom's house, accompanying the processions to the church and possibly playing for one of the real emotional high spots, the bride's farewell song (*cîntecul miresei*) to her family and friends, and to her maiden life. Whilst the marriage takes place within the church, the band plays for the young people, or those not invited to the feast, to dance in the street outside. Once the couple come out of the church there's another procession to wherever the wedding feast is being held – either in the village hall or the "tent" erected at the house of the bride or groom.

CLASSICAL MUSIC

Classical music was lavishly funded by the communist state, and still has far less elitist connotations than in the West. Most large towns have a philharmonic orchestra and/or an opera house, and tickets (available through the local *agenția teatrală*) are very cheap. Additionally, the Saxon communities have maintained a Germanic tradition of singing chorales by Bach and his contemporaries.

The first important composer of the Romanian national school was **Edvard Cavdella** (1841–1923), who was also a formidable violinist. Little known in the West, his works include the historical opera *Petru Rareş* and the romantic and lyrical *First Violin Concerto*, dedicated to and premiered by Enescu.

Although the composers Bartók, Ligeti and Xenakis were all born on Romanian soil, Romanian classical music remains virtually synonymous with **George Enescu**, born near Dorohoi in 1881. At the age of four he was studying with a local Gypsy violinist, Nicolas Chioru, and at the age of seven he was admitted to the Vienna Conservatoire, where he met Brahms and was present at the premiere of his clarinet quintet. Between 1894 and 1899 he studied under Fauré and Massenet at the Paris Conservatoire, before embarking on a three-fold career as composer, conductor and violinist. His *Romanian Rhapsodies* were first performed in 1903 and remain his most popular works; as the name implies, they are largely based on Romanian folk tunes. His *Third Violin Sonata* is his best chamber work and has a national flavour. His *First Symphony* (1906) was Brahmsian in style, but, although he remained a neo-romantic, later works also showed experimental features, such as the use of quarter-tones and a musical saw in his masterpiece, the opera *Oedipe*. He began work on this in 1910 and it was finally performed in 1936; it is the most comprehensive of treatments of the myth, covering Oedipus' entire life from birth to death, with no classical compression. There is a good modern recording (1989) featuring José van Dam.

By bad luck or bad planning, Enescu spent both world wars in Romania, the first as court violinist to Queen Marie and the second on his farm near Sinaia (in recognition of which the communists only collectivized two-thirds of his land). In between he spent most of his time in Paris, teaching violin at the École Normale de Musique (to Yehudi Menuhin and Ida Haendel, among others), and giving the premiere of Ravel's violin sonata in 1927. His recording, with the young

There the musicians will have a short break to eat and then play music all Saturday night, alternating songs to accompany the feast with dances to work off the effects of the food and large quantities of *ţuică*. There are even particular pieces for certain courses of the banquet when the soup, stuffed cabbage or roast meat are served.

Late in the evening comes the bride's dance (*jocul miresei*) when, in some villages, the guests dance with the bride in turn and offer money. Things usually wind down by dawn on Sunday; people wander off home or collapse in a field somewhere and then around lunchtime the music starts up again for another session until late in the evening.

With the trend towards larger and larger weddings all sorts of instruments have started to find their ways into bands. Most common is the piano accordion, which, like the *contra*, plays chords, though it lacks its rhythmic spring. Very often you can hear a clarinet or the slightly deeper and more reedy *taragot* which sounds wonderful in the open air. Sadly,

however, because young people have moved away to work in towns, they often demand the guitars, drums and electric keyboards of the urban groups at the banquets – along with appalling amplification, which is increasingly brought in, too, by traditional acoustic bands.

Some band leaders might regret the trend but they are obliged to provide what the people demand. They may play traditional melodies but with the newer instruments the quality of the music is often lost. Some groups like the marvellous **Pălatca** band stick unswervingly to the traditional line-up and are recognized as one of the great bands of Transylvania.

GYPSY BANDS

The band from Pălatca (Magyarpalatka), like most of the village musicians in Romania, are **Gypsies**. In the villages, Gypsy communities all tend to live along one particular street in the outskirts, often called Strada Muzicanţilor or Strada Lăutari – both of which translate as "Musicians' Street". Gypsy musicians will play for Romanian, Hungarian and Gypsy weddings

---

Menuhin, of the Bach *Double Concerto* remains one of the best available.

Again, after World War II he returned to Paris, and even after a stroke in 1954 refused to return to communist Romania, dying in Paris in 1955. He now lies in the Père-Lachaise cemetery: despite his opposition to communism, the regime nevertheless co-opted his name, christening orchestras and streets after him.

The best-known contemporary composer in Romania is the hugely prolific **Anatol Vieru**. He was born in Iaşi in 1926 and has composed in a modern but not avant-garde style, occasionally drawing on folk influences. Several of his works have been released internationally on CD.

Many of Romania's musicians have had more success abroad than in their home country. **Sergiu Celibidache**, born in Romania in 1912, studied in Berlin and in 1945 became conductor *pro tem* of the Berlin Philharmonic until Furtwängler was cleared of Nazi sympathies. He continued as assistant conductor in Berlin until 1952, going on to run the Swedish Radio Symphony Orchestra, the Stuttgart Radio Orchestra, and from 1980 the Munich Philharmonic, making his US debut only in 1984. Described as "transcendentally endowed", although not very interested in music outside the mainstream Germanic repertoire, he is also a

perfectionist, demanding up to eighteen rehearsals for some concerts; nevertheless he stopped making studio recordings in 1953. He is also a composer, with four symphonies and a piano concerto to his name.

Romania's best-known pianist is **Dinu Lipatti** (Enescu's godson), who had a mercurial talent and suffered an early death in 1950 from leukaemia. In his lifetime he was referred to as "God's chosen instrument". His recordings (just 5 CDs) have never been deleted, and one of them, made in Besançon just months before his death, is widely regarded as the best-ever live recital disc.

Contemporary musicians to look out for include **Alexandru Agache**, the sopranos **Leontina Vaduva** and **Angela Budlachu-Giurgiu**, and the conductors **Cristian Mandel** and **Horia Andrescu**. The violinist **Alex Bălanescu** left Romania in 1959, joining the Arditti Quartet and then in 1987 forming his own **Bălanescu Quartet**, playing works by David Byrne, Kraftwerk, Gavin Bryars and Michael Nyman as well as the established classics. He returned to Romania in 1991, and in 1994 released "Luminiţa" ("glimmer"; Mute STUMM 124), about the "so-called revolution", featuring drum machine and the sampled voice of Ceauşescu, alongside some fine folk-inflected string writing.

alike and they know almost instinctively the repertoire required. Children often play alongside their parents from an early age and grow up with the music in their blood.

Playing music can be an easy way to earn good money; the best bands command handsome fees, plus the odd chicken and bottles of *ţuică*. It's also an indication of the value of music in this society that the musicians are not only well rewarded but also well respected. When the old *primás* of the Pălatca band died all the people he had played for in the village came to pay their respects at his funeral.

It's difficult to highlight the best bands – there are dozens of them – but in addition to the Pălatca band I have heard great music from bands in the following villages of central Transylvania (the names are given in their Romanian form with the Hungarian in brackets): Vaida-Cămăraş (Vajdakamarás), Suatu (Magyarszovát), Sopuru de Cîmpie (Mezőszopor), Sîngeorz-Băi (Oláhszentgyörgy) and Sic (Szék), an almost totally Hungarian village and one of the great treasure houses of Hungarian music.

A glance at the engagement book of one of these bands will show them booked for months ahead. Yet most of them confine their playing to quite a small area as travel is relatively difficult. Some tunes are widely known right across Transylvania but many are distinctly local and a band playing too far from its home village will simply not know the repertoire. It will be interesting to see what happens now that local bands are travelling to Hungary and beyond on tour.

THE HUNGARIANS

There are about two million **Hungarians** in Transylvania and seven million Romanians, but it is the music of the Hungarian minority that has made most impact outside the region. The Hungarians consciously promoted the culture of their brethren in Transylvania to highlight their suffering under Ceauşescu. *Hungaroton*, the state label, produced a large number of excellent recordings while Budapest-based groups like **Muzsikás** have toured extensively and acted as cultural ambassadors for the music.

Transylvania has always held a very special place in Hungarian culture as it preserves archaic traditions and medieval settlement patterns that have disappeared in Hungary itself. As a minority during the Ceauşescu regime, the Hungarians felt threatened, and there was a deliberate effort to wear their traditional costumes, sing their songs and play their music as a statement of identity, even protest. These days, national costume and dances are much more visible amongst the Hungarian minority than the majority Romanians (other than in Maramureş).

REGIONAL STYLES

Within the overall Transylvanian musical language there are hundreds of local dialects: the style of playing a particular dance can vary literally from village to village. But there are some broad musical regions where the styles are distinct and recognizable.

Bartók gathered most of his Romanian material in the area around **Hunedoara**. The area is still musically very rich though, strangely enough, a recent musical survey found that virtually the entire repertoire had changed.

Further north is the area the Hungarians call **Kalotaszeg**, home to some of the most beautiful music in the region. This area lies along the main route from Cluj (Kolozsvár) to Hungary and Central Europe, and the influence of Western-style harmony shows itself in the sophisticated minor-key accompaniment – a development of the last twenty years. Kalotaszeg is famous for its men's dance, the *legényes*, and the slow *hajnali* songs performed in the early morning as a wedding feast dies down, which have a sad and melancholy character all their own. One of the best of all recordings of Transylvanian music includes both these forms, featuring the Gypsy *primás* **Sándor Fodor** from the village of Baciu (Kisbács), just west of Cluj. There is also some fine Romanian music in Sălaj county, in the north of this area, which can be heard in the villages or on a very fine Romanian recording of *jocuri* Sălajene (dances from Sălaj) by a small ensemble from Zalău.

Probably the richest area for music is known to the Romanians as **Cîmpia Transilvanei** and to the Hungarians as **Mezőség**. This is the Transylvanian Heath, north and east of Cluj – a poor, isolated region whose music preserves a much more primitive feel with strong major chords moving in idiosyncratic harmony.

Further east is the most densely populated Hungarian region, the **Székelyföld** (Székely Land). The Székelys, who speak a distinctive dialect of Hungarian, were the defenders of the eastern flanks of the Hungarian kingdom in the Middle Ages, when the Romanians, as landless peasants, counted for little. Rising up towards the Carpathians, their land becomes increasingly wild and mountainous, and the dance music is different once again, with eccentric ornamentation and very often a cimbalom in the band.

For Hungarian-speakers the songs are fascinating as they preserve old-style elements that survive nowhere else. In one village I heard a ballad about a terrible massacre of the Székelys by the Hapsburgs in 1764, sung as if it had happened yesterday. Fleeing this massacre, many Székelys fled over the Carpathians into Moldavia, where they preserved music and customs that are no longer found in the Székelyföld itself. During World War II, 14,000 Székelys were resettled in the south of Hungary. In those outer reaches, the string bands of Transylvania have given way to a solo violin or flute accompanying the dances.

MOLDAVIA & MARAMUREŞ

The Hungarian occupants of the remote pastoral regions east of the Carpathians are called the **Csángós**. Strictly speaking this is **Moldavia**, not Transylvania, and the music – with its archaic pipe and drum style – sounds wild and other-worldly, ruptured across the divide between Transylvania and the Balkans.

Hungarian records of the Csángós often feature music from the Ghimeş (Gyimes) valley, where you find peculiar duos of violin and *gardon* – an instrument shaped like a cello but played by hitting its strings with a stick. The fiddle playing is highly ornamented and the rhythms complex and irregular, showing the influence of Romanian music. Csángó songs are also of interest to Hungarians for their archaic qualities. The extraordinary Csángó singer **Ilona Nistor** from Oneşti (formerly Gheorghe Gheorghiu-Dej) in Bacău county has a growing reputation.

On the other side of Transylvania, sandwiched between Hungary, Ukraine and the Carpathians, are the regions of **Maramureş**

and **Oaş**, both areas of distinctive regional character. Village costumes are not just worn for best but for everyday life and the music includes magic songs and spells of incantation against sickness and the evil eye. You can still find traditional Sunday afternoon village dances, either on the streets or on wooden dance platforms. From birth, through courtship and marriage to death, life has a musical accompaniment.

The music of Maramureş, while recognizably Transylvanian, sounds closer to that of Romanians beyond the Carpathians. As often happens in the highland regions of Romania, here the music is played predominantly by Romanians, not Gypsies. With an instrumental group of violin, guitar (*zongoră*) and drum, it has a fairly primitive sound, lacking beguiling harmonies and with a repeated chord on the *zongoră* played as a drone. Hundreds of years ago much of the music of Europe probably sounded something like this.

WALLACHIA

As in Transylvania, most village bands in **Wallachia** are comprised of **Gypsies**: the group is generally named **Taraf** and then their village name. These *lăutari* (musicians) are professionals who play a vital function in village life at weddings and other celebrations: yet their music sounds altogether different from that of their Transylvanian counterparts. The word *taraf* comes from the Arabic and suggests the more oriental flavour of this music. Songs are often preceded by an instrumental improvisation called *taksim*, another name borrowed from the Middle East.

The lead instrument is, as ever, the fiddle, which is played in a highly ornamented style. The middle parts are taken by the *ţambal* (cimbalom), which fills out the harmony and adds a rippling to the texture. At the bottom is the double bass, ferociously plucked rather than bowed Transylvanian style. In the old days you'd always find a cobza (lute) in such bands, but their place has given way to the *ţambal*, guitar and accordion. The Gypsies are never slaves to tradition; the young ones particularly are always keen to try new instruments and adopt modish styles. The staple dances are the *horă*, *sîrbă* and *brîu* – all of which are danced in a circle.

In Romanian the word *cînta* means both "to sing" and "to play an instrument", and the *lăutari* of Wallachia usually do both. Whereas in Transylvania the bands play exclusively dance music, the musicians in the south of the country have an impressive repertoire of **epic songs and ballads** which they are called on to perform. These might be specific marriage songs or legendary tales like *Şarpele* (the snake) or exploits of the Haidouks, the Robin Hood brigands of Romanian history. One of the tunes you hear played by *lăutari* all over Romania is *Ciocîrlia* (The Lark), which has also become a concert piece for the stage ensembles. Reputedly based on a folk dance, it's an opportunity for virtuoso display, culminating in high squeaks and harmonics as the solo violin imitates birdsong, followed by the whole band swirling away in abandon on the opening theme.

Considering the wealth of village musicians in Romania it's significant that three of the very few recordings available feature the same *taraf* from the village of **Clejani**, southwest of Bucharest (just south of Vadu Lat station), although it's a village with some fifty professional musicians whose reputation has spread throughout the area. The appearance of the so-called **Taraf of Haidouks** from Clejani at the 1991 WOMAD festival caused a sensation as they played their wild and unmistakable music into the night and, when finally forced off stage, split into smaller groups to engage in persistent busking for the rest of the festival. Their debut recording, "Taraf de Haidouks", is extraordinary, packed full of truly virtuoso playing with incredible performances on violin, *ţambal* and accordion. It includes the "Ballad of the Dictator", (see box below) composed to a traditional melody by the 70-year-old fiddle player Nicolae Neascu, which tells of the dramatic fall of Nicolae Ceauşescu; a new addition to the age-old tradition of ballads addressed to the "Green leaf" (*Foaie verde* or *frunză verde*). They have since followed this up with an equally spellbinding album. Other famous Wallachian Gypsy bands include those from Mirsa, Dobroteşti, Suteşti and Brăila.

THE DOINĂ

The **doină** is a free-form, semi-improvised ancient song tradition. With poetic texts of grief, bitterness, separation and longing, it might be called the Romanian blues. Very often different texts are sung to the same melody, which may then take on a contrasting character. It is essentially private music, sung to oneself at moments of grief or reflection, although nowadays the songs are often performed by professional singers or in instrumental versions by Gypsy bands. Old doinăs of

---

Balada Conducatorului
(Ballad of the Dictator)

Green leaf, a thousand leaves
On this day of the 22nd
Here the time has returned
The one in which we can also live
Brother, live in fairness
Live in freedom

Green leaf, flower of the fields
There in Timişoara
What are the students doing?
Brother, they descend into the streets
Bringing with them banners
And cry "It is finished for the tyrant!"
What are the terrorists doing?
They pull out guns
Brother, they shoot at the people

Green leaf, flower of the fields
What are the students doing?

Into the cars they step
Towards Bucharest they head
In the streets they shout
"Come out, Romanian brothers
Let's wipe out the dictatorship!"

Ceauşescu hears them
His minister calls for
A helicopter which takes him away
What do the police do?
They follow in his steps
They bring him back in a tank
They lock him up in a room
And his trial begins
We take his blood pressure
And the judge condemns him
"Tyrant, you have destroyed Romania"

Nicolae Neascu of the *Taraf of Haidouks*

the traditional kind can still be found in Oltenia, between the Olt and Danube rivers in the south of the country. This one is typical:

I don't sing because I know how to sing
But because a certain thought is haunting me
I don't sing to boast of it
But my heart is bitter
I don't sing because I know how to sing
I'm singing to soothe my heart
Mine and that of the one who is listening to me.

LOST SHEEP

The pastoral way of life is fast disappearing and with it the traditional instrumental repertoire of the *fluier* (shepherd's flute). But there is one form – a sort of folk tone poem – that is still regularly played all over the country: **the shepherd who lost his sheep**. This song was referred to as early as the sixteenth century by the Hungarian poet Bálint Balassi. I've heard it on the flute in Moldavia, the violin in Transylvania and on the violin and gardon in Ghimeş. It begins with a sad, doină-like tune as the shepherd laments his lost flock. Then he sees his sheep in the distance and a merry dance tune takes over, only to return to the sad lament when he realizes it's just a clump of stones. Finally the sheep are found and the whole thing ends with a lively dance in celebration.

Some of the professional bands have adopted the lost sheep story and embroidered it so that during his search the shepherd meets a Turk, a Jew, a Bulgarian and so on. He asks each of them to sing him a song to ease his suffering and promises to pay them if they succeed. No one succeeds until he meets another shepherd who plays a *ciobaneasca* (shepherd's dance) and cheers him up. In the end he finds his sheep devoured by wolves.

THE PIPES OF PAN

Romania's best-known musician on the international stage is **Gheorghe Zamfir**, composer of the ethereal soundtrack of the film "Picnic at Hanging Rock". He plays *nai*, or **panpipes**, which are thought to have existed in Romania since ancient times – they're shown in a famous Roman bas-relief in Oltenia. The word *nai*, however, comes from Turkish or Arabic, so perhaps an indigenous instrument existed as well as a similar one brought by professional musicians through Constantinople.

In the eighteenth century "Wallachian" musicians were renowned abroad and the typical ensemble consisted of violin, *nai* and *cobza*. But by the end of the next century the *nai* had begun to disappear and after World War I only a handful of players were left. One of these was the legendary **Fanica Luca** (1894–1968), who taught Zamfir his traditional repertoire. Nowadays, Zamfir plays material from all over the place, often accompanied by the organ of Frenchman Marcel Cellier.

THE BANAT BEAT

The **Banat**, Romania's western corner, is ethnically very mixed, with communities of Hungarians, Serbs, Slovaks, Germans and Gypsies living alongside the Romanians. Its music is fast, furious and a relatively new phenomenon, having absorbed a lot from the *novokomponovana* music of neighbouring Serbia. It's extremely popular, played all the time on the national radio and by Gypsy bands everywhere. I suspect that its attraction is simply its fast, modern, urban sound, with saxophones and frequently erotic lyrics. The Silex recording of the **Taraf de Carancebeş** (*sic*) is a great introduction to this virtuoso style.

THE CEAUŞESCU LEGACY

Nicolae Ceauşescu's 25 years of dictatorship still hang like a dark shadow over Romania. The legacy extends, too, to some of the country's folk music, which was manipulated into a sort of "fakelore" to glorify the dictator and present the rich and picturesque past of the Romanian peasantry from whom Ceauşescu aimed to create the "New Man".

Huge sanitized displays called **Cîntarea Romaniei** (Song of Romania) were held in regional centres around the country with thousands of peasants dressed up in costume bussed out to picturesque hillsides to sing and dance. This was filmed, appallingly edited, and shown on television every Sunday (indeed, programmes of this kind, often lushly orchestrated with scores of strings, are still used to fill the odd half-hour gap in the schedule). The words of songs were often changed – removing anything deemed to be religious or that questioned the peasants' love of their labours, and replacing it with bland patriotic sentiments or hymns to peace.

This gave folklore a pretty bad name amongst the educated classes, though the peasants were hardly bothered by it at all. They just did what they were told for Cîntarea Romaniei and got on with their real music in the villages. The fact is that traditional music still flourishes throughout Romania – probably more than anywhere else in Europe – not thanks to Ceauşescu but despite him. The isola-

tion of the country and its almost medieval rural lifestyle have preserved traditions that have been modernized out of existence elsewhere. Luckily village systematization didn't progress very far, although the impact of earlier collectivization and forced resettlement of peasants badly affected traditional culture in some of the central provinces. Since the revolution, some musicologists have even hazarded a beneficial effect of Cîntarea Romaniei in reviving ballads, doinăs and other forms which were dying out. They are now concerned to get back to the original styles and even to rediscover the Christian dimensions of Romanian folk music.

As Romania slowly catches up with the rest of Europe, its rich musical traditions are bound to disappear. Already it is getting harder to hear traditional bands played at weddings. Doubtless the music will be maintained in an organized form, but the great joy of Romanian music now is its total spontaneity and authenticity.

DISCOGRAPHY

CDs are marked with an asterisk

TRANSYLVANIAN VILLAGE BANDS

Various Hungarian Music from Northern Mezőség (Hungaroton, Hungary). Four LPs featuring music from the villages of Bonţida (Bonchida), Răscruci (Válaszút), Buza (Búza), Fizeţul Gherlii (Ördöngösfüzes) and Suartu (Magyarszovát). Collected by Zoltán Kallós and György Martin, these are earthy performances of music that has become all the rage in Budapest.

*Various La Vraie Tradition de Transylvanie (Ocora, France). A good selection of peasant music from Maramureş and Transylvania.

*Various Musiques de Mariage de Maramureş (Ocora, France). One of the few recordings of Maramureş music, performed by three village wedding bands.

*Various Romania – Music for Strings from Transylvania (Chant du Monde, France). A fine collection of dance music played by village bands. Good to see Romanian music in a first-class release like this. Highly recommended.

*Sándor Fodor Hungarian Music from Transylvania (Hungaroton, Hungary). Music from Kalotaszeg including some Romanian dances. One of the essential Transylvanian records.

*Mihály Halmágyi Hungarian Music from Gyimes (Hungaroton, Hungary). Dance, wedding and funeral tunes played on fiddle and gardon. Strange and wild music. A great performance of "the shepherd and his lost sheep" with a running commentary.

*Szászcsávás Band Folk Music from Transylvania (Quintana/Harmonia Mundi, France). This is the real thing – a Gypsy band from the predominantly Hungarian village of Ceuaş (Szászcsávás). Great recòrding, wild playing plus some interesting Saxon and Gypsy tunes.

*Taraful Soporu de Cîmpie (Buda, France). From the village of Soporu, one of the fine Gypsy bands from the Cîmpia Transilvaniei.

HUNGARIAN TÁNCHÁZ GROUPS

*Various Musiques de Transylvanie (Fonti Musicale, Belgium). This is the best overall introduction to Transylvanian music, with a very good selection of pieces and performances.

*Béla Halmos Az a szép piros hajnal (Hungaroton, Hungary). One of the leading musicians of the Budapest táncház scene with a collection of music from various regions of Transylvania.

*Muzsikás *Máramaros* (Hannibal, UK). A fascinating CD from the top Hungarian group joined by two wonderful old Gypsy musicians on fiddle and cimbalom to explore the lost Jewish repertory of Transylvania, distinguishable by the oriental-sounding augmented intervals in the melody. Also *Blues for Transylvania* (Hannibal, UK), a fine selection of Hungarian music from Transylvania.

*Ökrös Ensemble *Transylvanian Portraits* (Koch, US). Another comprehensive guide to the various styles of Transylvania. The fiddle-playing of Csaba Ökrös on the last track is stunning.

*Ferenc Sebő *Folk Music from Lőrincréve* (Hungaroton, Hungary). Extraordinarily rich and beautiful music from the Maros-Küküllő region south of Cluj, with modern players re-creating the music as collected before World War II.

ROMANIAN GYPSY GROUPS

*Taraf de Carancebeş *Musiciens du Banat* (Silex, France). A five-piece band of saxophone, trumpet, clarinet, accordion and bass. Some stunning virtuoso playing, which is enough to explain the popularity of the Banat style.

*Taraf de Haidouks *Taraf de Haidouks* and *Honourable Brigands, Magic, Horses and Evil Eye* (Crammed Discs, Belgium). Both of these are essential recordings of virtuoso playing by Romanian musicians from Clejani in an ensemble of fiddles, accordions, *ţambal* and bass. Their earlier recording (as ***Les Lăutari de Clejani**) *Music of the Wallachian Gypsies* (Ocora, France) is another fine, if slightly less colourful collection of songs and dances.

*Trio Pandulescu *Trio Pandulescu* (Silex, France). This highly recommended trio features hot accordion playing from Vasile Pandelescu plus *ţambal* and bass. Brilliant music-making with delicate moments of real poetry and all the requisite fire.

ROMANIAN VILLAGE RECORDINGS

Various *Ballads and Festivals in Romania* (Chant du Monde, France). A scholarly collection of long ballads and a few dances from Wallachian villages. Good recordings and full texts in French.

*Various *Village Music from Romania* (VDE-Gallo, Switzerland). A three-CD box produced by the Geneva Ethnographic Museum. Archival recordings of specialized interest made by the Romanian musicologist Constantin Brăiloiu in 1933–43 on his travels around Moldavia, Oltenia and Transylvania; with detailed sleeve notes and lyrics.

OTHER RECORDINGS

*Dumitru Fărcaş & Marcel Cellier *Taragot et Orgue* (Disques Cellier 007014). Zamfir's accompanist with the leading player of the clarinet-like taragot.

*Gheorghe Zamfir & Marcel Cellier *L'Ame Roumaine* (Pierre Verany 750002, France). Popular panpipe music from Romania's most famous musician, with Marcel Cellier on organ.

*Various *Roumanie: polyphonie vocale des Aroumains* (Le Chant du Monde LUX 74803). CNRS/Musée de l'Homme recordings of the Romanians living in Dobrogea, Bulgaria and elsewhere in the Balkans. Hard-core ethnic stuff; melancholy unaccompanied vocal choruses.

*Various *YIKHES: Klezmer recordings from 1907–1939* (Trikont, Germany). "Jewish jazz" – remastered 78s, including a couple of 1910 tracks by Belf's Romanian Orchestra, virtually the only European Klezmer band of the period to have been recorded. Many Romanian musical forms like the *doina* have been absorbed into the Klezmer repertoire.

Simon Broughton

DRACULA AND VAMPIRES

Truth, legends and fiction swirl around the figure of Dracula like a cloak, and perceptions of him differ sharply. In Romania today, schoolbooks and historians extol him as a patriot and a champion of order in lawless times, while the outside world knows Dracula as the vampire count of a thousand cinematic fantasies derived from Bram Stoker's novel of 1897 – a spoof-figure or a ghoul. The disparity in images is easily explained, for while vampires feature in native folklore (see below), Romanians make no associations between them and the historical figure of Dracula, the Wallachian prince Vlad IV, known in his homeland as Vlad Ţepeş – Vlad the Impaler. During his lifetime (c1431–1476) Vlad achieved renown beyond Wallachia's borders as a successful fighter against the Turks and a ruthless ruler; his reputation for cruelty spread throughout Europe via the newly invented printing presses (whose pamphlets were the bestsellers of the fifteenth century) and the word of his political enemies – notably the Transylvanian Saxons. At this time, Vlad was not known as a vampire, although some charged that he was in league with the Devil.

VLAD ŢEPEŞ – THE HISTORICAL DRACULA

He was not very tall, but very stocky and strong, with a cold and terrible appearance, a strong and aquiline nose, swollen nostrils, a thin reddish face in which very long eyelashes framed large wide-open green eyes; the bushy black eyebrows made them appear threatening. His face and chin were shaven, but for a moustache. The swollen temples increased the bulk of his head. A bull's neck connected his head to his body from which black curly locks hung on his wide-shouldered person.

Such was the papal legate's impression of **Vlad Ţepeş** – then in his thirties and a prisoner at the court of Visegrád in Hungary. He had been born in Sighişoara and raised at Tîrgovişte after his father, Vlad Dracul, became Voivode of Wallachia in 1436. Young Vlad's privileged childhood effectively ended in 1444, when he and his brother Radu were sent by their father as hostages to Anatolia, to curry favour with the Turkish Sultan. By this move, Vlad Dracul incurred the enmity of János Hunyadi, prince of Transylvania, who arranged for Dracul to be murdered in 1447. Vlad and Radu were released by the Turks to be pawns in the struggle between their expanding empire, Hunyadi and the new ruler of Wallachia. The experience of five years of Turkish captivity and years of exile in Moldavia and Transylvania shaped Vlad's personality irrevocably, and educated him in guile and terrorism.

Seeking a vassal, Hunyadi helped Vlad to become **ruler of Wallachia** in 1456; but promptly died, leaving him dangerously exposed. Signing a defence pact and free trade agreement with the Saxons of Braşov, Vlad quickly decided that it was also prudent to pay an annual tribute of 10,000 gold ducats to the Sultan while he consolidated his power in Wallachia. For generations there, the boyar families had defied and frequently deposed their own rulers, including Vlad's father and his elder brother Mircea, whom they buried alive.

His method of law enforcement was simple: practically all crimes and individuals offending him were punished by death; and Vlad's customary means of execution was **impaling people**. Victims were bound spread-eagled while a stake was hammered up their rectum, and then were raised aloft and left to die in agony, for all to see. To test his subjects' honesty, Vlad disguised himself and moved amongst them; left coins in shops and overcompensated merchants who had been robbed; and slew all that failed the test. Foreigners reported the demise of theft, and Dracula symbolically placed a golden cup beside a lonely fountain for anyone to drink from and no one dared to take it away. On Easter Day in 1459, Vlad eliminated the potentially rebellious boyars en masse by inviting them and their families to dine at his palace; guards then entered and seized them, impaling many forthwith while the remainder were marched off to labour at Poienari. In a similar vein, he invited Wallachia's disabled, unemployed and workshy to feast with him at Tîrgovişte, and asked if they wished to be free of life's sufferings. Receiving an affirmative reply Dracula had them all burnt, justifying his action as a measure to ensure that none of his subjects should ever suffer from poverty or disability.

All this was but a ramp for Dracula's ambition to be the acknowledged ruler of a mighty power, which caused much feuding with the **Saxons** of Braşov, Sibiu and the Bîrsa Land. It began in 1457, when he accused them of supporting claimants to his throne, and decided to end the Saxon merchants' practice of trading freely throughout Wallachia. When they persisted, Dracula led his army through the Red Tower Pass to burn Saxon villages, and had any of their people found inside Wallachia impaled. In 1460, Vlad annihilated the forces of his rival, Dan III, who invaded with the support of Braşov; and on this occasion dined in a garden amongst the impaled bodies of his enemies, using a holy icon as a dish, according to the *Chronicon Mellicense*. A month later he attacked the Bîrsa Land, and impaled hundreds of townsfolk on Sprenghi Hill within sight of Braşov's defenders before marching off to ravage the Făgăraş region.

At the same time, Vlad plotted to turn **against the Turks** and form alliances with his cousin Ştefan in Moldavia, and the Hungarian monarchy. Having defaulted on payments of tribute for two years, and nailed the turbans of two emissaries to their heads when they refused to doff them, Dracula **declared war** by raiding Turkish garrisons from Vidin to Giurgiu. A massive army led by Sultan Mehmet II crossed the Danube into Wallachia in 1462, but found itself advancing through countryside denuded of inhabitants, food and water, "with the sun burning so that the armour of the *ghazzis* could well be used to cook kebabs". On the night of June 17 Dracula's army raided the Turkish camp inflicting heavy casualties, and a few days later the demoralized invaders approached Tîrgovişte only to recoil in horror. En route to the capital Vlad had prepared a forest of stakes 1km by 3km wide, upon which 20,000 Turkish and Bulgarian captives were impaled. Shattered by their losses and these terror tactics, the Turks retreated home in disorder.

Dracula's downfall has been attributed to the Saxons, who used every opportunity to support his enemies and defame him throughout Europe. Most likely they forged the implausible "treason note" (in which Vlad purportedly offered to help the Sultan capture Transylvania)

– the pretext for Mátyás Corvinus to order Dracula's arrest in November 1462. Until 1475, he was a "guest" at Visegrád, where Mátyás would introduce him to Turkish ambassadors to discomfort them; Wallachia's throne was occupied by Dracula's pliable brother Radu "The Handsome", who had once served as the Sultan's catamite. Released by Mátyás to continue the anti-Turkish struggle, Vlad resided for a year in Sibiu (where the townsfolk deemed it politic to allow him hospitality) and regained his throne in 1476. His triumph was short-lived, however, for Radu offered the boyars an alternative to "rule by the stake" and a chance to placate the Turks, which they seized gratefully. In circumstances that remain unclear (some say that a servant was bribed to slay him), Vlad was betrayed by the boyars and killed. His head disappeared – reputedly sent to the Sultan as a present – while the Impaler's decapitated body was buried inside the church at Snagov Monastery, where it remains today.

The lack of any inscription on Vlad's tomb and of any portraits of him in medieval church frescoes suggests that attempts were made, for many years afterwards, to erase the memory of Dracula in Romania, although in the Ceauşescu epoch, he was rehabilitated as a wise lawgiver and a fighter for national independence. Vlad's cruelties were minimized or forgiven, and apologists argued that impalement was widely practised by the Turks (as Vlad would have seen in his youth), and by Ştefan of Moldavia, besides being prescribed in the old Wallachian *Vlastares* penal code. In 1985 Ceauşescu's vile court poet Adrian Păunescu denounced Stoker's novel and the Dracula films as "only one page in a vast output of political pornography directed against us by our enemies", an attack "on the very idea of being a Romanian"; predictably the Hungarians were blamed for creating the vampire myth.

VAMPIRES

Horrible though his deeds were, Vlad was not accused of **vampirism** during his lifetime. However, vampires were an integral part of folklore in Eastern and Southeastern Europe, known as *vámpír* in Hungarian and *strigoi* in Romanian. Details of their habits and characteristics vary from place to place, but in their essentials are fairly similar. A vampire is an

undead corpse, animated by its spirit and with a body that fails to decay, no matter how long in the grave. Vampirism can be contagious or people might occasionally be born as vampires, bearing stigmata such as a dark-coloured spot on the head or a rudimentary tail. However a vampire is usually created when a person dies and the soul is unable to enter heaven or hell. The reason may be that the person has died in a "state of sin" – by suicide, for example, or holding heretical beliefs – or because the soul has been prevented from leaving the body. Hanging was a form of death dreaded by Romanians, who believed that tying the neck "forces the soul down outward"; while the Orthodox custom of shrouding mirrors in the home of the deceased was intended to prevent the spirit from being "trapped" by seeing its reflection. As Catholicism and Orthodoxy competed for adherents in the wake of the Ottoman withdrawal from the Balkans, priests also claimed that the cemetery of the opposing church was unconsecrated land, thereby raising the fear of vampires rising from the grave.

Once created, a vampire is almost immortal, and becomes a menace to the living. In Romanian folklore, vampires frequently return to their former homes at night, where they must be propitiated with offerings of food and drink, and excluded by smearing garlic around the doors and windows. Should a new-born baby lie within, it must be guarded until it is christened, lest a vampire sneak in and transform it into another vampire. Two nights of the year are especially perilous: **April 23**, St George's Day (when, as Jonathan Harker was warned in Bram Stoker's novel, "all the evil things in the world will have full sway") and **November 29**, the eve of St Andrew's Day. On the latter night, vampires rise with their coffins on their heads, lurk about their former homes, and then gather to fight each other with hempen whips at crossroads. Such places were considered to be unlucky, being infested by spirits called *lele* (Man's enemies). In Gypsy folklore, vampires (*Mulé*) also live at the exact moment of midday, when the sun casts no shadow. Gypsies must cease travelling, for at that instant *Mulé* control the roads, trees and everything else. Interestingly, Gypsies only fear their own *Mulé* – the ghosts and vampires of *gadjé* (non-Gypsies) are of no account.

The greatest danger was presented by **vampire epidemics**. Although in horror films and Bram Stoker's novel, vampires must bite their victims and suck blood to cause contagion, in Eastern European folklore the vampire's look or touch can suffice. A classic account refers to the Austro-Hungarian village of Haidam in the 1720s. There, before witnesses, a man dead ten years returned as a vampire to his son's cottage, touched him on the shoulder and then departed. The man died the next morning. Alarmed by this report and others relating how long-dead villagers were returning to suck their children's blood, the local military commander ordered several graves to be exhumed, within which were found corpses showing no signs of decay. All were incinerated to ashes – one of the classic methods of exterminating vampires. Another epidemic occurred in the village of Medvegia near Belgrade, between 1725 and 1731. A soldier claimed to have been attacked by a vampire while in Greece (where vampire legends also abound), and died upon his return home. Thereafter many villagers swore they had seen him at night, or had dreamt about him, and ten weeks later complained of inexplicable weakness. The body was exhumed, was found to have blood in its mouth, and had a stake driven through its heart. Despite this precaution there was an outbreak of vampirism a few years later, and of the fourteen corpses examined by a medical commission, twelve were found to be "unmistakably in the vampire condition" (undecayed). In 1899 Romanian peasants in Caraşova dug up thirty corpses and tore them to pieces to stop a diphtheria epidemic, and in 1909 a Transylvanian castle was burned down by locals who believed that a vampire emanating from it was causing the deaths of their children. Only recently, in 1988, outside Niş in southern Serbia, a thirteen year-old girl was killed by her family, who believed her to be a vampire.

Sceptics may dismiss vampires and vampirism entirely, but some of the related phenomena have rational or scientific explanations. The "return of the dead" can be explained by premature burial, which happened frequently in the past. Nor is the drinking of blood confined to legendary, supernatural creatures. Aside from the Masai tribe of Kenya – whose diet contains cattle blood mixed with milk – numerous examples can be found in the annals of criminology and psychopathology.

BRAM STOKER'S DRACULA

During the eighteenth century, numerous well-publicized incidents of vampirism sparked a **vampire craze in Europe**, with both lurid accounts and learned essays produced in quantity. The first respectable **literary work** on a vampire theme was Goethe's *The Bride of Corinth* (1797), soon followed by Polidori's *The Vampyre*, which arose out of the same blood-curdling holiday on Lake Geneva in 1816 that produced Mary Shelley's *Frankenstein*. Other variations followed, by Kleist, E. T. A. Hoffmann, Mérimée, Gogol, Dumas, Baudelaire, and Sheridan Le Fanu, whose *Carmilla* features a lesbian vampire in Styria.

These fired the imagination of **Bram Stoker** (1847–1912), an Anglo-Irish civil servant who became manager to the great actor Sir Henry Irving in 1878 and wrote a few other novels, all now justly forgotten. In 1890 he conceived the suitably *fin-de-siècle* idea of a vampire novel; initially it too was to be set in Styria, with an anti-hero called "Count Wampyr", but once he had unearthed the figure of Vlad Ţepeş during his detailed researches in the Reading Room of the British Museum, the setting moved east to Transylvania, and **Count Dracula** was born.

Stoker's fictional Count, who was a Székely, owed something to another historical Hungarian – the "Blood Countess", Elizabeth Báthori, born almost a century after Vlad's death – and was possibly influenced by the "Jack the Ripper" murders which happened a decade earlier in Whitechapel, where Stoker lived for a time while writing his book. Stoker delved deep into Romanian folklore, history and geography, and the book is a masterpiece in its mixture of fantasy and precise settings.

Other books on the same theme followed, but it was the advent of **cinema** and the horror film that has ensured the fame of Dracula. The silent *Nosferatu* is perhaps the greatest vampire film, but Coppola's *Bram Stoker's Dracula* is truest to its roots, even going so far as to include the historic Vlad Ţepeş in a prelude.

> Dracula buffs might like to contact the **British Dracula Association**, headed by Julia Kruk, 203 Wulfstan St, London W12 0AB (☎0181/749 2694) and Rob Leake (☎0181/853 1741). Their journal, *Voices from the Vaults*, concerns itself with the Gothic imagination and literature.

BOOKS

Since 1989, the surge in interest in Eastern Europe, and the particularly dramatic nature of Romania's revolution and its problems since then, have led to several excellent writers visiting in quick succession. In addition there is a wealth of nineteenth-century and early twentieth-century travellers' accounts, although much is out of print. Romanian literature is still under-represented in translation. Publishers details are given in the form (UK publisher/US publisher) where both exist; if books are published in one country only, this follows the publisher's name (eg Serpent's Tail, UK). University Press has been abbreviated to UP. Out of print titles are indicated (p/p).

TRAVELLERS' TALES

PRE-WAR

Hector Bolitho *Romania Under King Carol* (O/P). Reporting Romania's slide towards fascism from the Calea Victoriei, with ţuică glass and caviar close at hand, Bolitho established the style for a "Bright Lights of Bucharest" school of writing – gossipy, smug and cynical by turns.

Charles Boner *Transylvania: Its Products and its People* (O/P). Long-winded but useful nineteenth-century account: particularly informative on the Saxon and Magyar communities.

Emily Gerard *The Land Beyond the Forest* (O/P). One of the classic nineteenth-century accounts of Transylvania, written by an expatriate Scotswoman. Massive and rambling, but highly informative on folk customs, superstitions, proverbs and the like.

D. W. Hall *Romanian Furrow* (O/P). Discounting a few folk verses and some nice photos, this account of rural life hardly deserved King Carol's description of it as the "best book" about the Romanian peasantry in the 1930s.

Patrick Leigh Fermor *Between the Woods and the Water* (Penguin, UK & US). Transylvania provides the setting for the second volume in this unfolding, retrospective trilogy, based on Leigh Fermor's diaries for 1933–34, when he walked from Holland to Constantinople. His precocious zest for history and cultural diversity rose to the challenge of Transylvania's striking contrasts and obscurely turbulent past; the richness of his jewelled prose and the deluge of details are impressive, if not overwelmingly so.

Queen Marie of Romania *My Country* (O/P), *The Country that I Love* (O/P) and *The Story of My Life*, published as *Ordeal* in the US (3 vols; O/P) are all gushingly twee, and fail to convey the forceful character of this Edinburgh lass who won the hearts of Romania's people. Many of the photos are lovely, however, and the books do have a certain period charm.

Bernard Newman *Blue Danube* (O/P). Aside from a memorable encounter with some Gypsies near Orşova and a description of the Kazan Gorge, the Romanian chapters of this 1930s cycling epic contain little of interest.

Ethel Greening Pantazzi *Romania in Light and Shadow* (O/P). An amusing and affectionate book, by a Canadian woman who married a Romanian naval officer.

Maude Parkinson *Twenty Years in Romania* (O/P). Having gone there to teach, Parkinson grew to love the country and wrote this amusing testimonial, partly to raise Romanian prestige abroad during the disastrous years of the First World War.

Lion Phillimore *In the Carpathians* (O/P). A fascinating account of a journey by horsecart through the Maramureş and Székelyföld, by a proto-hippy who wants nothing but to commune with the mountains and the trees.

Sacheverell Sitwell *Romanian Journey* (O/P). Motoring around, the Sitwells were both politely appalled, and vaguely charmed, by Romania; but most of all seem to have been relieved that their gastronomic fortunes didn't suffer unduly. Nice colour plates in the original edition.

Walter Starkie *Raggle Taggle* (O/P). After his exploits in Hungary, Starkie tramped down through Transylvania to Bucharest, where his encounters with Gypsies and lowlife are recounted in a florid but quite amusing style. A secondhand-bookshop classic, occasionally found with the accompanying record of Starkie playing his fiddle.

Teresa Stratilesco *From Carpathians to Pindus* (O/P). Covers the same ground as Gerard, with an equally sharp eye for quirky details.

R. G. Waldeck *Athénée Palace Bucharest* (O/P). Subtitled "Hitler's New Order Comes to Romania", this captures the unease, corruption and hedonism of Bucharest before the outbreak of war. The machinations of Carol, the Iron Guard and Antonescu get a look in, but Waldeck's account is more an evocation of the times than a political study.

POST-WAR

Henry Baerlein, ed. *Romanian Scene* and *Romanian Oasis* (O/P). Two fine anthologies of travellers' tales in which most of the pre-war authors listed above are featured. Baerlein also wrote three turgid accounts of his own travels during the '30s: *Bessarabia and Beyond* (O/P), *And Then to Transylvania* (O/P) and *In Old Romania* (O/P).

Helena Drysdale *Looking for Gheorghe* (Sinclair-Stevenson, UK). A quest rather than a travel book, although the picture of Romanian life both before and after the revolution is spot-on. A search for a lost friend leads to unsavoury insights into life with the *Securitate* and finally to a hellish "mental hospital".

Leslie Gardiner *Curtain Calls* (O/P). A critical but never unsympathetic picture of Romania, Albania and Bulgaria emerges in this light-hearted account of Gardiner's visits during the '60s and early '70s. The Romanian chapters contain anecdotes concerning the pre-war monarchy, and a description of steamy Valcov in the Delta, where Gardiner made an unauthorized landing.

Jason Goodwin *On Foot to the Golden Horn* (Vintage, UK). Not exactly in the footsteps of Leigh Fermor, but nevertheless an engaging and well-informed writer walking from Gdansk to Istanbul in 1990 – almost half the book is in fact set in Transylvania. Very thoughtful, but

it's annoyingly hard to work out which are the author's opinions and which those of the characters he meets.

Brian Hall *Stealing from a Deep Place* (Minerva/Hill & Wang). Hall cycled through Hungary, Romania and Bulgaria in 1982 and produced a beautifully defined picture of the nonsense that communism had become, and of people's mechanisms for coping.

Georgina Harding *In Another Europe* (Sceptre, US & UK). Another cycle tour, this one in 1988. Slimmer than Hall's book but concentrating far more on Romania, with a more emotional response to Ceauşescu's follies.

Eva Hoffmann *Exit into History* (Heinemann/Viking). Not a patch on *Lost in Translation*, her superb account of being uprooted from Jewish Kraków to North America, but this tour of East-Central Europe in 1990 still yields seventy insightful pages on Romania.

Andrew MacKenzie *Romanian Journey* and *Dracula Country* (both O/P). *Romanian Journey's* dollops of history, architectural description and bland travelese wouldn't be so bad if MacKenzie didn't also whitewash the Ceauşescu regime, of which his strongest criticism was that there's "nothing soft" about it. *Dracula Country* is a more admirable book, as it doesn't purport to describe contemporary Romania and assembles interesting facts about folklore and Vlad the Impaler.

Rory MacLean *Stalin's Nose* (Flamingo/Little Brown). With its wonderfully surreal humour, this is not exactly a factual account, but it is a fundamentally serious book about the effects of World War II and communism all over Eastern Europe.

Claudio Magris *Danube* (Collins Harvill/Farrar, Straus, Giroux). One of the great travel books of recent years, full of scholarly anecdotes and subtle insights. Magris follows the Danube from source to sea, with sidetrips as far as Sighişoara.

Scott Malcolmson *Empire's Edge* (Faber, UK). A study of nationalism and nationhood since the changes of 1989 and 1991 in Bulgaria, Romania, Turkey and Uzbekistan. Malcolmson's rather dubious thesis is that moves towards ethnic homogenization, from the time of Eminescu onwards, have been driven by an image of European culture as rational, secular and above all white.

Dervla Murphy *Transylvania and Beyond* (Arrow/Charnwood, Ulverscroft). A more serious and analytical book than many of her others, tussling with the problems of immediately post-revolutionary Transylvania and its ethnic tensions in particular. Tellingly, she uses the Hungarian spelling "Rumania" throughout, and other spellings are erratic.

Peter O'Conner *Walking Good: Travels to Music in Hungary and Romania* (O/P). Another Irish fiddler in search of Gypsy music, forty years after Starkie. O'Conner's quest took him to Slobozia, Cojocna and Făgăraş, staying with local people a few years before this became illegal. Entertaining.

Ivor Porter *Operation Autonomous: with SOE in Wartime Romania* (O/P). Porter came to Olivia Manning's Bucharest in 1939 to do the job she gave to Guy Pringle, left in 1941 and returned in December 1943, to be captured at once – this is not only a fascinating account of the 1944 coup (including contacts with the West, covered up until 1989), but is also full of excellent background information on Romania in this period.

Giles Whittell *Lambada Country* (Phoenix, UK). Another cycle trip to Istanbul, at the same time as Jason Goodwin. Less than a quarter of the book is on Romania, but it's interesting and informative, particularly on Magyar attitudes.

HISTORY AND POLITICS

As well as the titles listed below, there's quite a collection of books on the changes of 1989 across Eastern Europe, well worth looking at if you're travelling around the region; they tend to treat Romania as the exception, the only one with a violent revolution. They include **Roger East** *Revolutions in Eastern Europe* (Pinter/St Martin's Press); **William Echikson** *Lighting the Night* (Sidgwick & Jackson/Morrow); **Mischa Glenny** *The Rebirth of History* (Penguin, US & UK); **Mark Frankland** *The Patriots' Revolution* (Sinclair-Stevenson/I R Dee); and **Gwyn Prins** *Spring in Winter* (Manchester UP/St Martin's Press). **John Simpson**'s *The Darkness Crumbles* (Hutchinson, UK), an updated version of his *Despatches from the Barricades*, is less analytical, but has a splendid first-hand account of dodging bullets during the Bucharest street fighting.

Mark Almond *The Rise and Fall of Nicolae and Elena Ceauşescu* (O/P). Definitive and very readable account by one of the best academics writing on Romania, though too kind to the sinister Silviu Brucan. Rather wayward footnotes and accents.

Dan Antal *Out of Romania* (Faber, UK). An insider's version of the now so familiar story: dreadful oppression under Ceauşescu, and even worse disillusion after the revolution. Well enough told by a sympathetic character.

Ed Behr *Kiss the Hand You Cannot Bite* (Hamish Hamilton/Random House). A good, populist account of the Ceauşescus' rise and fall.

Terence Elsberry *Marie of Romania* (Cassell/St Martin's Press). A colourful biography of Queen Marie.

Mary Ellen Fischer *Nicolae Ceauşescu, a Study in Political Leadership* (L. Rienner, UK & US). Academic, detailed and readable description of the system created by Ceauşescu that was soon to drag him down.

S. Fischer-Galaţi *Twentieth Century Rumania* (Colorado UP, US). An easy read with good illustrations, this complements Hale's book (see below) by providing more background, and is basically sympathetic to the changes that had happened since 1949.

George Galloway and Bob Wylie *Downfall* (Futura/Macdonald Futura). Unreliable – Labour MP Galloway has been well briefed by Iliescu and his aides and has fallen hook, line and sinker for their version of events.

Vlad Georgescu *The Romanians – A History* (Tauris/Ohio State UP). The best modern history in translation, although the importance of dissidents under Ceauşescu seems overstated. Georgescu, head of the Romanian Service of Radio Free Europe, died in 1988, but an epilogue covers the events of 1989.

Dinu Giurescu *The Razing of Romania's Past* (World Monuments Fund/US ICOMOS). Describes in painstaking detail the buildings destroyed by 1988 in Ceauşescu's megalomaniac prestige projects.

Julian Hale *Ceauşescu's Romania* (O/P). Readable and informative, albeit dated and overly optimistic.

C. Michael-Titus *The Magyar File* (Panopticum Press, UK). Takes up the cudgels on Romania's behalf, refuting evidence of discrimination against the Hungarian minority under Ceauşescu.

Dan Nelson *Romania After Tyranny* (Westview, UK & US). A collection of pieces by many of the big names in Romanian studies, but already looking dated.

Ion Pacepa *Red Horizons* (Heinemann/Regnery Gateway). A lurid, rambling "exposé" of the Ceauşescu regime, written by its former intelligence chief (who defected in 1978), describing disinformation and espionage abroad; corruption and perversions amongst the élite, and much else. Pacepa was deeply involved but reveals little about himself.

Prince Paul of Hohenzollern-Roumania *King Carol II, a life of my grandfather* (O/P). The nephew of the current King Mihai, Paul doesn't deny his grandfather's dreadful personal life, but attempts to rehabilitate him as a statesman placed by fate in an impossible position between Hitler and Stalin: plausible but not ultimately convincing.

Martyn Rady *Romania in Turmoil* (Tauris, UK). Wonderfully clear account of Ceauşescu's rise and fall, continuing to the end of 1991, which gives it an edge on the books rushed out in 1990. Recommended.

Nestor Ratesh *Romania: the Entangled Revolution* (Praeger, UK). A careful account of the revolution, laying out all the confusion that still surrounds events.

Ion Raţiu *Contemporary Romania* (Foreign Affairs Publications, UK). A generally negative portrayal of the system by an émigré who made a million in Britain and was to return after Ceauşescu's downfall to lead an opposition party.

George Schöpflin *The Hungarians of Rumania* (Minority Rights Group, UK). This careful presentation of the evidence on communist discrimination against the Magyars is worth reading.

R. W. Seton-Watson *A History of the Roumanians* (Cambridge UP, UK). Although it largely ignores social history and eschews atmospherics, and even the author admits his despair at the welter of dynastic details, it's still the classic English work on Romanian history before 1920. Seton-Watson's *Roumania and the Great War* (1915) and *The Rise of Nationality in the Balkans* (1917) somewhat influenced British policy in favour of the Successor States, and for this reason he attracted great hostility in Hungary.

John Sweeney *The Life and Evil Times of Nicolae Ceauşescu* (Hutchinson, UK). Not definitive, but worth reading.

László Tökes *With God, for the People* (Hodder & Stoughton/Lubrecht & Cramer). The autobiography of the man who lit the spark of the revolution and continues to be a thorn in the establishment's side, even as a bishop.

Richard Wurmbrand *In God's Underground* (Living Sacrifice Books, US). The memoirs of a Lutheran priest who spent many years incarcerated at Jilava, Craiova, Piteşti and other notorious prisons.

FOLKLORE

Romanian books on folklore and ethnography (of coffee-table book dimensions) are cheaper to buy and easier to find in Romania. The illustrations are often great, but many of the books have only garbled or touristic English summaries; however **Ion Milcea**'s *Sweet Bucovina* and **Maliţa & Banateanu**'s *From the Thesaurus of Traditional Popular Custom* (both published by Editura Sport-Turism, Bucharest) are safe recommendations. Massive books on the Saxon communities, beautifully produced in Germany, include *Die Siebenburgiooho Karpatenverein* (Wort und Welt, Thaur bei Innsbruck), *Siebenbürgen, ein Abendländisches Schicksal* by H. Zillich (Blauen Bucher) and *Kirchenburgen in die Siebenbürgen* by Hermann and Alida Fabini (Hermann Böhlwas). The best books on the Maramureş churches are *Monumente Istorice şi de Artă Religioasă din Erchiepiscopia Vadului, Feleacului şi Clujului* (Episcopate of Vad, Feleac and Cluj) which omits a few interesting places but is pretty definitive; and *Pictura Murală Maramureşeană* by Anca Pop-Braţu (Meridiane).

David Buxton *Wooden Churches of Eastern Europe* (Cambridge UP) A learned and thorough tome.

Gail Kligman *The Wedding of the Dead* (California UP, US) and *Căluş: Symbolic Transformation in Romanian Ritual* (Chicago UP, US). The first is a wonderful book if you want to know everything about the anthropology and rituals of one Maramureş village, leud. The second is a slim but interesting anthropological study of the Whitsun Căluş rite, which still lingers in parts of southern Romania.

Katherine Verdery *Transylvanian Villagers, three centuries of political, economic and ethnic change* (California UP, US). Based on fieldwork west of Sebeş – a duller area than Maramureş, but therefore more broadly applicable than Kligman's book, though not as readable.

DRACULA

Paul Barber *Vampires, Burial and Death: Folklore and Reality* (Yale UP, US). "A scholarly work on human decomposition and historical attitudes to it", which says it all.

Daniel Farson *The Man who wrote Dracula: a biography of Bram Stoker* (Michael Joseph, UK) Entertaining account of the life of the fictional Dracula's creator.

Radu Florescu & Raymond McNally *In Search of Dracula* (Hale/Graphics Society, NY) and *Dracula, a Biography* (Hale/Hawthorn) are founts of knowledge about the Impaler; while McNally's *Dracula was a Woman – The Blood Countess of Transylvania* (Hale, UK) divulges the perverted deeds of Elizabeth Báthori.

Christopher Frayling *Vampyres* (Faber, UK). Primarily a study of the vampire theme in literature and broader culture, but also a near-definitive review of the phenomenon itself.

Clive Leatherdale *Dracula, the Novel and the Legend* (Aquarian/Desert Island Books). More concerned with the novel than with the Romanian background.

Nicolae Stoicescu *Vlad Ţepeş, Prince of Wallachia* (Bucharest) is the standard Romanian biography of the Impaler, whom Stoicescu practically attempts to sanctify.

Bram Stoker *Dracula* (Penguin, UK & US). The Gothic horror original that launched a thousand movies. From a promising start with undertones of fetishism and menace in Dracula's Transylvanian castle, the tale degenerates into pathos before returning to Romania, and ending in a not too effective chase.

ROMANIAN LITERATURE

PROSE

Emil Cioran *On the Heights of Despair* (Chicago UP, US). A key early work (1934, reissued in 1992) by this nihilist anti-philosopher.

Petru Dumitriu *The Family Jewels; The Prodigals; Incognito* (all O/P). A literary prodigy lauded by the Party for his book *Dustless Highway*, Dumitriu fled Romania in 1960 and subsequently published two tales of dynastic ambition, followed by his masterpiece of moral and psychological exploration, set against the backdrop of the war and the communist takeover, *Incognito*.

Mircea Eliade *Shamanism* (Routledge/ Pantheon), *Youth without Youth* (Ohio State UP, US) and *Fantastic Tales* (Forest Books, UK). The first is the most interesting and informative example of the academic work for which he is internationally known. The latter two are fictions which don't quite match his reputation as a magical realist in the South American tradition, although this is partly the fault of the translation. His *Journals* are published in four volumes by Chicago UP, and *Les Roumains – Précis Historique* (a very slim history) is available in French in Romania.

Norman Manea *On Clowns – the Dictator and the Artist* (Faber/Grove Weidenfeld). Deported to the camps of Transnistria at the age of five, after the war Manea became an engineer and then an increasingly dissident writer, fleeing from Romania in 1986. This collection consists largely of over-intellectual musings on the nature of dictatorship and the subjected populace's complicity.

Herta Müller *The Passport* (Serpent's Tail/ Consort). Müller is a Schwab who left Romania in 1987. *The Passport* is a tale, in a distinctive staccato style, of the quest for permission to leave for Germany.

Dumitru Popescu *The Royal Hunt* (Quartet/ Ohio State UP). One of a sequence of seven volumes, this novel describes the way in which terror can overwhelm a community. Popescu is perhaps Romania's best-known contemporary novelist, and was president of the Writers' Union before the revolution.

Liviu Rebreanu *Uprising, Ion* and *The Forest of the Hanged* (Peter Owen/Ion Twayne, NY) comprise a panoramic picture of Romanian social life from the late nineteenth century to the First World War. *Uprising*, which deals with the 1907 peasant rebellion, shocked Romanian readers with its violent descriptions when it first appeared in 1933.

Elie Wiesel *Night* (Penguin/Discus). Wiesel was born in Sighet in 1928 and was deported to Auschwitz, where his family died, in 1944. After the war he pursued an academic career in the USA and was awarded the Nobel Peace Prize in 1986 for his work interpreting Judaism and the Holocaust. This slim book opens in the ghetto of Sighet, but soon moves to the death camps.

POETRY

Paul Celan *Selected Poems (1920–70)* (Penguin, UK). Romania's greatest poet, although writing in German, and one of the best of the twentieth century. Born in Bucovina in 1920, Celan survived the camps of Transnistria and emigrated to Paris. He committed suicide in 1970.

George Bacovia *Plumb/Lead* (Minerva, UK). With Arghezi he is the leading pre-war Romanian poet. Exquisite melancholy.

Maria Banuş *Demon in Brackets* (Forest Books/Dufour). Born in 1914, Banuş was involved with left-wing activities through the 1930s and 1940s, but her intimate lyricism remains popular today.

Petru Cârdu *The Trapped Strawberry* (Forest Books/Dufour). A Romanian-Yugoslav from Vršac, across the border south of Timişoara, Cârdu writes ironic poems in both Romanian and Serbo-Croat.

Ion Caraion *The Error of Being* (Forest Books/Dufour). A leading poet of the older generation, who composed many of his poems in the camps of World War II.

Nina Cassian *Call Yourself Alive?* and *Cheerleader for a Funeral* (Forest Books/Dufour). Savagely sensual and wickedly funny work from one of Romania's best poets.

Mircea Dinescu *Exile on a Peppercorn* (Forest Books/Dufour). Dinescu was a near-dissident before 1989 who was the first to announce the revolution on TV and was briefly co-opted onto the FSN Council.

Jon Miloş *Through The Needle's Eye* (Forest Books/Dufour). A Yugoslav-Romanian now living in Sweden, Miloş writes about universal social and environmental problems.

Marin Sorescu *Vlad Dracula the Impaler* (Forest Books/Dufour); *Let's Talk about the Weather* (Forest Books/Dufour); *Selected Poems 1965–73* (Bloodaxe, UK); *The Biggest Egg in the World* (Bloodaxe, UK). Sorescu's style is more ironic and accessible than that of many of his contemporaries and makes a good introduction to Romanian poetry.

Nichita Stănescu *Bas-Relief with Heroes* (Memphis State UP, US). Stănescu died aged fifty in 1982, but his prolific work (of which this is a selection) is still very influential.

Ion Stoica *As I Came to London one Midsummer's Day* (Forest Books/Dufour) and *Gates of the Moment* (Forest Books, Dufour). A poet of the older generation, now director of the Bucharest University Library, blending old and new influences.

Grete Tartler *Orient Express* (Oxford UP, UK). Another excellent Schwab writer, translated by Fleur Adcock.

Brenda Walker ed. *Anthology of Contemporary Romanian Poetry* (Forest Books/Dufour). Features the work of Romania's two best poets, Nina Cassian and Ana Blandiana.

FOREIGN NOVELISTS

Saul Bellow *The Dean's December* (Penguin/Harper & Row). The repression and poverty of Ceauşescu's Romania is contrasted with the hypocrisy and decadence of American society.

Olivia Manning *The Balkan Trilogy* (Mandarin/Penguin). The TV screening of *The Fortunes of War* has made Manning's epic story of thoroughly exasperating characters, initially set in Bucharest, widely known in Britain. The atmosphere of wartime Bucharest is well rendered in exquisite prose, but as an extended study of human relationships it's weakly constructed and eventually wearisome.

Gregor von Rezzori *Memoirs of an Anti-Semite* (Pan/Vintage) and *The Snows of Yesteryear* (Vantage/Knopf). The first is an account of growing up in the largely Romanian city of Czernowitz (Cernăuţi, now in Ukraine); the second is similar but more episodic.

Barbara Wilson *Trouble in Transylvania* (Virago/Seal Press). Inveterate traveller Cassandra Reilly goes to Sovata to investigate a murder, and gets the hots for most of the women she meets. Pretty strong on local colour in other respects.

LANGUAGE

Romanian is basically a Romance language with a grammar similar to Latin. This familial resemblance makes it easy for anyone who speaks French, Italian or (to a lesser extent) Spanish to recognize words and phrases in Romanian, even though its vocabulary also contains words of Dacian, Slav, Greek and Turkish origin, with more recent additions from French, German and English. German is widely understood – if not spoken – in the areas of Transylvania and the Banat traditionally inhabited by Saxons and Swabians; and many educated Romanians have learned the language for professional reasons, although the tendency amongst students nowadays is increasingly towards English. Foreigners who can muster any scrap of Hungarian will find it appreciated in the Magyar enclaves of Transylvania, but its use elsewhere invites hassle rather than sympathy, which is even more the case with Russian – a language that's greeted with derision by almost everyone except the Lipovani communities of the Delta.

Romanian **nouns** have three genders – masculine, feminine and neuter. **Adjectives** (usually placed after the word they describe) and **pronouns** always "agree" with the gender of the noun. *Mai* and *cel mai* are generally used to make comparatives and superlatives: eg. *ieftin* (cheap); *mai ieftin* (cheaper), *cel mai ieftin* (the cheapest). In Romanian the indefinite article "a" comes before the noun and is *un* for masculine and neuter words, *o* for feminine ones; the definite article "the" is added to the end of the noun: *-a* for feminine words, *-ul* or *-le* for masculine or neuter ones. The plural forms of nouns are slightly more complicated, but tend to end in *-i* or *-le*. **Verbs** are conjugated, so do not require pronouns such as "I" or "you", although these may be added for emphasis.

Pronunciation is likewise fairly straightforward. Words are usually, but not always, stressed on the syllable before last, and all letters are pronounced. However, certain letters change their sounds when combined with other ones. When speaking, Romanians tend to slur words together.

A "o" sound as in done.

Ă "er" sound as in mother; the combinations AU and ĂU resemble the sounds in how and go.

C is like "k" or as in country; except when it precedes certain letters: CE sounds like chest; CI sounds like cheek; CHE like kept; and CHI like keep.

E sounds as in ten; but at the start of a word it's pronounced as in year; while the combined EI sounds like bay or ray.

G is hard as in gust; except for the dipthongs GE which is like gesture; GI which is like jeans; GHE which is like guest; and GHI like gear.

I is as in feet; except for the vowel combinations IU as in you; IA as in yap; and IE as in yes.

LINGUISTIC POLITICS

The letter î replaced â when Stalin forced Romania to change the rules to make the language more Slavic in form, although a few exceptions such as România and Brâncuşi were allowed to survive. In 1994 the Romanian Academy decreed that î should revert to â, so that Tîrgu Mureş is officially Târgu Mureş, and Cîmpulung is now Câmpulung.

The rules (to do with whether words have a Latin root, where in the word the letter falls, and whether it follows a prefix) are too complex for most Romanians to follow, and as it is simpler for foreigners to cope with one accent on "i" (î) and one on "a" (ă) – Bîrgău rather than Bârgău, for example – and many signs and maps remain unchanged, we have decided to stick with the old form. However you should be aware of the potential for confusion.

Î (or Â) is pronounced midway between the o in lesson and the o in sort.

J is like the "s" in pleasure.

K only occurs in imported words like kilometre.

O is as in soft; except for OI, which is like boy, and OA as in quark.

R is always rolled.

Ş is slurred as in shop.

Ţ is a "ts" sound as in bits.

U sounds like book or good; but UA is pronounced as in quark.

W occurs in such foreign words as whisky and western.

In addition to the following language box, see the specialist vocabularies for eating and drinking (p.32) and hiking (p.41).

ROMANIAN WORDS AND PHRASES

Basics and Greetings

Yes, no, and	*da, nu, şi*	Good morning	*Bună dimineaţă*
Please, thank you	*Vă rog, mulţumesc*	Good day	*Bună ziua* (or *Servus*)
Sorry, excuse me	*Îmi pare rău, permiteţi-mi*	Good evening	*Bună seară*
		Good night	*Noapte bună*
Good, bad	*Bun, rău*	How are you?	*Ce mai faceţi?*
Do you speak English?	*Vorbiţi englezeste?*	What's your name?	*Cum vă numiţi?*
I don't understand	*Nu înţeleg*	Cheers!	*Noroc!* (literally Good Luck!)
Please speak slowly	*Vă rog să vorbiţi mai rar*		
Please write it down	*Scrieţi, vă rog*	Good, that's fine	*Bun, minunat* (*De acord* = it's agreed)
Say that again, please	*Vreţi să repetaţi, vă rog*		
I, we, you	*Eu, noi, dumneata* (*Tu* is informal)	Goodbye	*La revedere* (or *ciao, pa*)
		Bon voyage	*Drum bun* (literally "Good road")
Hello	*Salut*		
		Leave me alone!	*Lăsaţi-ma în pace!*

Directions and Accommodation

Where is..?/where are..?	*Unde este..?/unde sînt..?*	Twin beds	*două paturi*
The nearest	*cel mai aproape*	Double bed	*un pat dublu*
A (cheap) hotel	*un hotel (ieftin)*	For one person (alone)	*pentru o persoană (singura)*
Campsite	*loc de campare, popas*	Shower, bathroom	*duş, baie*
Toilet	*toaletă, WC*	There's no water	*Nu curge apă*
Is it far?	*Este departe?*	Hot, cold	*cald/fierbinte, frig/rece*
What bus must I take?	*Ce autobuz trebuie sa iau?*	How much per night?	*Cît costa pentru o noapte?*
Is there a footpath to..?	*Există potecă spre..?*	Is breakfast included?	*Micul dejun este inclus în preţ?*
Right, left, straight on	*Dreapta, stînga, dreapt înainte*	Have you nothing cheaper?	*Nu aveţi altceva mai ieftin?*
North, south, east, west	*Nord, sud, est, vest*		
Have you a room?	*Aveţi o cameră?*	Can you suggest another (a cheaper) hotel?	*Puteţi să-mi recomandaţi un alt hotel (un hotel mai ieftin)?*
With, without	*cu, fără*		

Signs

Arrival, departure	*Sosire, plecare*	Ladies' (Gents') WC	*WC femei (bărbaţi)*
Entrance, exit	*Intrare, leşire*	Waiting room	*Sală de aşteptare*
Vacant, occupied	*Liber, ocupat*	Operating, cancelled	*Circulă, anulat*
No vacancies	*Nu mai sînt locuri*	No smoking	*Fumatul oprit (Nefumatori)*
Open, closed	*Deschis, închis*		
Admission free	*Intrare gratuită*	No entry, danger	*Intrare interzisa, pericol*

Requests and Buying

I want (should like)...	*(Aş) vreau...*	Same again, please	*Încă un rînd, vă rog*
I don't want...	*Nu vreau...*	What's that?	*Ce este acesta?*
How much?	*Cît costă?*	Is it any good?	*Merita?*
A little (less)	*(Mai) puţn*	Bon appétit	*Poftă bună*
Is there...?	*Există.?*	Bill, receipt	*Notă, chitanţă*
Have you/do you sell..?	*Aveţi..?*	When will it be ready?	*Cînd este gata?*
Where can I buy..?	*Unde pot să cumpăr..?*	At once, we're in a	*Imediat, noi grăbim*
It's too expensive	*Este prea scump*	hurry	
Waiter, waitress	*Chelner, Chelneriţa*	What's the rate for the	*Care este cursul lirei*
What do you	*Ce îmi recomandaţi?*	pound/dollar?	*sterling/dolăruli?*
recommend?		Will you refund my	*Vă rog sa-mi daţi banii*
There's no more...	*S-a terminat...*	money?	*înapoi?*
Two glasses (bottles) of	*Două pahare (sticle) de*	Any letters for me?	*Aveţi vreo scrisoare*
beer	*bere*		*pentru mine?*

Getting Around

Does this bus go to the	*Autobuzul acesta*	When does the train	*Le ce ora pleacă trenul?*
train station?	*merge. la gară?*	leave?	
Bus terminal	*La autogară*	Two seats for...	*Două locuri pentru...*
Beach	*La plajă*	(tomorrow)	*(mîine)*
Into the centre	*În centru*	I want to reserve a	*Vreau sa rezerva loc de*
Does it stop at?	*Opreşte la.?*	sleeper (couchette)	*vagon de dormit (cu*
Has the last bus gone?	*A trecut ultimul*		*cuşete)*
	autobuz?	I want to change my	*Aş vreau să schimba*
I (want to) go to	*(Vreau să) merg la*	reservation to...	*rezervă pentru...*
Where are you going?	*Unde mergeţi?*	Is this the train for..?	*Acesta este trenul de..?*
Stop here (at...)	*Opriţi aici (la...)*	Where do I change?	*Unde schimb trenul?*
Is it a good road?	*Drumul este bun?*	Is there a boat from here	*Există curse de vapor de*
It isn't far	*Nu este departe*	to...?	*aici la..?*
Crossroads, bridge	*Intersecţie/răscruce,*	When does the next	*Cînd pleacă vaporul*
	pod	boat leave?	*următor?*
Which platform does	*De la ce peron pleacă*	Can I rent a (rowing)	*Pot să închiriez o barcă*
the train to... leave	*trenul către...?*	boat?	*(cu vişie)?*
from?		How much do you charge	*Cît costa ora/ziua?*
		by the hour/for the day?	

Time and Dates

What's the time?	*Ce oră este?*	Sunday	*Duminică*
It's early/late	*Este devreme/tîrziu*	January	*Ianuarie*
This morning	*Azi dimineaţă*	February	*Februarie*
Day, afternoon	*Zi, după masă*	March	*Martie*
Midday, midnight	*Amiază, miezul nopţii*	April	*Aprilie*
Evening, night	*Seară, noapte*	May	*Mai*
Today, yesterday	*Azi, astăzi, ieri*	June	*Iunie*
(day after) tomorrow	*(poi) mîine*	July	*Iulie*
Soon, never	*Curînd, niciodată*	August	*August*
Everyday	*În fiecare zi*	September	*Septembrie*
Monday	*Luni*	October	*Octombrie*
Tuesday	*Marţi*	November	*Noiembrie*
Wednesday	*Miercuri*	December	*Decembrie*
Thursday	*Joi*	New Year	*Anul Nou*
Friday	*Vineri*	Easter	*Paşte*
Saturday	*Sîmbătă*	Christmas	*Crăciun*

Numbers

1	un, una	11	unsprezece	21	douăzeci şi un/	500	cinci zece
2	doi, doua	12	doisprezece		una	1000	o mie
3	trei	13	treisprezece	30	treizeci	First, second	întîi, al
4	patru	14	paisprezece	40	patruzeci		doilea
5	cinci	15	cincisprezece	50	cincizeci	1 kilo	un kilo
6	şase	16	şaisprezece	60	şaizeci	a half	jumatăte
7	şapte	17	şaptsprezece	70	şaptzeci	a third	o treime
8	opt	18	optsprezece	80	optzeci	a quarter	sfert
9	nouă	19	nouăsprezece	90	nouăzeci	three quarters	trei
10	zece	20	douăzece	100	o sută		sferturi

ROMANIAN TERMS: A GLOSSARY

ALIMENTARĂ food store.

ARDEAL "forested land", the Romanian name for Transylvania.

BAIE bath, spa (plural *Băile*).

BISERICĂ church; **BISERICI DE LEMN**, wooden churches.

BIVOL buffalo, introduced from India by the Gypsies; **BIVOLARI** are buffalo-drovers (a Gypsy tribe).

BOYAR or *Boier* feudal lord.

BUCIUM (plural *Buciume*) alpine horn used by shepherds, also known as a *Tulnic*.

BULEVARDUL (*B-dul* or *Blvd.*) boulevard.

CALEA avenue.

CĂLUŞ traditional Whitsun fertility rite performed by *Căluşari* in rural Wallachia and southwestern Transylvania.

CAPRĂ masked "Goat dance" to celebrate the New Year.

CASĂ house.

CETATE fortress or citadel.

CHEI gorge.

CÎMPULUNG (or Câmpulung) meadow or long field, for which settlements like Cîmpulung Moldovenesc are named.

CLIŞARNITA towered guest house-cum-repository for treasures, found in Moldavian monasteries.

COMBINAT complex of factories

CSÁNGÓ Hungarian "Wanderers" from Transylvania who settled on the Moldavian side of the Carpathians.

DACIANS earliest established inhabitants of Romania, subjugated and colonized by the Romans during the first to fourth centuries AD.

DEAL hill.

DOINĂ traditional, usually plaintive Romanian folk song.

DRUM road; *Drum Naţional* highway.

ERDÉLY the Magyar name for Transylvania.

FSN *Frontul Salvării Naţional*, the National Salvation Front set up as an umbrella front during the revolution and soon transformed into a new government; Iliescu's wing split as the FDSN (Democratic Front of National Salvation) and then the PDSR (Democratic Socialist Party of Romania), while Roman's wing continued as the FSN before becoming the Partidul Democratic (FSN).

GADJÉ gypsy term for non-gypsies.

GRADINĂ garden.

GRIND raised area of accumulated silt in the Danube Delta.

GURĂ mouth.

HORĂ traditional village round dance.

HOSPODAR feudal prince of Moldavia .

ICONOSTASIS literally "icon-bearer", decorated screen in an Orthodox (or Uniate) church containing tiers of icons that separates sanctuary from nave and priest from congregation during Eucharist.

JUDEŢ county.

LAC lake.

LEGION or Iron Guard Romanian fascist movement, 1927–41.

LIPOVANI ethnic group living by fishing and gardening in the Danube Delta, descended from Russian "Old Believers".

LITORAL the coast.

MAGAZIN large store

MAGYARS Hungarians, roughly two million of whom live in Romania, mainly in Transylvania.

MĂNĂSTINEA monastery or convent.

MOARA mill.

MUNTENIA the eastern half of Wallachia, paradoxically not at all mountainous.

NAI pan-pipes.

NAOS nave or central part of an Orthodox church, lying below the central cupola and in front of the iconostasis.

NARTHEX entrance hall of an Orthodox church, often decorated with frescoes.

NATIONS or *Nationes* historically, the privileged groups in Transylvania.

NEDEIA village fair or festival characteristic of the mountain regions.

OLTENIA the western half of Wallachia, flanking the River Olt.

PĂDURE a wood.

PAS a mountain pass.

PCR *Partidul Communist Roman* – until 1989, the Romanian Communist Party (or RCP). Since reconstituted as the Socialist Party of Labour.

PEŞTERA cave.

PHANARIOTS Greek administrators, and later rulers of Moldavia and Wallachia during the centuries of Ottoman hegemony.

PIATRA stone or crag.

PIAŢA square; also a market.

PLAJĂ beach.

PLAUR floating reed islands, characteristic of the Delta.

POD bridge.

POIANA glade, meadow.

POPĂ (or *Preot*) Orthodox priest.

POTECA path.

PRONAOS see NARTHEX.

RĂSCOALA peasant rebellion; usually refers to the great uprising of 1907.

REGAT the "Old Kingdom", as Moldavia and Wallachia were known after they united in 1859.

RÎU river.

ROM Gypsies, who arrived in Romania during in medieval times.

SANCTUAR sanctuary or altar area of a church, behind the iconostasis.

SAT village.

SAXONS name given to Germans who settled in Transylvania from the twelfth century onwards.

SCHWABEN (Swabians) name given to Germans who settled in Banat in the eighteenth century; others who moved to Transylvania at this time are known as *Ländler*.

SECURITATE communist security police, now reborn as the SRI or Romanian Information Service.

SIEBENBURGEN Saxon name for Transylvania (literally, "seven towns").

ŞOSEAUA (Şos.) long tree-lined avenue.

STÎNA sheepfold.

STRADĂ (Str.) street.

SZÉKELY Hungarian-speaking ethnic group inhabiting parts of eastern Transylvania known as the Székelyföld.

ŢARA land, country (Romanian); Gypsy encampment.

TÎRG or *Tărg* market, fair or festival.

VAD ford.

VALE valley.

VĂTAF leader of Călușari dancers (Romanian); tribal chieftain (Gypsy).

VIRFU peak, mount.

VLACHS (or Wallachs) foreign name for the Romanians of Wallachia, Moldavia and Transylvania before the nineteenth century.

VOIVODE ruling prince of Transylvania or Wallachia.

AN A–Z OF ROMANIAN STREET NAMES

Romania shares in the European tradition of naming its streets after historical personages and dates, and these of course reflect the ruling ideology. Today most of the communist names, such as Lenin and Gheorghiu-Dej, have gone and been replaced by pre-war leaders such as Iuliu Maniu and Octavian Goga, although nine-teenth-century liberal-democratic figures such as Brătianu and Kogălniceanu remain acceptable. However, in Oradea and Tîrgu Mureş streets have been named after Antonescu, whose status remains unclear, and in Cluj and Tîrgu Mureş streets named after Hungarian heroes such as Petöfi now have Romanian names.

Vasile Alecsandri (1821–90) poet.

Ion Antonescu *Conducator* (war-time dictator).

Tudor Arghezi (1880–1967) poet.

Nicolae Bălcescu (1819–52) liberal politician, played a leading role in the 1848 revolution.

General Berthelot head of the French Military Mission which enabled Romania to survive World War I.

Lucian Blaga (1895–1961) philosopher, poet.

Ion Brătianu (1829–91) liberal politician, who invited Carol I to take the throne. Founder of a political dynasty, including his son **Ionel** (1864–1927), prime minister during World War I, **Vintila** (1867–1930), who succeeded his brother Ionel as leader of the Liberal Party, and **Constantin** (Dinu), leader of the Liberal Party from 1933, an ally of Maniu in the wartime opposition, condemned to life imprisonment, who died in prison in 1950.

Constantin Brîncoveanu (or Brâncoveanu) ruling prince of Wallachia 1688–1714, who generated an artistic renaissance.

George Călinescu (1899–1965) writer.

Dimitrie Cantemir (1673–1723) ruling prince of Moldavia 1710–11.

Ion Luca Caragiale (1852–1912) Romania's greatest dramatist.

George Coşbuc (1866–1918) poet.

Ion Creangă (1837–89) suspended deacon, author of folk tales known to every Romanian.

Alexandru Ioan Cuza ruler of united Wallachia and Moldavia 1859–1866.

Decebal Dacian ruler 87–106 AD.

Constantin Dobrogeanu-Gherea (1855–1920) literary critic, early socialist thinker.

Gheorghe Doja leader of 1514 revolt.

Ion Duca (1879–1933) Liberal prime minister assassinated by Iron Guard.

Mihail Eminescu (1850–89) the national poet.

George Enescu (1881–1955) the national composer.

Octavian Goga (1881–1939) poet, anti-Semitic prime minister 1937.

Bogdan Petriciu Haşdeu (1838–1907) linguist, historian.

Horea (Vasile Nicola-Ursu) leader of 1784 revolt, with Cloşca and Crişan.

Avram Iancu (1824–72) leader of 1848 revolt.

Iancu de Hunedoara ruler of Transylvania 1441–56, also Regent of Hungary.

Tache Ionescu leader of Romanian delegation at Paris Peace Conference 1918–20.

Nicolae Iorga (1871–1940) historian, founder of National Democratic Party 1910, assassinated by Iron Guard.

Panait Istraţi (1884-1935) writer.

Mihail Kogălniceanu liberal politician, played a leading role in the 1848 revolution, later Foreign Minister.

Gheorghe Lazăr (1779–1823) writer and educationalist.

Titu Maiorescu, literary critic, prime minister 1910–12.

Iuliu Maniu (1873–1953) prime minister, led anti-German resistance, died in prison.

Mátyás Corvinus son of Iancu de Hunedoara, king of Hungary 1458–90.

Samuil Micu co-author of *Supplex Libellus Valachorum* (1791), spoke at Field of Liberty (1848).

Mihai Viteazul ruling prince of Wallachia 1593–1601, also conquered Moldavia and Transylvania.

General Vasile Milea Defence Minister, committed "suicide" on December 22 1989 after refusing to order the army to open fire.

Matei Millo (1814–96) dramatist.

Mircea cel Bătrîn ruling prince of Wallachia 1386–1418.

Petru Rareş ruling prince of Wallachia 1527–38 and 1541–56.

Ciprian Porumbescu composer.

Emil Racoviţa founder of bio-speleology.

Liviu Rebreanu (1885–1944) novelist.

Mihail Sadoveanu (1880–1961) novelist, vice-president of Grand National Assembly (1948), president of Union of Writers (1949).

Andrei Şaguna bishop, elected leader at Field of Liberty (1848), first president of ASTRA.

Ştefan cel Mare ruling prince of Moldavia 1457–1504.

Nicolae Titulescu Finance Minister, Foreign Minister (1932–36), president of League of Nations, hated by the Axis.

Traian Roman emperor 98–117 AD, conquered Dacia 101–107.

Tudor Vladimirescu led 1821 revolt.

Vlad Ţepeş Vlad the Impaler, ruling prince of Wallachia 1456–76.

Aurel Vlaicu Romania's first aviator (1910).

INDEX

In Romania, the custom is to list a, i, s and t after ă, î, ş and ţ respectively, however, we have not distinguished between the two forms. Note also that î has been used instead of â.

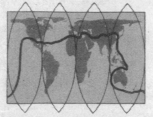

You are
A STUDENT

You travel
THE WORLD

You want
TO SAVE MONEY

Here's how

The International Student Identity Card

Available at Student Travel Offices Worldwide.

Entitles you to discounts and special services worldwide.